THE HISTORY OF BROADCASTING
IN THE UNITED KINGDOM
VOLUME III

THE
WAR OF WORDS

BY

ASA BRIGGS

D0208250

LONDON
OXFORD UNIVERSITY PRESS
NEW YORK TORONTO
1970

Oxford University Press, Ely House, London W.1

GLASGOW NEW YORK TORONTO MELBOURNE WELLINGTON
CAPE TOWN SALISBURY IBADAN NAIROBI DAR ES SALAAM LUSAKA ADDIS ABABA
BOMBAY CALCUTTA MADRAS KARACHI LAHORE DACCA
KUALA LUMPUR SINGAPORE HONG KONG TOKYO

© *Oxford University Press 1970*

384.5409
B854
v. 3

Made in Great Britain at the Pitman Press, Bath

This History is dedicated to

SIR BERESFORD CLARK
K.C.M.G., C.B.E.
(*1902–1968*)

*Controller successively of
the Overseas and the European Services
of the BBC during the war.*

ON A WIRELESS SET

Who is this coming to the microphone?
Is it the man again to cast his jest
New-minted on the garrulous unknown?
What sailor comes to answer our request?
What fair economist? What little street
Is emptied of its Joad this brain-sick hour
To prate of Plato old or Socrates?
What gardener talks of scarlet-veined beet,
Of onions, or the clotted cauliflower,
Or sounds the praise of upward-climbing peas?

O cubed shape! fair instrument! with wire
And knobs and shining dials over-wrought,
E'en now thy accents wake an old desire
And ancient echoes tease our wistful thought:
From aching memories of another day,
Too faint for dreams and well-nigh past recall,
We idly seek in midst of present woe
That golden time when thou again shalt say
Reuter is truth, truth Reuter—that is all
Ye know on earth and all ye need to know.

Punch, 17 May 1944

Director-General when war broke out, and the late Lady Violet Bonham Carter, one of the war-time Governors. Mr. T. W. Tallents allowed me, as he had done in connection with the second volume of this History, the fullest use of the valuable collection of his father's papers and press cuttings, and the late Sir Beresford Clark, link between pre-war, war-time and post-war BBC, to whom this volume is respectfully dedicated, lent me his Day Books and other papers. The late Mr. Douglas Ritchie showed me a manuscript copy of his war-time auto-biography, which sets out all the details of the BBC's famous war-time V campaign as he saw it. I was able to supplement this information from interviews with Mrs. Ian Black, Mr. Alan Bullock, Lord Ritchie Calder, M. Émile Delavenay, Mr. Martin Esslin, Mr. Malcolm Frost, Mr. and Mrs. Darsie Gillie, Sir Hugh Greene, M. Fernand Grenier, Sir John Lawrence, Mr. Tangye Lean, Mr. Leonard Miall, Mr. Noel Newsome, M. Michel Saint-Denis and other members of the BBC's French Service and Mr. F. L. M. Shepley. Mr. Carl Brinitzer kindly allowed me to see the proofs of his *Hier spricht London*, Mr. Bramsted placed the writing of his *Goebbels and National Socialist Propaganda* in perspective, and Mr. Gregory Macdonald lent me interesting letters exchanged between himself and the late Mr. Lindley Fraser. Mr. C. Macmillan organized an invaluable visit to the headquarters of the BBC's Monitoring Service at Caversham.

On other aspects of broadcasting I owe much to Sir Harold Bishop, who read the manuscript of this volume with as much meticulous attention as he read the manuscripts of volumes I and II; to my friend Mr. D. H. Clarke, who was at my right hand in the preparation of volumes I and II; to Mr. Norman Collins, who suggested the names of many other people I should see; to Mr. M. Dinwiddie, who sent me the typescript of his *Religion by Radio*; to Mr. Maurice Farquharson, who was always lively and encouraging; to Mr. John Green, who provided useful information about talks, particularly farming talks; to Mr. Harman Grisewood, whose own book also constitutes an important source; to Mr. Spike Hughes, with whom I talked about war-time songs; to the late Sir Basil Nicolls, with whom I was able to talk at length; to Mr. Roy Plomley, who sent me valuable material concerning commercial radio in

1939 and 1940; to Mr. Martin Pulling, Mr. R. C. Patrick, Mr. F. W. Alexander and other experts in sound recording; to Lord Radcliffe, who gave me an admirably lucid account of the problems of the war-time Ministry of Information; to Mr. E. C. Robbins, who read the manuscript with immense care; to Mr. A. P. Ryan, the central figure in many chapters of this story, and Sir Lindsay Wellington, with both of whom I have been able to discuss interpretation as well as information. Many members of particular BBC services have been able to comment on parts of the manuscript in its first form. They may not feel that the proportions of this volume are right, but everything that they have had to say has been taken fully into account.

I would never have been able to complete the volume had it not been for Miss M. S. Hodgson, the BBC's industrious and imaginative Archivist, and her staff, including Miss Marjorie Whitaker; and Mrs. Tamara Deutscher, who checked the book references and prepared the index. Always co-operative, always zealous and relentless in their search for strictly accurate information, they have assisted me at every stage. So too have Mr. D. P. Wolferstan, friend, colleague and guide; Miss Mary Jay, my indefatigable secretary; and Mrs. Vivienne Alistair and Mrs. Naomi Stuart, who helped to type the manuscript.

Lastly I would like to thank two distinguished proof readers —Mr. R. H. S. Crossman who spared time in his busy ministerial life not only to read but to make full comments (I hope that one day he will write his own account of the war years, for he played a most important and constructive part behind the scenes) and my friend Dr. Bryan Wilson of All Soul's College, Oxford, who also read the proofs of volumes I and II and has approached the study of this volume with the same scrupulous detachment.

ASA BRIGGS

University of Sussex, 1970

CONTENTS

LIST OF ILLUSTRATIONS

Items marked with an asterisk are reproduced by permission of the BBC.

PLATES

IN TEXT

I

PERSPECTIVES

The existence of broadcasting constitutes the main difference in propaganda between this War and the last.
The principal features of this new
development are the time element, the
universality of the medium and the
stamp of authority.

BBC Monitoring Service, *Weekly Analysis*,
3 Jan. 1940

1. Perspectives

WORDS do not win wars. Nonetheless, between 1939 and 1945 there was a prolonged war of words, which has sometimes been thought of less flatteringly as a 'wordy warfare',[1] in which the BBC took a leading part. The war of words is not the only interesting or important theme in the history of the war-time BBC, yet it is the theme which relates broadcasting directly to the political and military history of the war, to the great events which figure in the history books. This third volume in the history of British broadcasting is necessarily concerned, therefore, with something more than the impact of war on the BBC, an established institution which was, nonetheless, only seventeen years old, or on broadcasting as a rich and varied activity with a past and a future. It deals directly with the role of the BBC outside as well as inside Britain within the context of the general history of the Second World War.

This was an exciting role, often hectic, sometimes controversial. Yet the story is both complicated and neglected. Although many people working inside the crowded studios and corridors of the BBC thought and remarked how wonderful it would be when the full account of what was happening could be told,[2] most historians of the war have shared the view of some

---

[1] This is the title of Book III of R. Bruce Lockhart, *Comes the Reckoning* (1947).

[2] In November 1939 a deliberate attempt was made 'to collect the material for a history of the BBC in war time, whether written within the BBC or by an accredited outsider' (*Note by Maurice Farquharson, 9 Nov. 1939) and an Assistant was appointed to assemble and organize 'war archives'. In November 1941 the post lapsed and the BBC's Secretariat, headed by Farquharson, took up the job itself (*Note by Farquharson, 26 Nov. 1941). 'The use of broadcasting as an instrument of propaganda in this War is a subject that must await the historian,' the *BBC Handbook, 1941* stated on p. 9. The difficulties of recording information were freely admitted. Thus, in a note of 13 Jan. 1942 it is recorded that Harman Grisewood complained that much of the history of the European Service was not committed to paper. 'Material was not available on such subjects as BBC liaison through Political Warfare Executive with Allied Governments.' There were occasional references in the Press to the role of future historians. 'A grand and stirring story will one day be told of the BBC's share in the war effort,' the *Church Times*, for example, wrote on 22 April 1943. [An * in front of a footnote means that the letter or document is among the BBC's Records.]

of the top civil servants during the war and have either left the BBC out of the reckoning or dismissed it perfunctorily. An official British chart on the 'Organisation of War', passed by the censor in June 1942, did not include broadcasting at all. In a small square devoted to 'the Home Front', half the size of a square devoted to Labour and Production, it included 'Information' in a list of five items. Health, Education, and the Assistance Board constituted the first three, Information the fourth, and Pensions the fifth. In the six volumes of Winston Churchill's epic history there are less than ten references to the role of broadcasting or of the BBC, and none of these involve any comprehensive assessment. Churchill never referred either to his own war-time broadcasts, many of which have passed directly into history in their own right, or to the general influence of broadcasting on operations or on morale.

If the silence of historians may be explained, in part at least, by their difficulty in securing access to the relevant people or documents, Churchill's attitudes may be explained, in the first instance at least, in terms of his long-standing distaste for the pre-war Reithian BBC. He had broadcast only four times between 1934 and 1939, and even after 1945 he was to refuse to broadcast on at least nine occasions. There may, however, have been quite different and more profound reasons for his silence. Unlike Hitler, who wrote in *Mein Kampf* that 'in war time words are acts', Churchill was always far less interested in persuasion and propaganda than in the conduct of military operations. 'If words could kill, we would be dead already,' he told a radio audience as early as November 1939.[1]

This is not to say that Churchill did not possess what a French observer has called 'an innate sense of propaganda'.[2] As a British Intelligence chief has written, 'When he spoke or wrote a message it was always a deed, whereas when other Ministers spoke it was often only words.'[3] Or as Ed Murrow, one of the most effective of all broadcasters, has put it, 'he mobilized the English language and sent it into battle to steady his fellow countrymen and hearten those Europeans upon whom the long

[1] Broadcast of 12 Nov. 1939, 'Ten weeks of War'.
[2] J. de Launay, 'La guerre psychologique' in H. Bernard, G. A. Chevallez, R. Gheysens and J. de Launay, *Les Dossiers de la seconde guerre mondiale* (1964), p. 189.
[3] Bruce Lockhart, op. cit., p. 127.

dark night of tyranny had descended'.[1] Churchill's own view-point was simple. 'The people's will was resolute and remorse-less. I only expressed it. They had the lion's heart. I had the luck to be called upon to give the roar.'[2] Whatever others thought, he himself obviously did not consider that his own or any one else's broadcasting had played a critical part in the unfolding of the great drama of twentieth-century world war.

The silence of generals is understandable, for they were con-cerned essentially with front-line operations, even though it is strange that Montgomery, who does write about 'morale', does not mention broadcasting. There was, of course, one conspicu-ous exception. General de Gaulle dated the beginning of a 'new life' from the moment on 18 June 1940 when he broadcast from London his repudiation of Pétain's armistice agreement: 'as the irrevocable words flew out upon their way I felt within myself a life coming to an end'. Separated as he was from his own people, many of whom at first had never heard of his name, he acknowledged throughout his *Memoirs* that broadcasting, which he first approached in 1940 as a novice, had provided him with 'a powerful means of war'.[3]

Hitler, to return to the first and most obvious of the contrasts, had never been in any doubt about the matter. Like the other spokesmen of the National Socialist Party, he conceived of radio as a 'living bridge between leader and people'.[4] He not only recognized but exaggerated its value as an instrument of propaganda both at home and overseas. He had broadcast frequently between 1933 and 1939, although he had addressed his huge audiences mainly from party rallies not from studios, in complete contrast to F. D. Roosevelt, across the Atlantic, who carefully cultivated his famous 'fireside' style and liked to

---

[1] Murrow wrote these words on Churchill's eightieth birthday in 1954: they are reprinted in E. Bliss (ed.), *In Search of Light: The Broadcasts of Edward R. Murrow* (1968), p. 237.

[2] Quoted ibid., p. 237.

[3] C. de Gaulle, *The Call to Honour* (Eng. tr. 1955), pp. 89, 106.

[4] See H. L. Childs and J. B. Whitton (eds.), *Propaganda by Short Wave* (Princeton, 1943), p. 62. At the first Nazi radio exhibition in 1933, attended by Hitler, Goeb-bels had stated that radio would be to the twentieth century what the press had been to the nineteenth. (Quoted in E. K. Bramsted, *Goebbels and National Socialist Propaganda* (1965), p. 63.) A photograph of Hitler at the exhibition is printed in *BBC Year Book, 1934*, p. 294.

make his listeners feel that both they and he were at home.[1]
While Roosevelt acquired experience and proved himself a
most effective broadcaster, the Nazis pushed further their own
interest in radio. They were always fascinated by the relationship between modern technology and the mysteries of psychological manipulation, and they saw in radio 'the shock troop
of the National Socialist World Outlook', 'the most modern, the
strongest and the most revolutionary weapon which we possess
in the battle against an extinct world'. 'We spell radio with
three exclamation marks,' one of them remarked, 'because we
are possessed in it of a miraculous power.'[2]

The *mystique* of radio meant little to the British, although
they were highly skilled in its arts and in its techniques; and the
Director-General of the BBC, F. W. Ogilvie, who had been
appointed to his post as recently as 1938,[3] was an ex-academic,
who certainly did not conceive of his job as that of a propagandist. The BBC with its 4,889 employees in 1939 prided itself that
it was independent of the government of the day. In its foreign
programmes, which had been built up since the beginning of
the Empire services in 1932, it was dedicated to the idea of telling
the truth: when it turned to the Arab world, South America,
Germany and Italy in 1938 and 1939, it envisaged its task as
being above all else the start of a news operation. Goebbels, the
German Minister of Propaganda, served not as an example but
as a warning, and Nazi talk of 'fighting on the battlefields of the
mind' provoked little sense of the need for retaliation. The
insouciance was far less pronounced in September 1939 than it
had been a year earlier,[4] yet there was a deep-seated reluctance

---

[1] *Hitler in his Reichstag speech in December 1941 after the entry of the
United States into the war lampooned Roosevelt as 'that man, who, while our
soldiers are fighting in snow and ice, very tactfully likes to make his chats from the
fireside, the man who is the main culprit of this war'. (BBC Monitoring Service,
Weekly Analysis, 16 Dec. 1941.)

[2] E. Hadamowsky, *Der Rundfunk im Dienst der Volksführung* (1934), pp. 13, 19.
Cf. a broadcast of Goebbels (1 Dec. 1940) in which he described the German
Radio Service, RRG (*Reichsrundfunkgesellschaft*), as 'the most modern technical
instrument of the leadership of the people', and his introduction to H. Fritzsche,
Krieg den Kriegshetzern (1940).

[3] See A. Briggs, *The Golden Age of Wireless* (1965), p. 637.

[4] See below, pp. 141–58. There is a fascinating paper by Miss I. D. Benzie and
J. R. Morley, dated October 1939, which anticipated some of the ideas later
developed by Nazi broadcasters, including the use of enemy wavelengths, the
interruption of enemy programmes, and the creation of Nazi 'pretence' stations.

even to contemplate either 'deliberate perversion of the truth in order to maintain national morale',[1] a task with which the Nazis were thoroughly familiar, or to indulge in expensive efforts to win over people in other countries, a duty which the Nazis had imposed upon themselves in 1933.

It was from the Empire not from Westminster that the first cries of alarm about the deficiencies of British propaganda were heard. 'Newspapers reflecting strong feeling, nothing done to counteract German wireless propaganda,' a correspondent in New Delhi cabled home in October 1939. 'German programmes in English excellently received. Listeners await vainly for refutation from London or Delhi.'[2] The British Press was more eager to respond to the appeal than the Government. The *Daily Express*, which had told its readers on the eve of the struggle that there would be no war, was soon asking for 'one-man control'. There was a job at Broadcasting House for 'a master mind—a propagandist and a showman'.[3]

In September 1939 the propagandists and the showmen were all in Berlin, convinced believers in the myth that Allied propaganda had led to their 'betrayal' in 1918.[4] The master-mind was Dr. Goebbels, artful in juggling with the different media of communication which fell within his administration, keeping them moving by clever directives, and knowing that his Ministry and the Nazi Party were linked together in an intricate system of officials and agents.[5] His skill lay in his ability to play deliberately on predispositions and prejudices, contradictions and confusions. He knew that propaganda for home consumption and propaganda for overseas had to be thought out independently and that in neither case was the best propaganda

[1] *'War-Time Propaganda', an undated BBC Paper, probably written in December 1939.

[2] *Cable from a *Daily Telegraph* correspondent, 6 Oct. 1939.

[3] *Daily Express*, 2 Nov. 1939.

[4] They were probably influenced less by books like A. Ponsonby's *Falsehood in War-time* (1928) and S. Rogerson's *Propaganda in the Next War* (1938) than they were by the memories and myths of 'betrayal' in 1918. Hitler's interest in 'psychological dislocation of the enemy through revolutionary propaganda' was noted by H. Rauschning in his book *Germany's Revolution of Destruction* (1939).

[5] For a war-time British account of the network, see D. Sington and A. Weidenfeld, *The Goebbels Experiment* (1942), pp. 148 ff.

For more general signs of a shift in opinions, see A. J. Mackenzie, *Propaganda Room* (1938), ch. I.

necessarily that which set out to convince or convert. Propaganda was rather a form of 'direct action'.[1] Yet, the machine which he created was far less efficient than it appeared to be and the weaknesses behind his whole approach to propaganda itself were ultimately exposed. As the war continued, it became abundantly plain to German experts that propaganda could not be employed as 'scientifically' as some of its Nazi advocates had stated. Some German propaganda was as 'hysterically and emotionally uncontrolled as any propaganda in history'.[2] Some was very poorly co-ordinated, as different agencies, among which the Ministry of Propaganda and Ribbentrop's Foreign Office were only two, were drawn into rivalry with each other, a battle of authorities characteristic of the Third Reich.

German propaganda overseas had relatively little effect, indeed, except when it was closely geared to the operational needs of military campaigns, when words and deeds were in step. If more ambitious general notes were struck, as they were, for example, in the propaganda about a 'New European Order' in 1940 and 1941, the results were limited. Moreover, German propaganda to Britain was largely a failure. 'Haw-Haw' quickly built up a large audience, but as the war went on, he proved a diminishing asset.[3] Even in German home propaganda Goebbels found it difficult at critical moments to strike the same notes as the British had been able to strike with little fuss in 1940,[4] and the vulnerability of his propaganda became more manifest. He believed in words to the last, as did most of his fellow-countrymen, yet already by 1943 a broadcaster from London was able to tell the Germans that 'the silence of the drums and pipes today sounds almost louder and more impressive than the fanfares themselves used to do'.[5] 'The strategy of gloom', which Goebbels was forced to follow after 1943, carrying with it appeals to sacrifice and demands for 'total war', was

[1] This term is used in C. J. Rolo, *Radio Goes to War* (1943 edn.), p. 33.

[2] L. M. Fraser, *Propaganda* (1957), p. 52.

[3] See below, pp. 140–59, 230–7.

[4] See R. Semmler, *Goebbels the Man next to Hitler* (1947), p. 72. 'Just as a few of us admired the English when they stuck out in the autumn of 1940,' he told Berliners in 1943, 'so we have to stick out now. I reject indignantly the enemy allegations that we have weaker nerves than the Londoners.' (Article in *Völkischer Beobachter*, 4 Aug. 1943, quoted in Bramsted, op. cit., p. 427.)

[5] *BBC Feature, 'The Month of Fanfares', written and produced by H. Fischer, 26 July 1943.

not unsuccessful in influencing home audiences, yet just before the end he had to put his own trust primarily in luck, before ultimately reverting to nihilism.[1]

Goebbels is more interesting in the context of this book than Hitler, because it was he who managed the machine. Hitler, moreover, lapsed into radio silence just when Churchill reached the peak of his command of a medium the full importance of which he still did not appreciate. During the winter of 1942/3, Hitler spoke in public only once and the mere fact of being able to persuade him to broadcast in November 1943 was treated by Goebbels as a triumph.[2] During the last terrible ten months of the war, when the whole regime was in peril, he directly addressed the German people only three times and the last two messages were read for him by Goebbels.[3]

It is easy to see in retrospect, as Churchill always saw clearly at the time, that the long war, with its 'deep, slow-moving tides',[4] favoured the British, once they had allies, just as *Blitzkrieg*, military and psychological, had favoured the Germans. Above all, the BBC's emphasis on 'truth' and 'consistency', which came naturally to the broadcasters, produced long-term dividends as the war continued.[5] It had proved politically valuable, indeed, even in the short run, when the first disasters could not be glossed over. French propagandists provided a terrible warning before the fall of France of the dangers of unsubstantiated optimism,[6] and although there were moments when some people in Britain itself envied what

---

[1] There had always been an element of nihilism in his outlook, and in an entry in his Diary in 1926 he had written of 'the will to seek the last form for a people bound to perish'. (*Das Tagebuch von Josef Goebbels, 1925–6* (1961), p. 57.) See also Bramsted, op. cit., pp. 325–6, for his switches in propaganda; R. Semmler, *Goebbels, the Man next to Hitler* (1947); and L. W. Doob, 'Goebbels' Principles of Propaganda' in the *Public Opinion Quarterly*, vol. 14, no. 5 (1950).

[2] *Goebbels Tagebücher* (1948), p. 409. 'I had at last managed to put the Führer before the microphone for the first time since the Heroes' Commemoration Day. Now I can return to Berlin with my mind at ease.' Goebbels thought it significant also that Churchill was silent on the radio for nearly a year before his broadcast on 26 Feb. 1944.

[3] Z. A. B. Zeman, *Nazi Propaganda* (1964), p. 179.

[4] *This phrase of Churchill comes from his broadcast of 29 Nov. 1942.

[5] It was sometimes questioned by Goebbels. Thus, he remarked on the success of British propaganda in 'bombing' German towns in their communiqués. See his collection of war-time speeches, *Die Zeit ohne Beispiel* (1941), p. 365.

[6] See below, p. 227.

seemed to be the ruthless and relentless efficiency of the German propaganda machine,[1] the general feeling was well expressed in a book review of 1942—'our propaganda cannot be a mere copy of or retort in the manner of Goebbels'.[2] 'Totalitarian methods of propaganda,' Harold Nicolson, then Parliamentary Secretary to the Ministry of Information, wrote in 1941, 'are not only foolish as such but wholly inapplicable to a civilised community.' Even their external appeal was subject to a law of diminishing returns: their intellectual appeal was bound to turn against itself as soon as victories gave way to defeats. 'No permanent propaganda policy can in the modern world be based upon untruthfulness.'[3]

A year later, in the extended war, when the Japanese were winning their first dramatic victories in the Far East, the policy behind statements of this kind continued to be upheld. Lindley Fraser, the most prominent commentator of the BBC's German Service, admitted frankly in a talk to Germany that 'many of us in Great Britain are not satisfied about the way in which our strategy in the Far East has been conducted':[4] a German listener in a prisoner of war camp 'said to himself' when he heard this statement, 'if they can admit a catastrophe so openly they must be terribly strong'.[5] Churchill himself never made any attempt to pretend that things were better than they were, yet he usually exuded confidence. 'A speech broadcast by Mr. Churchill,' a New Zealand editor exclaimed, 'is as good as a new battleship.'[6]

By then, a 'League of Nations' of foreign refugees had assembled in the BBC's studios and offices in London, 'living, working and talking', as one of them put it, 'in a spirit of absolute independence'.[7] Each group had a distinctive life

---

[1] See below, pp. 222 ff. As late as 5 May 1945, a reviewer of E. Kris and H. Speier's book *German Radio Propaganda* (1944) remarked in the *Times Literary Supplement* that 'Goebbels is a bad man . . . but it is fair to allow that for a long time now he has been untiringly making the best of a very bad propaganda job'.

[2] *Tribune*, 26 June 1942, in a review of Otto Friedmann's *Broadcasting for Democracy*.

[3] *BBC Handbook, 1941*, p. 30.

[4] *BBC Sonderbericht, 26 June 1942, 'The Right to Criticize'.

[5] *BBC Script, 21 May 1963.

[6] *Letters received by the BBC.

[7] The Belgian, Victor de Laveleye, the pioneer of the V Sign, quoted in T. O. Beachcroft, *British Broadcasting* (1946), pp. 36-8.

of its own: each, indeed, had its own tensions, its own aspirations, its own gossip and its own style. Some groups were of very mixed political hues: all of them were influenced in their programmes and propaganda by the interplay of experience and personality. Year in, year out, the effort had to be made—and it was an effort which required great imagination—to establish and to maintain contact with people in countries about which there was often little precise or up-to-date information and where circumstances might change over-night. From battered war-time London the broadcasters had to reach shadowy, invisible audiences, many of them listening in terror of their lives, with one ear to what they were hearing and with the other to the enemy outside their doors. Broadcasting in such circumstances was a profoundly serious responsibility: it reached its heights when citizens spoke to fellow citizens cheerfully, hopefully, even enthusiastically. The British Government was in the background—with its own preoccupations and policies—yet the Government did not broadcast itself. Each group within the BBC might be influenced either by the policy of the British Government or by the policies of Allied Governments exiled in London. Yet each group had a measure of initiative and enterprise unknown to the team of broadcasters who worked under the orders of Goebbels in Berlin.

The sustaining effects of British broadcasting were noted almost everywhere as the war went on and as the BBC established a remarkable international reputation which it has never lost. The BBC was 'as beautiful as a Beethoven symphony —because Frenchmen were allowed to express disagreement with the British Government,' Léon Blum, the French Socialist leader, remarked after spending most of the war in a concentration camp. 'In a world of poison, the BBC became the great antiseptic.' 'The British broadcasts are more deadly than steel' was a German comment of 1942. 'If there is resistance in France, it is due to the BBC,' wrote André Philip, who had escaped from France to take part in de Gaulle's Government.[1]

The BBC's reputation was assured. Yet the last of these statements is surprisingly difficult to substantiate. The Second

[1] Quoted ibid., pp. 39 and 8.

World War has about it a Tolstoyan quality which makes it
impossible to write confidently of causes and consequences. The
relationship between the work of the BBC and the emergence
and growth of national resistance movements in Europe is a
vast subject which remains difficult to unravel. While there
is no doubt that the BBC was an indispensable 'source of
consolation'[1] to European listeners as the war went on, sometimes 'the only ray of hope',[2] its direct role, for instance in
providing specific guidance to resistance groups, varied from
country to country. There were particular events in the war
also which extended the scope of resistance more than any words
did, notably the entry of the USSR into the war in August 1941
which transformed the war situation in 'real' terms as well as in
terms of propaganda. What remains beyond doubt is that the
BBC itself did more than any other comparable agency both
to pull together different elements of resistance in each separate
European country—by giving news, the most important of all
its tasks, by providing ideas and inspiration, and at certain
stages by passing on operational orders—and to spread relevant
information between countries. The feeling of a generalized
'resistance' in Europe, a movement with some kind of 'solidarity',
owed much to BBC reports of what was happening, often
spontaneously, in scattered countries.

During the critical years of the war Noel Newsome, the
European News Editor, who had joined the Corporation at
the very beginning of the war, working from a Central News
Desk, concentrated on every kind of 'resistance' theme. It was
due to him as well as to the people within the separate sections
—some of whom turned to him for every kind of guidance,
others of whom were anxious to remain as independent of him
as of the Government itself—that the British, for all their initial
suspicion of propaganda, came to be looked upon as 'les
maîtres incomparables de la violence à froid et du dosage des
mots'.[3] The Germans themselves and their supporters in the
occupied countries came to acknowledge, albeit grudgingly,
British skill as the war went on. 'The British radio has to keep

---

[1] A phrase of a Roumanian listener (Notes collected after the war by the BBC's
External Broadcasting Audience Research Officer).

[2] Loc. cit. This was a phrase of a Hungarian listener.

[3] M. Mégret, *La guerre psychologique* (1956), p. 83.

our people in a state of alarm and jitters,' a pro-German French broadcaster exclaimed in March 1943. 'The job is well done.'[1] 'In spite of official circulars and the King's request,' a pro-German Danish newspaper wrote about the same time, 'the secret pro-British propaganda of teachers and clergymen and their incitement against the Axis powers is unlimited.'[2] Such indirect testimonials have been echoed by post-war historians who have claimed that British appreciation of audience psychology was more acute than that of the Americans and more sophisticated than that of the Russians. 'Il semble qu'après les hésitations du début,' one French historian has put it, 'les spécialistes britanniques soient arrivés à une efficacité plus grande que leurs collègues allemands. Cette victoire alliée dans la domaine de la guerre psychologique précéda sans doute la victoire militaire mais lui resta étroitement liée.'[3]

It is possible to trace the stages, each of which will be fully and critically examined within this volume, whereby the British were drawn into propaganda for Europe—tentative beginnings in 1939; fuller mobilization in 1940, with the introduction of programmes put out by foreign refugees in London; the V campaign of the spring and summer of 1941; the greatly improved co-ordination of propaganda activities in 1941 and in 1942, following the setting up by the Government of the Political Warfare Executive; the furnishing to the European 'underground' of news and advice from London; the giving of orders under the direction of SHAEF (Supreme Headquarters Allied Expeditionary Force) on the eve of D-Day in 1944; the linking of broadcasting, not least through broadcasts in German, to the final victory offensive.

Each of these stages needs critical examination, since there is ample room for continuing debate. The V campaign, thought by some to be 'brilliant, imaginative and successful', had its critics even at the time: it often seemed to be out of touch with

---

[1] Broadcast from Lyons National, 15 March 1943, quoted in *British Survey*, vol. IV, no. 23, 'The Battle of the Broadcasts'. He added, however, 'a few words of commonsense should be enough to dispose of these lies'.
[2] *Faedrelandet*, 3 Jan. 1943, quoted ibid.
[3] J. de Launay, loc. cit., p. 190.

operational realities.[1] There were grave difficulties confronting British broadcasters to Europe later on, when the opening of a 'Second Front' was delayed: 'We were clearly doing a big build,' one American editor put it in the early summer of 1943 after listening to BBC broadcasts during the previous year, 'and if after this the Allies did not land in Europe this year he was afraid that the disappointment and feeling of being let down would have very serious consequences.'[2] There was uneasiness also about the effects on British broadcasts to Germany of the Vansittart doctrine, set out in Vansittart's *Black Record* (1941), which drew no sharp distinction between Nazis and Germans,[3] of the official formula of 'unconditional surrender', and of the refusal to make a clear declaration of war aims. Some broadcasters like Hugh Carleton Greene, Head of the German Section, have argued that the 'unconditional surrender' formula, in particular, inhibited effective propaganda; others have claimed or implied that it mattered relatively little.[4]

The debate has moved into a wider range of subjects, including the relative influence of 'black' and of 'white' broadcasting. 'Black' broadcasting is 'pretence' broadcasting: it purported to come from behind the enemy lines—and there were at least sixty such stations during the war[5]—yet it was concocted at home. The BBC was pure white: the British 'black' or 'grey' stations were under the absolute control of the Political Warfare Executive.[6] In Germany Goebbels controlled the operations both of RRG (*Reichsrundfunkgesellschaft*) and of a whole range of 'black' stations. There was, on paper at least, unity of command. Sefton Delmer, a brilliant 'black broadcaster', has crossed swords both with Hugh Carleton Greene and with R. H. S. Crossman, who worked in the same organization, on the question of the relative

[1] See below, pp. 365–84.

[2] *Note by W. Horsfall Carter, the BBC's European Publicity Officer, 24 June 1943.

[3] See also Vansittart's article on 'Vansittartism' in the *Nineteenth Century*, May 1942.

[4] H. Carleton Greene, 'Psychological Warfare', a lecture delivered at the NATO Defence College in Paris on 9 Sept. 1959.

[5] This was the figure given by the American Foreign Broadcast Intelligence Service: it is quoted in E. Barnouw, *The Golden Web* (1968), p. 158.

[6] See below, p. 417 ff.

influence of the two British agencies—the BBC and the PWE-sponsored stations. He has suggested that many Service leaders saw special advantages in 'black' broadcasting which could be geared directly to Service requirements and for which they themselves were not officially responsible.[1] The BBC then and since has naturally emphasized the long-term importance of 'white' broadcasting which was open and above board. Indeed, it was suspicious not only of some of the arts of the black broadcasters but of some of the techniques of the 'creative planners' attached after 1943 to SHAEF, many of them with advertising experience rather than with detailed knowledge of broadcasting.

There was as much scope, therefore, for friction and for rivalry in the British as in the German war effort, and, as General Spears remarked to Duff Cooper in January 1941, 'one of our greatest weaknesses is a tendency of auxiliary bodies to follow a policy of their own independent of that settled by the main authority'.[2] Spears feared that the war could not be won if the habit became 'generalised'. In fact, however, the degree of initiative left both to the BBC and to the individual sections inside it liberated energy and stimulated imagination. The sense of a contest with Germans on every conceivable front can be discerned at almost every moment of the war. Behind the scenes, the Monitoring Service of the BBC, with no equally efficient German counterpart, grew from the humblest of beginnings to become a vast organization in its own right, supplying both BBC and PWE with invaluable information. The range of its activities was enormous and the skills and experience of the individuals who worked for it exceptionally varied. Already in the autumn of 1939 it was recognizing how complex the radio war had become: 'Germany has started bulletins in Swedish, Dutch and Turkish and has strengthened her output to India; Finland now broadcasts regularly in English and German; Radio Rome and also Ankara have been closely watching transmissions from Paris. Denmark appears to keep a keen watch on Russia.'[3] As the war went on through its

[1] See S. Delmer, *Black Boomerang* (1962), passim, and below, p. 276. He made a number of additional points in a reply to a review by R. H. S. Crossman in the *New Statesman*, 16 Dec. 1962. In 'black' broadcasting, he stated, 'intelligence, planning and production were all under one hat' (p. 222).

[2] Letter of 21 Jan. 1941.

[3] *BBC Monitoring Service, Weekly Analysis, 26 Nov. 1939.

many contrasting phases, the monitors watched it all, catching its immediacy, its intricacy, its subplots and its surprises.

The British began by thinking that the Nazis had a long-term propaganda plan, based on a tradition established in six years 'of controlling of public opinion, of distortion of facts and of a ruthlessness of mind which has not been developed in any other country to a similar extent'.[1] They noted the way in which Goebbels, who had used radio with great skill during the *Anschluss* crisis, started by treating the war 'as though it were another election campaign or party anniversary'.[2] By contrast, the British seemed to have to depend on improvisation. Bombs were falling on Warsaw and German armoured columns were moving deep into Poland before a BBC bulletin in Polish announced 'This is London'. In April 1940 Leif Konow was summoned to Broadcasting House to start the Norwegian programme on the day the Germans invaded Norway. The Danish and Dutch programmes began in the same improvised style. 'The BBC finds itself in a peculiarly difficult position,' the Corporation told the Kennet Committee on Manpower in October 1941, 'because its place in the modern state at war was not recognized until a year or so after the war had started. Had its place been recognized before the war or even on the outbreak of war many of the difficulties would be solved by now. Now the great possibilities of the BBC's Overseas Service in undermining the enemy's war effort are recognized by the Ministry of Information and in certain other quarters, but this recognition is very recent and it seems that its implications in terms of manpower and priorities are not fully appreciated even yet.'[3] Throughout 1941 the BBC was pressing hard for recognition as 'one of the essential weapons of the war'. 'Before the war and during its first year,' was the complaint, 'we constantly sought this recognition but without success . . . we never knew from one day to the next what [the] Ministry [of Information] would require of us.'[4]

[1] *BBC *Weekly Analysis of Foreign Programmes*, 19 Oct. 1939.
[2] Kris and Speier, op. cit., p. 14. It seemed ominous that on the day the Russo-German Pact was signed, one German radio station acted with great speed in offering a fifteen-minute concert of Russian music in place of a scheduled talk 'I accuse Moscow'. (E. Taylor, *The Strategy of Terror* (1940), p. 133.)
[3] *Notes for a meeting, 1 Oct. 1941; see also below, p. 276.
[4] *G. C. Beadle, then in charge of BBC administration (see below p. 354), to, E. St. J. Bamford, Ministry of Information, 23 Aug. 1941.

Two glosses must be made on these war-time assessments and complaints. First, we now realize that the Germans had no long-term plan. They depended on shifts of pace and mood and on tactical expedients. There are close parallels, therefore, between the economic history of the British and German war effort and the history of radio and its full utilization as a 'weapon of war'.[1] The German economy was not fully mobilized in 1939, 1940 and 1941 and, like propaganda, was 'geared for small-scale quick wars which would not unduly disturb her civilian standard of life': moreover, there were so many forces and counterforces within the German 'system' that a German General called it 'a war of all against all'.[2] Second, the BBC's grumbles, understandable though they were, overlooked one essential factor. If it had been turned into a 'weapon of war', it would not have retained the degree of independence it continued to prize. The 'black' broadcasters could set out to demoralize the Germans because they were geared to the war machine: the BBC gained in influence because it was always concerned with something more than demoralization.

Yet for all the differences between the British and German broadcasting structures and their role in 'the modern state at war', during the year 1942 the same kind of problems were confronting the broadcasters both in Britain and in Germany. How could they deal with setbacks or with defeats? By then both sides had these. How could they present the issues of what by then had become a wearing and protracted world war to their own citizens as well as to foreigners? For a time, the 'spiritual' seemed to matter less than the material. 'This is no war for throne and altar. This is a war for grain and bread, a plentiful breakfast, lunch, and dinner table,' Goebbels told his audience in May 1942.[3] 'Personal extravagance must be eliminated altogether,' Sir Stafford Cripps told his fellow-countrymen in Britain.[4] The delays associated with a war of attrition had to be explained to the impatient and to the excited. It was during this year, when the BBC was being 'reorganized',[5] that RRG was reorganized also: Hadamowsky,

[1] See B. H. Klein, *Germany's Economic Preparations for War* (1959) and A. S. Milward, *The German Economy at War* (1965).
[2] Milward, op. cit., pp. 190, 27. [3] Quoted in Kris and Speier, op. cit., p. 383.
[4] See A. J. P. Taylor, *English History, 1914–1945* (1965), p. 544.
[5] See below, p. 354.

Chief Organizer of the German radio, was transferred to a new post in June, and Fritzsche, a 'star' radio commentator, was given the new job of 'Delegate for the Control of the Political Aspect of Greater German Radio'. Goebbels himself found it necessary to approve the idea of a second national radio programme in lighter vein than the first. 'Good humor is important to the war effort,' he stated categorically for the first time, promising more light music and more entertainment as 'a war measure'.[1] In Britain, *ITMA* and the *Brains Trust* were at the peak of their remarkable popularity,[2] while CEMA, the Council for the Encouragement of Music and the Arts, and ENSA, the Entertainments National Service Association, were seeking to appeal to soldiers and civilians alike. In Britain, as in Germany, 'diversion' was seen as essential to full 'mobilization'. The war gripped whole societies as no war ever had done before.

For a time, therefore, the contrasting histories of British and German broadcasting criss-crossed and even coincided. Yet by 1943 the moment had passed. Initiative passed increasingly to the British who, whatever they might say—and rightly say— about independence, felt themselves as much 'under orders' as the Germans.[3] The staff of the BBC rose to its peak figure of 11,663 in March 1944—it employed 4,889 staff in September 1939—at the time when the staff of RRG and other German radio agencies, which had employed 4,800 people in 1939, had already begun to fall from its peak figure of about 10,000. BBC output in terms of programme hours had trebled and in terms of transmitter power had nearly quintupled. Moreover, the number of BBC foreign-language services had increased from 10 on the eve of the war, when the Germans were providing 36 such services, to 45 by the end of 1943, when the Germans provided 52. The Germans were beginning to face difficulties in organizing their foreign propaganda just at the time when the framework of the British effort had been strengthened and the drive of the British system was at its maximum. Goebbels offered his full support to Albert Speer, who sought with ability and determination to persuade

---

[1] Quoted in Kris and Speier, op. cit., pp. 55–6.
[2] See below pp. 527 ff.
[3] This phrase was used in the *BBC Handbook, 1941*, p. 10.

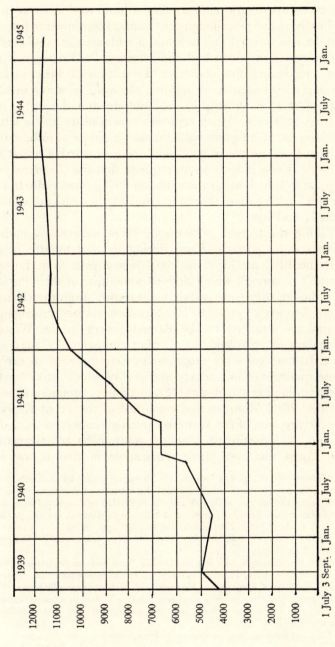

BBC STAFF 1939-1945

Germany to embark upon a policy of 'total war' in 1942, 1943, and early 1944,[1] yet, though the Germans continued to listen to him, he was worried that he could not inspire the same kind of public reactions which had characterized Britain when it too was at its darkest hour of danger. 'I sometimes feel that we lack the necessary initiative for fighting the war,' he wrote in May 1943 after a heavy air-raid on Duisburg and the end of the fighting in Tunis. 'Much criticism now appears in the letters reaching us. Morale among the masses is so low as to be rather serious. Even people of good will are now worried about the future.'[2] It was in such an atmosphere that the Germans were to go on to hear Hitler's voice, not on the German radio but on the BBC, telling them that Stalingrad would never fall when it actually had fallen.[3]

Taking the contest as a whole, there were many curious symmetries of pattern. Thus, during the last months of the war, the BBC produced its vivid *War Reports* from Europe, 'pictures in sound', which derived something of their inspiration, though they were certainly not a copy, from the German 'Front Reports' recorded by highly professionalized Propaganda Companies attached to the Armed Forces in the Western campaigns of 1940 and the Russian campaigns of 1941 and 1942. In both cases the programmes were designed to exploit 'those qualities of immediacy and reality which make broadcasting unique as a medium'.[4] 'From a purely professional point of view,' BBC Monitors had remarked of the Front Reports, 'the picture, say, of the Western campaign conveyed . . . day to day . . . constituted a unique journalistic achievement.'[5] *War Report* was even more remarkable in that it was less

[1] Milward, op. cit., p. 153. See also the important article by Goebbels in *Das Reich*, 19 June 1943. Speer himself realized the difficulty of implementing such a policy during the last part of the war and calculated that he committed 60 separate acts of high treason between January and May 1945 (Milward, op. cit., p. 188).

[2] L. P. Lochner (ed.), *The Goebbels Diaries* (1948), pp. 298–9.

[3] See L. Fraser, 'The BBC versus Dr. Goebbels', a talk to the Royal Empire Society, 18 April 1945.

[4] *BBC Monitoring Service Report, 'Outside Broadcasts on the German Home Service', 28 Sept. 1942. Fritzsche made much of the professional skill employed in the 'Front Report' programmes. He noted with pride, for example, how a record of the German entry into Belgium had been rushed to Vienna by a relay of runners, a motor cycle and two aeroplanes, and then telephoned from Vienna to Berlin (Kris and Speier, op. cit., p. 67).

[5] *BBC Monitoring Service Report, 28 Sept. 1942.

contrived, more direct and more regularly broadcast: it represented a kind of broadcasting which would have been inconceivable in Britain in 1939. It reflected, indeed, a far bigger set of changes, so big, indeed, that in June 1945 Sir Allan Powell, Chairman of the BBC's Governors, opened the meeting of the BBC's General Advisory Council, which had not been called together since the summer of 1939, with the words 'it seems almost in another era that we last met'.[1]

Before turning to the many different ways in which the war transformed the position of the BBC inside Britain, it is necessary to insist upon the fact that the Governors and Director-General of the BBC itself believed that the contest with Germany had been won not simply because of verbal eloquence or superior organization but because of superior principles. By the end of the war earlier Nazi talk of the 'power of radio' seemed in retrospect to be as wild and twisted as every other theme in Nazi philosophizing. 'Today,' the *BBC Year Book* stated in 1946, 'we can point to the history of broadcasting in Europe and say that certain good principles in broadcasting have defeated the worst possible principles.'[2] Long before the war ended, the Governors had reaffirmed that 'all foreign language services under their control' after the war would be 'objective and non-propagandist'.[3] Lindley Fraser, who had been willing to talk to Germans during the war about the seriousness of the position for Britain, put his hopes for the future, when freedom was secured,[4] in 'the reputation which the BBC has built up for itself . . . by a healthy realisation of the limits of propaganda' as an important factor in winning the peace.[5]

The organizational changes within the war-time BBC were so great that it was almost impossible for any one single BBC official, including the Director-General, to have an over-all

---

[2] *General Advisory Council, *Minutes*, June 1945; Report of discussion at a Meeting held on 13 June 1945.

[3] *BBC Year Book, 1946*, p. 7.

[4] *Board of Governors, *Minutes*, 14 Dec. 1944.

[5] Lord Halifax's broadcast of 22 July 1940 in reply to Hitler's 'peace proposals' in his speech of 19 July. See also below, p. 231.

[5] L. Fraser, 'The BBC versus Dr. Goebbels', talk to the Royal Empire Society, 18 April 1945. See also his little book *Propaganda* (1957).

view of the whole range of broadcasting problems and opportunities. In addition to the difficulties arising out of stratification—the perpetual and familiar, if sometimes exaggerated,
differences between the 'administrators' and the rest—there
were so many differences of function and location in the war-
time BBC that the sense of corporate unity was never easy to
maintain. Different divisions were widely scattered; as numbers
of staff grew, there was a majority of 'newcomers' in many
parts of the organization and the rhythms of work were
completely changed. Before the war some BBC employees, at
least, thought of Broadcasting House as 'an agreeable,
comfortable, cultured, leisured place, remote from the world
of business and struggle':[1] during the war one temporary
employee at least, George Orwell, thought of its atmosphere
as being 'something half way between a girls' school and a
lunatic asylum'.[2] A little more gently Lionel Fielden, who had
worked with the BBC in its pioneering days, said on his brief
return to the organization that 'I felt rather as if I had been
transferred from the Travellers' Club to the RAC'.[3]

It is notoriously difficult to recreate atmosphere, particularly
since opinions were just as divided at the time as memories are
selective and contradictory after the time. There were many
examples during the Second World War of what Orwell called
in another place 'huge bureaucratic machines of which we are
all part . . . beginning to work creakily because of their mere
size and their constant growth'.[4] The BBC was distinguished
from some of the others by the very substantial measure of
freedom left both to individual units and to individuals, by a
very real opportunity both for creative excitement and the
exchange of ideas, by the feeling of communication not only
with one's kind but with invisible audiences at home and
overseas, and by a sense of immediacy and urgency in relation
to the war effort. Indeed, to a young man, like Alan Bullock,

---

[1] J. Macleod, *A Job at the BBC* (1947), p. 48.

[2] A note in G. Orwell's war-time Diary, 14 March 1942, printed in S. Orwell
and I. Angus (eds.), *The Collected Essays, Journalism and Letters of George Orwell*,
vol. II (1968), p. 411. Yet see his letter written to the head of his section after his
resignation in September 1943, quoted ibid., pp. 315–16.

[3] L. Fielden, *The Natural Bent* (1960), p. 218.

[4] G. Orwell, *Poetry and the Microphone*, written 1943, published as New Saxon
Pamphlet, March 1945, printed in Orwell and Angus, op. cit., pp. 329–36.

who joined the European Service just before the storm broke in 1940, the war-time years in the BBC were 'the time of his life'.[1] He had a sense of 'being a historian, living through history, in history', and his account of the past dwells not on frustration but exhilaration. So too does Edgar Lustgarten's account of his nightly clashes with 'Haw-Haw' in the programme for English-speaking overseas listeners, *Listening Post*.[2] In a different sector of the BBC, Janet Quigley, Talks Producer, felt herself at the very centre of Britain's 'Home Front' and found war-time broadcasting a challenging and, at times, an exciting experience.

Almost all personal views were sectional views, and it was difficult to see around corners or even across corridors. Ogilvie, the first war-time Director-General, was never entirely at home in the organization which he had inherited from Reith and which by 1942 was very different in scale and shape from Reith's BBC. He had no desire to be 'a great white chief', and he disliked all the trappings of office. When he resigned in January 1942, the Governors stated bluntly and unanimously that 'the chief executive control of the BBC under war-time conditions called for different qualities and experience from those suited for peace-time control'.[3]

Ogilvie had been well served by many of the men whom he had inherited from the Reith regime—by his Deputy, Sir Cecil Graves, for example, by Sir Noel Ashbridge, the highly experienced and efficient Controller (Engineering), by Basil Nicolls, Controller (Programmes), by Sir Richard Maconachie (Talks), and by J. B. Clark, who had built up the BBC's Empire Service. There were also younger men of great promise who were obviously assured of an important place in the BBC of the future. The key figure, however, in the *haute politique* of the early years of war-time broadcasting, the man who felt that he knew more of its different bits and pieces than anyone else, was Sir Stephen Tallents, who had joined the BBC in 1936 as Controller (Public Relations) and had served for a time as Director-General Designate of the shadow Ministry

[1] *BBC Script, Alan Bullock, 'The Time of My Life', an interview with Derek Parker, 28 Jan. 1968.

[2] *BBC Script, 'The Time of My Life', 28 Dec. 1969.

[3] *Board of Governors, *Minutes*, 21 Jan. 1942.

of Information in 1938 and early 1939. Tallents was dropped
from this second post in the spring of 1939, but he was always
at Ogilvie's side in the first difficult days of the war when
Malcolm Frost was creating a 'monitoring and digesting'
service from scratch[1] and the BBC was adapting itself to war-
time needs more effectively than the Ministry of Information.
In May 1940 the post of Controller (Public Relations) disappeared, and Tallents became Controller (Overseas) at a
moment when it was evident that the overseas role of the BBC
would be enhanced out of all recognition.[2] He acted as Deputy
Director-General when Graves, the most experienced and most
conservative survivor of the Reithian hierarchy, who had been
appointed to the BBC in the distant days of 1926, was ill.

Tallents has left behind him a number of 'General Notes'
on 'The BBC in War-Time' which reveal how determined he
was, however strong the opposition, to survey the field of
broadcasting as a whole and not to look upon it as a collection
of separate parts. '*Sandbags* in the Hall,' the Notes begin, 'and
sentries', and one of the later chapter headings reads 'The Alien
Staff'. Tallents had an eye for colour and status, and this
section included such memorable remarks as 'The Hungarian
Unit. A duel averted by Duckworth Barker' and 'The Dutch
refugee Government . . . Our doubt about the size of the
studio chair and of the Queen's cushion'.[3] The Notes touch on
the increase in the number of foreign languages broadcast and
on the growth in transmitter power, a task which brought the
engineers into central areas of broadcasting policy making.[4]
They do not reveal, however, the hidden politics which influenced the BBC's position and which led to Tallents's disappearance from the BBC a few months before Ogilvie.
Undoubtedly Sir Allan Powell played an important part in this
period of tension and uncertainty, when the Intelligence services
were growing to a size and importance which dwarfed the BBC.

Before Tallents resigned, to be followed by Ogilvie, several

[1] Ogilvie asked Tallents to supervise this service. Ogilvie to Tallents, 5 Oct.
1939 (Tallents papers).
[2] He had much to do with the reorganization, as he stated in a 'Note of Proposals by S.G.T. on which the BBC was reorganised, May 1st 1940' (Tallents
papers). See below, pp. 257 ff.
[3] Tallents papers: Undated Notes for a History of the BBC in War-time.
[4] See below, pp. 63–5, 347, 355, 483–5.

attempts had been made by the Government to influence the organizational pattern of the BBC. They will be described fully in this volume. Yet they were all based on the frank recognition that the implications of broadcasting in war time were too far-reaching for one man to be able to survey them all, let alone to control them. Thus, when Ivone Kirkpatrick, an ex-diplomat, who had been interested in Britain's propaganda campaigns, became Foreign Adviser to the BBC in February 1941—very much of a newcomer in what was very much of a new and controversial post[1]—it was a necessary part of the arrangement that he should also have a counterpart on the Home side—A. P. Ryan, who became Home Adviser less than a month later. Unlike Kirkpatrick, Ryan knew the BBC from within. He had been appointed by Tallents in 1936, had been associated with him in the shadow Ministry of Information, and had become Controller (Home) in May 1940 when Tallents became Controller (Overseas). Ryan knew as much about the internal operations of the BBC as any man did in 1941, and after the large-scale reorganization in 1942 he was to serve as Controller (News). He stayed with the BBC in this position until 1947.

The coming of Kirkpatrick sealed the fate of Tallents. There was little love between the two men, and Tallents soon lost control of the system he had helped to create. In the meantime, it had been decided to introduce into the Corporation yet another new man, Robert Foot, who was to be the chief architect of the 'reorganization' of 1942, the biggest reshuffle of financial and administrative responsibilities since 1933,[2] which lasted until well after the end of the war. Foot was brought into Broadcasting House during the autumn of 1941 by Brendan Bracken, the Minister of Information. His brief was to inquire into and tidy up the whole organization, yet in his case also the Corporation proved far too big for him to find out quickly about every nook and cranny within it. Foot had been General Manager of the Gas Light and Coke Company, and he was accurately described as a 'businessman of wide experience'.[3] He was greatly helped in his inquiries by

---

[1] See below, pp. 332–4.
[2] See below, pp. 527 ff. See also Briggs, *The Golden Age of Wireless*, pp. 443–7.
[3] *Board of Governors, *Minutes*, 28 Oct. 1941. See below, pp. 359–61.

Gerald Beadle and by Thomas Lochhead, the BBC's Controller (Administration), formerly Chief Accountant, who was fully familiar with the tangled finances of the organization, yet he found the Corporation 'vast and complicated . . . without any real design or planning'.[1]

Before Foot had gone very far with his inquiries, he found himself appointed—new man though he was, or rather new man because he was—Joint Director-General of the BBC on Ogilvie's resignation. This was a very sharp break with the Reithian BBC, for although Reith had expressed complete lack of confidence in Ogilvie, he was even more resolutely opposed to Foot's inquiry and to Foot's appointment. Continuity was represented in a characteristically British way by the appointment of Sir Cecil Graves as the second Joint Director-General. The diarchy which they established was friendly and effective—Foot and Graves thought of themselves as 'partners and friends' and prided themselves on their 'complete understanding'[2]—yet it 'thoroughly baffled the staff'.[3] It was said, unfairly, at the time, that two Director-Generals were necessary, one to say Yes to the Minister of Information, the other to say No to the staff.[4] The very unfairness of the comment is a testimony to the difficulties of communication in an organization which by then employed over ten thousand people scattered in more than two hundred and fifty different establishments.[5]

Although the most difficult period in the constitutional history of the war-time BBC preceded the setting up of the diarchy, the diarchy itself did not last. Graves, who was more concerned than Foot with 'output' or 'production', as Foot preferred to call it, was forced to retire from the BBC on grounds of ill health in September 1943 after it had long become clear that he could not keep up with the pace and strain of the work.[6] For a time thereafter there was no division of labour and Foot

---

[1] Foot Manuscript, p. 139.

[2] See Foot's remarks about Graves in an obituary notice, *The Times*, 16 Jan. 1957.

[3] M. Gorham, *Sound and Fury* (1948), p. 109.

[4] Macleod, op. cit., p. 151.

[5] The 10,000 figure was reached between October and December 1941. For figures, see Appendix A.

[6] Foot Manuscript, p. 174.

reigned on his own. It was significant that he chose an engineer as his Deputy Director-General. Noel Ashbridge, Controller (Engineering), had first been appointed to the BBC, like Graves, in 1926, and in 1943 he inspired immense respect and prestige not only among engineers but among everyone who had worked intimately with him inside the BBC and on official committees. Foot was well aware that 'if the engineering staff at all levels had failed to provide efficiently for the really terrific expansion of broadcasting . . . or had failed to maintain [the service] without any serious interruption . . . not the most wonderful system of financial and administrative control, or the most highly expert programme staff could have saved it'.[1] He also knew that Ashbridge, like other senior officials of the pre-war BBC, was worried that the future of the service might be jeopardized by 'financial control and restrictions imposed by the Treasury'.[2]

Just as significant, nonetheless, as Foot's choice of Ashbridge was his effort to find outside the ranks of the BBC a man of ideas, drive, and influence who could deal with 'output'. Since he felt that he had been called to the BBC as a war-time task and he had no desire to stay there for ever, the choice that he made was of strategic importance not only in relation to the war but in relation to what was to come after it. It was of the utmost importance that he chose for the new job of Editor-in-Chief an experienced newspaper man, William Haley, who joined the BBC in November 1943; and it was Haley who succeeded Foot as Director-General in March 1944.[3] Thereafter, during the last stages of the war, the BBC had a Director-General who, like Reith, was interested in and had become knowledgeable about every aspect of the Corporation and who was at the same time by instinct and by policy outward-looking. Given the state of the war, he was more interested from the start in how the BBC would fare at the end of the war than in its pattern of war-time activities which by then had been securely established within a context of freedom.

In considering the pattern of activities in detail, it is important to note how little many employees of the BBC, let alone the

---

[1] Foot Manuscript, p. 176.
[2] Ibid., p. 177.
[3] See below, pp. 552-5.

people from outside who broadcast regularly, knew about the
haute politique of the Corporation. Charles Hill, the 'Radio
Doctor', has written convincingly of how he never came into
contact 'with the higher august échelons'. 'The responsibility
for talks rested entirely on the producer of a particular talk or
series and, because of the remarkably high quality of producers,
the system worked very well. . . . It is on the quality of those
at this level that success most depends.'[1] Many new people
entered the BBC at the producer level during the war as the
BBC lost much of the sense of 'self sufficiency' which had made
Broadcasting House something of an 'enclosed world' in 1939.[2]
It was characteristic of the war-time period, indeed, that the
BBC's Registry, which existed to serve the whole organization,
moved no less than five times.

Naturally there were tensions in the process, and concern
was often expressed about the effect of growth and movement
on the *esprit de corps* of the Corporation. 'A great many people
in the Corporation,' the Director of Publicity complained to
the Deputy Director-General in the summer of 1941, 'and
especially those who work outside London, lack a sense of
"common purpose"'; 'one-ness' he called it later. 'Many of
them are newcomers, drafted, it may be, to a remote part of
the country, and they have no knowledge of the extent and the
objective of the Corporation's war-time work, outside their
own circumscribed sphere of action. Old servants of the Corporation, used to working in London and now at one of our
outside bases, are worse off still. . . . There is, in certain
parts of the country, as our Welfare Officers will confirm, a
very definite spirit of antagonism between the veterans on the
staff and the newly fledged members. The result of this lack
of "bind" inside the Corporation structure is uncertainty
about the value of its work, some not altogether healthy criticism
about the BBC as an institution, and a certain absence of pride
in, and understanding of, the direction and the ideals which are
involved in the job which the Corporation has to do at the
present time.'[3]

---

[1] Lord Hill of Luton, *Both Sides of the Hill* (1964), p. 118.
[2] See H. Grisewood, *One Thing at a Time* (1968), p. 121.
[3] *Memorandum from the Director of Publicity, Kenneth Adam, to the Deputy
Director-General, 26 Sept. 1941.

The infusion of newcomers, particularly at the top, was a greater source of strength than some 'old servants of the Corporation' were usually prepared to admit; others within the Corporation welcomed the 'new hands' and the way in which the BBC was 'breaking into new fields, doing things in new ways, and making use of a lot of people who would never have come to the BBC but for the war'.[1] Whatever their attitudes, they were forced to admit that there had undoubtedly been a change in style. It was expressed lightly in a verse written by a member of the staff during the period:

> 'Once any taint of misdemeanour
> Upset the Corporation's tenour;
> But times have changed almost completely;
> 'Tis now no sin to sin discreetly;
> And final sign of moral falling—
> Evesham may say it's "London Calling".'

Evesham was one of the new war-time centres of BBC activity.[2] Wood Norton Hall, near Evesham, once the home of the Duke of Orleans, now nicknamed Hogsnorton in tribute to Gillie Potter, had been bought in April 1939, and it was to Evesham that the first party of BBC 'evacuees' moved on 29 August 1939. Soon afterwards the Variety and Religious Broadcasting Departments, along with the BBC orchestra, the Children's Hour team, and other sections of the Corporation, moved to Bristol. Administrators and programme makers were suddenly forced into closer relationships with each other than there had been since the early days of Savoy Hill: there were also close relations between engineers and administrators in the Premises and Equipment Liaison Committee.[3] While in Broadcasting House itself, therefore, the war was associated with sandbags, sentries, bunks in the basement and before long bombs, for the BBC as a whole it meant dispersal. There was, indeed, a whole sequence of moves, some of which are described in more detail in the history which follows. In April 1941 28.6 per cent of the total staff was still at Evesham, 12.9 per cent at Bristol, 6.2 per cent at Oxford, 6 per cent at Bangor,

---

[1] Gorham, op. cit., p. 101.
[2] See Briggs, *The Golden Age of Wireless*, p. 652.
[3] R. Wade, typewritten manuscript, 'Early Life in the BBC', ch. 9.

4.4 per cent at Manchester, and 4.1 per cent at Glasgow. Bedford was to be another centre—for Music and Religion. In London itself a whole range of buildings was used including 'Maida Vale', Bedford College, 200 Oxford Street and, after 1941, Bush House. The adventures of the staff either in blitzed London or in the remote provinces belong more to a picaresque novel—it is surprising that no such novel has been written—than to a general history, but it is impossible to understand the story without taking them into account. The first fortnight's menus at Bush House are said to have consisted almost entirely of coffee and kippers.[1] 'Do not confuse billets with lodgings,' the BBC's Defence Executive told the evacuated members of the staff tersely in 1940. 'The lodger is desirous and desired. You are a billetee; you probably don't want to live in a billet. Remember that it is even more probable that the billetor doesn't want you.'[2]

Given the dispersal, the influx of new members of staff and the timetable of war, it is not surprising that the BBC as a whole refused to take too seriously its twenty-first anniversary in 1943. The Director of Programme Planning, Godfrey Adams, who had started his BBC career as an announcer, insisted that while one or two of the early BBC broadcasts should be 're-created', emphasis should be placed throughout 'on the maturity of broadcasting which has now reached its majority, and not on its early babblings'. If there was to be any talk at all about the anniversary, 'let us have some grand broadcasting and serious talk about broadcasting, what it has to do and what it has done since it went to war at the comparatively youthful age of seventeen'.[3] A little nearer the appointed date—14 November[4]—he added, 'the event will probably be marked in programmes, but the size of the cake and the dimension of the candles will be dependent on other and possibly greater happenings in this big, big world'.[5]

[1] John Gray to the author, 29 April 1969.
[2] *Defence Executive to All Staff, 7 May 1940.
[3] *G. D. Adams to Nicolls, 6 April 1943.
[4] *There was protracted, voluminous, and somewhat acrimonious correspondence with a listener, as to whether this was the right date. The correspondent suggested 1 November, for on that date in 1922 licences were on sale, or 3 November, for then there had been a special broadcast demonstration from the Polytechnic, linking London, Birmingham, and Bristol.
[5] *Adams to J. E. C. Langham, 19 June 1943.

1. The Board of Governors, March 1943

(*a*) A Broadcast
by Churchill (in a
London pub)

(*b*) A Broadcast by
Churchill (in the
Trocadero
Restaurant)

(*c*) A School
Broadcast

2. Listening in 1941

(*a*) 'Try some of the German stations—we might get a crooner.'
Cartoon from *Punch*, 19 August 1942

(*b*) 'I always leave it tuned-in to Berlin—and waste the enemy's fuel.'
Cartoon from *Punch*, 16 December 1942

3. Cross Listening

(*a*) Churchill

(*b*) J. B. Priestley

4. At the Microphone

A Programme Policy Meeting formally decided that the anniversary should not receive great prominence.[1] It was aware that there had been such sharp breaks with pre-war broadcasting that there could be no straight return after the war ended to the conditions which had prevailed when it started. The appointment of Haley as Director-General in March 1944 coincided with a growing general interest in the role of a post-war BBC, which, as we have seen, was Haley's main concern even at the time. Because of the extent of the war-time transformation, he was able to think and to plan within a pattern which was already markedly different from that of 1939.

Because organizational changes in broadcasting during the war took place within a quite different governmental and administrative context from that of pre-war years, this third volume in the history of British broadcasting necessarily diverges from the two earlier volumes in its themes, in its range, and in its treatment. The pre-1939 BBC could be studied mainly on its own, with references, when necessary, to external relations with the Post Office and Treasury. By contrast, no account of what happened between 1939 and 1945 would be complete without persistent reference first to the Ministry of Information, which moved to Bloomsbury in September 1939 and which was concerned throughout the war with home broadcasting and, along with the Foreign Office and other agencies, with large sectors of overseas broadcasting; second, to a cluster of ministries and departments, some in London, some operating secretly in the country, which were responsible for the supervision or control of broadcasting to enemy countries; third, to those home ministries, like Food and Health, which were interested in good public relations; fourth, to the Armed Forces. At many points, indeed, the whole apparatus of government, greatly extended as it was, impinged more or less directly on the BBC.

In most of its activities the BBC was 'officially guided' by the Ministry of Information, yet the Ministry itself never fully established its claims until July 1941 when Brendan Bracken became Minister. On the eve of the change, Ryan, who knew

*Programme Policy Meeting, *Minutes*, 1 Oct. 1943.

as much about the Ministry as he did about the BBC, described it vividly as 'a sop to Cerberus', and added that 'the history of animal management contains no more dismal record of failure. No dog has been stopped barking by the Ministry of Information. The public are sceptical and unimpressed. It irritates the newspapers. Its relations with the BBC have not been happy. Government departments watch it with a jealous and distrustful eye. Parliament has not been impressed, and, if rumour speaks truly, it has not won the affections of the Cabinet. This is not the fault of the Ministry, but of the State.'[1] Its problems are not fully discussed in this volume—they would require an equally substantial history[2]—but in so far as they affected both the context and mood of broadcasting they can never be ignored.

Ministry and BBC—which might have been very closely interlocked if the first plans drawn up before the war had been followed[3]—shared the same purpose—'to explain the significance of events as they occur; to keep the essential issues before the nation; to inspire determination to see the war through; to reflect the personal experience of the man and woman in the front line; and to tell the ordinary citizen what he must do, and how and why, to cope with the practical problems that confront him in the new conditions of total war'.[4] In practice, however, there was room for both individual and institutional friction.

Relations were obviously at their best when there was a recognition of common interest—for example, in the collection and speedy dissemination of news; in the channelling of information through the Ministry and not through different Government departments; and in the assertion of the fundamental 'right to know and to know immediately all details as to the progress of the war'.[5] The fact that both BBC and Ministry

---

[1] *Ryan to Walter Monckton, 4 June 1941.
[2] There is no history of the Ministry in the Official Histories of the War.
[3] See below, p. 85.
[4] *Quoted in BBC Report to the General Advisory Council (1945), p. 3. BBC paper on War-time Propaganda, Dec. 1939: 'The Corporation regards the prosecution of the War as the most important objective of broadcasting at the present time ... [through] increasing generally the moral and material resources of the British public to bear the strain of war and to carry it through to a successful end.'
[5] *Ryan to Monckton, 10 Sept. 1941.

had common enemies—'statesmen, civil servants and leaders in the Fighting Services' who treated 'news as a nuisance' and propaganda as 'a cheap charlatan game'—very often drew them closer together.

Relations were obviously at their worst when the Government became uneasy about the constitutional position of the BBC, tried to urge the Ministry to establish tight control or even contemplated a complete take-over. 'Mutual exasperation' was then the order of the day.[1] There were many signs of this in 1940. When Churchill became Prime Minister, he asked Duff Cooper, his first Minister of Information, for a note for circulation to the Cabinet on the relations between the Ministry and the BBC.[2] Although Duff Cooper soon satisfied himself that 'machinery now exists' whereby 'complete control' could be exercised in relation to political subjects and news reporting,[3] complaints continued to be made during the autumn of 1940 at 'the higher levels of state' that the BBC was resistant to official directives.[4] Duff Cooper himself, when challenged in Parliament in March 1941, admitted that there had been a strong case ten months before for 'an entire re-organization of the system of foreign broadcasting' but went on to point out that 'it is difficult to reform your army on a new basis in the middle of the battle'.[5] In the course of further, often fierce, debates about British propaganda during the summer and autumn of 1941, the Parliamentary Secretary to the Ministry went further still in emphasizing the extent of control. When asked whether a remark he had made implied that the Governors of the BBC were no longer responsible for 'any part of the BBC's activities connected with the war', he replied laconically, 'I think that the Hon. Member may assume that that is what is intended by my answer.'[6]

[1] *Note by Ryan, 11 July 1941.
[2] *Ogilvie to Powell, 24 May 1940.
[3] *Hansard*, vol. 361, col. 1240. In a Memorandum of 20 May 1940 he wrote: 'The BBC have accepted hitherto and will continue to accept general guidance from the Ministry and will bow to our decisions, having made their observations.'
[4] See below, pp. 330–2.
[5] *Hansard*, vol. 370, col. 549. He began by saying that 'we are all aware that insufficient vision was shown before the war in making the necessary preparation for expansion in this direction, just as there was a lack of foresight in so many other directions'.
[6] *Hansard*, vol. 374, col. 583.

All such statements require to be put in their context: they must be subject also to serious qualifications as statements of fact even in relation to the times when they were made. The BBC knew that although it was bound by 'silken cords', which could sometimes feel like 'chains of iron',[1] it retained throughout the war a very substantial measure of independence. The year 1941 marked the low point in relations both with the Ministry and the Government, but even in that year, when much was in question besides the constitutional position of the BBC, most BBC employees, not least in the European Services, thought of themselves neither as government officials nor as paid 'propaganda warriors' but simply as broadcasters. Many of them were as critical of the Ministry of Information as some officials in the Ministry were of them. They believed that if the 'labour of policy determination' were undertaken more effectively at 'a high level', their own work as directors, producers, talks assistants and, above all, as purveyors of news would be even more productive than it was. They argued, indeed, that there was more 'technical equipment' and 'efficiency' in the Corporation than there was in Malet Street.[2]

From the time that Bracken took over and showed what a Minister of Information close to the Prime Minister and assisted by two very able secretaries—Bernard Sendall and Alan Hodge—and a supremely efficient Director-General, Sir Cyril Radcliffe, could do, there was no question of 'taking over' the BBC. There were further changes and 'reorganizations', but they were the result of reasoned decision-making on both sides not of uncertainty or panic. Confrontation gave way to co-operation. Gradually, as a sign of the new dispensation, functions previously exercised by the Ministry began to be passed back to the 'reorganized' BBC. In March 1942 Radcliffe suggested to Graves that the BBC should take over direct responsibility from the Ministry for the carrying out of broadcasting official government publicity on the home front,[3] and the Home Broadcasting Division of the Ministry which had been brought into existence during the early months of the

---

[1] A phrase of Sir Allan Powell, 8 Dec. 1943.

[2] *Memorandum from W. A. Sinclair to R. A. Rendall, 23 June 1941, passing on a copy of a paper he had written on 20 Nov. 1940.

[3] *Radcliffe to Graves, 23 March 1942.

war[1] 'off-loaded' much of its work on to a new Propaganda Unit set up within the BBC.[2] It was characteristic of the changed balance that this time the BBC—through Graves—urged that the Ministry should not give up all its powers. Ministerial broadcasts, he suggested, should continue to be the responsibility of the Ministry, since 'the past procedure has been a very convenient one as the Minister has been able to boom people off and to keep government departments in control'.[3]

The Minister himself chose the occasion of the twenty-first birthday celebrations of the BBC to assert the independence of the Corporation. 'Some people,' he said, 'think there is a great mystery between the Ministry of Information and the BBC. . . . I shall attempt to pierce that mystery. At the beginning of this war the Government were given power to interfere in the affairs of every institution in this country including the BBC. And though I am always willing to take responsibility for all the BBC's doings, I have refused to interfere in the policies of the Corporation. The Governors and many members of the staff often consult with the Ministry of Information and sometimes they condescend to ask us for our advice and we give it for what it is worth. But I can say from my own personal experience that no attempt has ever been made by the Government to influence the news-giving or any other programme of the BBC. In fact, I am constantly advising my friends in the BBC of the desirability of being independent and of being very tough with anyone who attempts to put pressure upon you.'[4]

Bracken was talking mainly about home broadcasting, and the Ministry of Information was not the only official agency concerned with 'guidance' and 'control'. At the beginning of the war a Department for Enemy Propaganda, Electra House, which had been set up in 1938, dealt with propaganda to Germany, with the Foreign Office, through its Political Intelligence Department (PID), enjoying the last word in relation to its operations. There was a change, however, in

[1] See below, pp. 101 ff.
[2] *Circulating Memorandum from the Director-General, 26 May; J. B. Clark to Foot and Graves, 17 June 1942.
[3] *Graves to Foot, 24 March 1942.
[4] *Brendan Bracken's Speech, 8 Dec. 1943.

the early summer of 1940 after Britain had been cut off from Western Europe. The Ministry of Economic Warfare now began to be directly involved in the complex of activities which came to be called 'political warfare' along with the operations of a newly founded Special Operations Executive, SOE. Until March 1942, therefore, when the system was changed, there was ample scope for divergences of opinion and tactics between Ministry of Information, Foreign Office, PID, and Ministry of Economic Warfare. There were times, indeed, when there was 'more political warfare on the home front than against the enemy'.[1]

In this story, as in that of the BBC, the year 1941 was critical. After protracted discussion in the Cabinet and what was often bitter argument in the House of Commons, Churchill initialled a new agreement about propaganda machinery in August 1941, one day after returning from his meeting with Roosevelt when they had signed the Atlantic Charter. The agreement provided for regular meetings between Eden, the Foreign Secretary, Dalton, the Minister of Economic Warfare, and Bracken, and for the institution of an operational committee under the chairmanship of Bruce Lockhart, a Foreign Office appointment. Early in 1942 when Dalton moved to the Board of Trade, responsibility shifted to the two other Ministers, and Political Warfare Executive (PWE) was formally constituted with Bruce Lockhart as Director. It included Rex Leeper, head of the Foreign Office's Political Intelligence Department, one of the first officials in Britain to interest himself in problems of propaganda, and Brigadier Dallas Brooks, head of the Military Wing of the Department for Enemy Propaganda, who had close ties with the Chiefs of Staff. A direct link with the BBC was established when Ivone Kirkpatrick, who, as we have seen, had been appointed Foreign Adviser to the BBC in February 1941, was invited to join the Executive. At the same time PWE moved into Bush House which by then housed the European Service of the BBC.[2]

PWE was never an easy organization to manage. It had diverse responsibilities and it called no men of diverse gifts. It depended for its success no flair and imagination as much as

---

[1] Bruce Lockhart, op. cit., p. 96.
[2] See below, p. 418.

on team work. 'Black' broadcasting alone required an unprecedented combination of talents. From the date of its foundation; however, the daily problems of European and Overseas 'white' broadcasting were handled more systematically than they had been before, with recognized, if not always accepted, routines. The drafting of 'directives' and the attempts to secure their implementation became such a regular feature of broadcasting policy that much of the detail of this volume is concerned with the relationships between PWE and the various Foreign Sections of the BBC. There were some problems which always confronted PWE which were very similar to problems confronted within the European and Overseas Services of the BBC. How far, for example, should it centralize its operations, how far should it regionalize them? Yet in retrospect it seems not only inevitable that there had to be *both* centralization and regionalization but that the very debate about such questions often produced the right kind of creative tension. PWE, like the Ministry of Information and the Psychological Warfare Division of SHAEF, which was first set up in Algiers in 1942,[1] deserves a history of its own, but it cannot be left out of the story told in this volume, even though its archives are still not open to examination.

In the tangle of dealings between on the one hand different services of the BBC and the BBC as a whole and on the other PWE, also sectionalized, the BBC had certain real advantages. It broadcast directly on a far bigger scale than the cluster of 'black' stations managed by PWE. It had to handle the news immediately as it came through, and in the case of overseas news, in particular, Newsome's directives and daily news conferences were impossible to 'control' by PWE. With Kirkpatrick in Bush House, the BBC was sure of something more than mere protection. PWE, of course, had advantages also, particularly direct access to all kinds of intelligence, fuller knowledge of operational criteria, and the ability to employ the most unorthodox or the most devious methods in the most complete secrecy and on a large scale.

In fact, fewer difficulties arose in practice in the relations

---

[1] See D. Lerner (ed.), *Sykewar, Psychological Warfare against Germany, D-Day to V.E. Day* (1949). PWD/SHAEF later moved with Eisenhower to London and its forward sections later moved to France. See below, pp. 673, 681.

between BBC and PWE than might have been expected.
Before PWE was set up, a German broadcasting expert,
Eduard Dietze, in what a BBC official called a 'pretty well
documented' article, had argued that by contrast with Germany
Britain had 'commissions and committees dealing with
questions [relating to foreign broadcasting] which call for
rapid and binding decisions by a single responsible person,
based, of course, on the opinion of experts'.[1] After 1942 there
was far less truth in the charge. During the last years of the
war PWD/SHAEF was the pivotal agency, gearing its operations directly to war needs, and it is significant that Newsome
left the BBC for SHAEF in 1944 to manage broadcasting
operations in recaptured Luxembourg.

On the home front, the BBC had intimate if sometimes
chequered relations with almost every department of the
administration, and there was certainly no Goebbels here to
survey the whole scene or to seek to pull the levers. In theory
the 'propaganda campaigns' which the ministries felt it necessary to launch—digging for victory, making do and mending,
'beating the coupon', anti-sneezing, keeping fit, recruiting
women for the Forces or for industry and so on—were the
responsibility of the Ministry of Information, but in practice
each Ministry had its Public Relations Division, and the
officials who worked there established their own relations
directly with people inside the BBC.[2] Broadcasting was
considered to be such an effective medium that it was easy to
forget that a radio audience is not necessarily a captive audience
and that a minister or a civil servant, however urgent his
message, is not necessarily a star broadcaster. That good
speakers were chosen and that some of them established their
reputation as a result was largely a tribute to producers inside
the BBC. The producers sometimes had to insist upon their
professional knowledge and experience even to the BBC's own

---

[1] *Farquharson commented on Dietze's article, which had appeared in *Rundfunk
Archiv*, April 1941, in a note of 15 Oct. 1941.

[2] *A BBC Circular on 'Facilities', Nov. 1943, describes the Facilities Unit
(London)—Liaison between Services, Ministries and the BBC. It refers to pro-
cedures 'in regard to permissions for broadcasts' affecting *inter alia* Fisheries, the
Merchant Navy, Agricultural Matters, Fuel Campaigns, Ministry of Production,
Ministry of Supply, Ministry of Aircraft Production and the Royal Family.

Board of Governors. Thus, George Barnes wrote bluntly in January 1942 that 'the success of a series of talks depends not upon the decision of a Board but on the enthusiasm which the producer is able to impart to his speaker'.[1]

The first moves of the war set the pattern. Thus, as early as 4 September 1939, John Green in the BBC's Talks Department was urging the need for 'farming and gardening talks', 'not a question of orders and instructions so much as of inspiration to cultivate', and Sir Richard Maconachie, the BBC's Director of Talks, who figures prominently in this volume, was reporting that he had told the Minister of Agriculture that initiatives should come from him or from the Cabinet through the Ministry of Information.[2] The Ministry of Health was even worried that the first war-time instructions which it had given to hospitals—to be sure that they did not fill up their beds with civilians when soldiers and air raid victims might need them urgently—were being implemented 'with excessive zeal'.[3] Gardening and health talks were to be among the BBC's war-time successes: so, too, were talks on food, notably the *Kitchen Front* series which started in June 1940.[4] There were in all, it was estimated, 1,196 war-time broadcasts on food.[5] Some other subjects seemed to suffer by comparison, and as the war went by the BBC itself tried to redress the balance. 'I feel the Board of Trade, mainly due to its own feebleness, has had rather a bad deal in the campaign field,' Miss Quigley wrote in 1943,[6] and although the BBC was aware that ineffectual Board of Trade propaganda might rebound on itself not on the Board of Trade,[7] soon afterwards a series of talks was launched.

In the case of each series of talks there had to be detailed

---

[1] *Barnes to Maconachie, 30 Jan. 1942. The Governors on this occasion expressed the opinion that the evening was not an appropriate time for discussing health (Maconachie to Graves, 31 Jan. 1942) and insisted on having a 'light' alternative on the BBC's second programme to a projected Home Service series on the Human Body.

[2] *Green to Maconachie, 4 Sept.; Maconachie to Green, 5 Sept. 1939.

[3] *Janet Quigley to Maconachie, 20 Sept. 1939.

[4] The first title suggested was 'The Food Front'. Howard Marshall, the well-known broadcaster, then working at the Ministry of Food, said that his Ministry was very keen on the title 'The Kitchen Front'. *(Marshall to Miss Quigley, 6 June 1940.) See below, p. 324.

[5] Jean Gordon to Dorothy Bridgman, 4 June 1945.

[6] *Miss Quigley to Maconachie, 2 April 1943.

[7] *Richard Sharp to Ryan, 9 June 1943.

discussion—sometimes not unlike the kind which now takes place in an advertising agency; consultation with outside bodies, like the Central Council for Health Education or the Women's Group on Public Welfare; and much coming and going with speakers, would-be speakers, and influential experts who knew the names of other speakers. The mood of war-time broadcasting in this huge area of concern is captured in odd phrases in surviving letters and memoranda. 'You will remember,' Miss Quigley wrote to Maconachie in April 1940, 'that when we originally discussed early morning talks, the subjects we agreed as probably suitable were health, holiness and marketing. Marketing we cover regularly. Holiness we attempt occasionally. But health so far has not been tried.'[1] It was later in the war that Charles Hill emerged as 'the Radio Doctor', insisting within the context of what he later called 'a siege economy [where] the perils were immense, and we all had a feeling that we belonged to one another',[2] that 'ill health is plugged, but health is not' and that 'it is no more possible to deal with health than it is to deal with economics in a few broadcasts, however clearly expressed and persuasively put'.[3]

'Sometimes I feel almost desperate now,' was one *cri de coeur* from inside the Ministry of Food in 1941, 'over the limitations of speakers and the alterations which are made by Colwyn Bay [headquarters of the Ministry] at the last moment. There is hardly anything left to talk about except oatmeal, carrots and potatoes.'[4] A few weeks later another Ministry official was inquiring about a sponsored talk being devoted to vegetables and not to scones.[5] Earlier in the war, on censorship grounds, the producer of *The Northcountry Woman*, a magazine programme produced in Manchester, was told to delete the sentence 'Even if pipes are still frozen and our families have colds there is some faint stirring of spring about'.[6]

The juxtaposition of campaign 'themes' and the difficulty

---

[1] *Miss Quigley to Maconachie, 22 April 1940.
[2] Lord Hill, op. cit., p. 107.
[3] *Hill to Barnes, then Director of Talks, 18 Nov. 1941.
[4] *Lionel Fielden, a well-known and experienced figure in broadcasting history, then employed in the Ministry of Food, to Miss Quigley, 11 Feb. 1941.
[5] *Letter of 16 Aug. 1941.
[6] *Barnes to Roger Wilson, 27 Jan. 1940.

of doing justice to them all, is illustrated in a note of 1943. 'Owing to the sudden indisposition of [the speaker] it is not possible to broadcast the "Mend and Make Do" programme at 6.30 p.m. in the Home Service this evening. You will remember that the request came from the Board of Trade. . . . This evening we have decided to repeat the Squander Bug programme, which was broadcast on 15 June. Fortunately this is recorded, and I gather that it was well liked by the National Savings Committee.'[1]

A study of the BBC's relations with the Home ministries is a necessary element in the social, if not in the administrative, history of the war. Relations between the BBC and the Armed Services, however, raised other questions, particularly concerning the flow of news. Military items broadcast both in Home and Foreign Language bulletins sometimes irritated the War Office, and in December 1940, for example, thirteen complaints relating to the period from February to October 1940 were transmitted to the BBC via the Director-General of the Ministry of Information.[2] At that time the BBC was broadcasting sixty news bulletins a day so that the number of complaints was proportionately less great than appeared on the surface. Formal liaison had been established with the War Office in January 1940, but the duties of the newly appointed Army Liaison Officer were not extended beyond the Overseas News Department until July 1940. Under Major R. S. P. Mackarness, who served in this office from March 1942 until December 1945, there was close co-operation concerning an increasingly wide variety of functions.[3]

In a different capacity Major A. E. (Eric) Maschwitz, who had joined the BBC in 1926 as a member of Outside Broadcasts, and who had served as editor of the *Radio Times* and left the Corporation in 1937 as Director of Variety, was Head of a War Office Broadcasting Section within the Army Directorate

[1] *James Langham, then Assistant Director Programme Planning, to Maconachie, 3 Aug. 1943.

[2] *F. Pick, then Director-General of the Ministry of Information (see below, pp. 330–2), to Ogilvie, 2 Dec. 1940.

[3] *Note by Major R. S. P. Mackarness on a Memorandum to Langham, 17 June 1942.

of Welfare and Education.[1] He had been employed earlier by
the Army as the officer in charge of the distribution of wireless
sets to the troops.[2] Maschwitz was involved in many War
Office assignments relating to Army entertainment at home and
overseas, but from January 1943 onwards an Army Broadcasting
Liaison Committee, meeting at first each week, dealt with
everything from the 'coordinated use of Army concert parties'
to a special series of not very popular broadcasts called 'The
Army Voice'.[3] From March 1944 onwards the Committee was
replaced by a new Inter-Services Advisory Committee which
included representatives of all three Services. Norman Collins,
one of the liveliest of the new men inside the BBC and Head of
its new General Overseas Service, was chairman.[4]

Because the Army covered such a cross-section of the nation
—it too had its 'old guard' and its newcomers—liaison inevitably
implied, as the war went on, discussion of a large range of
issues from recruitment and morale to specific items in entertainment and education.[5] Yet not all the earlier difficulties
in the handling of news about military operations were
successfully smoothed away. It seemed for a time, for example
in 1942, that GHQ (Middle East) was seeking unduly to
influence BBC assessments of the military situation in its
reporting of the conduct of operations.[6] Later in 1942 and
1943 there were problems in North Africa; and in 1944 and
1945 there were difficulties in Normandy,[7] while at the same
time complaints were being received from Generals Alexander,
Harding, and Leese in Italy that *War Report* had too much to
say about Normandy and too little about Italy.[8]

The BBC had fewer difficulties with the Air Ministry and
with the RAF than with the Army or with the Admiralty.

[1] See below, p. 134; *Major-General H. Willans to Graves, 20 June 1942.
[2] See E. Maschwitz, *No Chip on My Shoulder* (1957), p. 137.
[3] This programme started experimentally on 18 Oct. 1943 with the title 'War
Office Calling the Army'. Its predecessor had been 'John Hilton Talking', with
one of the best-known pre-war broadcasters turning his attention from unemployment and social welfare to Army morale.
[4] *Programme Policy Meeting, *Minutes*, 17 March 1944. See also below, p.
648.
[5] See below, pp. 311–13, 707.
[6] *Note by Ryan, 12 June 1942; Ryan to Radcliffe, 9 July 1942. See below,
p. 328.
[7] See below, p. 655.
[8] *Lord Burnham to Haley, July 1944.

Although there were early complaints about the lack of detail, particularly concerning losses, in RAF communiqués,[1] and later grumbles that air power was not being given enough attention in relation to the Mediterranean area,[2] the war ended with Air Marshal Sir Richard Peck thanking Ryan for the co-operative spirit in which the BBC had always treated RAF affairs.[3] By contrast, at many moments during the war relations between BBC and Admiralty had been far from co-operative, particularly during the early days, when Churchill was First Lord. The BBC was accused of 'unrelieved pessimism', and criticism of its bulletins was a feature of the meetings even of the War Cabinet. For its part, the BBC criticized the grudging divulgence of news on the part of the Admiralty. Relations improved as the war went on, and there were seldom any arguments concerning broadcasts relating to naval affairs or designed for men serving in the Navy. The only outstanding problem was making sure that news relating to the Navy could be broadcast as quickly as possible—good news as well as bad.

Changes in the attitude towards the broadcasting of the News—both on the part of the broadcasters and of listeners—were part of a bigger complex of changes which made the war-time years critical years in the history of broadcasting. However great the strains to which the BBC was subjected, these were years of advance both in the arts and techniques of radio. The Second World War was the first war in which broadcasting played a major part.[4] Less time had elapsed between the appearance of the national sound broadcasting systems and the outbreak of the war than has subsequently elapsed between the advent of television and the world of the 1970s. From our present vantage point the absence of television as a factor in the Second World War stands out: the war was a war of words rather than a war of images; and as André Malraux,

[1] *R. T. Clark, Senior News Editor, to Nicolls, 31 March 1940.
[2] *Moore to Wing-Cdr. Beauman, 17 May 1943.
[3] *Peck to Ryan, 13 Oct. 1945.
[4] Wireless telegraphy had been used on a strictly limited scale between 1914 and 1918—for espionage and intelligence, for communication across the lines of blockade, for the transmission of President Wilson's peace terms to the Germans, and for the first forays of Bolshevik propaganda.

who has always been keenly interested in techniques and arts of communication, has pointed out, until 1943 few even of the resistance leaders in France had any acquaintance with the face of de Gaulle, the man in whose name they were fighting.[1] In Britain itself the images were often blurred. At the time what was most obvious to contemporaries was the ubiquity of 'the radio war', the unleashing of 'all the tongues of Babel'. 'Three or four times as many stations as there were before the war now clamour to be heard. . . . A tour round the dial is an ear-splitting adventure.'[2] In August 1944 the BBC Monitoring Service was listening to about $1\frac{1}{4}$ million words a day— 300,000 of them in English—in 32 languages.[3] At its peak, it was itself sending out over 30,000 words in 'flash messages' to Government departments, including the War Cabinet, and to BBC News Departments.[4] Each day, indeed, according to Ritchie Calder, its written output in words was equivalent to that of two full-length novels. Daily British radio output in words amounted to 440,000 as early as 1942, 80,000 of them addressed to people at home.[5]

In such conditions it was inevitable not only that broad-casting output would be influenced from outside since it could be monitored by the enemy, but also that in the last resort it would be censored for reasons not of policy but of security. The weather was taboo; so, too, were precise references to places or in certain circumstances to people. John Snagge gave a commentary on a war-time boat race and never mentioned that he could not see how far Cambridge was ahead because the sun was in his eyes: yet Frances Day once made a

[1] A. Malraux, *Antimemoirs* (1968 Eng. tr.), p. 82.

[2] J. W. Drawbell, 'The Battle of the Air', Nov. 1943. For the first talk of a 'radio armaments race' during the 1930s, see S. S. Biro, 'The International Aspects of Radio Control' in *The Journal of Radio Law* (1932); W. Irwin, *Propaganda and the News* (1936); T. Grandin, *The Political Use of Radio* (1939); and A. Huth, *La Radiodiffusion, Puissance Mondiale* (1937).

[3] *C. E. Wakeham to Rendall, paper on the Monitoring Service, Post-War Planning, 16 Aug. 1944.

[4] *BBC Monitoring Service, *Monthly Progress Report* for July 1942. The peak in that record month was 31,383 words. Later peaks were in November 1943— 34,370 words, and in June 1944—41,205 words. Its *Daily Digest* reached a record of 190 pages in October 1942: the average number of words recorded in this summary was 100,000. It was distributed to approximately 600 people. (BBC Monitoring Service, Post-War Review, 29 March 1946.)

[5] *J. C. Thornton to Graves, 24 June 1942.

casual reference to General Montgomery's appearance at a London theatre when there was a censorship stop on reports that he was back in England from France.[1] Mr. Middleton in an unscripted gardening programme managed even to offend security criteria in the last sentences of a talk which was to have been rounded off, if more words were necessary, with references to lettuces and dahlias. 'Now a last word about carnations,' he said instead. 'Some of you find them difficult subjects, but it's because they like lots of lime, so cheer up, the way things are going at the moment there will soon be plenty of mortar rubble about. Just have another go.'[2] In the case of all unscripted programmes—and they were relatively rare— there was a 'switch censor', a censor sitting in the studio or in the control cubicle who could cut off a programme at once. It was the job of the switch censor to watch also for any deviations from prepared scripts: he was in a position to 'fade out' any programme 'instantaneously at need'.[3] The difficulties of switch censorship in some of the foreign-language programmes of the BBC were obvious enough, yet the rules were known to everyone inside the BBC, and everyone was expected to follow them faithfully.[4]

To the historian of British broadcasting the output of the British broadcasters, what was directly communicated over the air, subjected as it was to control and ultimately to censorship, deserves more attention than the institutional relationships between the BBC and other organizations, however much these set the terms in which broadcasting was carried on. Once again the Germans, with their very different balance of output, had their comments to make on the British situation. A German commentator told an Australian and Far Eastern audience in 1942 that 'London goes on with its radio programmes as if nothing had happened—people singing in the shelters; reports from a cricket match; nice and clever people make their talks; there is more dance music than before.' He added generously, 'we must respect them for all this'.[5]

The task of the historian must be to balance what was new

[1] Quoted in M. Gorham, *Sound and Fury* (1948), p. 113.
[2] Information supplied by John Green, Feb. 1969.
[3] *Note on Security prepared for the Ministry of Information, 10 June 1940.
[4] *Note on Security Censorship, 21 Nov. 1941.
[5] Quoted in Rolo, op. cit., p. 114.

and what was old in the war-time pattern of broadcasting. The pre-war philosophy of the BBC was often challenged, as we shall see, but it was not jettisoned. Nicolls, who believed that programme presentation should present the picture of a 'brisk, friendly and efficient BBC',[1] wrote as firmly in January 1941 as he might have done in 1931, that 'the BBC should constantly be trying to raise the standard of public taste, to create an appetite for items of minority appeal and to break down public resistance to certain types of programmes'.[2] The fact that many listeners were content simply 'to turn on the tap', 'a seemingly bad habit', could still be consciously exploited, as it had been to the full before 1939, to introduce them, say, to serious music.[3] The audience for radio drama actually doubled between 1939 and 1945; 'features' established themselves as a new art form with a very genuine sense of communication between creative artist and public.[4] These results were not accidental: they were carefully thought out. 'If broadcasting is not to confine itself perpetually to dance bands and variety programmes,' Lindsay Wellington wrote to Adrian Boult in October 1941, 'neither you nor we dare be frightened of applying to it a civilised and thoughtful scale of values.'[5] This was an important point to make in war time, and it fitted, of course, into a war where 'Art for the People' was canvassed more successfully by the Council for the Encouragement of Music and the Arts (CEMA) than it ever had been before.[6]

At the same time, there were big changes, signposts to a future more controversial than was realized during the war. The Forces Programme, started in February 1940, was a portent: it was to serve, indeed, as the forerunner of the

[1] *Memorandum by Nicolls, 4 April 1941.

[2] *Graves, Note on Presentation and Continuity, 22 Jan. 1941.

[3] *Ibid.

[4] There were changes in technique in this whole department of broadcasting as the multi-small-studio technique of presentation with elaborate dramatic control panels gave way increasingly to single-studio presentation with, if necessary, an adjacent narrator's studio.

[5] *Wellington to Boult, 2 Oct. 1941.

[6] See below, p. 311. For the general background of increasing public demand for the serious arts in war time, see A. Marwick, *Britain in the Century of Total War* (1968), pp. 298–300. See also the *Twentieth Annual Report of the Arts Council of Great Britain* (1961–2).

separately organized Light Programme which Haley was to launch on 29 July 1945. In a world starved of entertainment, it provided the kind of entertainment designed to appeal to very large numbers of people, and by the end of 1942 the audience listening to it was nearly half as large again as that which listened to the Home Service. 'All really minority material,' it was being emphasized, 'should be carried on the Home Service.'[1] The moral was to be drawn after the war in a world which was not starved of entertainment. Even during the war the 'lightening' of programmes had its critics as well as its supporters, and they were often very evenly balanced. A motion that 'the wireless encourages laziness' was defeated in Bradford in 1943 by 41 votes to 37, but a correspondent to a local newspaper did not allow the matter to stand there. 'While we all heartily agree that some BBC programmes have "taught us to endure, to clench our fists and grit our teeth",' he told his bigger audience, 'if one considers what the average person listens to on the Forces Programme, and this a more popular programme today, we cannot appreciate how "the radio has evoked latent talents in our island race".'[2]

The increased significance attached to news output during the war was also to raise controversial issues: it pointed rather to the post-war preoccupation with topicality than followed naturally from what had been the BBC's policy concerning News before 1939. During the 1920s and 1930s the BBC's News services had been authoritative but very restricted in scope and very cautious in tone, and tremendous care had been taken, above all else, not to be drawn into competition with the Press.[3] News talks had been introduced by Ralph Murray, but they were not an integral part of a news service. The change after 1939 was striking. 'Once the News was not of very great importance,' a BBC spokesman remarked, with not too much exaggeration, in 1944. 'Now it occupies the peak hours and has swept culture into the background.'[4] 'I never

[1] *Note by Nicolls, 3 March 1943.   [2] *Yorkshire Observer*, 30 March 1943.
[3] See Briggs, *The Golden Age of Wireless*, pp. 152–60.
[4] *Barrow News*, 8 April 1944, quoting an address by a local BBC representative.
*The first report of the Defence Sub-Committee of 11 Jan. 1939 envisaged an increase in the number of hours allotted to the News from 12 to 21 (80%) within a smaller number of hours for broadcasting as a whole. Talks were to be reduced by 77%, Drama and Features by 75%, and Variety by 60%. See below, p. 95.

read the newspapers. I hear all the news I want over the wireless,' a Kent listener explained.[1] Although the cogent argument continued to be used that since 'radio stimulates the desire for news', there was no conflict between BBC and Press,[2] H. G. Wells, who loved generalizations, spoke out boldly to a national conference in 1943 that 'the day of the newspaper was done'.[3] The nine o'clock News reached an audience of between 43 and 50 per cent of the total population,[4] and there were many times during the war when any snatch of news was more eagerly awaited than even the slickest entertainment.[5]

The change in attitudes, not least in the timing of the News, can best be pinpointed in specific examples. Thus, in an important Memorandum to Sir Walter Monckton in June 1940, Ryan, who had much to do with the war-time transformation, referred both to Home and Overseas News policy in language which certainly would not have been used inside the BBC before 1939:

The BBC News works under more sanctions, and therefore more slowly, as well as more accurately, than the Press. Foreign broadcasters work differently. This means that foreign radio stations, both European and American, are frequently ahead of the BBC. Such priority may, and often does, reach the British public, e.g. through Haw-Haw. A case in point is the resignation of M. Reynaud, which came over the tape in this country well before midnight on Sunday, and was used by the Americans and other foreign broadcasters forthwith. Had the BBC been a newspaper it would, without further reference to any outside authority, have given this news at midnight. In fact the news was not given, on the instruction of the Ministry of Information, and a number of telephone calls were immediately received from indignant listeners who had heard the French wireless and were disturbed by the silence of the BBC.

The BBC does not dispute the wisdom of such hold-ups, which are no doubt made judiciously and in the interests of accuracy, but

---

[1] *Tonbridge Free Press,* 8 Jan. 1943.

[2] *Advertisers' Weekly,* 29 April 1943.

[3] *World's Press News,* 25 March 1943. Cf. Hannen Swaffer, ibid., 22 July 1940: 'The defeat of journalism by the BBC continues—and will still go on unless newspaper proprietors take intelligent action.' See also *Journalist,* March 1944: 'Radio journalism has come to stay.'

[4] See the interesting article on 'Some Recent Trends in Listening' by R. J. E. Silvey in *BBC Year Book, 1946,* pp. 26–31.

[5] *The Times,* 28 Sept. 1943, had an interesting article on this subject.

they do show that British broadcasts already work under a handicap. If—and particularly at the present time—further handicaps are to be introduced for no better national reason than 'keeping the Press sweet', broadcasting will not be pulling its weight as a medium of national publicity.[1]

However great the handicaps—and they continued to be formidable throughout the war—there was a remarkable development in News techniques both in the domestic and even more in the overseas News services of the BBC—collecting information through war reporters; increasing the range of outside 'contacts'; introducing recorded insets into News programmes; experimenting with special News programmes; associating comment with fact; above all, gaining an enhanced sense of professionalism. Many of these developments, which had and have their critics, depended upon the introduction into the BBC of experienced journalists from outside, just as some of the developments in entertainment depended upon bringing into the BBC people who had been employed before the war in commercial radio. The 'medium' itself was looked at in a new way, a way which was not to be fully charted until years had elapsed. *War Report*, as we have seen, marked the triumph of a new technique. So, even earlier, did *Radio Newsreel* which was broadcast continuously from July 1940 onwards in the Overseas Services of the BBC. This programme, devised by Peter Pooley and Michael Barkway, was a programme *about* the news of the day. It was deliberately designed to suggest 'immediacy', seeking 'radiogenic stories' and 'sequences' and relying on slick continuity.[2] It, too, was to make its way into the Light Programme in 1945.

What was true of News was true also, in different measure, of Talks, already a BBC staple before 1939, although here the issues were even more complicated. The interest of government departments in getting their messages across to the public and the 'campaign' activities of the Ministry of Information have already been noted: the value of home broadcasting as a 'medium' was clearly appreciated in Whitehall. There was always a danger, however, as Ogilvie saw, that because of 'official' propaganda the BBC would become too closely

---

[1] *Ryan to Monckton, 17 June 1940.
[2] See below, p. 404.

identified with the Government in the eyes of ordinary listeners:[1] its very strength could become a weakness. Much was to be made after the war, indeed, about the fussy role of 'Auntie BBC', a term not employed during the pre-war years, and the fierceness of the reaction—Ogilvie shared it—was an indication of how great the war-time change had been.

Yet inside the BBC itself, the new responsibilities imposed upon the Corporation had seldom been allowed to become oppressive, and it was more often the broadcasters than their powerful clients who held the whip hand. The BBC was always suspicious of professional propagandists even during the early stages of the war when severe limitations were placed on its choice of broadcasters in the name of 'consensus'. 'The future student of history,' Maconachie, then Controller (Home), wrote in 1941, 'will surely be puzzled to find that in the second year of the war the use of such an obviously potent weapon as the microphone was still mainly dependent on the patriotism or good will of individuals who could be persuaded to undertake the broadcasting of talks in their spare time.'[2] During the later stages of the war, emphasis was deliberately placed on the stimulation of controversy. Critics might argue that 'in Broadcasting House we are constantly brought into contact with a wardrobe of swaddling clothes. There is a lack of the real air of energy and of freedom',[3] but that was not how either producers or administrators saw their task. '*To Start You Talking*', the title of a 1943 series for young people, was always one of the objects of the BBC's programme makers.[4] The talking included talk on the programmes themselves. Listener correspondence increased from 2,500 letters a week in 1939 to 4,500 a week in 1943, and there were some weeks when the figure exceeded 6,000.

[1] *Note appended to a letter from J. B. Clark to Maconachie, 26 Feb. 1941. Not every listener was percipient enough to see that 'blame' should be attached in case of doubt not to the BBC, but to the Ministry. (Letter to *The Grocer*, 8 Jan. 1944.)

[2] *BBC Handbook, 1941*, p. 65. For one individual's account, see W. Holt, *I Still Haven't Unpacked* (1953).

[3] *Free Europe*, 19 May 1944. Yet cf. W. L. Andrews in *The Newspaper World*, 10 April 1943: as the fortunes of war turned, it insisted on emphasizing that 'there were several sides to every public question or it would not be a public question'.

[4] See *The Times Educational Supplement*, 14 April 1945, for a review of the book *To Start You Talking*.

During both stages, there was as real and basic a contrast between the BBC and the German RRG in the way in which they dealt with home broadcasting as there was in the way in which they dealt with overseas broadcasting. The volume of serious music put out by RRG might be 'incomparably greater' than that offered by the BBC,[1] but as far as popular entertainment, talks and news were concerned the BBC was far less authoritarian and far less monolithic. German talks on food, cooking and gardening, not to speak of talks about the post-war future,[2]—all essential themes in a protracted war which brought in civilians as well as soldiers[3]—were designed to give orders rather than to stimulate thought or to promote voluntary action. Although the Army knew how to encourage initiative on the part of NCOs, national broadcasting often took the form of 'set pieces'. There was nothing like the interchange which started in the offices of talks assistants and producers inside Broadcasting House and continued until the very moment that programmes were broadcast. In Germany consensus was stressed throughout, and home broadcasting was concerned only with national solidarity. Indeed in the very last broadcast of the war, Count Schwerin von Krosigk, the last war-time Foreign Minister, spoke of 'the idea of the national community, which in the years of the war found its expression in the spirit of comradeship at the front and in readiness to help one another in all the distress which has afflicted the Homeland'.[4]

British broadcasting involved more than this. Through the art and imagination of British producers, indeed, new approaches to talks and discussion programmes were devised throughout the war—the 'Brains Trust' was the outstanding popular triumph[5]—which were to reach their highest point of development only after the carefully scrutinized and, if

---

[1] *Note by the Monitor, 27 June 1941. By contrast, there was little or no religious broadcasting in Germany. (*BBC Monitoring Service 'The Nazi Wireless at War', July 1941.)

[2] *The BBC Research Unit (Overseas) prepared as one of its Studies 'German Promises of Post-War Social Reform', 19 May 1941. Cf. Goebbels' broadcast on New Year's Eve 1944, quoted in Bramsted, op. cit., p. 365.

[3] 'Take cover', says one soldier to another in Evelyn Waugh's *The Sword of Honour*. 'You know, I think he's right', says a third. 'We'd better leave this to the civilians.'

[4] *BBC Monitoring Service, *Daily Digest*, 6 May 1945.

[5] See below, pp. 317-19.

necessary, censored scripts of war time gave way to the unscripted broadcasts of the post-war period. There were other
changes. One producer has stated that amongst the biggest
changes of the war was the permission to use alcohol as a
'conditioner'. Drinks were forbidden in the studio, but allowed,
subject to Corporation formalities, before and after broadcasts.[1] It became something of a cliché to say, while the members
of the Brains Trust were talking *before* a Brains Trust broadcast, 'If only *this* could have been broadcast.' And certainly
many brilliant orations which listeners never heard were
delivered in the Duty Room after the broadcast had ended.

Another big change was the increasing use of recordings, the
first stage in a technical revolution which was to produce its
full results only after the war. The Germans were far ahead of
the British during the war in this respect, a fact which was
confirmed by M. J. L. Pulling, a BBC engineer, when he visited
Germany in 1945 and reported on the development there of
the magnetophon sound-recording system, the origin of
modern tape recording.[2] During the war the BBC's Monitoring
Service had noted that the Germans knew how to cut and piece
together 'record strips', like films, and had pointed to 'the
possibilities of superimposing sound effects, of editing in general
and faking in particular'.[3] In fact, while the Germans used
recording for a multiplicity of purposes they did not exploit the
new techniques as much as they might have done; and it was
in Britain, where most of the recording was carried out on discs,
that ingenious use was made of snippets from Hitler's speeches.
5,000 discs were being used each week in 1943 as compared with
200 in 1939, and 7,000 in the week after D-Day. The number of
recording machines in use increased very substantially:[4]

[1] Note to the author by N. G. Luker, who later became Director of Talks, 7 Dec.
1962. See also B. Belfrage, *One Man in his Time* (1951), pp. 126–7.
[2] Note to the author by M. J. L. Pulling, then BBC Assistant Director of
Engineering, 26 Oct. 1965. For the American discovery of the tape recorder in
Germany, see E. Barnouw, *The Golden Web* (1968), p. 204. Plastic tape with a
ferrous oxide coating was far easier to manipulate than metal, which had previously
been used, and noise levels were substantially reduced by the application of a high
frequency alternating signal to the tape in addition to the sound modulation.
[3] *BBC Monitoring Service*, 'Outside Broadcasts on the German Home Service',
28 Sept. 1942.
[4] J. W. Godfrey, 'The History of BBC Sound Recording' in the *Journal of the
British Sound Recording Association*, vol. 6, no. 1, May 1959.

	1930	1939	1945
Steel Tape	2	6	8
Static Disc	–	6	70
Mobile Disc	–	6	28
Static Tape	–	–	4

A third change, influencing the techniques of radio, was the increasing use, originally for reasons of economy of space and manpower, of single-studio presentation in the production of plays and features. The pre-war system of production in a number of separate studios linked by an elaborate dramatic control panel was abandoned. There had been signs of a reaction against it even before the war began, and although its disappearance limited some of the experimental possibilities of radio production, the simplification of style had obvious advantages. BBC engineers did much to improve acoustics even when they had to use improvised materials, and although there were no war-time developments in the microphone, the employment in the scattered war-time studios, some of them scarcely suited to broadcasting, of a new type of amplifier, introduced just before the war, guaranteed a high technical standard of broadcasting.[1]

A fourth change was the introduction of the so-called 'continuity' system of presentation in the Overseas and Empire Services, a system which is still virtually unchanged and which, through BBC influence, has been established in the broadcasting services of almost every Commonwealth country. The pre-war practice of the BBC had been to allow over-runs and pauses between programmes, a practice that did not commend itself to the American networks and commercial stations that relayed many programmes from the BBC's North American service, especially during the bombing of London. For them, time was money, and exact timing had to be kept. The BBC insisted, therefore, on absolute punctuality in timing all programmes— something which, to begin with, not all speakers, and certainly few musicians, took kindly to. On the technical side, the

[1] Note to the author by F. W. Alexander, 5 Aug. 1965.

improvement in timing was complemented by the design of a special continuity studio, in which a single operator and an announcer, on opposite sides of the glass window, controlled the entire transmission, building the many separate programmes into a single entity, rather like a revue in which the different sketches and songs are presented in quick succession, linked by a compère and the orchestra. This 'continuity' system, with its precise timing and the provision of 'word-cues' from the announcer, was to prove invaluable in radio developments during the later stages of the war such as the Overseas Forces Programme and the Allied Expeditionary Forces Programme, where relay stations in the field had to enter and leave their parent BBC Service without using accurate clocks or engineering control lines. The pioneers in this development were Leslie Stokes, Tom Chalmers and R. T. B. Wynn, the latter one of the original broadcasting team at Writtle in the early 1920s, a symbol of continuity in himself.

Some of these changes behind the scenes in Britain are more difficult to chronicle, certainly more difficult to date precisely, than the changes which made their way into memoranda or which led to arguments with government departments. Taken together, however, they justified a remark made in a provincial newspaper in 1944 that 'so far as broadcasting is concerned, it cannot be said that the five years of war are "years that the locusts have eaten": this half decade has been a period of continuous advancement technically and even culturally.'[1]

Although much of the 'advancement' has to be related to what had gone before and what was to come after—in other words, it has to be seen in terms of a bigger time span than the war years themselves—there were a number of war-time assessments which, without benefit of hindsight, tried to relate the BBC's output to the whole background of culture and society during the war. In some respects, the most illuminating of these was by the well-known historian G. M. Young, who was frequently drawn into BBC affairs. In an article in the *Sunday Times*, written in 1943, he asked what the year 2043 would 'think of us' if the Governors of the BBC decided 'to lay up a

---

[1] *Birmingham Mail*, 12 April 1944.

week in 1943' for future scrutiny and instruction. 'Would the picture be fair and representative? Or to put it another way, suppose by some calamity all other records were lost, could I certify "A Week in 1943" to the historian in 2043 as first-class historic material?' Would it convey 'the intelligent conversation of 1943; the range of observation; the balance of interest; the things we noticed and didn't notice; the problems that puzzled us . . . the assumptions which turned out to be quite wrong; the sporting shots which turned out to be quite correct?'[1]

Unfortunately Young's questions were more interesting and comprehensive than the answers he gave to them. Instead of looking, for example, at the different reactions of different people according to age or class or district, he treated the population as if it consisted exclusively of readers of the *Sunday Times*: the very phrase 'first-class historic material' limits the curiosity of the cultural and social historian. Instead of trying to see whether the balance of BBC output reflected people's desire in war time to be entertained as well as informed or influenced, he left out entertainment altogether, paying no attention to significant shifts in taste or to the remarkable impact on all sections of society of a number of entertainment programmes, among which *ITMA* was outstanding. Instead of noting how in a war where science counted for more than it had done in any previous war the most powerful appeal to the public was the appeal to history, he had nothing to say about science and little to say about history.[2] Nor did he touch on the implications of the geographical spread of the war, which brought news of Russia and Japan and Malaysia straight into the kitchen. Instead, he surveyed BBC output from a strictly

---

[1] *Sunday Times*, 27 June 1943.

[2] *For German comment on the war as 'part of our historic past', there is ample evidence in the files of the BBC's Monitoring Service (e.g. 7 Oct. 1941). Darlan referred to Trafalgar, Radio Paris did not scruple to argue that collusion between British high finance and Leninist Russia went back to Cromwell and Peter the Great (ibid., 1 July 1941), and Stalin drew sharp contrasts between Hitler and Napoleon with as much care as German propagandists found meaningful comparisons—'Napoleon fought against the forces of reaction with the support of progressive elements. Hitler is leaning on reactionary forces in his fight against progress.' (Ibid., 11 Nov. 1941.) When Germany began to lose the war, Goebbels produced Frederick the Great as a model before he extolled the new range of V-Weapons. (Bramsted, op. cit., pp. 444–8.)

conservative point of view, struck above all else by what he considered 'the most reckless vilification of English institutions, the most grotesque distortions of English history and the most ignorant adulation of foreign achievements'. Pressed further, he maintained that much that was said about India, the Empire, Russia, the Public Schools or future arrangements for social security was wrong and irresponsible and would be bound to lead to 'disappointment and distrust'.[1] He was unimpressed also by a 'justification' of BBC Talks output on the part of 'one of the Ruling Elders' on the dubious grounds that 'we live in a progressive age'. Yet he ended by paying a great tribute to the handling of the News which had given the BBC 'a standing without rival on the European Continent'. 'What they say goes, and is whispered and copied, and carried by men and women and children at the risk often of their lives and the lives of their families from the Arctic to the Aegean. That is a great victory—I am not sure, if it is followed up, that 2043 will not regard it as our greatest victory.'

The Governors of the BBC were sufficiently worried about Young's criticisms to discuss them in detail at their Board meetings, and Foot, 'the Ruling Elder' to whom Young had referred, was told to write to Young to ask for a fuller explanation.[2] It is very difficult to catch the flavour of this discussion. Earlier in the war, in September 1941, Young had been offered £200 a year by the Governors 'to watch the English of our News bulletins', and in October 1942 the Governors had decided 'that his caustic comment is worth this small sum and that it should be continued for another year'.[3] Young had been expected to express views not so much on the content of News bulletins as on their language and style.[4] He had taken his responsibilities seriously and had written in detail not only about vocabulary, syntax, and imagery but about cadence— with elaborate cross-reference to *cursus planus, cursus velox* and *cursus tardus* in the Prayer Book. 'We shall have to await a simpler version of the *Quicunque vult servari* for broadcasters, according to Mr. Young,' Ryan commented aptly, 'before we

---

[1] *Sunday Times*, 27 June 1943; *Young to Foot, 3 July 1943.

[2] *Board of Governors, *Minutes*, 1 July 1943; Foot to Young, 2 July 1943.

[3] See H. Nicolson, *Diaries and Letters, 1939–45* (1967), p. 248.

[4] *Memorandum by Ogilvie, 30 Sept. 1941, describing a lunch attended by Bracken, Ronald Tree, Sir Malcolm Robertson, and Young.

can move from Faith to Works.'[1] Ryan greatly appreciated Young's gifts and Young appreciated Ryan's taste, not least in Latin quotations.[2] Other BBC officials were less polite. Young had ambitious ideas also of the BBC presenting its announcers with sheaves of documents from which they were to write their news bulletins rather than giving them official bulletins to read. Indeed, he was carrying into Broadcasting House his general views about history, emphasizing that history was in the making each day of the war. He was unhappy about the way in which the fall of Italy was reported in 1943,[3] but the reporting of the Normandy campaign fully satisfied him. 'May I say what superb history your creatures have been composing. Difficult: with lumps excised on what are no doubt good grounds— *Sicherheitsgrund*. But the clarity and balance of the narrative thrills me and for the first time in my life I have become a news-addict.'[4]

Ryan knew how to answer Young. 'When we think we have been reasonably colloquial, people say we were vulgar. When we feel we have been dignified they tell us we were pompous.'[5] On questions of style, indeed, as on questions of content, the BBC was easily attacked from two sides in a war where the English language, among so many other things, was under-going profound transformations. Characteristically George Orwell, who was one of Young's main targets, felt equally strongly both about the language and about the content of broadcasting. In his case, however, he wrote very critically of 'the BBC dialect' which working-class people 'instinctively dislike and cannot easily master',[6] and stated in 1944 that 'it is a nightly experience in any pub to see broadcast speeches and news bulletins make no impression on the average listener, because they are uttered in stilted bookish language, and, incidentally, in an upper-class accent'.[7] Like Young, however,

---

[1] *Ryan to Ogilvie, 9 Dec. 1941.

[2] Young to Ryan, 2 Oct. 1943: Mr. Ryan has kindly shown me a copy of this interesting letter and of the letter mentioned in the next footnote.

[3] Young to Ryan, 30 Sept. 1943.   [4] *Young to Ryan, 9 Sept. 1944.

[5] *Ryan to Young, 15 Sept. 1943.

[6] See his essay 'The English People', written in May 1944, and printed in S. Orwell and I. Angus, *The Collected Essays, Journalism and Letters of George Orwell*, vol. III, p. 28.

[7] Ibid., pp. 135–41, an interesting paper written for *Persuasion* on 'Propaganda and Demotic Speech'. Cf. Orwell and Young's ideas on Basic English, ibid., pp. 85–6, and G. M. Young, *Last Essays* (1950), pp. 78–96.

he vigorously defended the BBC's attitude to news and thought that it was its 'greatest victory'. 'The BBC as far as its News goes has gained immense prestige since about 1940,' he wrote in April 1944. ' "I heard it on the wireless" is now almost equivalent to "I know it must be true".'[1] 'Ask any refugee from Europe which of the belligerent radios is considered to be the most truthful. So also in Asia. Even in India where the population are so hostile they will not listen to British propaganda and will hardly listen to a British entertainment programme, they listen to BBC news because they believe it approximates to the truth.'[2]

Both Young and Orwell were better critics of language and better witnesses to the value of the News than they were to the range or balance of BBC programmes. They wanted the BBC to lean more definitely in one political direction than another;[3] and they were certainly not alone in this during a war when all 'progressives' longed for a new social order and many conservatives feared for the shape of things to come. The BBC, of its nature as much as through its circumstances, could neither catch every *nuance* of each of these extreme points of view nor appease suspicions. It was bound by the Government not to offer the use of the microphone to 'persons antagonistic to the war effort', but it tried, within the limits of the knowledge available to it, to select 'good broadcasters of all schools of thought able to hold the listeners' attention at home and overseas'.[4]

The logic of its position was not lost on everyone. In a 1943 debate in the House of Commons the ILP member, John McGovern, criticized the 'choice of propagandists by the BBC' and its failure to propagate all 'the different shades of opinion on political, social, religious and medical questions'. Yet Professor Gruffydd, while criticizing the BBC as 'over timid and over conventional', pointed out sensibly that 'the Right

---

[1] *Tribune*, 7 April 1944. A correspondent disagreed with this verdict (ibid., 21 April 1944). 'Would Orwell suggest that anybody now looks upon the BBC as they did in the days of Sir John Reith? Hardly.' Orwell stuck to his case.

[2] *Ibid., 21 April 1944.

[3] There is a devastating account of what happened inside the BBC to projects for any series of talks 'with some more or less definite propaganda line behind it' in Orwell and Angus (eds.), vol. II, p. 433.

[4] *Brief for the Minister of Information, 1 July 1943.

cannot accuse the BBC of being Bolshevist and the Left accuse them of being Fascist, and both *be right*. The simple truth must be obvious to all, that they are both wrong.'[1] McGovern himself admitted that it was necessary 'to weld together the forces of the nation', and his motion was defeated by 134 votes to 3. 'One cannot fail to have been impressed,' the BBC's Director of Secretariat wrote, 'with the high proportion of friendly comment on the BBC's work.'[2] When A. D. Lindsay, the Master of Balliol, publicly attacked the bias not of BBC talks but of news bulletins in 1944, Ryan replied in public, 'The extreme Right says from time to time that our bulletins are Red and enthusiasts on the other side condemn them for being reactionary. That, of course, is all in a day's work, but it is a little hard to get it from the author of *The Essentials of Democracy*.'[3]

Young and Orwell were both right from their different angles in relating the content of broadcasting to its tone. Quite apart from what they had to say, radio personalities acquired a popularity during the war second only to the heroes of statesmanship and the battlefield. Announcers were public figures, and it was a point of genuine interest in social history when Wilfred Pickles, a Yorkshire character actor, was brought down from Manchester to London to become a regular news reader.[4] His accent created as much of a stir—and almost as much controversy—as a war-time naval engagement. In assessing the significance of such an episode in terms of the whole range of BBC war-time output, Tom Harrisson, the founder of Mass Observation, was a more percipient and wide-ranging analyst and critic than either Young or Orwell. A frequent broadcaster both to the British and to overseas audiences, he wrote for part of the war a valuable weekly critique of BBC programmes for *The Observer*, and he collected regularly reactions to specific BBC programmes from his team of Mass Observation correspondents. 'This war,' he emphasized, 'has seen gigantic

[1] *Hansard*, vol. 388, cols. 835, 868. See below, p. 613.

[2] *Report by Farquharson to the Director-General, 12 April 1943. In preparing material for the debate the BBC had been anxious to collect evidence that 'we do not just slavishly follow the Government's lead'. (Note by J. C. Thornton, Assistant Director, Secretariat, Feb. 1943.)

[3] *Manchester Guardian*, 21, 22 Sept. 1944.

[4] See W. Pickles, *Between You and Me* (1949).

exploitations of the whispering ether.'[1] He realized how difficult it was in war time to secure genuine 'communication'—he was as interested in the language and style of communication as either Young or Orwell—and he tried to assess the forces making for national cohesion and for social stratification. He related the pattern of programmes to the movements of opinion throughout the many different phases of the war, asking, for example, about 'morale' in 1939 and 1940 and, as early as 1942, what people wanted life to be like after the end of the war.[2] He also recognized that entertainment programmes and the reactions to them were as significant for the student of social history as News or talks. He got near, therefore, to Young's prescription that historians should capture for posterity the preoccupations and prejudices of a particular sequence of generations. Finally, as a broadcaster himself, he was as sensitive as a writer–producer like Tangye Lean to the arts and techniques of radio—how a play was produced; how a script was rewritten; how recording might transform future broadcasting.[3] He was able, in consequence, to comment intelligently on such different matters as the relative lack of women's voices in a war where women counted for more than they had ever done in any previous war, or the effect of BBC 'games' and 'quizzes' on war-time domestic habits, or the likely popular reaction to BBC styles after the war. 'Many people,' he wrote in 1944, 'grew to like the Ovaltiney style before the war and would be glad to hear it back again.'[4]

There is likely to be no better source than Harrisson's papers and those of Mass Observation for the 'folklore' of broadcasting during the war. His version of what was happening may be compared with the accounts of an interesting though more highbrow discussion among the Governors of the BBC in the autumn of 1943. 'There is no consensus of opinion,' Harold Nicolson complained, 'even as to our target audience. Do we, for instance, aim mainly at the educated, the half-educated or the un-educated?' 'Cultural standards' had 'demonstrably declined' since the publication of the Ullswater Report in 1936.[5] 'The drive, impetus and conviction which are essential to the

---

[1] *The Observer*, 23 Aug. 1942.
[2] He gave interesting broadcasts on this subject on 20 July and 16 Sept.
[3] *The Observer*, 13 Sept. 1942.   [4] Article of 31 Dec. 1944.
[5] *Memorandum of 9 Sept. 1943.

direction of a great enterprise cannot be born of compromise,' Lady Violet Bonham Carter exclaimed.[1] 'In our approach to the public I think we have failed to take into account great changes that have come about in the character and outlook of the people, during the past few years,' Arthur Mann added.[2] All these matters were to acquire new significance after 1945.

Harrisson directs attention in all he writes not only to the arts but to the 'folklore' of war-time broadcasting. There was, however, an additional dimension to the history of war-time broadcasting which cannot be ignored. Broadcasting was only one element in the radio war, the first war in which radio was almost universally used by the Armed Forces, for purposes of defence as well as attack, by resistance movements as much as by governments. As Harrisson himself wrote in 1943, 'hundreds of thousands of Britons, Americans, Germans, have in the past five years learned to make, maintain and operate radio transmitting apparatus, solo-broadcasting complex messages and orders under any conditions (including battle) and over long distances. They *make* modern war. So we have a big potential of radio techniques.' The conclusion seemed to him to be that 'any Tom, Dick or Harry may start a Freedom Station in 1946. One person alone could run a local transmitter.'[3]

The deduction proved wrong: it may have been based on the parallel of the First World War after which thousands of radio amateurs trained during the war demanded regular broadcast programmes during the early 1920s. What was not wrong, however, was Harrisson's emphasis on the large numbers of people connected with various branches of radio engineering and operating during the war. Broadcasting was part of a 'vast and invisible web', which also included radar, the applied science of detecting and locating the range and whereabouts of any object by means of radio waves.[4] The British, forced on the defensive early in the war, made the most of some of their finest scientific brains who had been working on radar since

[1] *Note by Lady Violet Bonham Carter, 13 Sept. 1943.
[2] *Note by Mann, 3 Oct. 1943.
[3] *The Observer*, 19 Dec. 1943.
[4] See A. Price, *Instruments of Darkness* (1947); Sir Charles Webster and N. Frankland, *The Strategic Air Offensive against Germany*, 4 vols. (1961); A. P. Rowe, *One Story of Radar* (1948); and Sir Robert Watson Watt, *Three Steps to Victory* (1957).

1935, and by the time that the Germans introduced their own radio-controlled weapons the radio war, in its most general sense, had been won by the Allies. British telecommunications research went on to contribute to the success of the seaborne invasion of Europe in 1944. In the meantime, the development of radio devices had brought down Bomber Command losses to a level which the RAF and the Government felt able to countenance.[1]

It had been realized long before 1939 that broadcasting stations could be used by the enemy as accurate radio beacons, and from January 1936 onwards the BBC's Controller (Engineering), Ashbridge, and the man who was to be his successor, Harold Bishop, had sat on a technical sub-committee of the Imperial Defence Committee concerned with working out a mutually acceptable plan for broadcasting in war time, given this severe danger to national defence.[2] After long discussions, a BBC plan was accepted in July 1938 which provided for the grouping of high-power medium-wave transmitters into two geographical groups (Northern and Southern), each group using only one medium wavelength (449.1 and 391.1 metres), with a number of transmitters working on each wavelength at any given time. Enemy aircraft tuned to these wavelengths would not be able to obtain a reliable 'fix' on any transmitter, even supposing they knew its geographical location, until they were within about 25 miles range because of the pattern of radio interference resulting from the synchronized grouping. Within that range Fighter Command would have power to close down a transmitter, but because of 'synchronization' the listeners would continue to receive at night weak but intelligible indirect-ray signals from other transmitters using the same wavelength. Instructions concerning these arrangements were given to the Senior Control Room Engineer in Broadcasting House, and the closure of a transmitter in any part of the country was

[1] The British public was first told of radiolocation in June 1941, and advertisements appeared in 1942 asking for volunteers to work the apparatus. See M. Henslow, *The Miracle of Radio* (1946), p. 38.

[2] See Briggs, *The Golden Age of Wireless*, pp. 631 ff.; H. Bishop, 'The War-Time Activities of the Engineering Division of the BBC' in the *Journal of the Institution of Electrical Engineers*, vol. 94 (1947); L. W. Hayes, 'Never off the Air' in the *Radio Times*, 14 Dec. 1945.

carried out within a few seconds of the instruction being received. It proved necessary only once during the war for all the BBC transmitters to be closed down simultaneously. This was in sharp contrast with Germany where frequently during air raids all German transmitters were off the air.[1]

The BBC's basically simple but in practice highly effective method of operating transmitters entailed the development by BBC engineers of crystal drive equipment of high accuracy which would permit close synchronization without the use of line links. It was completed by the time of the Munich crisis and came into operation on 1 September 1939. Throughout the war it set the conditions of British broadcasting. At first, there was one single Home Service programme in place of the pre-war range. After February 1940 there were two alternative programmes, one of them for the Forces (373.1 metres).[2] Thereafter there were gradual relaxations, each of which was argued for inch by inch by Ashbridge in co-operative discussions with the Armed Forces.

To improve the quality and continuity of the British home broadcasting service, low-power transmitters were erected in big centres of population, the first of them in 1940 at Aberdeen, Liverpool, Stoke-on-Trent, and Nottingham. They were known as the 'H Group'; they had a service area of five to ten miles; they all transmitted the Home Service programme on 203.5 metres; and none of them was ever closed down until an 'Alert' signal was given in the areas in which they were situated. Most of them were built to the BBC's own design in small workshops in the Midlands, and by the end of 1941 there were sixty of them in operation. Mobile and semi-mobile transmitters were also employed: the first of these had in fact been ordered in 1938, and there were eight of them in use in the summer of 1940.[3] A wireless link was also installed in the London area which was capable of conveying the Home programme to any transmitter which had lost touch with the remainder of the BBC system. Although there were severe

[1] See below, p. 297.
[2] This wavelength was changed to 342.1 metres on 2 March 1941. The provision of the additional service was made possible by the introduction of a new type of aerial capable of providing a service at distances of over 150 miles without giving help to enemy aircraft.
[3] *R. T. B. Wynn to Bishop, 20 Aug. 1940.

strains when large-scale air attacks started in 1940, the system never broke down.

Building transmitters was an essential but difficult task in war time given shortages of men and materials: it was just as essential, moreover, for the expansion of the Overseas Services of the BBC by short wave as it was for domestic or European Services. There was, indeed, 'a war of transmitters', quickened in urgency after the Germans, who already had 'a natural advantage in their central position, acquired the radio transmitters of most of their erstwhile enemies'.[1] On the outbreak of the war Great Britain had five transmitters of 100 kilowatts or over and the Germans eight. By 1945 the total number of transmitters operated by the BBC had risen from 24 to 121, while the German figure had risen only to 50. The total number of engineers employed by the BBC had risen during the same period from 1,635 to 4,317, almost as high a figure as the total number of all BBC employees when war broke out.[2]

These were remarkable achievements since engineers were in short supply throughout the war and the BBC contributed many of its engineers in 1939 to other branches of the war effort. Moreover, the provision of any one transmitter usually entailed detailed and intricate decisions not only about engineering but about the economics of equipment, man-power, finance and, in some cases, lease-lend.[3] Two of the most interesting of the many stories of war-time engineering relate to the building of a long-wave station at Ottringham near Hull and to the acquisition by PWE of a medium-wave transmitter 'Aspidistra' which particularly concerned Churchill himself. These were the 'Big Berthas' of the Second World War.[4]

The full story of Aspidistra cannot be told, but even in outline the account of the acquisition of a 500-kilowatt RCA transmitter,

[1] *BBC European Intelligence Paper, 'The Transmitter War in Europe', 18 Feb. 1941.

[2] For the outline history of BBC engineering during the war, see H. Bishop, loc. cit. Allied transmitter strength increased, of course, in 1944 and 1945 as stations were captured from the Germans.

[3] There were also political issues involved, including the idea of building a network of local stations in the Mediterranean. When Captain Plugge, a representative of commercial radio, raised this and other questions about transmitters in Parliament in 1940, the BBC produced an important authoritative reply. (*Notes from Ashbridge to Wellington, with an accompanying letter, 9 Sept. 1940.)

[4] Rolo, op. cit., p. 13.

its erection in 1943 by Canadians at an underground site in Ashdown Forest, and its use, limited though it was, in international broadcasting operations, most of them outside the scope of the BBC, has an element of romance about it. Ottringham was a dream of Ashbridge which came true. He had asked as early as March 1940 for a long-wave station on the East Coast capable of delivering a strong enough signal to be picked up in Germany in daylight. The proposal was accepted reasonably quickly by the Ministry and the Cabinet, but the fall of France delayed its implementation. It was renewed in 1941, and a year later the station was opened. Ottringham was a huge station with four powerful transmitters which were housed in separate buildings with a central combining unit enabling two or more transmitters to be connected in parallel in order to increase the power. Ottringham operated thereafter as a unit in a synchronized group of long-wave stations—Brookmans Park (closed in September 1944), Daventry and Droitwich (both closed in December 1944).[1] The use of long-wave broadcasting, which had been suspended in September 1939 because Droitwich was then the only long-wave transmitter and synchronization was impossible, had been resumed in November 1941.

The provision of more short-wave transmitters, a matter of discussion before war broke out—the British were more or less on a par at that time with the Axis powers[2]—was not satisfactorily arranged until 1943, and there were vigorous arguments with the Army, PWE, and later the United States OWI (Office of War Information) before many political obstacles were removed and the location and use of the transmitters were approved. Four additional transmitters were ready for service by 1941 and 18 more by the end of 1943. These transmitters were associated with aerial systems designed to beam the programmes to any part of the world. There was protracted discussion in 1940 of the possibility of BBC short-wave transmitters being installed in Canada, but the proposal was not pressed. Commonwealth as much as British needs were thereafter

---

[1] Ottringham itself closed on 9 July 1945.

[2] *Note by Ashbridge, 9 Sept. 1940. In March 1942 (Ashbridge to Foot) Britain, with 14 high-power transmitters, 3 low-power transmitters, and 1 part-time high-power transmitter, was well placed also in relation to the United States.

taken into account in all discussions of distribution. All the figures relating to present and future transmitter power were regarded as strictly secret during the war and, despite parliamentary interest, details were never given.

While the 'battle for transmitters' involved somewhat similar considerations on both sides, there was as fundamental a difference in approach to one technical aspect of wireless policy—'jamming', interfering deliberately with wireless reception in enemy or neutral countries[1]—as there was in relation to the philosophy of propaganda. The Germans were always willing to 'jam' if it suited their purposes: when the Allies entered Naples in 1943 they found a whole battery of jamming stations capable of blotting out any 'undesirable programme' over a wide radius.[2] The British, unlike their Russian allies, never resorted to jamming as deliberate policy. Some British newspapers advocated such a policy.[3] The British Government, however, backed the BBC's engineers in resisting pressure to 'jam' even during the worst months of 1940.[4] Waste of valuable power and wavelengths was always emphasized: so too were the limitations of general jamming over large areas. More

[1] *An early example of reported 'jamming' was in 1936 when a radio appeal by the Empress of Abyssinia was said to have been jammed (*Sunday Mercury*, 19 April 1936). On the eve of the war a BBC official reported (1 Aug. 1939) that 'we are aware of a good deal of wilful jamming'. On 5 Jan. 1940 Major C. E. Wakeham told J. S. A. Salt that jamming has not 'greatly increased since the war'. By Feb. 1940, however, Ashbridge noted that 'interference is in general becoming definitely more widespread' (Ashbridge to Wellington, 29 Feb. 1940) and a note of 24 Oct. 1940 stated that 'the jamming situation has become steadily worse'. A report of Sept. 1941 stated that 'jamming is increasing both in intensity and widespread distribution'.

[2] *BBC Despatch from Frank Gillard, 11 Oct. 1943. 'The Fascist practice', he went on, 'seems to have been to have a number of powerful receiving sets set up in good listening positions round Naples, and each set connected by telephone to one or other of the jammers. Especially chosen linguists sit at these sets, monitoring all the programmes broadcast by the BBC European Service and by other Allied broadcasting organisations, such as for instance the United Nations radio in Algiers. As soon as any programmes [attracted their attention] particularly news bulletins from London the listening officer in Naples would pick up his telephone and order one or other of the local jammers to start working on such and such a wavelength.'

[3] For example, *Daily Sketch*, 25 May 1940.

[4] *BBC Security Measures Committee, *Minutes*, 19 June 1940. Ashbridge stated the alternative policies clearly in a memorandum of 25 Oct. 1940 in which he advocated 'continuing what we are now doing, that is transmitting each bulletin on as many different channels as possible', instead of using spare transmitters for jamming.

profoundly, it was argued that the country could only benefit in the long run from open and unimpeded radio reception. 'Jamming is really an admission of a bad cause. The jammer has a bad conscience. . . . He is afraid of the influence of the truth. . . . In our country we have no such fears and to jam broadcasts in English by the enemy might even be bad propaganda.'[1]

The relevant equations which were taken into account when assessing transmitter strengths or arguing whether or not retaliatory jamming—of the kind which Aspidistra permitted— should be attempted also involved wireless receiving sets which were in short supply in most countries for large parts of the Second World War. The ability of the broadcaster to 'get through' depended on the type, quality, and distribution of sets.

In Britain itself the situation was difficult. Nearly two million '19 Sets' were distributed to the British Forces for military purposes between 1940 and 1945,[2] and civilian demands were inevitably hard to meet. In 1942, one out of every five house-wives who tried to buy a high-tension battery, even in 'the best months', failed to do so, and just before Christmas the figure was one out of three.[3] Although the number of mains-driven receivers during the summer of 1943 was over 80 per cent in urban areas, it was only 64 per cent in rural areas, and large numbers of the listening public were having to restrict listening because of the shortage of dry batteries and the difficulties of getting wet batteries recharged.[4] Valves were also in short supply, although total production leapt from 12 million a year in 1940 to 35 million in 1944—a thousand-bomber raid meant a quarter of a million valves in use in the sky—and Radio Rentals reported that 'the demand for our service is, of course, far beyond anything with which we can cope'.[5] Sixty per cent of retailers suffered from a shortage of skilled labour for repair jobs.[6] In 1935 the radio industry was

[1] *BBC Statement on Jamming, 29 May 1940.

[2] M. Henslow, *The Miracle of Radio* (1946), p. 81.

[3] *Listener Research Bulletin, 10 April 1943, based on a Ministry of Information Social Survey.

[4] Ibid., 31 Aug. 1943.

[5] Speech by the Chairman of Radio Rentals as reported in *The Times*, 27 Jan. 1943.

[6] *Listener Research Report, 'Battery and Valve Supply and Wireless Repair Problems', March 1942.

producing 1,900,000 sets for use by ordinary listeners: the corresponding figure for 1943 was 50,000 sets.[1]

In an effort to deal with some of these problems, which were of concern to the Governors of the BBC,[2] the War Cabinet Production Planning Radio Committee, of which Ashbridge

1. War-time Utility Receiver, designed to Government specification
by Dr. G. D. Reynolds of Murphy Radio

was for a time a member, considered the possibility of producing a utility wireless set, and Foot asked for half a million such new sets in January 1943. There was an inevitable time lag. Indeed, by the time that production of non-branded utility sets began in July 1944—over 250,000 of them were subsequently manufactured—individual manufacturers were extremely keen to proceed with their own named models.[3] The thought of post-war competition was already influencing business plans.[4]

---

[1] Radio Industry Council, *The British Radio Industry in War and Peace* (1945), p. 11. The Radio Industry Council consisted of four associations—the British Radio Equipment Manufacturers' Association, the British Radio Valve Manufacturers' Association, the Radio Communications and Electronic Engineering Association, and the Radio Component Manufacturers' Association. It was said to have displayed 'a unity of policy and outlook never before achieved in radio, and rarely exceeded in other industries'.

[2] *Board of Governors, *Minutes*, 28 Jan., 18 Feb., 3 June 1943; Controllers' Conference, *Minutes*, 4 Nov. 1942, 6 Jan. 1943.

[3] Radio Committee, *Minutes*, 8 March 1945.

[4] In 1943 one radio manufacturer was advertising in 24 daily and Sunday newspapers and in the *Radio Times*. (*Electrical Trading*, Nov. 1943.)

The general sales position during the war has been summarized by the Radio Equipment Manufacturers' Association:[1]

	Manufacturers' Disposals	Utility Sales	Totals
1939	1,200,000	—	1,200,000
1940	800,000	—	800,000
1941	200,000	—	200,000
1942	110,000	—	110,000
1943	50,000	—	50,000
1944	30,000	90,000	120,000
1945	80,000	165,000	245,000

These figures clearly affected the distribution of wireless licences. While the habit of listening became more widespread in Britain than ever before, the total number of wireless licences fell for the first time since the introduction of broadcasting from 8,948,000 at the end of 1939 to 8,904,000 at the end of 1940, and 8,621,000 at the end of 1941. Thereafter numbers were held, and they reached nearly 10,000,000 at the end of 1945. The sale of the *Radio Times*, influenced though it was by war-time control of newsprint, showed a somewhat similar trend. Circulation went down slightly during the first years of the war, but from 1941 rose steadily. In 1943 average weekly net sales were over 3 million: in 1945 they exceeded 4 million.[2]

It is interesting to compare the position in Britain, where the distribution of wireless sets was treated as 'an affair of national, even imperial importance',[3] with that in Germany, where at the end of December 1941 there were 15,843,144 homes possessing wireless receiving sets. There were also large numbers of sets in collective use in factories. In the middle of the war,

[1] Note kindly supplied by D. I. Craig, statistician of the British Radio Equipment Manufacturers' Association, 6 June 1967.
[2] See Appendix B.
[3] *A. R. Burrows, 'War Time Prejudice to a National Service', 2 July 1942.

in 1942, set users were still said to be increasing, particularly in the rural areas.[1] Throughout the war, indeed, the Germans made every effort to extend home listening to their own RRG broadcasts—the eight or nine news bulletins each day, the *Zeitgeschehen* or News Reels, the *Frontberichte*, and the technical talks—while at the same time seeking to impose a ban, moral, legal, or technical, on listening to foreign stations.

As far as both British and German broadcasting to Europe was concerned—and here they were, as we have seen, in active hostility—details relating to the number and social distribution of wireless sets in each country were almost as important to the broadcasters as details relating to the number of transmitters which they could employ. Despite all the war-time difficulties of production there is ample evidence that in many countries, besides Germany, the number of sets in use increased. Yet the pattern was patchy. There were countries like Greece and Bulgaria, where there were very few sets (only 23,000 and 34,000 respectively in 1938), countries like Yugoslavia, where most of the pre-war sets (113,000 in all) were in the hands of the well-to-do sections of the population, and countries like Poland, where sets were deliberately confiscated by the Germans.[2] In Czechoslovakia, by contrast, 'radio density was high' (10.5 sets to 100 in Bohemia and Moravia in May 1939), and it was reported early during the war that 'everybody listens in, the whole nation, young and old, men, women and children, towns as well as hamlets'.[3] The number of sets increased sharply between 1938 and 1946, as it did in Denmark and Finland.[4] Despite all the German efforts to restrict or to forbid listening, both individual and group listening continued in Europe and overseas throughout the war. In Italy it was estimated that half the relatively small number of sets in use could receive short waves.[5]

[1] *Compendium of Planning Information, 7 April 1942.

[2] See below, p. 178.

[3] *BBC Overseas Intelligence Department, *Monthly Intelligence Report, Europe*, 8 July 1940.

[4] The 1945 figures are difficult to come by or, where they exist, to check. There were 704,000 sets in Denmark in 1938, 1,064,000 in 1946; 995,000 in Italy in 1938, 1,648,000 in 1946. The figures, subject to serious qualifications, have been provided by Asher Lee, the BBC's External Broadcasting Audience Research Officer. See Appendix C.

[5] *Supplement to 'The Transmitter War in Europe', 18 Feb. 1941.

There is no more fascinating aspect of the history of broad-casting during the war than that concerned with the efforts both of engineers and of producers to reach their audience and of specialists in listener research to assess their impact upon it. A report of January 1942 called 'Reception in Europe', one of a series, deals fully, for example, with the difficulties both in collecting evidence and in interpreting it. Tatsfield reported jamming of BBC broadcasts in Czech, Danish, Dutch, Flemish, French, German, Greek, Hungarian, Italian, Luxembourger, Norwegian, Polish, Roumanian, Serbo-Croat, Spanish, Turkish, and English, much of it local. In France, in particular, trans-missions were sometimes jammed so heavily as to become unintelligible. Heartening evidence was also reported that in Norway many people had kept their wireless sets despite attempts at confiscation. The report dealt with the difficult question of how often to change wavelengths for European programmes, with the absorbing question of what kind of voices could best penetrate all the enemy's attempts at inter-ference,[1] and with the extent of 'eavesdropping' to programmes not specifically designed for the audience in question.[2]

L. W. Hayes, Head of the Overseas and Engineering Information Department, was immensely knowledgeable about this vast range of subjects, all of them with an 'intelligence' angle: so too were many of the highly specialized monitoring engineers at Evesham, and later at Caversham and Crowsley in Oxfordshire near Reading. They meant little to most people in Britain, who were surprised when in October 1941 a mysterious voice, quickly nicknamed 'Funf'—after a character in *ITMA*—had the temerity to interrupt a news bulletin being read by Frank Phillips: 'Steady on, old man, you're reading too quickly for me.' Newsome thought that the inter-ruptions were 'in the true music hall tradition',[3] and Hayes believed that the best thing was to 'laugh it off',[4] yet the BBC quickly decided to cut out all intervals between programmes and

---

[1] *'Reception in Europe', 20 Jan. 1942.

[2] *A paper on jamming research concluded on 3 July 1942 that 'the vocal technique of the news reader is certainly more important than the quality of his voice'. Useful research was carried out in this field by J. W. Lawrence and V. D. Carse. Hugh Carleton Greene also produced valuable conclusions on the subject after a visit to Stockholm in 1942.   [3] *Newsome to Maconachie, 15 Oct. 1941.

[4] *Note by B. B. Chapman, 15 Oct. 1941.

stated diplomatically: 'Some listeners probably find them [the interruptions] amusing while others may be annoyed by them. We have already taken steps to reduce the effect of the interference, but should it become more troublesome we shall have to consider further and more drastic measures.'[1] Such measures did not prove necessary. The voice was stilled. The war continued.

There were many other 'intelligence' aspects of war-time broadcasting which were even more unfamiliar to British listeners in their homes. They did not know, for example, of the important contribution made by the BBC to the development of the 'Meaconing system'—relaying an enemy station through a BBC transmitter in order to confuse enemy aircraft seeking to use it for direction finding.[2] Lindemann wrote to Churchill in August 1940 of the possibility of sacrificing the home wireless for this purpose, but, though this supreme sacrifice was never made, the loan of a Daventry transmitter and the use of the pre-war television transmitter at Alexandra Palace for 'Domino' jamming of German aircraft range-finding proved highly successful in 1941.[3] The BBC's Monitoring Service was able also to collect invaluable information about the German morse service and Hellschreiber system—notification to the German Press of texts, releases, and censorship stops—and to tap telephone as well as broadcasting circuits.[4] Information collected from such sources had to be used, of course, with the greatest discretion, particularly as far as 'white' broadcasting was concerned.[5] Developments in electronics and missile technology since 1945, like developments since then in 'psychological warfare', enhance rather than detract from the significance of what happened in the radio war between 1939 and 1945. The war, we now realize, offered a foretaste of bigger things to come.

[1] *The Times*, 16 Oct. 1941.
[2] For the first Meacons, see Price, op. cit., pp. 34–5.   [3] Ibid., pp. 48–9.
[4] Monitoring of the DNB Hellschreiber service began on 23 Oct. 1941, was suspended on 1 Nov. 1941, and restarted in December. For morse, see *BBC Monitoring Service, Monthly Progress Report*, March, April 1942. The BBC itself ran a weekly morse service from August 1940 onwards, giving details of its regional programmes one week in advance. Morse news services for Europe were introduced in March 1942 after somewhat difficult negotiations with the Post Office.
[5] The 'black' stations had a differential advantage not only over the BBC but over RRG.

Our perspectives are necessarily different from those of 1939 to 1945, yet even during those years the controllers of broadcasting often looked at the war from what in terms of the history of the war were odd perspectives. This book, in consequence, opens what will sometimes seem to be a strange window on the world. For those of its readers who remember the war, selective memories of war-time broadcasting are more likely to colour the approach to the telling of the story as set out in these pages than an attempt to see it all in perspective. The war will be remembered not only for its great broadcasting landmarks, moments of shared experience, but for its songs and its slogans, its rhythms and its moods. Tommy Handley, Vera Lynn, Dr. Joad, J. B. Priestley and many others besides left their imprint on social history in a manner that people who never heard them at the time may well find difficult fully to understand. Recordings of their broadcasts, where they exist, have a Proustian quality which is still capable of stirring the strongest individual feelings. In years ahead, however, they will have to speak for themselves.

The account of broadcasting in war time which follows is chronological, and although, by necessity, it separates detailed examination of domestic themes from international aspects of broadcasting, it sets out to relate them to each other at each stage. It deals with the story in depth, explaining from documentary and oral evidence how and why particular decisions were made. The detail is often more relevant and illuminating than the broad generalization, for there have already been far too many generalizations about the Second World War to justify adding to or even repeating them. I have attempted throughout, as in the previous two volumes of this History, to avoid the temptation of looking at the past from the very fleeting vantage point of the present, nostalgic or otherwise. This attempt imposes certain canons of austerity: it also entails setting out and seeking to explain attitudes which may no longer be familiar or congenial. At the same time, it involves direct confrontation with forgotten or neglected experience.

Whether we have memories or not, many of the attitudes discussed and the millions of words in which they were clothed in war-time broadcasting should ideally be brought back to mind, of course, through the medium of the spoken word,

II

SITZKRIEG

In war the Board do not envisage the whole of broadcasting time being taken up by air raid warnings, notices and propaganda. They consider that it will be important to continue to provide as much entertainment and diversion as possible. It seems unnecessary, and even undesirable, that the Government should take the responsibility for day-to-day programme matters.

Memorandum on the Administration of the Broadcasting System in War, approved by the Board of Governors, 4 July 1939.

1. Behind the Scenes

FOR most Englishmen the Second World War began with a broadcast and an air-raid warning. On Sunday 3 September, at 11.15, in carefully measured tones, Neville Chamberlain, the Prime Minister, told listeners, most of them well prepared for the news, many of them anxious to have it confirmed, that Britain was at war with Germany and was fighting against 'evil things'. Within a few minutes the air-raid sirens sounded for the first time and people rushed to their shelters. There was an element of irony in both events. Not many months before, there had been rumours that Chamberlain believed that broadcasting had no part to play in modern war and should cease as soon as war broke out.[1] As for the sirens, they sounded a false alarm, and during the first months of the war, after the collapse of Poland, the main public danger was not a German air attack but national boredom.

The BBC had many assets in September 1939—a group of able people, particularly in engineering and production; a structure which allowed for considerable flexibility; a tested policy of telling the truth 'and nothing but the truth, even if the truth is horrible';[2] and, above all, a high sense of public

---

[1] As late as June 1938 the Government was still prepared to contemplate that 'ordinary broadcasting' would cease in time of war (*Report of a meeting held at the Post Office, 19 June 1938). 'If broadcasting had to be shut down, every alternative means of communication to the homes of the public would need careful consideration.' One alternative means—a large-scale 'wired' broadcasting system —was considered seriously by a sub-Committee of the Committee of Imperial Defence in 1939.

[2] *A comment by R. T. Clark, then the Home Service News Editor, April 1938, quoted in A. Briggs, *The Golden Age of Wireless* (1964), pp. 656–7. 'Telling the truth,' Clark maintained, was 'the only way to strengthen the morale of the people whose morale is worth strengthening.' For a critical episode in the history of the Arabic Service, see ibid., p. 404. J. B. Clark, then Head of the Empire Service, insisted in January 1938 that in all news bulletins, however concerned the Foreign Office might be about their repercussions, 'the *omission* of unwelcome *facts* of News and the consequent suppression of truth was counter to the Corporation's policy'. By February 1939, according to an Overseas Intelligence Department report on Arabic Broadcasts, 'the BBC Arabic broadcasts have established themselves firmly as being as nearly impartial as any institution can be'.

service, still associated with the name of Reith. Yet there had been many signs of tension, strain, and lack of leadership within the organization during the spring and summer of 1939.[1] Ogilvie had not been chosen as Director-General with war needs in mind, and when Sir Allan Powell became Chairman of the Governors in March 1939 no reference was made in his letter of appointment[2] or during the subsequent discussion in the House of Commons to his suitability for carrying the Corporation through months of preparation for war or for war itself.[3] Members of the House were as remote from realities as the Government. When Chamberlain spoke of Powell's 'rich experience', Jimmy Maxton asked him 'which of these bits of experience qualify this gentleman to arrange variety programmes?'[4]

In fact, there had been great confusion behind the scenes in the months before war broke out, and neither Powell nor Ogilvie was in a position in September 1939 to tell the public exactly what was happening. Some ministers believed that people would not 'bother to listen' to BBC programmes. 'Others pressed forward with streams of official exhortations and notices, calculated apparently to bring about this very result.'[5] Others tried to interfere with the content of broadcasting. On 25 August the Prime Minister's office had told the BBC not to broadcast a message from the National Council of Labour to the German people,[6] while on 2 September, during the eventful pre-war week-end, Sir John Simon, the

---

[1] See ibid., pp. 641 ff.

[2] *Major G. C. Tryon to Powell, 4 March 1939.

[3] Yet according to Viscount Bruce, who had been offered the post earlier, Chamberlain had told him that 'it was quite obvious war was coming'. (*Letter to Sir Ian Jacob, 15 May 1956.)

[4] *Hansard*, vol. 345, cols. 31–2. Powell's record involved no experience whatever of issues relevant to the BBC. From 1920 to 1930 he was Clerk to the Metropolitan Asylums Board, from 1930 to 1932 the organizer of the LCC's new department of Public Assistance, and from 1932 to 1939 a member of the Import Duties Advisory Committee.

[5] T. O. Beachcroft, *British Broadcasting* (1946), p. 25.

[6] See Briggs, op. cit., p. 650. The Foreign Office subsequently withdrew its objection, and the message of 25 Aug. was broadcast in full in the German Service on 30 Aug. On 20 Dec. Halifax accepted full responsibility for the incident. (*Letter to Ogilvie, 20 Dec. 1939.) The incident left a residue of resentment in the TUC and other bodies, and the TUC boycotted BBC talks until 1940. Sir Walter Citrine, its Secretary, continued to criticize many aspects of BBC policy and to refuse to take part in broadcasts.

Chancellor of the Exchequer, insisted by telephone on certain cuts being made in the BBC report of that day's parliamentary debate. There had also been a last-minute appeal to Halifax to allow a message from Chamberlain to the German people to be broadcast in German on the evening of Saturday 2 September. A broadcast from Germany had been monitored saying that listening to English radio stations would become illegal the following day and the BBC's German broadcasters wished to get their message out in time. Chamberlain was on his way from London to Chequers when Halifax was asked to give his authorization.

The BBC itself had made the most meticulous preparations for the dispersal of its staff and the introduction of the single programme, which was necessary for defence reasons. Yet it was inadequately equipped—mainly for reasons beyond its control—to cope with what actually happened in September 1939 and what had not been anticipated—the beginning of that curious kind of war which the Americans called 'phoney', the French 'cette drôle de guerre', and the Germans 'Sitzkrieg'.[1] Its operations were immediately restricted to two wavelengths, as had been planned, and part of the programme time even on those wavelengths was pre-empted for broadcasts in foreign languages. Neither entertainment nor information was easy to supply. Television, still a service for a tiny minority of twenty-five thousand viewers, 'would, of course, have been the ideal "black-out" entertainment', but it stopped suddenly 'without an *au revoir*' two days before war began.[2] The elaborately prepared but dull programme schedules made little appeal to the masses of radio listeners who were cut off from other sources of entertainment.[3] The Post Office had warned the Corporation with characteristic lack of imagination or foresight that if and

---

[1] See E. S. Turner, *The Phoney War on the Home Front* (1961), p. 180; R. Dorgelès, *La Drôle de Guerre* (1957). The Germans had issued censorship instructions on 25 Sept. 1939 that the word 'war' was to be used 'as sparingly as possible'. 'Preferably the expression "state of war" is to be used.' E. Kris and H. Speier, *German Radio Propaganda* (1944), p. 33. For a characteristically spirited personal gesture in Britain, see M. Gorham, *Sound and Fury* (1948), p. 89, where he describes the preparation of the first war-time number of the *Radio Times*: 'out of sheer reaction to the long use by the BBC of the evasive term "emergency", I used the word "war" in every second line'.

[2] *BBC Handbook, 1940*, p. 13.

[3] See below, pp. 96–7

4

when programmes were curtailed, the Post Office itself 'would wish on their part to curtail the income of the BBC'.[1]

The passion for 'news' was insatiable during the first days of the war in Poland, but there was confusion in the newly-founded Ministry of Information, suspicion in Press circles of the BBC entering into serious competition with the newspapers 'to their detriment',[2] and an inadequate sense within the BBC itself of the key importance of news as a major war-time service. There was no regular BBC foreign news service and no staff of foreign news correspondents. The two recording units—one under Richard Dimbleby in France (his first broadcast from France was not until 13 October) and one in London under Bernard Stubbs—had not yet begun to experiment with reporting techniques which were perfected later during the war. Immediately after the outbreak of war there were hourly news bulletins, but after a few weeks there was such a lack of news that their numbers were drastically reduced.[3] 'We feel certain that it is bad for the morale of the country,' a BBC official wrote, 'to create an expectation of news in the small hours. It seems much better that people should try to get their sleep and not feel that they will miss anything by doing so.'[4]

It is not surprising that by the last week of September Harold Nicolson was writing disconsolately in his Diary:

The effect of the black-out, the evacuation and the general dislocation has been bad for morale. The whole stage was set for an intensive and early attack by Germany which would have aroused our stubbornness. The Government had not foreseen a situation in which boredom and bewilderment would be the main elements; they concentrated upon coping with panic and had been faced with an anti-climax. They had not sufficient imagination to cope with that. We have all the apparatus of war conditions without war

[1] *Note by R. Jardine Brown, 12 July 1938.

[2] *Graves to Ogilvie, 18 July 1939, Note on an Interview with Waterfield.

[3] A pre-war agreement with the Newspaper Proprietors' Association prevented the BBC from regularly broadcasting news earlier than 6 p.m. or later than 2 a.m., although it was accepted that this understanding would not operate 'in the case of events of urgent national importance or of exceptional public interest'. There had been extra bulletins at the time of the Munich crisis. See A. Briggs, *The Birth of Broadcasting* (1961), pp. 172 ff. and *The Golden Age of Wireless* (1965), p. 159.

[4] *C. A. Siepmann to Waterfield, 13 Sept. 1939.

conditions. The result is general disillusion and grumbling, from which soil defeatism may grow.[1]

Foreign broadcasting got off to an equally difficult start. The BBC's Empire Service had celebrated its seventh birthday in 1939, yet less than two years had elapsed since the beginning of the Arabic Service, the first foreign language programmes transmitted from Britain. Spanish and Portuguese had followed, with French, German and Italian being added at the time of the Munich crisis in the autumn of 1938, but the BBC still lacked both transmitters and personnel to broadcast news bulletins in more than a limited number of languages. Even more seriously, there was still a running debate inside and outside the Corporation as to whether propaganda was 'a good thing'. The immediate pre-war mood, bleak and uninspired, was well expressed in the minutes of a meeting of the newly founded European Service held in June 1939:

Reported that at the present moment there was no special allowance for the European Service. Expenses must come out of the *Sonderberichte* (German broadcasts) allowance of £40 a week. The Foreign Office, however, had been approached by the D.G. for a further allowance of £75 a week.[2]

As far as broadcasts to Poland were concerned, the British Embassy in Warsaw reported only a few weeks before war broke out that 'no very useful purpose would be served by such broadcasts at present . . . Our offer to "propagandise" the Polish public might be thought impertinent by the Polish authorities who now, in fact, have an efficient and unbiased news service of their own . . . we should in any case be unable to compete, in the event of a radio war, with the very powerful German radio station next door which could obviously shout us down if they wished'.[3]

Ogilvie, the Director-General, himself believed on the eve of war that it would be a good idea to relay to Germany the famous 'song of the nightingale' in Bagley Woods as a token of

[1] H. Nicolson, *Diaries and Letters, 1939–1945* (1967), p. 36.
[2] *Minutes of a meeting of the European Service, 19 June 1939. *Sonderbericht* writers, however distinguished, were paid only 2 guineas for their contributions.
[3] *Undated note by J. B. Clark.

Britain's peace-loving intentions;[1] while Graves, the Deputy
Director-General, thought that 'it was necessary to give very
careful thought' to the implications of an extension of foreign
language broadcasting 'because of a risk of reprisals, German
listeners feeling we were propaganding, etc.'[2]

It was very difficult for the BBC in September 1939 to explain
to the home public or to the world precisely what had been
happening behind the scenes, what were its new terms of
reference, how its freedom had been restricted, why television
had been brought to such an abrupt standstill, why there was
only one home programme, and why the range of foreign
broadcasting remained so restricted. There were often the best
of reasons—particularly, of course, for synchronization—but
to have given an explanation would have involved a public
discussion of air defence, of transmitter strength and of the
organization and distribution of propaganda, all of which
topics had 'top secret' implications.[3] What made the position
much worse for the BBC, however, was that ministers responsible directly or indirectly for broadcasting policy were
unnecessarily evasive and left the BBC vulnerable to ill-
informed criticism. When, for example, Sir Edward Grigg,
the Parliamentary Secretary to the Ministry of Information,
was asked on 21 September why British broadcasting was
restricted to two wavelengths, he could only reply very lamely
that 'it would not be in the public interest to give an answer'.[4]
Many of the references of Lord Macmillan, the first Minister
of Information, to the BBC were 'inaccurate or derogatory or
lukewarm'.[5] Not surprisingly, the Director-General was
complaining as late as December 1939 that he could only

[1] Quoted in H. Grisewood, *One Thing at a Time* (1968), p. 130.
[2] *Note of an interview (on 6 July) between Graves and Lord Perth, 10 July
1939.
[3] For an example of an article in a responsible periodical which failed to
appreciate any of the reasons for the BBC's actions, see 'A Listener', 'The Political
Use of Broadcasting' in the *Political Quarterly*, June 1940. 'After six months of war
we are still being given only a single home programme . . . without the monopoly
it is doubtful if this lamentable state of affairs would have happened.' The writer
went on in the strongest language to blame the BBC for decisions which had been
taken not by the Corporation but by the Government.
[4] *Hansard*, vol. 351, col. 1077.
[5] *Farquharson to Ogilvie, 22 Dec. 1939. See below, pp. 100–1.

remember 'one occasion off-hand when the Government spokesman pointed—and that very half-heartedly—to the real cause of the trouble'.[1] He was doubtless referring to a passing reference by Sir Samuel Hoare in a House of Commons debate on 11 October to the fact that the 'danger of giving navigational aid to enemy aircraft' was 'the sole reason why there is at present only a single programme'.[2] What Hoare gave away then in the form of an aside should surely have been made into a substantive statement of policy, delivered far earlier.

The passion for secrecy was deep-seated and infectious. Before the war Graves had asked Sir Thomas Gardiner of the Post Office whether it would be desirable to warn local authorities that they would not be able to make much use of broadcasting in time of war as a medium for conveying urgent information and instruction to the people in their local areas for whom they were responsible. Gardiner had replied forbiddingly that 'war-time arrangements in relation to broadcasting are regarded as very secret, and I think it would be better not to say anything to local authorities that might lead them to inquire what is in mind'.[3]

The task of telling the public what was happening and for that matter of protecting the BBC might have been expected to fall on the newly formed Ministry of Information. Yet the Ministry not only lacked experience, drive and authority, but had changed considerably in conception in the months leading up to the outbreak of war. It had been decided as long ago as October 1935—by the Committee of Imperial Defence—that in time of war Government would assume 'effective control of broadcasting and the BBC',[4] and a year later the

---

[1] *Ogilvie to Lord Dufferin, 19 Dec. 1939; Ogilvie to Sir Edward Grigg, 16 Dec. 1939. 'The Government should at least make it *abundantly* clear to the public from *time to time* that they are themselves responsible for the war-time system of transmission which is at the root of our single programme, and therefore of most of such troubles as we have.' Grigg was the only Government spokesman during this period to give the BBC any encouragement. The other spokesmen, according to Ogilvie (16 Dec. 1939), were 'sub-tepid' in their remarks.

[2] *Hansard*, vol. 352, col. 395.

[3] *Graves to Gardiner, 15 Feb. 1939; Gardiner to Graves, 16 Feb. 1939.

[4] *Quoted in Graves to the Secretary of the Ministry of Health, 20 April 1939, asking for billeting reservations at Evesham, to which BBC sections were to be evacuated. There was no reply to this letter by 12 May when Graves wrote again. The reply finally arrived on 3 June.

Ullswater Committee had 'recognised' that 'in serious or national emergencies . . . full governmental control would be necessary over the BBC'.[1] In the same year it had been envisaged that the Ministry of Information would become responsible for 'censorship control over the programmes of the BBC'.[2] Reith and Sir Thomas Gardiner had reached agreement that, if war broke out, the Board of Governors of the BBC would go 'out of commission', that the BBC's Director-General and his deputy should become the only two Governors, and that the new Minister of Information should have power to prescribe broadcasting hours in war time and to give notice vetoing any broadcast matter, 'either particular or general'. In addition, 'regular contact' was envisaged between the Minister and the BBC's Director-General 'for other than censorship purposes'—an agreement which left the way open for an undefined measure of government control over broadcasting policy.[3]

Reith would doubtless have tried to interpret this understanding positively in the interests of the BBC, relying on the strength of his experience and the power of his personality. He would have also hoped that through Sir Stephen Tallents, who had served as the BBC's Controller (Public Relations) since 1936 and was nominated as the first Director-Designate of the Ministry of Information, he would be able to hold together BBC and Ministry. Yet Reith had left the BBC by the time that a formal deed of agreement was signed in August 1938 on behalf of the Postmaster General, R. C. Norman and C. H. G. Millis, two of the Governors, and Graves, the Deputy Director-General. It did not touch on the position of the Governors, but it set out that in case of national emergency the Postmaster General would inform the BBC in writing that most of his powers would pass to the Minister of Information, who *inter alia* could 'give notice vetoing any broadcast matter either particular or general' and 'approve the use of the stations for

---

[1] Cmd. 5091 (1936), *Report of the Broadcasting Committee*, para. 57.

[2] The decision to set up such a Ministry followed a report of a sub-committee of the Committee of Imperial Defence appointed in October 1935. Reith served on the sub-committee along with Sir Warren Fisher, Sir John Dill, Sir Robert Vansittart and others.

[3] See Briggs, op. cit., p. 632; Reith, *Into the Wind*, p. 305; *BBC Paper, 'The BBC and the Ministry of Information', 27 July 1938.

messages other than broadcast matter'.[1] It was on the basis of
this deed that the Postmaster General formally notified the BBC
on 5 September 1939 that the state of emergency existed.[2]

Between August 1938 and September 1939 there had been
many changes in the pattern as envisaged by Reith, and
although the BBC emerged on paper, at least, with a greater
measure of constitutional independence, what was irretrievably
lost was the possibility of an effective war-time interlocking
Directorate of BBC and Ministry. The first change was that
in January 1939 Tallents was asked to withdraw from the post
of Director-General Designate of the Ministry.[3] He was
replaced first by Sir Ernest Fass, the Public Trustee, who
because of ill health could devote little time to his duties, and
second, in June 1939, by Lord Perth, a diplomat.[4] Neither of
them knew anything about broadcasting. Nor did A. P.
Waterfield, the Deputy Director-General of the proposed
Ministry, the man with whom the BBC had most to do in the
critical weeks before war broke out. To make matters worse,
Waterfield was 'on loan', with 'no conveniences for official
letter writing', at the crucial time just before the Ministry
formally came into existence.[5] 'On the whole,' Waterfield wrote

[1] *Supplemental Deed of 3 Aug. 1938. The reference in the supplemental Deed
to 'the Minister' somewhat concerned the Chairman of Governors who thought
that it might possibly be construed as a Minister of Religion rather than of the
Government.

[2] *Sir Raymond Birchall to Ogilvie, 5 Sept. 1939.

[3] *Sir Samuel Hoare to Tallents, 16 Jan. 1939, thanking him for his services.
Sir Warren Fisher had thanked Ogilvie for Tallents's help in September 1938 in a
'really difficult situation' (letter of 24 Nov. 1938). Yet Tallents, who had written
a long memorandum on the activities of the Shadow Ministry, was no longer
thought to be the right man.

[4] *On 8 June 1939 Graves wrote to Ogilvie saying that he had arranged for
Ogilvie to meet the Director-General of the Ministry 'in about ten days or so,
as the gentleman in question has had to go off and rest under doctor's orders'. This
seems to have been a common occurrence with D.-G.s of the Ministry of Information. Perth himself was replaced by Sir Findlater Stewart a few days after war
broke out.

[5] *A. P. Waterfield to C. A. Siepmann, who was planning the schedule of
war-time programmes, 16 Aug. 1939. Siepmann had already had to warn him
(letter of 15 Aug. 1939) not to overdo official announcements on the radio. 'There
is one (proposed) announcement, for instance, dealing with evacuation which tells
mothers to send their children off to school, equipped with as many, I think, as
8 articles listed in the announcement. . . . I don't frankly believe that the average
working mother will take in such instructions, at any rate on a single reading.'

to an experienced broadcaster to whom he was offering a job in August 1939, 'we shall have close and constant contact with the BBC who will remain constitutionally independent, but will naturally act under Government instructions so far as may be necessary in matters that concern the national interest and the conduct of the war.'[1]

Functions changed as much as personalities. It was decided, for example, in March 1939, that censorship of BBC programmes should be transferred from the Ministry of Information to the BBC: the BBC Controller (Programmes) would act as Chief Censor, assisted by delegate censors to be appointed by him.[2] Censorship of news was to fall outside this arrangement, and 'political censorship' was to be exercised directly by the Director-General himself—in 'contact with' the Minister of Information. In place of an interlocking directorate at the highest level, there were to be links at a lower level, as there had been at the time of Munich, and members of BBC staff, several of them from the News Department, were seconded to the Ministry.[3]

As these and other domestic arrangements were being made, the Foreign Office, which had relaxed its inspection of the scripts of German and Italian broadcasts early in 1939,[4] delegated the control of propaganda to enemy countries in war time to a committee presided over by Sir Campbell

---

[1] Waterfield to Fielden, 1 Aug. 1939, quoted in *The Natural Bent* (1960), p. 206.

[2] *Note by Graves on Relationships with the Ministry of Information, 29 March 1939. Reith had envisaged that the Chief Executive Broadcasting Censor of the Control Division of the Ministry of Information would be a BBC official and that the Broadcasting Censors under him would all be BBC officials, seconded to the Ministry.

[3] By 25 Aug. 1939, when Ministry appointments were still in flux (*Note by Wellington), 38 people had been seconded from the BBC to the Ministry of Information. They included J. C. S. Macgregor, who later became head of the Broadcasting Division of the Ministry, Robert Kemp of the Features and Drama Department, a brilliant producer who returned in September, and N. G. Luker of the Talks Department, who subsequently became its head. The BBC had emphasized in May 1939 (*Wellington to Pym, 5 May 1939) that 'we are very anxious not to have to second people for the duration of a war'.

[4] *Exchange of views between Lord Halifax and Ogilvie, 1 Nov. 1938; statement by R. A. Butler in the House of Commons, 22 May 1939 (*Hansard*, vol. 347, cols. 1893–4). By July 1939 the chief complaint of the European News Department was not against outside control, but against the fact that there was lack of sufficient background information to put the BBC and Press diplomatic correspondents on equal terms.

Stuart, a veteran of Crewe House, the propaganda centre of the First World War.[1] Stuart's committee had met once by March 1939.[2] His plans for an 'Enemy Publicity organisation' included both broadcasting and leaflets from aeroplanes, and Ryan, Tallents's deputy, was appointed as liaison officer to assist him, '50 per cent our man', as Graves put it, '50 per cent Campbell Stuart's'.[3] He proposed to open his headquarters on September 1st at Electra House. Few people inside the BBC, even the people concerned with the *Sonderbericht* programmes, knew of the existence of Electra House when the war began.

Co-ordination of different agencies proved difficult to achieve even before the war had started; and Waterfield was upset when the Armed Services acted independently and, to his consternation, sent messages from Gort and Ironside direct to the BBC News Room 'on the personal instruction of the Secretary of State himself'.[4]

The Governors of the BBC had never learned at the time the full details of the Reith-Gardiner talks of June 1938. They had never been consulted when it was proposed that they would disappear once war started, and although they had been informed of this decision during the Munich crisis, they had made no observations, 'presumably because of the immediate threat of war'.[5] In June 1939, however, Sir Ian Fraser formally raised the important question whether it was advisable either in the interests of the BBC or of the nation for Ogilvie and Sir Cecil Graves, his deputy, both paid servants of the Corporation, to become the sole war-time Governors. At the same time, he argued, there were great objections to complete government control and direction.[6]

[1] See his book *Secrets of Crewe House* (1920).

[2] *Note by Graves, 29 March 1939. The meeting, attended also by Rex Leeper of the Foreign Office, met in January. Leeper was to be a most important figure in the subsequent story. [3] Ibid.

[4] *Waterfield to Graves, 4 Sept. 1939. He sent a 'fierce letter' to P. J. Grigg at the War Office asking him to see that in future 'the approved procedure is strictly adhered to'.

[5] *Board of Governors, *Minutes*, 28 Sept. 1938; Sir Ian Fraser, 'Memorandum on Control of Broadcasting', 27 June 1939. Fraser, who had become a Governor at the end of 1936, has set out his account of what happened in 1938 and 1939 in *Whereas I was Blind* (1942), pp. 162 ff.

[6] *'Memorandum on Control of Broadcasting', 27 June 1939; *Board of Governors, *Minutes*, 28 June, 6 July 1939.

The Governors discussed the proposed changes at their meeting on 6 July, when Ogilvie said that it would be best if he were to leave the room.[1] After formulating their views independently, they sent a deputation to meet Sir Horace Wilson, Chamberlain's confidential adviser, and Waterfield, at 10 Downing Street on 21 July. The arrangements, they complained, had been arrived at 'behind their backs'. While they would be prepared to resign *en bloc* if asked to do so or to accept a reduction in their numbers, they objected in principle to the promotion of 'officials' to be Governors. They added that although the Government might legitimately exert a closer control over broadcasting in war time than in peace time, 'the total eclipse of the independence of the Corporation would be widely regarded as a serious blow to liberty, and would create difficulties for the Government before the public opinion in the country'.[2]

Wilson was impressed by their arguments. When he suggested, however, that a compromise might be reached whereby there would be a small Board of Governors, consisting of the Chairman, the Vice-Chairman, the Director-General and the Deputy Director-General, the Governors reiterated their objection 'in principle' to making the two 'officials' Governors. 'Certain of the members of the Board felt,' they went on, 'that the chief executive officers, so far from gaining increased freedom of action by doubling the role of Governor and executive, might be hampered thereby.'[3] At last, after further talks between Ogilvie, Graves, and Wilson on 31 July—at which Ogilvie pointed out that any prolonged controversy between Governors and Government would entail 'very serious damage to the reputation of the BBC'[4]—the Government decided that

[1] *Ogilvie had first been informed of the proposed war-time arrangement by the Postmaster General on 27 Sept. 1938 before he took office. The Vice-Chairman, Millis, was at pains to tell him in July 1939 that the Governors had complete confidence in him. 'With the BBC's future in the hands of you, and Graves to assist you, I haven't a qualm in the world.' (Letter of 17 July 1939.) He added, however, 'You merely stepped into a state of affairs that already existed'. H. A. L. Fisher was less flattering and stated baldly in a letter of 19 July 1939 that 'the Governors are anxious for an exchange of views upon the subject with the appropriate ministers'.

[2] *Memorandum on an interview with Sir Horace Wilson, 21 July 1939.

[3] *Millis to Sir Horace Wilson, 27 July 1939, following a meeting of the Governors the day before.

[4] *Ogilvie to Millis, 31 July 1939.

in the event of war the Chairman and Vice-Chairman would be retained as Governors and that the constitutional position of the Director-General and his Deputy would not be changed.[1] Accordingly, two days after the outbreak of the war, when the Ministry of Information came into existence, an Order-in-Council was promulgated whereby Fisher, Fraser, J. J. Mallon, Viscountess Bridgeman and Margery Fry ceased to be Governors.[2] On 5 September Powell told Lord Macmillan that he accepted the direction of the Government 'in all matters pertaining to the war effort'.[3]

This was certainly not the last of the matter. The announcement of what had happened was not released publicly until 28 September. Chamberlain, under pressure several weeks after the event, made a foolishly terse statement in the House of Commons as to why the number of Governors had been reduced. 'This reduction was made in order to ensure the smooth and swift operation of the broadcasting system under war conditions.'[4] Clement Attlee, the Leader of the Opposition, was not appeased. 'The BBC,' he grumbled, 'has now become part of a bureaucratic machine at a time when it should be most clearly in touch with public opinion.'[5] Arthur Greenwood pursued the charge further a few weeks later when he accused the Government of being 'dishonest' about their *fait accompli* in getting rid of five Governors in one fell swoop.[6] A letter from Fisher to *The Times* kept the issue open. The 'dismissed Governors' had not approved of the new arrangement, he noted: they had merely acquiesced in it. 'The truth is,' Fisher went on, 'that, without

---

[1] *Wilson to Millis, 1 Aug. 1939, with copy to Graves. Millis to Wilson (1 Aug. 1939) and Graves to Wilson (2 Aug. 1939), expressed their satisfaction with the 'settlement'. Millis wrote also to Ogilvie on 1 August thanking him for his 'understanding and sympathetic attitude throughout', adding 'the confident hope that this situation—which was none of your making or of the Board's should not cast even a shadow on the unique relationship that exists between the Board and you and Graves. That is all that really matters.'

[2] *Board of Governors, *Minutes*, 24 Sept. 1939, describes how the Governors were told of the change.

[3] *Powell to Macmillan, 5 Sept. 1939. A document revising the Reith–Gardiner agreement, known as Document C, had been drafted in August 1939. (Waterfield to Graves, 4 Sept. 1939, referring to 'that formidable document known as Document C.)

[4] *Hansard*, vol. 351, col. 1491.

[5] Ibid., vol. 351, col. 1491.

[6] Ibid., vol. 352, col. 382.

the consultation of the Board of Governors, an Order-in-Council was prepared last year eliminating the Governors altogether in the event of war. It was only as a result of an energetic protest from the Governors, made when they were apprised of this arrangement, that the present arrangement was arrived at . . . [It is one] which they willingly accept as a temporary war-time measure, though it would not have occurred to them to suggest it, having regard to the general interests of the listening public.'[1]

Ogilvie was goaded by this letter into drafting a note of his own 'for record purposes' in which he queried the propriety of an ex-Governor revealing through the Press a Government plan which, good or bad, was strictly secret.[2] For the most part, however, he wisely kept his feelings to himself, even though they strongly influenced his attitudes during the last weeks of 1939 when suggestions were being made once more that the number of Governors should be increased.[3] By this time, indeed, Ogilvie was thoroughly unhappy not only about the way in which government departments were handling issues relating to broadcasting but also about their silence when the BBC itself was in no position to reply to criticisms made in ignorance of the true facts. In addition, therefore, to telling Sir Horace Wilson that if the number of Governors were increased the public would be encouraged in their belief that 'the war was never going to begin at home and that the war measures which broadcasting had taken were unnecessary', he moved over into a forthright, even truculent, attack. 'The BBC,' he went on, 'had gone through a very difficult time in the early days of the war, due mainly to acts of Government which the BBC could not even explain to the public—the transmission system

---

[1] *The Times*, 23 Oct. 1939. Miss Fry and Mallon had expressed their views less forcibly in the *Manchester Guardian*, 30 Sept. 1939, where they argued 'that the important thing was that the BBC Charter should be operated, and that the Corporation should not become a Government Department. We were agreed on that point and it has been conceded.'

[2] *Note by Ogilvie, 24 Oct. 1939; Tallents to Farquharson, 24 Oct. 1939.

[3] Creech Jones, then a backbench Labour M.P., asked a parliamentary question on the subject on 13 Dec. 1939 (*Hansard*, vol 355, cols. 1187–8). The BBC took the view that since the war might become 'more intensive' at any time in the future there was 'no sufficient reason for reversing a measure which was decided by all concerned'. (*Brief for the Minister of Information, agreed by Tallents, 12 Dec. 1939.)

(covered only by the blessed formula "national security"); Government mishandling of publicity regarding the change in the Governors, the failure of M.I.5 to O.K. our artists at reasonable speed; racketeering by Cabinet Ministers over their talks, the important restrictions upon the Opposition, etc. If the Governors were brought back now this would simply be regarded by the public as lack of confidence in the BBC and would be a further serious knock for us. . . . Reinstatement of the Governors now would be jam for Goebbels.'[1]

As Ogilvie implied, the reduction in the number of Governors and the change in his own position were merely two of many matters about which BBC and Government were at logger-heads during the first months of the war. The basic trouble, leaving on one side the unexpected character of the war itself, was that both the BBC and the Government had gone into the war uncertain of what their future relationship would be.

There were only two general guidelines. On 28 July in the House of Commons, Sir Samuel Hoare, who had been put in charge of the discussions about the role of the future Ministry of Information, made what looked like the one definitive statement about the future. The Government, he said, did not propose 'to take over the BBC in war time', but 'would treat broadcasting as we treat the Press and other methods of publicity, the Press and the films, and . . . leave the BBC to carry on . . . with a very close liaison between the Ministry of Information and the Broadcasting Corporation, with definite regulations as to how the work should be carried on'.[2] On the same day, free from all publicity, Waterfield telephoned Ogilvie that 'in matters of national interest or such as affect the conduct of the war the Corporation will naturally be prepared to act under the instructions of the Government. But the Government are anxious to do nothing which will affect the fundamental structure of the Corporation which they believe to be sound'.[3]

[1] *Record of interview with Sir Horace Wilson at Wilson's request, 29 Nov. 1939. Ogilvie also prepared a summary of exactly what had happened at different times in relation to the position of the Governors. This statement was signed by Powell and Millis on 8 Dec. 1939.

[2] *Hansard*, vol. 350, col. 1838.

[3] *Note of a telephone message from Waterfield, 28 July 1939.

Both assurances proved shaky, and it seemed to Ogilvie that a Ministry of Information memorandum called 'The Organisation of the Ministry', which clearly stated that there would be a 'Director of Radio' in the Ministry, unconnected with the BBC, gave colour to the popular belief that the Government had in effect taken over the BBC. Powell agreed with Ogilvie and directed attention to several discrepancies between the Ministry's memorandum and Hoare's statement. As a result of his criticisms, the Ministry, which conceded that its memorandum had been 'prepared hurriedly', changed the title 'Director of Radio and Communications' to 'Director of Radio Relations'.[1] Its spokesmen admitted that they would have to pay more attention to the 'tempo' as well as to the content of broadcasting, although Sir Kenneth Lee, the first Director of Radio Relations, knew little of the BBC and was quickly promoted in November to the Director-Generalship of the Ministry. H. G. G. Welch, formerly of the Post Office, took his place.[2]

While civil servants tried to establish new routines and ministers seemed uncertain or evasive about even the broad outlines of policy, events soon showed how difficult it was to carry on quietly the work of the BBC in war time. At the end of the first hectic twelve weeks Ogilvie produced a catalogue of complaints which was something in the nature of a *cri de coeur*. To understand fully what he said it is necessary to turn in greater detail to the sequence of trials and tribulations.

2. 'Twelve Weeks of War'

THE twelve weeks began in effect on Friday, 1 September 1939, two days before Chamberlain's broadcast, when orders had been signalled to every transmitting station and studio of the BBC to change over to war conditions. There were no hitches.

[1] *Record of a meeting between Powell, Ogilvie, Reith and Waterfield, 12 Sept. 1939.

[2] On matters of policy Ivison Macadam, Head of Publicity at the Ministry, was still thought of as the key figure. (*Lee to Ogilvie, 14 Nov. 1939.) Macadam ceased to be the 'contact man' early in 1940. (*Lee to Ogilvie, 13 Jan. 1940.)

The engineers carried out their plans quietly and efficiently, and large numbers of programme staff dispersed to sites outside London. The two wavelengths designated for home broadcasting came into operation, with 'synchronisation' of two groups of medium-wave transmitters.[1] This inevitably meant not only that the total number of hours of broadcasting output were curtailed—with, so it seemed, a consequent threat of redundancy to a large proportion of programme staff—but that listeners in many parts of the country would suffer from poor reception or worse reception than that to which they were accustomed. Most important of all, freedom of choice disappeared for home listeners. There was now only one programme.

If the war had immediately sprung to life and if, as had been expected, there had been large-scale attacks from the air, all these implications would have been quickly accepted. Credit would have been given to the Corporation for foresight and planning, for taking precautions which were not taken, for example, across the Channel in France. As it was, most home listeners, completely ignorant of what was happening behind the scenes, judged the BBC in terms not of its technical skill in switching from a peace-time to war-time service but, as they had always judged it, in terms of the appeal of its programmes. They were not satisfied.

The question of what to do with a single broadcasting service, a question posed earlier during the very first years of broadcasting,[2] had been discussed by a BBC sub-committee in relation to war-time conditions in the distant spring of 1938.[3] The committee included the Director of Programme Planning and the Director of Overseas Services, along with Colonel Stafford, the Defence Executive, and started with the premise that the listener's main preoccupation would 'presumably be with the reception of news, of official statements and instruction

[1] See above, p. 79.

[2] Briggs, *The Birth of Broadcasting* (1961), pp. 208 ff.

[3] *Reith had thought about the problems which this Committee faced earlier, when he envisaged that talks in war time would have to be largely of a utilitarian character to hold the interest of the public on that basis. (Draft Note on 'The Position of the BBC in War', July 1935.) Another undated memorandum, 'Protection against Air Attack' (1935), laid emphasis on the BBC maintaining 'the fortitude of the population, particularly in crowded and urban areas' and 'conceived that the broadcasting of programmes of music [sic] may be a very valuable factor to this end'. See Briggs, *The Golden Age of Wireless*, p. 630.

of all sorts'. News, therefore, in the committee's view, should be the chief programme item, laced with 'instruction', in a broadcasting day which would last from seven o'clock in the morning until midnight. Nonetheless, it was argued, entertainment could not be completely excluded, because of the need to maintain 'general morale', a need emphasized by the Home Office. To provide 'adequate distraction from the ordinary listeners' inevitable sense of strain, due regard should be paid *inter alia* to the importance of religion [note that this came first], varied entertainment and to the satisfaction derived from well-known personalities'. Half an hour was to be the maximum length of any programme. The Daily Service and Children's Hour were to remain as fixed points in the schedules. Outside broadcasts were considered to be particularly important, particularly 'sing-songs, concert parties, etc., from training camps', but only 'a very restricted field' was envisaged for talks and for drama and features, apart from topical war features if artists were available. It was agreed that some provision would have to be made for broadcasts in foreign languages, 'possibly on a slightly larger scale than that at present operated', and that in all programmes, far more material would have to be recorded, if only because of shortage both of staff and of artists. 'Our supply of commercial gramophone records is ample and up to date, but in view of the risk involved by centralised storage, we recommend that 1,000 assorted popular records should be despatched immediately to each of our Regional Offices to be kept for use in time of war.' Precautions would have to be taken throughout, it was felt, against enemy 'jamming'. 'Jamming the outgoing or incoming short-wave service would be somewhat easier than the jamming of the Home Service although even so it is not thought that an enemy could completely obliterate it'.[1]

Further reports in January 1939, this time from a different committee, suggested that there might be a 22 hours' service with two hours left over in the middle of the night for 'adjustment and maintenance'. Programmes would have to be 'simple', particularly at the beginning of hostilities, but 'their scope and entertainment value should be gradually increased as circumstances permit'. 'The maintenance of public morale should be

[1] *Interim report of the Sub-Committee on War-Time Programmes, May 1938.

the principal aim of war-time programmes.'[1] The balance of programme constituents in hours each week would be completely changed, as the following table shows:[2]

	Jan. 1939[2]	Envisaged for War time	Percentage Change
News	12	21	+75%
Talks	30	7	−77%
Music	110	70	−36%
Variety	60	24	−60%
Drama/Features	16	4	−75%
Outside Broadcasts	4	1	−75%
Schools	13	10	−23%
Children's Hour	16	4	−75%
Religion	16	6	−62%
Special Announcements	—	7	—
Total hours each week	277	154	−44%

It was in the light of the recommendations of this latter committee that the Director of Programme Planning, Charles Siepmann, had gone ahead with his plan for the period of unspecified length 'immediately following the outbreak of war', after which there would be 'a changeover to complete war-time planning'. In April 1939, therefore, a week's war-time programmes were planned in detail, with the necessary music and scripts and artists 'ready for action'. Not everything was settled, however. On the eve of the war, with the programmes prepared, Siepmann was complaining to Waterfield about 'the form of words' to be used in official notices, questioning the value or necessity of having one Admiralty announcement broadcast three times a day both in English and Gaelic[3] and, more seriously, considering to what extent local announcements could be fitted into one single national programme and by whose authority they should be broadcast: 'one has to contemplate the proposal for an announcement coming from some agitated local mayor whose sense of proportion may have failed him in a crisis.'[4]

[1] *Report of the Defence Sub-Committee on War-Time Programmes, 11 Jan. 1939.
[2] The hours figure for January 1939 was based on London plus regional output.
[3] *Siepmann to Waterfield, 15 Aug. 1939.
[4] *Waterfield to John Hilton, 30 Aug. 1939.

On the headings of Waterfield's official notepaper the word 'nucleus' had been typed after the title 'Ministry of Information': this disappeared, at last, on a letter of 10 September, when he sent on to Siepmann a copy of a letter from 'a very shrewd old lady of 82 years in Wales' who had listened to all the programmes during the week of crisis and 'had found the wireless a great comfort—it was everything to have news given frequently and always clearly and correct.'[1] The only trouble was that she had distinctly heard gramophone records 'at intervals during Mr. Chamberlain's speech'.

The BBC's earliest war-time programmes from 1 September onwards did not appeal to the public as much as they appealed to the old lady in Wales. The programmes consisted of ten daily news bulletins—there had been five before war broke out—and scores of official announcements, lasting for at least one hour a day, hundreds of gramophone records, pep talks by Ministers, of which there were thirteen before the end of the first week in October, and by civil servants, and large doses of Sandy Macpherson (23 in the first week and 22 in the second), unruffled and inviolate at the Theatre Organ.[2] At first, loud-speakers were rarely turned off, and new radio sets were installed in many places, including Parliament itself, which had hitherto eschewed them. The King's speech on 3 September, pronounced with 'depth of feeling' and asking his fellow countrymen 'to stand calm, firm and united in this time of trial', was thought to be reassuring and moving,[3] but thereafter complaints about other programmes multiplied.

The earliest criticisms were rueful; soon they became clamorous. With only churches and public houses open as places of public resort during the first days of war—George Bernard Shaw described the shutdown order on theatres, cinemas and concert halls as 'a master stroke of unimaginative stupidity'[4]—

---

[1] *Waterfield to Siepmann, 10 Sept. 1939.

[2] See the excellent account in his lively autobiography *Sandy Presents* (1950).

[3] It is printed in full in the *BBC Handbook, 1940*, pp. 35–36. See also J. W. Wheeler-Bennett, *King George VI* (1965), pp. 406–7. The Ministry of Information announced that a copy of the broadcast would be sent to every household in the land, but the King himself told the Prime Minister to forget this extravagant gesture after the Post Office had shuddered and there had been complaints that paper would be wasted.

[4] *The Times*, 5 Sept. 1939.

life gravitated back to the home, and broadcasting seemed inadequate either to reflect people's mood or to change it. In the light of what was to happen in 1940, when total war really began, it is interesting that a novel written by the greatest radio personality of 1940, J. B. Priestley, *Let the People Sing*, was one of the few projects planned in peace time to survive the new broadcasting arrangements. Yet it needed more than a novel in seventeen instalments to carry the public along in September 1939.

On Sunday 17 September a vigorous Press offensive against BBC war-time programmes started in the columns of the *Sunday Chronicle* and the *Sunday Referee*. The BBC, it was maintained, had missed a magnificent opportunity of proving its mettle. With a nation robbed of its theatre, cinema and concert halls 'and thirsting for the superb in music and drama, and the rib-tickling jokes of our drolls, what an opportunity was here— yet the BBC entertainments have been puerile'.[1] Marsland Gander, one of the most distinguished radio critics, agreed with the verdict;[2] and while the *Daily Mail* attacked 'the BBC Black-Out', Hannen Swaffer in the *Daily Herald* suggested that C. B. Cochran should immediately be put in charge of all entertainment programmes.[3] 'For God's sake, how long is the BBC to be allowed to broadcast its travesty of a programme which goes under the name of entertainment?' Peter Wilson demanded in the *Sunday Pictorial*.[4] 'I call this a scandal,' Collie Knox thundered. 'Never in its history has the BBC approached so near to slickness of organisation as in its disappearing trick to two refuges "somewhere in England" . . . In a twinkling, bang went all regional endeavour . . . bang went the contracts of hundreds of artists and instrumentalists, to say nothing of its own staff, and bang went the programmes back to the concert party, sand-shoe days of Savoy Hill.'[5]

The Press attack continued into October, with the weeklies and more specialized periodicals joining in, with Compton Mackenzie on the offensive in *The Gramophone*, and the *New Statesman* urging that the ordinary British listener should be

[1] *Sunday Chronicle* and *Sunday Referee*, 17 Sept. 1939.
[2] *Daily Telegraph*, 18 Sept. 1939.
[3] *Daily Mail*, 20 Sept. 1939; *Daily Herald*, 18 Sept. 1939.
[4] *Sunday Pictorial*, 24 Sept. 1939.
[5] *Daily Mail*, 22 Sept. 1939.

provided with an alternative programme collated from the BBC's own foreign broadcasts.[1] The attack soon moved into Parliament. 'There is a very wide criticism of broadcasting,' Attlee told the House on 26 September. 'I am not a habitual listener, but I must say that at times I feel depressed when I listen in. You should not be depressed by listening in.'[2] From the Government back benches Sir Arnold Wilson agreed with him. 'The BBC wants a thorough clearing out of . . . its present personnel and the substitution of men attuned as few of them are to the needs of war, with new ideas and a fresh outlook.'[3] On 11 October 1939 Arthur Greenwood could claim that he was speaking for Britain as he had been told he had done earlier during the debates about Britain going to war: 'I have myself had very little time to do as much listening in as many people, but I hear everywhere complaints about the "Weeping Will" programmes that have been given. We have to remember that in conditions of war, with the limitations there are in public entertainment outside our homes, the BBC becomes the main source of public entertainment for millions of people. In these days of train restrictions, lighting restrictions, restrictions here, there and everywhere, and the determination on the part of the Government to make the life of everybody as miserable as possible, it would be well if we could have some brighter entertainment from the BBC.' France had seventeen alternative programmes. Why not England? And why had no national leader broadcast a 'cheering' message—with the exception of Churchill a few days before? 'It is vital that the leaders of public opinion in this country should keep in constant touch with the people of this country. . . . We should have more broadcasts from the front and to the front. Why should we not hear the voice of the Commander-in-Chief over the wireless? Why should we not hear from the Tommy or the lance corporal, or the sergeant the story of the life he is leading out there? . . . The BBC should be less brief, more bright and more brotherly.'[4]

This wave of criticism, much of it justified, could not be

---

[1] *New Statesman*, 23 Sept. 1939; *The Gramophone*, Oct. 1939.
[2] *Hansard*, vol. 351, col. 1249.
[3] Ibid., col. 1255.
[4] *Hansard*, vol. 352, cols. 383–4.

countered adequately by the BBC on its own. It had been
foolish of the Corporation in September 1939, in an emergency
issue of the *Radio Times*, to congratulate listeners on the splendid
radio service they would continue to receive in war time,[1] and
a broadcast by Ogilvie himself on 8 September in which he
talked of continuing to 'give you our best possible service' did
not quite strike the right note.[2] Certainly there was a contrast
at this time between the mood of the people working 'like
beavers' inside the BBC,[3] often in the most difficult conditions—
all the first war programmes came from a stuffy little studio,
and Control Room was moved from the top floor of Broadcasting House to what was described as 'a wretched little cup-
board' below ground[4]—and the mood of listeners and critics.
Tom Harrisson, for example, was deeply concerned about a
failure to communicate which was expressed, he felt, both in
the language and style of presentation of programmes as well as
in their content.[5]

What few people fully appreciated was how unwilling to
communicate the Government was. 'For obvious reasons no
details can yet be disclosed' was a characteristic phrase in one
of Chamberlain's first statements about the war. In relation to
broadcasting, the Government persistently refused to explain
to the public and the Press why there was only one single home
programme and provided extraordinarily bleak answers in
Parliament to all questions relating to the BBC. The established
peace-time device of not answering in detail questions about

[1] *Radio Times*, Emergency Issue, on sale on 4 Sept. 1939. The copy with the
planned peace-time programmes for the first week in September had already gone
to press on the night of 31 Aug. War-time issue Number 2, a supplementary issue,
went to press on 5 Sept. 'The journal consequently established a record probably
unique in the story of weekly publications—that of having three press-days in one
week.' *BBC Handbook, 1940*, p. 42. (See also M. Gorham, *Sound and Fury* (1948), pp.
88–9, and *World's Press News*, 26 Nov. 1942.)

[2] He said that the BBC had had to plan to use a lot of gramophone records,
that the news service would be 'truthful and objective' and that as in the past the
broadcasting of religious services bore witness to 'the things of the spirit'.

[3] Gorham, op. cit., p. 88.

[4] J. Macleod, *A Job at the BBC* (1947), pp. 75–6. Macleod, critical though he
was of the BBC, looked back nostalgically to the first days of the war. 'In spite of
the limited programmes, it was admirable broadcasting, fresh and sincere and
human as in the earliest days of radio.'

[5] In a note of 7 Sept. 1939 he commented on the fact that there was 'no spark
of life' and no open acknowledgement of 'their special responsibility when all other
entertainments closed'. He also objected to the lack of home news.

BBC programmes was used by Chamberlain and his colleagues
to befog basic issues rather than to enlighten the public. One
of the least helpful remarks of the period, indeed, was Chamberlain's terse answer to a question from Sir Percy Harris in late
September: 'Will he see that some effort is made, now that the
Government are more responsible, to revert at least to the
standard of entertainment that existed before the war?' When
Chamberlain replied that 'conditions are very different from
what they were' and that it was not possible 'in present circumstances to maintain quite the same standard as before the
war', M.P.s called out 'Why?' and were given no answer.[1]
Nor did they get any answer from the Minister of Information,
Lord Macmillan.

The nadir in relations between the BBC and the rapidly
growing Ministry of Information was reached on 26 September,
when in answer to a direct challenge in the House of Lords
Macmillan said that he 'believed' the Board (of the BBC) had
'been more or less suspended and that the Chairman and Directors are in charge', but that he did not know 'exactly what the
control' was.[2] If the Minister of Information did not know
'exactly what the control was', how could the public be expected to know? Macmillan, in fact, added to the confusion by
implying that the BBC was 'independent' only as to 'shall I say,
the lighter parts of its programmes'.[3]

The Ministry of Information, as distinct from the Minister,
did little more to help the BBC in its home broadcasting during
the early weeks of the war. At the meeting of the Ministry's
Advisory Council on 15 September, when members were told
that the 'extremely complicated operation of synchronisation
had gone through quite smoothly', there was no discussion of
issues either helpful or harmful to the BBC and several members
of the committee strongly criticized the proposal, later to be
taken up by Greenwood, to allow members of the Forces to
broadcast anonymously. At the second meeting of the Council
the Chairman asked members for guidance as to what they

---

[1] *Hansard*, vol 351, col. 1493.

[2] *Official Reports, House of Lords*, vol. 114, cols. 1139–1140.

[3] Ibid. 'They must publish what is delivered to them authoritatively from the
Ministry of Information.' Macmillan also said in the House of Lords (vol. 114,
cols. 1280–1281) that 'you always have the privilege of not listening, which is one
of the greatest privileges I know in connection with the BBC'.

should talk about next.[1] In the meantime, the Ministry's Radio
Relations Division, to which two BBC officials, J. C. S. Macgregor and Andrew Stewart, had been seconded, insisted on
seeing in advance the names of all broadcasters, including
musicians,[2] a procedure not explained to the public which led
to such considerable delay that it seemed easiest for the BBC to
employ the same approved artists time and time again.[3] Outside broadcasts proved almost impossible to arrange, not only
for censorship reasons but because the Post Office lines, on
which such broadcasts depended, were unavoidably congested.
News releases to the BBC were delayed and on several occasions
their broadcasting was held up, with the embargo 'not to appear
before tomorrow morning's papers'.

The Press itself, for all its criticism of BBC programmes, was
not a neutral observer in all this. The Ministry insisted throughout that the BBC should not be allowed 'to prejudice the reasonable rights of the Press', and Macmillan himself took public
credit for the reduction in the number of BBC news bulletins.[4]
Particular objection was taken to the afternoon bulletin at four
o'clock, which was said to harm the interests of the proprietors
of evening newspapers. Although the BBC had emphasized
before war broke out that its desire to provide constant news
bulletins throughout did not spring from any ambition to compete with the Press but was simply based on a sense of the
national interest,[5] its assurances had been brushed aside.
Ogilvie believed that the Ministry was actually hampering the

[1] *Ministry of Information, Advisory Council, *Minutes*, 15 Sept. 1939. For the
unfortunate preoccupation of some people within the BBC with the 'smoothness'
of the arrangements, see Sir Stephen Tallents, 'British Broadcasting and the War',
in the *Atlantic Monthly*, March 1940, which begins: 'On the evening of Friday,
September 1st, 1939, Whitehall flashed through to the headquarters of the BBC in
Portland Place the order to take up its war stations. . . . Instantly, all over the
country, engineers unsealed and obeyed an intricate code of instructions.'

[2] See S. Macpherson, op. cit., p. 97: he was the only organist 'passed' by the
Ministry.

[3] Details of this system of control 'leaked' and were published in *The Star*, 26
Sept. 1939, and the following day Gale Pedrick wrote an article in *The Star* dealing
one by one with those criticisms made of the BBC for which it was not responsible.

[4] Lord Macmillan, *Official Reports, House of Lords*, vol. 114, cols. 1070-71, 14
Sept. 1939. He objected to the BBC 'stealing a march on the evening editions'.

[5] *Note of an interview between Graves and Waterfield, 18 July 1939. At the
second meeting of the Ministry of Information Advisory Council Ogilvie stressed
that 'fundamentally the BBC and the Press were not competitors; they were
friends and allies in a common cause'.

BBC in its relations with the Press, and on 20 September urged the Minister through Lee that the BBC and the Press should be left as in peace time to determine their own mutual relations and that the Ministry should be brought in only in the event of a disagreement.[1]

An acceptable pattern of war-time home broadcasting was not to take shape until the last four weeks of 1939, yet to see these early conflicts and dissatisfactions in perspective it is necessary to note that there was a marked improvement in BBC programmes after the beginning of October, an improvement for which the BBC itself was directly responsible. As the scattered departments of the BBC settled down to work, often in difficult conditions, careful stock was taken of how broadcasting should develop in war-time circumstances very different from those which had been expected. As early as mid-September, indeed, two Home Broadcasting Committees were set up, one internal and one with Ministry representation. It was at the second meeting of the first of these committees that Basil Nicolls, Controller (Programmes), announced a number of changes—a Sunday Children's Hour, more serious music, a weekly talk on the war, regular talks on 'foreign affairs', a series of 'actuality' programmes, a number of 'nostalgic features', and above all, a reduction in the number of gramophone records—along with the elimination of the word 'gramophone' from the *Radio Times*.[2] There was still a deadlock in dealings with the Newspaper and Periodicals Emergency Council which was asking for Dimbleby's 'war correspondence' to be held over each night until the following morning, but even this deadlock was soon to be overcome.[3] On 26 September Nicolls went on to mention that he had referred to Buckingham Palace the possibility of a

---

[1] *Home Broadcasting Committee, *Minutes*, 20 Sept. 1939. Lee and Welch of the Ministry of Information were present at this meeting, along with Macgregor and the BBC representatives. For the subsequent story, see below, pp. 308-9.

[2] *Home Broadcasting Committee (Internal), *Minutes*, 22 Sept. 1939.

[3] *Ibid. A five-year settlement was reached with the News Agencies in November (Memorandum by R. J. F. Howgill, 21 Nov. 1939); and on 7 Dec. 1939 an important meeting took place with the Newspaper Proprietors' Association and the Newspaper Society at which Ogilvie said 'he wished to make it abundantly clear that the BBC did not seek to damage newspaper or other interests'. 'A return to the pre-war arrangement in respect of news,' he went on, 'would seriously damage not only the reputation of the BBC, but, what was of far greater moment, the prestige of the nation as a whole.'

'Round the Empire' programme on Christmas Day culminating in a broadcast by the King.[1] Obviously the BBC was beginning to get back to normal again. Hallé concerts were scheduled again for October, but projected talks on 'men of the hour'— Stalin, for example, along with Hitler and Daladier—were turned down because it was 'felt impracticable to avoid partisanship and propaganda'.[2] It was also decided that 'foreign statesmen, including those in enemy countries' should be given 'normal courtesy titles' in all programmes—e.g. 'Herr Hitler', 'Marshal Goering', etc.—except in the reports of speeches in the House of Commons when the courtesy titles were omitted.[3] By 13 October the most familiar of all peace-time notes was struck when 'vulgarity' was being reported in Variety programmes.[4]

An attempt was made by Ogilvie himself to speed up the breakaway from the very special restrictions of the first few weeks of the war, though it was an attempt which created some interesting internal debate. On 6 October, when programmes were already improving, he could not be present at the Home Broadcasting Committee meeting and wrote a memorandum to Graves asking why programme items had been badly juxtaposed ('Ukulele Ike' immediately after a religious service; Chopin's 'Funeral March' as a fade-out for the Archbishop of York), why so much recorded material was still being used between 8.30 and 11 p.m., why there were so many repeats of programmes, and above all why gramophone records were still being used so freely as 'fillers'. 'It was agreed before the war that the first week of war would have to consist very largely of gramophone records, but that thereafter we should go live almost all along the line. It is now the fifth week of the war, and there are still 18¼ hours of gramophone records in this week's *Radio Times* apart from fill-ups . . . DPP [Director of Programme Planning] assures us that in the week beginning 15 October gramophone records will be down to six hours in the week. But seven weeks is a very long time from the beginning of the war and it will take us many more weeks after that to get clear of the hang-over in the public mind.'[5]

1 *Home Broadcasting Committee, *Minutes*, 26 Sept. 1939.
2 *Ibid., 29 Sept. 1939.   3 *Ibid., 6 Oct. 1939.   4 *Ibid., 13 Oct. 1939.
5 *Ogilvie to Graves and other members of the Home Broadcasting Committee, 5 Oct. 1939.

Siepmann, who was about to leave the BBC to take up a post at Harvard in November 1939, questioned not whether the Director-General should make such detailed comments on particular programmes, but whether the new Home Broadcasting Committee was the right instrument to scrutinize programmes and whether it could ever meet at the right time to influence policy. 'Programmes as broadcast derive initially from ideas, ideas which are sifted, reconciled and co-ordinated in a plan deriving its validity from considered principles and a continuing intention. . . . This work is so intricate, and involves so many people and so much time, that we only just win the race against the clock. The scheme was precarious in peace-time,[1] now in war-time it is even more so, complicated as it is by distribution of staff and inadequate communication. Control, more than ever in the past, is a one-man job, (in the last resort that of the Controller (Programmes)). . . . Now what has happened? There is superimposed a Committee which at a late hour reviews programmes and discusses both policy and detail. The work has already been done by experts (at Wednesday Programme meetings). . . . If this Committee can add anything of value to the work which has been done within the Programme Division, it seems a reflection on you and a reflection on us.' 'Cabinet control of programmes' was bad enough, but this particular committee, consisting largely of 'amateurs' and including, for example, the Controller (Engineering), was a 'Cabinet on which sit the wrong ministers'.[2]

Wellington, who had been Assistant Controller of Programmes since 1936, pursued the same line of argument. 'It is surely the function of Controller (Programmes) to control programme policy and practice in accordance with the general direction of the Director-General. You well know the ceaseless flow of enquiry, decision, direction, implicit in this function. How can C(P) possibly retain authority and the grasp of an infinitely complicated situation if he is reduced to wielding one vote on a committee of six in which he appears not to be credited with possessing any special professional knowledge of, or responsibility for programmes? . . . Why should the detailed

---

[1] For the peace-time system of programme planning, see Briggs, *The Golden Age of Wireless*, pp. 29–33.

[2] *Siepmann to Nicolls, 11 Oct. 1939.

working of any Division come to any Committee when a responsible Controller exists for the very purpose of understanding and controlling it? Little wonder that Heads of Departments get restive at delays, contradictory policy and a general sense of trying to move by hand the enormous and cumbrous machine. There is an alternative, isn't there? Wouldn't it be better for D.G. to deal in all programme matters with C(P) direct?'[1] Nicolls went on to take up the same point, this time specifically and directly with Ogilvie himself. Some of the issues which the Director-General had raised in his letter to Graves 'had already been dealt with by you with me at the meeting I had with you at 4.45 on Wednesday last. It seems to me to be a negation of all responsibility and efficiency if they are then to be dealt with by the Home Broadcasting Committee.'[2]

Ogilvie described this correspondence as the result of 'a curious misunderstanding'. In fact, it touched on fundamental issues of broadcasting. On the one side, the programme planners, with their long experience of broadcasting, were asking, even in war time, for autonomy. On the other side, though the case was never properly put, the Director-General was seeking something like 'direct control'. What was missing from the correspondence was the clear recognition on both sides that it was war time, that the debate followed the clamorous attack on BBC programmes, which had been given something of a political tinge, that the Director-General had a public role in war time as well as a part to play inside the organization. If Ogilvie did not appreciate the implications of all this, he was simply personalizing broadcasting politics.

The immediate upshot of the affair in October was the abolition of the two Home Broadcasting Committees and their replacement by a single Home Service Board consisting of the Director-General and Deputy Director-General, Ashbridge, Controller (Engineering), Nicolls, Controller (Programmes) and Tallents, Controller (Public Relations) 'to have control of programme policy'. Soon afterwards, the Midland Regional Director was added to represent regional opinion and to describe regional plans. Nicolls was to be responsible for the execution of the general line of approach. He was also to submit plans

[1] *Wellington to Nicolls, 10 Oct. 1939. [2] *Nicolls to Ogilvie, 11 Oct. 1939.

for programmes to the Board each week 'in as much detail as the Board may require'. The new Board had no difficulty in agreeing at once that 'propaganda, in the sense of perversion of the truth' was 'not in accordance with BBC policy' or that in the case of 'blitzkrieg' in the future not all 'escapist' talks would be cancelled as they had been when war broke out. It decided, however, that it needed more information about the detailed pattern of programmes before it could plan in general terms for the future.[1]

It was in the light of these discussions that Heads of major programme departments—Outside Broadcasts, Variety, Music, Schools, Features and Drama, Children's Hour and Talks—were asked to meet the new Board, one by one on a rota system, to explain their ideas and plans. Very quickly they were preparing detailed memoranda, even though this meant, in the words of Nicolls, that they had to do 'a good deal of thinking when they really have not time to do it'.[2] This somewhat grudging statement was an expression of genuine solicitude on the part of Nicolls for an over-worked and harassed staff.[3] Yet it was too negative. However great the additional burden imposed on the Heads of programme departments, the memoranda which they proposed were, for the most part, signposts to the future. In retrospect, they are invaluable to the historian. Taken together, they show that the 'improvement' in broadcasting which followed the jolt of the first weeks of war was not really a return to normal but rather the prelude to one of the richest and most exciting phases in the history of radio.

Outside Broadcasts, one of the first to report, noted that they had now 'come back into the programmes again', with 18 items a week (7 per cent) out of a total of 280. There were still grave limitations on the use of lines. The Post Office was asking that they should be used only after 7 p.m. on weekdays and 2 p.m. on Saturdays, and it was taking time and effort to establish the argument with the Post Office that 'a broadcast which has the chance of going into nine million homes has a pretty urgent claim on lines facilities'. Petrol rationing, too, would make

[1] *Home Service Board, *Minutes*, 3 Nov. 1939.

[2] *Nicolls to Ogilvie, 5 Nov. 1939.

[3] *Boult, then Director of Music, had written to Nicolls on 2 Nov. 'I would like to say that we feel it is quite impossible to get our ideas on paper with anything like adequate detail and thoroughness by November 10th.'

frequent 'out of the way broadcasts impossible'. As far as the content of outside broadcasting was concerned, there had been severe restrictions on sport, just as there had been on entertainment, and much of the glamour had gone out of such national sporting events as the Cesarewitch or the Cambridgeshire.

Consequently outside broadcasts of sport needed to be 'heavily pruned'. Concerts and opera had to be 'used more sparingly' because of their length, although 'camp concerts' were a 'new ingredient [which] on the whole seem to make up in heartiness what they lack in polish'. More could be done with composite, studio-broadcast 'anthologies', like *The World Goes By* or *Lucky Dip*. 'Religious Services', another item read, 'there is no scarcity of these.' The Outside Broadcasts Unit ended by asking for an expansion of its work on four grounds. First, outside broadcasting added greatly to variety of broadcasting material. Second, it gave the public 'a reassuring impression of normality'. Third, there was as much 'virtue in actuality' as ever. Fourth, 'Outside Broadcasts dealing with topicality give an impression of BBC resourcefulness and vitality'.[1]

This brief but sturdy document was closer to the heart of broadcasting than the earlier discussions of the Home Broadcasting Board. The Variety report which followed began, as might have been expected, with a survey of what had really happened in the first weeks of the war when the whole Variety Department had moved to Bristol and a repertory company of twenty-two performers and one orchestra working in one studio had set out to provide five to nine programmes a day, 'extremely simple', aimed entirely at the big public, and frankly designed to be largely cheerful 'background listening that didn't require much concentration between News Bulletins'.[2] The second week of operations had been far more difficult to organize than the first, and after a time 'the feeling of monotony' had been 'inevitable, as every show within these limitations—

[1] *Memorandum on Outside Broadcasts War-time Policy, 8 Nov. 1939.
[2] They had moved out of London a few hours before actually being given their pre-arranged cue for the move—an announcement in a News bulletin of the start of emergency programmes. 'Had the cue not come we would all have crept back to London and pretended we hadn't been out.' The first Bristol office of the Department was in the headmaster's house at Clifton College. See a vivid article by John Watt, 'How the BBC Went to War' in the *Sunday Dispatch*, 18 Feb. 1940.

from the *White Coons* to *Gentlemen You May Smoke*—had a tendency to sound the same, because the same people were in it'. Shows of a new type had been introduced with the same artists, like *Adolf in Blunderland*, but it had been very difficult to prepare such material at short notice. The Ministry of Information had held back for a time the engagement of a second repertory company, a necessary reinforcement, but throughout the second half of September there had been a marked improvement, following the return to the air in late September of *Band Waggon*, 'perhaps the most popular radio show of all time', with 'Big-Hearted Arthur' Askey and Richard Murdoch.[1] Additional studios had been acquired, rehearsal time had been increased, new staff had been engaged, and star names had been introduced. 'It is a little ironic that while the debate in the House of Commons on the "badness" of BBC programmes was in progress, Gracie Fields was actually on the air.' Much of the blame for what had happened was put squarely on the Ministry of Information. 'Ministry formalities caused us to miss our greatest opportunity when all the theatres were closed, and we could have got anybody under contract.' When the formalities were cleared, the theatres were open again.

By the time this report was being written, Ministry shackles had been removed and 'with a free selection of artists' the quality had enormously improved. 'The present output of Variety Department from the 6 o'clock News onwards, excluding dance music, varies between three and one show per night. . . . The types of entertainment vary as on a peacetime basis, and the week is sprinkled with dance music at the rate of eight to nine sessions a week for the weekly house band.' There were now three Variety studios, four bands, including 'the faithful Variety Orchestra' and the Dance Orchestra under Billy Ternent.

In future, the report went on, programmes could and should be carefully planned, with a very wide range, from straight Variety, such as *Music Hall, Garrison Theatre, Palace of Varieties* and *Sing Song*, across to straight dance music, with a broad span including musical comedies, revues, continuity shows such as *Band Waggon* and *ITMA*, cabaret, 'interest programmes'

---

[1] For the pre-war history of this programme, see Briggs, *The Golden Age of Wireless*, pp. 117–18, 255, 654.

such as *Strange to Relate* and *Scrapbook* ('reasonably intelligent entertainment . . . not sneered at by the multitude') and song-shows like *Songs from the Shows* and *Music Goes Round*. In any given week there should 'be some coverage of brow from low to high, the low naturally predominating'. Ogilvie under-lined this comment in pencil: he also wrote in pencil 'why at all?' after the sentence 'the Afternoon 5.30–6 programmes, of which we get a certain number allocated to us, are the most difficult to fill. It is hard to know what audience to cater for at this time except on Saturdays. For the late dinner public it is still light afternoon fare, and the high tea public have not yet got down to it.'

The conditions of broadcasting, the report rightly emphasized, did much to determine the scheme of what was being offered. Given one single programme, 'the old function of the Variety Department of being screamingly funny opposite a symphony concert' had disappeared. The main weight of Variety pro-grammes should be in the mid- and late-evening hours from 6 to midnight, when there should always be one big show and two subsidiary ones. A weekly round was envisaged. On Mondays there would always be *Monday Night at Eight* 'with the certain draws of Inspector Hornleigh, Puzzle Corner and the old *Monday Night at Seven* make-up'.[1] On Tuesday *ITMA* could go on the air: it is interesting that at this time *ITMA*, which was to be the greatest of war-time successes, could be described as a 'highly successful continuity show' which had not 'as yet' quite achieved 'the completely universal appeal of *Band Waggon*'.[2] On Wednesday there could be an alternation of *For Amusement Only* and single shows like *Kentucky Minstrels*, with the return of Robb Wilton, 'Mr. Muddlecombe'—also to become a symbol of the war—in a full-length show. On Thursday *Songs from the Shows*, *At the Billet Doux* and *Henry Hall's Guest Night*[3] could

[1] For the previous history of this programme, see Briggs, *The Golden Age of Wireless*, pp. 117, 119, 410. For the later weekly round, see below, p. 595.

[2] See Briggs, op. cit., p. 118.

[3] See H. Hall, *Here's to the Next Time* (1955), pp. 174–5, for the return of this programme. After the outbreak of war, Hall had tried to get into contact with Watt at Bristol, but 'they always said he was out'. His programme returned to the air in December just before the News, starting a long run 'which was perhaps the most successful period of the long years of its broadcasts'. Hall added rightly that the words 'From the stage of a theatre somewhere in England' gave the listening public a sense of atmosphere that could not be derived from a studio broadcast.

provide greater continuity than anything which yet existed on Fridays, 'the bits and pieces day of the week'. On Saturdays there would be *Band Waggon*, to be followed by *Garrison Theatre*, 'a music-hall programme with trimmings', which had already made its successful début in early November: it was based on an idea of Harry Pepper and Charles Shadwell's recollections of the Northern Command Garrison Theatre during the First World War. The programme included RSM Filtness, who had 'kept order' at the original Garrison Theatre, but it depended for its success on Jack Warner as the soldier-compère and Joan Winters as the 'little girl'.

The Variety memorandum contained planning proposals for what was to prove the solid core of war-time entertainment. It ended with an interesting discussion of two general points— one of which, as we have seen, had already been raised by the Board,[1] and one of which was to be raised time and time again by the Ministry of Information:[2] vulgarity and propaganda. 'It is our business to be vulgar in the Latin sense,' the memorandum stated, although, since the outbreak of the war, 'dirty lines had decreased almost out of existence', a continuation of a pre-war trend. On propaganda, while it was admitted that Variety offered a wide field for propaganda, direct or indirect, mainly the latter, it maintained 'conscious propaganda in entertainment is generally ineffectual because it is conscious. The criterion must still be entertainment value.' Syd Walker with his homely talks, 'possibly the only medium for direct propaganda', succeeded because he set out to entertain even when he was talking about evacuation. *Adolf in Blunderland* succeeded, likewise, because it was 'a piece of satiric entertainment, good or bad according to one's taste, and the propaganda aspect of it was, in its creation, entirely secondary to its topical satire'.[3] The Home Service Board accepted what was said in this report about propaganda—'permitted in Variety programmes as an unforced ingredient'—but on 'dirt' added succinctly: 'usual peace-time standards to be upheld'.[4]

---

[1] See above, p. 103.   [2] See below, pp. 167–8.

[3] *Report on Variety, 15 Nov. 1939. See Watt's article in the *Sunday Dispatch*, 18 Feb. 1940. During the early stages of the war practically any wisecrack about Goering or Goebbels—or 'jokes' like 'the higher the Führer'—would cause gusts of happy laughter.

[4] Home Service Board, *Minutes*, 24 Nov. 1939.

The report on Music, considered at the same set of meetings, was more a statement of aims and intentions than a detailed programme scheme, and needs to be supplemented from other sources. It raised issues about war-time broadcasting at the opposite end of the spectrum from the memorandum on Variety. Like the Variety Department, the Music Department had moved to Bristol on the outbreak of war and had faced some, though not all, of the same difficulties. During the first weeks of the war 'the musical world had been temporarily paralysed, partly on account of our momentary failure to fulfil the needs of the music-loving public'. Output had been restricted, and even when gramophone records were in such extended use regular peace-time musical features built on the compèred use of records had disappeared. There had been a recovery, however, and during the week when the report was written there were eighteen orchestral concerts in the single pro-gramme, eight of which were presented in evening or high-spot periods, and twenty-five recitals, eight of them in 'important listening periods'. Serious music occupied 26 hours, and light music (not including 'theatre organ, etc.') 21 hours. Light music, much of it still coming from London, some from the regions, posed few problems, and an 'emergency group', the Salon Orchestra, had quickly established its position. The first complete Gilbert and Sullivan opera ever to be broadcast, *Trial by Jury*, had been presented on 5 November.

Serious music, the report went on, if it were going to appeal to 'the infinitely wider audience' of war by becoming 'lighter', could do so not on the basis of 'compromise or half-hearted method', but only by 'a shortening of programmes where artistically possible and the vigorous ruling out of the mediocre both as regards music and performance'. It would still have to face the kind of Goering-like reaction briefly described by an aggrieved listener, 'when the word *Opus* is mentioned I switch off'.[1] The Wednesday Symphony Concerts would remain 'the backbone of our orchestral music policy'; indeed, the Depart-ment felt that 'the Music Department's peace-time plans for the 1939/40 season' still constituted 'an ideal scheme' which

[1] *BBC Handbook, 1940*, p. 20. Cf. the lady quoted on the same page in what reads very much like a pre-war joke: 'while she liked light music, she was "not much of a one for sympathy" '.

should be modified only when strictly necessary. International artists—and conductors—should be brought in whenever possible to avoid 'insularity', as Bruno Walter and Toscanini had been brought in during the winter and spring before war broke out. It was just as important in war time as in peace time 'to keep abreast—if not in advance—of the musical world . . . if music is to hold its place as a cultural force rather than a mere spiritual sop'. If the public demand was for 'an increased proportion of the classics', it was still necessary, nonetheless, to encourage new works. Attention should always be paid to minorities, and Saturday afternoon concerts, to be given before an invitation audience in Bristol, should 'keep alive and stimulate the interest in both modern musical developments and masterpieces of old music'.[1]

Nicolls supported the Music Department's contention that 'we should cater for minorities as reasonably as possible';[2] and the Home Service Board agreed in principle with most of the proposals set out in the report while insisting, with the majority in mind, that the terms 'recital' and 'chamber music' were to be avoided as much as possible in the billing of programmes.[3] The logic of a single home programme seemed to point inexorably at least to a careful choice of words in the presentation of programmes to the public.

The memorandum on Features and Drama, prepared by Val Gielgud, who was extremely unhappy about the move of his department from London and the difficulties which he had to face, was shorter and far more critical about what had already happened during the first weeks of war. 'Few aspects of broadcasting can have been more seriously handicapped. . . . The time limitation of the programme items to half an hour, the assumption that the single wavelength programme material automatically excluded anything that could by any stretch of imagination be labelled "highbrow"—and this label was at one moment applied to Shakespeare—cut at the roots of supply for a department whose listeners had always been a "minority" audience—considered literally vis-à-vis Music Hall.' Gielgud

[1] *Memorandum on Music Policy, 14 Nov. 1939. On 1 November the BBC had started to give regular concerts in the Colston Hall.
[2] *Note by Nicolls on the Memorandum, 16 Nov. 1939.
[3] *Home Service Board, *Minutes*, 17 Nov. 1939.

knew that in consequence his staff, stranded at Evesham, were underworked and almost mutinous and that Head Office had been far from sympathetic: 'not exactly encouraging,' he wrote in his diary on 11 September, 'to get a memorandum from Head Office saying that plays of greater length than half an hour are not for the present envisaged, and it is suggested they should be "of *Children's Hour* type".'[1]

Fortunately, by the end of September a more ambitious features and drama policy had been evolved, based on the need to supply first a 'contribution to the preservation of civilised culture in time of war' and second 'implicit or explicit propagandist contributions to national war-time activity'. 'Without ignoring in any way the demand for popular entertainment—from *Pickwick*, Wodehouse, Wells and Jacobs adaptations . . . and serials like *The Four Feathers* and *The Three Musketeers*, etc.—we should find every means to represent the classic drama—e.g. the Shakespearian sequences in St. George's Hall—and to retain the "pure radio" audience's good will with a proportion of definitely intelligent work on experimental lines.' If need be, this 'work' should be broadcast late in the evening at times 'too frequently allocated to popular items'.

There was little hint in this report of the future prominence of the feature programme as an 'art form' in time of war, although propagandist political features, like *The Spirit of Poland* and *The English Pageant* were mentioned—'programmes designed to stir directly the national pride of ourselves and our Allies without descending to a jingo level'—and implicitly propagandist items like *The Home Front* and *The Shadow of the Swastika* series were also described. The latter series, produced by Laurence Gilliam—with Professor Harold Temperley and E. L. Woodward as consultant experts—had been particularly highly praised, an opinion which was echoed by the Home Service Board, which felt that *The Four Feathers*—with a romantic formula acceptable 'even in war-time'—deserved to be accounted a success also.[2]

Unlike some of the reports prepared by other departments,

---

[1] Quoted in V. Gielgud, *Years in a Mirror* (1967), p. 97. Ten days later he wrote, 'We seem to be adopting American broadcasting methods and standards wholesale, and Adrian Boult is as cross about it as I am.' (Ibid., pp. 98–9.)

[2] *Home Service Board, *Minutes*, 1 Dec. 1939.

the paper produced by Gielgud, who believed passionately in high standards, could have been used to justify Chamberlain's comment in the House of Commons that standards had fallen and were still falling despite 'the non-materialisation of the expected Blitzkrieg'. Gielgud, indeed, was depressed and frustrated in the autumn of 1939. 'Owing to difficulties of studio accommodation and other technical handicaps, together with a considerably increased all-over dramatic output, [we have] deliberately lowered certain of our production standards.' 'Competent performance' was all that could be guaranteed or was expected from producers working with such limited rehearsal time as they were being permitted when the report was written.[1] There were rays of hope, however, when the department moved from Evesham to Manchester on 16 November, when St. George's Hall was opened for occasional London performances on 21 October, and when renewed opportunities were provided for hiring 'star actors like Henry Ainley and Leslie Banks'.

The memorandum on the *Children's Hour*—Gielgud would have appreciated this—was as long as the memorandum on Features and Drama. There had been a four-day break in the *Children's Hour* programme at the beginning of the war and the length of the programme had been subsequently reduced from an hour to half an hour. Nonetheless, the programme had now re-established itself, not completely centralized from Bristol, but on a regional basis, with programmes being transmitted each week from Scotland, the North of England and the West. (Wales was to follow in January.) It was admitted that it was 'extremely difficult to balance the claims of five Regions and yet preserve the continuity which has always been such a feature of the *Children's Hour*'. There had been no references to regional output in the Features and Drama memorandum.

The content of the *Children's Hour* programmes had obviously been carefully thought out, even at the highest level, as had the plan—worked out jointly with the Religious Department before the outbreak of war—to introduce a Sunday Children's Hour: this new service began on 29 October.[2] Reliance on 'old

---

[1] *Memorandum on Features and Drama, 21 Nov. 1939.

[2] *There was a separate memorandum by J. W. Welch, Director of Religious Broadcasting, on Religious Broadcasts to Schools, 24 November 1939. This advocated (successfully) a once-a-week religious service for schools ('An act of worship') at 9.10 a.m., a feature which continued after the war.

favourites' at the beginning of the war—*The Wind in the Willows*, *Toytown*, and talks by the Zoo Man, all designed to 'have a reassuring effect on listeners'—had given way to a somewhat more ambitious policy. Yet 'by common consent', it was stated, stories and plays 'bearing directly on the war have been avoided in *Children's Hour*, and jokes about the Nazi leaders have been sternly discouraged. The *Children's Hour* staff, urged thereto by the wishes of the Director-General, have been most anxious to avoid anything which would teach children to hate their enemies.' Given that 'quite large adult audiences habitually listen to the *Children's Hour*', there was a strong argument, it was maintained, for increasing its length to forty-five minutes.[1]

In contrast to the other reports, that on School Broadcasting could point to great success during the very first difficult phase of the war when School Broadcasting started at Wood Norton after only three days of war instead of in the planned 'Week 3'. 'Some of the best school broadcasts I have ever heard,' wrote Mary Somerville, the acknowledged authority, 'were given during the period, September 5th to 22nd.'[2] Twenty-two people, sharing two not over-large rooms, had dealt efficiently and imaginatively with a schools situation not envisaged before war broke out. Schools were not in session, and the audience consisted of children listening at home, in billets, in halls or barns, or even, while the weather lasted, in school playgrounds with a loudspeaker on the window sill. 'Each of our six daily items had, therefore, to be made complete in itself and directed to children as private individuals rather than as units of classes listening under the guidance of their teachers.' Even after the schools had reassembled there had been far less contact than before the war with the listening schools, and less information had come through from Education Officers. This made judgement more difficult. 'It has been a matter of frequent comment among all of us that, however much we, as producers, may enjoy the greater freedom we have had in experimenting we feel very much less sure of our ground in working under the present conditions.'

[1] *Memorandum on the Children's Hour, 13 Dec. 1939.
[2] For Mary Somerville and the tradition of school broadcasting see Briggs, *The Golden Age of Wireless*, pp. 189 ff.

A formal autumn programme—without the customary pamphlets—had been worked out as early as 9 September, but it had quickly been realized that because of unforeseen events it would have to stay very flexible. Far more schools were working normally than could possibly have been envisaged before the war broke out, for fewer children had been evacuated than had been expected, and there had already been a wide-spread drift back to the towns. 'Our educational commission now lies in the direction of providing as much normal fare as possible,' it was stated, but with certain additional series for 'children in the Neutral and the Evacuation areas, who are not attending school, in particular for junior children and infants who are being taught in small groups by visiting teachers'. Special attention also had to be paid to the 'Under Twenty Club', it was suggested, and the closest co-operation with youth organizations was recommended. The Board accepted this recommendation, with the proviso that the subjects to be discussed by the Club should be 'carefully chosen'.[1]

The whole of this report brings out the flexibility of active broadcasting at its best, its strong note of social responsibility, its willingness and ability to turn emergency into adventure. New ideas were propounded in it, and old ideas which had seemed impracticable in peace time were given a fresh airing.[2] Once again, however, the fear of propaganda was clearly expressed: 'We have been very careful to avoid in all pro-grammes anything of what we commonly call the "Churchill touch".' Unlike the Children's Hour memorandum, this School Broadcasting memorandum stated tartly that 'there is no escaping the fact that children are engrossed by the war'. Their interest was to be canalized not in programmes which satisfied 'the requests for more about the war, please', but in more modern history series and 'indirect propaganda along the lines set out in the Board of Education pamphlets on *The Schools in War-Time* on such matters as breaking new ground for vegetable growing or preparing for a better understanding

---

[1] *Home Service Board, *Minutes*, 8 Dec. 1939.

[2] *'We are turning one "Ann Driver" series,' wrote Mary Somerville, 'into a series for infants in home listening groups, which will include story material and verses for repetition as well as moving to music—(a new departure I have wanted to find room for ever since I studied a similar series in Japan in 1937).'

of new diets, or suggesting leisure time activities such as the use of library facilities and museums'.[1]

It is revealing to set this memorandum alongside that on Talks, where there was a parallel refusal to make plans too 'rigid' and a parallel reluctance to rest content with propaganda. 'It is now proposed to introduce subjects of "peacetime" interest, like Eric Newton's series *The Artist in the Witness Box* a series followed by BBC listening groups,' the report stated, even if it might prove necessary at the shortest notice to 'respond immediately to a change of conditions such as might be brought about by heavy air raids or other causes'. The Talks Department had been reduced in size on the outbreak of war—the Talks Executive and the Talks Booking Section had completely disappeared—'in the expectation that there would be little work for it to do', but by the end of September it had become abundantly clear first that there was plenty for it to do, and second that both the Ministry of Information and Parliament were particularly interested in what it was doing. While great difficulties had been encountered in getting approval for particular programmes and particular speakers selected by the BBC, there were incessant demands for programmes and talks from speakers suggested by the Ministry of Information, by government departments and political parties.[2] 'Ministers in rapid succession came to the microphone to describe the work and announce the plans of their departments. New regulations on a perplexing variety of subjects—from fish and coal to military service and gasoline—were reported and explained over the air.'[3] In many cases, the Ministers had demanded particular times and days for their broadcasts without paying any attention to considerations either of programme planning or of audience demand.[4]

A balanced policy for talks proved more difficult to secure

---

[1] *Memorandum on School Broadcasting, Autumn Term, 1939, 22 Nov. 1939.

[2] *Report on Talks, 31 Oct. 1939. 'The appreciation by Ministers and Government Departments generally of the superlative advantages offered by radio as a means of publicity in times of emergency is significant, and a sufficient answer to those who see in the competition of the Press a menace to the future of broadcasting.'

[3] Tallents, 'British Broadcasting and the War' in the *Atlantic Monthly*, March 1940.

[4] There had been troubles both with Churchill and Hore-Belisha in October and November. Churchill broadcast on 1 October and 12 November (on the latter occasion on 'Ten Weeks of War') and Hore-Belisha broadcast on 21 October.

during the first twelve weeks of war, as Ogilvie was still
complaining in November, than any other venture in broadcasting, with the possible exception of News policy, which was
still creating difficulties. The Liberal and Labour parties,

7.

Directions have been given by the Government
        to prepare for a war of at least three years.

That does not mean that victory may not be gained
                                in a shorter time.

How soon it will be gained
        depends upon how long Herr Hitler
            and his group of ~~gangsters,~~ wicked men

        whose hands are stained with blood
            and ~~sticky~~ with corruption,
                soiled
        can keep their grip upon the docile, unhappy German
                                                    people.

It was for Hitler to say when the war would begin,
        but it is not for him or his successors
            to say when it will end.

It began when he wanted it,
        and it will end only when we are convinced
            that he has had enough.

The Prime Minister has stated our war-aims
        in terms which cannot be bettered,
            and which cannot be too often repeated:-

        "To redeem Europe from the perpetual and recurring
        fear of German aggression, and enable the peoples
        of Europe to preserve their independence and their
        liberties."

That is what the British and French nations ~~people~~ are fighting for.

2. Extract from a broadcast by Churchill, 1 Oct. 1939: 'The First
Month of the War'. Original MS. corrected in Churchill's own hand.

supporting the war but opposing Chamberlain, resented the
Government's 'control of the air' and pressed hard for a
larger share of peak-hour talks, continuing, indeed, so to press
until after the fall of Chamberlain's government in May 1940.
On 9 October Sir Samuel Hoare had met Ogilvie, Lord
Macmillan and Sir Findlater Stewart to fix Wednesday evenings

for ministerial talks—with the Prime Minister's approval—
but discussions between Ogilvie, Attlee and Greenwood about
'Opposition time' at the end of October had been far less
satisfactory. Ogilvie's formula, 'equality to government and
non-government on Wednesdays, and a government pre-
ponderance of two to one on Saturdays' (alternate Saturdays
to be reserved, and the Labour Party and the Liberal Party
to be entitled to the same number of speakers) was unacceptable
to Attlee.[1] 'We have always taken up the position that on matters
of controversy, the Opposition should have equal rights with
the Government, and we should propose to adhere to the
same position if we should be in office. We are the official
Opposition. We cannot admit the claim of the Liberal Party
to an equality.'[2] Attlee also objected—in this case, too, not in
company with the Liberals—to Hoare's suggestion that Sundays should be the 'special preserve' of the Prime Minister,
who in case of emergency could broadcast, of course, at any
time he chose.

Given political difficulties of this kind, the BBC pressed
forward with plans for an 'independent' weekly commentary
on civil subjects on parallel lines to Major-General Sir Ernest
Swinton's *War Commentary*, which was first broadcast on
26 October.[3] Both German and American broadcasters seemed
to have great advantages through their ability to make quick
political points on the air. The idea of a commentary had first
been mooted in the Overseas Broadcasting Committee,[4] but it
was later taken up at successive meetings of the Home Service
Board. 'It seems a major weakness that we have nothing in our
Home Programme,' wrote Tallents, 'to correspond to (1)
American Commentators, whom a recent *Fortune* survey found
to be regarded as the most important source of news by about
56 per cent of those questioned (2) the considerable organisation which obviously lies behind the German commentaries,

---

[1] *Ogilvie to Hoare, 6 Dec. 1939.

[2] *Attlee to Ogilvie, 20 Dec. 1939. Ogilvie had seen Attlee, Greenwood and
Sir Archibald Sinclair in October. (Home Service Board *Minutes*, 3 Nov. 1939.)

[3] *The idea of the military broadcast had been accepted by the Home Broadcasting Committee on 22 September 1939 (Home Broadcasting Committee,
Minutes) and Swinton's name had been approved 'subject to tests of his broadcasting ability' on 26 September.

[4] This Board came into existence on 20 Sept. 1939. See below, pp. 180–1.

both Home and Overseas and (3) the machine which produces our own *Sonderberichte*'.[1]

As it was, this idea was not put into practice until February 1940, when it had widespread repercussions which continued long beyond 1940. In the first instance, both Nicolls and Maconachie, the Director of Talks, were extremely sceptical about its value. Having been put in charge of the co-ordination of all propaganda programmes, they remained very suspicious of all propaganda. They held that favourite American analogies were quite misleading and that the success of Hans Fritzsche's commentaries in Germany—they followed the German 8 p.m. main News bulletin—was irrelevant.[2] 'The proposal,' they concluded, 'should really be related to the whole talks output and not looked at in itself.'[3]

News, which perhaps significantly was not the subject of a separate memorandum during the first twelve weeks of war, was nonetheless considered by the Home Service Board on 30 October, when the 'virtues and defects' of the service were discussed, sharp criticisms were made of the order and presentation of particular news items in bulletins, and it was decided that in future copies of the 9 o'clock news scripts should be sent to members of the Board for their comments.[4] No attention was paid on this occasion to the first halting steps taken to include direct news reporting in BBC programmes, like the descriptions by eye-witnesses on 5 October of an attack on a German submarine and on 16 October of a German air raid on the Firth of Forth. Nor was there any discussion of the first BBC observers' 'front-line commentaries', like those on 13 October from the British Expeditionary Force in France, on 14 October from the R.A.F. in France, and 19 November from a minesweeper. In retrospect, these broadcasts stand out, along with the pioneer account by an R.A.F. officer of a flight over north-west Germany on 6 December. Yet Nicolls was unwilling to allow the broadcasting of the sound of the Maginot Line guns being fired after Dimbleby had made a recording of them.

---

[1] *Tallents to Graves, 28 Dec. 1939; Home Service Board, *Minutes*, 1 Dec. 1939: 'The possibility of a weekly commentary like Swinton's, but on civil subjects, to be actively explored.'   [2] See Kris and Speier, op. cit., pp. 70–1.

[3] *Note by Nicolls, 1 Jan. 1940.

[4] *Home Service Board, *Minutes*, 30 Oct. 1939.

At the time, what stood out was conflict about home news items, the difficult institutional relations not only with the Press but with government departments, particularly the Foreign Publicity Directorate of the Ministry of Information, headed by Charles Peake, and the Foreign Office itself.[1] In November 1939 the Foreign Office complained formally of the 'effect of Home News Bulletins in foreign countries'—BBC Home and Overseas News were strictly separated from each other— and suggested 'some form of centralised editorial control over *all* the news bulletins transmitted by the BBC'.[2] Eleven specific complaints were made as 'examples of BBC news embarrassing to His Majesty's Government', six of them relating to neutral countries. The Foreign Office went on to urge that a Board should be set up consisting of BBC and Foreign Office representatives.

Although the BBC, through Wellington, 'gently underlined the importance of maintaining BBC independence'—'I believe that the value of broadcasting as a medium for propaganda in all forms would tend to disappear if its integrity were compromised'[3]—all was not well inside the BBC's News organization at this time. The most important BBC official involved, the Senior News Editor, R. T. Clark, could not make an adequate defence against Foreign Office criticisms.[4] According to Nicolls, he was too 'preoccupied with administrative matters at this time', and he had already been criticized inside the BBC by Nicolls on 19 October and 2 November. 'After making all allowances for the scarcity of news in war time and the possibly

---

[1] H. R. Cummings was liaison officer between the BBC's Overseas News Service and the Foreign Publicity Directorate, and A. F. Haigh (from October) was liaison officer with the Foreign Office, dealing explicitly with broadcasts in foreign languages except German. Haigh was seconded from the Foreign Office. (*Salt to Ogilvie, 4 Oct. 1939; Perth to Graves, 4 Oct. 1939.) 'He and Cummings will be the sole channel of communication between the BBC, the Foreign Office, the Foreign Publicity Department and the Foreign Office News Division for all purposes concerning those Foreign Languages broadcasts.' At that time, there was no similar liaison with Home News, although both the Foreign Office News Department and the BBC were in contact through the Ministry of Information.

[2] *News Committee, *Minutes*, 2 Nov. 1939; R. A. Butler to Ogilvie, 20 Nov. 1939.

[3] *Wellington to Nicolls, 28 Nov. 1939.

[4] *He set out to rebut some of the charges made outside the BBC in a memorandum of 28 November 1939.

adverse influence of the Ministry of Information on the working of the news service,' Nicolls wrote on the latter occasion, 'the bulletins themselves have deteriorated in the last few weeks in a way that has chiefly suggested lack of control.'[1]

In the light of these criticisms, the Editor was provided with a Deputy and was relieved of some of his administrative duties on 3 November. These internal moves were not mentioned by Ogilvie in his reply to Butler; indeed, the BBC refused to rest on the defensive. Instead, Ogilvie pointed out that he could produce a long list of items on which the BBC 'had received contradictory advice from different departments of government or even different sections of the same Department'. At the same time, he thought that little useful purpose could be served by 'bandying of memoranda', and went on to suggest that the whole question of improving liaison should be discussed 'prospectively rather than retrospectively'.[2]

This letter reflected Ogilvie's general mood at the end of the first phase in war-time broadcasting. Having collected reports and memoranda from the different responsible officials within the BBC, he could pass from internal to external relationships. He was doubtless happy at the beginning of December to hear from Macgregor in the Ministry of Information that he now had 'markedly less to do to help the BBC in the Ministry' than he had to do during the early weeks of the war, that there were fewer 'silly questions' and that 'the whole machine is running more smoothly'.[3] He expressed himself equally happy about the introduction of a new daily war-time rhythm into broadcasting on 4 December with the new early morning prayers *Lift Up Your Hearts* and the new daily physical exercises *Up in the Morning Early*.[4] Christmas 1939 revealed how far the BBC had returned to its 'old self' again. The King duly broadcast and

---

[1] *Note by Nicolls, 2 Nov. 1939.

[2] *Record of telephone conversation between Ogilvie and Butler, 7 Dec. 1939. No further action seems to have been taken until the establishment of Home and Overseas Divisions at the end of April 1940. See below, p. 195.

[3] *Macgregor to Graves, 5 Dec. 1939. Macgregor suggested that there was no longer need for both him and Stewart to work in the Ministry. In fact, Stewart returned to duty in Scotland later in Dec. 1939. (Woodburn to Pym, 19 Dec. 1939).

[4] *These changes had been approved by the Home Service Board on 3 November 1939 (*Minutes*).

Gracie Fields sang in a concert from France.[1] On 31 December there was an evening service from Lambeth Palace with an address from the Archbishop of Canterbury.

The mood of the listening public was no longer by any means as critical as it had been in September, and the BBC was seeking diligently to gauge opinion on a regular listener-research basis. As early as 20 September, indeed, when the Press campaign against the BBC was at its height, the BBC's Control Board had agreed 'that we shall need guidance from Listener Research even more urgently than in time of peace'. Three main types of inquiry were proposed—into areas of defective reception, into the habits of listeners, given that 'evacuation, the black-out regulations and the changes in hours and nature of employment have clearly modified the habits of a vast number of households', and into 'the tastes and needs of listeners'.[2]

Concern for listeners in areas of defective reception had never been allowed to lapse during the autumn of 1939, and BBC engineers, headed by Ashbridge, were arguing behind the scenes with the Air Ministry about measures to improve listening conditions in places as 'far apart as Nottingham and Aberdeen'.[3] As for 'habits of listeners', a social survey undertaken by London Press Exchange interviewers had been conducted in October 1939: it was based on an inquiry into 3,450 urban homes.

R. J. E. Silvey, the Head of BBC's Listener Research Section, was in a position thereafter to tell his colleagues in detail about 'the listening day' and the way in which different social classes spent it. Whereas in homes where income was about £10 a week or more—the 'A' homes of 1939—only 9 per cent of listeners were up and about by 6.30 a.m., in homes where the

---

[1] For Christmas 1939, see Turner, op. cit., pp. 136–8. Oliver Stanley at the Board of Trade said 'that a little extra spending would do no harm', and though the Chancellor of the Exchequer, Sir John Simon, demurred, London and provincial hotel bookings were near normal and an advertising campaign was launched to popularize luxury French goods. For German radio at Christmas, see Kris and Speier, op. cit., pp. 336–9.

[2] *Tallents to Ogilvie, 'Listener Research', 20 Sept. 1939.

[3] *Home Broadcasting Committee (Internal), 26 Sept. 1939, 6 Oct. 1939. 'The need was again stressed for giving listeners fullest possible information about the reasons for indifferent reception conditions in war time.'

'breadwinner's income was less than £2. 10. 0. a week'—
the 'D' homes—three times as large a proportion were out of
bed. The time of going to bed showed contrasting differences.
At 11 o'clock at night over 21 per cent of listeners were still up
and about in 'A' homes, while less than 15 per cent in 'D' homes
had not gone to bed. Of the 9,000,000 licensed radio sets in the
country in 1939, about 600,000 were to be found in 'A' homes;
2,250,000 in 'B' homes, where incomes were between £10 and
£4 a week; 4,200,000 in 'C', where incomes were between £4
and £2. 10. 0. a week; and nearly 2,000,000 in 'D' homes.[1] Each
different social stratum posed different problems for broadcasters.

These facts and figures were obviously very relevant to the
interpretation of listeners' 'tastes and needs', and Silvey was
able late in 1939 to introduce new and improved machinery for
measuring the amount of listening. Plans for a 'continuous
survey' based on the postal distribution of questionnaires,
which would provide a daily 'listening barometer', had been
shelved on the outbreak of war.[2] The new plan, which involved
a survey, with 800 interviews each day, would make it possible
for results to be analysed far more quickly.[3] It was first brought
into operation on 3 December. Tallents, who had always been
keenly interested in listener research, was soon at pains to point
out, like his predecessors, that listening figures would not be
used to support arguments 'for an undue popularisation of our
programmes' or to suggest 'disagreeable comparisons' between
audiences attracted by individual Ministers or politicians.[4]
Yet the Ministry of Information envied the BBC's organization
and later in 1940 even dreamed of taking it over. 'Could we
not close down listener research and turn the staff over to the
improvement of our Home Intelligence Branch?'[5]

[1] The results are conveniently summarized in *BBC Handbook, 1940*, pp. 78–9.
[2] For the 'listening barometer' see Briggs, *The Golden Age of Wireless*, p. 278.
[3] *R. J. E. Silvey, 'Proposals for Listener Research in Wartime', 9 Nov. 1939;
Control Board, *Minutes*, 15 Nov. 1939.
[4] *Tallents to Silvey *via* Farquharson, 30 March 1940.
[5] *Pick, then Director-General of the Ministry, to Wellington, 25 Sept. 1940.
Pick, insensitive to so much, was particularly insensitive to the BBC's need for such
a service. (Pick to Wellington, 2 Oct. 1940: 'I doubt if in war time it can be
turned to any considerable value.') In the meantime, Mrs. Mary Adams, experienced in BBC affairs, who discussed the matter with Silvey in January 1940, had
begun to develop the Ministry's own Intelligence service 'to cover the trends of
public opinion about the war'. (Note by Farquharson, 30 Jan. 1940.)

In December 1939 the BBC was less interested in sociological intelligence than in programmes. The fact that there had been one programme only after the outbreak of war had made the new system of continuous audience measurement easier to operate, but it was evidence derived from the new system of listener research which was used to support the pressure for an alternative programme. The introduction of this new programme was the biggest new development in broadcasting since war had started, and the idea of it was beginning to dominate BBC thinking at the end of 1939 and the beginning of 1940.

3. An Alternative Programme

THE idea of an alternative programme had been mooted very soon after the synchronization scheme had come into operation, but at a meeting of Control Board at the end of September, Harold Bishop, the Assistant Controller (Engineering), told Ogilvie that 'the Air Ministry were adamant on the subject of a single programme and that there was no prospect of an alternative programme in the future'.[1]

In spite of this flat negative, Control Board did not drop the subject, which quickly became linked with the question of how best to entertain British troops stationed with the BEF in France.[2] Just as the home audience had been forced to get used to a kind of war they had never expected, so British soldiers across the Channel, who had anticipated going into battle almost at once, had been compelled to get used to living alongside Frenchmen rather than fighting Germans. The thought of a long 'siege' winter with little action clearly became a matter of concern to their superiors, and radio programmes were conceived as a means of securing 'the contentment and morale of the troops'.[3] Radio sets had quickly begun to appear in camps and billets in France at the same time as café notices

---

[1] *Control Board, *Minutes*, 30 Sept. 1939.

[2] *Ibid., 2 Oct., 14 Oct. 1939. Lee also raised this important issue on 10 October.

[3] *General F. Beaumont-Nesbitt to Ogilvie, 2 Feb. 1940.

reading 'Egg and Chips' and 'Hot Bathes' [*sic*]. At first, they were French sets, cheap and plentiful, with 'the scanty profits of canteen funds strained to the last franc to buy them'.[1] They could also be hired at about a hundred francs a month. Then in November 1939 the Nuffield Trust came forward with a grant for the provision of portable radio sets for the troops. BBC programmes, particularly news programmes, were keenly listened to, but there was no shortage of independent criticism of the fare being offered.

There was considerable listening also to Fécamp, Radio International, a French commercial station, supported by British capital, which continued to operate on 212 metres in the autumn of 1939 after Radio Luxembourg had closed on the outbreak of war.[2] It had an office at 37 Portland Place, broadcast for thirteen hours a day, and published a magazine, *Happy Listening*, which was distributed free to all units of the British forces on active service.[3] It too had celebrated Christmas 1939 with a message by Canon Pat McCormick at St. Martin-in-the-Fields, piano music from Charlie Kunz and 'singing and strumming' from George Formby and Tessie O'Shea. 'Breathing as ever the spirit of gay good fellowship and bright optimism,' it told its listeners, 'Radio International will broadcast the cheeriest of Christmas greetings to all its many thousands of listeners, but above all to the B.E.F. in France.'[4] It certainly attracted a good audience. 'The [Fécamp] programmes,' wrote Godfrey Adams, Nicolls' deputy, 'appear to bear all the stamp of having been carefully designed for the special audience, and a number of excellent artists in the light entertainment field are being used.'[5] Its Advisory Committee, the BEF Wireless Entertainment Committee, was presided over by Field-Marshal Lord Birdwood and included Captain

---

[1] Major R. Longland, BBC Liaison Officer with the Army, 'Listening with the Forces' in *BBC Handbook, 1941*, p. 94. Longland had been a member of the West Regional staff of the BBC at Bristol from 1938 to 1939.

[2] See Briggs, *The Golden Age of Wireless*, p. 369. On pp. 362–9 there is an assessment of its pre-war appeal. For Fécamp before the war, see also ibid., pp. 352 ff.

[3] It also broadcast propaganda in several languages and short commercial programmes in English.

[4] *Happy Listening*, Christmas Number, Dec. 1939.

[5] *Adams to Nicolls, 13 Dec. 1939. Adams had collected information from Cecilia Reeves in the Paris office of the BBC (Miss Reeves to Adams, 3 Jan. 1940: 'The Fécamp BEF programme is listened to morning, noon and night by the troops').

Leonard F. Plugge, M.P., Director of the International Broadcasting Company and one of the most stalwart protagonists of commercial radio.

Fear of commercial interests played a real though very minor part in the BBC's efforts to develop its own service for the BEF,[1] and there were French as well as British objections to Fécamp—relating, not least, to the nature of its broadcasts in German[2]—which weighed heavily against it. The British Armed Forces also applied pressure on the French for reasons of security to follow a similar system of synchronization of broadcast stations to that employed in Britain, while admitting that 'the exact point at which the military may issue an over-riding order, i.e. for the closing down of an unsynchronised station, like Fécamp, is vague'.[3] Viscount Gort and General Gamelin were 'very much opposed' to Fécamp, it was noted towards the end of the year.[4] In this context, a report prepared in December by Ryan called 'Broadcasting to the Troops in France' had special significance. Ryan, as liaison officer with Sir Campbell Stuart's propaganda group,[5] concerned himself with three questions—whether it was possible to provide a new service from BBC stations which could be heard by British troops in France; what arrangements could be made for providing listening sets in bulk for the troops; and, more delicately, how the type of sets issued to the troops could ensure that they would not permit listening to any other programmes except those provided by the BBC.

Ryan went on to discuss the possibility of an alternative BBC programme with Army and Air Force officers—Major-General Mason-Macfarlane on 3 December and Air Commodore Nutting a day later. Nutting stated that the RAF was no less anxious than the Army 'to have their troops

[1] The BBC also objected to a proposal from Northern Rediffusion Ltd. in Tyneside to organize a local gramophone record programme from 7 to 10 each evening for their 16,000 subscribers. (*C. Conner, Newcastle Director to Nicolls, 11 Nov. 1939.)

[2] *BBC Overseas Services Committee, *Minutes*, 7 Nov. 1939; Graves to Ogilvie, 21 Nov. 1939 expressing Sir Campbell Stuart's worries about the programme. Halifax had been in touch with the British Ambassador in Paris.

[3] *Report on Anglo-French Broadcasting Liaison by A. P. Ryan and Squadron-Leader Proctor Wilson, 18 Dec. 1939.

[4] *Note of meeting attended by Tallents and Langham, 21 Dec. 1939.

[5] See above, p. 87.

amused by broadcasting',[1] while Mason-Macfarlane more usefully proffered the good advice that a programme specially labelled 'for the BEF' would make the troops suspicious of it. It would be wiser, he went on, to put on an alternative, almost exclusively light, programme designed with the Army in mind but catering for listeners as a whole.[2] While the Air Ministry and the Admiralty made it clear that they did not share this view,[3] the BBC was in broad sympathy with it. 'This programme,' wrote Nicolls somewhat guardedly on 6 December, 'will also serve to provide an alternative to a good many listeners in this country, but it will be planned with the BEF as its primary objective.'[4] When the first announcements of the start of a new experimental service were prepared for the *Radio Times* and the Press at the end of December 1939, it was decided that no references were to be made at that stage to 'the scheme of a programme for the Forces' and that stress was to be laid rather on the idea of an 'alternative'.[5]

It was on 29 November that Control Board had agreed 'in principle' that 'plans should be prepared in all divisions for a special service for the fighting forces' and had passed on its recommendations to the main Board.[6] At this point, the title 'Services Programme' was being used inside the BBC.[7] Air

[1] *Ryan to Graves, 5 Dec. 1939.

[2] *Ryan to Graves, 3 Dec. 1939. The same point of view was put in London at a meeting at the War Office on 21 December.

[3] *Report on a meeting at the Air Ministry, 29 Dec. 1939; Report on a meeting at the Admiralty, 9 Jan. 1940.

[4] *Memorandum by Nicolls to Heads of Programme Producing Departments, 6 Dec. 1939. On 1 December Nicolls had written confidentially to Major-General J. H. Beith (Ian Hay), Director of Public Relations, War Office; this was followed by letters from Tallents to Beith, Sir Arthur Street, Deputy Under Secretary of State at the Air Ministry (14 Dec. 1939) and Sir Archibald Carter, Permanent Secretary of the Admiralty (17 Dec. 1939)—asking for guidance as to any special services which might be required by troops in France.

[5] *Note on Forthcoming Announcements Required, 18 Dec. 1939. The first Press announcement made on 3 January did refer to the Forces and the need for programmes 'suitable for active service listening'. 'Although the new programme is designed primarily for the Forces,' it went on, 'it is hoped that it will interest listeners at home as well.' See also the *Radio Times*, 5 Jan. 1940.

[6] *Control Board, *Minutes*, 29 Nov. 1939.

[7] *Tallents to Editor, *Radio Times*, 'Services Programme', 30 Nov. 1939, discussing publicity, *Radio Times* coverage and listener research. This title was later felt to be too comprehensive just as the title 'BEF Programme' was felt to be too narrow. The title 'Forces Programme' was chosen by Control Board. See *Minutes*, 3 Jan. 1940.

Ministry approval of the use of a wavelength of 342 metres for such a purpose had been announced on 6 December,[1] and reception tests on this wavelength had begun on 19 December using the Home Service programmes.

Daily experimental programmes followed from 7 January 1940, from 6 p.m. to 12.15 a.m. Some of the programmes were simultaneous broadcasts with the Home Service, but alternatives were introduced, particularly between 7 p.m. and 11.30 p.m., when the Home Service programme was 'considered to be unsuitable for the BEF'. During these contrasting periods, dance music, light music, theatre organ, variety and sporting programmes were broadcast. The first day's 'experimental' programme on 7 February included a concert by the BBC Salon Orchestra, conducted by Leslie Bridgewater, a song recital by Peter Dawson, and 'sessions' with Alfred Van Dam and his orchestra from the Gaumont Cinema, Kilburn, and with Mantovani. On 18 February, after more than two weeks' delay,[2] the alternative programme was extended to twelve hours a day—from 11 a.m. to 11 p.m.—and officially called the Forces Programme. Two wavelengths were now employed —342 from 8 p.m. to 11 p.m., 373 from 11 a.m. to 6 p.m., and both 342 and 373 from 6 p.m. to 8 p.m.[3] The programme on 18 February was more enterprising than that of the opening day and included a sports commentary by Raymond Glendenning from Lille on the football match between the French Army and the British Army, a performance by a concert party in France, and the first of a series of weekly News Letters. 'Bill and Bob' French lessons began two days later. By then Fécamp had been closed down on the orders of the French Command,[4] so that the BBC faced no competition. During the first months of the Service an average of £65 an hour was spent on original material.[5]

---

[1] *Control Board, *Minutes*, 6 Dec. 1939. The engineers had been engaged in discussions about wavelengths and air security for the past few weeks, with Ashbridge reporting on 17 November (Home Service Board, *Minutes*) that he was also meeting with difficulties from the Post Office, 'particularly in the form of side wind from the Relay Exchange interest'.

[2] *Wellington to the Post Office, 4 Jan. 1940. The grand 'opening date' had been deferred.

[3] 342 was used for the Home Service from 11 p.m. to 12.15 a.m.

[4] *Adams to Wellington, 9 Jan. 1940.

[5] *Adams to Nicolls, 14 Feb. 1940.

Throughout the gestation period and during the early weeks after the Forces Programme began, discussions continued with the War Office, the Air Ministry, and the Admiralty about the timing, content and presentation of programmes,[1] with the Admiralty taking the opportunity *en passant* to complain that in news bulletins 'a good deal of attention was given to the more pampered side of the Forces, while their own present desperately hard work had not been mentioned'.[2] The climax of these discussions was a fascinating report by Ryan on 'Listening in France'. This was followed on 29 January by a visit by Ogilvie to France to obtain first hand impressions of the reactions of officers, NCOs and men to BBC programmes.

Ryan had reported that the BBC medium-wave service could be heard day and night throughout the comparatively small region occupied by the BEF: that no unit was without sets, but that, with the exception of a few RAF stations, none had enough sets and that nearly all units were short of dry cell batteries; and that listening, unlike home listening, was invariably in groups, mainly during the evenings and for the breakfast and lunch time News. The troops listened a lot— with 'background listeners' in the majority. There were demands for 'more variety' and 'no heavy music', for extra doses of Gracie Fields, 'whose name was on many occasions bracketed with that of Mr. Winston Churchill as a popular turn', and for more broadcasts by artists who had actually appeared on the stage at 'live' Forces concerts.[3] Religion, drama and talks were never mentioned spontaneously at all by soldiers, and when questions on these subjects were pressed the answers were never encouraging. Padrés assured Ryan that they could not conceive of any billet where the set would not be turned off as soon as a religious service began. Plays were in such little demand that if they were to be introduced 'the will to listen would have to be worked up'. Talks would only be acceptable if they were topical and short.

[1] *Tallents, Langham and other BBC officials had a meeting at the War Office on 21 December, at the Air Ministry on 29 December and at the Admiralty on 9 January 1940.
[2] *Tallents to Nicolls, 11 Jan. 1940.
[3] *A. P. Ryan, 'Listening by the BEF', 23 Jan. 1940.

In brief, what the Forces wanted was a 'light' programme, and if any 'serious' items in it were to command support there would have to be an initial 'rousing of interest', a kind of 'gingering up'. Methods of announcing were relevant in this context. Announcers were expected to be more lively, even though, in Ryan's opinion, they should still speak 'authoritatively' and they should still be people who were 'obvious gentlemen'. He had heard everywhere that the men want to be talked to by 'a gentleman' and that 'the too matey approach' of Fécamp met only with 'derisive comments'.

The Fécamp model was defended, however, by General Ironside, the Chief of the Imperial General Staff, who after being given details of the first experimental BBC programme for the BEF said that this was not what they wanted. 'They delighted in the Fécamp programme.'[1] Ironside had complained earlier, as had the Adjutant-General, Sir Robert Gordon-Finlayson, about BBC delays in starting a full as distinct from an experimental service, and Major-General Beaumont-Nesbitt had agreed with them that 'the loss of the Fécamp programme . . . of the type which is most popular' was so serious that 'we are faced with a serious danger of a lowering of morale if we cannot provide at as early a date as possible the type of programme the troops really like and enjoy'.[2] In the meantime, Plugge made a strenuous but vain effort to have the Fécamp station reopened, sending round thirty thousand snowball postcards to BEF troops asking them to press for resumption of its service.[3]

One crucial decision had been taken by the BBC before these pleas were made, before Ryan wrote his report and before Ogilvie visited France. The Board of Governors had decided on 22 December that, following the example of Fécamp, the BBC's 'Sunday policy' should not be pursued in the planning

---

[1] *General Sir Edmund Ironside to Tallents, 25 Jan. 1940.
[2] *General F. Beaumont-Nesbitt to Ogilvie, 2 Feb. 1940.
[3] *Note by Ogilvie, 7 Feb. 1940. As late as 13 March 1940 Squadron-Leader Wilson, who was dealing with problems of radio liaison in Paris, reported that while 'the old Adam of Fécamp is buried at the moment' it had 'a pretty strong hope of resurrection'. The suggestion was put forward at an internal meeting in the Ministry of Information, attended by Ogilvie on 8 February 1940, that a private station should be opened—under the auspices of Lord Birdwood's committee in the Paris region. Ogilvie strenuously opposed this suggestion.

of the new service.[1] The broadcasting of original Variety
programmes on Sunday was still to be avoided, although there
was to be no objection to occasional repeats and to the inclusion
of both sport and dance music. J. W. Welch, the BBC's Director
of Religious Broadcasting, who was not present at the meetings
when this matter was discussed, telephoned Nicolls to express
his 'doubts and unhappiness' about this decision; he wrote a
memorandum objecting to the fact that the reversal of traditional policy was 'based on expediency and not on principle'
and arguing that the Central Religious Advisory Committee
ought to have been called together to discuss the new policy
before it became public.[2] 'I cannot see,' he went on, 'why we
should assume that because a few listeners have put on uniform
and crossed the Channel they should be considered different
persons religiously.'

It was at Welch's suggestion that it was decided that there
should be no live Variety programmes on Sundays,[3] but he
failed to carry the BBC on the bigger question. The decision
to broaden programmes, Ogilvie stressed, had been taken not
for reasons of expediency but out of 'a sense of duty to the
Forces in their special circumstances'.[4] There was no reason,
added Nicolls, why there should not be religious broadcasts
and dance music on the same day. Ogilvie took up Welch's
point that a 'constructive' Sunday policy in all BBC programmes was needed, not necessarily identical with the traditional policy: he suggested that 'for the moment'—a slippery
phrase—a new formula should be applied. First, Sunday
programmes should be 'different from weekday programmes,
particularly in presentation'; second, they should be of 'the
best quality in any department'; and third, they should be
'fortifying to the individual and a strengthening to the home'.[5]

---

[1] *Board of Governors, *Minutes*, 22 Dec. 1939. Home Board had agreed to this
a few days earlier (*Minutes*, 15 Dec. 1939). For changes in the attitudes to Sunday
policy on the eve of the war, see Briggs, *The Golden Age of Wireless*, p. 654.

[2] *Welch to Nicolls, 2 Jan. 1940. At the Home Service Board on 29 December
1939 (see *Minutes*) it had been agreed that Welch should see the Chairman of
CRAC, the Bishop of Winchester, and 'explain the position to him' so that 'the
Committee should in some appropriate way be informed of it'. (See also Tallents
to Farquharson, 29 Dec. 1939.)

[3] *Home Service Board, *Minutes*, 5 Jan. 1940.   [4] *Ibid. 12 Jan. 1940.

[5] *Welch to Nicolls, 'Forces Programme: Sunday Policy', 15 Jan. 1940. Welch
had submitted his general views on religious broadcasting to Home Service Board

Welch, however, was the only man who looked far ahead in 1940 and drew out the logic of what was happening. The fact that the BEF programme would provide a 'secular' alternative for home listeners surely meant that 'we shall not be able to return to our Sunday policy when the war ends'.[1]

Ogilvie was not prepared to look so far. No one, indeed, except Welch, looked into the future and faced the probability that the decision to start a 'light' programme for the Forces carried with it the ultimate implication of a peace-time light programme for everybody. Ryan, however, was prepared at least to look back and to acknowledge squarely the extent of the break with pre-war BBC policy which was being proposed. He insisted that the press release dealing with the start of the first full programme on 18 February should be worded far more dramatically than the carefully balanced announcement about the beginning of experimental programmes a few weeks earlier and was equally insistent on the need to present something more than 'a watered version of our peace-time programmes'. 'If we give them serious music, long plays or peace-time programme talks, they will not listen. We are quite entitled in peace time to say that we will leave the majority audience to the Luxembourgs for long periods, because we know that we have important minorities who wish for better things, and who have every right to be catered for by a body like ourselves which should deal in cultural as well as entertainment values. *But* our peace-time argument (which we shall never, I trust, surrender) completely breaks down when faced with the conditions prevailing over this new programme. So long as you have a minority for Bach, it is your duty to put Bach on. But when you know perfectly well that your listening curve will go down to zero, then Bach would be sheer intellectual snobbery.' The BBC was called upon to act as if it were still in competition with Fécamp. 'It is our duty as a public body

---

[1] *Welch to Nicolls, 2 Jan. 1940.

on 8 December. The Board had noted ominously that listener response figures to religious broadcasts were unexpectedly low and that there was danger of 'over saturation of the public'. In his new memorandum Welch attached 'very great value to the difference between Sunday and other days' as expressed in the difference of Sunday broadcasting from weekday broadcasting. *Scrapbook* was quite appropriate for Sundays—'it gives some sense of the past to a rootless generation'; *Garrison Theatre* was not.

enjoying monopoly rights from the State, to tackle our problems as vigorously and single-heartedly as we would if Fécamp was a commercial rival.'[1]

This kind of argument was to be used frequently inside the BBC long after 1940—and it had far-reaching social and cultural consequences—yet Ogilvie wrote simply on the top of the document 'I agree with Ryan's views'. What seemed to be the imperative needs of war counted solely in the making of the decision. And within less than a month Major Maschwitz was demanding that 'the Forces Programme should be made a unit on its own, run in healthy competition with, and on quite different lines from the Home Service'.[2]

Ogilvie's own visit to France to meet members of the BEF—he also met Noel Coward who told him plainly what he thought soldiers thought of BBC programmes—did little more than confirm the conclusions reached by Ryan and others,[3] but it was followed by a number of administrative changes and by organized listener research into BEF reactions to what was being offered. Major Longland was appointed BBC Liaison Officer with the BEF, and spent the next four months 'exploring the roads and lanes of France, running the BEF to earth'.

Sometimes the words 'I'm from the BBC' would produce the instant question 'Have you heard our dance band?' and a shout from outside one of the huts 'Turn out the band, quick, the BBC man's here'. Sometimes there were 'useful suggestions' such as 'Can't we have music before breakfast while we dress?', a frequently repeated question which eventually at the beginning of June led the BBC to push the Service back to 6.15 a.m. There were the usual differences of opinion among listeners—'more dance music, sir . . . don't listen to him, he's swing mad . . . it's organ music I like . . . nice bit of variety'. Longland was very much the officer, 'the bloke from GHQ', but he was both enterprising and sensitive, sending back to London 'a steady flow of answers to their questions about leisure hours, the best times for star items, and just when the minority tastes could be satisfied without robbing the majority of its entertainment'.[4]

---

[1] *Ryan to Tallents, 10 Feb. 1940.
[2] *Maschwitz to Adams, 18 Feb. 1940.   [3] See above p. 127.
[4] R. Longland, 'Listening with the Forces' in the *BBC Handbook, 1941*, pp. 94–8.

Organized listener research began with the enrolment of Forces correspondents in February and March 1940. They were a mixed group, recruited from BBC staff in the Forces, friends and acquaintances of the BBC staff, letter-writers to Broadcasting House and postal subscribers to *Radio Times* and *The Listener*. From March onwards they were sent weekly questionnaires concerning specific items in the Forces programme. RAF and Naval correspondents were recruited in the same way as Army correspondents, and in addition the Admiralty issued an order inviting each ship's company to nominate one representative to act as a correspondent with the BBC. The first programme specially designed for the Navy—*Naval Log*—was broadcast on 20 February, and *Air Log* followed a week later. Most of the programmes, however, were thought of primarily in terms of the needs of the BEF, and early in March a general questionnaire on listening conditions and programme preferences was sent to a random sample of the BEF, every two-hundredth man.

One of the first listener reports arriving on 26 February after the end of the first week's broadcast praised 'the great effort that has been made to give the BEF the type of programme that they enjoy': 60 per cent of the material had been 'good', 20 per cent 'fairly good', and 20 per cent 'on the dull side'. Against earlier forecasts, a play was singled out for special praise—'more of this type of entertainment might perhaps be given'—and while news bulletins were the most popular items, there was a demand for 'one news bulletin specially presented for the BEF in a brighter and more dramatic fashion than the ordinary bulletins'.[1] 'The thoughtful and keener men' were said to be listening intently to the French lessons: 'many men are friendly with French people and make use of French shops and are anxious to have a useful working knowledge of the language'. Talks, however, were not appreciated. 'They are all right for listeners at home,' one serviceman stated, 'but I don't think they are wanted by the men in France.' In general, 'too much of the Home Sweet Home stuff should not be included'.[2]

After several weeks, a fuller report was prepared by Listener Research. By then many new features had been introduced,

[1] *Capt. E. B. Butler to Squadron-Leader Wilson, 26 Feb. 1940.
[2] *Squadron-Leader F. C. Gillman to H. L. Morrow, 29 Feb. 1940.

including a special edition for the Forces of the *Radio Times*. *John Hilton Talking* carried the voice of one of Britain's best-known peace-time broadcasters, now a pillar of the Ministry of Information, directly to the Forces.[1] On 28 February Sandy Macpherson, the hero of the first home broadcasts during the period of 'emergency', began a new programme, *Sandy's Half Hour*, in which he played request tunes from men on active service: he had 1,500 requests from men in the BEF in less than a fortnight.[2] *Record Time*, a programme presented first by John Glyn-Jones and later to be popularized by Roy Rich, started soon afterwards, and there was the first great special occasion, an all-star Franco-British Concert, with Gracie Fields and Maurice Chevalier, from the Paris Opera House on 16 April. On 21 April a new series of programmes was introduced for the Indian Forces, announced a week earlier to the great satisfaction of Indian troops, whose 'delighted faces on hearing the news' were remembered by Longland as one of the special memories of the spring of 1940.[3]

'There is no doubt at all that the Programme for the Forces is immensely popular,' the Listener Research Report for the period from 21 April to 4 May began.[4] George Black, the great king of entertainment, had already noted its 'sentimental pull'.[5] Among unsolicited comments from members of the Forces themselves were widespread regret at the (temporary) passing of *Garrison Theatre*,[6] requests for more Doris Arnold gramo-phone recitals, further complaints that the Home News bulletin was 'too dismal' for the taste of the Forces, and 'some fear that the BBC may curtail the cheerfulness of Sunday pro-grammes in deference to Sunday observance pressure'. There

[1] *The series began on 20 February from Paris. Daily talks by Hilton had been suggested by the Ministry of Information, but the BBC resisted this, and the talks were put out only once a week. (Home Board, *Minutes*, 15 March, 20 March 1940.) The talks gained in popularity after a tough start. Of 27 comments on a Hilton talk, 7 said that it was very popular, 11 fairly popular, and 9 unpopular. 'The unpopular reports come, for the most part, from correspondents who say all speech, except News, is *ipso facto* unpopular.'

[2] *Summary of Listeners Opinion, 17–30 March 1940; Macpherson, op. cit., pp. 100–3.   [3] *Longland, op. cit., p. 98.

[4] *Summary of Listeners Opinion, 21 April–4 May 1940.

[5] *Home Board, *Minutes*, 16 Feb. 1940. Black had just had an interview with Ogilvie.

[6] The first recorded repeat of this show in the Forces Programme was on 18 February 1940.

were many demands for 'more Bing Crosby'[1] and embittered pleas for the use of 'more tact' arising from the playing of the popular song 'There's a boy coming home on leave' from two to five times a day when leave had already been cancelled. On songs in general there was no demand for marching songs, and 'crooners', particularly male crooners, were in favour because it was said that 'they help us to learn the words of the songs'.[2]

On most programmes opinions were healthily divided. There was already, indeed, a critical, if powerless, minority who thought the programmes were 'excessively light'. 'When asked why they do not do more selecting from the Home Service programme, the critics reply something as follows: the set is normally put on and left on the Forces Programme. If a less popular item comes on, it will be tolerated quietly for a minute or so and then somebody will say "Is anybody listening to this?" If anybody says "Yes", the item will stay on: if there is a negative or no reply, action is taken. In this way a minority then gets its chance. For a minority to take the initiative and suggest going *off* pleasant background music to something more stimulating on the Home programme is another matter altogether.'[3] The group nature of most listening was always emphasized. 'Could not request programmes be arranged not for individuals but for whole units, battalions, squadrons, and searchlight crews, etc.?' asked one listener. 'Ten or a hundred men would get a kick out of hearing something in whose choice they had participated, even if personally they had been voted down in the unit, and it would give the unit something to do working out their choice.'[4]

There are two interesting glosses on this report. In April 1940 Welch paid a five-day visit to the BEF and, as usual, produced a searching report which was completely free from platitudes. 'During the bitter and miserable winter which is just ending we were probably right in giving a Forces programme which was

[1] *Summary of Listeners Opinion, 17–30 March 1940.
[2] *Longland, op. cit., p. 96. The BBC was planning a War Songs Competition in March and April 1940. (Home Board, *Minutes*, 15 March, 5 April 1940.) For the 'more serious, patriotic' type of song the procedure was to be 'commissioning'. See also below, pp. 210, 577–9.
[3] *Summary of Listeners Opinion, 21 April–4 May 1940.
[4] *Ibid., 17–30 March 1940.

light, entertaining, and which asked little of the listeners. The BBC has got the goodwill of this audience.' So far so good, as was a warm tribute to Longland at the end of the report. Yet while Welch had found 'widespread satisfaction' with the Forces Programme, he added that he had not found 'real enthusiasm' for it. This was not simply because of the psychological effects of the 'bitter and miserable winter'. The just less than half-million who constituted 'the most homogeneous audience the BBC has ever been offered' were 'young, surprisingly literate (long, daily letters home are the rule), intelligent, not cranky, unbiased, not wedded to the familar and reminiscent, ready and eager for arguments in broadcasting. . . . The homogeneity, the sense of fellowship, and the passionate interest in home and home interests . . . are the three [essential] data about this Forces audience.' The Forces Programme did not meet all their aspirations.

This was a perceptive comment which prepares the reader for the later mood of 1940 after the war had burst into life. Soldiers were not to be passive agents of war, as they sometimes seemed to have been in the trenches between 1914 and 1918. Welch used the argument, of course, as a further reason for reiterating what he had already written about Sunday broadcasting. 'The more we live in France,' soldiers told him, 'the more British we feel, and now we appreciate the British Sunday and desperately want it to be different from other days. Sameness is the thing we hope to fight against, so for heaven's sake make Sunday *different* without making it dull.'[1]

The second gloss by Roger Wilson, then in Listener Research, is equally interesting. There were far more troops at home in Britain, he pointed out, than there were in France. 'Sentimentally, our first obligation is to those serving overseas. Practically, the matter does not appear to be as simple as that.' In Britain, many troops were scattered in small isolated A.A. posts 'living in unrelieved contact with an unchanging group' or concentrated in bigger units in small towns 'with only the most limited recreational opportunities'. 'The very difference of the Service conditions between these groups at home and abroad may well be worth attention from a programme point of view.' Wilson in this paper was also looking ahead—though

[1] *Welch, 'Report on visit to the Western Front', April 1940.

he had no intimation of it—to the problems of late 1940
when the Army was based in England and a far more enterprising policy for Forces broadcasting was needed than that
which had been canvassed in February. It was while the 'Bill
and Bob' technique of teaching French seemed to offer the
only useful educational opportunity in relation to Forces
broadcasting that Wilson wisely pointed out that the same techniques 'might be adapted to other subjects. French instruction
might be replaced by educational series examining other
informative material, designed to start discussion on other
subjects than the otherwise interminable war, sex and
sport.'[1]

Wilson's memorandum was not to bear fruit until after the
war really had become war, although the first talks about army
education had already begun a little earlier than the date when
he wrote.[2] In the meantime, the Forces Programme was being
listened to not only by far more servicemen in Britain than
servicemen in France but by far more civilians in Britain than
by servicemen in France and Britain put together. It really did
constitute a 'true alternative', although there was a great deal
of simultaneous broadcasting with the Home Service.

The steps whereby this home audience was built up are not
easy to chart. It was agreed almost at the start that there
should be 'trailing' of Forces programmes in the Home Service
—a device which the BBC was to develop in its post-war services
—and from March onwards the whole of a special page in the
Radio Times was devoted to it.[3] Whatever the contribution of
the Forces Programme to the morale of the troops, it made an
obvious contribution to home morale during the very long
winter when the British public showed that it was 'ready to
accept great sacrifices but not minor irritations'.[4] It was far
less under pressure from the Ministry of Information than the
Home Service and far more free from incessant attempts to
introduce open propaganda; and although all its potentialities
were not fully exploited in the early months of 1940 and were

[1] *Wilson to Tallents, 'Programme for the Forces', 17 April 1940.
[2] *Home Board, *Minutes*, 29 March 1940.
[3] *Ibid., 9 Feb. 1940; *Radio Times*, 15 March 1940.
[4] S. Hoare, *Nine Troubled Years* (1954), p. 418.

to be the subject of serious concern later in the year,[1] it very quickly became *the* popular programme.

From a vantage point two years later, Nicolls was to write disarmingly, 'Actually the Forces Programme has proved so popular with civilians that one of the BBC's difficulties has been the adjustment of the Home and Forces Programmes, considered as a pair, in such a way as to avoid the important informative talks and features in the Home Service being prejudiced by the greater popularity of the Forces Programme. The problem is eased by the fact that whatever the BBC may decide to do, listeners cannot be compelled to listen.'[2] Even from the vantage point of March 1940 the same landscape was visible with one difference—that in March 1940 there was another attractive programme to which both troops and civilians could listen and were listening, albeit only at certain limited times each day—the 'Lord Haw-Haw' programmes from Germany. The extent of the challenge—at least in the eyes of the BBC—is registered in an item in the March minutes of the Home Board: 'On DDG's suggestion, agreed that the *What's on Tomorrow* feature on the Forces Programme be moved, so as to enable a peak entertainment programme to start at 9.15 to attract listeners away from Haw-Haw.'[3]

4. A Second Alternative Programme

THE 'Haw-Haw' programmes from Germany were part of a pattern of German radio propaganda which had its origins in German policy long before William Joyce had left London for Berlin—with badly labelled luggage—on 26 August 1939. Yet, given the love of the British Press for personalizing policies and the atmosphere of boredom during the early months of the war, 'Haw-Haw' soon stole the headlines more than any BBC personality. The opening words of his programmes— 'Germany calling, Germany calling, Germany calling'—

---

[1] See below, p. 310.
[2] Nicolls, 'The Forces Programme' in *BBC Year Book, 1943*, p. 97.
[3] *Home Board, Minutes*, 29 March 1940.

quickly became catchwords, like snatches of dialogue from
ITMA. His broadcasts from Hamburg could be picked up on
almost any set, yet his reputation spread far and wide among
people who never once tuned in to his broadcasts.

The fact of being able to listen direct to what the 'enemy' was
saying—particularly in Haw-Haw's idiosyncratic accent—
quickly became something more than a joke as Haw-Haw built
up a regular audience. Radio critics might treat him as 'the
best entertainment in the blackout' and comedians might seek
—on the stage or before the microphone—to imitate the words
'Germany calling' (with varying degrees of success) or to sing
songs about 'Lord Haw-Haw, the Humbug of Hamburg,
the Comic of Eau-de-Cologne'.[1] Yet by Christmas 1939 both
the Ministry of Information and the War Office, not to speak
of hundreds of private individuals, were profoundly disturbed
about Haw-Haw's broadcasts and their likely effects. 'Thousands tune in to him to relieve the boredom and dullness of this
particular war,' wrote H. J. Ormerod, who called himself
'an ordinary member of the general public', to the Ministry
of Information, in January 1940.[2] 'Haw-Haw is as popular with
the British troops as with people at home,' Ryan wrote succinctly after his visit to France in the same month.[3]

German propaganda was manufactured in Berlin by a
complex and not always efficient machine managed by
Goebbels.[4] 'Haw-Haw' himself, however, was manufactured
not in Berlin but in Britain. One day before Joyce joined the
Reichsrundfunk on 11 September, General Sir Charles Grant
had already written to Ogilvie from Scottish Command
complaining of 'foul German propaganda' and asking if in
the BBC's foreign broadcasts 'the more obvious lies' were
being answered.[5] Within less than two months the question
was whether 'the more obvious lies' should be answered in
Home broadcasts, if necessary by 'a junior Mr. Churchill'.

[1] A revue called *Haw-Haw*, 'a new laughter show', ran at the Holborn Empire
during the summer of 1940.
[2] Letter to the Minister of Information, 12 Jan. 1940.
[3] *A. P. Ryan, 'Listening by the BEF', 23 Jan. 1940.
[4] See above, p. 7.
[5] *Lieut.-General Sir Charles Grant to Ogilvie, 10 Sept. 1939. Grant added
quickly that 'answering lies might be against the traditions of the BBC'. The main
theme of these early German broadcasts to Britain was that 'Germany is fighting
for the destruction of an injustice, while the others are fighting for its preservation.'

The omission of references in the *Radio Times* to the programme times of the nightly German mixture of news and topical talks —full details were given in *The Times*—surrounded them with 'mystery' and in the opinion of Melville Dinwiddie, the Scottish Director of the BBC, helped to increase their regular listeners. Could not 'Lord Haw-Haw', Dinwiddie went on, be 'flayed at the microphone, open and unabashed'?[1]

Joyce had been hired, with some misgivings, by Walter Kamm, the head of the German overseas short-wave service, at a time when the Germans were broadcasting nine news bulletins in English each day, and additional English 'voices' were urgently required. He joined a not very happy or co-operative team, and to begin with he had very little power or prestige. His voice was his fortune, an intriguing but puzzling voice, supercilious, soon notorious—'Cholmondeley-Plantagenet out of Christ Church', Harold Hobson called it; 'public-school Yorkshire' wrote a lesser authority.[2] He certainly sounded different from the stock BBC announcer. 'I imagine him,' wrote Jonah Barrington, the radio critic of the *Daily Express*, who invented his name, 'with a receding chin, a questing nose, thin yellow hair brushed back, a monocle, a vacant eye, a gardenia in his button-hole. Rather like P. G. Wodehouse's Bertie Wooster.'[3] Seldom could 'image' and reality have been less close to each other. On the day when 'Lord Haw-Haw' acquired his English title, Joyce, an apprentice news reader in Berlin, was given his first formal contract by the Germans.[4]

Yet it was the image which mattered. During the autumn of 1939 Englishmen had the choice of listening to a variety of foreign broadcasters. They could pick up a cockney voice from Moscow or, if they had powerful enough sets, they could hear English programmes from Chungking, ending with a rendering of *The British Grenadiers* played on Chinese instruments. They were still being exhorted by radio advertisements to 'get

[1] *Dinwiddie to Maconachie, 16 Nov. 1939.

[2] E. S. Turner, op. cit., p. 112. There were more sharply contrasting opinions about the voice than about the message. Charles Graves in the *Daily Mail*, for example, had scathing words for those who painted 'Haw-Haw' as a 'monocled ass'.

[3] *Daily Express*, 18 Sept. 1939. The *Sunday Dispatch* was the first of the other newspapers to take up the name.

[4] J. A. Cole, *Lord Haw-Haw—and William Joyce* (1964), p. 116.

Europe under your thumb' and to buy sets 'for *uncensored* short-wave news and entertaining programmes', since 'the rest of the world is transmitting in English day and night'.[1] From the galaxy of possible stars, Eastern and Western, Joyce, with his 'audacious naughtiness' and his 'barefaced lies', was quickly raised to fame. Indeed, people in Britain turned him into a smash hit before the Germans had given him a radio receiving set of his own, before he was granted access to any English newspapers, and before he was allowed to write his own scripts. At the very time when the BBC was under attack from many of the British newspapers, writers in the same newspapers were urging the public to listen to Haw-Haw. 'I urgently ask all of you who are able to listen to broadcasts from Germany to do so,' wrote Cassandra in the *Daily Mirror*.[2] 'The more people who tune in to the foreign propaganda experts, the greater the joy and the laughter,' wrote Barrington: 'healthy British laughter', he was still calling it at a Foyle's lunch as late as January 1940.[3]

Not everyone laughed, however, when the German radio rang a mock Lutine bell to announce the sinking of vessels in the British Merchant Navy. Percy Edgar, for one, the BBC's Midland Regional Director, who had been called in to attend the meetings of the BBC's Home Service Board to interpret the trends of provincial opinion, expressed concern 'at the amount of listening to German broadcasts of news in English' and thought 'they were having some effect'.[4] In Scotland, General Grant repeated his earlier warnings. The BBC's Monitoring Service noted in December 1939 how the Hamburg broadcasts had established 'a tradition of their own'. Their gross distortions always contained an element of truth, and they were clever enough to turn the allegations of yesterday into premises to cite today.[5]

Undoubtedly many of the complaints about Haw-Haw's broadcasts—and they soon began to pour in to the BBC— came from people who were alarmed by what they considered

[1] Turner, op. cit., pp. 109–10. A British Long-Distance Radio Club issued special certificates to readers who could produce 'verification cards' showing that they had listened to transmitting stations in five continents.

[2] *Daily Mirror*, 25 Sept. 1939.   [3] Cole, op. cit., p. 133.

[4] *Home Service Board, *Minutes*, 24 Nov. 1939.

[5] *BBC Monitoring Service, *Weekly Analysis*, 13 Dec. 1939.

his socially subversive message. All the rudiments of this message—even the language and the tone in which it was delivered—had been familiar before the war to tiny Fascist audiences at street corners. Joyce had belonged to a Fascist splinter group which found Mosley's language and style too restrained. Now his argument and manner became familiar to thousands of people sitting quietly in their own homes or in army camps. Joyce attacked with genuine relish 'the hyenas of international finance', criticized, sometimes with rich humour, as in his Orpington sketches, the 'decadent upper classes', expressed what seemed to be real concern for the plight of the ordinary people alarmed by 'the rising prices of food-stuffs',[1] dismissed democracy comprehensively as 'an elaborate system of make-believe under which you have the illusion of choosing your government', and referred hopefully from time to time to the possibility of a 'new system' within which 'the working men of England could exercise a formidable opinion'.

'The broadcasting is most insidious,' General Pile, head of the Anti-Aircraft Command complained, 'and is nothing more or less than an attempt to foment a social revolution.'[2] It would affect his Command more than any Command in England, 'for we are pretty bored in the evenings'. 'The BBC news bulletins were extremely dull, [and] when someone tunes in to Lord Haw-Haw, the whole room gets up and gathers round the wireless. After it is over, they go back to their games without comment.' Pile suggested that Haw-Haw should be answered directly on the BBC every night by a working man or 'by one of the very talented men who every Sunday take up their positions at Hyde Park Corner'. The one essential quality in the man responsible for a counterblast should be that 'the voice coming over the wireless should not be "Oxford"'.

Other correspondents thought that wit was more relevant than social class. A 'humorist', such as P. G. Wodehouse or Beachcomber, could best 'caricature His Lordship'.[3] The main thing, however, was that the British speaker should be able to render points quickly and wittily and to have the gift of apparent

[1] Women broadcasters were also called upon by the Germans to use the theme of 'the burden of rationing' in Britain, but none of them made an individual mark as a broadcaster.

[2] *Letter of 5 Dec. 1939.

[3] *Aylmer Vallance to Ogilvie, 11 Dec. 1939.

improvisation. Sections of the press began to support this point of view.[1] So, too, did Sir Robert Vansittart, who was to become the active war-time voice on all matters relating to aggressive anti-German propaganda. 'The Beaverbrook press has now repeated several times that we are wrong to let Lord Haw-Haw go unanswered,' he wrote on Foreign Office notepaper in December 1939. 'I think he should be shown up.'[2]

It says more about British society in 1939 than about German propaganda that 'Cholmondeley-Plantagenet out of Christ Church' could cause such alarm. The BBC's line, however, very forcefully expressed by Ogilvie, was that there should be no direct or regular replies to Haw-Haw. In answer to a mounting pile of letters of complaint, each one with its own suggestion of how best to deal with Haw-Haw, what had originally been natural inclination—'we are inclined to leave Hamburg alone, except for occasionally guying'[3]—became a deliberate, well-argued policy. 'We have all agreed that a permanent, regular refutation of German lies is not possible or desirable.'[4]

Yet there were sufficient critics of this policy in the Ministry of Information as well as in the Foreign Office for what had started as an attack on Haw-Haw to be diverted into an attack on Ogilvie and the BBC. At a December meeting of the Home Publicity Division of the Ministry of Information, for example, with John Hilton in the chair, it was argued powerfully that 'the German attack was mostly to the left and therefore there should be propaganda directed also to the left'. On this occasion, Maconachie, who had recently referred to the Ministry of Information as 'The Ministry of Propaganda',

---

[1] The climax of the Press campaign was reached in *Everybody's Weekly*, 10 Feb. 1940. It was now time, *Everybody's* wrote, to jam Haw-Haw. 'Would you invite a traitor into your house night after night?' A copy of this article was sent to Tallents by a Foreign Office official. 'Extravagant publicity,' wrote Raymond Burns in the *World's Press News*, 1 February 1940, had directed 'national attention to the only potentially dangerous system of enemy propaganda against this country's morale.' Haw-Haw made excellent use of a recording of a Churchill speech at Manchester in January 1940. (*BBC Monitoring Service, *Weekly Analysis*, 30 Jan. 1940.)

[2] *Vansittart, letter passed on to Ogilvie, 18 Dec. 1939.

[3] *Note by Nicolls, 27 Nov. 1939, in reply to a suggestion from the Engineer-in-Charge, Tatsfield, that there should be 'ridiculing of this German stuff' along with a weekly 'fun-feature' on it.

[4] *Nicolls to Maconachie, 13 Dec. 1939.

found it necessary to insist that he was 'completely opposed to the contradiction of particular statements, except in special circumstances, or to misdirected efforts to counter Haw-Haw's propaganda [which] might indeed do much to keep it alive and prominent'.[1]

Both Maconachie and Nicolls—with Ogilvie in the background—continued to question the policy of their critics inside the Ministry. 'Why should they know better than the BBC?'[2] The best answers to Haw-Haw were true news and good news. The sinking of the *Graf Spee* was the best counter-propaganda.[3] News, however, could be supplemented by serious programmes examining German propaganda themes and methods, like the monthly programme *The Voice of the Nazi*, and perhaps by weekly talks by regular commentators, dealing not only with topics which interested them but with issues of 'national importance' and with what John Hilton had called 'the philosophy and doctrine of the democratic way of living'.[4]

From the last of these ideas, which has been referred to earlier in a different context,[5] there developed in 1940 first the BBC's 'Onlooker' series and then the 'Postscripts', as they began to be called in March 1940. Even in its origins, the idea behind the Postscripts was as controversial as it was to prove to be in its implementation. Maconachie disliked it and thought it impractical, and Nicolls had doubts about it.[6] Ogilvie referred to it, however, in an authoritative letter to Campbell Stuart, written in December, in the course of which he dealt

---

[1] *Statement by Maconachie at a meeting of the Home Publicity Division of the Ministry of Information, 19 Dec. 1939; his reference to the Ministry is in a letter to Nicolls written on 2 December 1939.

[2] *Nicolls to Maconachie, 13 Dec. 1939.

[3] *Memorandum by Maconachie, 24 Dec. 1939. 'Since the reply of facts is a "long term" system of refutation,' he added, 'the success of false propaganda with any audience which has access to facts is essentially a "short term" affair.' He also favoured broadcasts emphasizing the superiority of democratic over totalitarian ideals.

[4] *Tallents to Graves on 'Commentator', 28 Dec. 1939.

[5] See above pp. 119–20.

[6] See below, p. 167. Maconachie believed that 'in the perspectives of the BBC's general output' there was not 'much ground left open to the general commentator, especially when it is borne in mind that large areas are already ruled out . . . e.g. party politics (practically non-existent) and criticism of foreign policy which (like certain other public questions) is largely excluded by censorship'. (*Maconachie to Nicolls, 1 Jan. 1940.)

with the advice which he had been offered by Vansittart and others. 'The Haw-Haw question is of great importance. We have never regarded it as the joke which it is supposed to be by some. . . . That Haw-Haw should be countered is, of course, agreed certainly; the only problem concerns the method.' After mentioning the idea of a regular speaker, Ogilvie added that 'there should be no undue publicity for Haw-Haw'. 'Why had *The Times* given the times and wave-lengths of his talks and why did M.P.s direct so much attention to him in the House?' Haw-Haw was not a person, but 'a well informed syndicate', and what he said was clever enough 'not to admit of easy answer'. Some of his talks about India or Pakistan or about the alleged sabotaging of the League of Nations in the last few years 'might have come straight from the *News Chronicle* or the *Manchester Guardian* . . . I doubt if even an F. E. Smith could take the air at 9.30 p.m. (let alone the other eight times) and make a success of it.' 'The Haw-Haw question,' he characteristically concluded—'merely [*sic*] makes it all the more important that the BBC's news service should be allowed to maintain its standards of truthfulness and speed.' The best defence was attack, and it should be attack in 'British terms not those of Haw-Haw's'.[1] Ogilvie wrote also in the same vigorous terms to Vansittart, and the latter replied equally vigorously that he was not convinced.[2]

The BBC had one other idea—appropriately it was an idea passed on by Tallents—to which Ogilvie referred also in his letters of justification. There should be a carefully organized piece of listener research to study just how *many* listened to Haw-Haw, how often, why and with what results. This was something which would be 'better done' by the BBC than by the

[1] *Ogilvie to Campbell Stuart, 26 Dec. 1939. Along with a copy of the letter sent to Sir Kenneth Lee (26 Dec. 1939), he added the covering note, 'If the Air Ministry continues trying to disguise losses on the wireless or if the Admiralty begins trying to disguise them (in the apparent interests of airmen or sailors or the home front) it will play straight into Haw-Haw's hands.'

[2] *Ogilvie to Vansittart, 26 Dec. 1939; Vansittart to Ogilvie, 27 Dec. 1939. A letter from Harold Hobson to *The Times* provoked Vansittart to write to Ogilvie again two days later reaffirming his own views. There were members of the Cabinet, too, who felt there should be a direct reply to Haw-Haw (Sir John Anderson to Ogilvie, 4 Jan. 1940). Campbell Stuart, however (letter of 28 Dec. 1939), accepted Ogilvie's thesis and added 'I agree profoundly with what you say and it is obvious that the matter can only be considered in conjunction with the whole question of broadcasting policy'.

Ministry of Information.[1] Silvey's experience, along with that
of Ernst Kris and Mark Abrams in the research section of the
Monitoring Service,[2] would be invaluable: together they
constituted 'a group particularly qualified to assist in the
psychological interpretation of the data'. Tallents had always
believed in listener research, and his proposal was accepted
by the Overseas Board in December.[3] Soon afterwards Silvey
began detailed inquiries which were to take shape in a
fascinating report on 'Hamburg Broadcast Propaganda: The
Extent and Effect of its Impact on the British Public during
mid-Winter 1939/40'.

An earlier survey in November 1939 by the British Institute
of Public Opinion, completed before Silvey and his colleagues
got to work, had shown that 50 per cent of those who listened to
foreign stations listened to German medium-wave broadcasts
in English from Hamburg and Bremen as compared with some
7 per cent before the war and as compared with 2 per cent who
listened to New York and 10 per cent who listened to Paris.
Moreover, listening to Hamburg and Bremen became progressively more popular with each step down the income scale,
whereas listening to Paris and New York on short-wave was
ordinarily more popular with the higher than with the lower
income group. Seven per cent of the BBC's own log-keepers
listened regularly to German news bulletins from Hamburg,
and there were signs that there had been a recent 'enormous
increase in the amount of listening'. Twenty seven per cent of
the British population were listening regularly to Haw-Haw.[4]

A bigger proportion still was to be drawn into listening to
Germany between the start and the termination of Silvey's
own inquiries. Indeed, an interim report prepared in January

[1] *Tallents to Ogilvie, 13 Dec. 1939. The Ministry pursued its own plans for
some time even though they overlapped with those of the BBC. (Macadam to
Ogilvie, 14 Dec. 1939.)

[2] Kris was later to be the joint author along with Hans Speier of the pioneer
study *German Radio Propaganda* (1944) which linked British research with the
important American research carried out in the New School of Social Research
from April 1941 onwards and the Research Project on Totalitarian Communication. Mark Abrams was beginning a distinguished career in opinion and market
research which was to make him an outstanding authority on the subject.

[3] *Overseas Board, *Minutes*, 14 Dec. 1939; Note by Ogilvie, 16 Dec. 1939.

[4] *Silvey to Tallents, 17 Nov. 1939. Salt, the BBC's Overseas Intelligence
Director, wrote to Charles Madge, 8 December 1939, asking him for his impressions of the problem.

1940 showed that during the previous month 30 per cent of adult listeners were tuning in to Hamburg. 'A typical 9 o'clock BBC news bulletin is listened to by 16,000,000 people, over 50 per cent of the listening public. If it is followed by a talk, this will be heard by 9,000,000. Of the other 7,000,000, 6,000,000 switch over to Hamburg, while the remaining million choose either some other programme or switch off.'[1]

In the light of these statistics, it is not surprising that the BBC decided deliberately to switch some of its most popular programmes to the period immediately after the 9 o'clock News. Putting on programmes like *Band Waggon* or Gracie Fields 'on each occasion when German material was broadcast' had already been felt to be the most effective way of limiting British interest in Hamburg and Bremen.[2] 'The onus must rest largely with you,' wrote the Director of Programme Planning to the Programme Organizer of the new Forces Programme, 'to provide as often as possible a really popular programme at this hour.'[3]

There were, however, many other interesting proposals to counter Haw-Haw during the winter months of 1939/40, not all of them put into effect. They ranged from the idea of putting on a Graham Greene play about the mind and motives of a traitor to that of introducing a new feature based on recordings of Haw-Haw punctuated with 'Stop' in *In Town Tonight* fashion, followed by a pungent riposte.[4] Most important of all, at a meeting on 2 January 1940 at the Ministry of Information to discuss 'propaganda from Hamburg', this time with the Minister in the chair, the idea of the weekly commentator was taken one step further. Vernon Bartlett's name was mentioned, and a few days later Charles Peake, 'with the blessing of the Foreign Office', wrote to Maconachie, who was

[1] *Interim Report, 'The Effect of Hamburg Propaganda in Great Britain', Jan. 1940.

[2] *Dinwiddie to Maconachie, 16 Nov. 1939.

[3] *Adams to Langham, 16 Jan. 1940. Some of the Home Service talks at this time, he added, were 'pretty dreary'. See also above, p. 140.

[4] *Gielgud to Nicolls, 17 Jan. 1940; L. Titchener to R. H. Eckersley, 9 Jan. 1940. There is also a note in the Monitoring Day Book, 27 March 1940: 'Home News enquired if they might have the tapes of Haw-Haw for their attempts at counter-propaganda. I said I could see no objection.' A pencilled query at the side 'What is the definition of Haw-Haw in this case?' was answered 'German Talks for England'.

reluctantly coming round to acceptance of the idea, referring to Karl Haushofer's weekly survey of the press on German radio before the war as a model. 'A very small committee', consisting of one representative of the Foreign Office, one of the Ministry of Information and one of the BBC, might meet with the commentator on the morning of the commentator's talk to draw up a script, which would then be given 'the imprint of his own style'.[1]

Although this particular procedure was never actually followed, the BBC's Home Service Board at its first January meeting not only approved the idea of appointing at once a weekly commentator who would 'counter German propaganda' but agreed to give the idea top priority over 'all other talks and proposals'. The terms 'commentary' and 'commentator' would be chosen 'to avoid suggestion of overt counter-propaganda'.[2] 'He will have some innocuous title,' Ogilvie wrote to Lee, 'as we thought it would be thoroughly bad policy to label the talks as specifically anti-Haw-Haw. The speaker is to be Norman Birkett.'[3]

Norman Birkett, the eminent lawyer, and not Vernon Bartlett, a very experienced broadcaster, was chosen for the job after extensive inquiries, chiefly because both the BBC and the Ministry of Information wished to keep unknown the identity of the commentator. Bartlett's voice was already familiar to millions of people, and while Birkett lacked broadcasting experience, he seemed to have the 'necessary qualifications' to establish himself over a period of time as a 'radio personality'. This, thought Commander King-Hall, who had been consulted on the matter, was the essential task—the building up of a microphone personality to whom everybody felt they must listen.[4] The reason why Birkett had not broadcast in peace time 'though so frequently proposed as a broadcaster, had probably been the Bar Council's objection to

[1] *Peake to Maconachie, 4 Jan. 1940.
[2] *Home Service Board, Minutes, 5 Jan. 1940.
[3] *Ogilvie to Lee, 18 Jan. 1940. Lee had written on 17 January saying that Barrington-Ward of The Times had suggested to the Minister of Information that twice-weekly talks in which Haw-Haw was answered 'indirectly and incidentally but nevertheless in definite terms' would be extremely valuable. Ogilvie endorsed this suggestion which, of course, was not new, as a 'valuable one'. (Ogilvie to Barrington-Ward, 18 Jan. 1940.)
[4] *Maconachie to Nicolls and Ogilvie, 15 Jan. 1940.

barristers broadcasting under their own names'.[1] In this case, however, his name was to be kept strictly secret. 'Will you please note,' Godfrey Adams wrote mysteriously on 19 January, 'that the weekly commentator is to be referred to as "Mr. X" in any internal memoranda dealing with the subject. His identity is to be regarded as strictly secret.'[2]

Birkett arranged to see Tallents on 10 January,[3] was 'immediately interested', asked for a 'devil' to help him, decided to accept the commission, and got down to work to prepare his first broadcast on 9 February. 'It is essential to be quite sure what the purpose of the new feature really is,' he wrote to Barnes, the BBC's Assistant Director of Talks, who had himself thought hard and long about how best to find an antidote to Haw-Haw. 'I have gathered what is desired is a weekly talk which would be of interest to listeners, but the real purpose behind it is to make authoritative answers to German propaganda in this country, without saying so, and without naming any particular broadcaster.' The title for the broadcast series presented 'some difficulty'. *Once a Week* was 'as good as any'. 'The Commentator' might be a good name for himself. His first talk on 9 February would obviously be 'of great importance' in relation to the winning of an audience. 'My own idea at the moment is that this talk must of necessity be rather general justifying a new voice on the wireless. . . . After a general introduction, some particular matter which has been the subject of a German broadcast ought to be dealt with simply, effectively and authoritatively. The conclusion should state that this will be a weekly feature, invite co-operation, and seek to leave a friendly personal atmosphere between speaker and audience. Thereafter each week should see some particular theme dealt with in the same way.'

Birkett foresaw certain difficulties. 'Many of the criticisms of Haw-Haw, for example, are directed to our domestic affairs. The unemployment figures, the conditions revealed by the Evacuation Scheme, the evasion of Income Tax, and similar matters are typical. Now these subjects are those which many

---

[1] *Maconachie to Wellington, 5 Jan. 1940.
[2] *Adams to H. J. G. Grisewood, 19 Jan. 1940.
[3] *Tallents to Ogilvie, 11 Jan. 1940. See also H. Montgomery Hyde, *Norman Birkett* (1964), p. 471.

social workers have examined for many years; and the Socialist party will be up in arms if they are dealt with in a way which runs counter to the policy they have long planned. Similarly, questions like the government of India, the treatment of native races, are highly controversial. . . . The question therefore whether each talk should receive approval before delivery by some authoritative body requires consideration. It would be fatal if some criticism arose that the talks were used for political propaganda at home. Whilst I myself could easily select a theme each week, I have a feeling that I ought not to do this on my own responsibility.'

Given this context, Birkett went on to ask how much latitude he would be allowed. 'For example, the German propaganda is directed to showing (i) German efficiency in economic activities and (ii) Britain's inefficiency in similar matters' and in drawing a contrast between 'the German system, as a most efficient "planned economy", and the British system based on competition and profit-seeking'. How could he deal, even obliquely, with Haw-Haw's references to rationing, to families of soldiers turned out of their homes, to the static figure of $1\frac{1}{2}$ million unemployed, and to living conditions in the Special Areas? 'What answers if any (and in what form) ought to be made are obviously matters of the highest importance, and could not be left to an individual; for they go to the root of controversial home politics and are really matters for the Government to decide.' Quite apart from all this, if an international debate with Haw-Haw was to start, 'very accurate information' would be essential. Should an official of the Ministry of Information supply information for the talks? 'It is vital to see clearly on what we are embarking before we commit ourselves to a course which may present great difficulties later.'[1]

This interesting letter does not seem to have been answered in detail, but on 31 January, Waterfield did the best he could in approved civil service manner and wrote to the Board of Education, the Ministries of Health, Food, Labour and Transport, the Home Office, the Board of Trade and the Unemployment Assistance Board, explaining that radio talks were to be given with the title *Once a Week* by an anonymous

[1] *Birkett to Barnes, 21 Jan. 1940.

speaker, designated 'by some such name as "Onlooker"'. 'This speaker will comment on passing events and, without making specific replies to the false statements of the Hamburg broadcasts, will put our side of the picture.' 'The purpose of this letter is to inform you that the BBC may have occasion to apply at very short notice for authoritative facts and statistics. . . . It is important that full information should be available as quickly as possible.' Each department should appoint a Liaison Officer to help with this project and with a further series of talks 'to show by comparison cross sections of national life in Germany and Britain'.[1]

Waterfield's instructions did not fully answer Birkett's questions, some of which had been raised by persons to whom the BBC turned before he was chosen and some of which, indeed, had been examined at length inside the BBC's own Talks Department. There Guy Burgess, among others, had joined with Maconachie, Barnes and John Green in protracted discussion. Bartlett had suggested sensibly that no one person but only a 'panel of broadcasters' would and could have the range of experience and opinions to cope with Haw-Haw, who, because of criticisms of the Government's social policy, had been turned in the eyes of many people into a kind of 'unofficial leader of His Majesty's Opposition'. Speakers should not be announced until they came before the microphone, and they should include J. B. Priestley, Howard Marshall, Harold Nicolson and Gerald Barry. The speakers 'should not hesitate to admit our own shortcomings', since the whole series should aim at 'reasonable explanation' rather than at 'exaggerated propaganda'.[2]

The germ of the famous 1940 Postscripts was present in this suggestion, but so too was the germ of the fierce argument which was to revolve round them. No single speaker in Britain in early 1940 could command the information or claim the role of spokesman in the confident style of Hans Fritzsche, the brilliant home commentator in Nazi Germany. Some of the difficulties were pointed out by G. L. Marshall, the Northern Ireland Director of the BBC. Marshall had recently met the

---

[1] *Waterfield wrote his letters to the different departments on 31 January 1940 (Wellington to Maconachie, 2 Feb. 1940).

[2] *Memorandum by Bartlett, 8 Jan. 1940.

Prime Minister of Northern Ireland who was concerned about the effects on working men of the Haw-Haw broadcasts and who had stressed that 'any counter attack to "Lord Haw-Haw" should emanate from Downing Street. Such a reply would carry much greater weight than any personal views by an individual.' These broadcasts should be supplemented by speakers recruited 'from the ranks of the labouring classes' [a startling phrase to obtrude in 1940]—such as young farmers, shipyard workers, etc.'[1]

Birkett went ahead on his own, however, assisted by Ministers when available, and by snippets of information from German broadcasts collected by the BBC's Monitoring Service.[2] Within the limits of his assignment, he proved, as his biographer states, 'an excellent booster for morale during the waiting period of the phoney war'.[3] Yet he never won the goodwill of the critics, and the audience for one of his talks, at least, was said to consist mainly of 'adolescents and middle-aged women'.[4] His performance neither quietened those who demanded 'the lie direct to Haw-Haw', nor those who believed that the answer to Haw-Haw was better entertainment.[5] Some listeners guessed Birkett's identity correctly, even though Haw-Haw himself remained unidentified throughout this period. Rosita Forbes was sure that Haw-Haw was Rolf Hoffman, who had studied at Glasgow University before the war.[6] Others were in no doubt he was Eduard Dietze. And from the security of the BBC Nicolls wrote with sublime confidence towards the end of February that it was 'quite clear'

[1] *Marshall to Maconachie, passed on to Ogilvie, 9 Jan. 1940. Haw-Haw's 'appeal' was wider than this. The North Regional Director, John Coatman, complained of the dangerous effects on *middle-class* households in the North of Haw-Haw's broadcasts, while the Countess of Harrowby wrote to Tallents on 22 February 1940 that a woman friend of a friend 'in the Potteries District has been completely won over' by Haw-Haw.

[2] For this Service, see below, pp. 187–90. Birkett's last trial script was described as 'promising'. (*Home Board, *Minutes*, 2 Feb. 1940.)

[3] Montgomery Hyde, op. cit., p. 471.

[4] *Home Service Board, *Minutes*, 5 April 1940.

[5] *Graves to Nicolls, 12 March 1940. 'There will always be a large body of people who will not listen to . . . the Onlooker who may listen to Haw-Haw but will certainly listen to attractive entertainment programmes. Hence my suggestion that simultaneous broadcast items at times when Haw-Haw is broadcasting are a mistake.' Nevertheless, there were protests when George Formby was put on the air at the same time as Haw-Haw in order 'to test audience reaction'. (Home Board, *Minutes*, 5 April 1940.) [6] *Sunday Dispatch*, 7 Jan. 1940.

that Haw-Haw was not Dietze, neither was he Baillie-Stewart nor William Joyce. 'I am personally quite certain he is a German and that we cannot say much about him being a traitor.'[1]

Vansittart did not identify him either, though he continued to press the case for tougher action to deal with him; 'Although I think it is easy to overrate Haw-Haw, I am convinced that the prevailing tendency is rather to underrate him.'[2] Likewise, Major Longland, from his vantage point with the BEF in France, expressed alarm that 'there is more or less consistent listening to Hamburg in the BEF, in officers' messes, men's canteens and *estaminets*. The DMI considers that this is a grave danger to morale and may in future be a very definite penetration point for enemy propaganda.'[3]

Silvey's report on listening to Hamburg, with information collected from 34,000 interviews and 750 questionnaires, appeared early in March and copies of it were sent by the Ministry of Information not only to their own Regional Information Offices but to Members of Parliament, who had taken a sustained interest in what Haw-Haw was saying. At the end of January, the report showed that out of every six adults in the British population one was a regular listener, three were occasional listeners and two never listened. (At that time four out of every six people—nearly twenty-three million people in all—were listening regularly to the BBC News.) Throughout January and February the habit of listening regularly had been on the decline, so that during the last days of February only two-thirds of the number were listening who had listened during the last week in January.[4]

'The black-out, the novelty of hearing the enemy, the desire to hear both sides and the insatiable appetite for news and the desire to be in the swim had all played their part both in building up Hamburg's audience and in holding it together (indeed for establishing it) as a familiar feature in the social

---

[1] *Nicolls to Macgregor, 21 Feb. 1940. For Dietze, see also above, p. 38.
[2] *Vansittart to Campbell Stuart, 4 March 1940; Campbell Stuart to Vansittart, 6 March 1940.
[3] *A report to Farquharson, acknowledged on 28 March 1940.
[4] *Farquharson to Press Representative, 20 March 1940: 'We have been keeping a watch as you know on the Hamburg audience and our information is that there has been a fairly steep decline in it.'

landscape.' As far as the 'typology' of those who listened to him was concerned—and this was the line of inquiry which had been pressed by Silvey and Abrams[1]—all types of persons listened but more men than women and more under 50s than over 50s. Against the weight of 'evidence' collected from letters, listening was more common in the upper income groups than in the lower income groups (incomes of £500 or more, 77.6 per cent; incomes of less than £200, 64.9 per cent). People with relatives in the Forces did not listen more than the rest. Analysis of a limited special sample of 5,000 interviews, organized by the British Institute of Public Opinion Research, showed that 17 per cent believed that the Hamburg broadcasts contained grains of truth or news scoops. (Out of the same sample 37 per cent believed Hitler had improved the living conditions of people in Germany before the war, 45 per cent that he had not, and 18 per cent had no opinion;[2] and 21 per cent were in favour of more things in Britain being rationed, 10 per cent were against all rationing, and 50 per cent were happy with things as they were.)[3] Yet in giving their reasons for listening to Hamburg, 58 per cent of the respondents said that they listened because Haw-Haw's version of the news was so fantastic that it was funny, 29 per cent because they wished to listen to the German point of view, 26 per cent because they hoped to get more news, and only 6 per cent because they thought he was so 'clever'.

Perhaps the most interesting result of the inquiry—although it does not seem as surprising now as it did at the time—was that the one outstanding feature of the Hamburg audience was its interest in public affairs. The average listener to the German broadcasts in English was a more politically conscious and politically sophisticated person than the average non-listener to Hamburg. He listened more regularly to BBC News and read more widely in newspapers, choosing the more serious papers. He had 'more often made up his mind than has the man who does not listen to Hamburg'. On the basis of the sample, 30

[1] *Salt to Silvey, 22 Feb. 1940: 'The object . . . is to see whether we can classify types of people who will react to given propaganda appeal' in a 'particular way'.

[2] Non-listeners to Hamburg to whom this question was put answered 22 per cent yes, 51 per cent no, 27 per cent no opinion.

[3] Non-listeners to Hamburg showed comparative figures of 17 per cent, 49 per cent and 11 per cent.

per cent of *The Times* readers had listened to Hamburg as against only 19 per cent of the readers of the *Daily Express*, 16 per cent of the readers of the *Daily Mirror* and 16 per cent of the readers of the *Daily Sketch*. Summing up, the report concluded that 'as compared with persons who do not listen to Hamburg, listeners to Hamburg are more conscious of such disunity as exists within the Empire, and more prepared to credit Hitler with positive social achievements. On these points they may be said to take up the view that Hamburg would wish them to take up. On the other hand, they are more favourable to rationing in this country and not materially more convinced than non-listeners to Hamburg that, whoever does gain from the war, it will not be the Nazis. On these points they take precisely the opposite view to that taken up by Hamburg propaganda.' Of course, the fact that the situation was static could not be left out of the picture. Joyce's voice and manner had given him 'some degree of immunity from the full force of British anger', but at the same time, 'it is safe to say that, as yet, widespread hatred of the enemy (as a whole) does not exist'. 'If there were widespread social discontent, this would be Hamburg's opportunity.'[1]

'Social discontent' seemed a more likely contingency to the authors of this report than the start of a real as distinct from a phoney war. This, indeed, is perhaps the most surprising point about the report today, when it is viewed in the light of what happened later in the year, in May 1940. It is a reminder of the importance of the generation later in the year of the 'Dunkirk spirit', just as significant in history as Dunkirk itself. A new consensus was to be achieved during the summer of 1940 which quickly ensured that Haw-Haw's earlier role became untenable. Indeed, at the time the report was being drafted the Germans were in the course of preparation for the kind of war that almost overnight would change Joyce's image in Britain.

Joyce's own personal position in Germany had also altered considerably early in 1940 when the Germans extended their 'black radio' organization, called Büro Concordia, under the direction of Dr. Erich Hetzler, the man who had originally

---

[1] *Listener Research Report, 'Hamburg Broadcast Propaganda: An Enquiry into the Extent and Effect of its Impact on the British Public during Mid-Winter 1939–40', 8 March 1940.

introduced Joyce to Kamm. The object of the exercise was to produce 'black radio' programmes purporting to come from native inhabitants of foreign countries, programmes designed deliberately to manipulate and to confuse. While Joyce was to continue his 'official' broadcasts on the Hamburg and Bremen medium wavelengths, he was also to take charge of the British section of black radio, working with the minimum of censorship and with considerable, though still limited, freedom of action.[1] He had access thereafter to the principal British daily papers—one day late—and to the main weeklies, although he was supplied with little information from the slender German monitoring services.[2] He was to work, moreover, within a general framework of radio directives issued to the black broadcasters each day following Goebbels's daily meetings. These meetings were attended by Hetzler's superior, Dr. Raskin.

Within this new scheme of reference, Joyce prepared the output of what eventually became during the course of 1940 a cluster of specialized stations, each designed to appeal to a different section of the British 'target' audience. The first of these, the New British Broadcasting Station, transmitting on short wave from East Prussia, began half-hour broadcasts in February 1940: it professed to be 'entirely run by British people who put their country above their own interest and are resolved to speak the truth for their country's sake'.[3] The broadcasts started with the signature tune 'Loch Lomond' and ended with the playing of a cracked record of 'God Save the King'. Far less restrained than the 'official' broadcasts, they were designed, like the more successful German black stations dealing with France, to disintegrate opinion before fighting began. The programmes of NBBS were monitored by the BBC, advertised by the Germans—posters appeared in London in May 1940—backed by pseudo-statistics ('anti-war opinion was 57.8 in Limehouse')[4] and discussed in Parliament,[5] but they could be picked up by only 38 per cent of British listeners equipped with

[1] The German black broadcasters had never been allowed to criticize Hitler or the Third Reich.
[2] *Wellington to Nicolls, 22 Feb. 1940.
[3] *BBC Monitoring Service, Weekly Analysis, 27 Feb. 1940.
[4] *Ibid., 9 April 1940.
[5] Cole, op. cit., pp. 137–8.

adequate apparatus,[1] and there is no evidence that they ever attracted a wide audience. Nor did the other 'black' stations—Workers' Challenge, the Christian Peace Movement and Radio Caledonia—added after fighting really had begun and, as part of the game of deception, taking up quite different and often hostile stances towards each other.[2]

In the meantime, the NBBS created far less public attention in Britain than the official broadcasts, and even they lost much of their appeal in the spring of 1940. On 10 May, the day the Germans invaded Holland, Belgium and Luxembourg, only 13.3 per cent of the population was listening to Hamburg. It was no longer necessary, thereafter, to counteract either the boredom or the apathy which had given Joyce his great chance, a chance which for the time being he had exploited more effectively than had seemed possible. Nor was it any longer necessary for the Ministry of Information to press the BBC into 'taking every opportunity of showing people that a real war is being waged even though the military situation is static and by showing them [it came as a superb anti-climax] that they are participating in it by collaborating in anti-gossip, road safety, food measures and the like'.[3]

5. Answering Back

'HOME propaganda' as envisaged by the Ministry of Information always had a slightly absurd air about it during the winter

---

[1] Captain Ramsay, who was later detained under Defence Regulation 18B, asked about it on 20 March 1940, and there were further questions on 3 April. The BBC brief for the official reply stated that 'the broadcasts came from a station in Germany and are being carefully watched'. When it was remarked that the station had few listeners, the further reply was given that 'the extent to which an audience is liable to grow depends largely upon the amount of publicity it receives'.

[2] See below, pp. 218–20. George Orwell, among others, was fascinated by and remained interested in this last aspect of the German 'black stations'. See his 'London letter' to Partisan Review, 1 Jan. 1942, printed in Orwell and Angus, op. cit., vol. II (1968), pp. 181–3. He was particularly sensitive to the curious interpenetrations of Fascism, Pacifism and left-wing ideologies.

[3] *Note of interview between Wellington and Farquharson, 18 March 1940.

and spring of 1939/40, when 'good citizenship' was all that there was to talk about. There was an inevitable sense of disproportion between ends and means when the rich resources of radio in war time were being thought of entirely in terms of 'anti-gossip, road safety, food measures and the like'. 'Billy Brown', the good citizen, described during this period in a poster

Billy Brown of London Town

Billy Brown's own highway Code
For blackouts is 'Stay off the Road'.
He'll never step out and begin
To meet a bus that's pulling in.
He doesn't wave his torch at night,
But 'flags' his bus with something white.
He never jostles in a queue,
But waits and takes his turn. Do you?

Printed for
London Transport

Billy Brown, the Good Citizen

3. Billy Brown of London Town

printed for London Transport,[1] was expected to possess heroic virtues that scarcely deserved lyrical treatment.

At the same time, BBC producers were applying themselves diligently, imaginatively and responsibly to a whole range of proposals of a new type. 'Although the urgency up to date has not been extreme,' Miss Quigley wrote to Maconachie early in November 1939, 'we have succeeded, I think, in keeping in touch with evacuation problems and so on, and have covered most of the obviously current health questions.'[2] Certainly Mrs. Brown was receiving as much attention from the BBC as Mr. Brown, and professional care was being taken in programmes relating to such difficult subjects as health, air raid precautions, food,[3] 'gossip' and savings to appeal not only to

[1] Turner, op. cit., p. 69.
[2] *Miss Quigley to Maconachie, 8 Nov. 1939.
[3] Gert and Daisy, for example, broadcast *The Kitchen Front* each weekday from 8 April to 20 April 1940.

well-to-do and to well-educated people but to 'the masses of
the population'. As in the case of considering who might best
reply to Haw-Haw, emphasis was being placed on the tone
as well as on the content of what was said. 'One of the cardinal
needs in our propaganda,' Andrew Stewart wrote in March
1940, 'is that it should be flexible enough to talk to people in
their own idioms of thought and speech.'[1] Regional variations
were also taken into account within the limits of the single
programme. *The Northcountry Woman*, a women's magazine programme for the North, was one of the first war casualties,
but it was restored later in September 1939. John Green,
dealing with agricultural problems, launched a 'country
problems' series which in 1940 was to take him to places as far
apart as Exeter, Preston and Coupar.

In all these connections, the BBC soon began to inspire
more confidence behind the scenes than the Ministry of
Information. There were, indeed, at least as many open attacks
in the Press on the Ministry as there were on the BBC—for
its over-staffing; for the content and style of its publicity;
above all, for the way in which it was spending public money
to advocate doing things which were already being done quite
spontaneously with far more grace and humour. If this was the
public reaction, those 'in the know' about the administrative
set-up felt that the Ministry lacked the power, the will and,
above all, the moral authority to co-ordinate the tangled web
even of information services. Nor were there many signs that
the Government as a whole was alive to its importance.

When Reith, with his unique BBC record, was appointed
Minister of Information early in January 1940, Chamberlain
gave him the vaguest of assignments and no secure guarantees
of backing. 'I asked what support there would be from him in,
for instance, re-establishing the authority and responsibilities
of the Ministry and in reassembling the various parts which had
been hived off, including press and censorship. No definite
reply; he was being very cautious: hoped there would not be
any "brawl".' He advised Reith to 'have a look around and
then tell him in a month or two what I wanted done'. 'As to the
BBC, it would to some extent come under my direction;
there was a great deal of dissatisfaction with it; but he hoped I

[1] *Note by A. Stewart, 8 March 1940.

would be gentle with it, and not use my knowledge of it to do things that another Minister could not do.'[1] In particular he told Reith that he did not want him to broadcast more than any other Minister.[2]

Reith's pages on his work as Minister make gloomy reading even in the general atmosphere of gloom which pervades *Into the Wind*. He had no shortage of ideas about what to do and, of course, no lack of energy or drive to do them, but he was doomed to labour in vain and ultimately to be dismissed from his place with the minimum of respect or even courtesy. His first meetings with Ogilvie were bound to be somewhat difficult. The ex-Director-General of the BBC who had made the BBC what it was—with 'intimate knowledge' of the BBC, which he had been told by the Prime Minister to use 'gently'— confronted a Director-General who was feeling all the strains of 'turning a far from happy BBC into something that it had never been, a new armament of war'.[3]

'Reith came to see me yesterday,' wrote Ogilvie on 23 February, 'the first time he had been in Broadcasting House since he left in 1938. I gave him a copy of the *BBC Handbook 1940* inscribed with greetings and best wishes from the old Firm.' Four points were discussed—'a daily series of talks of a "heartening kind", hitting at Haw-Haw, telling cheering stories of bravery in the Fighting Services or at home etc.';[4] the return of Campbell Stuart's 'Enemy Propaganda Unit' to the Ministry of Information;[5] an intensification of broadcasting to Germany, making it a whole-day operation and going

---

[1] J. C. W. Reith, *Into the Wind* (1949), p. 352.

[2] Letter from Lord Reith to the author, 23 Feb. 1965.

[3] *Ogilvie to Lee, 25 March 1940.

[4] *This was 'an urgent and personal request of Reith'. Ogilvie wrote guardedly, 'I said that I would have it considered here and taken up with the Ministry. I naturally did not commit myself to any undertaking.'

[5] See above, pp. 86–7. According to Ogilvie, Reith said that the 'return' of the unit was imminent and that Halifax had agreed. Yet this never happened and was not likely to happen. For a meeting between Campbell Stuart and Reith, see *Into the Wind*, pp. 352–4. There are minutes of a meeting at the Ministry of Information at which Reith, Lee, Monckton, Campbell Stuart and Ogilvie were present on 25 January 1940. 'The Minister asked the nature and degree of control Campbell Stuart had over the BBC in regard to enemy broadcasts and whether his control of enemy broadcasts was closer than the Ministry of Information's control of neutral broadcasts. It was explained that this was probably the case, owing to the fact that Campbell Stuart had been working with the BBC intimately for a longer period than the Ministry of Information.'

far beyond the broadcasting of news items and *Sonderberichte* to include 'concerts and entertainments etc. after the manner of Fécamp or Luxembourg';[1] and the constitutional relationships between BBC and Government in war time.

Ogilvie, who knew little of how Reith's mind worked, was surprised by the darting references to Fécamp and Luxembourg and even more by the general turn which the discussion took when Reith turned to the constitution of the BBC. Reith stuck to the views about the war-time constitution which he had urged in 1937 and 1938 before the structural changes after his resignation.[2] Things would have been easier if the BBC had been 'taken over', by which he obviously meant—Ogilvie had no insight into this—if the right kind of Director-General had been in a position of control with a direct line to Government. Ogilvie replied soberly that he was not interested in whether 'things were easy or difficult for the BBC and that it was a small price to pay for independence to have the occasional nuisance of carrying a Government baby' or to have to accept 'the racketeering between the Admiralty and the Foreign Office over the news of naval sinkings which he had quoted'. 'The fundamental point, in my view,' he went on, 'was that the constitutional independence of the BBC was of supreme importance, not only for the BBC as a body presumably continuing into peace time, but much more now for the Government and for the country at large. Democracy was one of the issues at stake in this war.' There was need for the BBC 'to diffuse with reasonable freedom views which did not conflict with the national interest, but were very far from being those of the Government itself', which, after all, 'was not an all-party Government'.

Reith continued to press and to probe Ogilvie. Surely the Overseas Services of the BBC should be thought of as 'a government institution'. Could they not perhaps best be handled directly by the Ministry of Information? Ogilvie replied that a diarchy in broadcasting would be damaging and would carry with it no compensating advantages in the national interest.

---

[1] 'I said,' Ogilvie replied, 'that the allocation of time in the foreign language services was fundamentally a matter for Government, and that of course our present schedules were based throughout upon specific Government advice.'

[2] See above, pp. 83-5.

There the remarkable interview ended. On leaving, Reith said that 'he had only been exploring the position in a personal, not an official, way'.[1] Yet the pressing and the probing continued. In a telephone conversation several days later Reith asked for Ogilvie's views on some 'concrete form of propaganda . . . some positive activity to which people might be urged', and Ogilvie replied that he doubted whether Home Front morale was bad. 'There might be an absence of cheerfulness, but there was plenty of determination.'[2] In exchange, Reith asked for Ogilvie's advice as to the line he should take if he were to make a broadcast, and Ogilvie told him, above all, to be 'genuine'. He added, perhaps by way of tit-for-tat, that the Minister should 'use the occasion to recover some of the goodwill which the Ministry of Information had lost at the start'.[3]

According to Reith, Ogilvie went on to consult his Chairman, Powell, who in turn consulted Sir Horace Wilson, and was given an assurance that the BBC would not be taken over by the Ministry of Information. When Reith was told this by Wilson on 1 April, he was concerned that the most important of all decisions relating to the BBC, that which he had been asked by Chamberlain to consider for himself, had been taken behind his back. This view was subsequently confirmed when he saw Chamberlain on 10 April and Chamberlain 'referred to the BBC as if there had never been any question of action to be settled'.[4] In fact, Reith was never called upon as Minister to reply to any debate in Parliament about the BBC.

One important administrative change inside the Ministry was made by Reith which strengthened the BBC's position. At his first meeting with Ogilvie and Powell, Reith had asked for a senior official of the BBC to be seconded to the Ministry.[5] Accordingly, Wellington was transferred to the Ministry in March 1940 as Director of Broadcasting Relations, a post of greater scope than that previously occupied by H. G. G. Welch

[1] *Note by Ogilvie on a meeting with Reith, 23 Feb. 1940; for Reith's account of the meeting, see *Into the Wind*, pp. 370–1.
[2] *Note by Ogilvie on a telephone conversation with Reith, 11 March 1940.
[3] *Ibid.
[4] *Into the Wind*, p. 370.
[5] Letter from Lord Reith to the author, 23 Feb. 1965.

or Lee.[1] Wellington was called upon to co-ordinate broadcasting problems, 'advising and organising in conjunction with the BBC and any other bodies concerned with broadcasting the dissemination through broadcast news of Government propaganda in all except enemy countries'.[2] His appointment was very much Reith's idea, and the BBC was anxious that it should not be followed by other similar appointments. From within the BBC Nicolls accepted the fact that a 'strong unit at the Ministry is far better from our point of view than a weak one', but he objected to the secondment to the Ministry of an additional experienced person from the BBC—R. A. Rendall or Harman Grisewood. There was an interesting exchange of views when Wellington stated that he needed 'a person of creative ability' alongside him who would take the load in all discussions concerning 'the best means of giving broadcasting effect to Government decisions'.[3] Nicolls replied that it was surely for the BBC itself to say what were the best means of giving 'broadcasting effect' to government decisions. 'Generally it doesn't seem to me desirable to let the balance shift over to the Ministry to this extent.'[4]

Wellington rightly believed that from his new post he could quietly protect the independence of the BBC—he realized the importance of Reith's pre-war arguments about interlocking[5]—and during the period of more than a year in which he served in his new post, the year of the opening up of the war, he did much to smooth out the difficulties which had arisen earlier between BBC and Ministry. 'We are making every effort to get a view of broadcasting generally accepted [in the Ministry],' he had written earlier, 'which is in line with the view of its functions and potential importance held by professional broadcasters. This will imply greater readiness of those in authority

[1] See above, p. 92.
[2] *The duties, which had been explained at an informal meeting at the Ministry on 18 January, with Reith in the chair and with Campbell Stuart and Ogilvie attending, were clearly set out in a memorandum from Graves to Nicolls, 9 April 1940. Ogilvie had first put forward his name on 16 January 1940 after speaking with Lee.
[3] *Another of his duties was 'to interpret from a broadcasting point of view all policy documents dealing with propaganda generally'.
[4] *Nicolls to Graves, 10 April 1940. Wellington remained unconvinced by this argument. (Graves to Ogilvie and Nicolls, 12 April 1940.)
[5] See above, pp. 83–5.

to play their proper part in broadcasting, particularly at moments of crisis, better and more consistent guidance from this Ministry on the propaganda policy to be pursued, more help to the BBC in overcoming the difficulties it meets in interpreting this policy.'[1]

While high-level exchange of views continued and Wellington found his bearings in his new post—no other BBC official was sent to join him—the pattern of war-time home broadcasting was being established. The Forces Programme was integrated into the new system, and the different Regions tried as best they could to reassert their claims to a share of Home Service time. The 'national needs' of Scotland, for example, were being pressed by Dinwiddie, the BBC's Regional Director in Glasgow, who complained that even after more Scottish programmes had been inserted into the single programme, the items constituted 'only a fraction of what is available in peace-time'.[2] *Lift Up Your Hearts* came from the Glasgow studio, but as Maurice Farquharson put it, 'the fact that English hearts had been uplifted at 7.55 a.m. for several months exclusively from Scotland, did not appear to secure the full recognition in Scottish breasts that it deserved'.[3] The magazine programme *In Britain Now* was designed to link speakers from all parts of the British Isles; *Family Album* described generations of Northern families drawn from life; and Ralph Wightman vividly portrayed market day in a town in the West Country.

For the most part, however, broadcasting was national, whether it came from London, Bristol, Manchester or Hogsnorton. While the producers in their scattered departments were looking for new material, Nicolls and Maconachie in Broadcasting House were determined that no one inside or outside the Ministry should go too far in turning the BBC into a propaganda agency. Serious discussions continued to take place on such questions as whether to broadcast occasional greyhound racing commentaries or on such familiar peacetime themes as how much to pay for the broadcasting of the

[1] *Wellington to Graves, 21 March 1940.
[2] *Dinwiddie to Nicolls, 9 Jan. 1940. There were legitimate grievances in Scotland concerned with indifferent reception particularly of the new Forces Programme. Dinwiddie also admitted to Tallents (letter of 17 Feb.) that 'the political situation in Scotland demands special treatment'.
[3] *Memorandum on a visit to Scotland by Ogilvie and Powell, 20 July 1940.

Grand National;[1] and there were further 'drastic warnings' to the staff of the Variety Department on the need to eliminate 'vulgarity' under 'threats of suspension'.[2]

Education was also a regular preoccupation, not least of Ogilvie,[3] while Maconachie, in particular, abandoned none of his reservations about propaganda, home or foreign. He had served on the Indian frontier before joining the BBC and he was convinced that if propaganda could be 'smelt' it lost its effect. 'Propaganda always involves great danger,' he wrote in December 1939, when schemes to answer Haw-Haw were being propounded, and he was 'rather afraid of a campaign based on short-term considerations'.[4] In a note to Nicolls two months later, he pleaded for a limitation of broadcast propaganda 'so as to avoid surfeiting the audience'. He had had his opinion confirmed when he overheard a passenger in a train say, 'Don't know what to believe these days. There's "Aw-Aw" and I reckon our wireless does propaganda too. There's not much difference between them. Everybody does it when they're at war.' According to Maconachie, Englishmen had a 'natural aversion to propaganda', and it was unfortunate, to say the least, that the BBC was obliged 'to broadcast material of a kind that is naturally disliked by the listener'. People tuned with relief to 'subjects not connected with the war', and these offered the best antidote to boredom.[5] If there had to be propaganda, it should be co-ordinated in one place, a view which Nicolls shared—with the important rider that the right place was the BBC itself.[6]

Reith himself, quite apart from his views about institutional relationships and the future of the BBC, had very definite ideas on 'the propaganda policy to be pursued', which he set

[1] *Home Service Board, _Minutes_, 12 Jan. 1940: '1939 fee of £350, no more to be offered for the Grand National race at Aintree.' 'Occasional greyhound racing commentaries ... but the detailed racing results still to be excluded from the News.'

[2] *Home Board, _Minutes_, 23 Feb. 1940.

[3] *Ibid., 29 March 1940. 'D.G. asked for advance consideration of the possibility of devoting more space, especially after the wavelength changes in the autumn, to educational matter, including serious music and literature in the Home Programme.'

[4] *Statement by Maconachie at a meeting of the Home Publicity Division of the Ministry of Information, 19 Dec. 1939.

[5] *Memorandum by Maconachie, 5 Feb. 1940.

[6] *Nicolls to Graves, 13 Feb. 1940.

out in March 1940 in a Cabinet paper, the first which he was asked to produce, called 'Notes on the Principles and Aims of British War-time Propaganda'.[1] The views of men like Macon-achie and many people inside the Ministry itself were pushed into the background. The real propaganda theme, as Reith saw it, was 'this is your war, the nation's war', a war which demanded a call to arms, a call to effort, and a call to sacrifice. The war had only just begun. Apathy was the great danger, for the war was a war of wills as well as of guns. 'In freedom, you must be as quick to discipline and self-surrender as men in the bonds of dictatorship.' Defeat would mean 'the end of life as we under-stand it in Western Europe' and 'a permanently disabled Britain'. Victory would mean 'a new world'—and here con-troversies would be bound to start if they had not started before—'Christian and not satanic, spiritual and not material'. 'You are fighting for justice and decency between man and man, nation and nation.'

The War Cabinet approved the Notes in place of a much more abstruse document before them[2]—Hoare said it was 'just what they should have been working to all along'[3]—but ironically it was not until Churchill became Prime Minister and Reith faded into the background that this approach to the public was followed. Reith himself, inexperienced in Govern-ment and for that matter in party politics, was unwilling to play politics on this question and refused to take the advice of Leo Amery, Beaverbrook and others that he should put in an 'ultimatum of requirements' which would enable the Ministry to fulfil the role which he believed was necessary.[4] Although he succeeded in smoothing over relations between the Ministry of Information and the official Opposition[5] at the same time as he was tightening up the internal organization of his Ministry, he was aloof from the group of politicians who were beginning to wage 'a war to begin war'.[6]

---

[1] The document is printed in full in *Into the Wind*, pp. 358–60.

[2] *Hood to Ogilvie, 7 March 1940.

[3] *Into the Wind*, p. 361.

[4] Ibid., p. 360. He was given good political advice by Stanley Baldwin in a remarkable letter of 31 January reprinted ibid., pp. 363–4.

[5] Ibid., pp. 365–6.

[6] L. S. Amery, *My Political Life*, vol. 3 (1955). Beaverbrook told Reith that he and Churchill were 'in the Government against the will of the Prime Minister: the country had demanded it'. (*Into the Wind*, p. 360).

In the meantime, therefore, while the war continued to
simmer gently, the Press was right in stating that Reith was
trying hard to be Minister of Information but *was not allowed
to be*.[1] As for Churchill, the BBC—like Chamberlain—
remained almost as suspicious of him as it had been before the
war. When he 'asked to speak' on 13 or 14 January, Nicolls
referred the matter to the Lord Privy Seal, indicating that
20 January was the 'first available date',[2] and it was not until
the Lord Privy Seal had failed to reply that the BBC itself
decided 'not to insist on the 20 January date at the cost of
engendering ill will'.[3] In the event, the 20th date stood.[4]

For all Reith's pleading, propaganda to enemy and occupied
countries, with widespread Intelligence implications—and at
this stage propaganda to Russia also—continued to remain the
province of Sir Campbell Stuart and Electra House.[5] Only
propaganda to neutral countries was the direct concern of the
Ministry. There were already, therefore, during the spring of
1940 many signs of the inter-departmental tension, conflict
and, equally serious, overlapping, which all writers on war-time
propaganda, with or without actual experience of it, whatever
their angle of approach, have been forced to stress. Part of the
the trouble lay in the Foreign Office, where there was reluctance
to delegate propaganda functions to any other agency. Part
of the trouble lay also, however, in a developing Intelligence
network, which was itself a sphere of rivalry and contention.
Compromises were almost impossible to achieve, and when
they were achieved it was almost impossible to work them out.
Reith was in deep waters, perhaps deeper than he knew, when
he was discussing with Halifax and Butler the possibility of an
intricate interlocking directorate, with Sir Walter Monckton
holding the double office of Deputy Under-Secretary in the
Foreign Office and Deputy Director-General of the Ministry
of Information, and with Stuart's work being transferred to the
Ministry.[6] Such a directorate would have challenged too

[1] Ibid., p. 360.
[2] *Home Service Board, *Minutes,* 29 Dec. 1939.
[3] *Ibid., 5 Jan. 1940.
[4] *Ibid., 19 Jan. 1940.
[5] For Reith's side of the story, see *Into the Wind,* pp. 361 ff.
[6] Ibid., pp. 362, 378. When Monckton was given both posts, Stuart retained
his separate domain.

many vested interests. Reith's reaction to the muddle was characteristic. 'What would Dr. Goebbels have thought of it all? I had been hailed as his opposite number, counterpart, arch-enemy. How he would have laughed—if he could have believed a tenth of what was happening here; at any rate it would have been a nice bed-time story for him, in almost daily instalments.'[1]

The BBC had been drawn into this maelstrom in five ways—first, through its role as a purveyor of propaganda, part of a cluster of media, with special relationships with France, the great ally, and the United States, the great neutral; second and more directly, through its foreign language broadcasting to enemy and occupied countries, Sir Campbell Stuart's domain; third, through the activities of a parallel body, the Joint Broadcasting Committee, which had been set up in 1939;[2] fourth, through the developing monitoring service; and fifth, and in some ways most seriously, through its task of supplying news not only to Britain but to the outside world.

The initial outlines of British war-time propaganda policy had been covered in the first speech delivered by Lord Macmillan as Minister of Information to the Advisory Council of the Ministry on 9 September 1939, when he declared that his 'canons for its guidance' included 'in dealing with Germany make clear that hostility is not to a people but to its rulers and their policy'; 'in dealing with the USA remember that their constitution is very different from ours; avoid pressing them or telling them what their duty is'; 'respect susceptibilities of certain countries and show particular caution in publicity directed to Italy, Japan and Russia'; 'give due prominence to achievements of our Allies, not suggest that we are doing everything'; 'this war is a crusade', 'belief in principles at stake' and we have 'no selfish aims for ourselves'.[3]

The BBC had operated within this framework throughout the winter and spring of 1939/40, although there were important changes of direction which were only slowly clarified. German policy—the subject of liaison between the BBC and

---

[1] *Into the Wind*, p. 367.
[2] See below, pp. 185-7.
[3] *Note by Ogilvie, who had attended the meeting, 7 Sept. 1939.

Electra House, not the Ministry, at meetings of a joint planning committee[1]—had first been discussed at the time of Munich, when it seemed axiomatic that there was a distinction between 'good' and 'bad' Germans. One 1939 *Sonderbericht* by Valentine Williams had made the most of 'good' Germans within the Army who were being purged by Nazi politicians. By April 1940, however, the axiom had been 'reviewed' and Nicolls was asking the authorities for a 'renewed ruling on the subject of drawing a distinction between the Nazi Government and the German people'. 'A tendency has recently been evident,' he wrote, 'for the distinction which the Prime Minister drew at the beginning of the war to become blurred, largely owing to the pressure of the French doctrine that they are all tarred with the same brush.'[2] Maconachie had been reluctant to include in the BBC programme a number of French scripts called *Verités sur l'Allemagne*, which followed the line that Nazism was merely 'the natural outcome of German character-istics', and argued forcefully that it was a matter of 'common-sense' that 'Hitlerism' and not 'the German people' should be deemed to be the enemy, particularly since Goebbels in his own interest wanted the British to assert that there was no such distinction. French distaste for 'soft stuff' and demand for a hard line only revealed their 'psychological error' and could generate 'a feeling of pessimism, if not defeatism'.[3] 'To make no distinction between the Nazi ruling clique and the German people may perhaps harden people in Germany still further,' the BBC Overseas Intelligence Department claimed in April, 'and help the Nazis to achieve the greater national solidarity towards which they constantly strive.'[4]

[1] The Liaison Officers were not expected to initiate action but to convey political guidance in the form of requests and to offer ideas about broadcasts in the form of suggestions. The BBC was responsible for the final arrangement of programmes and actual microphone practice. At first the Planning Committee met daily, then twice a week. There were also Electra House directives.

[2] *Nicolls to Wellington, 9 April 1940.

[3] *Maconachie to Nicolls, 5 April, 16 April 1940.

[4] *BBC Overseas Intelligence Department, *Monthly Intelligence Reports, Europe*, 15 April 1940. In BBC Monitoring Service, *Daily Digest of Foreign Broadcasts*, 20 April 1940, there is a quotation from a broadcast by Fritzsche: 'English war-mongers have dropped the cloak of ethics. . . . We like it much better when the English warmonger speaks about the ugly figures of the German past than when prop-agandists in London and Paris maintain that they now have to preserve the dignity of Schiller or Goethe because they have no longer a home in present-day Germany.'

By then, however, what Nicolls and Maconachie called 'French doctrine' had won support inside the British Cabinet and in the British Press and any possibilities of encouraging a German 'opposition' were being evaded. Before long, indeed, 'French doctrine' was to be crystallized into a distinctive British doctrine, 'Vansittartism'.[1] Wellington replied to Nicolls, therefore, that it was no longer possible to maintain any useful distinction between party and people, although if a revolutionary situation were to emerge in Germany at some future date, the distinction might have to be re-drawn.[2] From May onwards the term 'Nazi' was excluded from BBC news bulletins in German except when in the context of a quotation, and was used only sparingly elsewhere.[3] It is important to note that this change preceded the fall of the Chamberlain Government.

On two other related matters—a clear statement of war aims and the canvassing of a constructive social policy which would undermine much German propaganda to Britain—there was a further difference of opinion between Maconachie —and on these matters Reith was in agreement with him[4]— and the Government. The Government allowed nothing to be said about war aims which went further than the very general statement that after an Allied victory an unjust peace settlement would not be imposed upon the German people.[5] And as far as a constructive social policy was concerned, a matter for the Government itself, nothing of any value could be broadcast. The so-called 1940 mood was expressed in Government circles only after Chamberlain had fallen and the country had undergone the trial of Dunkirk.[6]

The implications of the review of British propaganda policy involved above all else broadcasts to Germany, yet in 1939 and

[1] See below, pp. 382–3.

[2] *Wellington to Nicolls, 17 April 1940.

[3] *Overseas Board, *Minutes*, 2 May, 9 May 1940.

[4] For Reith's view, see *Into the Wind*, p. 368. 'I had tried, without success and not for the last time to get something out of the Cabinet about post-war policy. It was needed for both this country and neutrals.' The first requirement for broadcasting was 'to state as positively as possible, and as often as possible, without prejudicing the effect, the aims and intentions of British policy'.

[5] *Wellington to Nicolls, 17 April 1940.

[6] The Labour Party's National Executive had put out a programme of war aims—itself general—in February 1940, and prayers were being said in churches in April 1940 'that from national penitence may spring a new zeal for social justice'. (Turner, op. cit., p. 185.)

early 1940 the BBC had been drawn also, through the prompt-ings of propaganda policy, into discussions with and about France and about the United States. There were BBC objections, indeed, when in September 1939 the British Embassy in Paris had discussed the appointment of broadcasting representatives from Britain directly with the Ministry of Information without consulting the BBC.[1] In November 1939, after preliminary contacts and meetings, some of them arranged by Campbell Stuart, Ryan had visited Paris for useful and friendly talks with the broadcasting authorities at a time when French broad-casting, which before the war had been 'something of a Cinderella in French political and social life',[2] was itself under review. Both policy and organization were being questioned when war broke out. The French instinct had been to close down foreign broadcasting and to use their stations to 'jam the enemy', a policy which both the BBC and the British Government refused to follow, and although the instinct had been suppressed and there had subsequently been regular transmission of official news bulletins in foreign languages, centralized from Paris under tight governmental control,[3] there were still many French broadcasters—and even more French soldiers—who favoured more jamming and fewer programmes. Friends of the Prime Minister, Daladier, were in the key positions in the broadcasting set-up, but there was also direct military influence through General Jullien, who was in close touch with General Gamelin. Some of the soldiers, indeed, had hoped just before the war began that they would be able to assert 'dictatorship in broadcasting', although they remained only 'one powerful element', with great potentialities for in-creasing their authority.

[1] *Overseas Broadcasting Committee, *Minutes*, 20 Sept. 1939. Graves and Ryan met Ivison Macadam of the Ministry of Information to discuss the role of the Ministry in this in November 1939 (Note by Graves, 1 Dec. 1939).

[2] *'The Government stations under the PTT,' Ryan added, 'did little com-parable to what has been done in England during the last ten or fifteen years towards working out a policy for radio as a national service.' (Report on 'Anglo-French Broadcasting Liaison' by A. P. Ryan and Squadron-Leader W. Proctor Wilson, 18 Dec. 1939.)

[3] *They were broadcasting in English, German, Polish, Czech, Slovak, Italian, Spanish, Dutch, Hungarian, Serbo-Croat, Roumanian, Bulgarian, Greek, Arabic, Turkish and Swedish. 'Russian has been considered and rejected for the same reasons as guided us in England.'

Jamming of Stuttgart, Cologne and Bremen continued, although the French were left in no doubt that the wisdom of this policy was challenged by the British, as was also the French refusal to synchronize the wavelengths of their stations in order to deny possible assistance to enemy aircraft.[1] (This matter had been discussed with the French as early as 1936.) Ashbridge and Hayes, from the engineering side of the BBC, visited France at the same time as Ryan and showed themselves just as interested as he was in the 'important clashes between French and British propaganda policies' and in the need for 'great efforts . . . to bring the propaganda of the two countries into line as in jamming or synchronization, on which their own views were clear and forthright'.[2]

Closer programme contacts with France began after a visit from Cecilia Reeves in January 1940,[3] but political issues remained a matter for discussion with Ministries and embassies. When Ogilvie himself visited Paris a month later, he had to pay a large number of business calls, without achieving any positive results: 'there was a sort of feeling that we are very sticky,' he added.[4] 'Broadcasting looms large in the discussions on propaganda which are held daily by British officials in Paris, both among themselves and with their French opposite numbers,' it was noted by Squadron-Leader Wilson, who had been in Paris since the early days of the war, 'but not all this activity is at the moment productive.' By then there were

[1] *There was partial synchronization in Northern France, with Fécamp upsetting the plan until it was closed down and with the question of extending synchronization to other parts of France not settled. (Report by A. P. Ryan and Squadron-Leader W. Proctor Wilson, 18 Dec. 1939.) See also above, p. 127.

[2] *Overseas Services Board, *Minutes*, 14 Dec. 1939.

[3] *Ibid., 11 Jan. 1940. A note was prepared on the subject, 16 Jan. 1940, listing 10 outgoing BBC programmes which had been relayed in France between 4 September and 14 January, 19 incoming programmes (they included Gracie Fields and Will Fyffe), 3 'cordial' exchange programmes (of which only one was Anglo-French, a concert of the Band of the Royal Air Force and the Garde Republicaine on 11 November), and 2 special programmes. In general, there was very little in the list of programmes to suggest real programme exchanges. It was out of these contacts that the batch of French scripts, including *Verités sur l'Allemagne*, arrived in London.

[4] *Note by Ogilvie, 7 Feb. 1940. At an informal meeting at the Ministry on 8 February it was agreed that co-ordination with the French was urgently needed so that both broadcasting systems could work in 'complete harmony'. Monckton also visited France in February and pressed for closer links with the French Ministry of Information.

fortnightly exchange programmes, *Vive la France*, and weekly talks by Robert St.-Jean. The French indicated also that they were prepared to reach an agreed policy on jamming, but at the same time began developing fifty small stations scattered through France for future jamming.[1] Full agreement about all these related matters had not been reached when the war in the West opened up in May.[2]

In the meantime, the BBC had shown that it was just as sensitive to links with the United States as it was to those with France, and although the flow of programme material from the United States had been suspended immediately after war broke out—with the exception of a reduced quota of talks by Raymond Gram Swing—facilities were given to American correspondents to broadcast direct from London to their own networks with the help of the BBC. From the United States, Felix Greene, the BBC's North American representative, wrote to London in October that 'it is of the greatest importance that the British people be not misled by false hopes and that they be accurately and frankly informed week by week as to the course of American opinion'.[3] While the amount of work in his office had been cut to such an extent that he was 'irked by idleness', nonetheless 'if the war drags on and American public opinion undergoes a change, it is not inconceivable that this country will enter the war [and] . . . for the BBC to find itself at that time without an office in America might be an aggravating embarrassment'.

Two months later on the eve of his recall, after the BBC had extended its American publicity rather than contracted it, Greene urged that if his successor were to be effective he should not be 'inflicted by the British upper-class manner which is taken here (quite often mistakenly) as insufferable arrogance'.[4] In fact, this danger was avoided when Gerald Cock, a highly energetic and imaginative BBC official, who had been Head of Television at the outbreak of war, replaced Greene in March 1940. Already R. H. Eckersley in London had set

[1] *'France and the BBC', report by Wilson and Ryan, 18 Dec. 1939; 'BBC Representation in Paris', 12 March 1940.
[2] See below, pp. 200 ff.
[3] *Greene to Graves, 16 Oct. 1939.
[4] *Greene to Graves, 18 Dec. 1939.

about arranging visits by American reporters to such different places as Coastal Command and a Conscientious Objectors' Tribunal and organizing interviews between representatives of the American broadcasting companies and persons actively engaged in the war, like the commander of the Polish submarine *Orzel* and two American survivors of the *Athenia*.[1] 'What about exploring the possibilities of providing similar facilities for neutrals?' asked Ogilvie.[2] London was said to be the 'easiest place' for an American reporter during the spring of 1940.[3] The first time that the Ministry of Information itself took a direct interest in BBC links with the USA—through its American Division headed by Sir Frederick Whyte—was in February 1940 when there was pressure for programmes designed with the American audience in mind 'during those hours when Americans might eavesdrop on the Canadian transmission'.[4] There was no service planned specially for the United States, however, until May 1940.[5]

Foreign language broadcasting, the third field in which the BBC was drawn into association with the Government, did not develop as rapidly during the first months of the war as the most active supporters of a vigorous British propaganda policy—including such people inside the BBC itself—wished, although there was much excitement at the time of the introduction of each new service.[6] One of the reasons for the relatively slow progress was a shortage of transmitters,[7] and Ashbridge, in particular, felt strongly that more aggressive action should be taken to 'increase our technical facilities for

[1] *Memorandum by R. H. Eckersley for Nicolls, 'Facilities for the American Broadcasting Companies', 25 Jan. 1940.

[2] *Ogilvie to Graves and Nicolls, 26 Jan. 1940. The American companies asked the BBC not to quote any of their commentators in BBC broadcasts to Germany. (Overseas Board, *Minutes*, 18 Jan. 1940.)

[3] For the account of an American reporter, see E. Sevareid, *Not So Wild a Dream* (1946).

[4] *Overseas Board, *Minutes*, 8 Feb. 1940.

[5] See below, pp. 403–4.

[6] A Foreign Language Committee, on which the Foreign Office was represented, met on several occasions in July and August 1939. Lord Perth asked the BBC to start Roumanian and Hungarian news bulletins in August 1939, at a time when British representatives in Warsaw and Belgrade were being asked whether bulletins in Polish and Serbo-Croat would be welcome. Spanish and Portuguese programmes, not for Latin America but for Spain and Portugal, had been inaugurated with the support of the embassies of the two countries in June 1939.

[7] See above, pp. 63–5.

transmitting propaganda'.[1] A second reason was a shortage of money, for each new language service introduced involved discussion about a supplementary budget. A third reason was the shortage of qualified people, particularly of English switch censors who could understand foreign languages and of English sub-editors. One man, for example, Michael Winch, was in charge of both the Polish and Czech news bulletins which began to be broadcast in September 1939. The Bulgarian Service, which the Ministry was most anxious to start, was extremely difficult to staff, even though 'more Bulgarians than had been anticipated had been found in England'; and the start of a Swedish Service, equally strongly pressed for, was held back by the lack of an organizer of 'suitable calibre'. There were also problems of priority. In December 1939 Ashbridge said that the BBC had to decide 'whether a complete medium-wave service day and night to the troops, or a good foreign language service' had the prior claim, and in January 1940, after it had been decided to go ahead with the Forces Programme, it proved necessary to draw up an 'order of urgency' list for foreign language broadcasting with Swedish first, Bulgarian second, and an increased number of German bulletins third.[2]

Thus, while the range of countries covered broadened substantially during 1939—six languages had been in use in January: fourteen were in use in December—the embryonic consolidated European Service, started in August 1939,[3] did not as yet command either the resources or the official backing to figure as prominently in the 'radio war' as the German RRG which had long been conceived of as 'the most ideal instrument of propaganda',[4] an instrument, above all, of attack. The BBC Overseas Service had grown out of its narrower Empire Service,[5] and since special obligations to the Empire continued to be recognized throughout the war, it had been felt necessary

---

[1] *Ashbridge wrote an important memorandum on the subject on 16 December 1939.

[2] *Overseas Broadcasting Committee, *Minutes*, 20 Sept. 1939; Overseas Services Committee, *Minutes*, 7 Nov., 1 Dec. 1939, 12 Jan. 1940; Overseas Services Board, *Minutes*, 21, 28 Dec. 1939.

[3] See Briggs, *The Golden Age of Wireless*, pp. 645–59, for pre-war developments.

[4] E. Hadamowsky, a high official of the German Propaganda Ministry, quoted in C. J. Rolo, *Radio Goes to War* (1943), p. 19. See also above, pp. 64–5.

[5] See Briggs, op. cit., pp. 369–410, 645–50.

to state in November 1939 that while the title 'Overseas Service' should always be used in place of the 'Empire Service', the merging of the Empire and Overseas Services should be made clear wherever possible.[1] The objective of a comprehensive Overseas Service, split into five or six units, was accepted in December 1939, although it could not be achieved at once because of shortage of wavelengths, staff accommodation and lines.[2]

That there was a demand for British news and for programmes not only in Canada or Australia but in Europe and overseas was never, of course, in doubt. A survey of Czech listening habits on the eve of the war[3] had revealed that among the 800,000 people with wireless sets in Bohemia and Moravia there was regular listening to BBC news in English and German, and a further survey showed that even in France BBC news in French, started at the time of Munich, along with German and Italian, had acquired a very large audience, particularly among the middle and professional classes.[4] The Polish Service, inaugurated by Count Raczynski, the Polish Ambassador, on 7 September, quickly made its mark with an 'agony column', giving details of the whereabouts of Polish refugees, but there were far fewer holders of wireless sets in Poland than in Czechoslovakia or France, and the Germans, who quite deliberately did not broadcast in Polish, made an effort to confiscate all Polish sets by February 1940. Those Poles who risked their lives and did listen wanted 'accurate news about actual events rather than to keep *au fait* with all political movements'.[5]

From Czechoslovakia, following the inauguration of Czech broadcasts by Jan Masaryk one day after the start of the BBC's Polish broadcasts, there were demands not only for news but for patriotic songs and material drawn from Czechoslovak history. 'Only those who know the people well,' wrote one correspondent, 'and who have experienced the pleasure they receive from hearing anything that is dear to their hearts being

[1] *Overseas Services Board, *Minutes*, 2 Nov. 1939.

[2] *Ibid., 21 Dec. 1939.

[3] *Memorandum, 'Foreign listening in Czechoslovakia', 25 Aug. 1939.

[4] *BBC Overseas Intelligence Department, *Monthly Intelligence Report, Europe*, 8 July 1940, p. 3.

[5] *Ibid.

broadcasted from London or Paris, will fully understand the value of this suggestion.'[1] Messages also came from countries to which the BBC did not broadcast. In January 1940, for example, twenty-one letters arrived from Holland asking for BBC news broadcasts in Dutch. Perhaps the 'star' broadcaster of this early *sitzkrieg* period was Masaryk, whose first broadcast began with the words 'The hour of retribution is here'. Masaryk was known in Czechoslovakia by his pet name of Honza, a character in a Czech fairy story often acted as a play called *The Tale of Honza*, and posters appeared in Prague windows with the notice 'Hear The Tale of Honza tonight at 9.30'. Weeks passed before the Germans realized what was meant.[2]

While audiences were being built up in particular countries, there was much 'cross-listening', a phenomenon which was to persist throughout the war. People listened not only to what was 'projected' deliberately at them, but also 'to what was projected at somebody else, and above all to what was projected for home consumption'. 'For instance, if an American journalist [and more than journalists were involved] wanted to get at the temper of Great Britain, he would pay little attention to what was being said to America, but very precise attention to what was being broadcast from Britain to Europe and to people at home.'[3]

Consistency, therefore, was as necessary in foreign broadcasting as objectivity, and although there were British critics of British policies who wanted British propaganda to carry with it the same kind of 'planned coherence' as German propaganda and to express the same preference for dramatic effect over consistency,[4] the 'official' line was rather to tell the same truth to everyone and to address even 'individual Germans' 'as an Englishman or Frenchman would speak to them if they could meet in a neutral café'. There was no room, it was

---

[1] *Ibid., 19 Feb. 1940.

[2] R. H. Bruce Lockhart, *Jan Masaryk* (1951), p. 32.

[3] *Statement by Ogilvie at a meeting of the Ministry of Information Advisory Council, 24 Oct. 1939. See also below, pp. 489–90.

[4] *Overseas Services Committee, *Minutes*, 12 Oct. 1939; see also Rolo, op. cit., p. 20. 'No propaganda without its *Dramaturgie*' had been a maxim of Dr. Raskin, an influential German broadcasting director. (*Handbuch des Deutschen Rundfunks* (1939/40).)

said, for 'ranting' in such an approach, while there was ample scope for 'virility, vigour and emotion'.[1] Difficulties persisted, for example in finding out the exact truth about the effect of RAF raids on Germany,[2] and the BBC's German Service was absolved from broadcasting Air Ministry bulletins in full; but in general the BBC built up its European audience and reputation on the candid presentation of the same basic news to all countries.

Its work was already under the direction of one of the most industrious, lively and imaginative of all its war-time recruits, Noel Newsome, European News Editor, who had joined the BBC from the *Daily Telegraph* just after the beginning of the war. Newsome was the central figure in the organization even before the great expansion of services which followed the fall of France.[3] While he and his colleagues were handicapped by the same difficulties in collecting and releasing news as bedevilled the Home Service,[4] it was significant that there were few complaints about the accuracy of overseas BBC News. Indeed, when Reith was appointed Minister of Information, the French Press chose the occasion to compare favourably British and French broadcasting. 'The initials BBC [quickly became] part and parcel of the daily vocabulary of French citizens.'[5]

The same recognition of the value of the BBC's European Services was, perhaps, slower to dawn in Britain itself, since they ate into the home listener's time and presented problems of priority there too,[6] yet from October 1939 onwards there was increased home publicity about the scope and value of overseas programmes and a brief statement was sent to the

---

[1] *Undated Memorandum by Ryan on 'The Principles of Propaganda as followed in Broadcasts to Germany', probably Feb. or March 1940.

[2] E. K. Bramsted, *Goebbels and National Socialist Propaganda* (1965), p. 290.

[3] See below, pp. 257–9.

[4] See below, pp. 308–9.

[5] *BBC Overseas Intelligence Department, *Monthly Intelligence Report, Europe*, 19 Feb., 21 March, 8 July 1940, quoting, *inter alia*, *Je Suis Partout* and *Paris Soir*, 26 Jan. 1940. Yet there were several surprising misconceptions about what the initials stood for. *Soleil Marseillais* called Tallents, the BBC's Controller (Public Relations), 'le directeur des Rapports Publics de la Big Broadcasts Company'.

[6] *Nicolls to Ogilvie and others, 16 Jan. 1940, when the claims of Welsh, Gaelic, German and Forces broadcasts were set side by side. 'The decision now required,' wrote Nicolls, 'is whether the Forces programme is to be sacrificed to the need for foreign propaganda on medium waves in daylight.'

Ministry of Information each day about the previous day's programmes—'news, . . . *Sonderberichte*, general talks etc.'[1] 'Many of the *Sonderberichte*,' Graves added, 'might provide excellent material for use in the Home Service.'[2]

The broadcasts in German, which had begun during the Czech crisis of September 1938, had already taken a new turn in March 1939 after the fall of Prague. News bulletins had been supplemented by the *Sonderberichte*, which, following discussions with Electra House, set out British views on international questions, and the number of straight political talks was doubled: many restraints, no longer called for, were laid aside and *Sonderberichte* writers, encouraged first by Ralph Murray and then by Leonard Miall, were able to permit themselves a far greater measure of freedom.[3] On the eve of the war a British visitor to Berlin was surprised to discover that his host's wife knew by heart the wavelengths and arrangements for BBC broadcasting to Germany and that, though they had no outside aerial, they had no difficulty in 'obtaining London after dark on their large set'.[4]

The range of BBC broadcasts in German was still narrow, however, and three new ideas were canvassed during the winter and spring of 1939/40—broadcasts appealing to special sections of the German audience, the use of a regular commentator, and religious broadcasts. Progress was slow, for different outside interests were involved. Thus, when in January 1940 there were representations from the TUC that German trade unionists in exile should broadcast to Germany, Electra House, while supporting the idea, insisted that each case should be considered on its own merits. Speakers, it insisted, should not be 'out of touch with thought in their country'.[5] The general policy of not employing German refugees to give talks or to take part in features, was to shape the pattern of broadcasting to Germany for the rest of the war.

At this time Electra House was also opposed to including insulting, brutal or facetious attacks on Hitler, and held that

---

[1] *Overseas Services Committee, *Minutes*, 19 Oct. 1939.
[2] *Ibid., 4 Jan. 1940.
[3] *Note by A. E. Barker, 21 July 1939.
[4] *H. H. Stewart to Frost, 25 Aug. 1939.
[5] *Overseas Services Committee, *Minutes*, 12 Jan. 1940.

there was plenty of evidence to suggest that the Germans were not enthusiastic about the consequences of the launching of a great offensive in the West. The less controversial idea of regular commentators, which was initiated by Electra House itself, was settled in February 1940, when Lindley Fraser, Professor of Political Economy at Aberdeen University, was appointed.[1] His regular commentaries became a feature of German broadcasting, and he himself became something of an expert on propaganda.[2] Another early speaker who was to broadcast regularly to Germany throughout the war was the Oxford don who had broadcast a number of *Sonderberichte*, including one on '*ersatz* Socialism' in October 1939. It was agreed in March 1940 that he should be used 'experimentally' as a morning speaker to German workers, provided that 'an alternative speaker of a different political colour' were also to be found.[3] Richard Crossman gave his first talk on 4 April, and Duncan Sandys, a speaker of a quite different political colour, followed on 24 April. Ogilvie was sufficiently interested in Crossman's broadcast to invite him for a talk about British programmes in German at the beginning of May 1940.[4] Before long, Crossman was to be very closely connected with the development of national propaganda on the basis of far more comprehensive Intelligence information than that available to the BBC. He remains one of the few people fully knowledgeable about both 'white' and 'black' broadcasting.

While broadcasting to Germany developed, at first with very little drama and certainly, and quite deliberately, with no attempt to discover a British counterpart to the highly successful Haw-Haw, the Germans continued, as they always had done, to treat listening to foreign radio as a crime. 'The man who consciously exposes himself [to foreign broadcasts] is dishonourable and is a fit subject for punishment . . . he cripples

---

[1] *Ibid., 8 Feb. 1940.

[2] See above, p. 21 and below, p. 278. See also his book *Propaganda* (1957). Miall successfully pressed in Feb. 1940 for Fraser to be given the opportunity to read the German press, to listen to Fritzsche, the German home broadcasting commentator, whenever possible, and to be '*au fait* with what the German listener and reader is getting at home'. (*Note to A. E. Barker, 7 Feb. 1940.)

[3] *Overseas Board, *Minutes*, 21 March 1940.

[4] *Ogilvie to Crossman, 22 April 1940.

himself spiritually and intellectually'.[1] As we have seen, a law
of September 1939 forbade all listening to foreign stations,
including neutral stations,[2] and *Deutschlandsender*, which gave a
full exposition of the law for German home listeners on 26
January 1940, emphasized first, that the ban extended to
musical items as well as news and second, that 'lack of understanding' of 'the nature of the programme' would not be
treated as an excuse when offenders were brought before the
Courts.[3] In some parts of Germany 'radio supervisors' were
appointed to spy on tenants in blocks of flats, and listeners to
foreign radio actually brought before the Courts—there were
225 convictions in March 1940—were publicized both on the
wireless and in the press. Fines were usually imposed, although in
Hamburg on 1 March 1940 two listeners were sentenced to five
years' penal servitude for listening to and discussing BBC news.[4]

That there was considerable listening to the BBC, even if
most of it was intermittent, was implied in Hitler's speeches of
30 January and 24 February in which he vigorously attacked
BBC news and British propaganda in general. The Nazis were,
however, in something of a dilemma. They encouraged every
German to buy a wireless set and on occasion issued cheap,
even free, radio sets, and although most of the sets were not
equipped for foreign listening, there was no really effective way
of preventing large numbers of Germans from listening to
Britain.

There were no similar efforts in Italy to check listening to
foreign stations before Italy finally entered the war, although
on the eve of her entry there was some jamming of BBC
bulletins. Throughout the winter and spring of 1939/40,

---

[1] See an article by Dr. Freissner in the official paper *Deutsche Justiz*, summarized
in *Frankische Kurier*, and *Neues Wiener Tageblatt*, 29 Jan. 1940. Goebbels called
listeners to foreign radio 'radio criminals' who were like soldiers who inflicted
wounds on themselves to incapacitate themselves for action (*BBC Monitoring
Service, *Weekly Analysis*, 20 Feb. 1940), and the term 'moral self-mutilation' was
in current use. Fritzsche gave less lurid reasons for banning foreign listening
(ibid., 6 Dec. 1939): 'Of course, the real reason why you are not allowed to listen
to foreign broadcasts is that we wish to spare you the tedium of listening every day
to silly English lies and ourselves the trouble of keeping up a stream of denials of
those lies from morn to eve.'

[2] Z. A. B. Zeman, *Nazi Propaganda* (1964), pp. 176–7. See above, p. 70.

[3] *BBC Overseas Intelligence Department, *Monthly Intelligence Report, Europe*,
19 Feb. 1940.

[4] Zeman, op. cit., p. 55.

therefore, there was a considerable growth in the Italian audience, with the British Embassy circulating details of programmes. The potential audience, however, was small, and there were fewer listeners in Italy as a percentage of the population than in any other Western country.[1] Colonel Stevens, a former British military attaché in Rome, began his weekly news commentaries to Italy on 22 December 1939: eventually, they were to be increased to four, and Stevens was to establish a reputation as 'the most popular figure in all Italy', 'Colonello Buonasera'.[2] In April 1940, however, at a time when the British were emphasizing that there was no fundamental clash of interests between Britain and Italy and that it was not a British war aim to smash Italian Fascism,[3] it was significant that many of the letters received from Italian listeners were hostile. 'It has not been possible for me to learn if my Government forbids listening to foreign broadcasts,' wrote one correspondent, at the start of an anti-Allied diatribe. Even the friendly listeners were friendly for what would eventually prove embarrassing reasons. 'I feel great sympathy for Great Britain and I should like you to be on the winning side in this war . . . and if Italy should go to war, I should like her to fight side by side with you to crush for ever that poisonous serpent that soils the earth! Down with Russia and her worthy friend! Hail to the Church and the King!'[4]

It must be remembered that this was, after all, the winter of the Russo-Finnish war. BBC broadcasts in Finnish began in March as part of a new 'Scandinavian hour', but Russian programmes were not started on the grounds that the demand for news from Britain was small, that the number of sets capable of receiving British broadcasts was also small, and that a large measure of control of listening was exercised in many blocks of flats.[5]

---

[1] Estimates varied from one million to two and a half million receivers, 2.4 to 6 per 100 inhabitants. Only 97,000, it was estimated, were owned by skilled urban workers, and less than 10,000 by agricultural workers.

[2] *See below, pp. 436–7.

[3] *An Italian Directive on these lines by Newsome survives. It is dated 27 April 1940.

[4] *BBC Overseas Intelligence Department, *Monthly Intelligence Report, Europe*, 15 April 1940. The BBC had used one right-wing commentator, C. M. Franzero, an Italian journalist, for a number of commentaries during this period.

[5] *Overseas Board, *Minutes*, 1 Feb. 1940.

In the whole field of overseas propaganda during this period, there was a further, if minor, complication for the BBC— the existence of a second body, the Joint Broadcasting Committee, known to those who knew anything of its existence at all as the JBC. The JBC was founded in the spring of 1939, nominally 'to promote international understanding by means of broadcasting'.[1] The Foreign Office was in the background, and Hilda Matheson, who had played an important part in the early history of the BBC,[2] was one of its chief public sponsors and later its Director. In fact, the main task of the JBC was to diffuse 'constructive' British propaganda, mainly through broadcast recordings, during a period of international tension, and Ryan provided the liaison with the BBC, some of whose officials were very doubtful about the new venture.[3] Particular thought was given by the JBC to the German situation, and it was envisaged by Miss Matheson that the JBC would have greater freedom than the BBC to develop propaganda for the German audience in the critical months of August and September.[4] Yet Ogilvie had no desire for the BBC to 'delegate its responsibility to others',[5] and Graves, for his part, stressed that listeners in Germany would not be so discriminating as to distinguish between BBC and other English efforts and that there would be times 'when joint coordination of plans will be essential'.[6]

There were meetings in July 1939 to discuss 'close liaison', yet liaison was never easy even after war broke out and after official instructions were issued that the main functions of the

[1] *Miss Matheson to the Director-General, Radiotjänst, Stockholm, 20 April 1939.

[2] See Briggs, *The Golden Age of Wireless*, pp. 124–7. See also Miss Matheson's book *Broadcasting* (1933) in the Home University Library and interesting notes written about her after her death in November 1940 in the *New Statesman*, 16 Nov. 1940 and *The Spectator*, 22 Nov. 1940 (the latter by V. Sackville-West).

[3] *J. B. Clark and R. D'A. Marriott had grave doubts from the start about its activities and felt that 'the BBC ought not to be thought party to this new propaganda activity' (Marriott to Clark, 25 April 1939). The Swedes wrote that they felt that 'we should continue to collaborate only with the BBC' (letter to Marriott of 3 May 1939).

[4] *Miss Matheson to Ogilvie, 19 July 1939. A JBC memorandum of this period (19 July 1939) stated, 'A long-term policy must be based on a conception of a new Europe, in which Germans, as well as others, can find satisfaction.'

[5] *Ogilvie to Graves, 24 July 1939.

[6] *Graves to Ryan, 14 July 1939.

JBC—an independent organization—were to prepare programmes first for clandestine distribution in enemy countries in
conjunction with Electra House and second for use in neutral and
friendly countries in conjunction with the Foreign Publicity
Division of the Ministry of Information.[1] India also came
within the terms of reference of the organization. The fact that
two BBC engineers were seconded to the JBC did not make
relations any easier, and the Ministry of Information had to
concern itself directly with the problem of 'coordination' as
early as November 1939.

There was certainly little willingness in the BBC to accept
the JBC view that the difference between the two organizations
was that the JBC was broadcasting indirectly through the
provision of recordings for use *in* foreign countries and by foreign
organizations while the BBC was broadcasting directly *to*
foreign countries.[2] The BBC wished, indeed, to build up its
own transcription service[3] and objected, moreover, to the fact
that because of limitations of finance and wavelengths it could
not itself transmit directly to audiences abroad 'feature programmes' of the type which the JBC was producing with what
seemed ample funds from Government and other sources.
Resentment grew as the JBC developed such activities as a
weekly news flash to Argentina—there was, after all, a regular
BBC Latin-American service—'actuality programmes' and
'sound pictures', one of its specialities, for Hungary, Bulgaria
and Yugoslavia, and even a weekly recorded talk in French on
facets of women's role in war time. 'I am sorry to appear
unduly persistent about the JBC problem,' wrote J. B. Clark
in January 1940, 'but there is increasing evidence to show that
their growing activities are bound to trespass on what we regard
as the BBC monopoly.'[4] 'A body which was formed in peace
time to do a small and well-defined piece of work,' Rendall
added, 'has in a very short space of time, created for itself,

[1] *A. Stewart to Graves, 9 Sept. 1939. Miss Matheson had written to Graves
about it on 12 April 1939, enlisting his name as a sponsor.

[2] The term 'broadcasting for use in foreign countries' was comprehensive. It
covered, for example, the smuggling of a Churchill speech into Italy on gramophone records as well as distribution of 'sound pictures' and 'sound magazines' for
use by foreign broadcasting companies in such diverse languages as Chinese,
Czech, Persian and Polish.

[3] See below, p. 344.

[4] *Clark to Nicolls and Graves, 30 Jan. 1940.

or solicited from Government Departments, a large volume of broadcasting work in a variety of different fields. Today that body is becoming a direct competitor with the Corporation in spite of the latter's monopoly status; moreover, it is to some extent recognized as an independent competitor by more than one Government Department. . . . Obstruction is silly, but as things stand today we are bound to feel jealous of our rights as the sole broadcasting authority.'[1] After Wellington's transfer to the Ministry of Information, some of the difficulties were smoothed over,[2] but the question of abolishing the JBC or subsuming it inside the BBC was not settled and was to arise again frequently during the months when the war sprang to life.[3]

So too were the crucial questions of monitoring with which the BBC had become concerned. The Monitoring Service had its remote origins at the time of the Italo-Abyssinian War during the winter of 1935.[4] When 'an enlarged scheme' was planned in the spring of 1939 with the support of the embryonic Ministry of Information,[5] Graves emphasized the need both for extra funds and for highly specialized staff,[6] but Waterfield

[1] *'Notes on the JBC' by R. A. Rendall, 12 Jan. 1940. See also Overseas Services Board, *Minutes*, 11 Jan. 1940: 'Decided that JBC activities should be investigated so that a definition can be drawn up as to their field of action vis à vis the BBC.'

[2] *Clark to Wellington, 10 April 1940.

[3] See below, p. 344. The issues also involved the whole war-time problem of recording. There was a serious shortage of recording equipment and of recording engineers. See below, pp. 326–7.

[4] Briggs, *The Golden Age of Wireless*, pp. 403, 652–3.

[5] *Fass to Graves, 22 March 1939, suggesting a discussion between Graves and J. B. Beresford, the Secretary of the University Grants Committee, then dealing with this range of questions, on 'the "monitoring" of foreign broadcasts'. Memorandum to Beresford, 14 April 1939: 'It seems highly desirable that there should be a separate monitoring staff composed of persons of suitable qualifications, functioning as a separate unit, independent of other broadcasting activities.'

[6] *Graves to Clark, 30 March 1939. In June 1938 selected news bulletins in English were being monitored at Tatsfield from Paris, Berlin, Rome, Prague, New York, Pittsburgh and Tokyo on a rota basis, along with Italian broadcasts in Arabic and a number of other broadcasts. 'Although the present service seems adequate from a general point of view,' it was stated then, 'a more intensive coverage might be of special advantage to Foreign Language Services News Editor and his staff. While the BBC's overseas news services are not propagandist in the tradition of the totalitarian states, the Foreign Language Service has perhaps a greater need than the Empire Service of giving straight positive and constructive antidotes both to general and particular tendencies in broadcast propaganda adverse to British imperial interests.' (Memorandum on the Monitoring of Foreign News Broadcasts, 27 June 1938.)

in the Ministry suggested that if monitoring would be of any use to the BBC itself, it should contribute to the cost.[1] The origins of the service were very humble. The BBC spent £810 on a wooden hut, six receivers and a number of aerials, hoping to recover the money from the Ministry later.[2] Waterfield, ignorant as ever of the likely needs of war-time broadcasting, duly questioned whether a twenty-four-hour service was really necessary;[3] and the BBC replied that monitoring was bound by its nature to be an expensive business.[4] R. D'A. Marriott, 'one of our ablest young men', was picked out as leader, with the expectation that he would have the same kind of liaison duties with the Ministry as Ryan had with Campbell Stuart.[5] Assisted by O. J. Whitley, Marriott organized a monitoring group which just before the outbreak of the war moved to Wood Norton,[6] and Malcolm Frost, whom Ogilvie asked to superintend operations, succeeded admirably in improvising services in London before the full implications of what was needed were generally realized inside or outside the BBC. It was Frost who first saw the need for effective analysis and speedy distribution. Work at Wood Norton very quickly expanded into a 'continuous rota of 24 hours a day, 7 days a week, with the help of recordings on wax cylinders'. Members of the staff were recruited mainly from foreigners resident in Britain, many of them men and women not only of great linguistic ability but of great intelligence, who were to be prominent in many walks of life after the end of the war. As their numbers grew, Wood Norton became a genuine international centre, almost a kind of international university.

Meanwhile, as further plans for a more comprehensive scheme were put forward by the BBC,[7] the basic principles of professional monitoring had been established within three

---

[1] *Waterfield to Graves, 25 May 1939.　　[2] *Bishop to Graves, 5 June 1939.
[3] *Note from J. B. Clark to Graves on a telephone conversation with Waterfield, 5 June 1939.　　[4] *Graves to Waterfield, 6 June 1939.
[5] *Graves to Waterfield, 7 June 1939.　　[6] *Note of 1 April 1939.
[7] *Overseas Services Committee, *Minutes*, 12 Oct. 1939. The Ministry of Information had not envisaged in September 1939 'the importance of this service not only to themselves but to other departments'. (Minutes of a meeting between Ogilvie and Waterfield, 12 Sept. 1939.) Efforts were made very early in the war to collect information about the early history of monitoring (for example, Farquharson to J. C. Thornton, 12 Feb. 1940; Note by E. Davies, 24 June 1940; Farquharson to Davies, 2 July 1940).

weeks of the outbreak of war. 'Ears became attuned to poor reception, . . . minds learned how to translate odd sounds into existing notions which fitted logically into the context. . . . While accuracy remained the permanent requirement, arrangements were made to increase speed.'[1] Steady nerves and stamina were in demand almost as much as linguistic skill and imagination. Attention was directed not only to routine monitoring but to special requests, determined by war needs, from the Foreign Office and other bodies. Thus, Russian and Finnish broadcasts were closely watched in November 1939, when particular checking was also demanded of German programmes to Czechoslovakia, South Africa, Turkey and Greece.[2] Finnish monitoring, on a large scale in February and March 1940, was drastically cut before the beginning of April.[3]

There was specialization almost from the start by function as well as by language, and important administrative changes took place in April 1940. By then, the main 'Reception Unit' had a staff of 131, of whom 62 were monitors, and a Special Listening Section had been set up 'to patrol the ether', check programme schedules and identify new stations. An Information Bureau, which became an independent unit under Major C. E. Wakeham, with a news branch under R. H. Baker, disseminated urgent and important excerpts from monitored material— and at the request of Electra House verbatim speeches by German leaders—to Government Departments in London, including the Cabinet, the Ministry of Information, the Foreign Office and the Service Ministries.[4] Material was also sent to BBC departments, some of which could use the relevant information and intelligence in framing news bulletins, talks and other programmes, and later to a short selective list of individuals.[5] In addition, an Editorial Unit, headed from April 1940 by J. Tudor Jones, produced a *Daily Digest of World Broadcasts*, a document of 100,000 to 150,000 words, and a

[1] *A. Goldberg, 'The Ears of Britain at War: Personal Impressions of the BBC Monitoring Service in War Time', Sept. 1945.

[2] *Overseas Services Committee, *Minutes*, 1 Dec. 1939.

[3] *Monitoring Service Liaison Committee, *Minutes*, 27 March 1940.

[4] *H. G. G. Welch to Frost, 20 Jan. 1940, replying to a letter from Frost to Welch, 20 Dec. 1940.

[5] *Overseas Services Committee, *Minutes*, 26 Oct. 1939; Overseas Services Board, *Minutes*, 2 Nov. 1939.

Daily Monitoring Report, a concise document of about 4,000 words. Finally, a small Research Section, set up in October 1939, produced a *Weekly Analysis* of foreign broadcasts, a series of 'intake reports', and a wide range of interesting working papers called 'Studies in Broadcast Propaganda'[1] on such diverse subjects as 'French Broadcasts from Hamburg', 'America and the War', 'Hans Fritzsche's Talks on the Deutschlandsender', and 'Regional References in English Broadcasts from Hamburg and Bremen'. It was possible from this mass of evidence to draw conclusions about the pattern of foreign broadcasting and propaganda which complemented other kinds of intelligence material gleaned from other sources. It was from monitoring sources, for instance, that the conclusion was quickly reached that the English talks from Germany were not the sole work of Haw-Haw but the 'work of a large body of experts working on specialised lines'.[2] Later in the war it was possible for Government Intelligence to prepare convincing versions of Goebbels's propaganda directions.

The work of the Monitoring Service—'ears to the sky'—was publicized at a Press Conference in November 1939. Teleprinters had not then been installed, but one hundred and fifty foreign news bulletins were already being monitored each day and 'new uses are being continually disclosed for the service and the material which it assembles'.[3] Top officers at the Ministry of Information were 'much impressed' by what they saw on a later visit to Wood Norton in April 1940.[4] Although there were many problems ahead, the BBC's Monitoring Service was one branch of the propaganda war effort where the British maintained a lead over the Germans. 'It was characteristic of the German radio,' wrote Tangye Lean later during the war, 'to prefer speaking to listening.'[5] In fact, Goebbels was very suspicious even of German government departments and ministers monitoring foreign broadcasts—he

[1] *Monitoring Service, *Monthly Progress Report*, April 1940.

[2] *Ibid., 14 Dec. 1939. The Monitoring Service had paid a tribute to the quality of German Monitoring in November 1939. 'Two hours and fifteen minutes after Mr. Churchill's speech it was caricatured on the German wireless. We admire the comprehensiveness of their monitoring service.' (*BBC Monitoring Service, *Weekly Analysis*, 21 Nov. 1939.)

[3] *Press Handout, Information from Overseas Broadcasts, 1 Nov. 1939.

[4] *Woodburn to Pym, 20 April 1940.

[5] E. Tangye Lean, *Voices in the Darkness* (1943), p. 182.

told the Minister of Science and Education that listening to foreign broadcasts was a rebellious occupation—and continued to resent the fact that the German Foreign Ministry under Ribbentrop maintained a modest monitoring service, which distributed a daily news letter.[1]

The BBC's own distribution of news brought it into the most difficult of all its intricate webs of relationships, and once again the problems were not settled by the time that the phoney war was over. When at the very first meeting of the Advisory Council of the Ministry of Information Lord Macmillan had laid down plainly that 'all British publicity should be truthful and objective' and that 'the dissemination of British news should be speedy and widespread', Philip Noel-Baker felt it necessary to add the warning that the Ministry of Information should never become a Ministry of Misinformation or Non-Information.[2] From the start, the Minister had too few powers, as Reith realized as soon as he took office. The BBC had too little scope also. Sir Edward Bridges might complain that BBC news was 'appallingly gloomy',[3] but his uneasiness about the method of reporting shipping losses could all too quickly become an argument for never reporting them at all, an argument which was used in February 1940 when attempts were made to stop the news of the sinking of the *Daring*. Nicolls had already conceded in January that distressing details were to be omitted, such as 'sunk in one minute', and had agreed that there should be a 'general mandate' to treat British sinkings with discretion.[4] It needed men of independent judgement, like Monckton, to recognize clearly that 'suppression in modern conditions fails' and that there was an international 'race for veracity'.[5] The BBC also faced recurring difficulties with the Air Ministry, the other Service department which was operationally active at this time and which was proposing in March 1940 to ban all broadcasts by serving RAF officers.[6]

[1] Zeman, op. cit., p. 177; *The Goebbels Diaries*, 24 Jan. 1942, p. 10.
[2] *Ministry of Information Advisory Council, *Minutes*, 7 Sept. 1939.
[3] *Ogilvie to Bridges, 26 Dec. 1939.
[4] *Nicolls to Ogilvie, 19 Jan. 1940. There had been a meeting in Lord Macmillan's office on 27 December 1939.
[5] *Monckton to Ogilvie, 27 Nov. 1939. The Germans made much of British delays in reporting shipping losses. (*BBC Monitoring Services, *Weekly Analysis*, 6 Dec. 1939.)   [6] *Home Service Board, *Minutes*, 29 March 1940.

Ogilvie turned to this range of problems, from which only Haw-Haw benefited, in a report for the Ministry of Information after six months of war, a counterpart to his report on the first twelve weeks of war.[1] He was anxious to identify, in the light of experience, 'such of the major reforms . . . required in the broadcasting field as depended for their successful accomplishment on full Government collaboration'. The BBC, he claimed, had set its own house in order. What was now needed was 'a real change of outlook' on the part of other people. 'The Service Departments should take most earnest account of the outstanding opportunities for victory or defeat in the world's mind which the radio commands.' Even 'honourable reluctance' to break with the tradition of Service reticence, to harass the bereaved, or to make statements on the radio before they were made first in Parliament might 'in the national interest have to yield to the paramount necessity of so declaring the British case that it may catch the ear of the world before the enemy has had time to forestall and distort it'.[2]

This report, which was approved by Ogilvie's senior colleagues,[3] began by examining the contrast between what people had thought would happen to radio before the war broke out and what had actually happened. It had been widely accepted before September 1939 that the broadcasting services of belligerents in time of war would be 'crippled in a cockpit of jamming and counter-jamming'. This had not happened. Instead, each belligerent had developed its radio services as working armaments of war. 'The BBC, with the approval of the Government, has ordered a powerful reinforcement of its transmitter resources. It has rapidly increased the number of languages which it employs, extended its machinery for ascertaining the effects of its services and developed a new organisation for following with alertness the broadcasting campaigns of other countries. It has gained much new experience

[1] See above, p. 92.

[2] *Ogilvie to Lee, 25 March 1940. Wellington backed the BBC. 'I can imagine . . . your comments on the subtle humour of being accused of broadcasting too little naval material and making misleading statements about naval matters, this from the Department which, in the eyes of the BBC, is more grudging than any other Government Department in the news it reluctantly divulges.' (Wellington to Nicolls, 27 March 1940.)

[3] *Tallents to Ogilvie, 24 March 1940, when it was stated that the Report had been approved by Tallents, Ashbridge, R. T. Clark, J. B. Clark and Maconachie.

during the last six months and will certainly gain much more as the war develops.'

What the Armed Services needed to do, the BBC argued, was not only to abandon their 'honourable reluctance' but positively to provide more broadcasts by naval, military and air experts on the lines of that given by Ernst Udet, Chief of the Technical Department of the German Air Ministry, to an American CBS audience on 8 January. According to the Head of the BBC American Liaision Unit, this broadcast had made a 'good impression' on the Americans and had encouraged them to believe that the Germans 'have more initiative in putting interesting talks about the war effort on the air than the British'. Yet when permission had been sought in London in March for Captain Woodhouse of the *Ajax* to broadcast to South America, it had been refused by the Admiralty 'in spite of repeated requests'.[1] News, too, had been withheld until after the Germans had broadcast it. There had been no prompt British report on the German raid of 16 March on Scapa Flow. The Germans had been able, therefore, to establish their own version of what had happened before any British statement was made.[2] Ed Murrow was one of the foreign correspondents who complained. 'My own attempt to see what the Germans did at Scapa Flow has also met with failure.

[1] *Eckersley to Ogilvie, 21 March 1940. Eckersley referred also to an interview between Jordan of NBC and Grand Admiral Raeder 'which had an effect on millions of listeners'. His efforts to get the British Admiralty to put on Sir Roger Keyes, 'a test case', had failed. 'We cannot afford to rest on old tradition,' wrote Eckersley, who knew what old tradition meant, 'but must play the enemy at his own game, or at any rate have a general policy.'

[2] The raid on Scapa Flow took place at 7.50 p.m. on 16 March 1940. At 3.40 a.m. on 17 March news of the raid was broadcast by Zeesen to America. The Monitoring Service collected this information. At 7.15 a.m. the Press Department of the Admiralty rang up the Home News Department and asked them to withhold the news of the raid until they could inform relatives of victims and issue their own bulletin. At 10.22 a.m. Radio Nantes quoted a German High Command Communiqué read over the German radio early that morning. At 12 noon a statement was issued by the Admiralty briefly describing the raid, and the statement was read in the BBC's 1 o'clock news bulletin. Reith also was annoyed by the general handling of the news of this raid. 'A spate of questions about what none of us knew had happened. The Ministry of Information forsooth.' (*Into the Wind*, p. 372.) The Germans made much of the British delay in giving details, pointing out that it had created an unfavourable impression not only in the United States but in Italy. (*BBC Monitoring Service, *Weekly Analysis*, 2 April 1940.) Fritzsche chose the occasion to speak of truth as a theme in propaganda.

So far as I know, no correspondent neutral or otherwise has visited Scapa since the raid.'[1]

In general, Ogilvie added, evidence collected by the Monitoring Service demonstrated clearly that 'British official reports tend to be less full than those of the enemy, and for that reason to fall short of maximum effectiveness abroad'. On only four occasions had British releases of 'important news' beaten German announcements—a British raid on the Kiel Canal on 4 September 1939; Chamberlain's statement about the *Rawalpindi* on 28 November; Churchill's announcement of the arrival of the first Canadian troops in Britain on 18 December; and Chamberlain's reference on 15 March 1940 to a British air raid on Germany while it was still in progress.[2] Ogilvie's complaints were echoed by the Press. While it is doubtless true that 'attackers' are always better placed than those they attack to organize the prompt release of news, nonetheless, as the *Evening Standard* put it eloquently, 'the old saying that a lie gets half way round the world before truth has time to get its boots on should be hung up in the office of every Government department'. 'Sealed lips are as dangerous as careless talk.'[3] And it was not only promptness which was at issue. 'The enemy wireless makes wider, prompter and more effective use of eye-witness reports than the British wireless has been able to do.'

The Government as a whole, the report went on, needed to clarify its approach to the use of radio. 'It is essential that a Government spokesman of unquestioned authority should be ready to broadcast promptly—or at least . . . to provide promptly the British interpretation of any important

---

[1] *Ed Murrow, Broadcast on 23 March 1940. The *Daily Telegraph*, 20 March, had a report headed 'US deceived by Nazi claims' which had been widely disseminated in the United States. On the same day, 19 March, that Chamberlain made a statement in the House of Commons on the raid (*Hansard*, vol. 358, col. 1844–5), describing it as a 'failure', the German radio broadcast that 'the rest of the world has no more faith in the official British War communiqués'. Yet a *Fortune* survey of December 1939 showed that at least at that date British news commanded more confidence in the USA than German or Italian news and slightly more than French news. There was, however, widespread scepticism about the truth of *all* war news.

[2] *M. Barkway (Empire News Editor) to Farquharson, 21 March 1940, complaining that even in relation to the night raid, pilots taking part in it were not allowed to broadcast until 'tonight, 48 hours after the first news of the raid'.

[3] *Evening Standard*, 20 March 1940.

international development.' Such an interpretation had been lacking at many crucial moments during the last few months, going back to 31 August 1939, when the German Government broadcast details of the sixteen points which it proposed for a Polish settlement. Most recently there had been no 'interpretation' of the announcement of the Russo-Finnish peace, first broadcast by Germany on the evening of 12 March.[1] 'The BBC cannot itself provide such interpretations,' Ogilvie stressed. 'It cannot secure through unofficial interpreters, at any rate without prompt authoritative guidance, the convincing world-wide impression which is at such moments essential.' He admitted the difficulties in the way of making such statements— Cabinet collective responsibility, Parliamentary control, relations with the Dominions, consultation with France. Yet, given the difficulties, he went on, it was essential to remember that 'it is part of the enemy's technique to time such events, so far as he can control them, so that they may take the Allies by surprise or catch their leaders in recess'. 'It appears essential that a Minister of the first authority, with experience at the microphone, whether it be a member of the War Cabinet or the Ministry of Information acting as the War Cabinet's mouthpiece, shall always be available, as against any sudden development, to interpret as promptly as the needs for collective consultation permit, British reactions and British policy by wireless to the world.'[2]

Ryan, who had wide experience in the world of news and of intelligence, was the main influence behind the Director-General's demand for a clearer and more authoritative policy at this time, and he was certainly one of the few people who could command the support to make such a policy feasible. Ogilvie asked for his return to the BBC in April 1940,[3] and duly secured it—Ryan becoming Controller (Home), a new appointment, on 22 April—while retaining his close links with outside official bodies. In the meantime, however—and Ryan's appointment should be seen against this background—the

[1] *Attempts, supported by the Ministry of Information, to get Lord Halifax to give a 'gong' talk on this occasion, had failed. (Home Board, *Minutes*, 15 March 1940.)

[2] *'Six Months of Radio War—Government Opportunities', Memorandum to Ogilvie, 25 March 1940.

[3] *Powell to Millis, 23 April 1940.

war had moved into a new phase with the Norwegian campaign beginning on 9 April, the first of a series of steps which were to transform the war and in the process to transfer political leadership to Churchill.

The Ministry of Information played little part in the Norwegian campaign, and rumours spread because there was too little official news, particularly from the Admiralty,[1] where Churchill was more optimistic in his early public statements than events warranted. When the decision was taken by the Supreme War Council on 27 April to withdraw from Norway, the BBC was not informed, nor was it informed when the editors of national newspapers were taken into the Government's confidence two or three days later.[2] The BBC once again, therefore, was left at the beginning and at the end of the campaign to face criticism which should more properly have been directed elsewhere. There were complications about the sending of a BBC correspondent—Stubbs or Ward—to Norway;[3] attacks in Parliament on the contents of home news bulletins on 10 April;[4] hurried improvisations, like the substitution of news in Norwegian on 9 April for news in Finnish in the time slot allotted to the latter (Finland had capitulated on 12 March);[5] and the hastily composed message in Danish broadcast the same day. This was written by Charles Peake at the Ministry of Information after it had been suggested by the London correspondent of *Politiken*, who had been forced to seek Lord Halifax's personal approval.[6]

Against this background, Newsome was complaining that the Government had tried during the last stages of the

[1] There had been an argument in January between Reith and Churchill as to whether news of naval losses should be released only once a week in a 'tabloid' statement.

[2] A. E. Barker to Tallents, 6 May 1940.

[3] *Home Board, *Minutes*, 12 April, 19 April, 26 April 1940.

[4] *Ibid., 12 April 1940. Swedish reports that the British had recaptured Bergen and Trondheim were quoted—as they were in *The Times*, 11 April 1940, although it was emphasized that they were unconfirmed. (D. F. Boyd to R. T. Clark, 24 April 1940.) At the same time, Boothby complained that the BBC should not have reported an Admiralty communiqué that two destroyers had been lost at Narvik on the grounds that 'it will spread alarm and despondency in every quarter'.

[5] *Overseas Board, *Minutes*, 7 March 1940, 11 April 1940.

[6] *J. Bennett, *British Broadcasting and the Danish Resistance Movement* (1966), pp. 1–2.

campaign to use the European News Service not to tell listeners the truth but to 'throw dust in the eyes of the enemy'. 'Owing to the fact that our treatment of the campaign was based on the assumption that it would be carried on, a false picture of the true situation was inevitably created and as inevitably has had a damaging effect on our reputation abroad for reliability.' 'I cannot but resent most strongly,' he went on, 'that we were used as a blind tool.'[1]

This was certainly not the lesson which the Government drew from the story of the Norwegian campaign. The BBC might see itself as 'the entirely innocent victim of strategic needs',[2] but there were people in the Cabinet who saw the BBC as 'an enemy within the gates'.[3] It was, moreover, still a very vulnerable target.

An informal hour-and-a-half meeting was held at the Ministry of Information on 22 April, and was attended not only by Ogilvie, Powell, Reith, Lee and Monckton, but by Sir Kingsley Wood, the Lord Privy Seal, and Sir Horace Wilson. All the misunderstandings came out into the open, with the BBC being forced into the defensive from the start. The fact that Churchill's speeches on Norway had created a bad impression not only in the United States but in Europe was overlooked:[4] the BBC was singled out for its own handling of news, most of which had been handed out to it. Reith questioned recent organizational changes within the Corporation, and Kingsley Wood attacked 'rather sweepingly' BBC news bulletins about events in Norway, criticizing *inter alia* the use made of 'unconfirmed statements' from Stockholm, all of which had been vetted by the Departments concerned. He also chose the occasion to attack 'pacifist sermons' broadcast in the Home Service and raised ominously the general question of 'whether all our [BBC] officials were sufficiently charged with patriotism and wisdom in dealing with the output of news and talks'—a matter which was duly taken up by the Governors of the BBC at their meeting on 24 April.[5] It was clear that the BBC was

[1] *Newsome to A. E. Barker, 5 May 1940.

[2] *A. E. Barker to Tallents, 6 May 1940.

[3] Reith, *Into the Wind*, p. 438.

[4] *BBC Monitoring Service, *Weekly Analysis*, 16 April 1940. 'One Jump Behind Again' was a characteristic American comment.

[5] *Powell to Millis, 23 April 1940.

being made the scapegoat for the failure of the Government to lead and to plan.

Before the full implications of this, almost the last, tangle of the phoney war were sorted out, the Germans invaded Holland, Belgium and Luxembourg on 10 May. The *Sitzkrieg* was over. The very last tangle was a disagreement on 26 April between the Ministry and Electra House as to whether the news bulletin at midnight should be in Dutch or German.[1]

---

[1] *Ogilvie to Wellington, 26 April 1940. Wellington to Ogilvie, 30 April 1940: 'I have not yet heard officially about the conflicting claims of the Ministry and of E.H. on the midnight period, but I shall do my best to resolve them for you.'

III

ATTACK AND DEFENCE

———

The day war broke out, my Missus looked at me and she said, 'What good are you?' I said, 'Who?' She said, 'You'. I said, 'How do you mean, what good am I?' She said, 'Well, you are too old for the Army, you couldn't get into the Navy, and they wouldn't have you in the Air Force, so what good are you?' I said, 'How do I know, I'll have to think.' . . . [So I joined the Home Guards.] The first day I got my uniform I went home and put it on—and the Missus looked at me and said, 'What are you supposed to be?' I said, 'Supposed to be? I'm one of the Home Guards.' She said, 'One of the Home Guards, what are the others like?' She said, 'What are you supposed to do?' I said, 'I'm supposed to stop Hitler's Army landing.' She said, 'What, YOU?' I said, 'No, not me, there's Bob Edwards, Charlie Evans, Billy Brightside—there's seven or eight of us, we're in a group, we're on guard in a little hut behind "The Dog and Pullet".'

ROBB WILTON (Radio Comedian)

1. Blitzkrieg

IN his broadcast of 30 March Churchill had warned his listeners that while all was quiet on the Western Front, 'more than a million German soldiers' were drawn up ready to attack at a few hours' notice all along the frontiers of Luxembourg, of Belgium and of Holland. 'At any moment these neutral countries may be subjected to an avalanche of steel and fire.'

The German armies moved on 10 May. The first radio messages came from Hilversum in Holland at 6.47 a.m.— 'large formation German planes flying westerly direction over Holland'.[1] At 8.5 a.m., German time, Goebbels read on the German radio the memoranda sent to the invaded countries; between 9 and 10 a.m. Hans Fritzsche followed with a list of carefully composed official announcements from the Ministry of the Interior and the German High Command; at 12 noon Hitler's Order of the Day was broadcast; and half an hour later the first German comments on the invasion were made. At 3 p.m. a talk was given on the details of the entry of troops into Luxembourg: it was repeated with additions at 5 p.m., including an interview with the pilot of a dive bomber. In the meantime there was an unremitting propaganda barrage in Dutch and French, employing a characteristic mixture of appeals and threats,[2] and both Dutch and Belgian stations were announcing details of mobilization and defence.

It would have been quite impossible even for the most intelligent monitor in any country outside Germany to have predicted either the time or the place of the new *Blitzkrieg* on the basis of radio evidence. 'Operation Yellow' had been put off many times, but there was no overture in May 1940. 'Broadcast indications of the direction of further German moves reveal an *embarras de richesse*,' the British Monitoring

---

[1] *BBC Monitoring Service, Editorial Bulletin*, 10 May 1940.
[2] *Appendix A to a BBC Paper, 'Broadcasting as a Weapon of War', 21 May 1940; BBC *Analysis of Foreign Broadcasts*, 12 May 1940.

Service had stated on 16 April. 'The Western Front, Holland, Belgium, and the Balkans and Sweden are all equally possible objectives, to judge from the evidence.'[1]

Between then and 10 May, attention to German plans in the West was diverted both by the German and by the Italian radio. Instead, the British were accused of seeking to 'enlarge the theatre of war', and there was talk of Allied efforts 'to spread the war to the Balkans and Mediterranean', with the warning that 'Allied plans might be camouflage for action in another direction'.[2] On 6 May the BBC's Monitoring Day Book had included a note that 'the greatest possible coverage of transmissions to and from the Balkans and Italy' was needed 'until further notice', and two days later there had been a further note that 'in view of the tension in the Balkans' tapes of all broadcasts to and from the Balkans were needed by the BBC's European News.[3] There were no wireless indications, therefore, of the imminence of *Blitzkrieg* in the West before the Hilversum broadcast on 10 May itself, except that the German psychological technique of projection—attributing your own schemes to the enemy—was carried far enough on 8 May for the German home radio to broadcast that 'nervousness and high tension in neutral states continue unabated. Over and over again the question is put: where will the British aggressor now act?'[4] In the meantime NBBS had been seeking on the eve of the invasion to rally opponents of the war effort in Britain. 'The time has come when those who really desire peace should not remain inactive,' was its message on 7 May. 'Those who wish to take part in a movement to stop the war must get in touch with any movement to end the war—even if its and their aims are not entirely in agreement.'[5]

This NBBS statement was heard by few listeners, although the Monitoring Service was soon collecting 'every phrase, however

---

[1] *Ibid., 16 April 1940. On 18 April 1940 the watchword for the Monitoring Service was 'watch the Danube' (*Editorial Bulletin*, 18 April 1940).

[2] *BBC *Analysis of Foreign Broadcasts*, 12 May 1940. See also the German Press Directives of 8 May and 9 May 1940 as printed in E. K. Bramsted, *Goebbels and National Socialist Propaganda* (1965), p. 235.

[3] *BBC, *Monitoring Day Book*, 6, 8 May 1940.

[4] Extracts from some of the key broadcasts between 8 May and 17 June 1940 are printed in E. Tangye Lean's interesting book *Voices in the Darkness* (1943), pp. 111–41.

[5] *BBC *Analysis of Foreign Broadcasts*, 12 May 1940.

scrappy' which NBBS broadcast.[1] Thousands of British listeners, however, heard Alvar Lidell announce at 10.45 a.m. on 10 May: 'This is the BBC Home Service—Here is a short news bulletin. The German Army invaded Holland and Belgium early this morning by land and by landings from parachutes. An appeal for help has been made to the Allied governments and GHQ says that Allied troops are moving to their support.'[2]

During the next few weeks there was a 'hunger for news' far more intense than there ever had been in any previous period of history. '"The News"—normally the 9 p.m. bulletin —became in most households an institution almost as sacrosanct as family prayers had once been.'[3] The six daily bulletins, read by announcers who now gave their names so that listeners could learn to recognize their voices[4]—a recognition that the source was more important than the medium or the message— were carefully compared with each other.[5] In the same period, a report on the reactions of soldiers, sailors and airmen to the Forces Programme stressed that for them too 'news bulletins are the only items followed with close attention these days (a point made again and again)'.[6] Events moved so quickly that there was also more cross listening to foreign news bulletins than there had ever been before, and comparisons were drawn here also. In many of the foreign broadcasts, not least the French news bulletins, it was difficult to separate news from propaganda, and there was a measure of additional confusion as

---

[1] *BBC Monitoring Service, *Editorial Bulletin*, 27 May 1940. A file was collected called 'Enemy Instructions for Rumour in Britain'.

[2] The Belgians had asked for Allied support in a broadcast from Brussels at 7.28 a.m. and the Dutch announced at 8.15 a.m. that 'our Allies are sending speedy help'. Rome did not announce the German moves in its 8 a.m. news bulletin.

[3] P. Fleming, *Invasion 1940* (1957 edn.), p. 107.

[4] *Home Board, *Minutes*, 12 July 1940. The Dutch wireless had warned its listeners before the collapse of Holland that no broadcast was authentic unless given in the voices of the known regular announcers. (*Manchester Guardian*, 11 May 1940.) The British move towards personalization was a popular one, 'the most popular of all the security measures introduced that summer' (E. J. Turner, *The Phoney War on the Home Front* (1961), p. 249).

[5] A suggestion in a letter to *The Spectator*, 12 July 1940, that so many bulletins were bad for the nerves won little support.

[6] *Programme for the Forces, Summary of Listener Opinion, 16–29 June 1940. On 30 May 50% of the population was estimated to have heard the BBC's 9 o'clock Home Service bulletin, 42% the 6 o'clock and 32% the 8 a.m. broadcast. Even the midnight news was listened to by 10%.

foreign stations passed into the hands of the Germans.[1] Confusion encouraged rumour which was itself a main constituent of many of the foreign programmes.

The Germans were temporarily placed, therefore, in a position—both as a result of the speed and success of their advance and of the limitations imposed by the Allied censorship systems—in which they could often give more up-to-date news about the progress of the war than the Allies. While their *Frontberichte*, designed for the home listener, were heralded by fanfares and supplemented by confident boasts that 'everywhere initiative is in German hands',[2] their foreign programmes needed no such dramatic effects to enhance the bare narrative. 'Hitler's predictions have come true while those of the Allies have not,' a BBC Intelligence Report noted in July 1940, 'and this has greatly damaged the prestige of British news.'[3] 'We shall in future broadcast news as well as commentaries,' an NBBS speaker declared on 25 May. 'We claim that we shall keep the public better informed than they [the BBC] do as to happenings both at home and abroad.'[4] Of course, NBBS deliberately mixed rumours with facts more noisily than Bremen, and from mid-May onwards coupled accounts of actual victories with threats of imminent invasion. It was time, NBBS had explained on 15 May, 'for the people of Britain to save themselves by rising and demanding peace before the final consummation of disaster'.[5]

[1] The first of these to be mentioned in the BBC's Monitoring Service *Editorial Bulletin* was Hilversum (15 May): 'In tomorrow's Digest Hilversum will appear in Part I of the Digest as a station under German control.'

[2] *The British avoided most of these trappings then and later, although they paid tribute to their 'authenticity, drama and human interest'. (*Appendix A to 'Broadcasting as a Weapon of War', 21 May 1940.) The news moved so fast, however, and there was such uncertainty about German intentions that preparations were made, for example, to add the Swiss national anthem to one of the few programmes of this type—the Sunday national anthems programme which included the Dutch and Belgian national anthems for the first time on 12 May. (*Home Service Board, *Minutes*, 10, 17 May 1940.) For the later history of this programme, see below, pp. 389–91.

[3] *BBC Overseas Intelligence Department, *Monthly Intelligence Report*, 8 July 1940. At the same time, great care was taken from the start not to introduce 'too optimistic a tone' into the news of the Netherlands and 'to avoid the difficulties which arose over the earlier Norwegian news'. (Report of telephone conversation between Ogilvie and Wellington, 11 May 1940).

[4] *BBC *Analysis of Foreign Broadcasts*, 28 May 1940.

[5] *Ibid., 21 May 1940.

Whatever the response to German propaganda in Europe—and in France there was an alarming response from a disunited people almost from the start of active hostilities[1]—the immediate British reaction to the opening up of the war was the replacement of Chamberlain by Churchill and the creation of a government of national unity. The Germans had concentrated on Mr. Churchill as their main enemy as early as September and October 1939 in the hope that what they called 'the Churchill problem' would divide rather than unite Britain.[2] '"Churchillism" not Hitlerism, should be destroyed.'[3] This thesis had been maintained throughout the winter of 1939/40, again with the assistance of the psychological technique of 'projection'; for example, after the *Altmark* incident in February 1940 Churchill was accused of organizing vicious attacks on unarmed German merchant seamen just as he had organized vicious attacks on unarmed Boers forty years before. He had not changed, it was said, since 1900.[4] Two months later, before he had become Prime Minister, Churchill was being described as the 'War Dictator',[5] and just after he had taken up his new post Dutch listeners to German radio were told that the move had not surprised Berlin. 'It is in line with the British policy that the biggest warmonger, Enemy No. 1, also becomes Minister No. 1.'[6]

Attacks on Churchill generated little response in Britain, and they carried even less danger after 10 May when Churchill expressed with firmness and eloquence what most of his fellow countrymen were feeling.[7] His first broadcast to the nation as Prime Minister—'Be ye men of valour'—was transmitted on 19 May, one day before the vanguard of the German Second Panzer Division reached the north of the Somme near

[1] See below, pp. 221 ff.

[2] *BBC Monitoring Service, Weekly Analysis, 19 Oct. 1939.

[3] *Ibid., 25 Oct. 1939.

[4] *BBC *Analysis of Foreign Broadcasts*, 20 Feb. 1940, reporting a talk in the German Home Service by Hans Fritzsche.

[5] *Ibid., 9 April 1940.

[6] Quoted in Tangye Lean, op. cit., pp. 112–13.

[7] *There is an interesting and characteristic comment reflecting Churchill's views in the BBC's Monitoring Service *Editorial Bulletin*, 17 May 1940: 'The British Prime Minister should always be called "the Prime Minister" and not "the Premier". "Premier" should be retained for the heads of foreign governments.'

Abbeville, thereby cutting the Allied armies in two. By the end of June his voice—and his views—had become familiar to all his countrymen, and 64 per cent of the adult population of the country heard his broadcast on 14 July.[1] 'I think that one of the reasons why one is stirred by his Elizabethan phrases,' Harold Nicolson wrote at the time, 'is that one feels the whole massive backing of power and resolve behind them, like a great fortress: they are never words for words' sake.'[2]

Although the role of the BBC during the 'strange months' of May and June 1940 was far more important than that of simply serving as a vehicle of government propaganda, its activities were very carefully watched both by politicians and civil servants. 'No one who is shown to belong to an organisation the policy of which is inconsistent with the national effort,' the Corporation maintained, 'or who is shown to have expressed views which are inconsistent with the national effort, may be invited to broadcast in any programme or to contribute material for broadcasting.'[3] Security measures were consequently tightened. The fact that two bogus announcements were broadcast on 13 May—the first instructing men in the RAF Volunteer Reserve who were on leave or doing civilian work to report to their bases, the second warning children to keep away from RAF premises in reception areas—was a sign of the dangers of accepting messages by telephone. Thereafter, all London announcements were routed through the Ministry of Information. It was with the same kind of consideration in mind that the peace-time SOS service was discontinued on 31 May. Staff were also told to keep their eyes open for any suspicious activities in Broadcasting House, which 'by its nature presents a vulnerable field for Fifth Column activities'.[4]

Some of the politicians who were forced to the forefront of the news in 1940 made their mark as broadcasters—Anthony Eden, for example, who broadcast the news of the setting up of the Local Defence Volunteers or 'Parashots', later called the Home Guard, on 14 May;[5] Herbert Morrison, new Minister

---

[1] *BBC Handbook, 1941*, p. 60.
[2] H. Nicolson, *Diaries and Letters, 1939-45* (1967), p. 93.
[3] *Note of 30 Aug. 1940, 'Broadcasting in War-time'.
[4] *Directive from the Director of Staff Administration, 12 June 1940.
[5] This and a later broadcast by Eden were said to have been greatly appreciated. (*BBC Home Board, *Minutes*, 28 June 1940.)

of Home Security, whose voice was unfamiliar to most listeners; and Lord Woolton, Minister of Food, who was keen to learn all the arts of what to him was a new medium. The new Minister of Information, Duff Cooper, who had been promised that 'the status of the Minister would be raised' and that he would be able to attend War Cabinet meetings 'in order that he should be fully informed upon everything that was taking place',[1] was said somewhat patronizingly within the BBC 'to have possibilities as a broadcaster' and to be 'willing to be drilled'.[2] He certainly took an active interest in everything which was happening and, despite some distaste for his own Ministry,[3] did what he could to encourage the BBC.

The Ministry had appointed a small Home Morale Emergency Committee on 22 May, proceeding on the assumption that it would be prudent to prepare for the worst, and it was under its aegis that official talks were called for to mitigate what it identified as five menaces to public calm—fear, confusion, suspicion, class feeling and defeatism. The first menace could best be overcome, it was suggested, not by exhortation but by specific guidance, not so much by words of comfort as by words of command.[4] Emphasis was placed on the importance of ensuring that citizens combined self-reliance with respect for air raid wardens and others upon whom local authority had been conferred, and to achieve this aim 'national guidance' was held to be necessary, if need be from men with national authority, notably General Ironside, the Chief of the Imperial General Staff. The second and third 'menaces' could be countered *inter alia* by broadcast addresses and by an intensified anti-rumour campaign designed to undermine the Hamburg broadcasts and the NBBS. A proposal to distribute two million pamphlets weighing fourteen tons was properly criticized by the Treasury. It was freely admitted that there would be other

[1] Duff Cooper, *Old Men Forget* (1953), p. 280.

[2] *BBC Home Service Board, *Minutes*, 17 May 1940.

[3] In *Old Men Forget*, he wrote that he was offered it 'almost as an apology' and described it as 'a monster, so large, so voluminous and so amorphous that no single man could cope with it' (ibid., p. 285). The Ministry reached a new peak of staffing in July 1940 (*Minutes of the Ministry of Information Policy Committee, 3 July 1940).

[4] The need for such guidance was emphasized by the Press. See, for example, an article in *The Times*, 1 July 1940, which argued that 'most of the grumbling is about insufficient direction'.

problems—for example, too many bad speakers coming to the microphone and too many official speakers coming with nothing to say[1]—but there were few doubts that given a 'guided' broadcasting policy public self-criticism would change into public self-praise. 'The public should and would be put into a bellicose and aggressive frame of mind.'

The attention specifically paid to the fourth menace—'class feeling'—is particularly interesting in retrospect, since Haw-Haw and the NBBS had done much to play on this theme, and Regional Intelligence Officers of the Ministry were reporting an increase in class resentment in various parts of the country. The BBC came directly into the picture in this connection, when it was argued more sharply than ever before that the predominance of cultured voices upon the wireless was danger-ous and that more working-class people should appear before the microphone.[2] Defeatism was obviously the final and most alarming of all the menaces, and steps would have to be taken, it was argued, not only to demonstrate as widely as possible how serious the ramifications of a German victory would be for *all* the population, but to consider whether there should not be some short and simple statement of war aims.[3]

The BBC did its best to work within the framework of this policy, as set out in a Draft Scheme for Broadcasting prepared by the Home Morale Emergency Committee,[4] but it extended it in places and, faced with a challenge, gave it a dimension of its own. 'Questions which were being widely discussed in April of this year,' Maconachie wrote, 'had come to seem

---

[1] *Barnes to Ryan, 25 May 1940.

[2] Attlee made this point, which was noted by Nicolson, who had much to do with the bolstering of morale. 'Attlee is worried about the BBC retaining its class voice and personnel and would like to see a far greater infiltration of working class speakers.' (*Diaries and Letters*, p. 99, entry for 3 July 1940.)

[3] *The Home Morale Emergency Committee reported on these lines to the Policy Committee of the Ministry of Information on 4 June. It was still anxious at this stage to restore faith in the strength and efficiency of the French armies. See below, p. 240.

[4] *There was also a tightening up of organizational links between the BBC and Ministry. Regular joint policy meetings were held each day from Monday to Friday and the Minister himself was present on certain days, usually Mondays and Thursdays, when an effort was made to deal with the most important broadcasting matters. (*Letter from Lee to Ogilvie, 21 May 1940.) Ogilvie replied in a letter to Lee on 23 May that he hoped to attend on Mondays and Thursdays and that Ryan would attend every day.

academic, if not trivial, by July, while certain matters like air raid precautions and first aid which in the early phases of the war appeared to be of practical interest only to the pessimist suddenly acquired a painfully topical importance.'[1] Along with statements about the effects of high explosive bombing, the dangers of parachute attack,[2] 'fifth column tricks',[3] air raid precaution talks (said to be 'popular')[4] and other official messages conveying specific instructions and advice on how to behave in an emergency, special efforts were made to foster 'the value of neighbourliness, the pooling of resources in a community—whether a village or a street—and practical forms of mutual help in times of a crisis'.[5] Programmes were overhauled to produce an 'aggressive attitude of mind towards invasion'.[6] 'In this war, unlike any other, defeat would mean extermination.'[7]

The Home Morale Emergency Committee seems to have overestimated the extent to which 'vigilant anticipation' needed to be generated from above, for as the month of May went by, villagers and townfolk throughout the country had little difficulty in concluding for themselves, without direction, that they were really in the front line.[8] The Committee worked on the assumption, however, probably in the light of the experience of the 'phoney war', that there was still 'a large section of the lower classes [*sic*] which believes that they would be just as well off under Hitler as under decaying capitalism'. This unsubstantiated statement had certainly been

[1] *BBC Handbook, 1941*, p. 64.

[2] *This matter had first been raised on 11 May (Report of a telephone conversation between Ogilvie and Wellington), when Wellington reported that a talk dealing with parachutists would soon be asked for but that the War Office had not yet made up 'their minds' as to the method of dealing with enemy parachutists by the public. An important meeting took place on that day between representatives of the War Office and the Ministry of Home Security to discuss plans which were subsequently dealt with in BBC news bulletins as well as in official messages.

[3] *Evening Standard*, 17 May 1940. 'Parachutists near Ostend are said to have had transparent parachutes and sky-blue uniform to make them semi-invisible during their descent.'

[4] *BBC Home Service Board, *Minutes*, 17 May 1940. Efforts were made also to raise the status of air raid wardens who were felt to have become 'figures of fun'.

[5] *Maconachie to Ryan, 28 May 1940.

[6] *Ibid.

[7] *Home Morale Committee, Draft Scheme for Broadcasting, undated memorandum.

[8] See P. Fleming, op. cit., Chapter 7, for an excellent account of 'John Bull at Bay'.

a main plank of NBBS propaganda and was to be even more of a plank of another German 'freedom' station, Workers' Challenge, which first went on the air, with unrestrained 'anti-capitalist propaganda', in July 1940.[1] Moreover, the Ministry of Information's diagnosis went on, 'there is a small but not negligible section of the middle classes which has not yet realised how near we are to defeat, hopes we won't make too harsh terms for the Germans, etc'. 'We recognise,' the draft concluded, 'that this point has been given much prominence already, but we must urge that repetition, however distasteful to a critical mind, is the essence of propaganda.'[2]

A further stage in the implementation of this diagnosis was an 'Anger Campaign', prepared in June, 'to heighten the intensity of the personal anger felt by the individual British citizen against the German people and Germany—as a factor in increasing the war effort and in preparing the British public for every emergency'. The reasoning behind this new campaign was dangerous. 'A good deal of the war-anger felt by the British people is not at present directed consciously against the Germans. It is our task to focus all war anger as directly as possible against the Germans and in such a way that it appears to come quite spontaneously from the people themselves. In other words, we want the people to feel that it is their anger which is growing of its own accord.'[3]

There is little evidence that the British people needed to be roused, and there remains long after the event the sense of something redundant if not repugnant in the idea that good,

---

[1] *'If we had our way we would dislocate the capitalists' necks' was the message on 21 July. The Monitoring Service identified the station 'as definitely not in Russia' on 12 July. It had been stated, however, at the Policy Committee of the Ministry of Information on 22 July that the station 'raises the Communist banner'. There is no evidence that it was listened to attentively by working-class people. Indeed Leonard Ingrams, at the heart of the Intelligence services, told Sefton Delmer that 'old ladies in Eastbourne and Torquay are listening to it avidly because it is using the foulest language ever'. (See Delmer, *Black Boomerang*, vol. II (1962), p. 38.)

[2] *Home Morale Emergency Committee, Draft Scheme for Broadcasting.

[3] *Report of the Ministry of Information General Production Division, 'Anger Campaign', referred to at the Ministry Policy Committee, 17 June 1940. The Germans also made anger a main theme of their own propaganda in late May and early June. 'Hate along the whole line is the outstanding new feature of this week's broadcast from Deutschlandsender.' (BBC *Analysis of Foreign Broadcasts*, 4 June 1940.)

rousing popular songs had to be prepared to stiffen morale or that specially commissioned articles had to be sponsored by twenty or thirty famous journalists including Godfrey Winn and J. B. Priestley. Even more repugnant was the admission that 'the difficulty of the problem is obvious, i.e., hammering at a theme, but without the public knowing that it is being influenced'.[1] The Ministry itself seems to have had some doubts, for after a long discussion in a Policy Committee meeting the discerning though unstartling conclusion was reached that 'it might merely be sufficient to impress the people that they were in fact angry'.[2]

Without prompting, the BBC had encouraged the writing of 'rousing popular songs' earlier in the year[3] and had offered Priestley an invitation broadcast on current events, following a series of Postscripts by the well-known barrister, Maurice Healy. They were looking for 'a contrast in voice, upbringing and outlook'.[4] Priestley was not well known as a broadcaster in Britain, and before the war radio had never seemed to him to be 'a very rewarding medium',[5] but very quickly his broadcasts became something of a national sensation. He had 'millions and millions of fans' and his 'mail arrived in bulging postbags'. 'Mr. Priestley's broadcasts are a privilege,' the *Daily Mail* noted. 'As the hours grow darker, so he grows brighter; and his common sense and Yorkshire stoicism, reflect the real and everlasting spirit of our race.'[6] In nineteen broadcasts between 5 June—a Wednesday—and 20 October, many of these immediately following the Sunday nine o'clock news, he built up an immense following, on average for each broadcast 31 per cent of the adult population. 'What is it that is giving

[1] *Machonachie to Ryan, 17 June 1940. A letter from a listener on 3 June 1940 attacked Harold Nicolson for making too much of rumour-mongering. 'Many of us', he added, 'look upon the Ministry of Information and the BBC as National Dangers far more than any Boche parachutists.'

[2] *Ministry of Information Policy Committee, 4 June 1940.

[3] *The suggestion had first been made by Lady Reading to Reith in February 1940, but was handled in a 'desultory way' until Nicolls prepared proposals for commissioning patriotic songs in July 1940. (Note of 17 July.) See below, pp. 577–8. Most of the 1939 patriotic efforts were dead by July 1940, among them Harry Roy's 'God bless you, Mr. Chamberlain'.

[4] *Note by Barnes, 6 May 1940.

[5] See his interesting preface to the recent American edition of his postscripts, *All England Listened* (1967), p. xiii.

[6] *Daily Mail*, 2 July 1940.

Mr. Priestley a radio following in this country which must be almost as big as Mr. Churchill's?' asked the *Yorkshire Post*, answering for itself that 'it is the sound of his voice that England finds so welcome and reassuring'.[1]

His strength, however, lay both in his voice and in his message. He sounded like 'a man of the people'. Describing things not only as they were but as they might be, he was able by instinct to combine general statements with vivid and specific detail about both people and things. 'The British listening public as a whole,' he recognized, 'responds immediately to any sincere attempt to use a little insight and to penetrate beneath the surface of this conflict.' 'Refer to a pie in a shop and there are pilgrimages to it.'[2] Although then and later he stated that he did not know what all the fuss was about,[3] he appreciated clearly enough that broadcasting had a very special role in 1940. It added to the vigour of his message that he believed also that 'the only people who do not seem aware of the terrific power of the broadcast word are the members of our War Cabinet' and that 'the official under-valuation of this great medium of communication and persuasion is . . . one of the most serious weaknesses of our war effort'.[4]

The fact that passages from his broadcasts soon roused suspicion in some official circles—Lord Davidson, who had been chairman of the Conservative Party during the 1920s, and Colonel Scorgie of the Ministry of Information complained about their content and tone—did nothing to detract from his popularity with most people. Among the 'stacks of letters' he received[5]—1,600 between June and October—only a few were critical.[6] It was only in September that serious concern began to be expressed about his 'left-wing views'.

[1] *Yorkshire Post*, 16 July 1940.

[2] See his brief preface to the published war-time version of *Postscripts* (1940), pp. vi and vii.

[3] J. B. Priestley, *Margin Released* (1962), p. 220.

[4] *Postscripts*, p. vi. When he was thanked by Duff Cooper for his services, he replied that Duff Cooper should have a 'showdown' with the Government about the relative importance of broadcasting and propaganda.

[5] *Priestley to Ogilvie, 2 Aug. 1940.

[6] *The Star*, 2 July 1940, commented that it was 'one of the small gains of the war that it brought to the microphone a man who does the job so well, both in his material and manner', but added that some people who 'raved' over his first broadcast—'a classic in every sense of the word'—were not nearly so pleased with his talk on 'Two-Ton Annie' on 30 June.

By then Maconachie was raising the same points which had been made by Birkett earlier in the year when he had first been invited to broadcast. Priestley has 'definite social and political views which he puts over in his broadcasts, and through these broadcasts, is, I think, exercising an important influence on what people are thinking. These views may be admirable or otherwise, but the question which I wish to raise is one of principle, whether any single person should be given the opportunity of acquiring such an influence to the exclusion of others who differ from him merely on the ground of his merits as a broadcaster which are, of course, very great.'[1]

The question of principle was to be raised on many occasions later, particularly in the age of television, yet the midsummer broadcasts of Priestley are an essential part of the social history of Britain in 1940, catching the mood, reflecting the temper. None of the alternative broadcasters later suggested to replace him after he had decided in October that he ought to stop broadcasting for a while[2]—Birkett again, Howard Marshall, Robert Donat, Leslie Howard, Frederick Hooper or A. P. Herbert—had anything like the same influence. It was recognized clearly in Broadcasting House that 'soft soap will not raise home morale' and that 'complacency in a regular weekly speaker is the attitude best calculated to irritate the public and create distrust in the Government and the BBC'.[3] One great man who did not catch the mood was Shaw, and there was a protracted argument about whether he should be allowed to broadcast at all. When he submitted a script early in June, the Ministry of Information refused to allow it to be broadcast. 'In view of G.B.S.'s amenability,' the BBC persisted, 'a further approach should be made to him.'[4] Shaw replied that he was still willing to broadcast, 'but not yet clear what to say',[5] but once again he was 'turned down by the Ministry'.[6]

Priestley hid nothing from his public. There were some signs,

[1] *Maconachie to Ryan, 6 Sept. 1940.

[2] *Priestley to Miss Wace, 9 Oct. 1940. He admitted that as well as feeling the strain he was 'more and more disappointed with the Government which does not make the big imaginative gestures needed at this juncture'.

[3] *Barnes to Maconachie, 10 July 1940.

[4] *BBC Home Board, *Minutes*, 14 June 1940.

[5] *Ibid., 28 June 1940. Part of a rejected earlier Shaw script is printed in D. Flower and J. Reeves (eds.), *The War 1939–1945* (1960), pp. 7–8.

[6] *Home Board, *Minutes*, 5 July 1940.

however, in these hectic weeks, when because of the use of
church bells as a warning of danger the recording of Bow
Bells as an interval signal was replaced by 'tick tock',[1] that the
BBC and the Ministry wished to keep from the British public
some of the details of the harsher side of war. On 17 May it
had been decided that in relation to the broadcasting of war
features 'the changing outlook of the country had to be watched',
along with 'the present policy of bringing the war home to
listeners by dramatisation of events',[2] the familiar German
pattern carried much further by Goebbels's PK units working
with the German armies at the front.[3] On 24 May, for example,
Ogilvie reported to the Home Board 'the Ministry view' that
while war feature programmes should not be discontinued,
'great care should be taken to guard against harrowing listeners'
feelings'. The Ministry wished the public 'to be spared
unnecessary frightening details'.[4] It also gave a ruling against
the dramatization of current events.[5] A BBC feature on Narvik,
first broadcast on Whit Monday and later in the Overseas
Service of the BBC on 30 May, had won the praise of the
Manchester Guardian and of the *Glasgow Herald*, but was so
bitterly attacked in Parliament by Sir Archibald Southby as
'a vulgarly sensational attempt at a dramatisation of a wonderful exploit' that Duff Cooper had to defend the whole position
of the BBC. Southby thundered about broadcasting officials
'who owe no allegiance to anyone but themselves and who
arrogate to themselves the right to do as they please'.[6] Val
Gielgud, who was the official most violently attacked, wrote
sensibly and responsibly about the BBC's position in a letter to
The Times,[7] and Duff Cooper had to remind Southby that there
were two sides to most questions.

In fact, the BBC's 'features' during the late spring and summer
of 1940 were among the Corporation's most remarkable

[1] *Ibid., 14 June 1940.
[2] *Ibid., 17 May 1940.
[3] For the PK units, see above, p. 20.
[4] *Home Board, *Minutes*, 24 May 1940. Wellington had told Nicolls four days
earlier to try 'to ensure that news bulletins are followed by cheerful and cheering
programmes as far as possible . . . especially in the early morning' (letter of 20
May).
[5] *Ibid., 7 June 1940.
[6] *Hansard*, vol. 361, col. 1234.
[7] *The Times*, 17 May 1940.

achievements of that year. 'The present situation,' wrote Gilliam, 'calls for every possible step we can take to stiffen the morale of the public.' Features with a 'heartening content' had a 'virile dynamic appeal to the attention and the emotions'. Seamen and airmen deserved special attention. So, too, did the patriotic themes of British history. Two historic programmes would be 'useful', Gilliam thought, when the battle in France began to rage—'a revival of *The Old Contemptibles*, a story of the retreat from Mons with the obvious moral that things were just as bad then and the tide turned', and *The Black Day of the German Army*, 8 August 1918: 'a script in preparation by Tom Wintringham could be ready inside a week'.[1]

Within this context, the news of Dunkirk made all earlier arguments out of date. On 24 May German armoured forces halted only a few miles from what was to become the British-French bridgehead at Dunkirk. The delay was disastrous for the Germans, for when their advance was resumed the British were prepared. From 27 May to 3 June fierce battle raged on the perimeter of Dunkirk. It took the Germans twelve days to move the twenty kilometres from Gravelines to Dunkirk, having moved 380 kilometres from Bastogne to Gravelines in fourteen days. From 10 May to 3 June seventy-five Dutch, Belgian, French and British divisions had been eliminated from the battle, but from the battered beaches of Dunkirk 338,226 men were embarked, including 224,717 British soldiers.[2] Their escape, brilliantly described at the time in the most effective of all Priestley's postscripts,[3] was a turning point in the war. Churchill was right to emphasize that 'the miracle of Dunkirk' was not a victory, but he was right also to draw from it the cheerful moral that Britain could not be defeated. Priestley ended his postscript with the same message. 'Our great grandchildren, when they learn how we began this war by snatching glory out of defeat, and then swept on to victory, may also learn how the little holiday steamers made an excursion to hell and came back glorious.'[4]

The BBC tried to make the most of Dunkirk. It pressed the

---

[1] *Gilliam to de Lotbinière, 22 May 1940.
[2] For a German account, see H. A. Jacobsen, *Dunkirchen* (1958).
[3] It is reprinted in *Postscripts*, pp. 1–4.
[4] Ibid., p. 4.

Minister of Information to allow it to bring to the microphone officers and men just back from France and to let them tell their own stories.[1] 'Simple eye witness accounts could be set against the background of the news . . . and of speeches made by the Prime Minister and Mr. Eden.' The BEF should be given its share of glory: 'day by day while BEF were fighting what presumably is one of the greatest defensive actions in military history, the News has been stressing RAF successes', and even the Air Ministry itself had said 'that it would be glad to take a back seat in favour of the BEF in the immediate future'.[2] On 14 June Ogilvie reported that Duff Cooper had granted explicit approval for a Dunkirk 'feature' a week later.[3] He added also that after Margesson had complained that the BBC had been remiss in not seeking permission to broadcast Churchill's Dunkirk speech in Parliament, he had asked in reply whether, since all previous BBC attempts to have speeches broadcast from the House of Commons had failed, Margesson would be willing to suggest 'new lines of approach'.[4]

There was a lighter side to the story of the 'strange summer' of 1940, or rather a continuing and never quite settled debate on 'lightness'. It is expressed in odd comments made in BBC Committees in May and June. 'Variety 11 May, vulgarity,' Home Board solemnly noted one day after the German attacks had begun.[5] On 31 May the possibility of removing racing results from their news setting was discussed, and it was decided to withdraw them from 8 June onwards, before the Government itself decided to ban all racing on 19 June. Yet the BBC had prepared itself and had at hand 'a recording of a commentary on an old Derby if the 1940 could not be broadcast live'.[6] The use of English words in German *lieder* was recommended—how many German *lieder* were broadcast in May 1940?—while at the same time the popular song 'We're gonna hang out the washing on the Siegfried Line' was deliberately dropped.[7] 'Better records' were to be used for the national

[1] *BBC Memorandum by A. P. Ryan, 'Broadcasting and the Returning B.E.F.', 31 May 1940. The Ministry was willing to co-operate. (Note of a telephone conversation, 1 June 1940.)   [2] *Ibid.
[3] It was never broadcast. (*Home Board, *Minutes*, 5 July 1940.)
[4] *Home Board, *Minutes*, 14 June 1940.
[5] *Ibid., 17 May 1940.   [6] *Ibid., 7 June 1940.
[7] *Ibid., 31 May, 14 June 1940.

anthems programme.[1] A weekly *Scottish Half Hour*, along with a fortnightly talk by a Scotsman, was expected to appeal to listeners over the border, and the Welsh Eisteddfod was to be rescued when it seemed that it might collapse.[2]

Religion figured prominently in all general discussions about broadcasting policy. 'Possibility of the King's message closing on a religious note' was examined at a meeting on 17 May,[3] although two weeks later it was decided that the scripts of all 'religious talks with political implications' were to be seen by Ryan and his deputy.[4] A speaker in *Lift Up Your Hearts* was said to have 'a voice out of keeping with the title of the programme'.[5] 'Consideration has to be given to the part that religion can play in the crisis,' it was noted later, 'and extra services of an intercessional kind may sometimes be appropriate.'[6]

The attack on 'frivolous' broadcasting, an attack which had its adherents in Parliament,[7] was pushed hard by Nicolls, and in a note on 'Programme Changes' sent out to all 'output departments' on 4 June, he began ominously with the words, 'Although now that Dunkirk has proved a moral victory, the immediate application of the policy is not so important, you may like to have a note of it for guidance on similar occasions in the future'. The policy was simple. 'The Corporation recognises the fact that a grave situation like the present should have some bearing on the day-to-day content of programmes. On the whole the effect should be towards a reduction in the trivial and the frivolous.' While 'recreational programmes' were doubtless necessary 'at a time when people are living under considerable stress and many of them working long hours', nevertheless both wavelengths, Home and Forces, should never be devoted simultaneously to 'frivolity'. Special care should always be taken to keep apart 'grave news' and 'light entertainment', if need be by the thirty-second silent interludes, and, if changes of programme had to be made at the last

---

[1] *Ibid., 21 June 1940.
[2] *Ibid., 26 July 1940; *BBC Handbook, 1941,* p. 16.
[3] *Home Board, *Minutes,* 17 May 1940.
[4] *Ibid., 31 May 1940.
[5] *Ibid.
[6] *Programme Directive by Nicolls, 4 June 1940.
[7] See below, pp. 577-9.

moment in the Home Service to avoid 'incongruities', an appropriate microphone announcement should be made on the following lines: 'Many of you may not be in the mood for *x* (which is available on the Forces Programme for those who want it) so instead we are . . . broadcasting *y*.' 'All this would show that the Corporation was alive to the feelings of the anxious listener as well as the listener who wants relaxation.' The main difficulty, of course, was that listeners would vary in their views about what constituted 'recreational programmes'. The range might extend, indeed, from a Beethoven symphony to a spelling bee—'with the smaller but more influential section of listeners despising the spelling bee and welcoming the symphony'.

The stilted language of this directive suggests that Nicolls did not find it easy to catch the so-called 'spirit of Dunkirk'. He fell back, however, as best he could, on traditional BBC policy. 'The Corporation must therefore effect a compromise which will give the maximum satisfaction and at the same time engender the least irritation.'[1] This policy obviously retained a core of common sense. Nicolls was not impressed by the fact that some Variety artists were claiming the special blessing of the Ministry of Information, saying that 'the Ministry likes their stuff'.[2] He knew too that the public could soon be put off by too much moralizing. 'Jack Warner did a turn about rumour on Sunday from the Hendon Rally and, as far as one can judge by wireless, he very nearly got the bird from the audience . . . Syd Walker's appeal the Sunday before last brought in only a few hundred pounds. This rather confirms our idea that he has been spoiling himself by his moral homilies.'[3] 'Any old rags, bottles or bones' was something more than a contribution to the salvage campaign, and there were limits to the use of Will Hay and Claude Hulbert as spokesmen of the campaign 'to stay put'. Variety artists should not be employed to advocate buying War Savings Certificates or carrying gas masks.[4]

At the same time, Nicolls and Maconachie were willing to

---

[1] *Programme Directive by Nicolls, 4 June 1940.
[2] *Nicolls to Wellington, 25 June 1940.
[3] *Nicolls to Stewart, 22 July 1940.
[4] *Nicolls to Wellington. 8 Aug. 1940.

admit within limits in June and July 1940 the need for indirect propaganda through 'incidental' references in programmes which were not primarily propagandist in character to such themes as the dangers of gossip and rumour and to the importance of 'extra production' and, until after the fall of France, to the strength of the British-French alliance.[1] Even Maconachie set to work in June on 'pithy wisecracks' which might serve as slogans, like 'Mouths Shut and Heads High: Long Tongues mean a Long War'.[2] Herbert Morrison's 'Go to it, and Keep at it' set the tone. It was wisely stressed, however, that the slogan 'Louder and Funnier' did not apply to what listeners should do with their wireless sets. 'Do not share your wireless with your neighbour.'[3]

With large numbers of shift workers sleeping through the daytime, this slogan, like so many of the rest, was a canon of a new civic morality. 'Put away your tin opener', for example, could be deduced from the gospel of 'digging for victory', which the Minister of Agriculture proclaimed at the Guildhall on 10 September[4] and which C. H. Middleton propagated every Sunday afternoon in his gardening talks. Yet something more was involved than civic morality: most of the slogans, not least those relating to agriculture, had powerful economic imperatives behind them, while they needed more than skilful public relations campaigns to put them across effectively by radio. A man like Middleton, who had established his reputa-tion as a broadcaster before the war, was an artist in his own right—easy in manner, on occasion acid in humour, always

[1] *Programme Directive by Nicolls, 7 June 1940. Nicolls insisted, however, that any propaganda admitted into such programmes had to take 'its place on merit as entertainment'.

[2] *There had been a long argument about whether the BBC should use slogans. The Ministry wanted broadcasting to be more vigorous and direct. 'Isn't it a little too polite and unpurposeful?' Wellington asked (letter to Ogilvie, 22 June 1940). 'Can we have its points made again and again in all sorts of ways for all sorts of audiences?' When Stewart complained on 20 July that the BBC was 'ignoring' instructions to broadcast slogans, de Lotbinière replied that 'the Ministry were not entitled to expect the BBC to follow this proposal as an instruction' (Memorandum to Nicolls, 20 July 1940).

[3] For the 'radio blare', see the *Manchester Guardian*, 19 June 1940, *The Star*, 6 July 1940, and the *Evening News*, 8 July 1940, with a story of a woman rushing to her next-door neighbour's with a dog whip to turn off a wireless.

[4] *John Green to Maconachie, 5 Sept. 1940, reported on this, also on a projected programme 'Rats on the Farm'. German broadcasters to the USA made fun of the *Kitchen Front* programmes (BBC *Analysis of Foreign Broadcasts*, 10 Dec. 1940).

capable of improvising, always conscious of his vast, if strictly limited, authority. Under Lord Hudson, Churchill's Minister of Agriculture, an Advisory Broadcasting Committee thrashed out every issue relating to war-time farming. John Green in the BBC Talks Department was himself a farming expert, something indeed of 'an agricultural philosopher',[1] and the Committee also included Alan Thompson, an expert on poultry, Anthony Hurd, a farmer in Whitehall, and for a time Donald McCullough, Public Relations Officer to the Ministry, who later became the star Question Master of the *Brains Trust*.

Industry was as obvious a target for the broadcasters in 1940 as agriculture, and every kind of topic and approach was discussed: straight talks were not the only or the main answer in seeking to achieve increased production. Whatever Lord Halifax might think of the irrelevance of home entertainment in the strategy of broadcasting, Lord Beaverbrook, the thrustful Minister of Aircraft Production, and Ernest Bevin, the Minister of Labour, had no doubts. *Music While You Work*, first broadcast on 23 June 1940 as a help to lessen strain, relieve monotony, and thereby increase efficiency,[2] took its place in the established war-time repertoire with full official approval, while Nicolls's policy of 'soft pedalling sport' to help increase production was turned on its head.[3] Control Board agreed in late July that there was no objection to the broadcasting of a cricket match or of boxing contests,[4] and Nicolls himself urged that 'the requirements of Overseas expansion should not be met at the expense of Home requirements'.[5]

As the summer went by, the Ministry itself relaxed some of its suspicions about too much entertainment. In language which was not so much stilted as elephantine, it suggested on 12 August that 'communal music and merry making' had their place in war time, a grim phrase which raised a few eyebrows in the BBC: 'it has to my ribald and irreverent mind,' wrote Ryan, 'an air of Morris Dances by the Whitehall Mummers

---

[1] A. Hurd, *A Farmer in Whitehall* (1951), p. 50. See ch. VII of this book on 'Press and Radio' for a general account of this side of the Ministry's work.

[2] *BBC Handbook, 1941*, p. 22. There is a brief history of the programme in the *BBC Handbook, 1945*, p. 60.

[3] *Programme Directive by Nicolls, 7 June 1940.

[4] *Control Board, *Minutes*, 17, 24 July 1940.

[5] *Home Board, *Minutes*, 30 Aug. 1940.

about it which is not the stuff to give the troops'.[1] Wellington replied that he felt the same about the phrase, but all that it meant was that it would be 'a good thing if some responsible ministers, preferably the Prime Minister, let it be known that the inhabitants of this country will not be doing wrong if they enjoy themselves and take advantage of whatever entertainments are offered. That, I hope, is where the BBC comes in with immense vigour and success.'[2] The Ministry, which had hitherto been at pains to emphasize that it was not a Ministry of Entertainment, was having to face up for the first time to the facts of protracted war, a war with full civilian participation and with the battle front in Britain itself.

How near the actual battle front had got to Britain was revealed in a controversial broadcast on 14 July by Charles Gardner, who witnessed and vividly reported on an air battle off Dover. 'It was quite dreadful,' one letter-writer complained. 'To broadcast a battle in which human lives are at stake is likening grim reality to that of a Derby scene.' Another listener, Major-General Guy Dawnay, described it in a letter to *The Times* as 'revolting to all decent citizens'.[3] Yet other newspapers defended 'inspiring reporting', the *Daily Mail* calling it 'grand' and the *Manchester Guardian* 'brilliantly exciting'.[4] Gaumont British Movietone secured film rights, and the Americans asked for a recording. Finally Ogilvie said that whatever the opposition, he had 'no intention of being browbeaten into a retreat to the safe regions of the colourless', and the BBC's Home Board, aware that the broadcast had been approved by the Ministry of Information before it was transmitted, commended it guardedly, 'subject to reservations on phraseology and technique'.[5] When Listener Research was asked to tabulate audience reactions, these were said to be strongly favourable.[6]

[1] *Ryan to Wellington, 15 Aug. 1940.

[2] *Wellington to Ryan, 22 Aug. 1940.

[3] *The Times*, 19 July 1940.

[4] *Daily Mail*, 16 July 1940; *Manchester Guardian*, 17 July 1940.

[5] *BBC Home Board, *Minutes*, 19 July 1940. Ryan told the Policy Committee of the Ministry of Information at its meeting on 30 July 1940 that 'the BBC thought the experiment well justified, and they would be ready to continue this kind of feature subject to very careful scrutiny'. Reactions to the broadcast were analysed in 'Postscript to Charles Gardner's Air Commentary, 12 Aug. 1940'.

[6] *BBC Home Board, *Minutes*, 26 July 1940.

Listener Research was thought to be particularly valuable at this time when indeed, there had, been a marked drop in listening figures at certain times of day[1] and when the public was making it clear that it wanted 'light and cheerful programmes'. When a random sample of over 2,000 listeners were asked 'When the news is grave, do you think the BBC should cut down Variety programmes?', 61 per cent said no and only 21 per cent yes. Further study revealed that the demand that Variety programmes should be reduced in number when the news was grave came mostly from those listeners who cared least for Variety at any time. The conclusion drawn—and it was perhaps a reassuring conclusion in the circumstances of the summer—was that 'a time of tension has the effect not of changing the normal tastes of the listening public, but of sharpening them'.[2]

2. Attack by Radio

WHILE Listener Research was examining the attitudes of the home audience, many analysts of opinion and of propaganda were soon pointing in the aftermath of the successful German *Blitzkrieg* to the successes of the German broadcasting machine and in particular to the skilful tactics employed in the defeat of France. The role of German radio propaganda to France during the period of *Sitzkrieg* was re-assessed in the light of the ultimate French collapse, and British procedures were often compared unfavourably with their German counterparts. 'British propaganda has had to counter [this] formidable onslaught on the European will to resist with inadequate technical means and, perhaps more important, with a propaganda policy which was not completely integrated either with

---

[1] *BBC Home Board, *Minutes*, 26 July 1940, when a decline of 5 per cent in the satisfaction curve came to be reported. The demand for entertainment was pointed to in Listener Research, *Weekly Report*, 24 July 1940.

[2] *Listener Research Bulletin, 9 May 1944. By the end of 1940, Home Board had decided that 'barometer and other evidence' should be a 'regular item on its agenda'. (*Home Board, *Minutes*, 13 Dec. 1940.)

the propaganda policy of our allies or with our own military strategy.'[1]

Five main reasons were given for the success of German propaganda, each of which seemed to have its relevance for British broadcasters and policy-makers. First, the situation in France had been specially favourable. 'The bacteria spread by German propaganda found in the French body politic favourable conditions in which to fester and corrupt the organisation in its vital parts.'[2] This state of affairs had existed since the political and social crises of the earlier 1930s, for there had been many signs in France of 'defeatism, incompetence and divided counsels at the head and an undermined morale among the rank-and-file'.[3] 'Countries,' it was argued somewhat superficially, 'seem to get the propaganda they deserve. . . . Against the Soviet Union, Hitler's Third Reich could find nothing effective to say and no one to say it; but against the static French Republic a single intelligent traitor who took his stand on the ramshackle ideology of the Third Reich could do damage.'[4] This argument, which has been repeated often since, had an element of hindsight about it. The fact that before the collapse a number of French correspondents to the BBC, including teachers, railway officials, workers and employers, had claimed that the influence of Stuttgart was 'negligible or even non-existent in their districts', was overlooked in assessments of this kind. So, too, was a BBC analyst's conclusion in early June 1940 that 'the invasion of French soil and the bombing of French cities appear to have put an end to any inclination to believe in German blandishments'.[5]

The second reason given for German propaganda successes was that they had one real radio 'star' in their propaganda to France, Ferdonnet, 'the traitor of Stuttgart', the journalist son of a Niort schoolteacher who was condemned to death in his absence by a French court.[6] 'Incomparably superior to

[1] *BBC Overseas Intelligence Department, *Monthly Intelligence Report, Europe*, 8 July 1940.   [2] *Ibid.

[3] *Ibid. For some of the current and subsequent explanations of the French crisis see S. M. Osgood (ed.), *The Fall of France, 1940, Causes and Responsibilities* (1965).

[4] E. Tangye Lean, *Voices in the Darkness* (1943), p. 105.

[5] *BBC Overseas Intelligence Department, *Monthly Intelligence Report, Europe*, 10 June 1940.

[6] He was condemned on 12 July 1940 and was duly executed on 4 Aug. 1945.

the English Lord Haw-Haw,' one British broadcaster said of him, 'his personality seems to have spread over the other talks and the news editing.'[1] 'Better informed than anyone else', he was also lively and interesting to listen to day-by-day.[2] Yet this judgement, again, must be qualified. If Ferdonnet was the chief voice, his influence was not paramount,[3] and he relied, above all, on a powerful organization composed largely of Germans who had lived in France, Belgium and Switzerland, and influenced by men like Otto Abetz, head of the German *Comité Français*, who later became Ambassador to Paris.[4] It was the strength of this organization which counted and the circumstances in which it operated, particularly in the static conditions on the Maginot Line, where it could appeal directly to French soldiers. All the German transmitters which broadcast in French had been deliberately grouped near the frontier where the French soldiers were massed, and so-called 'Front Radio' could be heard clearly by the weakest of receivers, including the home-made hyper-sensitive *Micro-soldat* radios which were extremely popular with French soldiers, as the drawing on page 224 from the magazine *Toute la Radio* shows.[5] The skill was unmistakable. Information, propaganda and direct appeals were adroitly interspersed with recorded songs by Tino Rossi and Lucienne Boyer, and ended with the words 'Bonne nuit, les gars. A bientôt'.[6]

The third reason given for the Germans' propaganda success was that they made the very most of the differences between Englishmen and Frenchmen and thereby split the Allies. France, the Stuttgart broadcasters had explained in

---

[1] Tangye Lean, op. cit., p. 104.

[2] His apparent omniscience may well have been exaggerated, as Haw-Haw's was to be (see below, p. 235). Yet it was emphasized by most writers at the time. See R. Dorgelès, *La Drôle de Guerre* (1957), p. 13; J. E. Whitton, 'War by Radio' in *Foreign Affairs*, April 1941.

[3] His main collaborator was Obrecht, 'Saint-Germain'.

[4] See O. Abetz, *Das offene Problem* (1951).

[5] The cheapest set capable of picking up English short-wave broadcasts cost £8. Among civilian listeners this implied, as a correspondent to the BBC from the south of France put it, 'that you have established wide contact with the well-to-do here and practically none with the less fortunate'. (*BBC Overseas Intelligence Department, *Monthly Intelligence Report, Europe*, 10 June 1940.)

[6] Dorgelès, op. cit., pp. 44–6. The most was made of information kept secret by the French, e.g. on visits of particular politicians to the Front; there were appeals to 'evacuate' and to 'save blood'.

every idiom and with every nuance, could only lose from its association with Britain. Lord Halifax, they had claimed, had become French Foreign Minister and the Quai d'Orsay had abdicated to 10 Downing Street:[1] meanwhile, they went on, every English soldier was a threat to the security of every

4. Eve of the Battle of France

French husband. 'Les Anglais donnent leurs machines, les Français leurs poitrines.' Every aspect of French anglophobia in 1940 can be traced back to the German broadcasts. Yet in this connection also it is important to note that the broadcasts said nothing which had not been said by Frenchmen themselves before 1939. An American analyst concluded in 1941, indeed, that 'pro-Nazi trends "made in France" were more important than the pro-Nazi trends imported from Germany', although the latter strengthened and supported the former, 'mingling with them and occasionally controlling them'.[2] In German

---

[1] See C. J. Rolo, *Radio goes to War* (1943), p. 68.

[2] *Dr. N. Muehlen, 'Observations on Nazi Propaganda and Public Opinion in France' sent to the BBC by John W. Wheeler-Bennett, 8 March 1941. There is a useful and balanced brief comment on propaganda themes in A. Horne, *To Lose a Battle* (1969), pp. 94–5.

broadcasts to France there was something for everyone, since pacifism, anti-semitism, anti-communism, anti-capitalism and anti-clericalism were exploited along with anti-British propaganda. The same technique of offering something for everyone could be traced in most German wireless propaganda, in relation, for example, to Norway, Holland and Belgium.[1]

The most also was made of rumours, even when conditions seemed quiet. Hore-Belisha's resignation as British War Minister in January 1940 had been forecast by Stuttgart one week before it was announced and made a great impression 'at the front'. The actual news of the resignation was broadcast by the Germans before it was broadcast by the British.[2] Such disparities had obvious effects on French opinion, not least among soldiers. French listeners to the BBC often stated openly that they compared BBC bulletins with those of Stuttgart.[3] The results of the comparison were not always reassuring. 'Stuttgart broadcasts,' a BBC Intelligence Report stated, 'succeeded precisely where the BBC failed to penetrate—namely with the workers and the soldiers.'[4]

The fourth reason given for German success was that as a result of the most careful study and research they had been able to follow up preparatory propaganda at precisely the right moment with a propaganda *Blitzkrieg* which coincided with their military offensive. Walter Schellenberg has described how radio broadcasts, ably directed by Dr. Adolf Raskin, then Director of Radio Saarbrücken, were deliberately designed at the critical moment to create the greatest possible fear and terror.[5] False news items were used to add to the chaos on the

---

[1] E. K. Bramsted, *Goebbels and National Socialist Propaganda* (1965), pp. 235 ff.

[2] The news of Hore-Belisha's resignation had been announced at 7 p.m. on 5 Jan. 1940, but the BBC was not allowed to broadcast it until the 6th. Deutschlandsender itself broadcast the news at 11 p.m. on the 5th. (*Clark to Nicolls, 8 Jan. 1940.) The Cabinet changes of 3 April 1940 were also broadcast by Deutschlandsender and by Hamburg before they were broadcast by the BBC. A stop on the broadcasting of the news was said to have been decided deliberately in the interests of the British Press. (*Nicolls to Ogilvie, 4 April 1940, reporting a conversation with a member of the Cabinet Office.) The same situation was to recur for the same reasons in June 1941.

[3] *BBC Overseas Intelligence Department, *Monthly Intelligence Report, Europe*, 21 March 1940.

[4] *Ibid., 8 July 1940.

[5] See E. Taylor, *The Strategy of Terror* (1940). At the same time the German Press was ordered 'to raise the fury against France and the detestation of her in
[*cont.*

roads, for example, and the most was made of every sign of the collapse of morale.[1] 'Fate has fulfilled itself,' French listeners were told by radio, for example, on 17 May. 'Panic reigns in Paris. Banks and savings banks are beleaguered by the public, while the Government's panic is shown in its hunt for hiding places in the provinces. At last it is understood in France to what degree the rulers have told lies to the nation. The French Army is streaming back in retreat while official quarters try to prove that such places as have not been named in the sober German communiqués are still in French hands. . . . If you have guns the rest follows.'[2] Throughout the brief campaign, comparisons were persistently made between the First and Second World Wars—'the German troops had achieved in a few weeks what could not be secured during the [entire] war of 1914–1918'[3]—and contrasts were also drawn between the decadence of French leadership and the brilliance of German leadership. There was relentless talk both of new and unknown weapons and of the ruthless and unflinching German will for victory.

Yet even the strength of this argument, which was much used at the time, must be considered critically. Throughout the hectic French campaign, Hitler never forgot that the ultimate outcome depended on Britain. During late May the German home radio devoted four times as much attention to Britain as to France, even when every tenth news item was a propaganda attack on the French.[4] Items about France on the German radio quickly gave way again to items about Britain after France fell; 'England,' in the words of Admiral Luetzow, 'which has been spared invasion since 1066, is now within reach of our guns, very near our planes and exposed to coastal warfare.'[5]

The fifth reason why German propaganda to France seemed

[1] See L. Hagen (ed.), *The Schellenberg Memoirs* (1956).
[2] Quoted in Tangye Lean, op. cit., p. 118.
[3] Press Directive, 14 June 1940, quoted ibid., p. 239.
[4] *BBC *Analysis of Foreign Broadcasts*, 21 May 1940.
[5] *Ibid., 2 July 1940. See also W. Shirer, *Berlin Diary* (1941), p. 375.

the German people to a peak'. (Secret Press Directive, 30 May 1940, quoted in Bramsted, op. cit., p. 238.) On 1 June the directive referred to France's 'sadistic and negroid methods', but greater restraint prevailed as victory drew near.

so successful in 1940 had direct relevance to the position of the BBC. Official French responses to German propaganda both during the preparatory phases and the *Blitzkrieg* had been either at best inadequate or at worst ill conceived. 'It is doubtful,' a BBC analyst wrote, 'whether the problems of the Home Front were ever faced.'[1] The French radio had never established a reputation for veracity;[2] it had followed the French poster campaign in making the most of what was to be the silliest of all phoney war-time slogans: 'We shall win because we are stronger.' When the crisis came, it alternated between wild exaggeration and deliberate evasion. 'Rien sur le bombardement de Havre; rien sur l'Espagne et l'Italie, rien sur l'évacuation probable de la colonie anglaise de Paris' were the characteristic censorship directives of 20 May.[3] At the same time, the desperate efforts which had been made to jam those German stations which were broadcasting in French were futile and generated increased animosity as the German armies advanced.[4] Before Paris was handed over to the Germans—appropriately enough by radio—and before Radio Stuttgart gloatingly broadcast a list of French radio employees who had been singled out for punishment as 'enemies of the Reich',[5] the French radio, itself in a state of near collapse, had begun to ignore news from Britain. The French public first heard the Armistice terms from the BBC, and there were very few references to the British offer of union which Churchill made on 16 June.[6] The last letters received by the BBC from France on the eve of the collapse reflected the new mood. Several listeners complained of the dangerous British habit of giving out too much news, a habit which had hitherto been warmly appreciated. Others violently attacked French politicians, and one, at least, betrayed an outburst of anglophobia. Quite a number of Frenchmen disapproved strongly of the talk by Jean Masson,

[1] *BBC Overseas Intelligence Department, *Monthly Intelligence Report, Europe*, 8 July 1940.

[2] See above, p. 173.

[3] A. Werth, *The Last Days of Paris* (1940), p. 62.

[4] There were reports of French soldiers listening to Brussels and even Rome for 'reliable news' when Stuttgart was jammed. (*BBC Overseas Intelligence Department, *Monthly Intelligence Report, Europe*, 14 May 1940.)

[5] Rolo, op. cit., p. 70.

[6] *BBC Overseas Intelligence Department, *Monthly Intelligence Report, Europe*, 8 July 1940.

the French radio representative in London, on the Miracle of
Dunkirk.[1]

The new French Government, headed by Marshal Pétain,
which came into power on 16 June, shared, for the most part,
most of these attitudes. Pétain, indeed, had been pessimistic
for weeks about the outcome of the battles and was convinced
not only that French defeat was inevitable but that the British
would be defeated also within a very short space of time.
Dominated by profound anglophobia, he faced the difficult
task of accommodating France in Hitler's Europe.[2]

Within this context, the German attack on France by radio
was reviewed almost in the form of a running commentary
during the summer of 1940. What was sometimes overlooked,
however, was the power of the military offensive itself. Given
the speed of the German advance, French propagandists,
however effective their techniques might have been, could have
done little, and German propagandists, subtle or crude, were
placed in an extremely powerful position to apply text-book
guidance. It is significant that in Holland, where Dutch radio
greeted the invasion firmly, issued messages clearly and
responsibly and countered German propaganda immediately,
there was no respite. The power situation was what counted.[3]
The conditions of defeat, however, influenced the subsequent
pattern and style of 'resistance'. France's 'strange' defeat left a
legacy of division and confusion. Holland's defeat, with no
element of 'strangeness' in it, left no obstacles to the ultimate
reassertion of national solidarity. All this, of course, was in the
unknown future.

For the British, two direct questions were posed at once.
First, was Britain's vulnerability in relation to German propaganda as great as that of France? It is in the light of this
question that the work of the Ministry of Information's Home
Morale Emergency Committee should be assessed. Second,
could British overseas propaganda be developed and extended
in a Europe large parts of which were now under direct enemy

---

[1] *Ibid. See below, p. 241.

[2] For his attitudes in June 1940, see H. Michel, *Vichy, Année 40* (1966), pp. 29 ff.

[3] There is a good account of Dutch reactions in 'D. Van der Heide', *My Sister and I* (1941). For the German side, see P. Leverkuehn, *German Military Intelligence* (1954).

control? 'Broadcasting,' it was recognized, 'is now our only means of addressing a great part of Europe and our only means of rapid and effective communication with most of the rest.'[1] Both questions had to be answered urgently. Britain itself seemed to face imminent attack, while in Europe it was felt that the whole of the BBC's European audience 'could easily be lost in a few weeks from now and the field left clear for German propaganda, whose efficiency will no longer be denied now that it has played so great a part in destroying France'.[2]

Some of the implications of the first question have already been examined. The replacement by Churchill of Chamberlain was in complete contrast to the replacement by Pétain of Reynaud. The defeat in France received far less attention in Britain than the miracle of Dunkirk. There was, indeed, a curious sense of exhilaration in seeming to stand alone. Fortunately, the BBC caught the mood more successfully than the Ministry of Information. At the time of crisis for Britain, the Ministry of Information, in the eyes of most Englishmen, was not strictly necessary, at least in its swollen form, and there was a healthy public reaction that honest Englishmen did not need to be 'guided'. Morale was strong and 'Cooper's snoopers', agents of the Ministry who listened in to and surveyed public opinion, were bitterly attacked in July and August in what began with 'the murmur of the tom-toms' in Fleet Street and ended in 'a menacing roar' in Parliament.[3] 'Whatever may be wrong with the Ministry of Information,' Sir Archibald Southby exclaimed, 'this country has not got the jitters and is perfectly happy. . . . Leave the people alone. They are not apathetic. They are worried, as everybody must be worried, by reason of the war, but they are not jittery or worried in a way which makes it necessary for people to be going round to find out exactly what they are thinking.'[4] The hard fact recorded by Duff Cooper—that only 2 per cent of the people

---

[1] *BBC Overseas Intelligence Department, *Monthly Intelligence Report, Europe*, 8 July 1940.   [2] *Ibid.

[3] Duff Cooper had been asked in Parliament on 17 July 1940 what steps were being taken to examine 'the effects on the public mind of propaganda made over the radio by persons employed to do so by his Department', and said 'no' in reply to a further question whether there was any sign of the discounting of Government propaganda because it was propaganda. (*Hansard*, vol. 363, col. 202.)

[4] *Hansard*, vol. 363, col. 1515 (1 Aug. 1940).

visited by his survey teams had objected to answering what were for the most part useful questions—seemed far less important in 1940 than the conviction held by most people during the lull between the Battle of France and the Battle of Britain that morale needed neither to be measured nor prompted. Indeed, the BBC postponed a talk by Silvey on listener research to avoid any danger of associating listener research with the activities of the Ministry.[1]

'Haw-Haw' and his colleagues certainly had little opportunity in such circumstances, whatever their earlier appeal, and an interesting BBC report on 'the propaganda attack on Britain after the fall of France' which was prepared in November 1940 began with the words: 'This is the study of an attack that failed.' 'From the fall of France to the beginning of October 1940, the German propaganda experts tried every device they knew to cause the fall of Britain.' The attack had various phases. First, the experts attempted to divide the country by suggesting that a reasonable peace was possible and only Churchill stood in the way. 'By continuing the war and by concentrating the invincible forces of German attack against the British Isles he is finally preventing saner men and saner counsels from extricating Britain from her hopeless position.'[2] The moral was intended to be 'Face the facts and cut your losses'. Yet the 'German propaganda experts' were never able to make the most of this line of attack since Hitler himself blew hot and cold on the idea of a peace offensive. The British, indeed, took the wind out of his sails after his so-called peace speech of 19 July, which in the opinion of Electra House, was designed primarily to appeal to German opinion.[3] Without prior consultation between Electra House and the Foreign Office, an immediate reply to the speech was prepared for Sefton Delmer to deliver; and within an hour of Hitler finishing his own broadcast, London hurled back his offers at him in such terms that there is said to have been consternation in propaganda circles in Berlin.[4]

[1] *Home Board, *Minutes*, 2 Aug. 1940.
[2] *BBC *Analysis of Foreign Broadcasts*, 25 June 1940.
[3] The speech was associated with a broader campaign involving cultural propaganda. Goebbels opened the Munich Art Exhibition with a catalogue of German artistic achievements in peace time. Dr. Funk made a speech on economic and political aspects of a New Europe on 25 July.
[4] See Delmer, op. cit., vol. II, pp. 16–17.

Halifax also broadcast, in different language—'awfully pious' it sounded to an American reporter in Berlin[1]—on 22 July making it clear that Britain would not negotiate 'until freedom was secure'. As early as 20 July Goebbels 'had the local press . . . break the news gently that apparently the Britons aren't having any' and by the 23rd there was resort once more to the 'projection' technique of propaganda—'Churchill's answer— cowardly murdering a defenceless population'.[2] German propaganda seemed to be rebounding against itself even in Germany: 'like a drug too often given, it is losing what little force it had'.[3]

In Britain public opinion needed neither Delmer nor Halifax to offer guidance. As A. J. P. Taylor has aptly written, 'Hitler was treated at this time as a devil or a joke. Either interpretation ruled out any thought of doing business with him.'[4] Certainly Haw-Haw was temperamentally and politically incapable of developing convincing peace propaganda at what might have been a critical moment, and he was left off the air for a few days and replaced by more persuasive German speakers, like Dietze, until Halifax made it clear that Britain was not interested in any compromise.[5]

Thereafter, a second phase of the German propaganda attack began with promises that the end of England would come 'not within a few years but within a few days'. Deliberate attempts were made to create panic and confusion, timed to coincide with mass bombing and with threats of invasion. 'Any day now, any moment indeed, the invasion of this country may begin with all its horror, bloodshed and destruction.'[6] So sure were the Germans of this familiar line of attack that they could broadcast confidently from Stuttgart that 'the evolution of the situation in England is very much like that of France before she collapsed'.[7] Yet such propaganda obviously depended on the ability of the German *Wehrmacht* to deliver decisive blows and when these blows were not forthcoming, propaganda inevitably once again rebounded on itself.

[1] W. Shirer, *Berlin Diary* (1941), p. 360.
[2] Shirer, op. cit., pp. 359–60.   [3] Ibid., p. 359.
[4] A. J. P. Taylor, *English History 1914–45* (1965), p. 489.
[5] J. A. Cole, *Lord Haw-Haw and William Joyce* (1964), p. 164.
[6] *NBBS Broadcast, 25 June 1940.
[7] *Stuttgart Broadcast, 29 July 1940.

There was a third phase of attack also which overlapped with the second. To mask the possible failure of the second phase, which the experts had to do by September—they had never, of course, been faced with a similar situation in France— they pursued a long-term campaign designed to suggest that Britain was bound eventually to lose the war, first, because the whole of Europe had been organized by Germany against her and, second, because Britain's social structure, economic organization and political system belonged to an age that had passed. 'Today a well-ordered Continent, armed to the teeth and commanding inexhaustible resources, confronts that disturber of the peace sent to her doom by her plutocratic leaders.'[1] The German High Command, it was added—just when the German High Command was not at all sure about what it wished to do—'view the war not as an exciting blood-sport, but as scientific work to be carried out with deadly precision'.[2] Priestley's broadcasts were on several occasions used as ammunition in relation to this third line of attack. 'The distress of poor sections of the British population and the acuteness of class divisions is aptly illustrated by Priestley's radio speech. What Priestley has seen and exposed in Western England is nothing new. It is one of the symptoms of senility of a long out-dated and unnecessary system.'[3]

German propaganda was always angled to particular strata of the population as well as phased in terms of a time-table. Thus, while Bremen and Hamburg were careful not to exagger-ate, the 'black stations' allowed themselves the utmost freedom to bully, cajole, threaten and intimidate. Workers' Challenge— 'against hunger and war'—attacked without restraint 'Churchill,

[1] *Deutschlandsender Broadcast, 31 Aug. 1940.
[2] *Bremen Broadcast, 10 Aug. 1940.
[3] *Deutschlandsender Broadcast, 7 Oct. 1940. This was a reference to a Priestley broadcast of 6 Oct. 1940 (J. B. Priestley, *Postscripts* (1940), pp. 86–90, 94) in which he argued that 'now is the time for our leaders to use a little imagination, to light beacons in this gathering darkness, to warm our hearts and set fire to our minds by proclaiming noble and universal aims; by so ordering affairs in this country that we might serve as an example to the world, not merely in courage and endurance, but in bold and hopeful planning for the future, releasing in us great creative forces'. This was not Priestley at his best, and he went on to talk of 'private incomes or pensions and all kinds of snobbish nonsense'. In his next post-script on 13 Oct., much more impressive, he dwelt again on the fact that 'far below, among the decent common folk, the graces and courtesies of life still flourish'.

Bevin, Attlee and the whole filthy, lousy gang who have betrayed you and exploited you', adding, with complete lack of authentic conviction, 'Don't worry about the coppers: they carry their guns about, but they haven't dared to use them against the workers.'[1] Bevin, Minister of Labour in the new Cabinet, was a favourite target—'Sir Ernie Bevin . . . Just think of the bloody rat sitting in his office, drawing his dough and telling us that we ought to work 84 blinking hours a week.'[2] There is no evidence that these broadcasts had any effect. In the meantime, Christian Peace Movement, first heard on 15 August, was quietly urging 'every good Christian to join in an effort to make the Government stop the war while there is something worth living for. Women are the greatest sufferers. You have most to lose. It is possible for you to bring the war to an end.'[3] Radio Caledonia, which demanded a separate peace with Scotland, made little of specific appeals to Scottish nationalism, although appeals to Flemish and Breton nationalists had figured in German summer programmes to Belgium and France.[4]

The varied German propaganda assault failed, although the interesting question must be asked whether the assault might have appeared in a quite different light if the Germans had actually invaded Britain and had attached 'the radio piston to a complete war machine' as they had done in France.[5] In May 1940 the Ministry of Information was concerned about the 'mischievous' NBBS broadcasts, particularly when they dealt with parachutists and fifth columns, and both it and the War Office were interested in reports that certain small broadcasting relay stations were relaying Lord Haw-Haw. The odd incident on 13 May when the BBC had had to withdraw a call for RAF reservists three hours after it had been announced left lingering doubts.[6] The BBC had received the text from the Air Ministry by telephone and it subsequently emerged

[1] *Workers' Challenge Broadcast, 18 Sept. 1940.
[2] *Ibid., 13 July 1940.
[3] *Christian Peace Movement Broadcast, 23 Sept. 1940; 15 Aug., the date of the first broadcast, coincided with the German air offensive (see below, pp. 284 ff.).
[4] *Voix de la Bretagne* had been active during the last days of French resistance. See also L. Jäckel, *La France dans L'Europe d'Hitler* (1968), pp. 74–6.
[5] See A. Horne's verdict on France (op. cit., p. 516): 'it was time that was the vital element which—more than weapons, even perhaps more than morale—France most lacked in 1940.'   [6] See above, p. 205.

that the Air Ministry knew nothing about the matter. Whether the incident was the result of a muddle or of sinister fifth-column activities was never quite clear.[1] There was certainly some evidence of fifth-column hysteria. The Security Executive headed by Lord Swinton to safeguard Britain's security also noted that the Germans were obtaining some British reactions to NBBS broadcasts within forty-eight hours of their delivery, but decided not to give unnecessary publicity to broadcasts which were being listened to only by a tiny minority. The Germans themselves clearly believed that it was useful to play on British class divisions which were real enough in 1940, yet they knew little of their precise political implications. Neither the Fascists nor the Communists had more than minimal support in 1940.[2] The People's Convention, in which D. N. Pritt was a leading figure, was to attract only strictly limited support early in 1941,[3] and most sections of the British Labour movement were bitterly opposed to Nazism throughout the war.[4]

The Germans believed also that it was most important to make the most of religious differences inside Britain, and the secret instructions which would have been issued under the auspices of the Gestapo to German intelligence and security forces landing in Britain included a note—*pace* Evelyn Waugh—that the records of the Religious Division of the Ministry of Information 'shall be secured without fail'.[5] In this approach

[1] See L. de Jong, *The German Fifth Column in the Second World War* (1956), pp. 97, 213.

[2] On 14 July 1940 Radio Moscow broadcast that 'the authorities are curtailing the liberties of the workers, searches are taking place and a special severity is being shown as regards Communist literature', but there was a more 'discreet' or 'non-committal' tone in Russian broadcasts even during the following week (*BBC Analysis of Foreign Broadcasts*, 16, 23 July 1940). After Hitler and his government had proclaimed a 'New Europe', Moscow emphasized that the USSR was the 'one socialist country', 'the most powerful unit in the world' (ibid., 13 Aug. 1940).

[3] The People's Convention was called in London in January 1941 with strong Communist backing. It was supported by 500 signatories from different sections of the Labour movement and, after urging in vague terms 'a people's peace that gets rid of the causes of war', it switched to support of the war after Russia's entry into it. N. See D. Pritt, *From Right to Left* (1965), pp. 245–87.

[4] See H. J. Laski, *Where Do We Go from Here?* (1941). An Independent Labour Party motion for a negotiated peace was defeated by 341 votes to 4 in the House of Commons in December 1940, and 'not a dog barked' when Morrison banned the *Daily Worker* in 1941. (Taylor, op. cit., p. 503.)

[5] The instructions set out in *Informationsheft GP.* are described in P. Fleming's *Invasion 1940* (1957 edn.), pp. 177 ff., 193.

they exaggerated the significance of pacifism in Britain which had undoubtedly assisted them during the period of appeasement before 1939. It is doubtful whether there would have been any substantial 'grass roots' support for the Germans in 1940, yet the British authorities, deeply concerned about a possible 'fifth column' which would resort to treachery and sabotage,[1] continued to watch carefully all German 'black' broadcasts, particularly those of NBBS, for code instructions. For the most part they found them wanting, even though one NBBS code message did figure in the Wolkoff case.[2]

What is beyond doubt is that during the summer of 1940 Haw-Haw's broadcasts ceased to appeal to most Englishmen— he had turned from Britain's 'biggest joke' to a 'danger to the nation'[3]—even though there was a remarkable burst of rumours based on what he was purported to have said with uncanny accuracy in his broadcasts.[4] Stories that he knew whether public clocks were running slow or fast at Cambridge, East Ham or Wolverhampton and whether road works were in progress at Orpington or Portsmouth were associated with more sinister claims that he knew all about troop movements and air raids before they took place, or that he had said that he 'had not forgotten' Ipswich or Ilford. In several prosecutions for rumour-mongering his name figured in the case,[5] and for a time an Anti-Haw-Haw League was sponsored by the *Daily Mirror*.[6]

---

[1] See ibid., pp. 53 ff., for the activities of the Invasion Warning Sub-Committee, an offshoot of the Joint Intelligence Committee, set up 31 May, and for the combination of anxiety, credulity and a sense of duty which led to many 'a humble Dr. Watson' being promoted, 'by the self importance which comes to patriots in an hour of crisis', to the status of a Sherlock Holmes (p. 60).

[2] For this case, see ibid., pp. 126–7. See also Earl Jowitt, *Some Were Spies* (1954).

[3] Bill Grieg in the *Daily Mirror*, quoted in J. A. Cole, op. cit., pp. 154–5.

[4] One of the first and most absurd rumours was that he had announced that Hitler would be crowned King of England on 15 Aug.

[5] Cole, op. cit., pp. 156–7. The tendency to attribute detailed local knowledge to German broadcasters had been noted as early as 1 Nov. 1939, when a Press Conference was held at the Ministry of Information on the subject. (*Note by Tallents, 1 Nov. 1939.) 'We are dealing with a new form of war scare rumour. People are using this effective formula because (1) they simply want to retail an interesting story; or (2) they have deceived themselves into believing that they have heard something which they have not heard; or (3) they have misheard something heard indistinctly not from a German station; or (4) because they are deliberately fomenting a word of mouth campaign in enemy interests for the purpose of disturbing the population.'

[6] It was wound up on 26 July 1940, 'having done its job'.

Many correspondents wrote to the BBC about such rumours, which were carefully examined by the monitoring analysts, but most of them were quite unsubstantiated and showed how many people were temperamentally unable to prevent themselves from making up and passing on good stories.[1] Haw-Haw, quite out of touch with British opinion, knew far less even about German plans and intentions than he might have done, just as Ferdonnet had probably also known less. Although the NBBS talked of secret weapons, including rockets and unmanned guided missiles, new gases and death rays, one-man tanks and even an atomic bomb, its organizers were not in the confidence of the German General Staff or of the Luftwaffe, and there is little evidence of close and detailed operational directions influencing the strident and frenzied German propaganda which increasingly alienated British listeners.[2] 'Cooper's Snoopers' reported, indeed, that during the summer of 1940 'his Lordship's audience had shrunk to a fraction of its former size'.[3] His emphasis on terror either angered or bored his audience.

The BBC Intelligence Report of November 1940 tried to draw the lesson from the welter of recent experience. 'The attack we have analysed was clearly a failure. The full reasons for that failure we shall not know until after the war. Some of the material collected suggests that the Germans relied on agents here whose support was, for various reasons, not forthcoming. [There is no evidence of this.] The fall of France caused many people who had enjoyed their winter Haw-Haw as a source of mirth or as a probe to thought to stop listening.' 'In the absence of defeat in battle, the German technique would probably fail against any country possessing a vigorous, healthy party system, and for three reasons. The range of

---

[1] E. S. Turner, op. cit., p. 111. *F. C. Mitchell of the London Press Agency wrote to Mark Abrams about one such rumour in the West Country on 14 Oct. 1940. After investigating the story, which had no foundation, Abrams replied on the 16th, 'I think the local police would be doing a very good job if they set about tracking this particular rumour to its source.' On 24 Dec. 1940 W. J. Howley wrote to Roy Macgregor that 'it is practically never possible to find someone who claims to have heard one of these broadcasts themselves. When exceptionally someone has been found, he has invariably been unable to produce a witness to corroborate him.'

[2] Cole, op. cit., p. 167.

[3] Rolo, op. cit., p. 61.

plausible misrepresentation is not unlike that with which a party member is familiar. Against plain lying, the party system will have provided protection or the political system could not have survived. A party system depends on the existence of a network of ideas and institutions in which the relationship between ideas and actions is continuously discussed and tested.'[1]

It is curious that so much weight was placed on the party system. Perhaps Ed Murrow got nearer to the truth. Recognizing that there was room for many opinions about the diplomatic, economic and military policy of the British government, he noted quietly before the great air blitz on London began how ordinary Londoners were made of stern stuff. 'They can take what is coming.'[2]

The BBC through its home broadcasting was to play an important part in the months of the Battle of Britain,[3] and although it was sometimes attacked in Parliament, it did not make the same mistakes as the French radio. Those M.P.s who believed that it should have been offering 'great music' rather than 'loose and debased' entertainment, that cinema organs were Hitler's secret weapon and that the public needed more and more rousing speeches,[4] were certainly far more out of touch with the public in 1940 than the enthusiastic team of producers inside the BBC. The policy actually followed—not, as we have seen, without question from inside the Corporation[5]—was designed to maintain a balance which one M.P. at least, George Muff, who represented Hull, rightly thought was sensible 'in these critical times'. 'When you switch on the wireless and you hear something that may be termed light, it certainly has a tendency, not exactly to exhilarate you, but it keeps what is wanted in these days, an even balance. Even *Garrison Theatre* had its good objects, it helped us to keep that balance. Let me confess that last night I was rather sorry that I was robbed of part of *Monday Night at Eight*.'[6]

[1] *Report on Propaganda Attack on Britain, 23 Nov. 1940.
[2] Broadcast of 18 Aug. 1940, quoted in E. Bliss (ed.), *In Search of Light. The Broadcasts of Edward R. Murrow* (1968), p. 29.
[3] See below, pp. 284 ff.
[4] See, for example, the speeches by Henry Strauss (*Hansard*, vol. 361, col. 465) and Sir Stanley Reed (ibid., col. 479).
[5] See above, pp. 109-10.
[6] *Hansard*, vol. 361, col. 495.

On the overseas front quite different tactics were necessary. There was still a serious shortage of transmitters, and as the Germans moved through Western Europe they added immensely to their strength. At the same time French overseas broadcasting to Poland, Czechoslovakia and other occupied countries ceased. There was also an acute shortage of people both to translate and to broadcast. Finally, although there had been changes in organization—Tallents had left his post as Controller (Public Relations) in March 1940 to become Controller (Overseas) and the former post was abolished— there was still need for far more substantial and far-reaching changes of structure and procedure. At first improvisation was necessary, and it was achieved, sometimes brilliantly. Later, however, there was to be a complete reorganization of British broadcasting to France and a new plan for broadcasting to Europe.[1]

One cardinal difference between British and French broadcasting policies was still emphasized. There was to be no jamming of Germany, however serious the situation.[2] Any jamming, it was held, would lead to reprisals, would stifle Britain's voice and would benefit the enemy more than Britain because Germany controlled more transmitters.[3] Sir Noel Ashbridge kept his nerve—and his common sense—when other schemes were suggested, for example, for interpolating propaganda of British origin on Hamburg, Bremen or other German wavelengths when they were closed down as a result of RAF bombing activity: so too did Duff Cooper. 'The main point is that this is a game which can be countered,' Ogilvie insisted. 'Whoever starts it invites reprisals.'[4] 'The suggestion that we should transmit in German on German wavelengths at a moment when German transmitters are off the air,' Duff Cooper wrote, 'has been many times before us. It has been seriously considered and examined from every point of view.

---

[1] See below, pp. 239 ff.

[2] *Even a paper of 28 May which foresaw the remote possibility of requisitioning radio sets if Britain was invaded—'a complete reversal of existing policy [which] would strike the public as a counsel of despair'—dismissed the policy of jamming, which, it pointed out, would give just as good direction-finding assistance to the enemy as intelligible broadcast programmes.

[3] *Paper of 28 May 1940 (for meeting of 30 May).

[4] *Ogilvie to Ralph Assheton, 30 July 1940.

The advice of the BBC has always been against any such operation. Germany can retaliate. It would be for those concerned with home morale to consider whether the possibility of retaliation by German transmitters transmitting in English on BBC home programme wavelengths is a factor of importance or not. . . . The risk and sacrifice must be weighed against the value of the propaganda which it is possible to put into Germany by this means. Propaganda by this means at a critical moment, it may be considered, would be of the greatest value; propaganda bearing no message beyond that which present policy and events allow might well not be considered worth the risk or sacrifice.'[1]

3. Britain and France

WHATEVER the case for or against intensive propaganda to Germany in June and July 1940, there was obviously need for urgent action in relation to France which passed quickly from friendship and alliance to non-belligerence and tacit hostility. It was from the BBC that the French first heard the news of the terms of the French Armistice. A few days earlier the Queen had broadcast in French to French women and de Gaulle had made his first—and, in retrospect, famous— broadcast to the French people one day after he had arrived post haste from Bordeaux.

During the months of *Sitzkrieg* followed by *Blitzkrieg* the BBC had built up a scattered audience in France, among whom there were certainly some French listeners who feared that contact between British and French Ministers of Information would inhibit the British from telling the whole truth.[2] The meeting of Duff Cooper and Frossard, the French Minister of Information, on 3 June was designed not only to express 'solidarity'[3] but to secure greater 'editorial coordination' of

---

[1] *Note of 24 July 1940.   [2] See above, p. 173.

[3] *In the light of this discussion Nicolls issued a Directive on 7 June 1940 stating that 'Anglo-French unity must be a matter of assumption and not argument' and that the term 'British war effort' should give way to the term 'Allied war effort'.

French and British broadcasts to foreign countries.[1] Weygand, it was rumoured, had given orders that French war communiqués should not be too explicit, and there were signs in Britain that the Ministry of Information was concerned lest the War Office should prejudice Anglo-French relations by reporting too starkly on the course of events. Eden's broadcast as War Minister on 2 June was thought to be too frank, and pressure, not wholly successful, was brought upon the War Office by the Ministry to change it. Not surprisingly, one of the last letters the BBC received from France before the Armistice warned against 'hiding things . . . in order not to upset us and to prevent us from worrying'.[2] The efforts to shore up Anglo-French relations, including bilingual announcements of certain programmes, the insertion of French items in the Forces Programme, and further exchange of programmes, had an air of unreality about them even to the participants. 'We felt,' Duff Cooper wrote later, 'like a party of the condemned playing at cards while awaiting the summons to the scaffold.'[3]

The most important aspect of the meetings was not the effort to watch 'French susceptibilities' with solicitude, but the plans to increase the number of BBC news bulletins in French, to lengthen the 8.15 news period, and to pay more attention to the needs of the French Colonial Empire.[4] Although by 10 June the scheme for more Anglo-French programmes was in abeyance, a daily fifteen-minute programme, *Ici la France*, inaugurated by Corbin, the French Ambassador, on 19 June, less than a week after the decision to launch it had been taken,

[1] *BBC Overseas Board, *Minutes*, 6 June 1940. An elaborate plan was drawn up for a Technical Commission in Paris with technicians and a language specialist from both countries and broadcasts from Paris and London prepared on a relay system. (*Note of 6 June.) 'The two Ministers also considered the possibility of a daily Anglo-French broadcast from London and from Paris by the Paris Radio.'
[2] *BBC Overseas Intelligence Department, *Monthly Intelligence Report, Europe*, 8 July 1940. All such correspondents were sent leaflets giving full details of the BBC's French Service. Another last-minute complaint was from a French woman listener who objected to 'ridiculous clownery' in a BBC Variety programme just before a serious news bulletin in French.
[3] Duff Cooper, *Old Men Forget* (1953), p. 281; *Home Board, *Minutes*, 14 June 1940.
[4] *BBC Overseas Board, *Minutes*, 13 June, 20 June 1940. At the meeting of 27 June Wellington expressed the Ministry of Information's appreciation of the development of the experimental French Service.

provided a link between the pre-Armistice and the post-Armistice period. It was a programme more or less freely in the hands of the French themselves, but it had its French critics. 'Do you think it is the slightest consolation to us to be told that Hitler will never penetrate "the secret gardens of France"?' one Frenchman wrote to the BBC. 'Hitler doesn't give a damn for all this. Since you talk so much about "eternal France" in an effort to make us forget the shame and misery of a "temporary" France, let us be reminded of the days when the spirit of France was able to retain its greatness even in the darkest hours.'[1]

Masson, the official representative of the French radio in London, gave many broadcasts in May and June, not only on big events, notably Dunkirk,[2] but on such topics as war production and the new British emergency powers.[3] After line communication with France came to an end during the German advance, it was he who suggested the daily programme which became *Ici la France*. He continued to supply material for this programme, the length of which had been increased from fifteen to thirty minutes, even after he had been recalled to France—for political reasons—immediately after de Gaulle's broadcast of 18 June and was awaiting transport to take him back.

The first de Gaulle speech was a landmark mainly in retrospect. On 17 June, Pétain had made his first broadcast to the French nation, announcing his taking over of political power, and his intention to sue for the end of hostilities.[4]

---

[1] *BBC Overseas Intelligence Department, *Monthly Intelligence Report, Europe*, 8 July 1940.

[2] See above, pp. 227–8.

[3] *Letter from Tallents to Ryan, 31 May 1940; MoI Policy Committee, *Minutes*, 10 June 1940.

[4] 'Je fais à la France le don de ma personne pour atténuer son malheur,' Pétain explained. Edward Ward described, as a BBC correspondent, French reactions to this broadcast in a talk given on 21 June 1940. 'The effect of his words was terrible. A Frenchman lunching at the next table broke down and covered his face in his hands.' Tangye Lean wrote also (*Voices in the Darkness*, p. 139) of how a French listener commented that 'we listened to the cold, quivering tones of a tired old man'. This, however, was not the general reaction. See Michel, op. cit., for a very full account of Pétain's attitudes and influence. 'L'autorité du maréchal Pétain fut acceptée par tous, plus qu'avec résignation, avec soulagement et espoir' (p. 414). 'A l'été de 1940 la France était tout entière pétainiste' (p. 415). British attitudes were irrelevant, and the British Commander in France, General Alan Brooke, did not learn of the broadcast until after it had been delivered. (See R. Mengin, *No Laurels for de Gaulle* (1967), pp. 58–9.)

It was in the light of this speech that the British War Cabinet, not without argument, decided just before eight o'clock on the evening of 18 June that General de Gaulle should be allowed to broadcast a talk.[1] The BBC was told simply that a French General—unnamed—would be arriving at the studio, and Elizabeth Barker and Leonard Miall, who escorted him for the first time to a BBC studio, were unaware, as most BBC officials were, of the full historical significance of the occasion.[2] De Gaulle appeared 'calm but tense'. Like Pétain, he emphasized the first person singular and talked of assuming a 'national task', the responsibility for keeping alive the spirit of France, but, in complete contrast to Pétain, he set the French situation in its world context and stated frankly that he had no doubts about the need to continue with the fight. 'The very factors that brought about our defeat may one day lead us to victory.' 'The France of French resistance should not, and would not be extinguished.' De Gaulle's talk, which was not recorded, was trailed in the 8.15 news bulletin and went on the air at 10 p.m.[3] How many listeners heard him is uncertain. What is certain is that they were a tiny fraction of Pétain's audience a day earlier.[4]

Although the first reaction from the French Minister of Foreign Affairs to de Gaulle's broadcast was relatively mild—Baudouin asked Corbin, the French Ambassador in London, to tell the British that it would be 'un geste inimical' to permit a French officer to broadcast appeals against its decisions[5]—Masson was immediately recalled by telegram to France, where later in the year he was for a time placed in charge of the direction of Vichy radio. In London there were conflicting currents of opinion, not least among Frenchmen,[6] both about

[1] E. L. Woodward, *British Foreign Policy in the Second World War* (1962), p. 75.

[2] Note by Elizabeth Barker: when de Gaulle's importance was recognized quite soon afterwards, Tallents rebuked Miss Barker for not wearing stockings.

[3] *J. B. Clark to A. E. Barker, 19 June 1940. See also *Jean Oberlé vous parle* (1945), pp. 28–30. De Gaulle in his *Memoirs* and Robert Mengin in his book give the time wrongly as 6 p.m. See also *Le Figaro littéraire*, 17–23 June 1965.

[4] Miss Reeves lived in France after the war for over twenty years before she met anyone who had actually heard this first broadcast (oral evidence). Letter from Miall who was there, 1 June 1967. De Gaulle had complained that his first broadcast was not recorded.

[5] Quoted in Michel, op. cit., p. 227. See also Woodward, op. cit., p. 75.

[6] See the highly individualistic account in Mengin, op. cit., and the French version of this book, from which it has been adapted as well as translated, *De Gaulle à Londres* (1965). See also A. Crawley, *De Gaulle* (1969), pp. 119–20.

General de Gaulle's role and his prospects. Yet de Gaulle broadcast again on the 19th—he had announced this without warning on the air the day before, technically a breach of censorship—and this time he was given a glass of sherry by Ogilvie. At almost the same time Émile Delavenay, the BBC's Assistant European Intelligence Director, was ordering the Monitoring Service to 'telephone a "flash" at any hour of the day or night of anything indicating that the French Government as such no longer exists'.[1] Bordeaux was not clearly audible at Wood Norton,[2] yet there were reports both of the jamming of the BBC and of announcements on the French radio of at least one BBC programme in French.

So long as Churchill and his colleagues believed that it was necessary to continue to communicate with Bordeaux, even if it was through 'the bars of the cage', and that the French Overseas Empire might continue to fight, great circumspection was shown in allowing de Gaulle to proceed further with his broadcasts. 'So long as we can hope to get any good out of the French Government,' Duff Cooper stated, 'we must not criticise it.' On a rather different plane, J. B. Clark warned that frequent repetitions of the same appeal by the General would not necessarily improve his position.[3] After the signing of the Armistice at Compiègne on 22 June, however, the position had clearly changed, and it was duly noted that Article 14 of the Armistice, never put into effect,[4] provided that the French radio should close down. De Gaulle broadcast, with the approval of the War Cabinet, again on the 22nd and 23rd, when he announced that he was forming a French National Committee,[5] on the 24th, on the 26th, on the 27th, and on the 28th, when he was able to state that the British Government

---

[1] *BBC *Monitoring Day Book*, 19 June 1940.

[2] *Ibid., 23 June 1940.

[3] *Clark to Barker and Tallents, 19 June 1940.

[4] E. Jäckel, *La France dans l'Europe de Hitler* (1968), pp. 104–6. See also A. R. Rahn's book *Ruheloses Leben* (1949). There was often confusion between his office and that of Abetz (see Jäckel, pp. 109–10, 149). On 29 Aug., the Vichy Government obtained permission to broadcast one programme service for the Occupied Zone, subject to German political and military censorship. (Michel, op. cit., p. 177).

[5] There were difficulties about the BBC's news bulletin on this subject on the 23rd. These led to talks at the Foreign Office, and there were further problems on the 24th. As late as the 26th the situation was still confused.

had recognized him as 'the leader of all free Frenchmen wherever they may be'.[1] From 18 July onwards five minutes were
allowed each day to the Free French for a broadcast immediately preceding *Ici la France* called at first *Liberté, Égalité,
Fraternité,* and later, with an eye on Vichy, *Honneur et Patrie.*[2]

These talks were subject to security censorship by the Ministry
of Information, but not to any political directive. 'As for us,'
de Gaulle wrote later, 'we determined to speak only on our
own account. . . . I never accepted any supervision, nor
even any foreign advice.'[3] The precedent for allowing this
measure of freedom was provided by the 'free time' allowed to
American broadcasters earlier in the war. It was emphasized,
however, in the Ministry of Information, where Raymond
Mortimer, a confirmed friend of France, did everything he
could to maintain and foster a spirit of co-operation, that, on
grounds of availability of time alone, while 'all possible facilities
should be given to the French . . . applications from other
refugee Governments should be treated with reserve'.[4] 'Full
authority has been given for doing all that can be done to
advance the aims of General de Gaulle,' Wellington wrote to
Tallents on 10 July.[5]

The subsequent broadcasts were sometimes made—on
grand occasions—by General de Gaulle himself, sometimes by
guest French speakers, including at a later stage of the war
recent arrivals from France. For the most part, however, they
were given by Maurice Schumann, a young second lieutenant
who had worked as a journalist in London, spoke impeccable
English and had made his way from St. Jean-de-Luz to
England: he was 'discovered' by Mortimer. De Gaulle chose
Schumann as his main radio spokesman, and on more than

[1] Woodward, op. cit., p. 77. De Gaulle broadcast again on 13 July, 23 July and
3 Aug.

[2] *Note by Tallents, 13 July 1940. Memorandum by A. E. Barker, 17 July 1940.
De Gaulle would have preferred three periods of fifteen minutes a week. (Overseas
Board, *Minutes*, 11 July 1940.)

[3] C. de Gaulle, *Mémoires de guerre* (1954 edn.), vol. 1, p. 165. Liaison between
de Gaulle and the BBC during 1940 was *via* the European News Editor, Newsome,
for all questions relating to News and *via* the French Service Organizer—M.
Russell Page—for all programme questions. (*BBC Overseas Board, *Minutes*,
29 Aug. 1940.)

[4] *BBC Overseas Board, *Minutes*, 20 June 1940. 'Free time' was given to the
Dutch 'Radio Oranje', from 28 July onwards. See below, p. 267.

[5] *Wellington to Tallents, 10 July 1940.

Honour, common sense, the interests of the
country demand that all free Frenchmen should
continue the fight wherever they are and by whatever
means they can. It is therefore necessary
to group wherever this can be done the greatest
possible French force. Everything which can be
gathered together in military units and in
means to produce armaments should be organised
wherever there are any such.

I, General de Gaulle, undertake this national
task here, in England

I invite all Frenchmen of the land armies,
of the naval forces and of the air forces, I invite
the engineers and the specialist workmen of the
armament industry who may find themselves on
British territory or who can come there, to join
me for this purpose.

I ..
I invite the leaders, the soldiers, the sailors,
the airmen of the French forces, on land, on sea and
in the air wherever they may find themselves to get
into touch with me. I invite all French people
who wish to remain free to listen to me and to follow
me.

Long live France free in honour and in independence.

I shall speak again to-morrow on the London
Radio.

5. Extract from a contemporary English translation of a broadcast
by General de Gaulle on 22 June 1940

twelve hundred evenings Schumann spoke to France anonymously for five minutes. The initial announcement changed
as the war went on, from 'Voici le porte-parole des Français
libres' to 'Voici le porte-parole de la France libre' and
eventually 'Voici le porte-parole de la France combattante'.
'We will never forget,' Georges Duhamel, the novelist, wrote
after the war, 'the familiar voice of Maurice Schumann,
which if we come back in a thousand years will always remind
us of our sufferings and our hopes during the bitter years.'[1]

While de Gaulle was able through these developments to
make his name known in France—he was sentenced to death
in his absence by the Vichy Government early in August[2]—
the BBC expanded its French Service in quite a different
direction. Just before the collapse of France, when everything
was in the melting pot, a French listener made a suggestion
to the BBC which was to be exploited with great success.
'You should take a leaf out of Dr. Goebbels' book,' he wrote,
'and study the special needs of the French public in the matter
of presentation. You must now flood France with truthful
news in order to counteract German propaganda which will
have an even greater and more subversive effect now that the
French radio will be silent. To this end you must get together
in London a team of well-qualified Frenchmen for at least
twelve hours a day. . . . These broadcasts must be edited by
Frenchmen with a thorough knowledge of public opinion in
France. These French editors must also listen in to German
transmissions in French in order to be able to deny them.
Such broadcasts from London have a very vital part to play.
They must keep up French morale. They must inspire con-
fidence in our final victory.'[3]

The recruitment of a team of Frenchmen who were to
establish themselves as some of the most remarkable broadcasters of the war took place under great pressure in July and

---

[1] Quoted in J.-L. Crémieux-Brilhac, 'Les Emissions françaises à la BBC pendant
la guerre' in *Histoire de la deuxième guerre mondiale*, No. 1, 1950, p. 76. This extremely
useful article has a number of small but important errors in it. For the subsequent
history of these broadcasts, see below, pp. 448 ff. See also M. Schumann, *Honneur
et Patrie* (1945).

[2] *BBC Monitoring Day Book*, 2 Aug. 1940.

[3] *BBC Overseas Intelligence Department, *Monthly Intelligence Report, Europe*,
8 July 1940.

August 1940: Miss Reeves and Darsie Gillie, who had recently returned from France and had been appointed to the French desk of the European News Service, played an important part in selecting them. Gillie himself, a man of great intelligence and of strong feelings, was to be one of the key figures in the making of the BBC's policy towards France, a policy which did not always follow lines which were fully approved of by the Foreign Office. Likewise, the members of the French 'team' certainly did not always follow lines which were fully approved of by de Gaulle. The French Service not only had a spirit of sturdy independence but a distinctive epigrammatic humour. 'The very soul of French wit has fled to London,' a Frenchman remarked later in the war.[1] It was through the individual and complementary qualities of the members of the 'team' and the imagination with which the team was deployed that the BBC's French programmes were transformed. As a result the German radio, which had played its part in the defeat in France, 'lost as spectacularly as it had previously won'.[2] The outward symbol of defeat was to be the dynamiting of the long-wave transmitter of Radio Paris close to the demarcation line between Occupied and Unoccupied France in May 1942. The real defeat came much earlier, however, during the summer and autumn of 1940 itself.

Two of the first French broadcasters who later joined the permanent team were young journalists, Pierre Maillaud, then working for Havas,[3] and Yves Morvan. Maillaud, who was to broadcast under the name of Pierre Bourdan, was recommended to the BBC by the Ministry of Information and was taught to use the microphone by Miss Reeves, who consulted Ed Murrow before teaching him. He arrived while Masson was still at Broadcasting House and the French Government was still at Bordeaux, and he was so bitterly opposed to the actions taken by Pétain's Government that he was involved in a fracas with Masson and challenged him to a duel. His attacks on Pétain were so direct that they met with criticism from Frenchmen in London and for a time, excellent

[1] Quoted in Tangye Lean, op. cit., p. 161.
[2] Ibid., p. 142.
[3] When Havas ceased to operate, he started the Agence France Presse which functioned throughout the war in London.

broadcaster though he was proving to be, his talks were dropped. Morvan, who became far better known under his pseudonym, Jean Marin, was actually brought to the microphone by Masson, although he was a strong supporter of de Gaulle from the start. A Catholic *bourgeois* from Brittany, he had a quite different background and outlook from Maillaud, who was a radical from the Midi.[1]

Maillaud and Morvan were joined on 2 July by Michel Saint-Denis, the first Frenchman to be given a full-time post inside the BBC. He had served as a French Army Liaison Officer with the British Expeditionary Force in France and had been evacuated from Dunkirk *via* Weymouth. A nephew of Jacques Copeau, he had already established a brilliant reputation as a theatre producer and as Director of the *Compagnie des Quinze*. Very quickly, under the pseudonym of Jacques Duchesne, he became *animateur* of the French radio team. Approaching broadcasting as an artist rather than as a politician—in politics he was basically conservative—he applied to it the kind of genius which it so often lacks. The result was not only an effective programme for France in the hour of her greatest need but a feast of radio at its most original and best. Denis Johnston, the playwright, noted how Duchesne and his colleagues, who had started with virtually no experience of broadcasting, treated the 'mike like an old friend'.[2] 'With a message to give and enough theatrical experience to invent original ways of giving it,' Tangye Lean wrote during the war, 'half an hour's propaganda became more exciting in his hands than any other radio programme I had heard. Neither content nor means of presentation gave the listener a chance to switch off; themes were attacked from all angles, originally, wittily, musically, in dialogue.'[3]

The other members of the team, who were recruited for the most part in June and July 1940, were Pierre Lefèvre, another young actor and a pupil of Duchesne, Jean Oberlé, a painter whom he also knew—a brilliant *raconteur*, he was to become the *enfant terrible* of the group—Maurice van Moppès, a draughtsman and a friend of Oberlé, Jacques Brunius ('Borel'), a film

---

[1] Marin now heads Agence France Presse.
[2] Note from Miss Reeves.
[3] Tangye Lean, op. cit., p. 157.

scriptwriter and a socialist, and Edouard Merens, a musician. In the background, along with Gillie, was Russell Page, who was appointed French Service Organizer on 1 August and who believed as passionately as any Frenchman in the past and future of France.[1] The first genuinely new products of the French team were *Les Trois Amis*, a weekly discussion about current affairs between Duchesne, Bourdan and Oberlé, which began on 18 July, and *La Petite Académie*, a weekly forum on phrases and expressions of current interest, starring an imaginary President, Brunius, an archivist, Duchesne, a rapporteur, Oberlé, and a permanent secretary, van Moppès, accompanied by his dog Musso, Pierre Lefèvre. This programme began on 1 September. Both these items were to become staple fare in the half-hour programme *Les Français parlent aux Français*, the successor of *Ici la France*, which was first broadcast on 6 September—to the French Empire as well as metropolitan France.

As the years went by, this programme became more and more 'professional', although an air of spontaneity, rare in sound broadcasting at that time, remained to the last— 22 October 1944. News commentaries were blended with music, talks and slogans, many of them catching musical ditties which provided 'natural breaks' in which other items might be discussed by the listeners. Occasionally, as on 21 October 1940, when Churchill broadcast to France in French, or in late 1941, when the Germans were beginning to shoot innocent French hostages, there was a change of style and mood. In general, however, the programme was entertaining rather than 'heavy' and propagandist not in a crude but in a highly subtle and sophisticated manner. The first slogan employed was characteristic. 'J'aime mieux voir les Anglais chez eux que les Allemands chez nous.' The need to allow the maximum freedom to Duchesne and his team was fully recognized by Raymond Mortimer and by Oliver Harvey in the Ministry of Information. A sensible distinction was drawn by them between 'political direction' and 'broadcasting practice'.[2]

The Churchill broadcast has been vividly recalled by

[1] Somerset Maugham was considered for an important post but was reported 'not available'. (*Overseas Board, *Minutes*, 18, 25 July 1940.)

[2] *Note by J. B. Clark on French Liaison, 20 Nov. 1940.

Duchesne.[1] He lunched and dined frugally with the Prime Minister with the noise of German planes in the background and with Churchill talking passionately not only of Hitler but of Pétain—'always been a defeatist'. After being forced to adjourn to the air raid shelter, the task of translating Churchill's words into French began. 'I want to be understood as I am,' Churchill emphasized, 'not as you are, not even as the French language is. Don't make it sound too correct.' When the translation was completed, it was typed, like all Churchill's broadcasts of this period, like a poem in free verse,[2] with exceptionally large letters. The rehearsal was as illuminating to Duchesne as the translation. 'If I spoke perfect French,' Churchill remarked, 'they wouldn't like it very much.' And so the broadcast went on the air with its powerful opening, 'C'est moi, Churchill, qui vous parle'.[3]

Between the inauguration of the extended French Service and Churchill's broadcast there had already been several twists and turns in Anglo-French relations,[4] and the Vichy Government had resumed a range of broadcasting activities.[5] These were organized in competition with German-controlled stations in Paris and other towns in Occupied France which for their part continued to devote much of their effort to anti-Vichy radical and revolutionary propaganda.[6] The French Service in London might make the jibe

'Depuis Strasbourg jusqu'à Biarritz
La radio est aux mains des Fritz',

but there were marked differences of tone and style, if less of news, between Vichy and Radio Paris, the latter with its *Coq Gaulois* call sign and its programme *Les Français de France parlent aux Emigrés* as a rejoinder to *Les Français parlent aux*

[1] *BBC script, 'A Day with Churchill', 30 Nov. 1959. This talk was given on Churchill's 85th birthday.

[2] See above, p. 118.

[3] *Ogilvie congratulated Churchill on a broadcast which came through 'superbly' (Letter of 22 Oct. 1940).

[4] A. D. Hytier, *Two Years of French Foreign Policy, Vichy 1940–42* (1958).

[5] Rolo, *Radio Goes to War* (1943), pp. 73–4, describes how it later developed world propaganda, including appeals to French Canadian separatists and anti-United States broadcasts designed for South America.

[6] See an entry in General Halder's *Kriegstagebuch* (1962–4) for 1 Aug. 1940 in which he stated that the Vichy Government was very sensitive to attacks made upon it by the German-controlled Paris radio.

Français. There is little sign, however, that Radio Paris, for all its glitter, ever secured a hold on French listeners. Radio Vichy, dull though it might be immediately after the Armistice, was different. In the summer of 1940 there was widespread support for Pétain along with widespread suspicion of or distaste for Britain, and Vichy broadcasts, particularly Pétain's broadcasts, were listened to with genuine interest. Yet, by the winter, when the controllers of the Vichy radio had begun to show intelligence and skill in keeping down the volume of propaganda and increasing the number of hours devoted to broadcasts for youth,[1] there were the first real signs of dissatisfaction both with Pétain and his régime.

At first there was little general listening to the BBC in France. The Germans were on their best behaviour and conditions were reasonably relaxed. A refugee from France said that he never spoke with anyone who heard a BBC broadcast in France between June and September 1940.[2] By October and November, however, there were a few signs that the BBC was already beginning directly to influence French opinion. For many people, indeed, listening to British broadcasts was the first act of resistance.[3] The publication of pamphlets and broadcasts based on BBC broadcasts sometimes followed. 'At the beginning,' the French socialist, André Philip, wrote during the war about the origins of the French resistance, 'the BBC was everything. We needed help from outside, and the BBC gave that help.'[4]

Little distinction was drawn in France, then or later, between the News in French, the Free French programme managed directly by de Gaulle, and the general programme of the Duchesne team, and for all the political differences—some of them were more than nuances—between the different individuals concerned in broadcasting from London, they were all thought to be carrying a 'Gaullist' message. There were some Frenchmen at this time who believed also that there was

[1] For Vichy's 'doctrine of youth', see Michel, op. cit., pp. 127–9.

[2] Muehlen, op. cit. He added that while de Gaulle was mentioned occasionally by the official French Press, 'as long as I was in France, there was no talk about him'.

[3] Michel, op. cit., p. 416. See also his *Les Mouvements Clandestins en Europe* (1961), p. 13 and *Histoire de la Résistance 1940–1944* (1950), p. 61.

[4] Tangye Lean, op. cit., p. 149. See also H. Amoureux, *La vie des français sous l'occupation* (1961), p. 535.

little real difference between Pétain and de Gaulle. Despite the death sentence on the General, they both seemed to be patriots in tacit collusion with each other, the one waiting in France, the other preparing in England. 'We do not like to hear you speak slightingly of Marshal Pétain whom we respect and admire,' a correspondent wrote in September, regretting that de Gaulle was not in France to help him with the task of 'purification'.[1] Other Frenchmen were sceptical about everything. 'People listen to London,' wrote a correspondent in October 1940. 'They don't know who is telling the truth. They wait. They are building up their individual opinion. We have all been so duped by the papers and by wireless that we don't believe in anything completely any more.'[2]

As Britain showed that she was not going to be defeated quickly—Pétain had been sure of her imminent defeat—the BBC's programmes undoubtedly gained in importance. They gained still further when the Battle of Britain revealed that the British could take it. A letter received by Pierre Bourdan and posted in Paris on 29 September spoke of the continuing French hope to be delivered by 'our Allies'. 'If only you could see us listening to your broadcasts,' he went on, 'we only live for that.' The letter ended with the sentence: 'If this reaches you, how will I ever know?'[3] A month later another correspondent stressed that since the continued resistance of the English, 'the Germans are becoming more and more nervous and irritable'.[4]

Yet the official British attitude towards Pétain remained cautious throughout the year. After the attack on the French fleet at Mers-el-Kebir on 3 July had further alienated many Frenchmen and had led directly to the breaking-off of diplomatic relations between Britain and Vichy,[5] there were efforts to be conciliatory. The world had been shown that Britain remained firm in its resolution to fight,[6] and de Gaulle had to

[1] *BBC European Department, *Monthly Intelligence Report, Europe*, 30 Sept. 1940.
[2] Quoted ibid., Nov. 1940.
[3] Note by Miss Reeves.
[4] *BBC European Department, *Monthly Intelligence Report, Europe*, 28 Oct. 1940.
[5] Woodward, op. cit., pp. 92–3.
[6] There were many favourable American comments on this move (*BBC *Analysis of Foreign Broadcasts*, 9 July 1940) and Ciano in his *Diary* hailed it as a proof of British 'fighting spirit'. The event produced consternation among Frenchmen and among British Francophiles. (See Mengin, op. cit., pp. 93 ff: Michel, op. cit.,

face up to its more complex consequences. Maurice Schumann, indeed, made his BBC début on 3 July, before becoming de Gaulle's *porte-parole*, with the preparation of a talk on Mers-el-Kebir which was read for him by another speaker. While the British Government was anxious not to provoke open hostility in France, within the BBC itself Miss Reeves was advised by Ed Murrow around this time that unless the utmost care were taken not to attack the person of Pétain, however much his policies were attacked, there would be such a rupture with France that it would be difficult to make up for it for years ahead. Newsome shared this view, which was also enshrined in Ministry of Information directives on 17 July. 'We should continue to be polite to Pétain personally but may be derisive about the men of Vichy.'[1]

Great importance was placed on the value of straight news to France, free from the language of propaganda. At the same time, talks specifically addressed to French workers, an idea of Jack Sandford, formerly *Daily Herald* correspondent in Paris, William Pickles of the London School of Economics, and Henri Hauck, Labour attaché at the French Embassy,[2] were broadcast in dawn bulletins from August onwards. Attempts by the Free French to increase their amount of 'free time' were resisted.[3] Anxieties remained about anti-French feeling in Britain, which had concerned the Ministry of Information in May and which it had then believed could best be countered by arranging special talks and programmes, including a broadcast by Reynaud. Until the fall of France doubts about

---

[1] *Programme Directive No. 25 by Nicolls, 19 July 1940. The same directives included a warning 'to be careful not to show any partiality' as between Roosevelt and Wendell Willkie if Roosevelt was nominated as a Presidential candidate in the United States. At the end of 1940 (Woodward, op. cit., p. 91) information received by the Foreign Office suggested that the use of the term 'Vichy Government' in BBC talks was causing offence in Vichy, and it was decided to introduce the term 'Government of Marshal Pétain'.

[2] For the later ramifications of these talks, see below, p. 450.

[3] *Overseas Board, *Minutes*, 14 Nov. 1940. The report was from Commandant Massip, de Gaulle's representative, who dealt with Intelligence arrangements on what was thought to be a 'satisfactory basis'. (Overseas Board, *Minutes*, 22 Aug. 1940.)

---

p. 236.) The Germans in a week of extensive propaganda to France made the most of the end of the Franco-British alliance. Russian radio reported the event with anti-British undertones and made no comment on the political composition and stance of the Pétain Government.

the French Government's attitudes were to be ascribed to German propaganda.[1]

Subsequent attitudes towards Pétain registered, though not necessarily directly, the far from simple course of diplomatic relations between Vichy French, Germans, British and Free French.[2] Mers-el-Kebir had stimulated every kind of Anglophobia which Sir Ronald Campbell, the British Ambassador to France, had noted in leading political circles during the days before the Armistice.[3] The abortive Anglo-French attack on Dakar on 23 September, following on the rallying to the support of de Gaulle of several of the French African colonies, provided a powerful impetus to closer Franco-German collaboration,[4] and the meeting between Pétain and Hitler at Montoire on 24 October 1940, extremely limited though it was in its effects, proclaimed full collaboration as a deliberate political objective.[5] By contrast, the dismissal of Laval from the French Government on 13 December 1940, which followed although it was not motivated by renewed Anglo-French contacts earlier in the month,[6] seemed to show that there was still an entry into the cage. Pétain himself used the Vichy radio to announce Laval's dismissal before any consultation had taken place with the Germans.[7]

Collaboration as a policy could never command the support of all Frenchmen and even some of those who were tempted to give it a chance were quickly disillusioned about the lack of correspondence between idea and reality. BBC broadcasts began, therefore, to produce a definite listener response; and by the end of 1940 it could be claimed that 'listening to our broadcasts appears to be general all over France'.[8] In August 101 letters from France had been received, 24 from Occupied

---

[1] *Maconachie to Salmon and Luker, 12 July 1940. At a Policy Committee of the Ministry in May most speakers had argued that British action in relation to anti-French feeling depended on the success or reverse of the French in the military operations.   [2] Hytier, op. cit., and Woodward, op. cit., pp. 91 ff.

[3] See F. Charles-Roux's fascinating account *Cinq mois tragiques aux Affaires Étrangères* (1949); Woodward, op. cit., pp. 68 ff., 101.

[4] W. S. Churchill, *The Second World War*, vol. II (1954), pp. 419–37, and C. de Gaulle, *The Call to Honour* (1955), p. 119.

[5] Michel, op. cit., pp. 305 ff.; Jäckel, op. cit., ch. 7.

[6] Woodward, op. cit., pp. 95 ff.

[7] Jäckel, op. cit., p. 207. Foreign Office views of what was happening were influenced by Pétain's broadcasts, e.g., an important announcement of 30 Oct.

[8] *BBC European Department, *Monthly Intelligence Report, Europe*, 23 Dec. 1940.

(a) A U.S. Serviceman in the City of London, interviewed by Robin Duff, 1942

(b) A Chelsea Pensioner, interviewed by Wynford Vaughan Thomas, 1941

5. Battle of Britain Interviews

(a) 'News in Norwegian—don't want to listen to that, do we?' *Punch*, 7 April 1943

(b) 'I wonder how many of you spotted the mistake in yesterday's recipe?' *Punch*, 15 December 1943

(c) '. . . and in the beautiful second movement comes a passage in which the strings make a last appeal to us to use cold water for washing.' *Punch*, 12 August 1942

7. Home-Front Listening

(*a*) Ed Murrow
interviews a
British Seaman

(*b*) BBC Recording
Engineer on board
a Minesweeper

(*c*) Art Feldman
(NBC) with BBC
Recording Engineer
in a Flying
Fortress

8. Sounds of War

France; 82 were received in September, 23 from Occupied France (with only 35 of the 82 specifically addressed to the BBC and the rest intercepted by the Censorship); and 79 were quite specifically addressed to the BBC in October. While the French Empire seemed to be 'still dominated by a paralysing attitude of wait and see on the part of officials anxious to preserve their positions and colonists who do not visualise the present or future very clearly',[1] there were French listeners to *Les Français parlent aux Français*, which was said to enjoy 'general popularity', who, conscious of no nuances of political difference, wrote enthusiastically: 'May Joan of Arc and the Cross of Lorraine which adorns the flag of General de Gaulle sustain your courage and our own.'[2]

The Paris correspondent of *Ya* noted in October, the month of Montoire, 'a veritable pandemonium of British radios pouring news through balconies, windows and patios'.[3] There was no evidence at this stage of prosecutions for listening offences in the Occupied Zone, but it was significant that on 28 October Vichy imposed a ban on public listening to foreign, by which was meant British, broadcasts devoted to 'une propagande antinationale'. The penalty was six days' to six months' imprisonment, with fines varying from 16 to 1,000 francs, together with confiscation of the sets.[4] Private listening was obviously considerable and there were reports of local booms in the sale of short-wave sets, at Clermont-Ferrand, for example: at the same time, there was heavy jamming of the British broadcasts on the medium waves, and the BBC was forced to give 'microphone instructions' to its broadcasters in French. 'References to the *radiophonique* quality or otherwise of particular speakers' were 'growing more frequent',[5] with de Gaulle's voice 'continually referred to as more *radiophonique* than those

[1] *Ibid.

[2] *Letter from Montpellier, 14 Oct. 1940, quoted in BBC European Department, *Monthly Intelligence Report, Europe*, 23 Dec. 1940.

[3] Quoted in the *Daily Telegraph*, 30 Oct. 1940. Cf. *L'Action Française*, 10 Oct. 'The English radio is in full blast. At 8.15 p.m. it can be heard in certain streets, all windows open.' Maurras attacked the BBC's 'golden tongues' and 'radio impostors'. For De Gaulle's appeal see M. Baudot, *L'opinion publique sous l'occupation* (1960), p. 83.

[4] Michel, op. cit., p. 139. See also p. 150 for the underlying philosophy as represented by Pétain.

[5] *BBC European Department, *Monthly Intelligence Report, Europe*, Nov. 1940.

of the regular speakers'.[1] There were urgent requests for more broadcasts by de Gaulle, including one from the staff of a hairdressing establishment at Marseilles, and signs that the News was most popular with peasants and workers and *Les Français parlent aux Français* with 'the better educated listeners'. Song slogans caught on—for example, 'Radio Paris ment' and 'Un Armistice ce n'est qu'un Armistice'—and were being hummed in places as far apart as Brittany and the Alpes Maritimes.[2]

A writer in *The Times* attributed the recent transformation of spirit—before Montoire—to 'the native sanity of the French' rather than to the efficiency of British propaganda,[3] and German ineptitude played its part certainly as much as open counter-German propaganda.[4] Yet the volume of BBC evidence relating to French reactions to British broadcasts was so substantial in November that it was decided to issue special audience surveys of France a week in advance of the *Monthly Intelligence Report* on Europe as a whole.[5] Fortified by the first real British military success of the year—Wavell's capture of Sidi Barrani on 12 December—and proud of the fact that German bombs which destroyed their studio on 9 December did not interrupt their programmes,[6] the French *équipe* was in particularly cheerful spirits at the end of 1940. It was in the knowledge that France was responding to the London broadcasts that Maurice Schumann—on behalf of de Gaulle and with the approval of the Ministry of Information[7]—told his listeners across the Channel to stay in their homes for one hour

[1] A Swedish journalist reported from France on 16 Sept.: 'One can often hear General de Gaulle's voice through open windows in French houses and hundreds of thousands of French people already know his voice.' De Gaulle sent his first agent to France within a month of the Armistice (M. R. D. Foot, *SOE in France* (1966), p. 151).

[2] *Ya* quoted by Radio Méditerranée, 31 Oct. 1940. The Germans had reintroduced slogans into the Radio Paris programmes and Vichy was copying the style of *Les Français parlent aux Français*. (*BBC European Department, *Monthly Intelligence Report, Europe*, 28 Oct. 1940.) 'Vichy imitates. Paris parodies.' (Ibid., 21 Jan. 1941.)

[3] *The Times*, 18 Oct. 1940.　　　　　[4] Foot, op. cit., pp. 135–6.

[5] *BBC European Department, *Monthly Intelligence Report, Europe*, Nov. 1940.

[6] *BBC script for the Twenty-First Anniversary Programme of the French Service, 27 Sept. 1959.

[7] *Overseas Board, *Minutes*, 19 Dec. 1940. 'The decision to adopt the proposal would rest with the Ministry of Information, and it would be made clear that the idea was sponsored by the Free French movement.'

between two o'clock and three o'clock on New Year's Day 1941, the first attempt at an organized demonstration of resistance. Broadcasting from London, it seemed, was beginning to enter an operational stage.

4. Counterattack

THE reorganizing of British broadcasting to France during the summer and autumn of 1940 was part of a much bigger, though still untidy and incomplete, reorganization of BBC overseas services. The psychology was aggressive rather than defensive. 'I'd like to see England take the offensive on the air as everywhere else,' wrote an American listener to a BBC official in the dark days of early June.[1] 'Our overseas broadcasting takes little account of the persons who may hear it and above all whose sympathy we wish to secure.' The 'voice of the people here' should be heard throughout the world.[2]

The European News Editor certainly needed no prodding, and throughout this period of German advance across Europe Newsome inspired everyone with his infectious zest and drive. He had strong views as well as strong feelings, and a 'candid rhymester' in the *Overseas Service Rag* who knew how strong feelings had been and could be about British foreign policy, penned the appropriate lines in July 1940: 'Something tells me that slight friction there might be if Mr. N-v-ll- Ch-mb-rl-n had occasion to visit this office of Eur.N.E.'[3] Newsome was one of nature's anti-Chamberlainites, always looking to the future not to the past. He determined

---

[1] *Quoted in B. Meredith to Rendall, 3 June 1940.

[2] *B. Meredith to P. Pooley, 3 June 1940. A small sub-committee had been set up late in May to scrutinize 'possible broadcast offensives' (Overseas Board, *Minutes*, 30 May 1940). A sub-committee to consider proposals made internally or externally for the use of broadcasting in 'abnormal ways'—primarily for enemy propaganda—was set up under Salt's chairmanship in June. (*Letter from J. B. Clark to Griffin, 30 June 1940.)

[3] *The Overseas Service Rag* is undated, although it was not without historical sense. 'When future historians, poring over the records of our day, discover a musty copy of this Rag,' the editor remarked, 'well may they murmur "Was this their finest hour?"'

that the BBC should resolutely place all its emphasis on 'our moral and material capacity not only to defend ourselves but to strike at the enemy' and on 'our moral and material fitness to keep alive in conquered Europe the spirit of resistance to conquest by brute force and eventually to lead to a great uprising of the peoples against a morally and spiritually bankrupt tyranny whose actual material strength is waning'.[1]

By October, when German bombs were falling on London, the feeling, even inside the BBC, that the German propaganda machine was immeasurably superior to the British had evaporated. 'British broadcasting,' it was claimed, 'has in the last three months clinched a major victory . . . credit is due also to the Germans themselves for the telling propaganda they have done for Great Britain by untiringly prophesying a collapse that never came, yet the evidence is conclusive that British broadcasting, by an offensive strategy of propaganda, has made the most of Hitler's first military defeat.' Belief in BBC news had been restored, for it had been shown that the Germans exaggerated. At the same time, it was maintained, many Europeans who had been despondent in July had begun to doubt whether Germany would eventually win the war. What was needed at once, it was suggested, was an intensification of the campaign 'to lead people to desire an anti-Nazi revolution rather than to fear it'—to provide them with the 'concrete facts, slogans, symbols, allusions, martyrs'. 'Now is the time to get across to him, while London also is in the front line and the enemy's propaganda makes us look braver than we are.'[2] There was also a need to state war aims, to relate what was happening socially inside Britain to what would happen later everywhere in Europe.[3] 'The German radio's sensitiveness to any prominent statement linking British victory with social progress shows the advantages of going further.'[4] To succeed, 'the BBC clearly needs a policy to put across a picture of what Britain intends to do with victory'.

---

[1] *European News Editor, Directive, 8 July 1940. There was no counterpart to these directives in the Home News service of the BBC. (See above, p. 121.)

[2] *BBC European Department, *Monthly Intelligence Report, Europe,* 28 Oct. 1940.

[3] *Ibid. The theme is taken up also in Studies in Broadcast Propaganda, No. 18, 'Germany's War Aims: the new Europe'.

[4] Deutschlandsender on 9 Aug. had called any British claims to approve of any kind of socialism 'hypocrisy'.

While Newsome's enthusiasm was limitless—and necessary—there were times when the mood of this period, which was to be carried to its climax in the V campaign of 1941, was absurdly optimistic and completely out of touch with reality. It could be seriously argued by the BBC's Intelligence service that 'many people in Germany had not reached the stage of desiring an anti-Nazi revolution [*sic*]',[1] when it is clear in retrospect that there were very few of them indeed who had. Moreover, there was little recognition of the close relationship between military success and the collapse of enemy morale. Although the *Monthly Intelligence Report* for October made the valid point that offensive propaganda was disastrous if military events fell short of it, it was absurd to pretend, for all the German failure to invade Britain, that Goebbels had now made the same mistake as the British made in Norway.[2] The possibilities of a general European revolt against Hitler in the summer and autumn of 1940 were smaller even than the possibilities of a German invasion of Britain. It was in a mood of euphoria that Ogilvie, the BBC's Director-General, of all people, was urging as early as June 1940—before the German failure to invade Britain had become manifest—that as part of a 'go tough policy in Western Europe, the BBC should adopt the motto "Every patriot a saboteur"'. 'A civilian population which is not actively hindering the enemy,' he went on, 'are [*sic*] in effect traitors to the common cause.'[3]

It was fortunate that in practice British propaganda did not swing during the strange circumstances of the summer of 1940 towards this frantic extreme. While it was accepted, as it never had been earlier, that a 'comprehensive and unified plan of campaigning propaganda was necessary',[4] at a meeting held to discuss Ogilvie's proposals the more sensible view prevailed that 'premature efforts led to the execution by the Germans of the best people before the time was ripe'.[5] The main lines of propaganda were being decided upon, indeed, outside the BBC by a growing Intelligence service located in the

[1] *BBC European Department, *Monthly Intelligence Report, Europe*, 28 Oct. 1940.
[2] *Ibid. [3] *Ogilvie to Tallents, Kirkpatrick and others, 24 June 1940.
[4] *Overseas Board, *Minutes*, 11 July 1940.
[5] *Report of a meeting held at the BBC, 28 June 1940. Kirkpatrick was present, so too were Mortimer and other representatives of the Ministry of Information, and Newsome.

Bedfordshire countryside; and one of its representatives told Ogilvie bluntly first that there was no need to 'arouse' Scandinavia, and second that in Poland and Czechoslovakia, which Ogilvie had singled out for special praise on the grounds that they were 'not lying down', 'the policy hitherto adopted had been to tell the people to bide their time'. Before people should be told to hide their corn, to put sugar in petrol tanks or to block canals, Europeans as a whole would have to be assured 'about the character of Britain's war effort'. It would have to be clear, indeed, that Germany was 'on the hop'.

Germany, of course, was not 'on the hop' in 1940, and a quite different propaganda strategy was needed—long-term rather than short-term, psychological rather than operational—from that suggested by Ogilvie. The first practical step inside the BBC was the reorganization of the European-language services which was agreed upon late in June[1] and implemented on 19 July with the appointment of J. S. A. Salt, formerly Deputy Director of Overseas Intelligence, as Director of European Services. Tallents remained Controller (Overseas) and J. B. Clark Assistant Controller, while Newsome retained full responsibility for all European News and News talks, under the general direction of A. E. Barker, the Overseas News Editor. Salt, a supremely honest man never without ideas, was in charge of programmes.[2] He was backed by a small staff, including J. W. Lawrence, who was responsible for planning, R. J. T. Griffin, who became head of Intelligence, and V. Duckworth Barker, the European Language Supervisor. Salt was responsible also for the team of translators and announcers.

This was still a modest complement to run two European programmes from 30 June onwards, a step which was made possible by the provision of additional transmitters.[3] Moreover, there were difficulties in getting adequate finance, and, not least because the national Intelligence services were expanding at the same time, in securing, retaining and accommodating

[1] *Overseas Board, *Minutes*, 20 June 1940.
[2] For the ending of this division which lasted until 1 Dec. 1941, see below, p. 342.
[3] *'The European Service, a Proposal for the Development of European Departments', 31 Aug. 1940. Two notes by J. B. Clark on 'The Splitting of the European Service', 21 June 1940 and 'Winter time schedules', 31 July 1940.

experienced staff.[1] These were vividly expressed in a note by Duckworth Barker headed 'Smart Boy Wanted' in October 1940. It was necessary, wrote Barker, to 'campaign against the theory that I stand to other sections in the office of a nursery gardener who tends his seedlings through the difficult period in the hope that their first flower will catch the eye of some passing stranger and send his hand to his pocket'.[2]

'News,' Salt believed, 'ranks first in any foreign service. The aim throughout must be to create and maintain an unrivalled reputation for prompt and reliable news. A further aim must be to make each separate [European] service sensitive to the special needs and circumstances of the different audiences to which it is addressed.'[3] Yet he was troubled by the deliberate division, which he felt amounted to 'segregation', between News and Programmes; and considered that in the French Service, despite its successes, there was a danger of 'the lack of any comprehensive policy'.[4] In the best pre-war BBC tradition, he wanted a wide range of talks as well as of news bulletins. He pressed hard, therefore, for the appointment of a talks assistant and a talks producer in the French section.[5] He hoped that there would also be an increase in the specialized staffing of other sections, on the grounds that 'the British broadcasting service to Europe should not be less thoroughly equipped for an offensive than the naval, military and air services, and its equipment should be part of the resolute and methodical preparation for the campaigns of 1941 and 1942 for which the Prime Minister asked on 20 August'.[6]

Yet by November 1940, when a further expansion—'a triple expansion'—of the European Services was being planned,[7] Salt had realized how difficult his plans were to implement and was complaining that 'the present system gives rise to certain serious difficulties in coordination, and complicates our relations with the Ministry of Information and other Government Departments'. From the time of taking office he had been caught up in a mesh of unresolved difficulties involving

[1] *BBC Overseas Board, *Minutes*, 19 Sept. 1940.
[2] *Duckworth Barker to Salt, 5 Oct. 1940.   [3] *BBC Handbook, 1941*, p. 40.
[4] *Salt to Tallents, 25 Nov. 1940.
[5] *Overseas Board, *Minutes*, 28 Nov. 1940.
[6] *Memorandum on the British Broadcasting Service to Europe, 31 Aug. 1940.
[7] See below, pp. 345–65; *Overseas Board, *Minutes*, 14 Nov. 1940.

programme schedules, transmitters, recording equipment, lines, the recruitment and training of staff, the provision of accommodation and, not least, finance, including dollar exchange.[1] His approach was different from that of Newsome, and he had been entangled awkwardly in institutional wrangles with Electra House concerning the German Service, with the *émigré* governments in London about extended 'free time',[2] with Sir Samuel Hoare about broadcasts to Spain,[3] and with the Foreign Office about the policy implications of almost everything which he was doing or wanted to do. Detailed lists of 'complaints' from the Foreign Office had been submitted to the BBC on 23 July and 30 October, and there had been one particularly irritating contretemps with Lord Halifax. The Foreign Secretary had grumbled at the height of the blitz—he admitted later 'without full knowledge' of the circumstances— that there had been 'too much interference lately with the schedule of the foreign broadcasts of the BBC'. Mentioning Portugal specifically, he told Duff Cooper that 'even if some of the Home Entertainment had to be curtailed I think this ought to be considered, if it is the only way of bringing back the foreign broadcast schedule to something like its normal condition'.[4]

Duff Cooper supported the BBC in this 'crisis', pointing out that Broadcasting House was 'in the battlefield' and that it was with the greatest possible reluctance that the BBC had had temporarily to compress its two European schedules, so recently introduced, into one 'in order to reduce to the minimum the

---

[1] *These different items were summarized by Tallents at the Overseas Board. (Ibid., 21 Nov. 1940.)

[2] *Overseas Board, *Minutes*, 23 May 1940, when it was reported that requests by *émigré* governments for the right to broadcast official announcements should go through either the Foreign Office or the Ministry of Information.

[3] *Sir Samuel Hoare, British Ambassador in Madrid, to Ogilvie, 22 July 1940: 'The Press here is *entirely* German. The radio, therefore, is our only hope.' See also his *Ambassador on Special Mission* (1946), p. 68, in which he quotes a letter he wrote to Halifax on 27 Sept. 1940 saying that he had been urged by some people in the Spanish Foreign Office to counteract German propaganda through the BBC. The British Embassy circulated copies of the BBC Spanish news twice a day in Madrid. For arguments about the content of Spanish broadcasts, see below, pp. 478-9.

[4] *Halifax to Duff Cooper, 26 Sept. 1940. He had been sent a telegram by the British Ambassador in Lisbon who reported that after a change in timing many Portuguese thought they had lost their programme altogether.

proportion of the staff concentrated in one place'.[1] 'The enemy,' he told Halifax, 'have paid particular attention to Broadcasting House and the BBC on two recent occasions were ordered to evacuate the building.'[2] In the following month Broadcasting House was to be bombed,[3] but in the meantime Ogilvie had to call on Halifax at the Foreign Office to clear up what he called 'a ridiculous and tiresome misunderstanding'.[4] In the light of the explanation given Halifax apologized for his letter.[5]

In such circumstances, the introduction of each new foreign service was a complex and arduous question with repercussions on the programme schedules for existing services and sometimes protracted arguments about priorities which the Ministry of Information seldom handled very sympathetically. While Halifax was concerned about Portugal,[6] the Ministry was pleading for more time for Spain[7] and for second bulletins in Roumanian and Serbo-Croat,[8] suggesting a mid-afternoon Polish bulletin at a time when an Italian bulletin was on the air,[9] and changing its mind about the timing of a Hungarian bulletin in such a way that it ended by suggesting precisely the same proposal which it had angrily turned down when it had been made at the start by the BBC.[10] 'It is most undesirable for us to regard revision of schedules as a game which can be played daily or weekly,' J. B. Clark, the Assistant Controller (Overseas), objected sensibly; he raised specific points such as likely Norwegian resentment if they lost their most important bulletin along with the general point of the distaste of listeners

[1] *BBC European Department, *Monthly Intelligence Report, Europe*, 30 Sept. 1940, gives the details of the cuts. The BBC itself noted that a prominent Czech had expressed the fear that the sudden reduction in all the European Service would lead many people to think: 'London is going the way of Paris'.

[2] *Duff Cooper to Halifax, 30 Sept. 1940.

[3] See below, pp. 294–5.

[4] *Note by Ogilvie, 3 Oct. 1940.

[5] *Overseas Board, *Minutes*, 10 Oct. 1940.

[6] The Overseas Board made a proposal in September 1940 to appoint a BBC representative in Lisbon, but no suitable candidate could be found. (*BBC Overseas Board, *Minutes*, 25 July, 26 Sept., 3 Oct. 1940.)

[7] 'La Voz de Londres' was inaugurated on 17 Nov. 1940 by J. H. P. Marks.

[8] *J. B. Clark to Salt and others, 2 Oct. 1940. The Roumanian Service was cut back to ten minutes on 19 Sept. 1940, as was the Serbo-Croat Service.

[9] *Miss I. D. Benzie to Clark, 1 Oct. 1940.

[10] *Overseas Board, *Minutes*, 24 Oct. 1940; Miss Benzie to Clark, 10 Oct. 1940; Clark to Salt and others, 10 Oct. 1940.

everywhere for 'complex shuffling'. 'We cannot lightly re-time the Danish without the concurrence of other important interests.'[1] With his remarkable capacity for identifying the relevant pressures, Clark saw a danger that Polish interests in the Ministry might be 'so strongly pressed that they overshadow some of the other interests (for example, Scandinavian). This is no doubt a reflection of the strength of the personalities involved.'[2]

On 15 October it was necessary to hold a meeting between Salt and Lawrence on behalf of the BBC and Michael Stewart and Miss Benzie of the Ministry to try to clarify the position. The BBC representatives expressed the view strongly that changes in programme schedules should only be made with the utmost caution. 'Effective broadcasting,' they argued, 'depends on the inculcation of listening habits, and any change, however well "trailed", is bound to lose us a proportion of the audience.' The Ministry representatives 'admitted the general validity of these and other points, but stressed the importance of the considerations which had led them to make the original proposals'.[3] Two days later it was the BBC, not the Ministry, which was proposing more news bulletins in Serbo-Croat. 'Yugoslavia is already almost encircled by the Axis and is subject to very heavy diplomatic pressure. It may become an occupied country in the near future.' The BBC asked also for an extension of the time devoted to Danish broadcasts: 'the economic importance of Denmark and the recent stiffening of morale in that country suggest that 10 minutes a day is not an adequate service for Denmark.'[4]

Yugoslavia was to break with Hitler in March 1941, incidentally opening up a new and fascinating phase in BBC overseas broadcasting,[5] but the tone of broadcasting to Denmark

---

[1] *Ibid. A listener in Yugoslavia wrote on 9 Oct. that 'I am very annoyed with the BBC for changing the time of their broadcasts every now and then. You may tell them that it is a very bad sort of propaganda.' (BBC European Department, *Monthly Intelligence Report, Europe*. Undated, probably Nov. 1940.)

[2] *Clark to Salt, 10 Oct. 1940. On 12 Dec. 1940 Salt complained in a letter to Wellington of the Ministry's relative inattention to Norway although 'the country is getting near to open revolt'.

[3] *Note of a meeting held in the BBC, 15 Oct. 1940.

[4] *Lawrence to Salt, 17 Oct. 1940. The number of Serbo-Croat bulletins rose from 1 to 7 during the period from September 1940 to April 1941.

[5] See below, pp. 462–6.

remained extremely cautious even after a few daring attacks were made on 'Perfidious Scavenius', the Foreign Minister in Stauning's Copenhagen Government, in February 1941.[1] In the meantime, the Ministry pressed for an Albanian programme after Italy had invaded Greece through Albania on 28 October, and the service began on 13 November. Salt thought it 'would have flattery value only, as the upper classes who possessed sets could understand broadcasts in Turkish, Greek or Italian'.[2] There were, in fact, only three thousand wireless sets in the whole of Albania, and after the Greeks had driven back the Italians across the Albanian frontier, the BBC found it very difficult to present them to the Albanians in the role of liberators. The Greek Service itself, with George Angeloglou as editor, was to go through many vicissitudes later during the war,[3] but Caclamanos, former Greek Ambassador in London and a friend of Venizelos, gave stirring commentaries after the Italian attack and special messages were broadcast from King George VI and from leading British politicians. There was talk at this time also of broadcasts to Russia,[4] and H. G. Wells envisaged broadcasts of news and views aimed directly at Stalin and his entourage. The Foreign Office disapproved,[5] and Tallents recorded his own view that such broadcasts 'might well fulfil the historic function of an Arabian night's entertainment for the tyrant'.[6]

Many of the problems of expanding the different language services—each with its own distinctive problems—can be illustrated from the history of the Dutch, Belgian and Norwegian services. The Dutch Service had started on 11 April with a 15-minute daily bulletin: it should have started earlier but was 'held up for weeks owing to the Ministry's failure to produce a specialist sub-editor'.[7] The time chosen, 5.0–5.15 p.m., was one, Newsome grumbled, when 'the average Dutchman is not at home', but after the German invasion of Holland an extra

[1] See J. Bennett, *British Broadcasting and the Danish Resistance Movement* (1966), p. 27.

[2] *Overseas Board, *Minutes*, 31 Oct. 1940.   [3] See below, pp. 461–2.

[4] *Overseas Board, *Minutes*, 31 Oct. 1940. A few days earlier Tallents had talked to Sir Maurice Peterson of the Ministry of Information about the idea (Tallents to Ogilvie, 28 Aug. 1940).

[5] *Peterson to Tallents, 18 Oct. 1940.

[6] *Note by Tallents on a meeting with H. G. Wells, 1 Sept. 1940.

[7] *A. E. Barker to J. B. Clark, 20 March 1940.

bulletin had been added in the late evening.[1] Negotiations with VARA, one of the four main Dutch programme broadcasting companies, had preceded the entry of Holland into the war.[2] Yet after the Dutch collapse the BBC, while sympathetic, refused to deal separately with two VARA directors who had escaped, J. W. Lebon and M. Sluyser,[3] and entered into negotiations with Dr. J. Pelt, head of the Dutch Press Service in London, who was recommended by Professor Gerbrandy, the Dutch Minister of Justice.[4] At a joint meeting, the Ministry of Information pressed the BBC to accept Pelt as an adviser on the content and style of the BBC's bulletins; and after the surprised BBC representatives had pointed out that this would be against the Ministry's policy of exercising great caution in allowing exiled governments to acquire separate facilities for broadcasting, they were told somewhat sharply that 'the Ministry rather deplored BBC resistance to suggestions that they put forward in relation to broadcasting'.[5]

On 6 June Gerbrandy and Pelt formally asked Ogilvie and Tallents for 'free time', which they had been promised in Paris by the French before the collapse of France on a scale which they could not then utilize.[6] Two weeks later they produced a detailed 'scheme for a Dutch broadcast' designed 'to counteract the German moral penetration in the Netherlands and . . . the defeatist sentiments that may possibly arise in the Dutch people'.[7] It would include an initial broadcast

---

[1] See above, p. 198.

[2] On 17 April a representative of VARA (Vereeniging van Arbeiders Radio Amateurs) had visited J. B. Clark to see whether after an invasion a group of broadcasters from this concern could be evacuated to Britain, but the BBC refused to deal solely with one company. The others were AVRO (Algemeene Vereeniging Radio Omroep), sponsored by business interests, KRO (Katholiche Radio Omroep), sponsored by Roman Catholic interests and NCRV (Nederland Christelijke Radio Vereeniging), sponsored by Protestant interests. (*Record of Interview by J. B. Clark, 17 April 1940.)

[3] They were the only two members of VARA's staff who succeeded in escaping, although in February 1939 they had transferred some of their capital to London in case of invasion. (*Note of meeting with J. B. Clark, 24 May 1940.)

[4] *Tallents to Clark, 20 May 1940.

[5] *Note of a discussion between Miss Benzie, Clark, Newsome and A. E. Barker, 4 June 1940.   [6] *Note by Tallents of Meeting, 6 June 1940.

[7] *'A Scheme for a Dutch Broadcast', offered to Tallents on 19 June 1940. It was pointed out that one advantage of the service was that it could be rebroadcast in the Netherlands East Indies where there was a law forbidding the rebroadcasting of *foreign* broadcasts.

by the Queen, a political radio diary to be presented four times a week, a 'Mail letter' from Batavia, a weekly broadcast by a Dutch Cabinet Minister, and a *pot-pourri* of Dutch songs. Reginald Foort, the cinema organist, was said (by a happy coincidence) to be 'very popular with the Dutch people'. In addition to making this detailed proposal for a programme of their own, Gerbrandy and Pelt asked to be kept fully informed about the content of the BBC programmes in Dutch.

The Ministry was keen, for reasons which are not entirely clear, to allow the Dutch Government separate time for broadcasting, even though the particular time they proposed was useless for listeners in the Dutch East Indies.[1] Perhaps its officials were influenced by the fact that Hilversum, which had passed under German control,[2] claimed the co-operation of the four Dutch companies and was anxious to secure rebroadcasting arrangements from Batavia. The Ministry certainly made the most of the argument, which it did not apply at that time to any other country, that in order to get full propaganda value broadcasts should be dissociated as far as possible from the British Government and associated as far as possible with the national government in exile. There was apparently a debate behind the scenes as to whether the *émigré* governments were so tarred with the 'appeasement' brush that they should not be given direct broadcasting facilities of the kind some of them had already enjoyed in Paris before the fall of France.[3] Different governments were to be treated in different ways. After a meeting of the Ministry's Policy Committee on 1 July,[4] therefore, free time was conceded to the Dutch on 9 July. It was explicitly stated that it did not constitute a precedent, that scripts in Dutch should be sent for scrutiny to the Ministry, and no straight entertainment would be broadcast by the Dutch during their daily fifteen minutes.[5] Radio Oranje, as the new

---

[1] *Clark to Tallents, reporting a telephone conversation with Wellington, 26 June 1940.

[2] See above, p. 200. There were reports of a boycott of German-controlled stations. (*BBC Overseas Intelligence Department, *Monthly Intelligence Report, Europe*, 5 Aug. 1940.)

[3] See T. Barman, *Diplomatic Correspondent* (1968), pp. 102–3.

[4] *There had been previous discussions on 26 June, 27 June and 1 July 1940, during which Kirkpatrick had put forward the Dutch requests with full backing from Lord Perth: there is also a letter on the subject from Lee to Ogilvie, 18 July 1940.

[5] There had been objections from Lord Swinton who was in charge of a

[cont.

programme was called, duly took the air on 28 July, with a broadcast by Queen Wilhelmina.

BBC European programme makers thought that the first Radio Oranje programmes were dull and uninspiring[1]—'trying to fill a daily quarter of an hour with the haphazard musings of a few tired old men'[2]—and there was considerable tension between a lively and intransigent BBC Dutch News section, which broadcast three news bulletins each day, and a somewhat stiff and unimaginative Radio Oranje team. 'Great difficulty' was caused also by 'the lack of understanding among Dutch Ministers of certain essentials of broadcasting technique'.[3] Even though telegrams of congratulation reached London from Dutchmen abroad,[4] and there were encouraging signs of widespread passive resistance to the Germans in Holland itself,[5] difficulties were to persist in 1941 and 1942, some of them of a more serious kind.[6]

The history of the Belgian Service, one of a number of new services introduced in the autumn of 1940, was quite different. As early as May 1940, Tallents had quoted a Ministry of Information view that the destruction of Belgian transmitters 'raised at once the question of the service we could give to Belgium',[7] but nearly a month later, after the Belgian Government had fled to France, nothing more had been achieved than the recognition that the BBC had to bear 'Belgian interests

---

[1] *The first programme was planned at a meeting in Broadcasting House on 19 July 1940. No payment was to be made by the Dutch for the use of studios and equipment, but the Dutch were to pay their own speakers, writers, and technicians. A further programme was added on 9 Dec. 1940, and this pattern persisted until the end of the war.

[2] *Elston, the BBC's Sub-Editor for Dutch News, to A. E. Barker, 4 Sept. 1940. Elston himself was strongly criticized for his own programmes. (Letter from de Sausmarez of the Ministry of Information to Salt, 27 Aug. 1940.)

[3] *Tallents to Kirkpatrick, 9 Aug. 1940. Cf. Overseas Board, *Minutes*, 8 Aug. 1940: 'Weaknesses of present Radio Oranje service noted: proposals for offering friendly assistance with a view to improvement reported.'

[4] *BBC Overseas Intelligence Department, *Monthly Intelligence Report, Europe*, 5 Aug. 1940.

[5] *Daily Telegraph*, 19 Oct. 1940.   [6] See below, pp. 472–3.

[7] *Tallents to Ogilvie, 15 May 1940; Overseas Board, *Minutes*, 23 May 1940. A meeting was held on 18 May between Clark, Miss Benzie and others at which a special Belgian Service was discussed.

---

committee dealing with security operations (including uses of codes in broadcasting) and who did not accept the proposal until 9 July. The Dutch offered the use of their station at Curaçao as a *quid pro quo*.

in mind when compiling our French and Dutch bulletins'.[1] The difficult political and constitutional situation in which the Belgian Government found itself after King Leopold had decided to stay in occupied Belgium[2] did not make it possible for the Belgians to secure 'free time', although the first Cabinet Minister to arrive in Britain gave a broadcast on 23 June. 'If possible,' the Ministry of Information argued, 'a Belgian service should be started before the formation of a refugee Belgian Government in Britain.'[3] The conditions of the 'collapse' of European countries obviously influenced the attitude of the Ministry towards subsequent broadcasting arrangements, and the Belgians were treated quite differently from the Dutch. In 1941 the Foreign Office was to try to persuade the Ministry to follow a more open policy of the kind which the Ministry itself had pressed on the BBC in its early dealings with the Dutch.[4]

The first programme specifically designed for Belgium was launched on 28 September, the anniversary of the final offensive in Flanders during the First World War. A 10-minute programme presented alternately in French and Flemish— Radio Belgique or Radio Belgie—was designed by Victor de Laveleye, who was later to play the initiatory role in the V campaign,[5] and Nand Geersens, who used the pseudonym of Jan Moedwil. The Flemish programme was listened to by many Dutch listeners, some of whom preferred it to Radio Oranje. Both programmes, however, had begun to establish an audience, despite all the difficulties, by the end of 1940. There had been some complaints from Belgium of the 'bombastic tone' and 'hollow proclamations' of the Free French programme,[6] and the 'more sober' approach of Radio Belgique was immediately appreciated.

[1] *J. B. Clark to Marriott, 8 June 1940; BBC Overseas Intelligence Department, *Monthly Intelligence Report, Europe*, 5 Aug. 1940: 'There is need for special broadcasts for Belgium.'

[2] *The Times*, 4 Oct. 1940. Belgian ministers were on the move during the late summer and early autumn of 1940 while the King remained in Belgium. No contact was made with the Germans, and after the fall of France the Pétain Government refused to give them any facilities.

[3] *Overseas Board, *Minutes*, 22 Aug. 1940.

[4] See below, pp. 473–4.

[5] See below, pp. 365–84.

[6] *BBC Overseas Intelligence Department, *Monthly Intelligence Report, Europe*, 28 Oct. 1940.

The Norwegian Service, started in the most dramatic and difficult of all circumstances,[1] had been managed from 6 May by Denis Winther, a businessman who stayed as head of the section until after the war. Although he was assisted by a Norwegian broadcaster, Olav Rytter, who had started working with the BBC while there was still a chance that fighting in Norway would continue,[2] the Norwegian State Broadcasting Authority pressed in June and July 1940 for a more active and varied Norwegian Service directly controlled by Norwegians. Its Chairman, Dr. Raestad, and its Director, Dr. Sommerfelt, wanted to use 'the National Norwegian Government machinery' and to set up an Advisory Council to assist Toralv Øksnevad, the former head of its News Department, who arrived in Britain in August as Director-Designate of Programmes.[3] The Ministry of Information considered this proposal alongside the proposal of the Dutch Government, but was far less willing to concede time unless the Norwegians agreed to embark on active propaganda. 'Snakes and ladders galore here,' commented Ogilvie.[4] 'I have been rather terrified by the Raestad-Sommerfelt memorandum,' J. B. Clark added, 'for they have conceived an elaborate organisation without any proper outlet. . . . It will, however, make our work impossible if, in addition to the Foreign Office, Ministry, Services, and other departmental contacts all giving directions on the service, we are expected to collaborate with an organisation of the size contemplated by the Norwegians which has no proper *raison d'être*.'[5]

Relations between Raestad and Sommerfelt on the one hand and the BBC on the other were not improved by the vigorous attack made by Norwegians in London on 'disheartening' BBC programmes to Norway for which, it was argued, Norwegians would be bound to hold the Norwegian Government responsible. 'We fear,' they concluded in a letter which they also sent to Halifax, 'that in the interest of our common cause we must

[1] See above, p. 16.
[2] *Record of an interview, 3 June 1940.
[3] *Report by Tallents of an interview between Ogilvie, Tallents, Raestad and Sommerfelt, 21 June 1940; Memorandum by Raestad and Sommerfelt, 3 July 1940; Overseas Board, *Minutes*, 22 Aug. 1940.
[4] *Note addressed to Tallents on a carbon copy of a letter of 6 July to Raestad acknowledging the Memorandum of 3 July 1940.
[5] *Clark to Tallents, 10 July 1940.

advise the Norwegian Government to ask you to discontinue
the Norwegian broadcasts altogether if the service cannot be
profoundly modified.'[1] This protest went as far as Churchill,
who told Ogilvie to take steps without delay to deal with the
situation.[2] Despite this initiative from the top, Ogilvie was
still concerned not to upset the Ministry of Information which
was trying to restrict free time[3] or the Swinton Committee
which was treating a further extension of free time to any
government as prejudicial to national security. There were
further problems bound up with Norwegian politics and the
degree of support which the Norwegian Government in London
commanded in Norway itself. Yet the Overseas Board followed
Ogilvie's and Tallents' advice and expressed a preference for
giving the Norwegians free time rather than broadcasting
'unacceptable programmes'.[4] After further consultation with
the Ministry an offer was made to the Norwegians of a daily
15-minute programme on 25 July.[5] Ogilvie explained in a
letter to Churchill on 29 July some of the reasons for delay and
the nature of the offer which was now being made.

The outcome of these extremely confused exchanges was an
agreement reached on 28 August at Broadcasting House.
The Norwegians did not secure free time on the same lines as
the Dutch—Øksnevad himself came out against it—and
instead Øksnevad and Rytter were seconded to the BBC,
responsible to Barker for news bulletins and to Salt for programmes, while still being paid their salaries by the Norwegian
Government.[6] What had started in such confusion ended
triumphantly, for the agreement whereby the BBC took
maximum assistance from the Norwegians while retaining
final control was to last throughout the war. By the autumn of
1940 everybody in Oslo was said to be trying to hear the
London broadcast,[7] and by the end of the year it was the BBC,

---

[1] Norwegians in London also attacked the Bergen accent of the announcers.
(*Report of a dinner party sent to A. E. Barker, July 1940. Raestad and Sommerfelt to Ogilvie, 16 July 1940.)
   [2] *Halifax to Ogilvie, 20 July 1940; Churchill to Ogilvie, 28 July 1940.
   [3] See above, p. 244.   [4] *Overseas Board, *Minutes*, 18 July 1940.
   [5] *Report of a meeting between Kirkpatrick, Wellington, Tallents and Clark
in a letter from Tallents to Kirkpatrick, 25 July 1940.
   [6] *Report of a meeting between Clark (in the chair), Barker, Salt, Sommerfelt,
Øksnevad, Miss Benzie and Kenny, 28 Aug. 1940.
   [7] *The Times*, 1 Nov. 1940.

as we have seen, which was pressing the Ministry not to overlook the special needs of Norway as its resistance movement grew.[1] When Raestad and Sommerfelt met Tallents in December, they expressed complete satisfaction with the Norwegian Service.[2]

While these three new services were being developed in such contrasting ways, the Polish and Czech Services also underwent strains and tensions during the summer and autumn of 1940, particularly after the suspension of the French services to Poland and Czechoslovakia before the fall of France. In March 1940 the Director of Polskie Radio in Paris had visited London at the invitation of the BBC and it had been agreed that the Wednesday and Saturday London programmes in Polish should each include a section sponsored by the Polish Government.[3] The BBC's main interest at this time was to improve its own news service to Poland, the service which was of main interest in Poland;[4] the main interest of the Poles was to secure genuinely free time both for an 'Agony Column' and for propaganda. Further Polish efforts to secure the full text of all Polish broadcasts, preferably in advance, were unsuccessful during the busy summer,[5] but the Poles went on to appoint a liaison officer with the BBC, Count Jan Balinski-Jundzill of the Polish Research Centre.[6] Despite considerable pressure, they failed in 1940 to secure free time on the same lines as the Dutch.[7]

The Czechs did not officially seek free time at this stage, although they were interested in setting up a joint consultative committee on broadcasting with the Poles[8] after Beneš had been recognized by the British as head of a provisional Czechoslovak Government on 3 July.[9] There were reports that the Czechs were a 'nation of disarmed resisters',[10] and a broadcast by Beneš on 21 September was said to have given 'calm to

[1] See above, p. 260.
[2] *Overseas Board, *Minutes*, 5 Dec. 1940.
[3] *BBC Press Release, 27 April 1940.
[4] See above, p. 177.
[5] *Overseas Board, *Minutes*, 27 June 1940.
[6] *Ibid., 21 Nov. 1940.
[7] *A. E. Barker to Wellington, 30 July 1940.
[8] *Overseas Board, *Minutes*, 18 July 1940.
[9] For the complex negotiations, see R. Bruce Lockhart, *Comes the Reckoning* (1947), pp. 94 ff., 712–20.
[10] *BBC European Department, *Monthly Intelligence Report, Europe*, 2 Sept. 1940.

everybody and filled them again with self-confidence'.[1] There was heavy German jamming of the broadcasts in Czech,[2] and it was an ex-minister of the pre-Munich Czechoslovak Government who advised that a person 'intimately familiar with Czech matters should always be at hand in the BBC' to retort at once to German allegations dangerous to the Czech state of mind. He should always scrutinize Czech news broadcasts from London with regard to their 'probable effect' on Czech listeners.[3] The cruelly suppressed Czech revolt on 17 November 1939 had shown the dangers of premature political action.

Broadcasts to Germany during this period remained the special province not of the Ministry of Information but of Electra House. Yet the Italians were always treated differently. Before the Italian declaration of war on 11 June, British broadcasts in Italian were already being jammed,[4] but after the fall of France an evening bulletin in Italian was beamed from London to Cairo and rebroadcast.[5] The BBC found it difficult indeed to build up an effective broadcasting team to exploit the situation, particularly after Italians were interned, with other enemy aliens, in the Isle of Man on 16 May; and as late as December 1940 Salt was complaining that no tests of new staff had been possible since June and that the existing staff was 'morally and physically exhausted'.[6] There were grumbles from the Ministry of Information that the news bulletins, edited from July 1940 to January 1941 by Cecil Sprigge, were 'too dry and not presented with sufficient attention to the present needs of an Italian audience'.[7] In the meantime, Colonel Stevens continued to build up his reputation even when circumstances were far from propitious.

[1] *Message from a Czech listener, ibid., 30 Sept. 1940. The same report claimed that the Germans were devoting more care to their Czech broadcasts. 'Crude propaganda and childish cabaret has given place to long explanatory meditations on topical events.'

[2] *Ibid., 28 Oct. 1940.

[3] *Ibid., 8 July 1940.

[4] See above, p. 71.

[5] Plans had been made before the fall of France to rebroadcast from Radio Méditerranée, a French commercial station at Antibes. Cairo started its own Italian news service in October 1940.

[6] *Salt to J. B. Clark, 21 Dec. 1940; J. C. Jeaffreson to Duckworth Barker, undated.

[7] *Peterson to Tallents, 9 Dec. 1940.

The German Service faced even more serious difficulties during the summer and early autumn of 1940. The decision not to employ German *émigrés* except as announcers or away from the microphone—a policy diametrically opposed to that followed in the French Service and, of course, in the 'black' radio stations—did not prevent a 'crisis in morale' in the German Service when the Press launched an unpleasant campaign against all enemy aliens in May and June 1940. The crisis heightened when enemy aliens were taken into custody and large numbers of them transported to Canada and Australia. 'Country saved from the Fifth Column Scab' was the *Daily Herald* headline.[1] The Nazi victories in Europe shocked and alarmed all anti-Nazi Germans living in England, and after the fall of Boulogne, it was reported that 'several members of the unit, in a state of great despondency, professed themselves unable to work until better news came'.[2] The final 'crisis of morale' came when on the visit of the King and Queen to Broadcasting House even refugee broadcasters who had been fully screened were not allowed near the royal visitors.[3] In such conditions, it proved difficult to recruit well-qualified new staff.[4] Indeed, the same conditions which so greatly assisted the French section of the BBC in June and July 1940 worked irresistibly against the German section.

At the same time, there were strong differences of opinion within the section and between the BBC and Electra House on major aspects of policy. Some centred on the employment of F. A. Voigt, the hard-hitting but controversial journalist.[5] Others were more fundamental. Before leaving Britain for Canada ten days after the fall of France, Campbell Stuart had complained that 'since Electra House had had difficulty in getting the BBC to do many things that they wanted, it

---

[1] *Daily Herald*, 17 May 1940.

[2] *Duckworth Barker to A. E. Barker and others, 31 May 1940.

[3] Leonard Miall told the Queen that the German Section was 'where we do the dirty work; where our colleagues try and raise their listeners' morale, we try and lower it'.

[4] *Overseas Board, *Minutes*, 24 Oct. 1940.

[5] *Ibid., 9 May 1940, for the first appearance of Voigt's name. Voigt was backed by Campbell Stuart. 'Confirmed that BBC had the right to turn down scripts or speakers from the broadcasting point of view, and that in any case Voigt might be ruled out as a speaker on the score of his voice.' It was agreed (*ibid., 23 May) that Voigt should be used occasionally but not regularly.

should be determined who had the deciding voice in such matters'.[1] Tallents's view was that the BBC should be more than 'parrots acting to the dictation of Electra House', but Ivone Kirkpatrick of the Foreign Office, who was to play such an important part in the later war-time history of the BBC, was influential behind the scenes and felt that far stronger control of the BBC was necessary. A somewhat untidy rearrangement of official responsibilities followed a succession of meetings in July and August, culminating in the appointment of Hugh Dalton, Minister of Economic Warfare, as Chairman of a new Special Operations Executive—with Vansittart to assist him;[2] in the resignation of Campbell Stuart, who had known 'every landmark and every dangerous shoal in Whitehall'[3] in the Chamberlain period but who was not at ease in a Churchill régime; in Leeper taking charge of the 'country' operations of Electra House with David Bowes-Lyon as his deputy; and in an uneasy division of labour in London between Dalton and Duff Cooper, the Minister of Information, who agreed to share the responsibilities for different kinds of propaganda to enemy countries.

The BBC's German section was left in a weak position institutionally as a result of these changes. Yet in the context of Europe as a whole, the rearrangements permitted a new and more realistic approach to sabotage and subversion—'the stimulation of the subversive tendencies already latent in most countries'[4]—and to political warfare. The national Intelligence system was far more comprehensive, of course, than that of the BBC, and Rex Leeper, Director of Enemy Propaganda,[5] also ranked as head of the Political Intelligence Department of the Foreign Office. There were many obstacles in the way of efficient planning, yet it was during this period of limited reconstruction that many critical decisions were taken, for example, those in relation to 'black broadcasting', with

---

[1] *Tallents to Ogilvie, 4 June 1940, following a meeting with Monckton, Campbell Stuart and Valentine Williams at the Foreign Office.

[2] M. R. D. Foot, *S.O.E. in France* (1966), p. 8. Chamberlain arranged the final details of the scheme.   [3] Barman, op. cit., p. 114.

[4] Foot, op. cit., p. 9, quoting a War Cabinet decision of September 1940. Churchill's directive to Dalton was brief and simple: 'And now set Europe ablaze.' (H. Dalton, *The Fateful Years* (1957), p. 366.)

[5] H. Dalton, *Call Back Yesterday* (1953), p. 220. Leeper's opposite number was Gladwyn Jebb, Dalton's Chief Executive Officer.

Leeper, Brigadier Brooks, head of the Military Wing of the Department for Enemy Propaganda, Valentine Williams, Crossman and, later, Sefton Delmer organizing from Woburn the 'freedom radios'—'research units' was their cover name—which pretended that they were broadcasting from inside Hitler's Europe.[1]

Crossman was in charge of German operations, and he had definite ideas of his own about what form both 'white' and 'black' broadcasting to Germany should take. Until the appointment in October 1940 of Hugh Carleton Greene as the BBC's German editor[2]—he had previously been the Berlin correspondent of the *Daily Telegraph*—the BBC's German organization was too weak to deal effectively with Electra House on terms which would permit it any effective initiative of its own. In face of Voigt's opinion that the German news bulletins should be 'absolutely cold, without comment' and with no 'propagandist intention', Newsome had insisted on 'skilful and subtle presentation',[3] but there was little scope for a wide range of non-news programmes until November 1940 when the need for a BBC German programme unit was finally accepted.[4] A March of Time programme—*Vormarsch der Freiheit*—was introduced in the autumn, and plans were made to develop programmes specially designed for the German forces in the new year.[5] A new series of liaison meetings between the representatives of the BBC and Electra House started in October 1940, with a daily news and news talks meeting, a weekly meeting to discuss general directives, and a fortnightly meeting to discuss general programme questions.[6]

The opening up of new perspectives was becoming plain

---

[1] S. Delmer, *Black Boomerang*, vol. II (1962), pp. 36 ff.; R. Bruce Lockhart, op. cit., pp. 169 ff. See also below, p. 426.

[2] Negotiations to secure Greene had started in August 1940. For his appointment and its consequences, see below, pp. 425–31.

[3] *German Planning Committee, Minutes*, 12 July 1940.

[4] *Overseas Board, Minutes*, 14 Nov. 1940; German Broadcasting Committee, *Minutes*, 16 Nov. 1940. See also minutes of meetings of 1 and 29 Nov. 1940 for an attempt to borrow Delmer from Electra House to run the programme.

[5] *For the *March of Time* idea, see Overseas Board, *Minutes*, 31 Oct. 1940. The idea of a Forces programme was first mooted at a meeting on 2 Nov. 1940. There were many difficulties to overcome, not least at the War Office. (Overseas Board, *Minutes*, 5 Dec. 1940.) An 'agricultural review' was first broadcast on 2 Oct. 1940.

[6] *Overseas Board, Minutes*, 17 Oct. 1940.

in a number of memoranda penned by Duckworth Barker and sent to Salt in October 1940. 'We should consider running a regular feature designed partly to play on the homesickness of German troops and partly to spread uneasiness among them regarding the course of events in Germany and the fate of their own people. . . . This object might be attained by the creation of a typical German family whose comments on the situation, doubts and disillusionments could be broadcast in the form of a weekly conversation.'[1] Such an idea was, of course, far more limited than the idea behind *Les Français parlent aux Français*; given the continuing ban on the use of aliens, the German Service still had to be developed on the basis of ideas submitted mainly by Englishmen.[2] There were, however, many ideas submitted by refugees from Germany, particularly members of the BBC's Monitoring Service.[3] 'At present,' Barker complained to Salt, 'we draw on the great reserves of knowledge possessed by monitoring in only an haphazard fashion. I should like to press that you might acquire the full-time services of two German monitors specially trained to note linguistic points and items likely to help in building German feature programmes.'[4] Salt himself believed that 'the E.H. method of organisation has suffered inevitably from being so far removed from the microphone and the result is that the technical possibilities of broadcasting have never been explored'.[5]

There is very little substantial evidence concerning the German response to BBC broadcasts during the course of these institutional vicissitudes. Intelligence reports about the 'demoralisation of German troops of occupation' were obviously exaggerated,[6] but there were signs of defensive notes being

---

[1] *Duckworth Barker to Salt, 17 Oct. 1940.

[2] *Duckworth Barker also suggested in a memorandum of 28 Oct. 1940 a weekly comic feature called 'Hitler's Weekly Address to his Troops'.

[3] George Weidenfeld, for example, submitted an index of German propaganda items which might form the basis for counter propaganda. The items included 'characteristic extracts from speeches by Nazi leaders, revealing the empty, redundant and purposely vague phraseology of the Third Reich' and characteristic items concerning the New Order in Europe or other predictions relating to the National Socialist Millennium.

[4] *Duckworth Barker to Salt, 15 Nov. 1940.

[5] *Salt to Oliver Harvey, 28 Sept. 1940.

[6] *BBC European Department, *Monthly Intelligence Report, Europe*, 28 Oct., 23 Dec. 1940.

struck in German home propaganda for the first time. An article in a German magazine claimed that 'British lies' were becoming 'more systematic' and that the standard of announcing had recently improved.[1] Yet Lindley Fraser was not yet able to match Fritzsche,[2] and in general there was a lack of punch in the content and style of the programmes which cannot have made them appealing to any sizeable German audience. One of the most effective of the speakers was 'Frau Wernicke', played by Annemarie Haase, with a script for German women written by Bruno Adler. A 'private report' smuggled in from Germany at the end of 1940 suggested 'that Frau Wernicke is much admired by the Propaganda Ministry, who rate her as excellent and effective propaganda; and it is possible that they may have been thinking of her . . . when they decided to inaugurate their regional transmissions'.[3] Such reports generated qualified optimism. It was claimed, indeed, that 'if only British broadcasting were set a definite objective, it would be able to plan its campaign with more hope of success than the Germans ever had, for our German audience in the occupied countries is more receptive than was the Germans' audience of civilians in Britain'.[4]

There was to be far more talk before the war was over of the need for a 'definite objective'. In the meantime, behind the BBC's counterattack was a strengthening and expansion of the BBC's Monitoring Service. There was also an effort, which in the long run was checked, to create a large-scale BBC Intelligence organization of its own. Research and Intelligence figured prominently in the discussions of 1940 on the grounds that 'Germany's broadcasts were based on an Intelligence Service and on the thorough sociological study of the listeners of each country' and that the BBC, for its part, should 'collect promptly and sift not only the actual reactions of listeners but their local grievances and leanings'.[5]

[1] *Die Woche*, 16 Oct. 1940.
[2] *BBC Overseas Intelligence Department, *Monthly Intelligence Report, Europe*, 5 Aug. 1940. 'Lindley Fraser is vigorous without being abusive, but may approach his conclusions too obviously. . . . There is a strong case to be made out in favour of developing some British equivalents to Fritzsche.'
[3] *BBC European Department, *Monthly Intelligence Report, Europe*, 23 Dec. 1940.
[4] *Ibid.
[5] *BBC Overseas Intelligence Department, *Monthly Intelligence Report, Europe*, 5 Aug. 1940.

The Research Unit had been duly extended in April 1940 to include a number of specialists trained to apply research methods to the production of outgoing propaganda. Soon afterwards, in the light of the German attack on the West, new estimates to expand the BBC's Monitoring Service 'to meet the changed war situation' were quickly approved,[1] and Duff Cooper was one of a group of official visitors who inspected Wood Norton during the German *Blitzkrieg*. Temporary monitoring units were also brought into existence in London, and a War Office monitoring unit, soon to be called the Y Unit, was moved from South-East England to Evesham.[2] An outgoing teleprinter service to the Admiralty, the Air Ministry, the War Office, the Foreign Office, the Ministry of Information, Electra House and the Home Office began to function, although at first there were numerous mechanical breakdowns.[3] News was flashed through to the appropriate recipient with unprecedented speed. Thus, Mussolini's declaration of war was received in the Admiralty within four minutes of his Rome broadcast announcing it, ten minutes ahead of all other news services.[4]

Routines were further streamlined in June and July when the number of members of the monitoring staff rose to over 150, of whom almost two-thirds were practising monitors, some of them 'roving monitors' dealing not with particular programmes but particular areas. The Editorial Unit began to prepare a daily statement on trends in enemy propaganda and on points for broadcasters to America, including Murrow and the American broadcasters themselves, as well as a basic monitoring report and a report for the War Cabinet. Special surveys were also made by the Research Unit on such topics as 'Broadcasts for the French Listener'[5] and 'German Propaganda on a New European Order'. In September the Ministry of Economic Warfare—with its Intelligence functions—was added to the

---

[1] *Overseas Board, *Minutes*, 16 May 1940. A few members of the Overseas Intelligence Department were transferred in the interim period. The Monitoring Service had noted on 9 May (Monitoring Service, *Editorial Bulletin*) that 'there has been more evidence in the past few days of the increasing use by German radio propaganda of a monitoring service apparently very similar to our own'.

[2] *Tallents to Graves, 14 May 1940; Frost to Tallents, 20 May 1940.

[3] *BBC Monitoring Service, *Monthly Progress Report*, May 1940.

[4] *Ibid., June 1940.

[5] *Ibid., July 1940.

list of recipients of information, along with the Czech Government.[1] Particular attention was paid during this period to 'the New Europe' as conceived by Germany. 'Please watch this theme and all reactions to it,' monitors were told on 29 July and 2 August.[2] Churchill himself used material collected by the Monitoring Service in his broadcast of 8 October.[3]

The Monitoring Service was directly linked also with the News service of the BBC. Newsome said on 11 May that he found monitoring news flashes 'invaluable' in preparing news bulletins for Europe, and on the same day Colonel Stevens was ordering tape of those broadcast from Rome.[4] The European Service was also using news supplied by various agencies—Associated Press, BUP, Exchange Telegraph and Reuter—but it wanted any information Evesham could supply from Havas and from Stefani the Italian Agency.[5] 'Stories which offer obvious possibilities of anti-German or Italian propaganda to the United States' were also in demand, to be used by 'speakers such as Vernon Bartlett, J. B. Priestley and Megan Lloyd George'.[6] A few weeks later Barkway of Empire News was asking for 'any monitoring reports on Tokyo'.[7]

To complete this account of the British counterattack, it is necessary to turn briefly from Europe, the centre of the drama, to the outlying parts of the world which watched what was happening as fascinated or horrified spectators. In Latin America, events in France gave 'a terrible shock to public opinion', and it was felt to be essential by British representatives in Spain that the British point of view should be expressed as forcibly and as frequently as possible.[8] In the Middle East and North Africa, while French policy had not been in all respects popular in the Arab countries, 'the military collapse of France was a serious blow to confidence in the success of the

---

[1] *Ibid., Sept. 1940.

[2] *BBC Monitoring Service, *Editorial Bulletin*, 29 July, 2 Aug. 1940.

[3] *Ibid. There is also a note in BBC Monitoring Service, *Editorial Bulletin*, 12 Oct. 1940: 'The Digest helps Mr. Churchill.' Churchill had been given the figure of the tonnage of German bombs dropped on Britain by the Monitoring Service via the Air Ministry.

[4] *BBC *Monitoring Day Book*, 14 May 1940.

[5] *Ibid., 4 June 1940.

[6] *Ibid., 12 June 1940.   [7] *Ibid., 22 July 1940.

[8] *BBC Overseas Intelligence Department, *Monthly Intelligence Report, Latin America, Spain and Portugal*, 15 July 1940.

Allied cause',[1] and Churchill himself was anxious that the full resources of broadcasting should be used to restore morale.[2] A second BBC news bulletin in Arabic was introduced at once, a new Palestinian announcer was appointed, steps were taken to explore the possibilities of broadcasts in North African dialects,[3] and efforts were made to co-ordinate policy and propaganda in relation not only to broadcasting but to the Press and the cinema. The same kind of problems arose as were being posed in discussions of European broadcasting. 'Those responsible for German and Italian broadcasts are quite obviously supplied with the most detailed and up-to-date information available to their governments concerning the political situation in the countries to which their propaganda is addressed. In this respect the BBC Arabic Service is at a disadvantage.'[4]

While most of the difficulties confronting the Latin American services were dictated by the course of historical events and Latin American reactions to them,[5] BBC broadcasts in Arabic were subject to sharp, even acrimonious, criticism from Professor Rushbrook Williams in the Ministry of Information[6] and from the British Foreign Office itself. The Germans were making much of the fact that they had always sympathized with the Arab cause 'and hoped that the Arabs would one day regain their position in the world consistent with the honour of their race and their great history'.[7] To counter propaganda of this kind, it was suggested, specialists should be enlisted to assist the Arabic News Editor, Donald Stephenson, and the

---

[1] *BBC Overseas Intelligence Department, *Monthly Intelligence Report, Arab Countries*, 22 July 1940.

[2] *Report of a meeting held on 13 Aug. 1940. 'Broadcasts to North-West and West Africa should be carried to the highest point.'

[3] *S. Hillelson, Note on Planning of the Arabic Service, 18 July 1940. 'It is a matter for serious consideration whether the BBC should not inaugurate broadcasts in Moroccan or Algerian Arabic.' It was impossible to start these services in 1940. The Moroccan appointed was arrested in Tangier in November 1940 for 'speaking against Spain in a local café'.

[4] *BBC Overseas Intelligence Department, *Monthly Intelligence Report, Arab Countries*, 19 Aug. 1940.

[5] *BBC Overseas Intelligence Department, *Monthly Intelligence Report, Latin America*, undated, probably Oct. 1940. In the Latin American Press Dakar was compared with the Norwegian expedition.

[6] For Rushbrook Williams's later role in the BBC, see below, pp. 499–500.

[7] *German broadcast in Arabic, 21 Oct. 1940.

Programme Organizer.[1] Harold Nicolson told Ogilvie of criticisms made by R. A. Butler of the running of the existing service,[2] and pressed for some 'definite decision' in order that Duff Cooper might reply to 'the criticisms which pour in from our representatives in the Middle East'.[3]

Although the BBC made a reasoned defence of its policies within the limits of its resources—Donald Stephenson wrote an impressive 'broad review' of what was happening[4]—and went on in September 1940 to co-ordinate its Arabic, Persian and Turkish services, with S. Hillelson as Director,[5] the current of criticism was not checked. Clearly there were many influential critics who continued to query the BBC's view that, above all else, it should provide the Arab (a doubtful type when generalized) with the day's news, however salted or gilded, and that there should be no copying of the 'unrestrained deluge' of the German broadcasts from Zeesen. In early November Duff Cooper sent to Ogilvie a copy of a telegram from Eden, the Secretary of State for War, who was out in the Middle East and who was being told on all sides that BBC news bulletins in Arabic were repeating unconfirmed rumours from enemy sources and showing lack of 'virility and incisiveness' as compared with bulletins in Turkish.[6] He added that the Prime Minister himself was much concerned and demanded an explanation. Eden and Duff Cooper were so disturbed with

---

[1] *Note of a meeting between Tallents, Clark, Rushbrook Williams and Dr. Arberry, 2 July 1940; S. Hillelson, Suggestions for a Planning and Research Board, 5 July 1940; exchange of letters between Barbour and Rushbrook Williams, 25, 29 July, 7, 9 Aug. 1940; J. B. Clark to Wellington, 21 Aug. 1940; Wellington to Clark, 22 Aug. 1940.

[2] *Nicolson to Ogilvie, 8 July 1940. There had been strong criticisms earlier in the year. German broadcasts in Arabic were said to make a successful appeal to 'the semi-educated and illiterate classes', and the British were said not to take enough account of 'Arab mentality'. (*BBC Overseas Intelligence Department, Memorandum on the Arabic Service, 17 May 1940).

[3] *Nicolson to Tallents, 11 July 1940. There had been criticisms from Glubb Pasha who sketched out an outline of an ideal programme for the Transjordanian Bedouins which the BBC thought would be most unsuitable for sophisticated audiences in Syria, Egypt and the Sudan.

[4] *Stephenson to J. B. Clark, 12 July 1940.

[5] He was appointed Assistant Director on 9 Sept. and Director on 5 Oct. Stephenson became Near East News Editor on 7 Oct., and Assistant Director on 1 April 1941.

[6] *Duff Cooper to Ogilvie, 7 Nov. 1940. For Eden's visits to the Middle East, see The Earl of Avon, Memoirs: The Reckoning (1965), pp. 169–70.

what they were being told that they suggested that the Ministry of Information should take over all foreign broadcasting.

The argument was part of a much larger war-time argument, and there were elements in it which anticipated debates at a much later stage in the history of broadcasting.[1] The Cabinet decided to set up a committee under Kingsley Wood to examine what changes, if any, were necessary in the constitution and management of the BBC to ensure fuller governmental control. For its part, the BBC could find no traces of unconfirmed rumour in its Arabic broadcasts, nor could it detect any evidence of deviation from British foreign policy.[2] In a series of exchanges between Ogilvie and Frank Pick, the Director-General of the Ministry of Information—he had succeeded Lord Perth on 12 August 1940—Pick explained that Downing Street was disturbed by the Eden telegram and painted a dark picture of the issues involved. He added, nonetheless, that much of the criticism was unfair and prejudiced. 'The trouble is that our masters, the politicians in the Cabinet, will not stop to reflect upon the situation.'[3]

The effort more closely to control the BBC continued,[4] but the problems of the Near East Services were resolved, temporarily, at least, on 19 November at a meeting attended by representatives of the BBC, the Ministry of Information and the Foreign Office. The main conclusions were that the fortnightly interdepartmental meetings on the Arabic Service should now be held weekly and that the BBC should produce a comprehensive memorandum on the principles and layout of the Service. Hillelson produced a general memorandum a few weeks later which gives a concise and vivid description of the Arabic Service and its senior staff at that time.[5] News and propaganda were being supplemented by entertainment in an effort to 'attract and hold the attention of an audience not primarily interested in news and politics'. It was also suggested

[1] See H. Grisewood, *One Thing at a Time* (1968).

[2] *Ogilvie to Duff Cooper, 8 Nov. 1940. Regular meetings were held at the Ministry of Information to deal with the Near East. They were attended by Rushbrook Williams and by representatives of the Foreign Office and of PID. Ogilvie claimed that 'the best possible broadcasting as a fighting service is the only thing for which we are working'.

[3] *Tallents to Ogilvie, 16 Nov. 1940; Pick to Tallents, 18 Nov. 1940.

[4] See below, pp. 329 ff.

[5] *Memorandum on the Arabic Service of the BBC, 10 Dec. 1940.

in the same month that there should be a permanent BBC representative based in Cairo.[1]

By the time that these suggestions were being made, the war had moved to North Africa. Another kind of counter-attack had at last begun. To understand the role of broadcasting, both domestic and international, in the crowded year of 1940, however, it is necessary to go back in time to the Battle of Britain, for it was that battle which was decisive in relation to the whole history, psychological as well as military, of the Second World War.

5. The Battle of Britain

WHILE such intensive efforts were being made to mobilize opinion in Europe and other parts of the world during the summer and autumn of 1940, Britain was alone. The presence of Allied governments and foreign forces on British soil provided more of a consolation than a support. As the summer went by, the possibility of invasion always seemed real.

Yet events remained surprising. The Battle of Britain, the beginning of which Churchill announced in his 'finest hour' speech of 18 June, was an air battle, not a land battle. It was a battle, moreover, between élites and not between 'masses'. And while the Germans seemed assured that they would win it—'it will take between a fortnight and a month to smash the enemy air force,' General Stapf wrote to his colleague General Halder, on 11 July[2]—it ended in a British victory. In relation to the history of the Second World War as a whole, it was decisive: as a Belgian writer has written simply in retrospect, 'la victoire dans le ciel d'Angleterre a sauvé le monde'.[3]

It is possible to note also in retrospect how confused and indecisive German thinking and planning were during this

---

[1] *J. B. Clark to Wellington, 20 Dec. 1940.
[2] Quoted in D. Richards, *Royal Air Force, 1939–1945*, vol. 1, (1953) p. 155.
[3] H. Bernard, 'Les tournants militaires' in *Les Dossiers de la seconde guerre mondiale* (1964), p. 33.

critical period, how much precious time was wasted at the moment of greatest opportunity, and how the attack itself strengthened British civil defence.[1] The tactics of German broadcasters were far less effective in these circumstances than they had been during the *Blitzkrieg* in Holland, Belgium and France. The Germans continued to draw a distinction between the 'plutocratic', 'war-mongering' British Government and the British people itself,[2] but since they lacked any clear idea of the vacillations of German military and political leadership or of the range of possible invasion dates, they were just as ill-equipped psychologically and politically to cope with Hitler's military plans as they had been to cope with his brief but ambivalent 'peace gestures'. They certainly did not know to what extent an air attack on Britain—'Operation Eagle'—was itself designed to serve as a prelude to a direct assault by sea and land—'Operation Sea Lion'. The final German Home Service broadcast on the armistice negotiations at Compiègne had ended with the playing of *We Sail Against England*. Yet on 4 August Deutschlandsender had to deny that there was any inconsistency in the simultaneous threat of a war of attrition and Goering's declaration that the Luftwaffe was getting ready for a total war on England. The language was more reassuring than realistic. 'We see no inconsistency whatever. Everything will be done at the right time.'[3]

Nonetheless, it was ominous for Englishmen, in the light of what had happened earlier on the eve of the Battle of France, that on 12 and 13 August, when the Air Battle of Britain began in earnest,[4] the Germans made no attempt to suggest to their own home listeners that a decisive operation was beginning: indeed, they placed more emphasis on the blockade than on the air attack. Fritzsche told his audience on 17 August that 'we have

---

[1] T. Taylor, *The Breaking Wave* (1967); P. Fleming, *Invasion 1940* (1957), pp. 197–201; and T. H. O'Brien, *Civil Defence* (1955).

[2] See above, pp. 232–3: German Press Directive for 8 Aug. 1940; E. K. Bramsted, *Goebbels and National Socialist Propaganda* (1965), p. 240.

[3] L. Kris and H. Speier, *German Radio Propaganda* (1944), pp. 388–9.

[4] The war-time British account given by the Air Ministry in its *The First Great Air Battle in History* (1941) treated the period from 8 Aug. to 23 Aug. as Phase I (Objects of Attack, Shipping and Ports). Phase II lasted from 24 Aug. to 5 Sept. (Objects of Attack: Inland Fighter Aerodromes, Aircraft Factories and Residential sections). Phase III (6 Sept. to 5 Oct.) was the assault on industry and on London. Phase IV (6 Oct. to 31 Oct.) was an attack on London and scattered objectives.

never asserted that all that was needed to make the British Empire collapse was a push with the finger'.[1] The German Press, along with the radio, was warned not to issue special bulletins—*Sondermeldungen*—announcing or promising any kind of 'knockout blow'.[2]

There was a contrast, of course, between what German home listeners were told and what the British were told in talks from Germany. NBBS stated as a 'straight' news item on 14 August that parachutists were landing near Birmingham, Manchester and Glasgow and were being sheltered by fifth columnists. Yet the German Home Service also tried out satire in making such comments as 'the most fashionable sickness in England is parachutist fever' or 'the English plutocracy is resorting to the maxim that it is easier to die when drunk than sober'.[3] There were stories on NBBS and Workers' Challenge about organized groups of disgruntled British workers who were opposed to the war mustering themselves in workshops, factories, mines and dockyards. Yet in the German Home Service the main emphasis was on British dread of what would happen. 'The English fear of an impending German military invasion is weighing like a huge nightmare on the inhabitants of the British Isles.'[4]

The original date set for Operation Sea Lion was 15 August, but although British G.H.Q. knew of this date, no special precautions were taken except for the cancellation of a training exercise.[5] The day came and went. On 7 September, three days after Hitler had pledged himself in public to invasion, the NBBS was assuring its listeners that 'Hitler may at any hour give orders for the invasion to begin'[6] and Press Chief Dietrich had moved his headquarters to the French coast ready for the 'historic moment'. On the same day, the British issued the order 'Cromwell', the alert was sounded, the church bells were rung, and the Home Guard stood to arms. The

---

[1] *BBC *Analysis of Foreign Broadcasts*, 20 Aug. 1940. See also Bramsted, op. cit., pp. 240 ff.

[2] Press Directives for 20 July, 6 Aug. and 11 Aug. 1940, printed in Bramsted, op. cit., p. 240.   [3] Kris and Speier, op. cit., p. 301.   [4] Ibid., p. 302.

[5] P. Fleming, op. cit., p. 257. It was on 16 July that Hitler directed that preparations for invasion should go ahead.

[6] An NBBS speaker said on 6 Sept. 'I lay down the main lines of action and co-ordinate activities throughout the country. It is up to you to use originality and enterprise.' On the 9th he added that the Fifth Column was ready.

alert remained in force until 19 September, while in the mean-time the German air attack was switched to London. 'The fact that the raids were now under the personal command of Goering,' NBBS warned on 10 September, 'can only be interpreted as the definite beginning of the invasion.'

A new date for Operation Sea Lion was fixed—21 September. Once again the day came and went—as did a third selected date, 27 September, when invasion was postponed 'until further notice'. On 12 October the decision was taken to cancel any invasion plans for the rest of the winter. In effect, if not in intention, Operation Eagle had gone forward on its own. To the British, war in the autumn of 1940 meant not war against invaders but the air 'blitz', the kind of war, indeed, which had been forecast before 1939 and in terms of which the first precautions had been taken.

While the 'Battle of Britain' raged—the Germans were later to deny that it ever took place[1]—the world had the opportunity of comparing two accounts of what was happening. The Americans wrote dramatically of a 'battle of the communiqués'. The history of this battle is at least as confused as that of any battle in history. What is clear at once is that neither side produced accurate statistics, and what becomes clear almost at once is that the reception given to the statistics in different parts of the world was influenced by far more than the simple desire to know the truth. The figures of air losses as given at the time by the British and the Germans are set out in the following table (p. 288) which compares them with the actual losses.

Peter Fleming has calculated that, all in all, between 10 July and 31 October the British over-stated their case by 55 per cent and the Germans by 234 per cent.[2] In itself this gap is wide. The immediate reaction to the statistics as offered at the time must be assessed, however, in terms of psychology as much as of arithmetic. In Britain, where the Air Ministry never implied that the figures released each day were pro-visional, the statistics had an important psychological effect on a country fighting for its life: they inspired 'not only the fighter pilots but the whole nation to still greater miracles of effort'.[3]

---

[1] Kris and Speier, op. cit., p. 389.   [2] Fleming, op. cit., p. 231.
[3] Richards, op. cit., pp. 170-1; see also B. Collier, *The Defence of the United Kingdom* (1957) and *The Battle of Britain* (1962).

British and German Losses—16 August–6 September 1940[1]

August:	BRITISH LOSSES as reported by			GERMAN LOSSES as reported by		
	BBC	Deutsch-land-sender	Actual	BBC	Deutsch-land-sender	Actual
16	22	92	21	75	31	45
17	nil	5	nil	1	1	4
18	22	147	27	152	36	71
19	3	5	3	6	2	6
20	2	10	2	8	3	6
21	1	7	1	13	6	13
22	4	11	5	10	2	2
23	nil	7	nil	3	2	5
24	19	64	22	50	20	39
25	13	72	16	55	14	20
26	15	70	31	47	21	41
27	nil	3	nil	3	1	3
28	14	44	20	28	15	30
29	9	21	9	10	7	17
30	25	98	25	62	34	36
31	37	133	39	88	32	41
September:						
1	15	62	15	25	9	14
2	20	93	31	55	23	35
3	15	†	16	25	†	16
4	17	57	17	54	17	25
5	20	46	20	39	16	23
6	19	67	23	46	24	35

† Not available.

[1] *This table is based on BBC Monitoring Service reports, Home Service news bulletins, and D. Wood and D. Dempster, *The Narrow Margin* (1961), Chapters 15 and 16. Richards, op. cit., p. 191 has an invaluable table of weekly statistics which also gives production figures.

In the table as printed, actual British losses and those quoted from BBC bulletins do not include aircraft destroyed on the ground, for which the German High Command made the following claims within the day's totals:

16 August	23 (the actual number was considerably greater, but many of them were trainers: see *The Narrow Margin*, pp. 285–6).
18 August	23 (this figure also included planes destroyed in A.A. fire).
24 August	7 (this figure also included planes destroyed in A.A. fire).
26 August	9
31 August	14
1 September	10
2 September	4
4 September	2
6 September	13

BBC figures and figures of actual losses do not include the small number of British aircraft lost in operations against Germany and occupied Europe. These losses were included in the German High Command communiqués.

Some anxiety had been expressed earlier in the summer that too little was being said about British air losses, and Vernon Bartlett had been asked, like Joubert, to explain how casualties to enemy aircraft were checked and verified.[1] Yet by the time the air battle began, the emphasis had shifted to 'the marvellous spadework which has gone into the production of our air fighting machine'.[2] The heat and excitement of the battle stirred the public to pride rather than to analysis.

In Germany, where the public was told that Churchill systematically reversed the figures given in the German communiqués,[3] stories of the battle were handled so carefully from the start that the way was prepared by propagandists for something like the final outcome. At first, the emphasis was on the size of the attack. 'The first absolute air war in history is being fought over England,' Air General Quade proclaimed on 24 August.[4] Comment of this type remained predominant during the first and second phases of the offensive when the Germans made their biggest mistake of the battle by switching their attack from fighter stations to other targets. During the third phase, the mass bombing of London,[5] the main theme of German propaganda was no longer German power but German retribution: attention was focused on the 'un-provoked' British bombing of Berlin on 25/26 August and on successive nights.[6] It was not until 7 September, three days after Hitler had said that he would reduce London to chaos, that the Germans reported that 'this afternoon the Luftwaffe attacked for the first time the city and port of London with considerable forces'. German planes, they went on, had 'chased through the night sky like comets' and pounded 'with relentless violence'.[7] 'The Day of Judgement' was at hand. 'London would become a second Warsaw.'[8]

---

[1] *Maconachie to Ryan, 14 Aug. 1940.

[2] *Ryan to Edgar, 23 Aug. 1940.   [3] Kris and Speier, op. cit., p. 393.

[4] *BBC *Analysis of Foreign Broadcasts*, 27 Aug. 1940.

[5] Fritzsche had said earlier that Londoners could sit safely in their shelters, knowing that they were far away from military objectives.

[6] Richards, op. cit., p. 182.

[7] In his speech of 4 Sept. he promised that 'if the British Air Force drop 2 or 3 or 4,000 bombs in one night, we will drop 150, 180, 230,000' (*BBC *Analysis of Foreign Broadcasts*, 10 Sept. 1940; Richards, op. cit., pp. 183–4; Kris and Speier, op. cit., p. 399).

[8] *BBC *Analysis of Foreign Broadcasts*, 15 Oct. 1940.

Yet as it became clear that the heavy German attacks on London in early September, personally conducted by Goering himself,[1] were not achieving their intended effect, the gap between what was being said by the Germans over the air and what was actually happening in London widened alarmingly. British morale was not cracking, yet Deutschlandsender was reporting that 'stories of panic and flight recall the flights of the civilian population from Belgium and Northern France before the offensive of German troops'.[2] This was the first time during the war that German home listeners were being given a completely unreal picture of what was happening abroad. As the number of new aircraft emerging from British factories each week was beginning to exceed the number lost and as the Germans were being forced to shift from day attacks to night attacks, 'a measure of Fighter Command's triumph',[3] effective retribution seemed as unlikely as complete victory.

15 September, in retrospect, was the day of the greatest British victory: the British lost 26 aeroplanes and the Germans between 50 and 60. At the time, the extent of the victory was grossly inflated—the British claimed 185 German losses as against 25 of their own—but the Germans, who claimed 79 British losses, themselves conceded that they had lost 43 aircraft, a bigger figure than on any previous day of the Battle.[4] From this time onwards, Goebbels and his colleagues had to face the fact that the Luftwaffe had not been successful in establishing the degree of overwhelming air superiority which would have permitted Operation Eagle, with or without Operation Sea Lion, to destroy Britain. There had to be a change of tone, therefore, both for overseas and home audiences. 'The German attack on England,' a German broadcaster to South America put it on 4 October, 'is chiefly

[1] One of the raids was accompanied by the star broadcasting expert Hadamowsky, who vividly described in a broadcast of 11 Sept. 1940 a 'city which can no longer find any rest'. (Kris and Speier, op. cit., pp. 400–1.)

[2] *BBC *Analysis of Foreign Broadcasts*, 17 Sept. 1940: Deutschlandsender broadcast of 10 Sept. NBBS was describing with relish the heavy casualties, the panic, the profiteering, the administrative chaos and the threat of epidemic and of revolution.

[3] Richards, op. cit., p. 193.

[4] Fritzsche attacked the figure of 185 as wildly inaccurate: Kris and Speier in 1944 took the figure as true without any attempt at criticism. The fact that Fritzsche quoted the precise figure given by the British was itself significant. He was able to make the most of it because he knew it did not make sense.

important from the point of view of war economy; less important from the purely military point of view.'[1] Deutschlandsender itself began to speak more dispassionately of 'the nerves and endurance of Londoners' (21 September) and their 'remarkable resistance and tenacity' (18 September), while Fritzsche, who had made much of the social tensions created by bombing—'the poor are left homeless while the plutocrats shelter in safety or leave the city altogether'—was driven to admit on 17 September that 'London, now at the mercy of German bombs, is still unable to free itself from the spell of the upper classes who have ruled there for centuries'.[2] 'France collapsed when her army was beaten,' Radio Hamburg reported on 21 October. 'There is no such possibility of bringing about a collapse of Britain.'[3] It was left to Fritzsche to rationalize the situation. 'We Germans have never prophesied immediate victories as the English did. . . . We have only declared that victory—the date of which nobody can tell—will be ours.'[4] The BBC monitors noted correctly that by the beginning of November, 'in its range of appeal and subject matter the argument of the Hamburg group of stations is tending to return to its position in the period of static war which preceded the invasion of Scandinavia'.[5]

To some neutral countries, particularly the United States, German propaganda became as distasteful during the Battle of Britain as British resistance became inspiring. Yet particularly during the early stages of the battle the Germans struggled hard to convince the world that 'England has not only lost the greatest air battle there has been but also the greatest propaganda battle', and that 'naturally [sic] the German, not the English, reports of recent air battles are believed in the world'.[6] The Ministry of Information had been so 'irreparably discredited', they went on, 'that even Churchill himself had

---

[1] *BBC Research Unit (Overseas) Report No. 87 (1941).

[2] *BBC *Analysis of Foreign Broadcasts*, 24 Sept. 1940.

[3] *BBC *Analysis of Foreign Broadcasts*, 29 Oct. 1940.

[4] Quoted in Kris and Speier, op. cit., p. 402. Later in June 1941 Fritzsche was to pooh-pooh British 'drivel about the alleged German air battle over England' and to describe it as 'fantasies told by British firesides . . . to conceal the failure of the RAF from the last autumn up till now' (ibid., pp. 389–90).

[5] *BBC *Analysis of Foreign Broadcasts*, 5 Nov. 1940. See also Bramsted, op. cit., pp. 242–3.

[6] Kris and Speier, op. cit., p. 393.

by-passed it' and instead was now using the Air Ministry and
the Ministry of Home Security as 'mouthpieces for his lies
about the air raids'. They also referred back to 'British lies'
about Bergen and Trondheim during the Norwegian campaign.
Inevitably, therefore, as the battle went on, the Germans found
themselves facing unanticipated difficulties in their overseas
propaganda. The tables were turned by mid-September. As
the Germans began to accuse the British of living in a 'world of
illusions' and of refusing to face up to the hard facts of German
power, there were many people outside Britain who were
beginning to think that it was the Germans who were living
in a world of illusions if they believed they could smash Britain.
There were some commentators also who anticipated Chester
Wilmot's verdict that Hitler had suffered his first great failure,
of far greater ultimate consequence than all his victories.[1]
Later in the war, in October 1942, Hitler was to justify the German failure to defeat Britain in 1940 by arguing that 'the
settling of accounts' with England would have tied down the
whole of the German Luftwaffe at a time when in his rear
'there was standing a state already getting ready to go against
us at such a moment'.[2] He was, indeed, already looking not
West but East as the autumn went by, and his first famous
'Barbarossa' directive concerning Russia was issued on 18
December.

One main reason why the British account of what was happening was more acceptable at the time in the United States
than the German account was the skill, the integrity and,
above all, the courage of American commentators in London.
Earlier in the year, when 'America Firsters' were mustering
their strength and turning to advertising agencies to plan radio
programmes, complete with celestial choirs, in an effort to
prevent any American aid to Britain[3]—a pro-British publicity
campaign was launched in the United States. The events of
September and October 1940 spoke louder than words,
particularly when they were interpreted in the stirring words,
hot, immediate words, of Ed Murrow and his fellow-corres-
pondents. 'You burned the city of London in our houses,'

---

[1] C. Wilmot, *The Struggle for Europe* (1966), p. 59. For current comment in
1940 see *BBC Analysis of Foreign Broadcasts*, 22 Oct. 1940.
[2] Quoted in Kris and Speier, op. cit., p. 389.   [3] *Broadcasting*, 15 Oct. 1940.

Archibald MacLeish was to write to Ed Murrow later, 'and we felt the flames that burned it. You laid the dead of London at our doors and we knew the dead were our dead—were all men's dead—were mankind's dead—and ours.'[1] The policy of allowing American correspondents to inspect the scenes of raids, to talk to wide cross-sections of the population and to have free access to the microphone was abundantly justified.

The occasional critical note in American broadcasts added to the sense of veracity: Raymond Gram Swing, among others, complained of the slowness of Air Ministry reporting. A broadcast by Duff Cooper on 3 August in which he had spoken with excessive zeal of the 'eagerness' of the British for more German bombers to come had been particularly strongly criticized: in Ed Murrow's words, 'the Minister's time might have been better spent in getting a few of his despatches through the censors in time to make the headlines of the New York newspapers'. Murrow was always prepared, as Priestley was, to praise individual courage while criticizing social or political ineptitude. 'There is room for many opinions about the diplomatic, economic and military policy of the British government,' he declared on 18 August. 'This country is still ruled by a class.' Yet 'if the people who rule Britain are made of the same stuff as the little people I have seen today, then the defence of Britain will be something of which men will speak with awe and admiration so long as the English language survives.'[2] As the 'blitz' continued, Murrow, brave, resourceful, superbly articulate, was always in the thick of it: so too was Fred Bate, the London representative of NBC, who after being injured when a landmine exploded in Portland Place on 8 December 1940 still tried to get into Broadcasting House to read his script.

Broadcasting House was a landmark—and a target—in the German attack on London. It had become something of a fortress during the months of invasion scare, when orders from the Commander-in-Chief, Home Forces, and from Fighter Command were given priority over directives from the Ministry

[1] Quoted in F. W. Friendly, *Due to Circumstances Beyond our Control* (1967), p. xvi.
[2] E. Bliss (ed.), *In Search of Light* (1968), p. 29.

of Information.[1] Even before the beginnings of the Home Guard groups of volunteers had been assembled to patrol the studios and corridors. They wore arm bands, carried torches and were armed with truncheons. Later, the BBC's own Home Guard, which was to carry out its duties efficiently and enthusiastically for the rest of the war—it had to be reminded very early in its history that broadcasting came first[2]—was very effectively mobilized before the air blitz began. By then, the central Control Room, the News Studio and the Emergency News Room had all been transferred to the sub-basement and the Defence Room had been sealed off with an iron door protected by armed guards: the door bore a notice saying that anyone who did not show a pass would be shot at sight.

Every effort was made, therefore, to 'carry on' the broadcasting service during 'the aerial attack on London'.[3] Before Broadcasting House was bombed for the first time—on 15 October—there had already been several serious 'incidents', each of which was recorded faithfully by Ralph Wade, who was in charge of all the BBC's London premises throughout the blitz. St. George's Hall, with its nationally known BBC Theatre Organ, had already been gutted by incendiary bombs on 25 September;[4] there had been a daylight raid on Tatsfield Receiving Station on 3 October; and on 14 October the upper floors of Beaumont Mews, Marylebone High Street, the BBC Publications office before the war, had also been destroyed by fire.

The 500-pound time bomb which landed on Broadcasting House on 15 October was a direct hit. It entered by a window on the seventh floor, crashed through the walls of the fifth floor, and came to rest in the Music Library on the third floor. It caused so much damage in its transit that staff did not realize at once that it had not exploded: an order to clear the Tower was not given soon enough to save the lives of a number

[1] The 'Document C' Committee, which had drawn up BBC war plans, had been reconstructed with enlarged terms of reference in May 1940 and held eleven meetings under Waterfield's chairmanship between 11 May and 15 July 1940.

[2] *Control Board, *Minutes*, 22 Aug. 1940.

[3] *A special meeting of Control Board was held on 17 Sept. 1940 to deal with this subject.

[4] It had been unoccupied since the Variety Department moved to Bristol. See above, p. 107.

of employees on the third and fifth floors—seven in all, four men and three women (four were in the Monitoring Service).[1] Such severe damage was done to the Tower that it took a year to repair the structure and three years to restore the studios.[2] The BBC's Home Service did not interrupt its programmes on this or any other occasion. The explosion took place when Bruce Belfrage was reading the nine o'clock News. Listeners in their homes heard a distant thud, a slight pause, the whispered words 'Are you all right?' and Bruce Belfrage continuing as if nothing had happened.

More serious damage still was done in the late evening of Sunday 8 December when a landmine exploded in the centre of Portland Place. A policeman was killed in the street, a car parked outside Broadcasting House was set on fire, and the building was shaken by blast, ravaged by fires which could not be put out for seven hours, and deluged with water. According to an eye witness, a BBC engineer, L. D. Macgregor, who has left an unforgettable account of the incident, Broadcasting House resembled 'a scene from Dante's *Inferno*'.[3] Marmaduke Tudsbery, the BBC's Civil Engineer, arrived on the scene soon after the bombing. 'The rest of the story,' he wrote characteristically, 'is commonplace (in war time!); it remains only to say that I didn't see my bed again that night.' Broadcasting House he had regarded as 'my building, on which I had, with others, lavished so much care in its planning and construction only a few years before'. He had now become one of London's office-less. 'Instead of my handsome 7th floor office in B.H. now a wreck, I've to be content with a rat-trap in a small building nearby: Egton House.'[4]

BBC engineers did a superb job repairing apparatus and wires and ensuring that broadcasting went on. So too did the producers, announcers and artists. During those difficult weeks people lived and slept (on a ticket basis) in Broadcasting House, took their meals there, and shared their gossip and

[1] *A Committee of Enquiry was instituted, and produced a report with five appendices dealing with Evidence, Narrative, Fatal Casualties, Payments and Recommendations. See B. Belfrage, *One Man in His Time* (1951), pp. 111–12.

[2] *M. T. Tudsbery to D. H. Clarke, 6 June 1965.

[3] The passage is quoted in D. Flower and J. Reeves, *The War, 1939–1945* (1960), p. 144; see also C. FitzGibbon, *The Blitz* (1957).

[4] *Note by Tudsbery, Dec. 1940.

ideas. The Concert Hall became a great dormitory, 'a discreet curtain of blankets being suspended across the room to divide the sexes'. 'I used to wonder,' Freddy Grisewood has written, 'what Sir John Reith, with his strict views about propriety, would think if he were to see all those men and women strewn about the floor on their mattresses with so flimsy a dividing line between them.'[1] And it was not only the Concert Hall which had changed. 'An air of uncertainty hovered about the interior of Broadcasting House at night. . . . When opening a door, no matter what the room, one never quite knew what to expect.'[2] Just outside Broadcasting House an armoured car was waiting every night to take the news reader to the Maida Vale studios if it was not possible to carry on from Broadcasting House.

That continuity was maintained was a tribute to engineers outside London as well as at Broadcasting House and to the provincial BBC staffs, some of whom were also subject to heavy German raids. Birmingham offices were damaged on 18 October; the Adderley Park transmitter totally destroyed on 19 November 1940; the Swansea studio and headquarters burnt down on 21 February 1941; and 35/37 Whiteladies Road, Bristol destroyed on 17 March 1941.[3] It says much for the years of careful preparation that whatever troubles befell, the system of synchronization worked smoothly. The Air Ministry might order certain stations to be closed down, as had been anticipated—during the period of invasion scare it had been decided optimistically that if any transmitters were in danger of capture by invading Germans they should not be destroyed 'since it is believed such capture would be a temporary occupation only'[4]—yet the Home Service went on uninterrupted, heard in all parts of the country with no regional isolation.[5] Fears that the Germans might fill the air with false news and false instructions on BBC wavelengths never materialized.[6] The

---

[1] F. Grisewood, *My Story of the BBC* (1959), p. 121.   [2] Ibid., p. 122.

[3] When Bristol was subjected to heavy German attacks, it was decided that large numbers of BBC staff, beginning with the Variety Department, should be transferred to other parts of the country. (*Control Board, *Minutes*, 9, 10 Dec. 1940.)   [4] *Note of 6 June 1940.

[5] Steps had been taken in the summer to determine the role of Regional Commissioners in the event of regional isolation. (*Home Board, *Minutes*, 7, 21, 28 June, 5 July 1940.)

[6] Detailed plans were made to deal with such contingencies, including diffusion of programmes and the use of short waves. (*Ibid., 30 Aug., 13 Sept. 1940.)

only way in which air raids affected listening in the home was that there was a sudden loss of volume and a deterioration of quality when the local station had to close down and the same programme was being received from a more distant station in the same group. Such a change was usually an indication that the air raid siren was about to wail. Even the loss of volume and deterioration of quality were checked as the BBC quickly and without fuss built large numbers of low-power transmitters to meet the needs of large centres of population. They were able to carry on when high-power transmitters were out of action and could work until enemy aircraft were very close indeed. There were ten of them in use by 10 November 1940.[1]

The success of this operation contrasts with the failure of the German Home Service to maintain continuous broadcasting, even though British raids on Germany in 1940 never reached the dimensions of German raids on Britain. Many medium-wave German stations were regularly closed early in the evening, and on a bad day, like 21 October, all but four German and German-controlled long and medium-wave stations in Europe were off the air for a significant period.[2]

During the blitz BBC programme output never reverted, even when danger was greatest, to the dull model of September 1939, and there was never any necessity, as at one time seemed possible, to return to one single home programme.[3] Of course the programme planners faced a particularly difficult dilemma when the future was so uncertain—whether to plan eight weeks ahead, as in peace time, which often meant running the risk of seeing their work thrown away at the eleventh hour, or whether to improvise and reveal to a public which wanted mixed fare and good fare inevitable signs of lack of arrangement and haste.

The demand for 'topicality' persisted, with the nine o'clock News as popular as ever, even after the beginning of heavy air

---

[1] See above, p. 63.

[2] *BBC *Monitoring Day Book*, 3 Sept., 21 Oct. 1940; Miss Benzie to Salt, 31 Oct. 1940: 'We fear that it isn't generally realised here that the German Service has been drastically curtailed . . . by closing down so many of their medium-wave stations at 7.15.'

[3] *Home Board, *Minutes*, 12 July 1940. Reducing staff and simplifying administration were two of the reasons given for reverting to a single programme.

raids.[1] Greater 'punch' and 'vigour' were introduced into the news bulletins,[2] yet bulletins dealing with the scale and effects of the blitz were severely censored. Since the BBC, like the Press, had to avoid giving useful information to the Germans, it was forced to use vague phrases like 'a district in North London', 'considerable damage to house property' and 'many casualties, some fatal'. Nonetheless, 'human-interest programmes' were devised to show how London and other cities were weathering the air attack, some of them designed with an eye on an overseas as well as a home audience. Outstanding among them were two specifically overseas programmes, *London After Dark* and *London Carries On*, broadcast during air raids at night from various points in the capital, with the background sound of London's anti-aircraft barrage in action. *The People of Coventry*, which followed the heavy German attack on the city in November, was said to have been 'superbly done'.[3] Although there were some signs by then that the American public was becoming less interested in air raids as such—'they had lost their news value'[4] —concern was strong in Britain and the Empire. The defence of Britain was dramatized for British home listeners in *Spitfires over Britain*, *Watchers of the Sky*, and *Balloon Barrage*, while these programmes were deliberately balanced by other features seeking to show that Britain was not simply on the defensive. *Bombers over Berlin* dealt with British air initiatives; *The Patrol of the 'Salmon'* and *Swept Channels* were concerned with Britain's naval activities on which long-range victory was said to depend.

The 'patriotic' theme predominated throughout home broadcasting during this period. *Napoleon Couldn't Do It* by L. du Garde Peach was presented as a 'topical parallel' during the first week of September, along with a special children's

---

[1] *Ryan to Pick, 24 Oct. 1940.

[2] *Home Board, *Minutes*, 28 June 1940. An effort was made to break away from the language of official statements. Announcers also became Programme Assistants. See Belfrage, op. cit., pp. 114–20.

[3] *Letter from a listener to A. Stewart, 28 Nov. 1940.

[4] *BBC *Analysis of Foreign Broadcasts*, 12 Nov. 1940. Fritzsche treated the raid on Coventry as retaliation for the British attack on a 'sacred shrine' in Munich and as a necessary attack on a great armaments centre. (Ibid., 19 Nov. 1940.) Later what had happened to Coventry was treated as a warning of what would happen elsewhere. NBBS reported that the police in Coventry had to keep the people from lynching Herbert Morrison, adding hopefully, 'it wouldn't take many raids like this to start a revolution'. (17 Nov. 1940.)

programme commemorating the outbreak of the war called
To Thee My Country and *Men of Mettle* dealing with heroes of
the war. These were followed by *They Went To It*, 'stories of
civilian courage from the regions', and Francis Dillon's *Jack
the Giant Killer*. A. L. Rowse broadcast on 'patriotism', and
Princess Elizabeth made her first broadcast—in Children's
Hour—on Sunday 13 October, with Princess Margaret adding
'Goodnight' at the end. Steps were taken also to prepare a
Churchill programme based on his life and his writings and—
the *caveat* was necessary—to be approved by him.[1]

Yet after all the debates of the summer[2] the pattern of
broadcasting allowed for entertainment as well as for instruction,
and German propagandists were as far from the truth in
arguing that BBC output consisted mainly of recordings 'put
on to keep up the spirit of the public when all else fails' as they
were in talking about the blitz itself.[3] Recordings of talks by
evening speakers were permitted because of travel difficulties,[4]
yet not only was there a severe shortage of recording equipment but all the old pre-war preferences for 'live programmes'
still persisted. Fritzsche might challenge the view that 'the
transmission of light dance music in a dark hour was proof of
unshakeable stability in adversity' on the grounds that 'it
was possible to put on a dance record on a gramophone even
with trembling hands'.[5] Others among his colleagues were
genuinely impressed by the BBC's trust in 'gaiety in the grimness'.[6] Cicely Courtneidge, Flanagan and Allen, Evelyn Laye,
John McCormack, Sir Harry Lauder, Binnie Hale, Jack
Buchanan, Max Miller, Sonnie Hale, Jessie Matthews,
Gracie Fields, Joan Winters, George Formby and Leslie
Henson were some of the entertainment stars of the last
months of 1940. *Band Waggon*, with Askey and Murdoch, and
Garrison Theatre were such favourites that they were recorded
well in advance, not for security reasons but because of the
war-time preoccupations of their principal artists; and *Hi
Gang*, a brand new show with an American team—Vic Oliver,

---

[1] *Note of 30 Aug. 1940; BBC Home Board, *Minutes*, 8 Nov. 1940.
[2] See above, pp. 216 ff.
[3] *BBC Monitoring Service, *Weekly Analysis*, 24 Sept. 1940.
[4] *Home Board, *Minutes*, 20 Sept. 1940.
[5] *BBC *Analysis of Foreign Broadcasts*, 10 Dec. 1940.
[6] This was the title of the chapter on Variety in the *BBC Handbook, 1941*, pp. 72–5.

Bebe Daniels and Ben Lyon—was such a success that by the end of the year, following pre-war precedents,[1] it was moved from the studio to the stage.[2]

Meanwhile, as a counterpart to 'gaiety in the grimness', religion served as 'a very present help in time of trouble'. Sunday 8 October was observed as a National Day of Prayer,[3] and the BBC was caught up in the entanglements of a well-backed public campaign to secure 'a dedicated minute' of silence before the nine o'clock News.[4] The campaign, which was pressed on the BBC by Captain Margesson—with the support of Churchill[5]—led the BBC to set up a powerful Advisory Committee to consider the question. It included Margesson, the Archbishop of York, Lord Macmillan, Major J. J. Astor and Miss Margaret Bondfield. In the light of the Committee's report, it was decided to broadcast the chimes of Big Ben, which lasted for a minute, before the nine o'clock News in place of the Greenwich time signal and to leave listeners to decide for themselves whether this interval, 'the Big Ben minute', was 'dedicated' or not. The sponsors of the scheme were not fully satisfied with this compromise, even though Big Ben had become a national symbol and it had been agreed that it should be broadcast live even at the risk of gunfire accompaniment.[6] An attempt to restore the Bow Bells interval signal was unsuccessful after the War Office had protested.[7]

The BBC Handbook for 1940 gave estimated average audiences for eleven well-known series of programmes in

---

[1] See Briggs, *The Golden Age of Wireless* (1965), pp. 115 ff.

[2] *Home Board, *Minutes*, 20 Dec. 1940. It ran for a year until 18 May 1941, and was started again in Nov. 1941.

[3] Another sad event in the history of religious broadcasting was the death of the Rev. Pat McCormick, Vicar of St. Martin-in-the-Fields, in Oct. 1940. For his role in broadcasting, see R. J. Northcott, *Pat McCormick* (1941).

[4] The idea had first been mooted very early in the war (see a letter in *The Scotsman*, 15 Nov. 1940). For the launching of the big campaign, see *The Times*, 8 Nov. 1940. Waldron Smithers, who wrote regularly and boringly to the BBC on every subject, was a staunch supporter (see *Truth*, 30 May 1941).

[5] *Home Board, *Minutes*, 4 Oct. 1940.

[6] *Ibid., 1 Nov., 22 Nov. 1940. For continuing pressure from Margesson, see ibid., 20 Dec. 1940, 7 Feb. 1941. The pamphlet of the 'Big Ben Movement' called *The Spiritual Front* is said to have sold 70,000 copies. See also the *Manchester Guardian*, 28 June 1941.

[7] *Home Board, *Minutes*, 20 Dec. 1940. The six pips which the BBC described as 'Greenwich time' no longer came from Greenwich after the bombing of the Greenwich Observatory. (*The Star*, 16 Dec. 1940.)

October 1940. Saturday night Variety was listened to by nearly eleven million people, almost a third of the entire population. *War Commentary* was heard by over seven millions, and *American Commentary* by six. *The Kitchen Front*, the series for housewives 'on what to eat and how to cook it', broadcast with the co-operation of the Ministry of Food, commanded an audience of well over five millions, and *The World Goes By* three-and-three-quarter millions. The Wednesday symphony concert, which was a permanent feature of the broadcast week, along with the Sunday afternoon concert, usually attracted an audience of over two-and-a-half millions, and a short session of evening prayers, broadcast three times a week in the late evening, was heard by a million-and-a-quarter listeners.[1]

Christmas 1940 was very different from Christmas 1939.[2] The King did not broadcast, nor did President Roosevelt, whose name also had been mentioned as a possibility.[3] The

Estimated Average Audiences for Eleven Well-known Series in October 1940	
Saturday Night Variety 8–9 p.m.	10,700,000
'War Commentary' Thursdays 9.20 p.m.	7,200,000
'American Commentary' Alternate Sats. 9.20 p.m.	5,800,000
'The Kitchen Front' (Talks) Daily 8.15 a.m.	5,400,000
'The World Goes By' Wednesdays 6.45 p.m.	3,750,000
'Music While You Work' Daily 10.30 a.m.	3,500,000
'The Week's Good Cause' Sundays 8.40 p.m.	3,250,000
'In Your Garden' (Talks) Sundays 2.15 p.m.	2,950,000
The Daily Service 10.15 a.m.	2,850,000
Wednesday Symphony Concert 8–9 p.m.	2,650,000
Evening Prayers Tues., Weds., Thurs. 10.15 p.m.	1,230,000

[1] *BBC Handbook, 1941*, pp. 78–80. The decision to produce this Handbook was taken in the middle of the blitz. (*Control Board, *Minutes*, 27 Sept. 1940.)

[2] See above, pp. 122–3.

[3] *Home Board, *Minutes*, 6 Dec. 1940. Duff Cooper opposed the suggestion. (Ibid., 29 Nov. 1940.)

IV

WORLD WAR

━━━━━━

In a war involving whole peoples, winter is bound to increase propaganda's share of the strain: this second winter of war may even make propaganda the decisive weapon.

BBC European Department, *Monthly Intelligence Report, Europe*, Nov. 1940

A year of events of historical significance is nearing its end. A year of the greatest decisions lies ahead.

HITLER, 11 December 1941

1. 'Sounds of War'

THE pattern of home broadcasting did not change significantly after the autumn of 1940 and the second winter of the war. It had been recognized explicitly by the Ministry of Information in May 1940 that 'the war is likely to be a long and hard struggle, and that our long-term policy should therefore continue unchanged except in so far as our activities have to be temporarily diverted to action designed to achieve an immediate effect'.[1] There were no such 'temporary diversions' between Christmas 1940 and the crucial entry of Russia into the war on 22 June 1941, although the news from abroad, coupled with continuing German bombing attacks, was often sufficiently dispiriting to threaten morale. 'We discuss the possible decline of morale,' wrote Harold Nicolson in May 1941, after a meeting of the Ministry's Home Planning Committee. 'It is true that nobody actually speaks of the possibility of defeat or surrender but this silence is a bad sign of repression. . . . Morale is good—but it is rather like the Emperor's clothes.'[2]

It has been argued in retrospect, that Hitler's Balkan campaign, which opened with his attack on Yugoslavia and Greece on 6 April 1941, postponed by critical weeks the start of his long-premeditated Russian campaign.[3] Leopold Amery had broadcast a remarkable talk in Serbo-Croat before the Royal Yugoslav Government, which wished to ratify a pact with Hitler, was forced to resign, and his salute to the 'fighting spirit' of Yugoslavia undoubtedly helped to inspire the group in Belgrade which engineered the *coup d'état*. He had broadcast with the full support of Churchill whom he telephoned when the Ministry of Information was proving cautious in its approach to a neutral

[1] *Ministry of Information Policy Committee, *Minutes*, 27 May 1940. Cf. the later and more limited German realization of the same point. Five years, it was said, was the only date-line by which Hitler felt bound. (*Das Reich*, 29 Sept. 1940, quoted in Bramsted, op. cit., p. 242.)

[2] H. Nicolson, *Diaries and Letters*, vol. II (1967), p. 165: entry for 8 May 1940. Wellington had urged at Home Board (*Minutes*, 7 Feb. 1941) that steps should be taken to counter the 'no worse off under Hitler type of defeatism'. A documentary feature on defeatism was planned. (Ibid., 7 March 1941.)

[3] See above, p. 292; G. von Blumentritt *et al.*, *The Fatal Decisions* (1956).

country, and his speech was amended to make it stronger in
tone as he and Leonard Miall descended in the lift to the
underground studios.[1] Yet it was the subsequent rapid collapse
of Yugoslavia[2] and the British failure to afford adequate
material assistance to the Greeks which affected British opinion.
Successes in East Africa and Iraq and the sinking of the
Bismarck[3] provided little consolation, particularly since the
Germans, led by Rommel, soon regained all Cyrenaica, which
had been captured from the Italians, with the exception of
beleaguered Tobruk. Hitler's decision to send German troops
to North Africa in February 1941 had opened up a new kind
of desert war, something of a war within a war, very different
in character from the war of 1914 to 1918 or from the war
which had raged in Europe in 1940.

In these circumstances, fears were often expressed that Haw-
Haw was coming into his own again. At the beginning of the
year, he was concentrating on the intractability of Britain's
domestic problems: by June 1941, he was ranging widely over
international questions. On 12 February he became a German
citizen, and on 3 April he divulged his identity to the British
public. Thereafter he was described on the German radio as
'William Joyce, otherwise known as Lord Haw-Haw'.[4] The
BBC was anxious—in so far as it took open notice of him at all—
to emphasize that his 'output' was 'the work of a syndicate
which combs the British Press and other services for reliable
information which in turn covers much less reliable information
and comment'.[5] Letters continued to pour in, however,

---

[1] There were interesting comments on the speech in the English newspapers
on 27 March. See, for example, *The Star*, which reported a conversation between
Amery and a reporter. 'When I suggested that his broadcast had had an effect on
the course of events Mr. Amery said "I won't take any credit for that, although
they do know me very well out there".'

[2] Philip Noel-Baker broadcast a postscript on Yugoslavia on 5 April, and a
feature *Salute to Yugoslavia* was broadcast, after the Foreign Office had seen the
script, on 6 April.

[3] Listeners heard the story of the attack on the *Bismarck* in a series of bulletins
culminating in a midnight bulletin on 27 May 1941, and a recording of a speech
on the subject by the First Lord of the Admiralty at a lunch in London was broadcast in the United States. Deutschlandsender broadcast the news at 10 p.m. on
the 27th followed by an interval of silence. A programme on 'The End of the
Bismarck' was broadcast on 5 June 1941.

[4] J. A. Cole, *Lord Haw-Haw—and William Joyce* (1964), pp. 176, 190-1.

[5] *Kirkpatrick to Rendall, 12 May 1941.

complaining that he was not being adequately answered. 'I listened in to Haw-Haw last night,' a letter of 16 January 1941 began, 'one of his better efforts, I thought. He had a list of ten points which Britain—so he said—would find impossible of solution after the war: building, labour, employment, health, etc. I tried to listen as though I had never heard him before. I was impressed by the methodical arrangement of his material and the (apparently) logical sequence of his argument. Had I been a stranger to his wiles I might perhaps have succumbed to him—until the moment when he attacked Churchill. Then suddenly I had the feeling . . . he was just a "chap with an axe to grind speaking for a nation trying to put something over on me". When he went on to attack the Jews this feeling was strengthened, and he ended up by totally antagonizing me and undoing the effect he had so carefully built up.'[1]

Reports of Haw-Haw's uncanny accuracy—he was said to have referred in detail to places as different and as far apart as Andover and Worcester[2]—and of the continuing interest shown by sailors and soldiers in his broadcasts[3] led the Ministry of Information to appoint a sub-committee to examine and assess the effects of enemy propaganda in English,[4] and Powell told Ogilvie a few weeks later that 'certain sections in Whitehall' continued to be worried 'by what they believe to be the extent and effects of British listening to Haw-Haw'.[5] Ogilvie in turn asked Silvey to report on the position. He replied soberly that 'the great craze for listening to Haw-Haw' was 'a thing of the past' and that 'a recrudescence of . . . prodigious listening is extremely remote unless the whole context of the war undergoes a radical change'. It was all too easy to get worried, even in Whitehall, 'on the strength of the testimony of one's wife's cousin's gardener'. Haw-Haw still had some listeners, of course. A number of them were Fascists. Others

[1] *Unsigned letter of 16 Jan. 1941.
[2] *There is a BBC list of places named in Haw-Haw rumours. In a note to J. B. Clark of 27 June 1941, Marriott pointed out once again that there was no real evidence for any of the rumours.
[3] *Letter of 26 March 1941 in which a Captain referred to 'the avidity with which the sailors tune in to German broadcasts in English'.
[4] *A. Stewart to Maconachie, 28 March 1941.
[5] *Ogilvie to Nicolls, 20 April 1941.

were listeners with 'an insatiable appetite for news'. 'In so far as our own News Bulletins are regarded or come to be regarded as untrue, inadequate, or tardy, people turn, or will turn to other news in English to some extent. . . . In so far as people think that there is news of military operations in Greece or North Africa which they are not hearing from the BBC, they will inevitably be tempted to go elsewhere in the hope of hearing it.'[1]

Unfortunately, there continued to be problems in the handling of News during the spring and early summer of 1941. The six bulletins a day were based on news collected from official communiqués, News Agency reports and the BBC's own observers, and there was ample scope for misunderstanding between the Government and the BBC. In October 1940, Ryan, who had by then been handling home news for six months, noted that 'important people in Parliament and the Civil Service sincerely lack confidence in the BBC'. They claimed that it resented official directives and only accepted them reluctantly or after argument and that it was seeking to compete for 'scoops' with the newspapers 'instead of realising that what is heard on the wireless goes immediately all round the world and is regarded everywhere, however it may be qualified, as the voice of the British Government'. These were old charges, and Ryan believed that they were unfounded. He also believed that the 'rational handling of News' should be regarded positively as 'a fourth arm in this war'.[2]

If members of the Government and the Armed Forces continued to criticize the BBC—and Wavell was often critical of reports on the North African fighting—the BBC itself continued to have counter charges to make. Conflicting orders came from different departments,[3] and all too frequently there was a 'stop' on important news which the Germans were able to exploit. Much of the criticism was based on hearsay and gossip. Some of Wavell's charges against the BBC should have been made against the War Office. It was absurd policy not to announce the British landings in Greece in April 1941 until after the Germans had told the world—and Britain; yet Wavell and the Foreign Secretary took joint responsibility

---

[1] *Memorandum by Silvey, 29 April 1941.
[2] *Memorandum of 20 Nov. 1940, 'The BBC and Official Contacts'.
[3] *Note by Ogilvie on a meeting with R. A. Butler, 25 Nov. 1940.

for this decision on the grounds that an early announcement might provoke a German invasion which had already been planned. Ryan rightly observed that 'we go to great public expense to set up an international broadcast news service and then gratuitously sap its strength'.[1] Likewise, there was no reason at all, except a desire on the part of the Government to placate the Press, why news of important Cabinet changes, like those made on 29 June 1941, should be held back until after they had already been broadcast by Deutschlandsender and Stockholm.[2]

The most trivial of all the governmental criticisms of the BBC, but one expressed in the highest quarters and passed on by Nicolson,[3] was that a tone of 'sarcasm, irony, boasting and jocosity' was sometimes introduced by the news readers. The charge was answered in a long memorandum by R. T. Clark, the Senior News Editor, in which he stated tartly that 'except when the Foreign Office has desired or approved it, e.g., in a comment on a Hitler speech, this had, in obedience to instructions, been steadily avoided by *us*'.[4] Nicolson, however, was not fully satisfied. 'I wish the BBC were less sensitive,' he wrote. 'Then one could get down to work together in that spirit of real collaboration which I ardently desire. But when we try to take your hands you look down to make quite sure we are not treading on your toes.'[5]

Arguments of this kind were part of a bigger cluster of arguments about the relationship between the BBC and the Ministry of Information and between the Ministry of Information and other government departments.[6] During the winter of

---

[1] *Note on Release of News by Ryan, 6 April 1941.

[2] *Tallents to Ogilvie, 30 June 1941. The same situation had occurred in April 1940 (Nicolls to Ogilvie, 4 April 1940). Monckton tried in vain to have the ban lifted in June 1941.

[3] *Home Board, *Minutes*, 25 April 1941. A parliamentary question about 'the inclusion of inappropriate animadversions in the news items broadcast' was asked on 24 April (*Hansard*, vol. 371, col. 257). In his reply Nicolson stated that 'the BBC do not include in their news bulletins any commentaries which are not either supplied or approved by responsible Departments'.

[4] *Home Board, *Minutes*, 31 Jan. 1941, include the first reference to this subject which was often to recur. 'Mr. Nicolson reported MoI view that irony had lately been evident in BBC Home News bulletins, and was undesirable. Noted that Foreign Office communiqués sometimes contained sarcastic comment.' See also ibid., 18 April 1941.

[5] *Nicolson to Ogilvie, 8 May 1941.   [6] See below, pp. 329 ff.

1940/41 and the spring and early summer of 1941, however, the BBC did much entirely on its own initiative. It also showed that it could be self-critical. The Home and Forces Programmes developed naturally as contrasting 'alternatives' which could be received in Britain 'for the most part equally easily . . . by civilian and service listeners'. If the second Programme was 'lighter' than the first, the theory behind the contrast remained that while there was no difference between soldiers' and civilians' tastes, there was a real difference between listening conditions in the home on the one hand and the canteen and the barrack room on the other. It was insisted that there should be 'an easy switch for civilian and service listener alike, from Home to Forces and back again to Home'. The object of the programme planners, it was maintained, was 'to combine tradition with enterprise'.[1]

A remarkably self-critical committee on the Forces Programme, headed by Godfrey Adams and including Lionel Fielden, Eric Maschwitz and Andrew Stewart of the Ministry of Information, had reported in September 1940.[2] It had consulted, among others, Sir James Grigg, Permanent Under-Secretary of State for War, General Sir John Brown, head of the Directorate of Army Welfare,[3] and representatives of the Navy and Air Force, yet it insisted from the outset on non-interference from outside on the grounds that any interference tended 'to clog the actual process of broadcasting'. In line with many previous BBC committees, it expressed alarm at 'renunciation of broadcasting standards'. 'We do not believe that creative work of any real value can be successfully accomplished unless the creator has a sense of pride and responsibility in his individual task.' Complaining comprehensively of the lack of direction, lack of co-ordination, lack of checking, lack of responsibility and even lack of *esprit de corps*—'we cannot but feel that the spirit of team work and purpose, once a

---

[1] *BBC Handbook, 1942*, pp. 28, 33.

[2] *Report of the Forces Programme Committee, 30 Sept. 1940. Its secretary was N. Hutchison.

[3] *Adams to General Sir John Brown, 3 Sept. 1940. 'We feel that the first and most important step is to establish, as Sir James Grigg suggested, some machinery for continuous contact so that any proposals or plans made by us shall be dove-tailed into the plans of your department and guided by it.' An Inter-Services meeting took place on 20 Sept. 1940. See also above, p. 41.

feature of the Corporation, has almost disappeared'—it went on to demand greater speed and imagination in presentation,[1] more improvisation on the part of announcers, and a far wider range of programmes both in entertainment and in education. 'The coming winter is likely to be a time of waiting and preparation, with the British public sick for action.' The main difficulty was that the word 'education' by itself had a 'depressing effect' and that the demand for light entertainment already exceeded the supply.

Nevertheless, the outline of a Forces Educational programme was prepared and costed,[2] and discussions with the War Office on this subject continued.[3] A Central Advisory Council for Education in H.M. Forces had been formed in January 1940 and had examined the possibilities of and the resources available for Forces Education later in the year,[4] and a new scheme had begun to be put into effect from the end of September.[5] The BBC co-operated to the full, and as early as November had launched its initial discussions on what was then called 'an Educational Programme for the Forces'.[6] A demonstration broadcast was attended by Service representatives, and an Army instruction was issued to encourage listening.[7] It was decided, however, that neither the word 'Army' nor the word 'education' should be used in relation to any new set of programmes,[8] and a bi-weekly series called *Forces Reconnaissance*, first broadcast on 4 February 1941, dealt broadly with such different topics as the people and problems of the USA and the Commonwealth and new methods of warfare. This series preceded the setting up by the Army Council of the Army Bureau of Current Affairs in September 1941.[9]

---

[1] *Home Board insisted (*Minutes*, 24 Jan. 1941) that this did not mean American slickness. 'American methods had never been regarded as the model, although they might be suitable for some Departments.'

[2] *Ibid., 8, 21 Nov. 1940.   [3] *Ibid., 20 Dec. 1940.

[4] *BBC Handbook, 1942*, p. 66; T. H. Hawkins and L. J. F. Brimble, *Adult Education, The Record of the British Army* (1947), pp. 99–100. The BBC's Central Committee for Group Listening was represented from the start on the new Central Advisory Council.

[5] Ibid., p. 105.   [6] *Home Board, *Minutes*, 22 Nov. 1940.

[7] *Ibid., 24 Jan. 1941. At this time both the R.A.F. and the Navy were said to be 'interested'.

[8] *Ibid., 3 Jan. 1941. 'Mention the word "education" and you scare off 90% of the men,' one observer commented. See Hawkins and Brimble, op. cit., p. 160.

[9] Ibid., pp. 119, 158 ff.

As far as entertainment was concerned, the BBC never found it easy to co-operate with ENSA, the Entertainments National Service Association based on Drury Lane and directed by Basil Dean.[1] ENSA was concerned not only with entertainment for the Forces and for munitions workers but with a weekly *ENSA Half Hour*, which had first been broadcast in March 1940—it had as its signature tune *Let the People Sing*—and with *Break for Music*, which was organized by a cavalcade moving from factory to factory. The BBC found it far more difficult to co-operate with ENSA on broadcasts for home audiences than for troops overseas—Cecil Madden's relations with Dean were better than those of any other BBC official[2]—and there were almost continuous wrangles between ENSA and the Corporation both about initiative and style. Who should lay down rules about what was suitable for broadcasting? Dean had accused the BBC in August 1940 of seeking to 'cut out martial ardour' from ENSA broadcasts, and a few months later had got into a dispute about including fanfares, Shakespeare quotations and *Land of Hope and Glory* in one highly controversial *ENSA Half Hour*.[3] There were further wrangles about publicity—Who took credit for what?[4]—and about payments to artists.[5] All these wrangles were duly recalled in February 1941 when the BBC's Home Board noted that ENSA had decided to set up a Broadcasting Advisory Council without consulting the BBC.[6] The step was described as 'very objectionable', but ENSA for its part insisted through the Chairman of its new Advisory Council, Sir Herbert Dunnico, that 'no discourtesy had been intended'. The sole purpose of the Committee was to criticize ENSA broadcasts and to point out their

---

[1] See Basil Dean's long and interesting book, *The Theatre at War* (1956), which tells the story of ENSA, as he saw it, of the opposition encountered and of the achievements it had to its credit. An Inter-Departmental Committee, appointed in the autumn of 1940 and presided over by Lord May, examined the future of ENSA and reported in March 1941.

[2] See below, pp. 568 ff. *London Carries On* first went on the air early in 1941.

[3] *Ogilvie to Nicolls, 27 May 1940; de Lotbinière to Nicolls, 28 May 1940. Originally John Sharman, a BBC producer, was in charge of this programme. See also Dean, op. cit., pp. 274–5.

[4] Dean was often accused of 'slanging' the Corporation. (*Standing to Nicolls, 22 July 1940.)

[5] *D. H. Clarke, Memorandum of 3 Feb. 1942, 'Business Relations with ENSA'.

[6] *Home Board, *Minutes*, 28 Feb. 1941.

defects.[1] Ogilvie's acceptance of this 'assurance' was tempered by his remark that 'the Corporation must bear the sole responsibility for the quality of its output'.[2]

During the next few months, there were many signs of mutual jealousy, recrimination and confusion. The BBC has never found it easy to get on with bodies which make independent broadcasting claims of their own, yet ENSA, itself subject to almost incessant public criticism, was right to insist that it was in a special position because of its mandate from HMG to carry out 'a national service in a particular field'.[3] Behind the constitutional controversy, however, was a producers' argument at a much lower level about what constituted good radio material. Only two days after Ogilvie had somewhat modified the BBC's original position that the Corporation wanted control of ENSA programmes and had drawn lessons from religious broadcasting, suggesting as a criterion the concept of 'reasonable control',[4] the Director of Outside Broadcasts, Michael Standing, rejected an *ENSA Half Hour* script as 'amateurish'. Nicolls and Graves, who were consulted, were even more forthright.[5] Not long afterwards Ogilvie and Dean were dealing with each other once more as 'protagonists'.[6] Although they both tried to agree upon a list of 'working rules', tensions persisted into 1942.[7] They were reported even to the Board of Governors. 'ENSA impatient of BBC supervision of their broadcasts; poor quality of material.'[8] ENSA, for its part, had its own Broadcasting Executive, with W. Macqueen-Pope as first Director of Programmes, Roger Ould as Manager, Stephen Williams, who had worked with Radio Luxembourg, as

[1] *Dunnico to Ogilvie, 19 March 1941.
[2] *Ogilvie to Dunnico, 24 March 1941.
[3] *Notes of a meeting held on 25 July 1941. Ogilvie, Graves, Nicolls, Maconachie, Standing and Farquharson represented the BBC, and Dunnico, Sir Louis Sterling, Sydney Walton and Cyril Asquith represented ENSA. It is important to bear in mind that ENSA had a wide range of tasks to carry out. In the broadcasting field alone it was involved in 940 'live' broadcasts between March 1940 and May 1945 (Dean, op. cit., p. 285).
[4] *Dunnico to Ogilvie, 29 July 1941.
[5] *Standing to Nicolls, 31 July 1941. Notes by Nicolls and Graves were appended.
[6] *Nicolls to Tallents, 26 Aug. 1941.
[7] *The 'rules' are set out in a memorandum of 12 Sept. 1941 and in Dean, op. cit., p. 276.
[8] *BBC Board of Governors, *Minutes*, 11 Sept. 1941.

Broadcasting Officer and Margaret Harper-Nelson as Senior
Secretary and later Deputy to Ould. Relations were far from
satisfactory there, too, and the atmosphere was often 'cloudy
with disputation'.[1]

Not all outside entertainment posed so many problems.
Workers' Playtime, which was first broadcast on 31 May 1941,
originated from discussions between Ernest Bevin, the Minister
of Labour, and John Watt—what Watt called 'a big hook-up'.[2]
A few months earlier, Watt had suggested taking *Garrison
Theatre* to a factory, but his suggestion had not been accepted
by the management.[3] Bevin adopted the idea with enthusiasm,
calling the programme 'a great work for a great people'.[4]
The first broadcast came from a factory at Wrexham, the
initial schedule of six weeks was soon increased to six months,
and by the end of the year three programmes were being
broadcast each week.[5] Other new shows of a related kind were
Factory Canteen and *Works Wonders* in which the workers themselves provided the talent. The reactions of this new kind of
audience unmistakably influenced other new ventures in
entertainment in 1941, notably *Happidrome* with Harry Korris
as Mr. Lovejoy, Cecil Frederick as Ramsbottom and Vincent
Robinson as Enoch.

Along with *Ack-Ack, Beer-Beer* broadcasts, originally designed
in May 1940 for men and women of the anti-aircraft, balloon-
barrage and searchlight units[6]—this programme celebrated its
centenary in the middle of 1942—*Happidrome* had the widest
possible popular appeal. The song 'We three' was known
throughout the country. In style and content, the programme
contrasted sharply with *Hi Gang*, which returned to the air in
November after a summer break, and a number of recorded
American Variety programmes, particularly *Broadway Calling*,

---

[1] Dean, op. cit., pp. 271, 273–4.

[2] *Watt to Standing, 14 May 1941.

[3] *Daily Mirror*, 22 Nov. 1940.

[4] *Recorded message by Bevin who inaugurated the new series with a personal
statement on 28 Oct. 1941. For Bevin's interest in ENSA, see Dean, op. cit., pp.
128–39.

[5] *BBC Handbook, 1942*, p. 43.

[6] At first, this programme had an educational content, and it was not transferred to the Variety Department until October 1940. The programme was highly
successful by the autumn of 1941, as a memorandum by its producers (10 Sept.
1941) shows.

which introduced British audiences to Jack Benny and Bob
Hope shows. Thereafter there were to be two distinct strands
in war-time Variety, one essentially British provincial and one
American. The old national favourites persisted, of course—
Music Hall, Eight Bells, Kentucky Minstrels and *At the Pig and
Whistle*—while Tommy Handley, after a short and less successful series of nostalgic summer programmes, *Its That Sand Again*,
returned in September in *ITMA* which was to become the
the 'classic' programme of the war.[1]

Another new programme with a remarkable future ahead of
it was Victor Sylvester's *Dancing Club*, which combined efficient
instruction with the smoothest of entertainment.[2] It appealed
immediately to the Forces, for whom special entertainment
programmes continued to be produced—*Tom, Dick and Harry*,
dealing with the off-duty adventures of a soldier, a sailor
and an airman; *Women at War*, designed specially for women in
the Services; *The Blue Peter; Under the Red Duster* and *Ship's
Company*, written by two sailors,[3] setting out to interest both the
Royal Navy and the Merchant Navy; and *Irish Half Hour*,
which reached a far wider audience than the large number of
men and women from Eire in the Services, the same audience
which enjoyed the lowbrow humour of Arthur Lucan and
Kitty McShane in *Old Mother Riley Takes the Air*. *Irish Half
Hour* was opposed at first by the Northern Ireland Government,
but John Betjeman, then serving in the office of the British
High Commissioner in Dublin, rallied to its defence. He
claimed, indeed, that it had a large audience in Eire, which
listened frequently to the Forces Programme on the grounds that
'it is not BBC, and, therefore, not propaganda'.[4]

Several of these programmes reached Forces overseas under

---

[1] *The suggestion had been made to Nicolls as early as 10 Jan. 1941 (Memorandum from Madden) that recordings of American shows should be broadcast
'on which a fortune is spent in scripting'. This 'germ of an idea' was to grow so fast
that there were serious doubts about the policy later in the war. See below, p. 567.

[2] There were twenty dance band programmes a week in 1941. Geraldo was
responsible for one of the most popular of them. Ken Johnson, along with several
members of his band, was killed in a 1941 air raid. The BBC Theatre Organ was
another air raid casualty in the spring.

[3] Signalman Wright and Leading Writer Blackburn also wrote *Libertymen,
Fall In* which was broadcast in Dec. 1941.

[4] *Later there was a serious shortage of batteries in Eire (letter from Betjeman
to Nicolls, 19 Jan. 1942, with its forceful plea 'get more Zinc for Eire').

the intelligent and energetic auspices of Cecil Madden's BBC Empire Entertainments Unit which had been set up in April 1940. About fifty to sixty programmes a week were sent out, ranging from Freddy Grisewood's *Your Cup of Tea* for soldiers fighting in North Africa—the rattle of genuine tea cups was a background noise—to *Over to You* and many other individual message and request programmes which are still remembered by thousands of ex-servicemen. *Home Town* was compèred by the Cockney actor Ronnie Shiner; *Record Time* was devised and presented by Roy Rich; and Vera Lynn was establishing her unique reputation as the 'sweetheart of the Forces'.[1] In reverse, *Greetings from Cairo* consisted of messages, recorded by courtesy of Egyptian State Broadcasting, from men serving in the Middle East. The relatives and friends to whom the messages were addressed were notified by the BBC before the broadcast so that they could arrange to listen.[2]

The success of some of these ventures, particularly with troops serving in the desert, depended on achieving a sense of personal communication. 'Hearing your voice on the wireless gave me a wonderful thrill' was a characteristic personal response. Vera Lynn was exceptionally successful in the art of appealing not only to soldiers as a group but to the individual soldier lonely in the midst of battle, homesick before the battle began. At the same time, Army camps were places where it was easy and natural to express solidarity of collective reaction. After broadcasting for the first time to the Gibraltar Garrison Joan Gilbert received a typical cable—'Fifty military police acting spokesmen all ranks Gibraltar report programme smash hit everyone wildly excited suggest extension immediately.'[3]

The programme planners of Forces broadcasts had to appreciate the psychology both of the distant serviceman and of his family at home. They needed creative ideas about new broadcasting series, however, if they were to avoid the staleness of persistent repetition. Among the specific proposals for

[1] See below, pp. 578–9.
[2] There were also limited programmes from Canadians, West Indians, Maltese, South Africans, Rhodesians, Australians and New Zealanders. See *BBC Handbook, 1942*, p. 71. See also below, pp. 492–4.
[3] Quoted ibid., p. 71.

popular programmes listed by the Forces Committee during the autumn of 1940[1]—before the beginning of the war of movement with its thrusts and counter-thrusts in North Africa— were two daily features, *What the Papers Say* and *Topics of the Day*, the latter based on a successful German programme; a British counterpart, not necessarily of the same type, to the popular American question-and-answer programme, *Information Please*;[2] a widening range of inter-Service competitions; the founding of an inter-Allied radio club—'a real *Café Colette* at which members of all British, Imperial and Allied Services should meet before the microphone for singing, dancing, cross-talk and general friendliness';[3] a 'Call to Britain Week', 'the intention being to use religious services, speech, drama, features and music to "put across" the spiritual issues involved in the present war'—the Director of Religious Broadcasting commented refreshingly that 'he was not very clear how this could be done or how far the Christian issue could be identified with the National Cause'—and a family or Forces serial. The Committee was inclined to consider it a pity that the first important family serial for some time—*At the Armstrongs*— should have been handed over to Schools Department; 'there was a big need for a cheerful, good-humoured, down to earth sort of family characters . . .' handled as 'general entertainment'.[4]

Not all the ideas set out in this Report were taken up at once—it was not until 1948 that *Mrs. Dale's Diary*, which established a nation-wide reputation as a daily serial, was first broadcast—yet one at least was to take its place in every social history of the war. The idea behind *Information Please* was that of a request programme for information on all subjects, frequently

[1] *Report of 30 Sept. 1940.

[2] Fielden was particularly interested in this idea, as were Maschwitz, Andrew Stewart and Donald McCullough, who was then a Duty Officer in the Ministry of Information (*Stewart to Adams, 20 Dec. 1943).

[3] Grigg told the Committee that this was a suggestion 'that would interest the Prime Minister enormously, as he had the cause of the Allied troops very close to his heart'.

[4] *At the Armstrongs* was taken off the air in June 1941 (*Home Board, *Minutes*, 20 June 1941), but it reappeared later under the title *With the Armstrongs Again*. Many youth organizations were said to have listened in groups to this programme (*BBC Handbook, 1942*, p. 67). The programme alternated with that of the *Eighteen and Under Club*.

with a 'strong vein of the serious', supplied over the microphone in 'pithy, entertaining and authentic form' by a panel of well-known experts.[1] The idea was transformed by Howard Thomas, who had joined the BBC in October 1940, into the idea of the *Brains Trust*.[2] 'Serious in intention, light in character', as Watt, the Director of Variety, described it, it was the responsibility from the start of Variety. Thomas had worked before the war for three years in commercial radio and had later been a producer of *Ack-Ack, Beer-Beer*. He was joined in 1940 by Douglas Cleverdon, the West Region Features producer.[3] The really long-term partnership began when Donald McCullough, who had been head of an advertising agency before moving first to the Ministry of Information and then to the Ministry of Agriculture,[4] was chosen as 'question master', a term coined by Thomas. Three 'guests'—C. E. M. Joad, Julian Huxley and Commander A. B. Campbell— were then selected from an initial list of twenty-seven names and a short list of fourteen. The original association of these three men was 'largely accidental', yet as Joad himself put it, 'the combination proved unexpectedly effective. The public liked to hear the scrapping which Huxley and I brought to the discussion of such questions as the relation between the brain and the mind; it liked still more to hear Campbell keeping up his end with both of us.'[5]

The programme first went on the air with the title *Any Questions* on 1 January 1941, with no one able to answer the first question, completely factual, put by an RAF sergeant, 'What are the seven wonders of the world?' McCullough believed that the first programme would be the last, yet the *Daily Mail* commented prophetically the next day that the programme promised to become one of the most popular of radio features. The first emphasis on factual questions and answers, reflected in an effort to associate the *Encyclopaedia*

[1] *Report of 30 Sept. 1940.

[2] Home Board approved the idea in November (*Home Board, *Minutes*, 1 Nov. 1940).

[3] *The combination of Thomas and Cleverdon was designed to ensure that 'the balance between intellectualism [*sic*] and entertainment might be preserved' (*Watt to Nicolls, 15 May 1941).

[4] See above, p. 219.

[5] C. E. M. Joad, 'The Brains Trust: A Retrospect' in the *New Statesman*, 27 May 1944.

Britannica with the programme,[1] was quickly forgotten, and the topics discussed became general and speculative. Within a few weeks the programme was reported to be 'shaping well'[2] and thirty questions a day were being received at Broadcasting House—there had been only fifteen in all after the first programme[3]—and the series went on for eighty-four weekly broadcasts without a break.

Its success depended not only on the remarkable and varied abilities of the personalities in the broadcasting teams, but on the originality, drive and leadership of Thomas, who trusted and warmed to his audience and thought of his programme as 'a trailer of knowledge'. Yet even he did not expect that 'we were about to blow some of the cobwebs from the minds of a considerable part of the nation' and that the term 'Brains Trust' would soon become a household word and would be applied to Army Brains Trusts and Rotary Brains Trusts alike. 'The number of people calling themselves "Brains Trusts" must be enormous', one writer was to put it before long. 'From Joad, Hogg and Co. down to the Little Piddlington Allotments Brains Trust, there is infinite variety.'[4]

The programme was promoted to Sunday afternoon on 13 April 1941 (in the Forces Programme), and reached a peak audience of 29% of the population aged sixteen and over on 21 December 1943 and a peak weekly correspondence of 4,400 letters. Questions were to be asked about it in Parliament.[5] The reason for public interest was that 'from the beginning it was accomplishing what it set out to do—to make listeners sit up and think'. The fact that, as Thomas put it, 'little more than that was ever intended' was almost a guarantee that it would not run into some of the difficulties which confronted other programmes designed to 'make listeners sit up and think in wartime'.[6] Yet its success was a testimony, as Joad said, both to

---

[1] *Memoranda of 26 Nov., 12 Dec. 1940.

[2] *Home Board, *Minutes*, 7 Feb. 1941. 'Members of the Home Board to listen if possible.'

[3] *Note by Nicolls, 19 Aug. 1942, based on information from Howard Thomas.

[4] *Truth*, 4 Feb. 1944, in a review of a book by 'Democrat' called *Be Your Own Brains Trust*.

[5] See below, p. 563.

[6] The story of the programme is told in H. Thomas, *Britain's Brains Trust* (1944). See also below, pp. 560–4.

'the accumulated fund of unexpended seriousness' in the population as a whole and to 'the failure of popular education to
satisfy the people's needs or to win their interests'.[1]

Most of the difficulties in attempting to get people to sit up
and think were met, some of them dramatically, when J. B.
Priestley proceeded to his second series of Postcripts which
began on 26 January 1941. In November he had proposed a
set of six fortnightly feature programmes under the general
title of *The Long Road Home*—dealing with 'Freedom', 'Security',
'Money', 'The Enemies', 'Two Types of Great Men' and
'The Kingdom of Heaven'—and the Minister of Information had given his approval 'subject to clear understanding
that Priestley would not be allowed greater liberty in this setting
than in others'.[2] Ogilvie felt that the synopsis 'strayed so
undeniably into politics that the whole idea should be rejected',[3]
but it was Priestley himself who suggested that since the
presentation of the programmes would be very complicated
because of staffing difficulties, a series of talks would be more
suitable. He was not happy about the term 'postscript', but he
wanted the Sunday night spot.[4] Monckton, Ogilvie and Ryan
approved the new plan,[5] and Priestley set to work to prepare talks
which quite deliberately were to be longer than the previous series
and which would have 'more bite'. They were also to be more
'aggressively democratic in feeling and tone'.[6] The war would
not last long, Priestley believed, if the country could discover
'a short clear creed' to send 'a trumpet call round the world'.[7]

Priestley had continued to broadcast—with outstanding
success[8]—to the United States during the autumn of 1940, but,

[1] Joad, loc. cit.; cf. Listener Research Paper, 12 July 1941: 'it does seem to be
appreciated as education in a palatable form'.

[2] *Home Board, *Minutes*, 29 Nov. 1940; 'The Long Road Home', Note by
Gilliam, 2 Dec. 1940.

[3] *Ogilvie to Duff Cooper, 11 Dec. 1940; Note by Tallents, who concurred,
21 Dec. 1940. Monckton approved of the series.

[4] *Priestley to Ryan, 3 Jan. 1941; Priestley to Ogilvie, 3 Jan. 1941. He thought
that the term 'postscript' suggested something too official, and he felt that the
character of the postscripts had changed so much since his 'retirement' that he
would have to wrench them back very sharply if they continued to be given this
name.   [5] *Ryan to Ogilvie, 9 Jan. 1941.

[6] Priestley, *All England Listened* (1967), p. xviii.

[7] *Broadcast of 26 Jan. 1941.

[8] *Tallents to Macgregor, 24 Dec. 1940. Very favourable reports had also
come in from Canada.

despite or because of his immense popularity in Britain, there had been so much criticism from inside and outside the BBC about the last broadcasts in his previous series[1] that it was clear from the outset that the new talks would not meet with universal approval. In fact, a deputation from the 1922 Committee almost immediately protested to Duff Cooper about Priestley's reappearance at the microphone, and Churchill himself, who had been arguing forcefully that the less his ministers broadcast the better, complained that the first postcript expressed views on war aims which were in conflict with those of the Prime Minister.[2] At the same time, there were many messages of support for Priestley.[3] Duff Cooper stoutly defended Priestley's right to broadcast, but he did not think he should give more than six postscripts in a series.[4] Later, he insisted in more general terms that future policy in relation to Postscripts should be that the speakers should vary and no one should be signed up on a long-term basis.[5] Ryan insisted that there was no difference

[1] See above, pp. 211–12. To put the criticism in perspective, it is necessary also to take note of Press comment late in 1940. 'It is almost a national calamity that he should be silent in these dangerous and fateful hours' (letter to *Time and Tide*, 9 Nov. 1940); 'We shall never know how much this country owed to Mr. Priestley last summer. . . . For those dangerous months when the Gestapo arrived in Paris he was unmistakably a great man' (Graham Greene in the *Spectator*, 13 Dec. 1940); 'The Government ought to appoint Mr. Priestley Director-General of Broadcasting' (*Nottingham Guardian*, 3 Dec. 1940).

[2] *Ryan to Ogilvie, 29 Jan. 1941. It should be noted that Churchill also suggested an embargo on future broadcasts by the Minister of Shipping.

[3] *After his first broadcast in the new series he received a thousand appreciative letters and two hundred which were critical. The second postscript showed that two hundred were appreciative and one hundred critical. 'Isn't it queer "they" allow Priestley to broadcast again when his ideas are so "unofficial",' wrote one listener, 'but isn't it grand?' Sir Archibald Southby attacked the broadcasts on the air. A Listener Research Report (25 Feb. 1941) showed that Priestley's postscript 'Meditations in a Railway Train' was approved of by seventeen listeners out of twenty.

[4] *Duff Cooper had deleted two passages from one of Priestley's overseas broadcasts on the grounds that German propaganda to the United States suggested that Britain was 'going Bolshevik' and that this suggestion might be confirmed from the two passages in question. (*Note by Tallents, 9 March 1941; Ogilvie to Tallents, 10 March 1941.) He also questioned passages in one home postscript. Priestley in fact gave eight postscripts in all, and lunched with Duff Cooper before the last.

[5] *He followed the same policy later in the year in refusing to allow Vernon Bartlett to give a series (*Home Board, *Minutes*, 25 April 1941). Ogilvie had seen Monckton about the series on 24 April 1941 and urged that the Minister should take full responsibility for his decision. The initiative for choosing future postscript broadcasters lay with the BBC, but the Minister had to approve the list 'from time to time'. (*Home Board, *Minutes*, 2 May 1941.)

of opinion between the Ministry and the BBC concerning this new approach.[1]

Priestley was extremely unhappy about the outcome of this second series of Postscripts—he was replaced by A. P. Herbert —and held the Ministry of Information mainly responsible. He refused thereafter to do 'occasional' postscripts and told the BBC it was wrecking its most successful talks feature.[2] It was plain, however, that there was a real conflict of views in 1941 between Priestley and the Government not only about domestic social policy but about international war aims. Efforts had been made to persuade Priestley to follow up his 1940 broadcasts with a campaign of public meetings,[3] and although at first he refused, he later on helped to found and served as Chairman of the '1941 Committee', a body with a strong 'progressive' political purpose.[4] The Committee was described soon afterwards, in the idiom of the period, as a 'sort of leftist Brains Trust'.[5] In a preliminary statement called *We must Win*, it demanded a proclamation of national 'ideas and objectives'. By contrast, Churchill, backed by the Cabinet, refused to make any declaration on war aims, on the grounds that 'precise aims would be compromising whereas vague principles would disappoint'.[6] Incidentally, he thereby jettisoned a propaganda statement which had been prepared laboriously by Harold Nicolson and Lord Halifax. He also upset many people inside the BBC, including Ogilvie, who were concerned either with home morale or with foreign propaganda. Even the Conservative Lord Davidson, who argued that 'the

---

[1] *Ryan to Monckton, 18 March 1941. Yet the Home Board *Minutes*, 21 March 1941, stated flatly: 'Priestley series stopping . . . on instructions of Minister.'

[2] *Priestley to Ogilvie, 22 May 1941. Yet Priestley prepared a feature programme later in the year called *Listen to my Notebook*.

[3] Sir Richard Acland to Priestley, 5 Oct. 1940; Priestley to Acland, 9 Nov. 1940, in the Acland Papers. (I owe this reference to Mr. Angus Calder.) Acland published his book *The Forward March* in March 1941, and later on set up a movement with this name.

[4] The setting up of the new committee was announced in the *Evening Standard*, 16 Jan. 1941. 'The suggested titles,' the report stated, 'are "The Total War Society" and "The 1941 Committee". I think Mr. Priestley will find something better than these.' A BBC official wrote tersely in ink opposite the press cutting 'This looks bad'.

[5] R. Reynolds, *Survey of the Left* in *Left*, Oct. 1942.

[6] Nicolson, op. cit., p. 139; entry for 22 Jan. 1941. Churchill had a record audience of 70% for his broadcast of 9 Feb. 1941. (*Home Board, *Minutes*, 28 Feb. 1941.)

average man is not in the least interested in hypothetical peace aims', had been anxious that the BBC should broadcast programmes early in 1941 'concerned with the future of our country and the material conditions—expressed in terms of housing, employment, education, etc., that will arise in the new Britain which must be built when victory has been achieved'.[1]

Few of these items figured prominently in the output of the BBC Talks Department in 1941, although one series late in the year, *Making Plans*, dealt with some of the issues. Millis, the Vice-Chairman of the Governors, expressed alarm in January 1941 that BBC programmes were giving 'a distorted picture of British social conditions' and 'ignoring the great advances made up to the outbreak of war',[2] but there was little justification for this expression of opinion. The main emphasis in talks policy continued to be placed on home issues and on the war itself. As in the past, relations with different Ministries had their ups and downs, and propaganda was always in danger of being over-played: 'it is not really business, even from the Ministry of Information's point of view,' Maconachie claimed in April 1941, as he had done so many times before, 'to have so many campaigns running at the same time. How mutually destructive high-spot broadcasts of a propaganda kind can be was made abundantly clear on a recent Sunday when President Roosevelt's great speech was broadcast in full, Mr. Bevin announced the Government's new policy on manpower, and Mr. Herbert Morrison launched the Invasion Campaign—all on the same day.'[3]

Agricultural broadcasts did much to acquaint farmers, sometimes organized into discussion groups, with the need to extend the acreage of ploughed land, to save imported feeding stuffs, to set up pig clubs: the very most was being made of voluntary effort and participation. *Backs to the Land*, chaired by John Morgan, M.P., was the title of the highly successful Saturday series, not 'Back to the Land', the original title which had been proposed and which John Green rightly felt had too many nostalgic echoes of 'three acres and a cow' to be rousing enough for war time. The series prospered, as did British

---

[1] *Note of 30 Oct. 1940.
[2] *Board of Governors, *Minutes*, 29 Jan. 1941.
[3] *Maconachie to Ryan, 11 April 1941.

agriculture. Food programmes were sometimes more tricky. Miss Quigley, who had pioneered *The Kitchen Front*, moved over to other programmes, mainly for women in the Forces, in the autumn of 1941. At that time, 'the line of responsibility between the Ministry of Food and the BBC still had not been clearly drawn'.[1] *The Kitchen Front* was the BBC's own responsibility, but 'as a matter of courtesy' the Talks Department, which took endless pains in its choice of speakers and themes, showed all scripts dealing with food questions to the Ministry before they were broadcast. 'We cannot . . . afford to allow things to be said in Talks about food,' wrote Barnes, Maconachie's Director of Talks, 'which are contrary to the policy of the Ministry of Food.'[2]

Miss Quigley's new programme *Women at War* was first broadcast in October 1941, complete with a 'Brainteaser's Trust' as one of its components. 'Beauty Hints' were another. A good audience was soon built up, although there had been considerable scepticism as to whether ATS girls would be as receptive as hill farmers or even busy housewives. 'The results of suggesting any talks are most depressing, as you thought,' one ATS officer had reported from a local unit. 'The wireless blares all the time in the recreation room at a deafening pitch . . . but as soon as a talk comes on they switch off.' The only talk that had ever succeeded was one giving accurate dancing instructions.[3]

The immediate events of war received most attention in talks, as might have been expected—the violence of the 'Battle of the Atlantic', which preoccupied Churchill and which reached its first peak between March and July 1941; the successive steps, particularly Lend-Lease, mooted in December 1940, put into effect in March 1941, which turned American aid into a reality; the RAF strategic bombing offensive, 'the effects of which were seriously overrated';[4] a poison gas threat which never materialized, but which was discussed methodically

---

[1] *Barnes to Howard Marshall, 5 Sept. 1941; Marshall to Barnes, 5 Sept. 1941.
[2] *Directive by Barnes, 12 Dec. 1941.
[3] *Alison Settle to Miss Quigley, 10 Oct. 1941, reporting a conversation.
[4] See C. Webster and N. Frankland, *The Strategic Air Offensive against Germany* (1961), vol. I. See also *BBC Home Board, *Minutes*, 11 July 1941: 'In view of physical possibility of inserting recording apparatus in "Flying Fortress" aircraft, C.(E) to explore possibility of obtaining effective programme material.'

by one of the BBC's most experienced broadcasters, John Snagge;[1] Empire politics, with Mackenzie King, Menzies, Curtin, Peter Fraser, General Smuts and others broadcasting either direct from London or in recordings from their own countries; and the new economic controls—on 1 June, for example, Oliver Lyttelton introduced clothes rationing by radio.[2]

Old broadcasting favourites like John Hilton, Middleton and Freddy Grisewood, star of *The World Goes By*, were joined by new ones, some of whom made their mark immediately, like Quentin Reynolds with his personal messages to Dr. Goebbels and Mr. Schickelgruber,[3] or seaman Frank Laskier, completely unknown by name to listeners, who described vividly the daily struggle between the Merchant Navy and the U-Boat.[4] Although Churchill recorded a record peak audience (77 per cent of the population over the age of sixteen) for his broadcast on 27 April, there were more and more 'news talks' during the year by 'ordinary people'—soldiers, sailors, airmen and civil defence workers. 'These,' it was claimed, 'are the men and women with the great stories to tell during our generation.'[5] The stories were thought to speak for themselves. Slogans were explicitly excluded as 'fill-ups'; it was felt that they would set the wrong tone.[6]

In relation both to talks and to news, recording gained greatly in importance in 1941. The Forces Programme Committee had rightly complained that there was a tendency inside the BBC, despite all the pressures, to regard recording as comparatively unimportant, 'a sort of ugly duckling of

[1] *Home Board, *Minutes*, 31 Jan. 1941: 'C(H) reported Government directive that programmes should draw public attention indirectly and, without being alarmist, to necessity of anti-gas precautions.'

[2] For futher broadcasts about clothes, see below, p. 559.

[3] *There were troubles behind the scenes in relation to at least one of the talks by Reynolds. Churchill insisted that there should be no programme references to Rudolf Hess, who had landed by air in Britain on 11 May 1941 (Home Board, *Minutes*, 30 May 1941), and after a passage relating to Hess had been deleted by the BBC on Kirkpatrick's advice, Reynolds reinstated it. Kirkpatrick upheld his objection and referred the question to Duff Cooper (ibid., 27 June 1941). Hitler also placed an embargo on broadcast references to Hess. See also below, p. 428.

[4] Sir Walter Citrine refused to give a talk in an Empire series by Trade Union leaders on the grounds that the script would be censored. (*Home Board, *Minutes*, 7 March 1941.)

[5] *BBC Handbook, 1942*, p. 58.   [6] *Home Board, *Minutes*, 28 Feb. 1941.

administration and engineering'.[1] Trained staff knowledgeable about recording techniques were not being reserved from military service; the acquisition of essential materials and the prevention of wastage in their use was not being centrally controlled; research towards the provision of synthetic substitutes for increasingly rare materials was not being pursued; there was no exchange of experience between different organizations concerned with the same kind of work, particularly the JBC and the BBC;[2] and, worst of all, irreplaceable apparatus was being exposed to air raids and was in imminent peril of destruction.

These were serious and controversial charges, and a sub-committee was set up by the Control Board in October 1940 'to enquire into the general position of recording and to report'.[3] It reported in December 1940, and its main recommendations were accepted.[4] A new Recording Services Committee was created, consisting of three senior officers from the Engineering, Programmes, and Administrative Divisions—Martin Pulling, Lynton Fletcher, and Derek Hetley. The Committee was 'to provide a working scheme and to bring it into force as quickly as possible, and thereafter to supervise the question of recording services and to frame plans for development'.[5] There was much for the Committee to do. An increased use of recording was undoubtedly necessary for six reasons—to avoid calling performers to the studios during air raids or at night when air raids were likely to take place; to provide a reserve of material if broadcasting broke down; to cope with some of the problems created by censorship; to permit the increased development of outside reporting, including news commentaries; to facilitate export of programmes overseas; and to serve the needs of the Monitoring Service.

At the same time, there were special war-time problems relating to the supply and maintenance of equipment.[6] The

[1] See above, pp. 52–3. *Report of the Forces Programme Committee, 30 Sept. 1940.   [2] See above, pp. 185–7, for the JBC.

[3] *Control Board, Minutes, 16 Oct. 1940.

[4] *Controller (Engineering) demurred at the proposal that the Senior Officer taking charge of recording functions in the Programme Division should be called Recorded Programmes Director (ibid., 2 Jan. 1941).

[5] *Ibid., 18 Dec. 1940.

[6] *There was also a serious shortage of valve supplies by Nov. 1940. See Control Board, Minutes, 13, 20 Nov. 1940. It was stated in Jan. 1940 that the Treasury

use of the Phillips-Miller system, imperfect though it was,[1] had been extended to the limit before the collapse of Holland, where the equipment was produced, and Belgium, where the film was manufactured; thereafter European supplies were cut off. The Marconi-Stille system used tape made of a special steel manufactured in Sweden, supplies of which were always precarious. Disc systems seemed most hopeful, for there were at least two firms producing discs in Britain whose output might be increased, and several American sources of supply. There was something of an impasse, however, as Ashbridge reported in February 1941 that 'the quality of disc recordings was not now seriously below pre-war level nor likely to be materially improved. Further supplies of film or tape recording equipment were unobtainable.'[2] It was not until 1942 that a satisfactory long-term plan of development for the disc system was introduced.[3]

Meanwhile, mobile recording was bringing distant war into the home, and ninety 'news talks' a month were being broadcast in 1941.[4] The Eritrean and Abyssinian campaigns provided the few victories which thrilled listeners in the spring of 1941; and they could hear Bruce Anderson of the South African Broadcasting Corporation reporting on the Battle of the Mahda Pass, Dimbleby broadcasting from Keren, and, some days after the event, a recorded account of the entry into Addis Ababa on 5 May of Haile Selassie, the first victim of Axis aggression to be restored to his position.[5] Details of the return of British troops from Greece and Crete were also recorded, and Chester Wilmot of the Australian Broadcasting Commission

[1] For the system and its disadvantages, see Briggs, *The Golden Age of Wireless*, pp. 102–3.

[2] *Home Board, Minutes, 21 Feb. 1941. At the next meeting he reported loss of a consignment of film from the USA.

[3] The JBC (see above, p. 185) was a competitor of the BBC for disc equipment. It was taken over in 1941.

[4] *BBC Handbook, 1942*, p. 56.

[5] The Abyssinian campaign raised the question of whether or not the Abyssinian National Anthem should be broadcast in the Allied Anthem programme (*Home Board, Minutes, 11 April 1941). Nicolls was asked to investigate the 'authenticity' of the Anthem recorded. Later it was reported (ibid., 25 April 1941) that a choral version of the Anthem was 'in hand'.

had given its approval to the construction of a new factory for valve supplies in Britain, with the BBC to have the first call on its output (ibid., 31 Jan. 1941).

was already a well-known voice from the Western Desert. So too was Edward Ward until he was captured by the Italians.[1]

While the development of News policy during this period raised most of the issues which arise in News broadcasting at any time,[2] it would be a mistake to conclude that the pattern and volume of news recording were in any sense similar to those of post-1945 broadcasting. Recording, indeed, whether overseas, at sea, or at home—with men like Godfrey Talbot, Robin Duff, Michael Reynolds and Robert Dunnett experimenting successfully with the medium—was thought of not as a mainstay but as 'an invaluable assistant at moments of emergency'. 'But, of course,' the *BBC Handbook* for 1942 stated, 'the majority of news talks are either spoken directly to the listener through the microphone or they are recorded at one of the stations of the BBC. (If they are recorded, the listener is always so informed).'[3] The 'but', the 'of course' and the brackets are all significant. Much of the pre-war suspicion of recording lingered.[4] And there was a deliberate refusal to imitate the German techniques developed by the radio units of Goebbels's Propaganda Korps.[5] 'The aim,' the BBC put it, 'is not to broadcast an artistic reconstruction of an event but a truthful account which may also bring to the listener the words and sounds recorded at the time. Nothing is put into a news talk that is not true—not even the addition of a sound which did not come exactly in the right place.'[6]

The Press was interested in 1941 in other aspects of 'the sounds of war'. The *Daily Herald* reported on 19 May that BBC technicians had been taking 'sound pictures' of a London blitz to be used in the treatment of soldiers suffering from war nerves.[7] More practically, ARP demonstrations included BBC

---

[1] *At Home Board (*Minutes*, 10 Jan. 1941), it was reported that Dimbleby was now in Cairo and Ward on his way to the Front. Dimbleby was authorized to purchase a car in Egypt 'up to £250' (ibid., 17 Jan. 1941).

[2] There were signs, for example, that attempts were being made to use Dimbleby as a specially 'inspired' war correspondent: this policy stopped in 1942 (*Letter to Ryan, 25 July 1942).

[3] *BBC Handbook, 1942*, p. 58.   [4] See Briggs, op. cit., pp. 101–3.

[5] See above, pp. 20, 213.   [6] *BBC Handbook, 1942*, p. 59.

[7] *Daily Herald*, 19 May 1941. On 10 Feb. 1941, the *Daily Sketch* had written that people who knew nothing of the blitz could hear it if the BBC decided to 'put it on'. For the medical experiments, see the *British Medical Journal*, 2 Aug. 1941. Dr. A. E. Carver, a nerve specialist, recommended that the BBC should

recordings of 'five hundred pound bombs screaming down within thirty yards' of Civil Defence leaders.[1] Throughout 1941 the war, even when it became a world war after the entry into it of Russia in June and the United States in December, remained a war of the home front where, as Priestley commented in one of his postscripts, elderly civilians might suffer more than young soldiers. Nerves counted and so too did morale. 'Harry Strauss attacks me,' Harold Nicolson wrote in his diary on 16 December—five days earlier he had noted that 'our nerves are not as good as they were'—'on the grounds that the BBC is almost wholly left-wing. The Conservative view is never presented. It is difficult to tell him that most of the right-wing people make bad broadcasters. Let them find their own Priestley.'[2] It was a fair comment. In its News the BBC remained as objective as any broadcasting corporation ever could be; in presenting views, it had to rely upon the nation as it was, people's opinions as they were, and whatever talent was available, all within a frame set not by itself but by the Ministry of Information.

2. Controllers and Controlled

THE frame mattered more than the general public realized. 'Up to a point,' Ogilvie had written feelingly to Herbert Morrison in June 1940, 'the BBC can render a useful public service by being a good-natured Aunt Sally at which members of the public can relieve themselves of their nerves at times like these—especially in the absence of the standard Aunt Sallies of party politics. But only up to a point.'[3] Later in 1940 and

---

[1] *Leicester Mercury*, 18 Sept. 1941; *Leicester Evening Mail*, 18 Sept. 1941. See also the *Oxford Mail*, 26 Sept. 1941.

[2] H. Nicolson, *Diaries and Letters*, p. 197.

[3] *Ogilvie to Morrison, 18 June 1940. Ogilvie was complaining of a news comment in the *Daily Herald*, 31 May 1940.

---

broadcast a weekly concert of blitz noises in order to accustom the public to the din (*Daily Mirror*, 20 Oct. 1941). The *Yorkshire Post* (23 Oct. 1941) was sceptical. Could not music serve the purpose equally well? 'Nor is the repertoire of loud music so limited that any cynic could justly propose leaving the whole plan to Wagner.'

in the course of 1941 far greater danger lay in the fact that
the BBC was becoming a good-natured Aunt Sally of the
Ministry of Information and the Cabinet.

There had been a substantial reorganization of the Ministry
of Information in August 1940,[1] and further moves towards
reorganization were made during the energetic and controversial but very brief Director-Generalship of Frank Pick,
who had moved earlier in 1940 from the London Passenger
Transport Board to join Reith for a short spell at the Ministry
of Transport.[2] Pick proposed to set up a 'Broadcasting Division'
as one of the twenty-three divisions within the Ministry[3]—
there were to be six main departments—and clearly envisaged
a much closer control of BBC activities than there had been
during 1939 and earlier in 1940. He interested himself in the
authorship and content of the Postscripts, suggested a weekly
lunch presided over by Ogilvie where Postscript speakers
could meet representatives of the Ministry of Information,
and urged that quite apart from a weekly talk by ministers 'it
ought to be open to the Ministry of Information to nominate
one additional talk every week if required'.[4]

Pick was concerned also about the pattern of overseas
broadcasting, as was the Cabinet, and planned to appoint a
Regional Officer in the Ministry of Information for every
Regional Editor inside the BBC. Unaware, however, of the
institutional intricacies of the national propaganda network
and insensitive to his own limitations, he tended to ignore what
was actually happening and to make suggestions which had
already been adopted or general remarks which could not be
substantiated. He began and ended all his letters in green ink.
In September 1940 he asked the BBC bluntly 'whether we are
carrying out any propaganda abroad which is worth anything'.[5]

---

[1] See above, pp. 161 ff.

[2] J. C. W. Reith, *Into the Wind* (1949), pp. 387–8. When Pick moved to the
Ministry of Information, Reith told him frankly that 'the work was not in his line
and that he and Cooper would not get on together'.

[3] Bamford thought that 23 or 24 divisions were far too many, and later in the
year (Meeting of the Ministry of Information Policy Committee, 21 Nov. 1940)
Duff Cooper himself argued that perhaps Pick had taken too much on his own
shoulders. At the same meeting Lord Davidson had pressed for a small Board to
advise the Minister.

[4] Pick to Ryan, 28 Oct. 1940. I am grateful to Mr. Ryan for letting me see this
letter.   [5] *Wellington to Ogilvie, 28 Sept. 1940.

He went further still two months later when he told Ogilvie with even greater bluntness that the Government would end by 'taking over the BBC'.[1]

Ogilvie had seen Duff Cooper a few days earlier and neither he nor his Chairman had formed the impression that such a fundamental change was likely. They had been warned of Eden's dissatisfaction with the Arabic Service, had been informed of the setting up of a Cabinet Committee, with Kingsley Wood in the chair, to inquire into the position of the BBC,[2] and had had it put to them that the BBC's Controller (Overseas) might become 'an official of the Ministry'. Yet Duff Cooper had added that he had explained to Churchill that the BBC had done everything which he had asked it to do and nothing which he had asked it not to do.[3] With equal bluntness, therefore, Ogilvie replied to Pick that his [Pick's] attitude to the BBC and to broadcasting affairs generally was 'wholly mistaken and inefficient'. In the space of three months he had twice tried to induce Wellington to abolish the BBC's Listener Research Department; he had described the Forces Programme as 'something absurd which ought never to have been established'; he had criticized foreign-language programmes without reading the scripts; and he had failed to press for adequate numbers of transmitters and expert personnel to permit the BBC to carry out its essential tasks. 'Neither the Ministry nor the BBC mattered in comparison with the national cause, and it was the business of both of us to see how we could help together to advance it; considering any means whatever (including, if necessary, taking over the BBC) without prejudice and without rushing about with head down like a bull.'[4]

Although there were some members of the Government who were, as always, unhappy about the 'special position' of the

---

[1] *Note by Ogilvie, 22 Nov. 1940.

[2] See above, p. 283.

[3] *Note by Ogilvie, 21 Nov. 1940. Duff Cooper had stated in the House of Commons on 11 June 1940 that he had found the authorities of the BBC 'perfectly willing and eager to accept my advice and guidance ... I have satisfied myself that machinery now exists whereby I can exercise complete control over what is said on important political matters.' (*Hansard*, vol. 361, col. 1240.) Duff Cooper had earlier reported this to the Cabinet on 20 May 1940.

[4] *Note by Ogilvie, 22 Nov. 1940. See also Memorandum, 'Government and BBC in Wartime', 26 Nov. 1940, handed to Duff Cooper by Powell and Ogilvie, 28 Nov. 1940.

BBC—according to Reith, Churchill himself spoke of the BBC at this time as 'an enemy within the gates, doing more harm than good'[1]—others besides Duff Cooper were far more appreciative. R. A. Butler, for example, who had passed on many 'complaints' from the Foreign Office,[2] thought that any idea of the Government taking over the BBC would not be in the best interests even of the Government; since, he stated, the BBC was 'a microcosm of the problems of efficient government in a democracy', he wished Ogilvie well in solving them.[3]

The Government did not 'take over' the BBC. Yet it did not agree with Powell and Ogilvie that a Broadcasting Council should be appointed to assist the Minister of Information in providing a 'fully coordinated and positive direction of propaganda'.[4] Instead, following the recommendation of the Kingsley Wood Committee, it proposed the appointment of two new 'Advisers' to the BBC, one to deal mainly with home affairs as General Adviser, the other to deal with foreign affairs. This proposal was passed on to the BBC on 31 December by Sir Walter Monckton,[5] who had succeeded Pick as Director-General of the Ministry of Information on 14 December.[6] According to Monckton, the Minister of Information expected that in the ordinary course of events the advice of the two Advisers would be accepted, but he added that there would be the right of appeal to the Minister in case of any difference. It cannot be said that the BBC welcomed even this carefully qualified proposal. Ogilvie replied that the idea of a 'General Adviser' was completely new,[7] and, on behalf of the Governors, Powell expressed fears that the persons

---

[1] Reith, op. cit., p. 438.

[2] See above, pp. 281–2. He wrote an important memorandum on the subject of relations between the BBC and the Foreign Office on 30 Oct. 1940.

[3] *Note by Ogilvie, 25 Nov. 1940.

[4] *Memorandum, 'Government and BBC in Wartime', 26 Nov. 1940. The Council would have had the Minister in the chair and would have included representatives of the Foreign Office, the Services, and the Ministry of Home Security.   [5] *Monckton to Ogilvie, 31 Dec. 1940.

[6] Ministry of Information Official Circular, 14 Dec. 1940. Colonel Scorgie became Deputy Director-General. *Pick wrote to Ogilvie on 13 Dec. 1940, 'I am afraid we did not see eye to eye altogether while I was here, but we had the good fortune not to fall out. I merely write to thank you for the amiable way in which you have taken some of the criticisms of the BBC, which perhaps I put a little unkindly. However, now I shall be merely an ordinary listener to the BBC.'

[7] *Note on an interview between Ogilvie and Monckton, 1 Jan. 1941.

appointed would be able to range freely and without check over the whole field of the Corporation's activities and administration.[1] At the same time, Monckton, with characteristic care for other people's sensibilities, explained reassuringly that there was no intention to supersede the Governors or the Director-General and that the only purpose of the proposed moves was to strengthen the machinery by which the Ministry's directives on news and propaganda could be given to the BBC.

At a further meeting on 21 January at which Monckton, Wellington, Powell, Ogilvie and Tallents were present, Duff Cooper himself explained that the appointment of the Advisers was necessary in war time when the Government needed to exercise control over broadcasting matters which might affect the conduct of the war. He reaffirmed, however, that the Government had avoided and would not propose any change in the status of the BBC and that at the end of the war 'normal relations would be resumed'. As for the role and functions of the Advisers, these would 'be largely determined by experience'.[2] Doubts remained on the BBC's side, and Ogilvie pressed for the term 'General Adviser' to be dropped and for the two Advisers to be called Home Policy Adviser and Foreign Policy Adviser respectively.[3] Meanwhile Tallents noted hopefully that the Empire was excluded from the new system of control.[4] Duff Cooper passed on Ogilvie's observations to the Cabinet, and announced in the House of Commons early in February that two governmental Advisers, each an official of the Ministry of Information, would be appointed, 'one on general topics, and home policy more particularly, and one on foreign policy'.[5]

Ivone Kirkpatrick, 'considered to be one of Lord Halifax's best men', took over the second post on 3 February.[6] He was a 'new man' to the BBC, although he had recently shown great interest in broadcasting problems. Aged 44, he combined wide diplomatic experience with agility and ambition. 'He

---

[1] *Note by Powell, 4 Jan. 1941.

[2] *Note by Tallents of a meeting, 21 Jan. 1940. Duff Cooper was accompanied by Monckton, and Powell and Ogilvie by Tallents.

[3] *Ogilvie to Powell and Tallents, 24 Jan. 1941.

[4] *Note by Tallents, 25 Jan. 1941.

[5] *Hansard*, vol. 368, col. 1184. See also ibid., vol. 369, col. 1272, where he told a questioner first that the appointment of two official advisers would 'increase the control exercised by the Government' and second that 'the Government's policy has been to maintain the independence of the BBC'.   [6] *Letter of 1 Feb. 1941.

was quickwitted and surefooted like a mountain animal,'
Harman Grisewood, who was soon to work closely with him,
has written, 'with a good head for heights and well used to
rough weather. Despite his manicured "Mayfair" appearance
there was little of the diplomat in him. He won his points by
attack rather than by persuasion. Military brusqueries came
easier to him than urbanity.'[1]

It was clear that Kirkpatrick's arrival presaged new times
for the BBC as well as new men, and few people inside the
Corporation were as willing to be impressed as Grisewood.
Yet Kirkpatrick began by writing disarmingly to Tallents,
whose personal position was most affected by the new appointment, that no one was more conscious than he was of 'the
appalling difficulty of the BBC foreign service. Mistakes real
or wholly imaginary are ventilated, but no one bestows a
thought on the thousands of things well done. . . . I am
happy to think I won't be amongst strangers.'[2] Tallents
hoped, indeed, at this time that Kirkpatrick would be
'practically helpful' to the Corporation. Kirkpatrick, he
pointed out, had access through his previous work not only
to Ministers, particularly the Foreign Secretary—Eden was
interested in his appointment and was impatient that he
should take it up quickly—but to the Chiefs of Staff; he would
be able to secure quick decisions on important issues from the
highest authorities; and there was a good chance that he would
be able to harmonize interests which seemed to conflict with
those of outside bodies.[3] In fact, however, Kirkpatrick's
appointment meant that Tallents, who might at one time have
been Director-General of the Ministry of Information and who
had deliberately abandoned Public Relations for the more
pressing problems of Overseas broadcasting in May 1940,[4] was
on the way out of the BBC which he had always hoped that
he would eventually direct. Although he did not leave until
September 1941, the die had long been cast, and by then also,
after much coming and going, there had been a major reshuffle
of people and functions.[5]

---

[1] H. Grisewood, *One Thing at a Time* (1968), p. 134.
[2] *Kirkpatrick to Tallents, 28 Jan. 1941.
[3] *Tallents to Ogilvie and Powell, 1 Feb. 1941.   [4] See above, p. 238.
[5] See below, pp. 339–42.

Ryan, who was given the Home Broadcasting post on 5 March, a few weeks after Kirkpatrick's appointment, was no stranger to the BBC. Brought in originally by Tallents, with whom he had worked closely before 1935,[1] he had served as as Liaison Officer to Sir Campbell Stuart and from March 1940 as Controller (Home): throughout the whole of this period, indeed, he had been the leading figure in most of the BBC's dealings with the Ministry and with the Armed Forces. His war-time record with the BBC was impressive, therefore, long before March 1941. Duff Cooper delayed offering him the new post on the grounds that some Cabinet Ministers might take exception to appointing someone from inside the BBC instead of seeking an Adviser from outside.[2] Any objections were quickly overcome, however, and on 5 March 1941 in a most complicated arrangement Monckton asked Ogilvie to release Ryan from duty with the BBC so that he could be seconded to the Ministry of Information in order that he could in turn be seconded as General Adviser to the BBC.[3]

If Kirkpatrick's appointment carried with it a threat to Tallents, Ryan's appointment certainly carried with it a threat to Ogilvie. The Director-General remained most unhappy about Ryan's title and the wide range of duties which it was stated that he would discharge; he feared, indeed, that Ryan would become an Inspector rather than Adviser. 'Bottlenecks' would be created which would bring much of the work of the BBC 'to a dead stop'.[4] When Ryan wrote to Ogilvie on 3 April asking that the sending to him of Control Board Minutes should be regularized 'as you agreed', Ogilvie replied tersely 'I agreed to no such thing'.[5] Difficulties with Ryan appeared to have been smoothed over by the end of the year, but it was Ogilvie who was eventually to disappear—after Tallents—in January 1942.[6]

[1] See Briggs, *The Golden Age of Wireless* (1965), pp. 19, 266, 269, 652.
[2] *Monckton to Ogilvie, 13 Feb. 1941.
[3] *Ogilvie's Secretary to Ogilvie, reporting telephone message from Lord Hood, 5 March 1941; Monckton to Ogilvie, 5 March 1941.
[4] *Draft Note by Ogilvie, 14 April 1941.
[5] *Ryan to Ogilvie, 3 April 1941; note by Ogilvie in red ink.
[6] See below, p. 345. As a consequence of Ryan's appointment as General Adviser, Maconachie became Controller (Home) and Barnes Director of Talks. Roger Armfelt became Assistant Controller (Home) in Sept. 1941.

The process of 'smoothing over' involved far more, indeed, than good relationships between particular people. There were very big changes in the institutional structure between the time that the Advisers were appointed and Ogilvie left. First in time was the reconstitution to full strength in April 1941 of the BBC's Board of Governors which had been reduced from seven members to two after the outbreak of war.[1] Powell and Millis were joined by Sir Ian Fraser, Dr. J. J. Mallon, Lady Violet Bonham Carter and Arthur Mann, the former editor of the *Yorkshire Post*. Thereafter there was an effective counterpoise both to the Ministry and the Cabinet and on occasion through Lady Violet Bonham Carter to Churchill himself. The Governors were further strengthened in July 1941 by the addition of Harold Nicolson, who after a ministerial reshuffle lost his post as Parliamentary Secretary to the Ministry of Information. Nicolson's disappointment at being dismissed was not eased by a tactless and ill-founded remark by his successor Ernest Thurtle, Labour M.P. for Shoreditch, that the BBC Governors had no war-time function,[2] but he soon settled down happily to his new BBC responsibilities. Brendan Bracken, who took Duff Cooper's place as Minister of Information at the same time as Nicolson left in the second big change of the year, soon disclaimed Thurtle's statement, and stated categorically in the House of Commons that 'the Governors act as trustees to the public and Parliament for the maintenance of the integrity and high standards of British broadcasting. They have always recognised that in war time it is necessary and right that the Government should control the policy of the BBC in matters affecting the war effort, the publication of news, and the conduct of propaganda. Subject to this measure of control, the Governors in addition to their responsibility as trustees, remain in charge of the administration and technical services of the Corporation, and of the expenditure of the moneys voted to it by this House.'[3]

[1] See above, pp. 88–9.
[2] H. Nicolson, *Diaries and Letters, 1939–45*, p. 180.
[3] *Hansard*, vol. 374, cols. 1917, 1918. When the number of Governors was restored, Duff Cooper had replied 'Yes, Sir, certainly' to a supplementary question in the House as to whether, 'within the reasonable restrictions of war, this enlightened Board of Governors will be allowed to exercise genuine freedom'. (*Hansard*, vol. 370, col. 991.)

Bracken, lively and intelligent, showed far more understanding of the BBC's point of view than any previous Minister
of Information, and his continued presence in this post until
the end of the war—close in mood, spirit and friendship to
Churchill—served thereafter to stabilize the constitutional
position of the BBC. Moreover, from 1 August 1941 onwards
his Deputy Director-General was Cyril Radcliffe, whose great
gifts were fully employed in harness, and the Ministry was
generally and effectively reorganized.[1] Yet something of the
success of the new arrangements rested on the experience
and sense of independence displayed by the Governors of the
Corporation, probably a more able and lively team than any
before them. Nicolson himself, whatever his limitations as a
politician, was an attentive, civilized and receptive Governor,
and Lady Violet Bonham Carter, as brilliant as she was
determined, refused from the start 'to be treated merely as a
figure-head'.[2] Fraser, different in outlook and opinion from
the rest, had always been tough and independent: he had
protested vehemently about the reduction in the number of
Governors in 1939;[3] and he was now able to put forward the
BBC's case in the House of Commons, since under a war-time
House of Commons Disqualification (Temporary Provisions)
Act he was allowed to sit in Parliament as representative for the
Lonsdale Division of Lancashire while at the same time serving
as Governor of the BBC.[4] In July 1941, for example, he spoke
forthrightly in a House of Commons debate both about the
BBC and the Ministry of Information, stressing, perhaps for the
first time in Parliament, their interdependence rather than their
rivalry. 'I doubt if the Ministry of Information itself has the
power it ought to have,' Fraser argued, 'and I am sure broadcasting suffers from this. Great development has taken place in
broadcasting, but it might have been greater and might have
been swifter if the Minister, to whom we have to go for approval

[1] Bernard Sendall and Alan Hodge came in as Bracken's private secretaries.
Colonel Scorgie moved over to the Mines Department. Later in the month
Kenneth Grubb became Controller of the Ministry's Overseas Division with
responsibilities for all parts of the world other than the Empire and the United
States. See below, p. 352.

[2] Nicolson, op. cit., p. 183, entry for 13 Aug. 1941.

[3] See above, p. 87.

[4] See I. Fraser, *Whereas I was Blind* (1942), p. 167. He was elected to Parliament
in April 1941.

and to help us obtain priorities of labour, materials, and equipment, was in a stronger position.'

Fraser went on to tell the story of 'how we wasted weeks getting consent to look in certain parts of the country for sites for stations and then further weeks negotiating with the Post Office about lines, the Office of Works about securing priority or requisitioning, the Ministry of Supply about materials, the Armed Forces about interference'. He ended with the observation that 'if the House saw the details of this struggle as I have seen them, they would, I am sure, feel as I do that the time has come to put broadcasting under a Minister the importance of whose office is fully realised'.[1] He might have added, had he known it, that during the blackest days of 1940, when battle headquarters had been set up in Broadcasting House, there had been a remarkable proposal to requisition parts of Broadcasting House for the use of other government departments. This suggestion was put forward at a meeting between Powell, Ogilvie, Lord Beaverbrook and, strange though it might seem, Reith, who was then Minister of Works.[2]

Mann, another new Governor, was less of a public figure than Fraser, but he held strong views about the presentation of news and talks and had proved his independence and strength of character when as editor of the *Yorkshire Post* he had attacked the Munich Agreement of 1938: immediately after taking office as a Governor he wrote forcefully that the independence of the BBC had to be preserved and that it was 'the responsibility and duty of the Governors to ensure it'. 'A democracy functions with any hope of success only if the people are well informed as to the events upon which the Executive take their decisions and if the Executive is subjected to free and open criticism.'[3]

Powell's role is more difficult to assess. He had been consulted frequently behind the scenes during the period when the number of Governors had been reduced, and private talks which he was to have with Bracken during the autumn of

---

[1] *Hansard*, vol. 372, cols. 1595–1600.

[2] *Control Board, *Minutes*, 6 Nov. 1940. The meeting took place on 2 Nov. Ogilvie consulted the Minister of Information, the Foreign Secretary and Greenwood, the last-named promising to take it to the Cabinet. See the laconic comment in Reith, *Into the Wind* (1949), p. 411, 'Broadcasting House only just escaped'.

[3] *Note by Mann, 1 May 1941.

1941 were of key importance in the story of the fall first of Tallents and then of Ogilvie. To some people, indeed, he was not so much the man who made the new arrangements work as the *éminence grise*, the Chairman who became more important at the critical moment than the Director-General. Mann might talk of democracy, but his own Chairman could move very quietly indeed behind the scenes with very few people knowing what he was doing.

Undoubtedly Powell's actions, like those of Kirkpatrick, were influenced by bigger changes still in the pattern of Intelligence agencies which the War Cabinet agreed upon in June 1941. The development of the Political Warfare Executive (PWE),[1] announced to Parliament in September 1941,[2] followed highly critical debates about British propaganda overseas, during which Duff Cooper had had to defend the arrangement whereby the Foreign Secretary laid down the foreign policy of the country 'while the Minister in charge of propaganda' attempted 'to put this policy over to the countries concerned'.[3] 'Cooperation between Government Departments would obviously become impossible,' Duff Cooper told one questioner, 'if all inter-Departmental communications were to be made public.'[4] After taking over Duff Cooper's post, Bracken plunged vigorously into the discussions about a new PWE set-up, more professionally organized and allowing far greater unity of command, telling Parliament that in the meantime 'the organisation of the various foreign services of the BBC is under review'.[5] Powell was obviously aware of the main outline of what was happening. 'His [Kirkpatrick's] time,' he wrote in September 1941, 'will largely be taken up by his daily association with PWE and by the supervision of

[1] See above, pp. 36–8.

[2] *Hansard*, vol. 374, cols. 293–4. In May 1941 (see ibid., vol. 371, cols. 1255–6), Churchill had replied to a questioner that several departments were concerned with propaganda to foreign countries and that if the Minister of Information or the Minister of Economic Warfare could not answer any question relating to propaganda he himself would do so.

[3] Ibid., vol. 372, col. 1620.   [4] Ibid., vol. 373, col. 581.

[5] Ibid., vol. 373, col. 2108. Cf. ibid., vol. 374, col. 295: the Prime Minister replied to one questioner that 'the small anonymous [PWE] executive' would 'probably concentrate some of their earliest attention on this point'. The BBC's comments on one of the most important debates on propaganda are set out in a note by *Thornton to Ogilvie, 3 July 1941.

the carrying of their policy into effect right up to the micro-phone.'[1] Bracken thanked him for the 'energetic part' he had played in ensuring the success of the new regime.[2]

Before the BBC's internal rearrangements were agreed upon, the Governors as a whole demonstrated that they could stand up for themselves as a Board. When Thurtle, insensitive as ever, made a statement in the House of Commons in October 1941 that the Governors were not concerned with the war-effort of the BBC and were only concerned with culture and entertainment—the statement recalled some of the sillier statements of the *Sitzkrieg*[3]—the Chairman and the Governors of the BBC protested sharply to Bracken, who replied that Thurtle would not be allowed in future to answer questions about the BBC. Even this categorical reply did not satisfy the Board. 'We are not content with this, and point out that if what Thurtle said was really BBC policy, then we are not worth collectively £7,000 a year of Government money.'[4]

The Board was directly concerned with the negotiations about the future role of the BBC's 'Advisers',[5] seeking to draft alternative job specifications to those prepared by the Ministry.[6] They were soon presented, however, with cogent and telling advice both from Ryan and from Kirkpatrick themselves. By September 1941 Ryan was complaining that unless the Advisers also became BBC Controllers with executive authority inside the BBC as well as responsibility to the Ministry of Information, the BBC would never run efficiently.[7] 'The immediate step,' Ryan went on, 'is to put the two Advisers in as Controllers, still with direct access to the Director-General and DDG of the Ministry of Information and attending the Ministry of Information Executive Board. . . . As Controllers in the BBC the two Advisers would, of course, deal on general BBC Control Board matters through the Director-General of the BBC.'[8]

---

[1] *Powell to Bracken, 18 Sept. 1941.
[2] *Bracken to Powell, 22 Sept. 1941.   [3] See above, pp. 84 ff.
[4] Nicolson, op. cit., p. 187, entry for 9 Oct. 1941. 'I wish you were my Under Secretary,' Bracken told Nicolson a fortnight later. 'What fun we should have.' (Quoted ibid., p. 189.)
[5] *Board of Governors, *Minutes*, 22 April 1941.
[6] *Ibid., 26 June 1941.
[7] *Ryan to Radcliffe, 10 Sept. 1941.
[8] *Memorandum by Ryan, 22 Sept. 1941.

Kirkpatrick also had come to realize that there was far more to be said for controlling than for advising. He was unhappy about proposals for the further reconstruction of the BBC's European Service which were being mooted by Salt throughout the spring and summer of 1941 and made his views as clearly felt as those of Ryan. He believed that the most urgent task was to co-ordinate News and other programme output and to devote detailed attention to 'the direction of propaganda',[1] and later in the year, after PWE had been established, wrote very critically of the state of affairs inside the BBC when he arrived. 'Before the creation of PWE . . . the Director of European Services [Salt] was virtually controller of the European Service except that he did not control the News staff. The latter was responsible to the Overseas News Editor [A. E. Barker] who in turn was responsible only to the Overseas Controller [Tallents]. Thus under this organisation News was not coordinated with Talks or Features—provided nothing harmful was put on the air, Talks and Features staff, who were responsible only to Salt, could put out anything they pleased without regard to the opinion or output of the News Editors. Worse still, News Editors were not in a position to criticise the translation of their own bulletins since the translators were responsible only to Salt and could decline to receive instructions or criticism from the News Editors.'[2]

Kirkpatrick put his trust not in Salt but in Newsome, and he resisted all Salt's attempts to organize the European Service 'on a divisional or quasi-divisional basis',[3] to become Controller (European Services) and to have appointed two Assistant Controllers, one dealing with Policy and one with Management. Others inside the BBC doubted whether Salt had the experience to run such a complex organization, while recognizing that 'the time has come for a major operation'.[4] 'I cannot avoid the feeling,' J. B. Clark, Assistant Controller

[1] *Salt to A. E. Barker, 10 March 1941, commenting on a memorandum from Kirkpatrick. Salt claimed that the memorandum repeated points he had made earlier in Dec. 1940. (See above, p. 261.)
[2] *Note by Kirkpatrick, 21 Oct. 1941.
[3] *Salt to Tallents, 16 Dec. 1940; Salt to Barker, 10 March 1941; Salt's notes on Kirkpatrick's views on 'Organisation of European Service', 10 March; Salt to Tallents, 29 Aug. 1941.
[4] *J. B. Clark to Tallents, 4 April 1941.

(Overseas) wrote to Tallents in May 1941,[1] 'that the European staff is being developed on inflated and ill-controlled lines.' Two months later, after a scheme had been prepared which involved the raising of Salt's status (along with that of Rendall, the Director of the Empire Service) to that of a Head of a Branch with subordinate Directors, Graves, the Deputy Director-General, opposed the recommendation: 'I have a high opinion of Salt's ability,' he remarked, 'as I think most of us have, but I don't feel he is a good organiser.'[2]

The upshot of months of discussion which lowered the morale of many of the people working loyally with Salt[3] was Kirkpatrick's appointment as Controller (European Services) in October 1941. The appointment entailed the full separation of the BBC's foreign Services into European and Overseas. Salt lost his place, and was transferred to the United States in December 1941 as Assistant North American Director.[4] Tallents disappeared from the Corporation, and the 'insider' who emerged with enlarged authority was J. B. Clark, who had been Tallents's Assistant Controller. Meticulous, thorough, immensely experienced in BBC affairs and deeply devoted to the Corporation, Clark now became Controller (Overseas).[5]

The critical decision to separate the foreign Services into two had been put to Bracken by Powell in September 1941,[6] and after some hesitation on the part of the Ministry, Clark's appointment was approved.[7] Clark had made it clear before he was appointed that he was unhappy about the way in which important decisions were being taken inside the BBC without his being consulted: indeed, on behalf of Salt and Rendall as well as of himself he expressed 'our common misgivings about the manner in which our former Controller [Tallents]

[1] *Clark to Tallents, 14 May 1941.

[2] *Graves to Tallents, 25 July 1941.

[3] *Tallents to Ogilvie, 8 Sept. 1941. Salt put forward many different schemes of reorganization, including the one outlined above, on p. 261.

[4] See below, p. 408. *On 8 Oct. 1941 he had written to Clark saying that Kirkpatrick should 'come out into the open' as to why he did not want to work with him. Some people inside the BBC never forgave Kirkpatrick for his 'intrigues'.

[5] *The reorganization was promulgated by Ogilvie on 9 Oct. 1941 in a note headed 'Wartime Organisation'. At the same time Ryan's appointment as Controller (News Coordination) was announced. See below, pp. 535–6.

[6] *Powell to Bracken, 27 Sept. 1941.

[7] *Bracken to Powell, 2 Oct. 1941; Powell to Bracken, 8 Oct. 1941.

has been relieved of his position'.[1] He obviously resented the appointment of Government nominees as BBC Controllers. Yet what led to the final decision to appoint him Controller (Overseas) was the Government's insistence that there should be a basic transformation. It was on 11 September 1941, an important date, that Powell told the Governors that he had met Bracken at the latter's request 'when the Minister had indicated his concern at the management of the Overseas Division and his view that, owing to the fact that this Service was in considerable part outside the pre-war activities of the Corporation and was directly paid for by the Government as part of the war effort, the Government was entitled to satisfy itself through the Minister as to the efficiency of the organisation both as to cost and personnel'.[2]

Clark, who disliked even the slightest threat of 'intervention' in the affairs of the BBC, could not have been expected to approve of the logic behind the argument that he who pays the piper calls the tune. Yet he was to survive all the newcomers, and eventually in 1944 when Kirkpatrick left the BBC was to take his place as Controller (European Services).[3] Meanwhile, Kirkpatrick established his own position confidently and with increasing authority, even vis-à-vis PWE. Salt had found it impossible to provide a generally acceptable candidate for a deputy: Kirkpatrick soon found Harman Grisewood, then Assistant Director of Programme Planning, who became Assistant Controller (European Services) at the end of October. Yet there was an element of irony in Kirkpatrick's own position. He insisted categorically that 'the European Division will derive its policy instruction, through its Controller, from the Government's new Political Warfare Executive which, as announced by the Prime Minister, is responsible to the Minister of Information and the Minister of Economic Warfare. This institution will be translated into broadcasting terms by the Director of Propaganda [Newsome] and conveyed to the Staff in his directives and by other means.'[4] At the same time, the directives were never universally to be obeyed. And although he produced a blueprint in which he envisaged the new

[1] *Clark to Ogilvie, 24 Sept. 1941, enclosing a memorandum 'Principles affecting the War-time Organisation of Overseas Services'.
[2] *Board of Governors, *Minutes*, 11 Sept. 1941.   [3] See below, p. 682.
[4] *Note on the Organisation of the European Division, 21 Oct. 1941.

European Division having three departments—Propaganda, Intelligence and Organisation[1]—with a 'central production group' and seventeen 'national output sections'—English, German, Italian, French, Norwegian, Scandinavian (other than Norway), Polish, Czech, Dutch, Belgian, Greek, Yugoslav, Bulgarian, Hungarian, Roumanian, Albanian and Luxembourger—he was never to secure the degree of centralization he wished. There were to be many bitter arguments about Intelligence, and his proposal that the BBC's department of Intelligence would include nineteen Regional Intelligence Officers, Research, Records and Information, was never to be implemented.[2]

Earlier in 1941 there had been protracted debate before the Joint Broadcasting Committee (JBC) had been finally assimilated into the BBC, to form the nucleus of a new BBC Transcription Service.[3] The debate was less intense, however, than that which followed the setting up in October 1941 of a subcommittee headed by Sir Leonard Browett to investigate 'overlapping' between PWE and BBC Intelligence.[4] It carried

[1] The Department of Organisation was to concern itself with presentation, including liaison with the Engineering Department, language staffing, microphone techniques, publicity, and planning ('to ensure that the right steps are taken at the right time to avoid growing pains').

[2] *See below, pp. 423–5. It is interesting to compare this programme organization with that suggested by Salt (*Memorandum of 27 June 1941), in which he envisaged eight main regional services, each run by a Service Director, controlled by four central Directors, for Planning, Propaganda, Production and Management.

[3] *Note by Tallents, outlining the possibilities of the transfer, 9 Jan. 1941; Overseas Board, *Minutes*, 9 Jan. 1941; Bamford (Ministry of Information) to Ogilvie, 12 March 1941, agreeing in principle to the transfer; Clark to Wellington, 26 March 1941, setting out some of the difficulties; Bamford to Clinton-Baddeley, 6 March, who had directed the JBC since Miss Matheson's death at the end of Oct. 1940; Clark to Tallents, 1 April 1941; Memorandum from H. J. Dunkerley, 15 April; JBC: 'A Note on General Organisation', 30 April. During the last stages of the discussions, the role of JBC as a recording agency led to a series of interesting arguments about recording facilities and developments. The BBC formally took control of and responsibility for the activities of the JBC on 1 July 1941. The first estimates of the London Transcription Service were prepared in Aug. 1941.

[4] *Bracken to Powell, 22 Sept. 1941, announcing the appointment of a committee; David Stephens (PID) to Powell, 8 Oct. 1941, announcing that Browett had been chosen as chairman. David Bowes-Lyon represented PWE and J. B. Clark the BBC. J. B. Clark to Rendall on the object of the committee, 4 Nov. 1941: 'it should be a matter of primary concern for us to ensure that our Intelligence and related units make the maximum use of all external sources of information and do not, beyond the point of absolute necessity, duplicate work which is being done outside.'

out its inquiries while Kirkpatrick was reorganizing the BBC's European Services and it gave an immediate blessing to 'regional' rather than 'functional' organization of the BBC's European staff 'so long as the work was properly coordinated'.[1] Yet its final report, which appeared in November 1941, seemed to Kirkpatrick, at least, to press 'regionalization' too far. There would be far too many Controllers. 'A year's experience in the BBC' had taught him that the best men should be free to act without too many restraints, as Newsome had acted in relation to European News. Too much regional control would carry with it the danger of 'creeping paralysis'.[2] The strength of Newsome was that his language was English, and he looked at Europe free from any regional blinkers.

The problems were not all solved, nor were the changes yet all over. They were to reach their dramatic climax with the resignation of Ogilvie in February 1942 and with a further and this time more thorough reorganization of PWE in the same month. Before turning to the next stages of the story of the controllers and the controlled, however, it is necessary as a preliminary to turn back in time to the set of earlier decisions which determined the total foreign output of the BBC against a background of protracted and extended war. In January 1941 the Minister of Information invited the BBC to put forward proposals for a large extension of its overseas services and to frame them on the assumption that all priorities in the supply of equipment, accommodation, labour and staff would be forthcoming. 'Triple expansion' was to be the watchword, and the fate of this enterprise must be treated as a leading theme in the history of the years 1941 and 1942.

3. 'Triple Expansion'

THE idea of a large-scale extension of BBC overseas services had first taken shape in the autumn of 1940, when it was clear that

---

[1] *Browett Committee, Interim Report, 25 Oct. 1941. After the publication of the final report there were talks on Bush House between Walter Adams, General Secretary of PWE, and Grisewood.

[2] *Kirkpatrick to Bruce Lockhart, 22 Nov. 1941.

the volume of foreign-language broadcasting was in danger of actually falling.[1] 'It is a lamentable fact,' Vernon Bartlett had complained early in December 1940, 'that at present less time is devoted to broadcasting in foreign languages than was the case a year ago, yet you have all those European countries which have come under Nazi domination and which can only be reached by the spoken word.'[2] The BBC admitted that the amount of time devoted to European languages had been slightly reduced, while pointing out first that 31 foreign languages were now being employed instead of 17 and second that the amount of world service broadcasting to countries outside Europe had considerably increased.[3] Nonetheless, both the Corporation and the Government were concerned about the obvious deficiencies. Following a decision of the War Cabinet on 30 December 1940, therefore, the Ministry of Information invited the BBC to put forward specific proposals with a view to a 'possible trebling of present output',[4] and accordingly a memorandum from the BBC was duly presented to the Minister in mid-January 1941.

'Triple expansion' was believed to be necessary for a number of reasons, set out in the following order—to enable the BBC 'with enhanced power to convey to all parts of the world truthful news and a prompt, clear and insistent exposition of British policy'; 'with growing force to counter and discredit the enemy cause within the enemy countries and among populations subject to enemy occupation'; 'to bring Britain closer to the various parts of the Empire, to British Forces serving abroad, to British ships at sea and to the United States'; 'to encourage the Allies . . . and serve, better than it can at present . . . Allied Governments now seated in London'; and 'to present the British cause persistently and convincingly to neutral countries'. This imposing list was related to the needs of peace as well as to the ends of war. The importance of each item, it was urged, 'seems bound to grow as the war proceeds, bound again to take on a fresh significance when the other forms of national armament are unleashed during peace

[1] See above, pp. 262–3.
[2] *Hansard*, vol. 367, col. 589.
[3] *Unsigned Memorandum of 11 Dec. 1940.
[4] *Monckton to Powell, 31 Dec. 1940; Control Board, *Minutes*, 8 Jan. 1941; Note on the Extension of the BBC's Overseas Services, 14 Jan. 1941.

negotiations and during the period of European re-settlement which must follow a British victory'.

Expansion entailed more transmitters, increased numbers of staff and additional buildings in order to secure greater output, including almost non-stop transmissions to France, Germany and Italy, and greater discrimination to cater for the special points of view and tastes of particular audiences. In tabular form the projected output represented expansion in all sectors:

	Current Daily Output	Projected Daily Output
1. World Service	23	53
2. Latin-American Service	4	11½
3. Near-Eastern Service	2¼	6
4. European Service	19½	82
Total hours	48¾	152½

It was recognized that some of the 18 additional transmitters required to increase output would have to be bought from producers in the United States; that the 2,750 new staff would have to be recruited at a time of labour shortage and mobilization; and that most of the buildings would have to be improvised and scattered, although most of them should be preferably situated in London. The project would involve a capital outlay of at least £2,300,000 and a recurrent expenditure of over £2,000,000. Finally, it was acknowledged that ideally there should be 'parallel developments in the British Dominions and Colonies'. 'The existence of British territories in all parts of the world provides an opportunity for establishing an Imperial broadcasting network with a coverage with which no other country could compete.'[1]

This ambitious paper was considered at a short meeting held at the Ministry of Information on 22 January 1941 with Monckton in the chair. Lord Davidson expressed particular interest in the Empire scheme, and Ashbridge estimated that

[1] *Note on the Extension of the BBC's Overseas Services, 14 Jan. 1961.

£500,000 of dollar exchange would be necessary if the scheme was to work. Even then, he went on, there would be a fifteen month delay before any appreciable new expansion could be achieved in overseas programmes, since this would be the minimum period required to manufacture and instal one station of six transmitters. Most pertinently, Monckton expressed the view that the proposals as a whole would have the greatest appeal if he could state categorically that the expenditure might well shorten the war by a month. He noted also that even though the projected expenditure was only a fraction of the daily expenditure of the Armed Forces, the scheme could only be effective if the Cabinet took a direct interest in the matter of priorities. It might be wisest, therefore, he suggested, to lobby the Foreign Office, the Board of Trade, the Ministry of Economic Warfare and—this was a necessary political addition—Beaverbrook's Ministry of Aircraft Production. Churchill's own personal interest was also felt to be essential.[1] The lobbying duly went on behind the scenes, the Ministry of Information's Policy Committee supported the proposals at its meeting on 30 January, and a fuller series of BBC estimates was prepared for the Treasury, the one vital ministry which had not been mentioned.

Monckton sent on a copy of the fuller estimates to the Treasury on 18 February and, after three prods from Powell and Ogilvie,[2] at last received a favourable reply on 9 May 1941. 'The expenditure involved in the scheme is very large but we recognise the importance of strengthening the BBC overseas services, and we are prepared to give general financial blessing to the scheme as outlined in your letter.'[3] Between February and May the signing of Lend-Lease had improved the country's dollar position, and it was recognized that, while twelve of the additional transmitters required could be manufactured in Britain—an order for these could be put in at once—the rest would have to come from American producers with the orders placed through the British Purchasing Commission in Washington. On one proposal only was the Treasury

---

[1] *Note by Tallents, 22 Jan. 1941.
[2] *Ogilvie to Monckton, 21 March; Ogilvie to Duff Cooper 7 April, 1 May 1941.
[3] *Sir Alan Barlow to Monckton, 9 May 1941.

reluctant—that of providing a BBC transmitter in Canada[1]—and on this particular question the BBC itself had had its own reservations.

The substance of this very favourable reply was communicated to Ogilvie, who was asked to work out a plan in detail in collaboration with the Broadcasting Division of the Ministry of Information.[2] For the next few months, when so many issues of organization were being discussed in Broadcasting House and in Malet Street, a special Overseas Expansion Committee[3] concerned itself with the detail, which was also examined carefully at every relevant level of the Corporation. There were, however, two main sets of general difficulties in the way. First, the BBC was not exempted from the Essential Work Order of 1941, and found it difficult to maintain, let alone to increase, its key staff. The numbers of its staff had risen from 4,889 in September 1939 to 7,142 in April 1941: it felt, however, that if it was to carry out its tasks efficiently it needed complete exemption from military and industrial service for its existing staff without having to argue about individual cases, the power to retain staff on a compulsory basis for the duration of the war, the authority to conscript people for service with the BBC, and, not least important, the withdrawal from the Forces of a very limited number of individuals out of the 700 BBC employees then serving.[4]

Second, there were peculiar problems associated with buildings.[5] Premises leased by the BBC outside London were widely scattered and varied in quality; and Wood Norton was a large and for a time almost independently run centre.[6]

---

[1] The BBC quickly decided not to erect a transmitter in Canada. (*Overseas Board, *Minutes*, 15 May 1941.)

[2] *Monckton to Ogilvie, 13 May 1941.

[3] *Control Board *Minutes*, 21 May 1941. It included Ashbridge, Tallents and Lochhead and was under the chairmanship of Graves.

[4] *Note by Powell, 7 April 1941. See also a further letter enclosing a memorandum on the same subject from Powell to Duff Cooper, 8 July 1941. 'Either the broadcasting service is essential to the conduct of the war, in which case the BBC should be given its men and not compelled to waste the time of key men in unprofitable bargaining, or else the Government thinks that other services more urgently need the men. In the latter case it is submitted that the BBC cannot carry out its commission.'   [5] *Overseas Board, *Minutes*, 20 March 1941.

[6] In July 1941 the Symphony Orchestra, the Music Department and the Theatre Orchestra were transferred to Bedford, where they remained until shortly after the end of the war.

In London itself, which during the summer of 1941 was still thought to be highly vulnerable to German attack, there was fierce competition for all available buildings. There had been serious and spectacular bomb damage in houses near Broadcasting House in a raid on 16/17 April 1941, and on 10 May in the last big raid of the blitz a considerable part of Bedford College, which the BBC had leased, was destroyed. On the same night a heavy explosive bomb also landed on the Peter Robinson building, 200 Oxford Street, where Overseas Services of the BBC operated: fortunately it did not explode. A high explosive bomb landed also on the BBC's premises at Maida Vale which had been used by the European Services: there was one casualty, and extensive damage was done. It was in the aftermath of the blitz and with fears of what might still be in store—even a German atomic bomb[1]—that a meeting of the Home Defence Executive, presided over by Findlater Stewart on 24 June and attended by representatives of the Ministry of Home Security, the Air Ministry, London Region and the Chief of General Staff Home Forces, agreed that because of continued dangers of air attack additional accommodation should be sought not in central London as had been previously envisaged[2] but on the periphery, 'even though some administrative inconvenience might be caused thereby'.[3] One large site with dispersed buildings was thought preferable despite the possibility of attack by dive bombers.[4]

The BBC received no immediate satisfaction in relation to either of these two sets of difficulties, although it went ahead at once with the ordering of transmitters and the re-scheduling of output. At a meeting with Duff Cooper in early June 1941 the BBC representatives were driven once again to complain that there was 'insufficient recognition of broadcasting as a vital part of the war effort' and 'inadequate machinery of

[1] For some of the doubts on this subject, as expressed by the Maud Committee in 1941, see M. Gowing, *Britain and Atomic Energy, 1939-1945* (1964), p. 78. By March 1941 the atomic bomb had ceased to be a matter simply of scientific speculation. (Ibid., p. 68.)

[2] *Powell to Duff Cooper, 12 May 1941; Control Board, *Minutes*, 25 June 1941.

[3] *Ogilvie to Monckton, 1 July 1941. Monckton approved of the plan to site activities on the periphery (Monckton to Ogilvie, 17 July 1941).

[4] *Overseas Expansion Committee, *Minutes*, 22 July 1941; Control Board, *Minutes*, 23 July 1941. No official reply to this proposal had been received by the end of the month.

(*a*) Workers' Playtime

(*b*) Bing Crosby
and Tommy
Handley

10. Light Entertainment

(*a*) Women Technical Assistants prepare a Steel Tape Recording Machine

(*b*) The London Transcription Service

(*c*) Marking a Passage in a Recorded Speech by Hitler

9. Broadcasting Techniques

(a) A European News Copy Taster dictates a News 'Flash'

(b) BBC Monitoring Service: the Editorial Room

11. Behind the News

(a) King George VI

(b) General
de Gaulle

(c) The Soviet
Ambassador,
M. Maisky

12. A Trio of Broadcasters

Government for measuring broadcasting against other national claims'.[1] Duff Cooper felt that there were no differences of opinion with the BBC on policy,[2] yet it soon became clear that several Members of Parliament, notably Philip Noel-Baker, were even more disgruntled with the rate of progress already achieved than was the BBC itself. 'Our whole propaganda energies, especially through wireless,' he maintained, 'should be multiplied tenfold and at whatever cost.' If the war were to be shortened by one day as a result of effective propaganda— Monckton's earlier criterion—ten million pounds would be saved.[3] As it was, Dr. Goebbels had signed on 1,200 people whom he wanted for one job only—to sell his 'New Order' to the United States. In Britain, there were too few people and too few resources. Moreover, Noel-Baker went on, the conditions in which people worked were often deplorable. The European Services, for example, were housed in what he described for security reasons as 'the black hole of Tooting Bec': 'there are far too many people for the cubic space available and there is no present hope of any change, expansion or relief'.[4]

Rightly or wrongly the BBC thought that Noel-Baker's intention was not to help the BBC but to embarrass it and to embarrass Ogilvie in particular. In preparing its brief for the parliamentary debate, therefore, it made the most of what had actually been achieved in the way of expansion since September 1939—the acquisition of 48 additional premises, 27 of them in London, and the sharp increase of 560% in the Corporation's Overseas Services staff. Nonetheless, it was forced to point out as its own conclusion that 'the whole initiative and pressure in the matter of the provision of new stations and transmitters before and since the war has been taken by the BBC, and they have been met month after month with delays and adjournments—some, no doubt, inevitable, but not attributable in any shape or form to the BBC'.[5] Duff Cooper in his reply to

---

[1] *Notes for a meeting in May 1941. See also above, p. 16.
[2] *Duff Cooper to Powell, 17 June 1941.
[3] *Hansard*, vol. 372, col. 1601.   [4] Ibid., col. 1603.
[5] *Note by the Chairman, 24 June 1941. 'He [Noel-Baker] may even say,' the Note added, 'that Ogilvie is unfit for his job. He is going to attack them for their dilatoriness in regard to the accommodation problem and their lack of foresight regarding the provision of transmitters. . . . The facts are . . . that the whole initiative and pressure in the matter of the provision of new stations and transmitters

[cont.

the parliamentary debate went out of his way in his turn to exonerate the BBC from direct responsibility for relatively slow progress. 'It is imperative that the foreign service should operate from London in suitable buildings, but it is only rarely that there is such accommodation available in Central London. . . . The BBC, not being strictly a Government Department, have not had their fair share of priority, but hon. gentlemen must not blame the authorities in charge of the BBC. They have not to pay for themselves, and they have no reason for economy or parsimony. They are doing their best, and the difficulties are very great.'[1] He did not add that some of the misunderstanding arose from 'the necessity for secrecy': this rather than 'lack of foresight' remained a source of parliamentary confusion.[2]

These points were discussed further at a meeting between the Governors and Duff Cooper on 17 July 1941, when Duff Cooper himself confessed that he had not been able to bring home to people 'in high quarters' the importance of broadcasting and somewhat helplessly urged individual Governors who had personal contacts with any ministers to make the most of them. He also said, perhaps for the first time, that there had sometimes been hesitation on the part of the BBC to carry out the Ministry's directives.[3] The discussion was not restricted to such issues: it brought in also many of those other elements of open dissatisfaction which have already been considered[4]— notably dissatisfaction with the organization of news and of propaganda. Since the course of the discussion revealed how weak Duff Cooper's position was and how great were the frustrations he felt, it was obvious that the BBC needed a new dispensation if it were to be fully mobilized. The new dispensation was not long in coming. The following day Duff Cooper was transferred to the Duchy of Lancaster,[5] and Bracken, his successor, was soon reported by Harold Nicolson to be 'sacking everybody at the Ministry'.[6] Bracken was

[1] *Hansard*, vol. 372, cols. 1620–1.
[2] *Note by the Chairman, 24 June 1941.
[3] *Board of Governors, *Minutes*, 17 July 1941.
[4] See above, pp. 257 ff.   [5] See above, p. 336.
[6] H. Nicolson, *Diaries and Letters* (1967), p. 183: entry for 29 July 1941.

before and since the war has been taken by the BBC.' If during the debate there were to be any attack on the Director-General, this would be 'strongly resented by the Governors'.

certainly anxious, this time with Churchill's full support, to establish what the real broadcasting priorities were. 'How is our big broadcasting station which is to override foreign broadcasts getting on?' Churchill asked on 31 August. 'There was a long delay in setting about it, but I understand that the fullest priorities had been given.'[1] 'Perhaps you will be good enough to tell me,' Bracken wrote to Powell a few days later, 'whether you are satisfied by priorities which have been given?'[2]

In fact, while the idea of a possible take-over of the BBC's foreign services receded with Bracken's appointment, the BBC was faced in the autumn of 1941 with an aggravation of the situation in relation to all its earlier plans for triple expansion. It succeeded in increasing the range and volume of its overseas output—at the end of the year it was broadcasting in 40 languages instead of 32 at the beginning and for nearly 231 hours a week instead of 145[3]—but it had got nowhere near the targets it had set itself in January. At least four drafts of a triple expansion schedule were prepared by early August 1941,[4] but the continuing obstacles to any substantial increase of output, even to the maintenance of output in relation to the critically important European Service, were set out with disturbing candour in a memorandum of that month. 'Expansion has been carried out in anticipation of improvements in accommodation and equipment which have not always materialised. This has had a cumulative effect on working conditions, with the result that a reduction in output is necessary if a general deterioration of the propaganda effort is to be avoided.' Accommodation at Bush House, to which the first European Service staff had moved in January,[5] was so over-crowded that it impaired health and efficiency, while recording facilities were so inadequate that they prevented proper programming.[6] There was indeed a characteristically ill-tempered note in discussions at this time concerning the use of the recording facilities inherited from the JBC.[7]

[1] *Note from the Prime Minister, 31 Aug. 1941.
[2] *Bracken to Powell, 2 Sept. 1941. See below, p. 358.
[3] BBC Handbook, 1942, p. 5.
[4] *The fourth draft was ready on 2 Aug. 1941. See also the paper by C. Lawson-Reece, Supervisor of Overseas Planning, 'Policy for the Expansion of European Services', 12 June 1941. [5] *Overseas Board, Minutes, 16 Jan. 1941.
[6] *Note by J. W. Lawrence, 'Propaganda, Fighting Power and Efficiency', 5 Aug. 1941. [7] *For the take-over of JBC, see above, p. 344.

Whether or not the BBC 'leadership' itself was responsible for what was wrong by not insisting that this deplorable state of affairs should be changed,[1] it contributed to a continued sense of crisis in the autumn of 1941. There was certainly a lack of crispness and consistency in its approach to its own problems. There were also deep differences about personalities, including Tallents, before he left, and to an increasing extent Ogilvie himself. The administrative machine passed into the willing hands of Beadle, the BBC's West Regional Director, during the autumn of 1940—he became Acting Controller (Administration) after Lochhead was taken ill in the autumn of 1940—and Beadle soon came to the conclusion that 'the internal management' was chaotic. Changes were made in 1941—some of them were greatly resented by a few old officials of the Corporation—but Beadle believed that 'bold and experienced leadership . . . unhappily lacking' was necessary if there was to be 'a radical adaptation of the administrative machine . . . to keep pace with the tremendous demands being made upon it'.[2]

Matters seemed to be coming to a head in September 1941 when the Production Executive gave instructions to all government departments on the Prime Minister's orders 'to examine their building programmes with a view to the drastic curtailment of projects which, however important in themselves, could be dispensed with'.[3] The BBC was given one day's notice on 10 September to inform the Ministry of Works and Buildings of cuts it proposed to make in relation to the triple expansion scheme.[4] Monckton confessed that it was 'extremely tiresome' that neither the BBC nor the Ministry of Information had been given adequate notice,[5] yet the fact that the BBC

[1] *The *Minutes* of the Overseas Board record a whole series of disappointments and delays in the BBC's building and repairs schemes at Bush House (e.g. 23, 30 Jan., 6 Feb., 24 April 1941). Lady Violet Bonham Carter pressed questions about lay-out at the Board of Governors' Meeting, 22 April 1941.

[2] G. C. Beadle, *Television, A Critical Review* (1963), p. 29. After Beadle had taken over the post of Acting Controller (Administration) the Accounts Department, under the Chief Accountant G. H. Dunbar, passed in November 1941 from the responsibility of Controller (Administration) to that of Controller (Finance). Lochhead worked from an office in Oxfordshire, where the BBC Accounts Department was evacuated, and attended weekly meetings of the Control Board.

[3] *Ogilvie to Monckton, 10 Sept. 1941.

[4] *Ibid.

[5] *Monckton to Ogilvie, 11 Sept. 1941.

responded at once with a brief paper showing that the original estimates of January 1941 were no longer relevant provided some justification, at least, in the circumstances of 1941, for a governmental review of the position. The financial position was thoroughly unsatisfactory. Transmitters and plant had been ordered to secure a trebling of output, but little had been done about extra accommodation. £2,800,000 was now thought to be necessary for new building construction which would raise the capital cost of the whole triple expansion scheme to £5 million. Estimates and facts diverged alarmingly. It is significant that it needed the pressure of a general Government directive for this greatly enhanced figure to be released.

It was perhaps equally significant that Ogilvie cut the ground from under his own feet by conceding at once that it was unrealistic to go ahead with the scheme as a 'practical proposition'.[1] He recognized 'present labour and material supply problems' and 'the great difficulties of securing the specialised staff necessary to implement the triple expansion', thereby failing to respond to the growing demand inside the BBC itself for assertive leadership. His answer, indeed, concluded on a flat and uninspiring note. 'The BBC does not recommend any reduction in the number of transmitters agreed and already ordered, but recognises that considerable reductions in capital cost of office and studio premises could be made without preventing a limited expansion of, and improvement in, the output of its news and talks propaganda for overseas consumption.'[2] Given this reply, it is scarcely surprising that the Ministry itself did not feel able to go even as far as the BBC wished,[3] and the Corporation was left to proceed with a stage-by-stage development, which marked, in effect, the end of the bold scheme for triple expansion as it had originally been put forward.[4]

Undoubtedly, the financial and administrative confusions of the early autumn and the inability of the BBC and the Ministry to secure the objectives which they had themselves laid down

[1] *Control Board, *Minutes*, 17 Sept. 1941.
[2] *Note by Ogilvie, attached to his letter to Monckton, 10 Sept. 1941.
[3] *Monckton to Ogilvie, 11 Sept. 1941.
[4] *Ogilvie to Monckton, 19 Sept. 1941; Monckton to Ogilvie, 26 Sept. 1941; Overseas Expansion Committee, *Minutes*, 8, 15 Sept. 1941; Control Board, *Minutes*, 17 Sept. 1941.

earlier contributed substantially to the pressure of events which led to the replacement of Ogilvie as Director-General in January 1942.[1] Seven episodes illustrate the growing sense both of frustration and of uncertainty. First, the idea of an Empire Broadcasting Network, close to Tallents's heart, was abandoned: no good purpose, it was argued officially, would be served by the official launching of an ambitious programme of imperial broadcasting co-operation.[2] Second, Tallents, who had long been at Ogilvie's side and who had acted as Deputy Director-General when Graves was ill, as he often was, disappeared from the Corporation altogether in September 1941, as we have seen, following the creation of PWE and the reorganization of the BBC's overseas services:[3] there had been, indeed, a 'revolt of the barons' inside the BBC against him. Third, there was an aggravation of the complaints, some of them very damaging, that while the BBC had been scrambling for more pennies it had not done its best for the European Service staff who had been working in Bush House since 17 March. The move of PWE staff there in September focused attention on their position, and PWE complained directly to the Minister.[4] Ogilvie might argue that 'in spite of our joint efforts [the BBC's and the Ministry of Information's], increases in accommodation have only become available piecemeal and after long delays; and that even when accommodation has become available, further time had inevitably to elapse while it was equipped with the technical apparatus of broadcasting', but it seemed, rightly or wrongly, to Bracken that there had been a lack of drive, given the BBC's own sense of its priorities.[5]

Fourth, it was, to say the least, unfortunate for the 'image' of the BBC that, despite all its propaganda, the Twenty-Fourth Report of the Select Committee on National Expenditure could seriously suggest that, in order to economize on coal,

[1] See below, pp. 361–5.　　　[2] *Note by Tallents, 8 Sept. 1941.
[3] See above, pp. 339 ff. Tallents was subsequently associated with the Board of Trade in organizing the fuel rationing scheme.
[4] *Control Board, Minutes, 1 Oct. 1941. At this meeting Ogilvie read out the letter from PWE. The meeting agreed that the onus of further demands should be thrown on PWE.
[5] *Stephens to Bracken, 20 Sept. 1941; Ogilvie to Radcliffe, 6 Oct. 1941. Ogilvie had visited Bush House with Duff Cooper in March 1941, when they had agreed that overcrowding was likely there in the future. (Control Board, Minutes, 26 March 1941.)

gas and electricity, it would be wise to close down home broadcasting say at ten o'clock in the evening and to cut out the eight a.m. News and possibly the whole morning programme. The fatuity of this report, with proposals which Bracken rightly described as 'disastrous',[1] was no tribute to the abilities or imagination of a war-time Parliamentary Select Committee, yet it certainly showed how ineffective the BBC had been in justifying its special role on the 'home front'.[2] It was left to the Corporation to point out, again almost apologetically, that 'a strong argument against the Select Committee proposal is that, if any of the BBC's news bulletins were dropped, the enemy would almost certainly put on a bulletin in English to take its place'.[3]

Fifth, while the Kennet Committee on Manpower, which had been appointed on 1 April 1941, agreed that the reservation age in the BBC should be raised to 35 for people engaged in administrative and executive grade work, it refused to allow this concession to people in professional grades.[4] Despite all the special pleading earlier in the year on the part of the BBC and written and oral evidence given to 'the Committee', Kennet insisted that 'the rule that men of military age must be released, for whom adequate substitutes can be found or trained, must under present conditions be nation-wide in its application'.[5] The BBC once again had failed to establish its case. Sixth, there was enforced retreat all along the line in relation to premises. Plans to extend development on a site at Aldenham had been shelved earlier. There was to be much further discussion of the plans, but there was no sign of any immediate action.[6]

[1] *Bracken to Powell, 9 Oct. 1941. See House of Commons Paper 123 (Session 1940–1941), *Twenty-Fourth Report from the Select Committee on National Expenditure*, 23 Oct. 1941.

[2] *Note by Graves, 19 Nov. 1941, pointing out that the discontinuation of broadcasting at 10.30 p.m. at most could save .55 per cent of total fuel consumption during five winter months. Robert Foot, who knew about fuel, had confirmed that a meeting of the National Gas and Electricity Committee had agreed that so little saving would result from cuts in broadcasting that they could not be justified on those grounds.   [3] *Ibid.

[4] *There is an important paper on the dealings of the BBC with the Kennet Committee, written in December 1944 by W. R. Baker, who had been appointed War Services Officer in 1940.

[5] *Lord Terrington to Ogilvie, 10 Nov. 1941.

[6] *Overseas Expansion Committee, *Minutes*, 11 Nov. 1941.

Seventh, there was an argument even about transmitters. Approval had been given in September to the building of the new long and medium-wave station at Ottringham,[1] but the Production Executive decided in October 1941 that it could not grant priority to the construction of new short-wave stations for which contracts had already been placed. 'Rightly or wrongly,' Bracken told Ogilvie, 'they argue that there is no item in the BBC list of plant which in present circumstances requires such high priority and they say that the best procedure is to work the needs of the BBC item by item into their proper place in the planned production of the contractors concerned.' Bracken himself was clearly unhappy about this verdict, although he doubted the value of seeking to challenge it immediately: he suggested, indeed, to Ogilvie that it might be wise if the BBC were to appoint a Controller of Development, who could concern himself exclusively with the preparation of plans and their advocacy in official circles.[2] Ogilvie replied on behalf of the Governors that weeks of delay were clearly inevitable and that as things were there would be little likelihood of new short-wave stations being ready before the spring of 1943. There was no need for a Controller of Development: 'our Engineering Division is adequately staffed for the work if the manufacturers could be enabled by Government action to give us the necessary deliveries'.[3] After Bracken had insisted that he required a detailed statement if he was to persuade the Prime Minister to override the Production Executive,[4] Ogilvie went on to have prepared a special memorandum setting out once more the detailed case which had been presented on so many previous occasions. The proposals were eventually accepted, but the strain on Ogilvie had been apparent throughout.

Each of these seven episodes was revealing in itself. Together, they ensured that the bold scheme of January 1941, which had been prepared at the request of the Ministry of Information, was never fully put into effect. They culminated, however, in a more radical and, as it turned out, decisive debate about finance and organization which came into the open in November

---

[1] *Bracken to Powell, 2 Sept. 1941; Ogilvie to Bracken, 4 Sept. 1941.
[2] *Bracken to Ogilvie, 7 Oct. 1941.
[3] *Ogilvie to Bracken, 9 Oct. 1941.
[4] *Bracken to Ogilvie, 20 Oct. 1941.

1941. Earlier in the year, in July, the Public Accounts Committee had begun to take an interest in the complex war-time finances of the BBC,[1] and in October Bracken had summoned Robert Foot, General Manager of the Gas, Light and Coke Company, to meet him and had asked him to spend three months inside the BBC as 'General Adviser on War-Time Organisation', investigating its administrative and financial systems. After three months of hard effort, he said, Foot could go back in peace to his 'bloody gas'. He added that he was deeply concerned that because of lack of adequate financial control inside the BBC the Treasury was interfering too much and assuming too much responsibility. 'The pre-war administrative and financial systems had been outgrown, had become top-heavy and were no longer adequate to cope with an entirely different situation. . . . The Governors were worried, the Government was worried, and something had to be done about it.'[2]

After Foot had met the Governors informally[3] and had agreed to undertake the assignment—Bracken in thanking him said that he deserved the George Cross—he found that Lochhead's appointment as Controller (Finance) greatly simplified the BBC's financial operations, which were beginning almost for the first time to interest the Press. 'Axe Man appointed to prune BBC' was one headline. The day Foot arrived in Broadcasting House, the first telephone call he received—to his immense surprise, even to his immense alarm—was not from anyone inside the BBC but from Reith, the great voice from the BBC's past, who suggested that the only thing that it was necessary for him to do if he wished to tighten the BBC's organization was to get rid of the Director-General. Foot had met Reith only once before—and then only casually and uneasily—and they were never to establish working relations with each other.

Foot arrived in Broadcasting House on 1 November, and four days later the Chairman of the Governors, who had had talks with Bracken, received an official letter from Radcliffe pointing out that the Minister had noted that there had been

---

[1] *Control Board, *Minutes*, 27 Aug. 1941.
[2] Foot Manuscript, p. 118.
[3] *BBC Board of Governors, *Minutes*, 28 Oct. 1941.

heavy overspending that year both on the Home and Forces Programmes—£150,000 in one quarter—and an unexplained increase in programme costs.[1] Two weeks later in a further letter Radcliffe probed more deeply into the BBC's finances. New expenditure for 1941/2 was forecast at about £7,500,000: the Parliamentary vote, based on estimates prepared at the end of 1940, was £5,600,000. 'This excess of £1,900,000, which is foreshadowed,' he wrote, 'would be conspicuously large in any event. I understand, however, that to a considerable extent the excess represents additions to the Corporation's expenditure for which no specific financial authority has been given by the Ministry or the Treasury. If this is so, it will be no easy matter to satisfy the Treasury and Parliament that additional funds should be provided on this scale.' This second letter concluded with a demand for the most careful scrutiny of all existing plans for 1941/2 and for the introduction of an improved system of financial control.[2] There were to be further conflicts, concerned this time with capital grants relating to the acquisition of property without explicit Treasury sanction.[3]

Inside the BBC, Lochhead had prepared a detailed paper on financial control: it had been drafted, he said, with the object of reviewing the position internally, but, because of Treasury interest, it now acquired public significance. 'A radical change in outlook and procedure' was in his view necessary. 'The aim should be that no expenditure is authorised which is not covered by a complete estimate approved internally and by the Ministry. . . . At present, individual operations of the service are not controlled so as to show how expenditure on each unit compares with its output.'[4] In working out his plans for reorganization, therefore, Foot found it easy to co-operate both with Lochhead and with Beadle. They told him at once that they were deeply concerned about the position, that a major reorganization was urgently necessary, and that they would help him with it. In sharp contrast, Ogilvie said that he had

---

[1] *Bracken to Powell, 5 Nov. 1941. A Note had been prepared inside the Ministry by H. G. G. Welch on 10 Oct. 1941 on the Ministry Control of BBC Expenditure. The BBC replied to the note about programme costs (Note of 25 Nov. 1941), stating that fees and travel costs had risen along with 'quality'.

[2] *Radcliffe to Powell, 20 Nov. 1941.

[3] *Powell to Radcliffe, 10 Dec. 1941; Radcliffe to Powell, 15 Dec. 1941.

[4] *Note on Financial Control, 1 Nov. 1941.

no experience in business management and was not particularly interested in it.[1] He nonetheless signed a letter to all BBC Controllers announcing that pending the completion of Foot's report, a special committee consisting of Foot, himself and Graves, who had once again been ill and absent from the BBC, with Maurice Farquharson as Secretary, would 'exercise immediate control of any proposals which will involve additional expenditure in any direction'. 'It is not intended,' he explained, 'that economy should be exercised in such a way as to impair the efficiency of the service ... but it must be realised that subject only to this, there is a duty upon everyone throughout the whole Corporation not only to be personally mindful of the need for economy but actually to put economy into practice in every way within his or her scope and responsibility.'[2]

Before Foot's full proposals for 'reorganization' were put into effect, Ogilvie had resigned on 27 January 1942, and Foot had replaced him in a diarchy of Directors-General with Graves, the most senior and the most conservative of BBC officials, at his side. There was one final and dramatic crisis—on a different subject—before Ogilvie left.

The idea of moving the staff of the Monitoring Service from Wood Norton to Caversham had been notified to the staff in August 1941, when London's vulnerability was being discussed secretly in official circles and it was felt that the monitoring staff at Wood Norton had expanded to such an extent that the use of Evesham as a transmission centre in the event of London being evacuated was being prejudiced. Ogilvie considered the case for the move without taking into account the anxiety which was openly expressed by many people working at Wood Norton about future living conditions and financial arrangements at Caversham.[3] Subsequently there were long discussions about other possible sites,[4] and great uncertainty prevailed about future plans both for siting and organization.

Serious divergence of views soon became apparent between Ogilvie and the highly efficient and responsible young BBC officers on the spot—Marriott, the Director of the Monitoring

---

[1] Foot Manuscript, p. 138.   [2] *Note by Ogilvie, 19 Dec. 1941.
[3] *Monitoring Service Liaison Committee, *Minutes*, 27 Aug. 1941.
[4] *Ibid., 23 Sept., 7 Oct. 1941; Control Board, *Minutes*, 21 Aug.; Control Board (Administration), *Minutes*, 15 Oct. 1941; Report by Marriott, 15 Sept. 1941, on a site at Crowsley.

Service, who had been considered a few weeks earlier for a key position in a new European Services structure as devised by Salt[1] and Oliver Whitley, the Chief Monitoring Supervisor, both of whom were to have distinguished post-war careers with the BBC, and John Shankland, the head of the Monitoring Y Unit, who was later killed in action in the Royal Navy. They all felt that invaluable monitoring staff would be lost if a move were made to Caversham, where problems of accommodation would be acute; they also disagreed with the engineers about the conditions under which weak long-distance signals would be received there by the monitors. J. B. Clark strongly supported the three 'rebels', whom he described as 'experts' whose considered opinion should be allowed to carry the greatest possible weight.[2] Graves also was uneasy about Ogilvie's apparent indifference to substantial criticism, and even after consulting Frost, who had been so intimately concerned with the launching of the Monitoring Service in 1939[3] and who felt that the 'rebels' should obey orders in war time, he remained uneasy. Although Control Board reaffirmed its decision to move the Monitoring Service to Caversham, and Ogilvie wrote tartly to Clark that 'decisions are not open for reconsideration, without fresh evidence, simply because they are disliked by the particular parties concerned',[4] the matter was far from settled. When Ogilvie visited Wood Norton to explain to the monitoring staff what was happening, he kept both Marriott and Whitley out of the meeting, and later on they accused him of not telling the truth. In the Board of Governors Harold Nicolson took up the rebels' case, stressing that the Monitoring Service was 'one of the most brilliant and important departments of the BBC' and that if its success was jeopardized the BBC might well be accused of 'obstruction' by the Government.[5]

The Governors carefully considered the details of the case,

---

[1] See above, p. 341. Marriott had been appointed Head of the Monitoring Service on 28 June 1940, and Director of a separate department on 23 Sept. 1940.

[2] *J. B. Clark to Ogilvie, 16 Oct. 1941; *Control Board (Administration), *Minutes*, 15 Oct. 1941.

[3] Graves consulted Frost about the possibility of his returning to the BBC, but after a number of further consultations, including one with J. B. Clark, he decided not to return.

[4] See above, p. 361. *Ogilvie to Clark, 28 Oct. 1941.

[5] *Nicolson to Powell, 5 Nov. 1941.

concluding somewhat ambiguously first that when Governors heard complaints from staff they should report the complaints to the Director-General and second that the Director-General should report major changes in policy or personnel to the Chairman before implementing them.[1] They were clearly not prepared to support Ogilvie in the enforcement of 'discipline' or to treat as axiomatic that when he gave an 'order' it should be obeyed. As for the three 'rebels', they all resigned from the BBC and joined the Forces—Shankland leaving on 20 December, Marriott on 29 January and Whitley on 30 January. By the last of these dates Ogilvie himself had gone. There is no doubt that the three 'rebels' were completely out of sympathy with him, that they felt that he had little real understanding of their problems, and that they recognized that by resigning they helped to bring about his downfall. Nicolson also felt that Ogilvie had to go, though for somewhat different reasons. In a characteristic note in his diary he wrote on 26 January 1942: 'To Grosvenor House where we have a hush meeting of the BBC Board. We decide to retire Ogilvie and put Graves and Foot as Joint Directors-General in his place. I am sure that this is right, as Ogilvie is too noble a character for rough war-work. Yet I mind deeply in a way. This clever, high-minded man being pushed aside. I hate it. But I agree.'[2]

In January 1942 the Press was preoccupied with bad news from the Western Desert and from the Far East and paid relatively little attention in days of newsprint shortage to Ogilvie's 'fall'. The *Daily Express*, however, gave to the news item the headline 'Mr. Ogilvie leaves BBC: Differences with M.o.I.' and the *Daily Herald* referred to the 'interference from Whitehall' which had compelled Ogilvie to leave.[3] Both papers saw the resignation as a change pointing to 'complete control of home broadcasting by the Ministry of Information and by the Minister'. The *Evening News* spoke of 'a complete victory for the M.o.I.'. 'Once war broke out it was obvious that the control of the Corporation would largely pass out of the hands of its

---

[1] *Board of Governors, *Minutes*, 6, 13 Nov., 4 Dec. 1941. They set up a sub-committee to consider the case, consisting of Nicolson, Fraser and Foot. It made its recommendations on 13 November.

[2] Nicolson, op. cit., p. 207.

[3] *Daily Express*, 27 Jan. 1942; *Daily Herald*, 27 Jan. 1942.

Governors';[1] at last the control had become absolute. Ogilvie had not seen eye to eye either with the Governors or with Bracken: it was inevitable that he had to go. The following day *The Times* in its fifth leading article expressed rather vague alarm that the integrity of the BBC might be in jeopardy.[2] Yet the political correspondent of the *Daily Telegraph* was nearer the truth when he reported that he understood that the new system of dual control would not involve any change in the relations between the Minister of Information and the BBC and that the appointments had been made by the Governors on their own initiative and not at the instigation of the Ministry of Information.[3]

Bracken made this clear in the House of Commons. Ogilvie had not been sacked: he had resigned. It was not his business, he said, to delve into the domestic affairs of the BBC. 'The House cannot have it every way. Either they want the Governors to have a certain amount of independence or they want the BBC to be an appendage of the Ministry of Information, which would be a very bad thing.'[4] He certainly believed this, as his later actions were to show. Foot was equally certain. 'Before our appointment there is no doubt that whatever Ogilvie's personal ideas and hopes may have been, the BBC was drifting nearer and nearer to control by the Government and if the change had not been made the drift would undoubtedly have continued simply because the BBC's own internal organisation was not sufficiently strong and efficient to enable it to manage its own affairs, whether financial or otherwise, without any considerable interference.'[5]

A few of the newspapers were less worried about personalities than about programmes. A writer in *The Star* drew a sharp contrast. 'Mr. Ogilvie has always held that we should be kept as cheerful as possible during war time, and that we should have all the entertainment we could. . . . Mr. Robert Foot . . . comes from the world of business and regards the growth of the BBC's staff and the extent of its entertaining activities as an

---

[1] *Evening News*, 27 Jan. 1942.
[2] *The Times*, 28 Jan. 1942.
[3] *Daily Telegraph*, 28 Jan 1942.
[4] *Hansard*, vol. 377, cols. 1165–6.
[5] Foot Manuscript, p. 141.

expensive item that ought to be cut down.'[1] In complete contrast, a writer in the *Daily Mail* suggested that the change would mean 'a new deal' and 'better shows'.[2] Such comments were very superficial, and no newspaper referred to the tangled network of overseas services which the BBC had extended in 1941 within the limits of its powers and within a separate financial vote. Ogilvie remained, as he always had been during his years at the BBC, civilized and disarming. A month after he left the BBC, he wrote to Ryan, who had sent him a friendly and touching note after his resignation, addressing him for the first time as Patrick 'now that we're no longer officially connected' and stating simply—or perhaps not so simply, given the telling inverted commas—'I "resigned" from the BBC with keen regret—even in order to "facilitate reorganisation", as the phrase was!—and with the happiest memories of all work and dealings with the staff . . . I had looked forward to more and other work . . . with you.'[3]

This letter offers a glimpse of Ogilvie as a man. Yet the story of his eclipse and of the questions of finance, organization and reorganization which led to it were and are less interesting intrinsically or in relation to the history of the war than the BBC's first real effort at large-scale overseas propaganda in 1941—the V campaign—and the entirely new situation which confronted the BBC when Russia and the United States entered the war. There was ample room here also for dispute, serious and trivial, before a new pattern was established in 1942 which, like the new pattern of finance and administration, was to survive until the end of the war.

4. V for Victory

THE internal crisis in the BBC and the protracted discussion about the organization of propaganda were overshadowed in

---

[1] *The Star*, 27 Jan. 1942.
[2] *Daily Mail*, 28 Jan. 1942.
[3] Ogilvie to Ryan, 10 March 1942. I am grateful to Mr. Ryan for the use of this letter.

most people's eyes by what was perhaps the best-known of all the BBC's propaganda activities during the war, the V for Victory campaign, which was launched in January 1941. Its effectiveness has subsequently been doubted.[1] At the time, however, it caught the imagination not only of the European audiences to which it was addressed but of people in Britain who learned about what was going on from broadcast features and from newspaper articles. The campaign certainly worried the Germans sufficiently to make them claim the letter V as their own symbol and to seek to dispose of British propaganda not by ignoring it or resisting it but by homeopathy. 'When the history of the war is written,' an American reporter commented in 1943, 'it seems likely that the V campaign will appear as something more than a propaganda stunt. It has certainly done much to make the people of occupied countries conscious of their national and international solidarity. Experience has shown that nothing can stop what Goebbels has called "the intellectual invasion of the Continent by the British radio", an invasion of which the letter V was the symbol.'[2] 'Nearly everywhere in Europe,' the *BBC Handbook* stated in its brief summary of the campaign, 'resolute people expect leadership from British broadcasts and are ready to act on them.'[3]

There are many aspects of the V campaign which were not known to listeners during the war, but listeners were given a broad outline which was historically accurate. The choice of the V symbol was 'the result of trial and error combined with a certain amount of elementary planning'.[4] Victor de Laveleye, the BBC's Belgian Programme Organizer, introduced what was quickly to become a European symbol within a strictly Belgian context in January 1941. In a broadcast on 14 January, he suggested to his compatriots that V was an appropriate 'rallying emblem' because it was the first letter both of the French word *Victoire* and the Flemish word *Vrijheid*. Since it was also the first letter of the English word Victory—and for that matter of his own Christian name—it was 'the perfect symbol of Anglo-Belgian understanding'.

---

[1] See above, p. 13.
[2] C. J. Rolo, *Radio Goes to War* (1943), p. 141.
[3] *BBC Handbook, 1942*, p. 25.
[4] Rolo, op. cit., p. 136.

De Laveleye's initiative was entirely his own, and he had no wider purpose than that of appealing to Belgians. A BBC commentator had noted that as early as August 1940 Belgians were using a 'thumbs up' sign and were adopting 'pro-British fashions',[1] and de Laveleye believed, as did Newsome and his Assistant News Editor, Douglas Ritchie, that there was a general need in European propaganda for slogans, gestures and visual emblems.[2] What he did not foresee was the speed with which his broadcast of 14 January would lead to action not only in Belgium but in France and Holland. News quickly arrived from Belgium that pro-British sympathizers had changed the initials on placards and posters of the pro-German Flemish separatist organization VNV into VVV, adding for good measure the initials RAF, while on 22 January the BBC received its first letter about the V sign from a channel port in occupied France. 'Multitudes of little "V"s appear on all sides for as *La France Libre* is listened to every evening, so *Radio Belgique* of London is followed with the same interest.' A further letter from Normandy, which arrived in February, described how, in the words of the correspondent, 'as soon as the Belgians gave their friends the "V" as a rallying sign, I went out and chalked "V"s on the walls.'[3]

The introduction of the V campaign coincided with overt signs of increased 'resistance' in Europe. The 'stay at home on 1 January' appeal of the Gaullists[4] had marked the beginning of the attempt to stage demonstrations in France, and it was followed by attempts on the part of the BBC to 'give the French a feeling of conspiracy, a feeling that they were part of the show'. There were signs also in Holland and in Norway of open resistance—in Holland, student protests and in February 1941 mass strikes in Amsterdam[5]—and in Norway, the growth of

---

[1] *BBC European Department, *Monthly Intelligence Report, Europe*, 2 Sept. 1940.
[2] *Ibid., Nov. 1940.
[3] *BBC Studies of European Audiences, 'The V Campaign', 8 Oct. 1941. This study provides the fullest extant account of the chronology of the campaign.
[4] See above, pp. 256–7.
[5] See L. de Jong, 'Anti-Nazi Resistance in the Netherlands' in *European Resistance Movements, 1939–1945, A Report of the First International Conference on the History of Resistance Movements* (1960), pp. 140–1, and W. Warmbrunn, *The Dutch Under German Occupation* (1963), pp. 106–11. There is a Dutch monograph, *De Februari-Staking* (1954). There is a useful brief article by J. Marres, 'Nazi Overlords' in *The History of the Second World War* (ed. B. Pitt), vol. 2, no. 6.

MILORG, an indigenous military resistance movement founded by men who for the most part had themselves taken part in 1940 in the brief war against the Germans.[1] It was in the light of evidence of this kind that Emile Delavenay, Assistant European Intelligence Director, pressed for an extension of the V campaign, that a special programme in *Les Français parlent aux Français* series was devoted to the V sign on 22 March, that a programme followed for Holland on 9 April, and that a month later the European Service as a whole took up the campaign, thereby giving it a quite new dimension.

By then, there were ample signs of its success in France. On 24 March an American correspondent at Vichy cabled that 'for several nights' anti-German inscriptions had become so numerous at Moulins that severe punishment was inflicted on the town by the Germans. Three days later a letter from Marseilles reported that there was 'not a single space' without V signs on walls, pavements and doors, and a letter from the Marne department on 28 March claimed 'Nothing but Vs and still more Vs everywhere on the walls, on the roads, telegraph posts, etc.'. 'It was an avalanche of Vs everywhere even on vehicles and on the roads,' a correspondent from Argentière added. At Tarbes, the birthplace of Foch, V signs were interspersed with slogans like 'France for the French: Send the Boches back to Bocheland' and 'Tarbes gave birth to a Victor: She does not want a Collaborator'. On 1 April Radio Paris announced ominously that in order to put an end to the 'recrudescence of inscriptions etc. on the walls of Paris' offenders would be prosecuted in the magistrates' courts, and four days later *Le Petit Parisien* announced that 6,200 notices had been sent to property owners, *concierges* and others, holding them responsible for the activities of 'idiotic calligraphists'. There were also attacks on the advice given by BBC broadcasters urging Frenchmen to hoard nickel coins.[2]

Before the BBC extended the V campaign, there were already

---

[1] S. Kjelstadli, 'The Resistance Movement in Norway and the Allies' in *European Resistance Movements, 1939–1945, Second Conference Report* (1964), p. 325. *Nationen* (Oslo), 5 March 1941, reported savage sentences in Norway for acts of sabotage and 'insulting behaviour'.

[2] *Reports from Copenhagen also referred to the Danes hoarding copper coins, 'perhaps acting on advice given in the BBC's Danish broadcasts'. (BBC Studies of European Audiences, 'The V Campaign', 8 Oct. 1941.)

two signs of the kind of serious problems it was to pose—the
possibility of encouraging severe German repression and the
danger of precipitating premature action on the part of
'resisters'. A Paris broadcast on 29 April 1941 began, 'Silly
people, you can take up your chalks again, and put—in full
this time—the word you began so well—"Victims"—in blood
red letters'.[1] On 2 May a letter arrived at Broadcasting House
from Unoccupied France which asked in sombre fashion,
'many speak of revolt . . . but what can we do? We have no
weapons . . . It is true that we still have chalk, which allows
us to draw "V"'s and the Cross of Lorraine everywhere.'[2]

Pressure from inside the BBC to extend the V campaign
came from Newsome and Ritchie. The former believed passionately that it was necessary to prepare 'a really positive and
constructive plan to offer the world as an alternative to the
New Order offered by Hitler' and that a 'moral approach'
would rouse Europe.[3] The latter argued more specifically in
January 1941 that the time had come 'to consider a clear and
co-ordinated policy in regard to what we want the oppressed
Peoples to do and how we should persuade them to do it'. An
'underground army' should be mobilized, and the Germans
should be told about it 'in the hope of making their flesh creep'.[4]

Kirkpatrick was in broad sympathy with Newsome's
purpose and recognized his abilities. Indeed, soon after he
arrived in the BBC, he pressed hard for a rearrangement of
functions within the BBC's European Service which would
enable Newsome to take charge of a separate propaganda
section to ensure 'unified control of output'.[5] Kirkpatrick had
access to all sources of military and civil Intelligence, however,
inside and outside the BBC, and while he promised Ritchie
that he would discuss his paper on sabotage with 'the soldiery',[6]
he was aware that a BBC propaganda policy which was not

[1] *Ibid.
[2] *Ibid.
[3] *N. Newsome, 'British War Aims', 27 Feb. 1941; 'A Plan and Basis for
Propaganda', 4 May 1941; 'A Turning Point in Broadcasting to Europe', 8 Oct.
1941; 'Political Warfare', 23 Sept. 1941.
[4] *D. Ritchie, 'The Underground Army', Jan. 1941.
[5] *I. Kirkpatrick, Note on Proposed Organisation of Overseas Propaganda
Department, 27 Feb. 1941; Note by Tallents on a meeting held on 4 March 1941
to discuss the proposal. See also above, p. 341.
[6] Kirkpatrick to Ritchie, 6 Feb. 1941 (Ritchie papers).

co-ordinated with the activities of SOE could do more harm than good. He continued to back Newsome in face of Salt's scepticism about 'an Overseas Propaganda Department outside the normal channels of authority',[1] yet at the same time prevaricated when Ritchie wrote to him about the need to proclaim 'total war' to be followed by a 'total peace'.

Ritchie summarized his views in a paper called 'Broadcasting as a New Weapon of War' which he circulated on 4 May. Its message was bold, even brash: 'When the British Government gives the word, the BBC will cause riots and destruction in every city in Europe.' Less than two weeks later, after a meeting in Bush House, an 'unofficial' committee, later known as the V Committee, was set up under his chairmanship, 'to encourage, develop and coordinate British broadcasts to enemy occupied countries about action against the Germans'.[2] It first met on 26 May, when it pledged itself '(a) to create the frame of mind in which our listeners will feel themselves part of a great army (b) to give instructions to this army that will be good for its morale and bad for the morale of the German garrisons and (c) to give suggestions and instructions to the Occupied Countries which will greatly increase Germany's economic difficulties'.[3]

Among those present were de Laveleye, Griffin, Gillie, Denis Brogan, John Lawrence and John Rayner of the Ministry of Economic Warfare, the only non-BBC representative, who, according to Ritchie, was 'only interested in the economic embarrassment of the enemy'.[4] Like Newsome, Ritchie emphasized the importance of acting within 'a European framework', 'Europe against the Germans'. He was convinced that 'nationalism was an anachronism' and that he was defending 'good against evil'. The fact that he knew little or nothing about the activities of SOE or of the Ministry of Economic Warfare did not inhibit him: there are signs, indeed, that although he did not 'wish us to compromise ourselves with the authorities',[5] the official indifference towards his plans

---

[1] *Salt to Tallents, 24 Feb. 1941; Observations on Mr. Kirkpatrick's scheme, March 1941, unsigned.
[2] *European Board, *Minutes*, 16 May 1941.
[3] *BBC Studies of European Audiences, 'The V Campaign', 8 Oct. 1941.
[4] *Ritchie to Lawson-Reece, 24 June 1941.
[5] *Ibid.

displayed outside the BBC stimulated him into even greater enthusiasm. He was unworried also by the possibility of 'trouble with the Allied governments': the only effective way of mobilizing Europe, he felt, was by encouraging 'leadership in London'. He found inspiration also in the activities of NBBS which had already 'tried out' some of his ideas 'on us'.[1]

Enthusiasm of this order was rewarded when Ritchie was selected to broadcast anonymously to English-speaking listeners in Europe as 'Colonel Britton'. The English-language service was chosen for two reasons—first, it was, of course, Ritchie's own language, and, second, it was easier for Newsome to influence the policy of the European programme in English, including the News, than it would have been to control the foreign-language programmes, each of which had links with the Ministry of Information or with Electra House. The four-minute broadcast on 6 June was announced as 'a regular feature in which Colonel Britton will deal with points in correspondence . . . from . . . the occupied countries'. It was practical in emphasis, not political. An element of mystery was also deliberately cultivated. When later on an American reporter obtained permission to interview 'Britton', it was on the strict understanding that the Colonel would remain concealed behind a lofty partition.[2] In fact, Ritchie, thirty-six years old, had neither the appearance nor the outlook of a colonel. His great strength was tenacity of purpose, and he had even more occasion to reveal this quality in his dealings with the authorities in Britain than in his broadcasts to European resistance movements.

The V Committee backed Ritchie fully, extending the campaign to advocate 'gentle' disruptive activities in Europe, like encouraging more travel in order to upset the transport system, more consumption of food to harass the organizers of rationing systems and more misuse of official forms to trouble the ubiquitous bureaucrats. The Committee also exploited the V sound as much as the V sign. On 27 June the morse · · · — was broadcast, followed by the opening theme of Beethoven's Fifth Symphony, and on 28 June the V sound on drums

---

[1] *Ibid. Note by Lawson-Reece.
[2] Rolo, op. cit. (1943 edn.), p. 138.

became the station identification and interval signal throughout
the BBC's European Service.[1] Broadcasters in various languages
explained how every daily sound could be made into a V.
School-teachers could call their children to order by clapping
their hands in a V rhythm; blacksmiths could hammer out V
tunes on their anvils; even trains could suggest that they were
moving in V time. Europe responded. There was a story on
6 July that records of the Fifth Symphony had been played 'in
error' by Radio Hilversum. On 14 July Radio Moscow broadcast a talk in Russian about how people in Occupied Europe
'not only see the V sign, but hear it in the knock on the door,
the whistles of railway engines, the pealing of church bells'.[2]

To define clear-cut purposes for the V campaign was far
more difficult than to establish a new European fashion, and
although Ritchie was taken along to see Major Desmond
Morton, Churchill's confidential adviser, and Sir Edward
Grigg, he was not informed about operational aspects of
propaganda. There were problems, therefore, when the V
Committee went ahead with the idea of staging a demonstration in Paris on 14 July. 'Until July 14th,' Ritchie broadcast
on 4 July, 'let the Underground Army go underground, and
let the knocking be very quiet knocking.' The Ministry of
Information was unhappy about broadcasts in French which
repeated this advice—so, too, were de Gaulle and some of the
other Allied Governments—and after seeing Kirkpatrick
Ritchie had to cancel the plans and substitute a new date,
20 July.[3] He was clever enough in his broadcasts to make this

---

[1] Preoccupation with music as propaganda can be traced throughout the year.
London Calling Europe began with Purcell's Trumpet Voluntary, 'a theme which,
without being bombastic, inspires confidence and a feeling of unshakable strength.
To link the items together, a passage from Beethoven's Fifth Symphony (the 'V'
rhythm) is faded up.' (*Weekly Bulletin of BBC Broadcasts to Europe*, 17 July 1941.)
A sanguine Language Supervisor suggested as early as August 1941 that 'now that
Hitler's armies are again on the plod (in Russia) I wonder if your department
could make use of Gounod's *Funeral March for a Marionette*. Except for a buoyant
passage in the middle, it seems to me the march could serve very effectively either
as a lead-in or as lead-out to some feature, or else as a *leit motif* to suggest a horde
of puppets tramping mechanically and wearily to their doom.' (*Note of 15 Aug.
1941.)

[2] *BBC Studies of European Audiences, 'The V Campaign', 8 Oct. 1941.

[3] *Overseas Board, *Minutes*, 10 July 1941. 'Mr. Kirkpatrick reported the
campaign would be launched on the 20th vice 14th July in view of feeling amongst
Refugee Allied Governments against linking start with France.'

change of plan sound genuinely operational, and once again to widen the campaign to comprise all Europe. He also secured *via* Kirkpatrick a message from Churchill which was broadcast to Europe on 19 July: 'The V sign is the symbol of the un-conquerable will of the people of the occupied territories and a portent of the fate awaiting the Nazi tyranny. So long as the people of Europe continue to refuse all collaboration with the invader, it is sure that his cause will perish and that Europe will be liberated.'

Before 20 July dawned, the V campaign had taken its most remarkable twist. Impressed by the way in which V signs and sounds were spreading throughout Europe, Goebbels and the German propaganda machine decided to appropriate the letter V for themselves. Oslo, Hilversum and several other German-controlled stations began deliberately to broadcast the opening bars of Beethoven's Fifth Symphony as part of their station signals: so too did the German Home Service, which broadcast a concert conducted by Furtwängler on 16 July which included the whole of Beethoven's Fifth. On 17 July Fritzsche devoted one of his home talks to 'V for Viktoria', 'the old German victory cry', the rallying call of all peoples of Europe 'united in the struggle against Bolshevism'. 'What people are seeking,' he declared, 'is some small sign showing that they belong to the community that is being founded in the struggle.' At the same time, German directives to exploit the V sign flashed throughout Europe. *Prager Abend* appeared with a huge V covering its front page, and one of Prague's main streets was renamed Victoria Street; *Fritt Volk* in Oslo proclaimed that the letter V denoted 'a German victory on all fronts', and huge V streamers appeared outside the main hotels. Berlin newspapers printed articles on their own V campaign, although it lasted for only a very short time in Germany itself.[1] In Amsterdam a thirty-foot banner was hung from Queen Wilhelmina's palace bearing the words ' "V" for victory which Germany is winning for all Europe on all fronts', and in Paris the Germans placed a huge V sign on the Eiffel Tower.

---

[1] *BBC *Weekly Analysis of Foreign Broadcasts*, 29 July 1941. The BBC decided that it would not hold back the development of its campaign on the grounds that the Germans were imitating it (*Overseas Board, *Minutes*, 17 July 1941).

German skill neutralized the V sign, although for weeks there was confusion throughout Europe—except in Italy, where no effort was made to enter the campaign—as to what it meant. In Unoccupied France, where there was 'a frenzy of "V"'s', it obviously meant support of Britain, and when the RAF raided Nantes French resisters marked out on the ground a V in oil lamps:[1] in Paris V was a German symbol, with the German-controlled radio praising 'a little tank driver' who first thought of the idea and decorated his vehicle with a huge V surrounded by laurels and swastikas. In Holland pro-British groups wore white Vs and pro-German groups orange Vs. In Norway the Norwegians added 'H 7'—for Haakon the Seventh—to their Vs,[2] and in other parts of Europe the initials RAF were appended. In Yugoslavia the sign was used in anti-German riots on 28 July, and in Budapest and Sofia the sign was used by anti-German groups. In Germany itself there was some confusion. Radio Bremen in English admitted on 27 July that 'it was the English who started this "V" business, just as they started the war', but a home broadcaster on 22 July remarked that 'Duff Cooper has been brazenly trying to appropriate the German Victory sign "V"'. From London Newsome replied in one of his 'Man in the Street' talks. 'The conquered, oppressed, disarmed and pillaged peoples of Europe have inflicted a crushing defeat on their conquerors and oppressors. They have forced the Germans into the ridiculous position of being compelled to adopt as their own the symbol of Europe's resistance, the V sign. . . . Soon, perhaps, the Germans will be forced to pretend that the letters RAF stand for the Luftwaffe, that the Cross of Lorraine is a new type of Swastika . . . that there never was a Third Reich, that Hitler's war was a myth.'[3]

In Britain, outside the range of German manœuvres, the campaign attracted great attention in the Press. As many V

---

[1] *Daily Telegraph*, 23 July 1941.

[2] There had been considerable confusion in Norway, for one day after Fritzsche's broadcast about 'V for Viktoria', Lunde, the Norwegian Minister of Propaganda in Quisling's cabinet, attacked Norwegians who followed their 'foreign masters' and scribbled 'V' signs everywhere. (*BBC *Weekly Analysis of Foreign Broadcasts*, 22 July 1941.)

[3] *The 'Man in the Street' talks to Europe* (1945), pp. 12–13. This talk was broadcast on 19 July 1941.

signs were chalked on the walls as in France, and over six
hundred letters were received by the BBC from listeners who
suggested that badges, brooches, studs and earrings could be
fashioned in the shape of a V. Eggs, runner beans and pea pods
were displayed in the shape of Vs. In Leicester it was decided
to display a large V on the city's Clock Tower.[1] Mass Observation called the public reaction to the campaign 'the biggest
civilian war reaction since "Pots to Planes" and LDV recruiting'. Not surprisingly, 'Britton', whose broadcasts, unlike
other overseas broadcasts, were distributed to the Press as
hand-outs, was hailed as 'the Scarlet Pimpernel of the Radio'.[2]
Churchill himself began to give the V sign on every occasion,
and advertisers proved as eager to take up the message as
politicians. Nonetheless, great concern was being expressed
behind the scenes that the campaign could do more harm
than good. Bracken, who had become Minister of Information on 20 July 1941,[3] told Parliament that the Ministry
regarded the campaign as 'a sort of *Lift Up Your Hearts* signal
to the oppressed people of Europe', yet Leeper was pressing
that SOE should have exclusive responsibility for subversive
propaganda in Europe and that the BBC should not be allowed
to act 'on its own'.

In the neutral United States the V sign quickly caught on—
Wendell Willkie wore a tie pin in the shape of a V—but in
neutral Stockholm it was noted more soberly that 'Britain's
propaganda campaign—V for Victory—has had rather a mild
effect except that everybody is talking about it'.[4] In Spain
and Portugal there were said to be instances of listeners
laughing at German claims to have invented the V sign, and a
Swiss newspaper correctly assigned the responsibility for the
beginning of the campaign to de Laveleye.[5]

---

[1] *Farquharson to Maconachie, 1 Aug. 1941.

[2] *Daily Express*, 14 July 1941. Cf. *Daily Mail*, 14 July 1941. 'Britton's talks are
not controlled by the War Office but by the Ministry of Information. Yet, even
the Ministry do not know what he meant by his last broadcast.' Later (*Overseas
Board, *Minutes*, 31 July 1941) it was decided to treat the V campaign cautiously
in Home Service programmes and not to introduce an interval V signal for the
Home Service. This policy had been agreed upon at the Ministry of Information
Policy Committee on 24 July.

[3] See above, p. 336.   [4] *Aftonbladet*, 22 July 1941.

[5] *BBC Studies of European Audiences, 'The V Campaign', 8 Oct. 1941;
Die Weltwoche, 11 Sept. 1941.

During the late summer and autumn of 1941, acts of sabotage were increasing throughout Europe, some of them under SOE auspices. The first two successful SOE operations had been conducted earlier in the year, one party being dropped into Poland, the second into Northern France to sabotage a German airfield. Further activities in Yugoslavia and Greece revealed some of the logistic and political complications.[1] As SOE became increasingly active and involved, Ritchie's private enterprise inevitably was curbed, if not fully controlled. He had broadcast on 26 July that 'the "V" army' had 'dictated a course of conduct to the Germans' and 'imposed its will' upon them, but soon afterwards a Coordination Committee on Operational Policy tried to impose its will upon him. It was ready, however, to back him in a further broadcasting campaign to persuade Europe to 'go slow', which he announced in a broadcast on 22 August. This was followed by a broadcast on the same theme by Ernest Bevin on 5 September, the playing of the Tortoise Dance from Saint-Saëns's *Carnival des Animaux* and the nomination of 15 September as 'Tortoise Day'.[2]

Yet the Coordination Committee saw Ritchie's role as 'psychological' rather than operational. As a result of the reorganization of the BBC's European Services and the emergence of PWE, a new propaganda framework was created;[3] and the final meeting of the BBC V Committee was held on 1 October. A few days later a new PWE V Committee met under Bruce Lockhart's chairmanship. 'Britton' continued to broadcast until May 1942—he broadcast on 21 December 1941 asking his listeners 'to make 1942 our first victory year'—but he was clearly unhappy at what he thought was a loss of official enthusiasm for his ideas. In a letter to Kirkpatrick in December 1941 he asked somewhat forlornly 'whether anything can be done to save from early extinction the "V" campaign, which

[1] See F. W. Deakin, 'Great Britain and the European Resistance' in *Proceedings of the Second International Conference on the History of Resistance Movements* (1964), pp. 102–4. The 'Quisling' press often attributed activities to the British which were spontaneous. It was a crude propagandist exaggeration, for example, for the Belgian *De National Socialist* to write on 9 Aug. that 'sabotage indubitably exists . . . Belgium is ruled by the British Intelligence Service'.

[2] On 19 Sept. 1941 he told his audience that 'the time has now come for a wide extension of the "V" radio groups', and a week later gave advice on the construction of frame aerials and the best means of defeating jamming.

[3] See below, pp. 417 ff.

had such startling successes so long as it was run inside the
BBC'. The campaign, he went on more forcefully, had created
'a new conception of broadcasting and of its potentialities'
and had established broadcasting as a 'new weapon of war'.
The new Regional Directors of PWE, 'by design or by chance',
had allowed the campaign to drop and 'while professing that
they had no wish to kill the campaign have, in fact, done their
best to kill it'.[1]

There is little doubt that this assessment was correct, though
higher powers than the Regional Directors were ultimately
responsible. Indeed, before PWE came into existence steps
had already been taken 'to syndicate Ritchie's material as a
means of maintaining quality and control'.[2] The entrance of
Russia and America into the war further changed both the
perspectives of resistance groups and the operational time-
table. What 'Britton' was saying in English to Europeans
as a whole might be suitable for one part of Europe and not
for another. Gillie was as uneasy as the PWE Regional Director
or de Gaulle was about broadcasts which might not catch the
'mood of France', and so too were many of the other heads of
BBC foreign-language sections. 'Mentality and methods of
resistance vary a great deal from country to country,' Elizabeth
Barker wrote sensibly to Ritchie in May 1941. 'Would it not
be better to start first with individual "exercises" in individual
countries—things which would be particularly suited to that
type of people, and perhaps are already being practised by
them all on a small scale? Then, at a later stage, by means of
telling the various countries about each others' exercises it
would be possible gradually to build up a "European consciousness". If we try to rush the "European consciousness" we
might well fail, or at the most produce something rather arti-
ficial which might not stand up to the strain.'[3] She emphasized

---

[1] Ritchie to Kirkpatrick, 2 Dec. 1941 (Ritchie papers).

[2] *Overseas Board, *Minutes*, 24 July 1941. It was decided then also not to
publicize 'Britton' as an individual.

[3] *Miss E. Barker to Ritchie, 7 May 1941. There is also an interesting and
percipient note by Alan Bullock, 8 May 1941, about the research implications of
Ritchie's plan. 'We shall need a great deal of information about economic and
military movements and conditions, in order to decide what orders to give to our
Allies. Most of this information or instructions based upon it, will of course come
from MEW, and the different Services Departments. We need to research carefully
[cont.

also that it was absolutely necessary to co-operate 'to a certain extent with the Allied Governments'. By the end of 1941 these views were widely current inside the BBC. In addition, there were many people in Bush House who believed that Ritchie exaggerated the significance of the English-speaking groups in Europe, pointing out that only 8 per cent of the Norwegians, 9 per cent of the Dutch, 1.5 per cent of the French, and .5 per cent of the Czechs and Serbs spoke English.

Outside the BBC, other elements contributed to the currents of criticism. Ritchie's optimism about the outcome of the war was out of line with the 'realism' of Army and Navy officers who foresaw a long struggle and knew that an immediate landing in Europe was out of the question; and the military events of early 1942 involving the sharpest reverses since 1940 checked all 'premature' hopes. SOE, moreover, had its own immediate plans, and it did not wish to communicate them to Ritchie. These were 'facts' of the situation which not only stopped the V campaign but muzzled 'Britton'. If one man was to play the key role, it was not to be he.[1] Nonetheless, after his broadcasts were brought to an end on the orders of PWE in May 1942,[2] Ritchie was congratulated by Bruce Lockhart on 'a campaign which achieved remarkable success in capturing the imagination of the whole world and which I understand was mainly your own idea'.[3]

In October 1941 the BBC made its own tentative assessment of the degree of success of the campaign as far as Czechoslovakia, Poland, Yugoslavia and Norway were concerned. Shortly after the first effects of the V campaign in Belgium and France

[1] A Ministry of Information official had written to him sympathetically in May 1941 after he had produced his *Broadcasting as a New Weapon of War*. He said he had sent a copy of the paper to the War Office with the comment, 'the only fundamental point in which we differ is that you want a committee to run it, and I want one man regardless of the particular clothes he wears'. (Ritchie papers.)

[2] In his last 1942 broadcast of the 'Britton' series Ritchie told his audience that 'the most critical period of the war is now nearly on us'. He broadcast again, however, on Christmas Day 1942, and in 1944, on this occasion as a member of the staff of SHAEF. See below, p. 643.

[3] Bruce Lockhart to Ritchie, 8 May 1942. (Ritchie papers.)

into what has already been done in each of the occupied countries. . . . As we learn more of what each group of patriots is doing, so we can vary our instructions to fit in with the opportunities and skill of the different groups. It might be worthwhile [also] to investigate former campaigns of resistance—e.g. the Belgians 1914–18 . . . [or] the Yugoslavs under Austrian rule.'

had been noted, a message was sent to underground leaders in Czechoslovakia asking if the campaign should be extended to that country. No answer was received, but at the time of the Yugoslav *coup d'état* it was reported that the letter V was in use in Prague, and the V campaign began to be directed there. Severe repression—500 wireless sets were said to have been confiscated by the Germans in the little town of Tabor— did not check the subsequent 'go slow' campaign or acts of sabotage. Yet BBC analysts could not draw any conclusions about the critical issue of whether Czech 'outbreaks' were spontaneous, 'timed by local leaders who weighed the risk' or 'due to radio leadership from Moscow or London'. The most that they would say—and it was probably too much— was that 'British radio leadership is a supporting line upon which the Czech front line can fall back if German reprisals smash the organised leadership on the spot'.[1] Jan Masaryk had told Ogilvie earlier in 1941 that he had 'almost daily evidence of how anxiously the London broadcasts are listened to in our country',[2] but it was Hitler's attack on Russia, followed by the immediate Soviet recognition of the Czech Government in exile and the setting up by the Czech Communists of a Revolutionary Committee in August, which was of decisive importance in broadening the Czech resistance 'front' and multiplying resistance activities.[3] By the time Reinhard Heydrich became 'Deputy Protector' of the Czechs in September 1941, the beginning of a terrible period of repression, the Czech resistance had passed into a quite new phase.

In Poland the V campaign had been sufficiently successful for the Germans to insist that large Vs should be printed on the front pages of German-controlled newspapers, and a German court felt it necessary to acquit an inhabitant of Warsaw who had been accused of pasting a V on a stranger's attaché case.[4] There was widespread sabotage during the summer and

---

[1] *BBC Studies of European Audiences, 'The V Campaign', 8 Oct. 1941.

[2] *Masaryk to Ogilvie, 20 Jan. 1941. Later in the year Prague Radio warned against 'incitements of the Czech-speaking Jews in London'. (*BBC *Analysis of Foreign Broadcasts*, 7 Oct. 1941.)

[3] H. Michel, *Les Mouvements Clandestins en Europe* (1961), pp. 89–90.

[4] *Nowy Kurier Czestochowski*, 27 July 1941, quoted in 'The V Campaign', 8 Oct. 1941.

autumn of 1941, culminating in a proclamation by the German
Governor Frank that all saboteurs would be shot and those
aiding or abetting them would be sentenced to life imprisonment.[1] Caution about the implications of counselling resistance
movements to resort to sabotage had been clearly expressed
in relation to broadcasting to Denmark and other countries
in August 1941. 'Our policy for the moment about appeals for
sabotage', PID stated in that month, 'might be summed up as
follows. We ourselves are not making appeals for sabotage (news
talks should be watched to see that we do not). We should
be extremely discreet in using anyone else's appeals for sabotage. . . . We should report, with discretion, sabotage that is
actually taking place.'[2]

More ample evidence was arriving by then from Yugoslavia
than from Poland, and on 8 August 1941 the Croatian Foreign
Office in Zagreb referred directly to BBC efforts to promote
insurrection: specifically, the Corporation was blamed for
disturbances in a concentration camp at Kerestinec. At that
time Yugoslavia was being subjected to a propaganda barrage
from Moscow, and the BBC analysts showed little real understanding of the developing complexities of rival resistance
movements there. Their conclusion that 'although our broadcasts were certainly not intended to provoke outbursts there,
the "V" campaign had had a most serious influence in Croatia'
was not substantiated. There was an obvious contrast, which
they ignored, between the fierce quality of Croat resistance and
Colonel Britton's relatively mild suggestions, and there was an
equally striking contrast, which they also misrepresented,
between the British broadcasts to Yugoslavia and those from
Moscow. 'There is at present no evidence that Croats and Serbs
on the spot felt the contrast,' the BBC's over-optimistic evalua-
tion went on, 'and resented it—on the contrary, in spite of
some confusion over the German adoption of the "V", the
British campaign may well have helped to give the guerillas
and saboteurs in Yugoslavia a feeling of unity with the peoples
of the other occupied countries, for although our propaganda
lagged behind the reality, Axis propagandists persistently
blamed British intrigue for the unrest in Yugoslavia.'[3]

[1] *Ibid.   [2] Quoted in Bennett, op. cit., p. 49.
[3] *BBC Studies of European Audiences, 'The V Campaign', 8 Oct. 1941.

This naive comment brings out some of the limitation of BBC Intelligence assessments. The Yugoslav Communist Party was setting up its military committees in May and June 1941, and Communist partisan activity began in July: it was reported to London and to the Comintern in Moscow. Already, too, there was a separate anti-Communist centre of leadership and organization in Yugoslavia, associated with General Mihailović, who was in touch with London.[1] Relations between the two bodies 'on the spot' and with the Yugoslav Government in exile in London were to complicate the pattern of BBC broadcasting to Yugoslavia. Political issues were crisscrossed also by national issues. Serbs, Croats and Slovenes all wanted to use the BBC to put forward their own point of view, and much time was taken up in trying to persuade them to divide the available time fairly. Both the Croats in the émigré Yugoslav Government in London and the Communist partisans in Yugoslavia attacked the BBC on a number of occasions for serving as the tool of the Serbs. In this complicated situation it was clear that 'Colonel Britton' was no more than one small voice. Nor could he in any sense influence the local situation which had reached the point by September that German-controlled politicians were giving guerilla fighters three days to 'leave the forest and the rifle and return to their homes'.[2]

The same considerations were true to a lesser extent of Norway, where SOE apparently wanted to move more quickly than MILORG and to secure a 'secret army' willing to engage in immediate action.[3] The intricacies of Norwegian resistance politics were concealed from the BBC at the time, but were perhaps implicit in a letter received from Norway in May 1941: 'the time will come when thousands of young Norwegians will run to the mountains and there dig up the weapons which were never handed over to the Germans and which the Germans have never been able to find. We are working here in secret

[1] See D. Plenca, 'Le Mouvement de Libération Nationale en Yougoslavie et les Alliés' in *Proceedings of the Second International Conference on the History of Resistance Movements* (1964), pp. 468 ff; Deakin, 'Great Britain and the European Resistance', ibid., pp. 103, 105.

[2] *BBC Analysis of Foreign Broadcasts*, 16 Sept. 1941. The order was given on 14 Sept.

[3] S. Kjelstadli, op cit., pp. 326–7. There was an attempted general strike in Oslo on 10 September. The Germans declared a state of emergency, and two trade union leaders were executed.

and the result will be a great help when you from England come back to drive the Germans out.'[1]

In retrospect, three obvious points stand out. First, the Germans retained the initiative in the summer and early autumn of 1941. Second, the entry of Russia into the war had a far greater impact on the history of European resistance movements than psychological propaganda from London, and by the end of the year had changed the German mood.[2] Third, the British Government itself had no desire to extend the V campaign along the political lines implicit in Ritchie and Newsome's approach.

The last of these points can be disposed of most easily. There was no more interest in formulating British 'war aims' at the end of 1941 than there had been at the beginning.[3] The Atlantic Charter of August 1941, issued as a Press release, was both too vague and too general to provide a clarion call, and Goebbels could dispose of it effectively—in so far as it had any bearing on German attitudes and policies—by replying to it equally generally, bitterly, and even venomously.[4] Nor was there any sign that the Charter had any greater appeal in other parts of Europe, except as a guarantee that the United States, not then at war, was pledged to the victory of the Allies.

Alongside the public and private discussions inside Britain about the implications of the V campaign there were parallel discussions about 'Vansittartism' which raised even sharper differences of opinion and feeling. The question of whether to draw any distinction between the German Government and the German people was a crucial question in the formulation not only of propaganda policy vis-à-vis Germany but of propaganda policy vis-à-vis Europe. 'Every possible view exists on this subject,' A. V. Hill wrote succinctly in the middle of 1941, 'and the average of them all is just about zero.'[5] Monckton and Radcliffe might argue forcefully for more co-ordinated,

[1] *BBC Studies of European Audiences, 'The V Campaign', 8 Oct. 1941.

[2] See below, pp. 398–9. Yet there is evidence that the Communists had clearly played a leading role in the February strike in Holland.

[3] See above, pp. 321–3.

[4] *Das Reich*, 17 Aug. 1941; *BBC *Analysis of Foreign Broadcasts*, 19 Aug. 1941, reported a Deutschlandsender *riposte* to the British 'bragging offensive'. 'We don't want to win the war by propaganda. We have the German Armed Forces and we can afford to take the propaganda front lightly.'

[5] *A. V. Hill, Note on Propaganda to Germany, July 1941.

decisive and prompt propaganda—and their argument was to lead to the creation and development of PWE[1]—but the content of British propaganda was never determined as crisply as the machinery for disseminating it. As Ogilvie noted in a reply to Hill, the 'Nazi vs German issue' already had 'a most interesting history'. 'At times', it was 'a battle of shadows: at times—and, as I think, more often—[it was] an issue fundamental to the philosophy of life and to the winning both of the war and the peace.'[2]

Of course, the Germans were never as disturbed by any kind of British propaganda in the summer and early autumn of 1941 as British analysts believed. They retained the initiative. An interesting article in a 'Quisling' newspaper referring to the postponement of Britton's 'demonstration' advertised for 14 July showed how the situation was viewed not only by them but by their sympathizers in the occupied countries. 'It is foolish of the BBC,' a Dutch 'Quisling' paper wrote, 'to announce that an important fact will take place on 14 July and then to postpone it for a week. One may assume that London did not consider a parachute attack or they would not have broadcast it beforehand, and any way it would be doomed to failure . . . we conclude it was intended to excite public opinion in occupied territories with a view to creating incidents. Thanks to the commonsense of the occupying forces serious conflicts were averted, as the Amsterdam events were not directly concerned with military matters, although the forces took direct action. Many Dutchmen dislike the food situation as a restriction on individual liberty, but hatred between different national groups and general disorder is only increased if the London broadcasts continue. Nothing much can be achieved, as a few thousand police would restore order, and the German military authorities would remain unconcerned.'[3]

If there was a touch of complacency in this statement, it was only a touch, and historians have shown in relation to Holland at least that there were fewer expressions of anti-German sentiment in the period after the repression of the

[1] *W. Monckton and C. Radcliffe, 'Memorandum on Propaganda Policy', June 1941. See also below, pp. 417 ff., 692–3.
[2] *Ogilvie to Hill, 26 July 1941. See also above, pp. 14, 171–2; below, pp. 693–4.
[3] *Volk en Vaterland*, 19 July 1941, quoted in *BBC Studies of European Audiences, 'The V Campaign', 8 Oct. 1941.

February strike than there had been during the previous ten months.[1] There was certainly more than a corresponding touch of exaggeration in a BBC comment that the evidence of German troops being confined to barracks in some places in Europe on 14 July was a sign that 'British broadcasting, by use of the "V" campaign, had forced German propaganda into making a major blunder'.[2] 'If the British really believe we have as few Germans in the occupied countries as they say, why do they wait to disembark on the Continent and obtain easy successes?' the Vichy radio pertinently asked in September 1941.[3]

The entry of Russia into the war on 22 June 1941—in the midst of the V campaign—was such a dominating event in the military history of the whole war and in the history of European resistance movements that it forces the V campaign into the margin of history. Immediately, groups of people who had at best pursued equivocal policies or at worst had refused to mobilize against the German occupying forces not only were drawn into the struggle but attempted to lead it. Thereafter, British broadcasting was to operate in a quite new kind of situation, a situation which called not so much for single-minded daring as for subtle assessment and complex organization. The implications of that great event, followed as it was by the second great event of the extended war—the entry of the United States into the struggle in early December—were so far-reaching that they made most earlier political happenings seem little more than an exciting prelude.

5. Russia and the United States

In March 1941 Goebbels had written that 'the fanfares for proclaiming Special Announcements [*Sondermeldungen*] are already being polished. Front and Home Front are awaiting

---

[1] Warmbrunn, op. cit., p. 112.
[2] Quoted in *BBC Studies of European Audiences, 'The 'V' Campaign', 8 Oct. 1941.
[3] *BBC *Analysis of Foreign Broadcasts*, 9 Sept. 1941.

the command of the Führer.'[1] At that time it was not clear to the Germans or to anyone else what the content of *Sondermeldungen* would be. Hitler had taken his decision to invade Russia before the end of 1940,[2] but the news of 22 June 1941 came as much as a surprise to the German masses as it did to the people of Britain or Occupied Europe. There had been speculation, rumours, leaks and Intelligence reports,[3] of course, but throughout the European broadcasting services, as among the population at large, there was a sense of shock.

On 26 May Radio Moscow had given a preview of its home programmes for June, concentrating on economic questions and the All-Union Agricultural Exhibition;[4] and although 'war preparedness', particularly anti-aircraft artillery activities and ARP, figured prominently in Russian programmes on the eve of the invasion, the BBC's Monitoring Service concluded one week before Hitler struck that 'there is no foundation in Russian broadcasts for the speculation . . . on the possibilities of a conflict between Berlin and Moscow'.[5] On 21 June most of the Russian programmes were devoted to students' summer work and workers' summer holidays. 'Up to the last,' it was reported by the monitors, 'Radio Moscow, both in home and foreign transmissions observed what the Continent would have described as "un calme tout Britannique" or as Moscow put it "a quiet Bolshevik manner".'[6] Yet the tone changed as abruptly as the content after a broadcast by Molotov on 22 June. 'People steeled in labour will not shrink from the privations of war. They will also be able to crush the enemy on the battlefield.' Patriotism and solidarity were the main themes, and there were appeals to 'Russia our Fatherland'. The slogans began to appear along with the songs and poems. 'Hitler started this war, Stalin will end it.'[7]

The Germans, who had made the most of Britain's disaster in Crete, the climax of the ill-fated Greek campaign, drawing

---

[1] Article in *Das Reich*, 9 March 1941, quoted in Bramsted, op. cit., p. 243.
[2] See above, p. 292.
[3] For some of them, see W. S. Churchill, *The Second World War*, vol. III (1950), pp. 317 ff. Hess's flight to Britain on 11 May sparked off many of the rumours and speculations.
[4] *BBC *Analysis of Foreign Broadcasts*, 3 June 1941.
[5] *Ibid., 17 June 1941.
[6] *Ibid., 24 June 1941.
[7] *Ibid.

the pertinent moral that there were no longer any islands,[1] dwelt more on the United States than on the Soviet Union in their immediate pre-invasion broadcasts: following some of their own precedents, they actually reduced the amount of attention previously devoted to Russia in their broadcasts.[2] Once the move had been made, however, the idea of a great crusade was proclaimed: the Bolsheviks were described as sub-human leaders of beastly hordes and the Germans as 'the true saviours of European culture and civilisation from the threat of the political underworld'.[3] Detailed news was carefully held back until 29 June, when in a fascinating theatrical performance the fanfares sounded and no less than twelve Special Announcements were read dramatically over the radio with intervals of music every quarter of an hour. In the meantime, the public had been battered with general propaganda.

American commentators in Europe were divided in their reactions to Hitler's move.[4] Some thought that the burden on Britain would be lightened and that Hitler had made a 'colossal' blunder in becoming engaged in a war on two fronts; yet Martin Agronsky, NBC representative in Ankara, broadcasting several days before the attack took place, told Americans that if Hitler invaded Russia it would be one of the most popular things he had done. 'Perhaps Hitler, one of the great political psychologists of our time, regards an anti-Bolshevik war as the only thing left which can turn the conquered people's hate of Nazism into an expression of the general hatred of Bolshevism.'[5]

There was certainly some radio evidence to support this view, not only from Bucharest and Budapest and Helsinki,

---

[1] *Ibid., 3 June 1941; E. Kris and H. Speier, *German Radio Propaganda* (1944), p. 302.　　[2] Ibid., p. 304.

[3] Bramsted, op. cit., pp. 244–5. For the briefest of periods it was stressed, as in June 1940, that the Russians had been planning an attack on Germany, 'to stab the German people in the back', and that the Germans had taken the necessary counter-action.

[4] The invasion provided ready arguments both for America's isolationists and its anti-isolationists. The former said that America should not intervene because the Russian war meant either that the Axis would be beaten anyway or that America should not help to save Europe for Communism. The latter maintained that a 'supreme opportunity' had been presented for America to intervene, 'an opportunity which, if not seized, would never recur'.

[5] *Broadcast from Ankara, 16 June 1941, quoted in BBC *Analysis of Foreign Broadcasts*, 24 June 1941.

but from Vichy France, where there was a burst of indignation against British activities in Syria. Darlan was making the most of anti-Bolshevism during the week before Hitler's invasion of Russia. Pro-Russian Communists and pro-British Gaullists, he argued, shared the same aim—'to create disorder in our country, increase the misery of the population and prevent the regeneration of France'.[1] The same line was taken by the Spaniards.[2] The German propagandists made as much as they possibly could of 'European consciousness' and of the claim that they were not only protecting Europe but preparing for the creation eventually of a highly organized European economy, a *Grosswirtschaftsraum*: they pushed this idea particularly hard, indeed, in their broadcasts to the United States. In broadcasts of 29 June and 30 June the main theme was 'Europe's unanimity'.[3] Joyce, who had heard of the imminent attack on Russia only through an information leak, struck a somewhat different note in his broadcasts to England, both on NBBS and on Hamburg. 'Can anyone deny the fiasco of the old order? Certainly nobody in England; for the distressed areas, the misery of unemployment, the decline of industry, shipping and commerce are proofs of the Old Disorder.'[4]

In Britain Churchill himself responded at once to the dramatic news, and his famous broadcast of Sunday, 22 June, which he had worked on for a whole day,[5] was reported—

---

[1] *Ibid., 17 June 1941, referring to broadcasts of 13 June 1941.

[2] *Ibid., 1 July 1941. 'This enormous battle,' Radio Malaga stated, 'is a prolongation of the three years' war carried out on Spanish soil.' By contrast, the Italians made little use of this approach, and their star commentator, Ansaldo, made no attempt to present the war as a crusade.

[3] The campaign continued with varying tempo. 'Something like a European consciousness appears for the first time in history,' Deutschlandsender stated in October, 'a feeling of Continental community which is displayed by the progressive minorities of nearly all European nations.' (*BBC *Analysis of Foreign Broadcasts*, 14 Oct. 1941.)

[4] *Hamburg in English, 29 June 1941, quoted ibid., 1 July 1941. Workers' Challenge blamed Churchill for extending the war and 'engineering' Socialist Russia's entry into a capitalist struggle. Kris and Speier, op. cit., pp. 306–7, point, however, to the interesting shift in stereotypes describing Germany and her allies before and after 22 June. Before 22 June emphasis was placed on 'young' nations and 'new order': after 22 June it was on Germany as 'old' and on the claims of 'tradition' and 'history'.

[5] See Churchill, op. cit., p. 331. He quotes an account by Colville, his private secretary, of what exactly happened on this day. He had, in fact, been thinking about his broadcast for several days.

with some omissions—to the Russian people at five o'clock on Monday morning. 'Hitler,' he exclaimed, 'is a monster of wickedness, insatiable in his lust for blood.' Moreover, he was 'in continual motion, striking first in one place and then in another'. 'The Russian danger,' he insisted, 'is our danger', adding that Britain would provide 'any technical or economic assistance' to Russia within its power. 'The cause of any Russian fighting for his hearth and home is the cause of free men and free peoples in every quarter of the world.' Churchill did not conceal his fear that Russia might be beaten, but he left the impression, as he always did, that the war as a whole could not be lost.

Much has been made of Churchill's distaste for Communism, and of the effort it must have taken him to welcome Russia as an ally. The day before the attack, indeed, he had remarked that 'if Hitler invaded Hell, I would make at least a favourable reference to the Devil in the House of Commons', and in the broadcast itself he explained that no one had been a more consistent opponent of Communism that he had been for the last twenty-five years and that he would 'unsay nothing'. He had always drawn a distinction, however, between Soviet Communism and Russian national interest. In fact, in his very first war-time broadcast of 1 October 1939, long before he became Prime Minister, he had referred to Russian policy as 'a riddle wrapped in a mystery inside an enigma' with national interest as the possible key. 'It cannot be in accordance with the interest or the safety of Russia that Nazi Germany should plant itself upon the shores of the Black Sea or that it should overrun the Balkan states and subjugate the Slavonic peoples of South-Eastern Europe. That would be contrary to the life-interests of Russia. But here the interests of Russia fall into the same channel as the interests of Britain and France.' On the eve of the German attack on Russia Churchill had warned Stalin. He said in his broadcast of 22 June that it was one of the 'characteristics' of the war that it would bring a country such as Russia into it. He was sure—and it was a consolation to him—that it was a further characteristic of the war that the United States would come into it also. His broadcast of 22 June had almost as much significance in the United States as in Britain for it was 'the first weighty comment on the new situation that the American people heard'.[1]

There was a widespread opinion in Britain and the United States in June 1941 that Russia would be quickly defeated. Nicolson, like Sir Stafford Cripps in Moscow, spoke of three weeks: experts in the War Office spoke of ten days.[2] Not surprisingly, therefore, the Planning Executive of the Ministry of Information discussed schemes for reinforcing home morale in the event of a Russian collapse[3] and held meetings to discuss what propaganda Britain should put out to America in the event of a complete German victory.[4] By then, however, the ten days had long been up and the first three weeks were over. Stalin on 3 July had delivered his first war-time broadcast to his people about 'scorched earth' and 'partisan warfare'. During this exciting period of immense uncertainty, when the Russian armies were being pushed further and further back and British listeners were learning dozens of place names which they had never heard before,[5] an element of farce crept into the discussions inside the BBC and the Ministry about Russia.

It centred—not by accident—on the popular programme *National Anthems of the Allies*, which was broadcast before what was still the great broadcasting event of the week, the nine o'clock News on Sunday evening, the evening when the Russian news broke.[6] To get round the difficulty of having to broadcast the Internationale, the very sound of which disturbed some people inside the BBC and the Ministry, it was proposed that the whole programme should be dropped.[7] Nicolls was not in favour of doing this,[8] and a search began for an acceptable alternative Russian 'contribution'—Kol Slaven or the Kutusov 1812 March. The recordings proved unsuitable, and the Russian

[1] M. Gorham, *Sound and Fury* (1948), p. 109.

[2] H. Nicolson, *Diaries and Letters* (1967), p. 174, entry for 22 June 1941. He described Churchill's speech as a 'masterpiece'.

[3] Ibid., p. 176, entry for 30 June 1941.

[4] Ibid., p. 178, entry for 18 July 1941.

[5] They were pronounced not as the Russians pronounced them but on a compromise system: see J. Macleod, *A Job at the BBC* (1947), p. 111, for some of the difficulties.

[6] *There had been problems about the playing of other national anthems (see above, p. 327). It was decided, for example, to play the Luxembourg anthem only once every six weeks. (Overseas Board, *Minutes*, 20 February 1941.)

[7] *Ibid., 26 June 1941.

[8] *Nicolls to Ogilvie, 30 June 1941.

Press Attaché strongly advised that the Internationale should be played after a rebroadcast of Stalin's speech of 3 July.[1] It was not. The result was that questions were asked in Parliament; Tallents was drawn into the unenviable position of arguing with stiff if strict correctness that Russia was not an 'Allied Power' and that only the anthems of allies were played; and Lord Snell, on behalf of the Government, had to pontificate that 'the decision of policy in this matter rests with the Ministry of Information, which, however, consults the Foreign Office where suitable, and feels obliged to follow its views, for example, as regards the playing of anthems of countries not officially allied to us'.[2] Not surprisingly, Nicolls began to regret his first refusal to drop the National Anthems programme. After stating firmly that 'monkeying about' with the anthem in whatever form will not be a 'successful evasion of the Russian issue', he concluded that it would be better to abolish them [the anthems] altogether than 'start doing one or two of them at a time in the setting of a little feature', the latest effort at compromise.[3]

Much time and energy at the highest levels continued to be devoted to the issue. Duff Cooper himself recommended on 12 July that the Kutusov 1812 March should be played the following day, but the BBC discovered that the only available record was broken to pieces.[4] On the morning of the 13th the Foreign Office intervened to ask the pertinent question whether the failure of the BBC to play the Internationale that evening 'would make the BBC look ridiculous', but Eden refused to try to persuade Churchill to change his 'emphatic' opinion that the Internationale should never be played. In fact, the Kutusov 1812 March was played on 13 July. On the following

---

[1] *Griffin to J. B. Clark, 4 July 1941.

[2] *Note by Tallents, 6 July 1941. *Hansard*, vol. 373, cols. 161–2, 583–4. 'Could not the Minister arrange to have the National Anthem of the Soviet Union sung and played in this House?' asked Gallacher, the Communist M.P. The Policy Committee of the Ministry of Information had discussed on 19 June—before Russia came into the war—some of the implications of Russia not being an ally: 'Should "the Red Flag" [*sic*] he played on Sunday evenings?' was one of them. It was anticipated that there would be 'large diversities' in viewpoints about a full alliance. Churchill set to work at once, however, to establish a war alliance. (*The Second World War*, vol. III, p. 341.)

[3] *Nicolls to Ogilvie, 8 July 1941.

[4] *Note by Tallents, 13 July 1941.

day Ryan, on behalf of Duff Cooper, announced briskly that the National Anthems programme as a whole would be dropped. 'Hereafter and beginning on Sunday next, July 20th, one country is to be taken each week, and a selection played of its rousing, gay and patriotic airs, exclusive of its National Anthem.' France was to be taken the following Sunday and Russia the Sunday after that. Ryan emphasized that both the Internationale and The Red Flag were to be excluded from the Russian selection.[1] The result of this change was that the audience listening to the Home Service at 8.45 p.m. on Sunday evenings was halved.[2]

Many months of war were to elapse before the Internationale was played.[3] The controversy, absurd though it was, reflected the uneasiness with which many people in high places viewed the entry of Russia into the war. In lower places also there was some confusion. Mass Observation reported that under half of the people whose views they had collected were glad that the attack on Russia *had* taken place, most of them giving the obvious reason that it would take some of the pressure off Britain and that it would reinforce the 'great alliance', a few hoping that two dictatorships would destroy each other. Only a small minority expected Russia to win. A surprisingly large proportion, however, regretted that the war had drawn in yet another country, where in Churchill's own phrase 'maidens laugh and children play'. 'They'll be fighting in heaven presently' was one comment.[4] 'The war is becoming a world war, although every nation has made sacrifices to limit it,' the BBC's Intelligence Report for August 1941 noted.[5]

The entry of Russia into the struggle 'altered the values and relationships of the war'.[6] It raised four sets of important questions for the BBC—first, what should be said about the new

[1] *Ryan to Powell, 14 July 1941.
[2] *Note by Nicolls, 16 Feb. 1942. The national airs of Australia, for example, were listened to by only a third of the audience listening to the National Anthems programme. Nicolls was somewhat contemptuous of African and Asian airs: 'there has crept in an element of comedy for the ordinary listener, who does not understand half-tone scales and exotic instruments and who is not roused to frenzy by the beat of the tom-tom.'
[3] See below, pp. 393–4.
[4] Mass Observation Report, June 1941.
[5] *BBC *Monthly Intelligence Report, Europe*, 16 Aug. 1941.
[6] Churchill, op. cit., p. 337.

war in home programmes; second, should a British war correspondent be sent to Russia; third, should there be a BBC foreign-language service in Russian; fourth, what changes, if any, should be made in British overseas propaganda? The first question was answered cautiously. Nicolls wrote that 'five days after Hitler's attack the position was "delicate", not because of lack of British goodwill but because of Russian sensitivities'. 'For the present, therefore, any reference to Russia must be very carefully considered, and referred if necessary. Variety gags and jokes and the use of Russian-sounding names or Communist titles should normally be avoided.'[1]

'Projection of Russia' was bound to provoke political argument, and the Foreign Office had its own views on what could and should not be done.[2] Maconachie argued against talks or features on Russian political history but in favour of talks on Russian 'cultural achievements'. Guy Burgess, also in the Talks Department, supported this view. So too did Maisky, the Soviet Ambassador.[3] Maconachie rightly pointed out that 'if we suddenly become appreciative of the Russian system and way of life, we might easily provoke cynical and hostile reactions from our audience'. He cited Cassandra's comment (in the *Daily Mirror*) on the fact that '20,000 people in Moscow had attended prayers for a Russian victory, after the constant denunciations of the Soviet regime as "Godless"'.[4] Even the cultural achievements were carefully sifted at first: talks and features about science and the theatre were allowed, books and films were to be handled with discretion.[5] By the early part of August, however, the position was sufficiently clarified to permit broadcasting on a very wide range of topics.[6] Churchill was now in direct communication with Stalin, whom the BBC decided—appropriately or otherwise—to refer to as 'Monsieur Stalin' from 11 August onwards.[7]

When it became obvious that the Russians were courageously resisting the Germans, a wave of pro-Russian feeling began to

---

[1] *Nicolls, Programme Directive, no. 61, 27 June 1941.

[2] *Tallents to Nicolls, 5 July 1941; Overseas Board, *Minutes*, 3 July 1941.

[3] *Maconachie to Barnes, 10 July 1941, following a talk with Lady Violet Bonham Carter who had met Maisky.

[4] *Maconachie to Barnes, 6 July 1941.

[5] *Kirkpatrick to Barnes, 22 July 1941, with a note by Barnes.

[6] *Note of 6 Aug. 1941.   [7] *Maconachie to R. T. Clark, 11 Aug. 1941.

sweep Britain.[1] It was particularly prominent in reactions to cinema news reels, in the leaders in the *Daily Express*, in the Tanks for Russia Week, which began on 22 September and on Red Army Days, and in Mrs. Churchill's Aid for Russia appeal; but it also affected everything from pop music—'Lovely Russian Rose'—to political protest—'Open the Second Front Now'— which reached its peak in 1942.[2] The mood was to persist not only after the eventual opening of the Second Front in 1944 but after the first open signs of Anglo-Russian political and diplomatic differences in 1944 and 1945.[3]

The BBC played its part in this story.[4] It broadcast *Eugene Onyegin*; it produced an adaptation by Louis MacNeice of the film *Alexander Nevsky*, with music by Prokofiev, and a biography by the same author called 'Dr. Tchekov'; it presented *The Three Sisters* and *Squaring the Circle*; it arranged talks by Maisky, the Soviet Ambassador, by Eric Godfrey ('I worked in a Soviet Factory'), by Tom Barker on the Kuznetz Basin, by Sir John Russell on the Caucasus, and by Sir Bernard Pares; it introduced British music lovers to Shostakovich and Khachaturian as well as offering more Rachmaninov, Borodin, Balakirev, and of course, Tchaikovsky; it provided Russian marches and folk-songs, often recorded by famous Russian choirs; and it presented one whole 'Russia Night' in which Cecil McGivern, one of the BBC's most talented writer-producers, collaborated with Joseph Macleod, the announcer, who was interested in all things Russian.[5] It was Macleod who read over the air Alexander Werth's *Russian Commentary*, a programme with considerable popular appeal which was instituted at short notice in July 1942. In this context it was not surprising that the playing of the Internationale was permitted from

---

[1] *It was noted by a CBS correspondent in London (BBC Monitoring Service *Weekly Analysis*, 9 Sept. 1941): 'The British people are anxious to give Russia the fullest possible help and there is widespread feeling that so far not nearly enough has been done.'

[2] See below, p. 411. See also K. Young, *Churchill and Beaverbrook* (1966), pp. 211 ff.; T. Higgins, *Winston Churchill and the Second Front* (1957).

[3] For an interesting account of the story as seen by Thomas Barman who joined the British Embassy in Moscow as First Secretary in September 1943, see his *Diplomatic Correspondent* (1968).

[4] *Overseas Board, *Minutes*, 17 July 1941: 'Reported that projection of Russia by cultural programmes was in hand.'

[5] J. Macleod, op. cit., p. 133.

22 January 1942 onwards,[1] and that of the Red Flag soon afterwards.[2]

It was far easier, whatever the complications, to put on programmes about Russia than it was to secure broadcasting facilities from Russia. This, indeed, was one aspect of the situation which could never be fully communicated to the British public. Dimbleby asked in July 1941 to be transferred to Russia from North Africa,[3] but the request was turned down and Sir Stafford Cripps reported soon afterwards from Moscow that it would be difficult for any correspondent to get good eye-witness facilities.[4] The BBC persisted, with Maconachie pointing out sensibly that he did not like the idea of 'the greatest war in history ending with the BBC record for reportage consisting of Ward and Dimbleby in the Middle East and no one in Russia': a correspondent would be worth while, he went on, even if he merely broadcast 'Soviet handouts with such discretion as he is able to exercise'.[5] The matter was referred back again to Bracken and from Bracken to Cripps, and it was decided at the beginning of August 1941 to send out Vernon Bartlett, by far the most experienced of all the BBC's foreign broadcasters and the pioneer of all work in this field.[6] Bartlett was well disposed to the Soviet Union and wanted to make his assignment a success, but he was so beset by irksome censorship restrictions and lack of Russian interest in his mission, that he had to return with his hopes unfulfilled.[7] An October visit to Moscow by Monckton did not solve the difficulties,[8] and talks at Kuibyshev with Vishinsky and Lozovsky, the head of Soviet radio, were as abortive as all previous and, as it proved, later talks. Technical liaison with

---

[1] *Ryan to Foot, 22 Jan. 1942: 'We are asked not to overdo it, and only to play it when the occasion really does call for it.' (Nicolls, Programme Directive, no. 75, 25 Feb. 1942.)

[2] *Adam to Miss Ferguson, 15 Oct. 1942. For later programmes, see below, p. 411.   [3] *Home Board, Minutes, 4 July 1941.

[4] *Ryan to Maconachie, 23 July 1941.   [5] *Maconachie to Ryan, 23 July 1941.

[6] *Overseas Board, Minutes, 31 July 1941. Bartlett agreed, at Bracken's request, on 30 July. For Bartlett's earlier career, see Briggs, The Golden Age of Wireless, pp. 146–7.

[7] *Overseas Board, Minutes, 17 Sept. 1941. Report by Bartlett on his visit, 10 Oct. 1941. See some of his comments in Advertisers' Weekly, 2 Oct. 1941. Barman discusses his visit in his book, p. 165.

[8] *Note by Ogilvie, 2 Oct. 1941, saying that he had asked Monckton to give Bartlett the greetings of the BBC.

the Russians, Ashbridge told Monckton in October 1941, was also 'very poor, practically non-existent'.[1] Propaganda liaison was even more difficult to achieve, though there was some exchange of information.[2]

Although John Lawrence was appointed Press Attaché in Moscow in February 1942, the BBC, unlike the Americans,[3] never obtained permission to send a correspondent to Moscow. A few press correspondents, notably Alexander Werth, wrote commentaries and a substantial amount of Russian material was subsequently to be used in the BBC's European Services[4]— Ilya Ehrenburg, for example, was to give weekly talks in French—yet the British public for the most part got its news and views from Russia with far less sense either of detail or of immediacy than its news and views from the United States. Of Lozovsky it was rightly said that 'he speaks only what he wants the world to know'.[5] Exchanges were restricted mainly to messages of goodwill from groups like factory workers, nurses and schoolteachers. In Moscow itself a close watch was kept on foreigners, and it was never easy even for seasoned observers 'to test the movement of opinion against the propaganda-soaked pages of the Soviet newspapers'.[6] Although, from the other side, the BBC took the initiative early in 1942 in supplying the Russians with BBC transcriptions, the London Transcription Service, which had incorporated the old JBC,[7] had no Russian section.[8] There were differences of opinion also between the BBC and the Ministry of Information's Russian Section about what was 'suitable', and no precise information ever came in about whether or not the Russians used any of the material sent.

[1] *Ashbridge to Monckton, 3 Oct. 1941. The same point was made in a letter from Hayes to Lawrence, 4 Feb. 1942.   [2] Barman, op. cit., pp. 112–13.
[3] CBS had Larry Lesueur in Moscow. For the CBS team, see P. W. White, *News on the Air* (1947).
[4] The effort to get permission for Werth to broadcast direct failed, although he did broadcast one such commentary in June 1943. On 3 July 1943 Maconachie wrote to Barnes that 'C(N) can get no further at all, nor can the Foreign Office help towards inducing the Soviet authorities to show greater cooperation'. There was talk of replacing Werth in November 1944.
[5] *News Chronicle*, 17 Sept. 1941. For later complaints of Russian secrecy, see the *Daily Mail*, 3 Jan. 1942.
[6] T. G. Barman, 'Moscow during the War' in *The Listener*, 10 Oct. 1968.
[7] See above, p. 344.
[8] *C. Conner to Griffin, 5 Oct. 1942.

As far as broadcasts in Russian to Russia were concerned, here also there was a complete *impasse*. There had once again been discussion of a Russian Service earlier in 1941: two talks a week on military matters were requested by the Ministry of Information at the suggestion of Cripps, and steps had been taken to appoint an Intelligence Officer to prepare plans.[1] There had also been discussion about the possibilities of special broadcasts in Ukrainian.[2] Nonetheless, Andrew Rothstein, the TASS correspondent in London, thought that the Russians would not welcome such broadcasts 'unless they contained a big element of self-criticism',[3] and this proved to be a correct assessment even after 22 June. Churchill's speech of that day was broadcast in Russian—on short wave—but there was so little time for preparation that the Slavonic Languages Supervisor, N. Gubsky, who had never broadcast before, had to translate it as he went along.[4] The following day, when Eden broached the subject of a regular service with Maisky, the latter 'shied like a young colt and remarked darkly that it was an extremely delicate question'.[5]

Before it was finally decided on grounds of high policy not to start a Russian Service,[6] the BBC produced a most interesting and responsible paper called 'Broadcasting in Russian: Some Relevant Facts' in which it was stated that broadcasts in Russian would reach 'a large and eager audience'. The Moscow broadcast of parts of Churchill's speech had been cheered by a large crowd,[7] and subsequent news of RAF exploits had been received with great appreciation. Broadcasts from London, it

[1] *Overseas Board, *Minutes*, 27 Feb., 13 March 1941; see also above, pp. 184, 265. Miss Benzie to J. B. Clark, 15 Jan. 1941; Clark to Mrs. Stewart, 31 Jan.; Mrs. Stewart to Clark, 24 Feb.; Salt to Wellington, 5, 12 Feb.

[2] Clark to Wellington, 5 March 1940; Griffin, 'Some Implications of Broadcasting in Ukrainian', 19 May 1941; Miss Benzie to Clark, 9 May 1941.

[3] *Lawrence to Salt, 30 May 1941.

[4] *Tallents to Ogilvie, 27 June 1941. Staff numbers were being built up at that time with a view to starting regular broadcasts. (Overseas Board, *Minutes*, 26 June 1941.)

[5] *Kirkpatrick to Tallents, 24 June 1941: Kirkpatrick had earlier declared himself opposed to broadcasts in Russian on several grounds, one being basic—that since radios had been confiscated in the Soviet Union 'there were no receiving sets' (note of 14 June 1941). This also was Duff Cooper's view (letter to Ogilvie, 30 June, congratulating the BBC on the Churchill translation). Overseas Board noted Agency reports about the collection of sets (*Minutes*, 3 July 1941).

[6] *Ibid., 17 July 1941.

[7] *Manchester Guardian*, 28 June 1941.

was maintained, would have a big part to play 'in overcoming a total separation of nearly twenty-five years'. The Germans were already broadcasting in Russian and in Ukrainian, claiming recklessly at the same time that their Army was revolutionary and that they wished to restore private ownership of land. British broadcasts should be complementary to those of the Russians. 'If the Germans should disorganise badly the Russian radio, the primary requirement would be news bulletins, as many and as full as possible. But at the moment, the Russian radio gives its home front one of the fullest and most objective news services in the world.' Russia needed, above all else, to be told what Britain was doing to help them, and Russian officials in London should be employed to give eye-witness accounts and commentaries. Music, literature and news about science should be broadcast also. 'Broadcasting on these lines would not be easy,' it was admitted, 'since any sham would show through.'[1]

It is sad that this bold but thoroughly practical scheme could not be put through. As it was, the Foreign Office decided against it[2] and the Russians disapproved of it.[3] Lozovsky showed as little enthusiasm for the idea, wrote Bartlett, as he did for any suggestion 'which might lead to the slightest infiltration of British ideas into the USSR'.[4] There were no broadcasts in Russian from London for the rest of the war, except for a weekly fifteen-minutes newsletter which was broadcast with the co-operation of TASS from 7 October 1942 until 26 May 1943.[5]

While BBC broadcasts in Russian were ruled out, efforts were made to 'project Russia' as well as Britain in BBC overseas programmes. 'Although we are not [yet] allowed to broadcast in Russian,' Salt remarked in July 1941, 'it is clear from a study of Russian broadcasting . . . that they are particularly susceptible to the flattery value of our performing their plays,

[1] *'Broadcasting in Russian', 10 July 1941.

[2] *Overseas Board, *Minutes*, 17 July 1941.

[3] *The Foreign Office asked Sir Archibald Clark Kerr, the new Ambassador, to broach the subject with the Russians in April 1942.

[4] *Report by Bartlett, 10 Oct. 1941.

[5] *European Divisional Meeting, *Minutes*, 24 Aug. 1942. 'If the Soviet army defeats the German armies, Britain's share in the peace may largely depend on whether British broadcasting can keep Europe's landlubber millions aware of other forces besides the Red Army and of other hopes than Soviet leadership.' (BBC *Monthly Intelligence Report, Europe*, 16 Aug. 1941.)

music, etc.'[1] In fact, however, the Russians were scarcely dependent on such aids: they very quickly extended their own overseas propaganda, and, using quite different methods from the BBC, tried to out-shout the Germans and to jam Berlin radio. As early as August 1941 they broke into the German Home News Service with comments like 'lies, lies' and 'don't you believe it':[2] the strange voice they employed was quickly nicknamed 'Ivan the Terrible' and 'Mick the Mad Russian'. The Germans for their part tried to jam Moscow radio and set up a Russian 'freedom station' on NBBS lines early in August 1941: it accused Stalin of trying to sell out to the British.[3]

Breaking into enemy programmes, which had often been suggested to the BBC,[4] was briefly tried by the Germans on the BBC's Home Service—the 'Voice' attracted a good deal of Press interest[5]—but at best it was a gimmick. Far more effective even in Russian radio strategy were the general programmes which always drew a sharp distinction between the 'Fascists' and the German people and which deliberately encouraged more tough resistance in the occupied countries, including large-scale sabotage, than either Electra House or Ritchie had ever scrupled to do. Atrocity stories were repeated in gruesome detail, special attention was paid at first to Yugoslavia and to Poland, and direct appeals were made to saboteurs and resistance movements. Broadcasts to Holland mentioned collaborators by name, and broadcasts to France talked of guerilla warfare.[6] 'Our war for the freedom of our country,' it was stated, 'will blend with the war of the peoples of Europe for their independence and democratic freedom.'[7] In the

[1] *Salt to Nicolls, 29 July 1941; BBC *Monthly Intelligence Report, Europe*, 16 Aug. 1941.

[2] *BBC *Weekly Analysis of Foreign Broadcasts, Europe*, 26 Aug. 1941. Deutschland-sender replied on 24 Aug. that 'this form of wireless warfare is nothing new. We used it during the Polish campaign and later. . . . Suitable counter-measures against the Bolshevik attempts at interference are in progress.'

[3] *Ibid., 5 Aug. 1941; C. J. Rolo, *Radio Goes to War* (1943), pp. 159–60.

[4] *See above, p. 6. Bracken had been sent a letter on the subject on 3 Sept. 1941; in a letter to Bracken of 5 Sept., Ashbridge reiterated British policy not to jam, while adding 'we have always borne in mind the possibility of employing . . . other methods' if war circumstances necessitated or favoured them.

[5] See above, pp. 71–2.

[6] *BBC *Weekly Analysis of Foreign Broadcasts*, 1 July, 22 July 1941. (For an early call for sabotage in Poland, see the *Daily Mail*, 12 July 1941.)

[7] *Ibid., 19 Aug. 1941.

meantime, anti-German groups were broadening the range of their activities during the late summer of 1941, and by September BBC monitors were noting a deliberate and careful gradation in Soviet references to resistance. 'They speak of discontent in Rumania and Hungary, describe sabotage in Yugoslavia and Czechoslovakia, give accounts of the moral resistance of Norwegian trade unionists and in the case of France report the growing activities of French patriots.'[1]

The Germans began to pay increasing attention in their broadcasting to signs of resistance, complaining of an alliance between the Comintern and the British Secret Service. They even noted a danger of infection in Germany itself as the Russian winter approached. 'We Germans would be miserable creatures,' Fritzsche exclaimed on 23 September, 'if we did not keep the Englishmen away from our back door also.'[2] Hitler himself turned to these themes in his speech of 8 November at the traditional celebrations in honour of the Nazi 'martyrs'. This speech was not broadcast, and the Germans, unlike the Danes, were given only short and carefully selected extracts on the German radio. The following passage was omitted from the German version: 'And then there are the most stupid hopes of the lot, that an insurrection or a revolution will break out in Germany. Such people as might make a revolution do not exist here any longer.'[3]

It is impossible either to understand or to evaluate the growth of resistance in Europe during these months when 'Fortress Europe' was being transformed into 'Prison Europe' without taking into account the failure of the Germans not only to crush Russia as quickly as they had planned, but to live up to their own exaggerated propaganda claims. 'The enemy already lies defeated and cannot rise again,' Hitler stated categorically in his famous Order of the Day from his Eastern Headquarters on 2 October, relayed to the public a week later, and in his speech of 3 October.[4] 'The Soviet Union is finished militarily,' Otto Dietrich told German and foreign journalists on the same

---

[1] *Ibid., 23 Sept. 1941.
[2] *Ibid., 30 Sept. 1941.
[3] *Ibid., 11 Nov. 1941.
[4] Kris and Speier, op. cit., p. 373.

day that Hitler's order was released. 'The English dream of a war on two fronts has definitely come to an end.'[1] Goebbels, who realized the dangers of such talk and foresaw future reverses on the Russian front,[2] provided alternative propaganda which gained in independence and in importance as the earlier exaggerations became apparent. Yet while much of the new propaganda was effective in its German context—notably the Winter Help campaign, *Winterhilfespende*, which brought about a definite improvement in morale[3]—European opinion was directly affected by the German failure both of deeds and of words. The Anti-Comintern Conference, followed by the signing of the Anti-Comintern Pact in November 1941, might be hailed as 'the manifestation of a world front such as history has never seen before',[4] but Ribbentrop found it necessary to add after the Pact had been signed that 'in our times of motors, tanks and Stukas, revolts in occupied territories are impossible from the outset'.[5]

The signing of the Pact was followed soon afterwards by the fall of Rostov to the Russians, the first occasion during the war that the Germans had had to announce an important reverse in land fighting. 'The English draw far-reaching conclusions from this insignificant event,' Zeesen told Rommel's German army in North Africa. 'They also hope that it will shake the morale of the German troops. If that were so, what would be left of the English after their glorious retreats which in every case took the form of headlong flights?'[6] This was comment for the men of the desert. Yet in Berlin itself Goebbels was noting how 'really amusing' it was to see all the German ministers one by one approaching the Führer asking his permission to listen to foreign radio stations,[7] and recognizing

[1] Bramsted, op. cit., p. 246.

[2] Kris and Speier, op. cit., p. 374; Bramsted, op. cit., p. 247, where there is a reference to 'Dietrich's gaffe' which Goebbels exploited. 'Goebbels,' Bramsted writes, 'anticipated the reverse in Russia by several weeks.'

[3] Ibid., p. 248.

[4] *Paris Radio, 24 Nov. 1941, quoted in BBC *Weekly Analysis of Foreign Broadcasts*, 2 Dec. 1941.

[5] *Ibid. Cf. a comment of Radio Moscow quoted ibid., 27 Oct. 1941: 'The real war has only just begun with the fight for Moscow.'

[6] *Ibid., 2 Dec. 1941.

[7] L. P. Lochner (ed.), *The Goebbels Diaries* (1948), p. 57. He criticized German home radio at this time. A musical director-general had been temporarily placed in charge of the entertainment programme and was offering the Germans nothing

frankly that Quisling, who was appointed Norwegian puppet premier early in 1942, 'is hated violently in the entire enemy world and is now the target for vile calumny'.[1]

Goebbels admitted equally frankly that the German people underwent a great inner change at this time as the promised decision in Russia did not mature and as the war entered a new phase which, he suggested, resembled in some ways that of the third year of World War I.[2] He wrote in his diary in February 1942 that since 'we . . . must envisage operations of longer duration [we] are accordingly compelled to change our slogans and our policies fundamentally'.[3] There was still consolation, of course, in the fact that the British, in his view, were even more pessimistic and gloomy when confronted with the first disasters of the new war in the Far East.[4]

The war had spread to the Far East in early December 1941 when the United States was drawn into what was plainly by now a 'world struggle', what an Italian commentator called a 'terrifying inter-continental drama which hangs over hundreds of millions of people in the farthest of lands'.[5] The German propaganda machine had long prepared the Germans for this eventuality,[6] and news of the early Japanese successes provided something of a diversion from the news of the Russian front. The story of the attack on Pearl Harbour was received, like the story of Hitler's attack on Russia, on a Sunday— 7 December. 'As a result of the new developments in the Far East,' a German military commentator remarked in a broadcast of the following day, 'the attention of the whole world, including ourselves, will be concentrated to a high degree on the operations in the Pacific area.'[7] On 11 December Germany

---

[1] Ibid., p. 30.   [2] Ibid., p. 38.   [3] Ibid., p. 61.

[4] See below, pp. 499–500. For the 'symmetrical pattern', see above, pp. 17–18.

[5] *BBC *Weekly Analysis of Foreign Broadcasts*, 9 Dec. 1941.

[6] So too had the Russian propaganda machine. 'The realisation that we are not alone, that we have on our side Britain and the USA lends us courage', Moscow radio broadcast on 1 Nov. (*Ibid., 4 Nov. 1941.) Yet it was noted also that there was no Second Front. 'There are at present no British or US armies of any kind on the Continent of Europe.' (Ibid., 11 Nov. 1941.)

[7] *Ibid., 16 Dec. 1941.

---

but symphonic music. 'People of this type,' Goebbels wrote, 'usually sit in an ivory tower and don't know what the common man wants and what he needs most.' (Ibid., p. 31.) See also above, pp. 18, 51.

and Italy declared war against the United States. Roosevelt had long been regarded and described as a 'gangster':[1] it was not necessary to do anything more than gloat over the remarkable early Japanese successes. In Russia, it was stated by contrast, if with caution, that it was the Japanese who had behaved in a 'gangster-like manner', that the USSR, the USA, China and Great Britain constituted a most powerful bloc with inexhaustible reserves, and that while Japan's reserves would exhaust themselves, those of the United States would grow.[2]

The BBC, which had been concerned throughout the whole of the previous year with the strengthening of the 'special link' with the United States, was as ready for the event as the Germans; and certainly Churchill did not need any time to prepare his broadcast on the subject, as he had needed time in June. The news of the actual attack, given at 9 p.m., might have 'dumbfounded' British listeners, but for Churchill the news meant simply that 'we had won after all . . . Britain would live . . . Hitler's fate was sealed. . . . As for the Japanese they would be ground to powder. All the rest was merely the proper application of overwhelming force.' Roosevelt's speech to Congress on 8 December, listened to by 79 per cent of all homes in the United States, was relayed to Britain and heard by millions of listeners on this side of the Atlantic.[3]

The next few weeks were to be some of the most difficult and testing that Churchill ever faced. Nonetheless, there was a real sense in which Anglo-American understanding had been canvassed with more warmth to the British people before the United States entered the war than Anglo-Russian understanding was officially canvassed even after the USSR came into the war. The NBC and CBS reporters in London had provided a non-stop flow of news comments and more general programmes, such as CBS's *Round Britain*

[1] *Ibid., 4 Nov. 1941. 'Roosevelt says he can overthrow the New Order in Europe. That is where he is wrong. Just as we cannot divert the Amazon into the Spree, so he cannot divert the Spree into the Amazon. . . . He will at best succeed in incorporating the remnants of the British Empire into the USA.' The German Home Service broadcast announcing Pearl Harbour stated that 'Warmonger No. 1 has at last attained his goal and has succeeded in bringing the war to his people' (ibid., 9 Dec. 1941).

[2] *Ibid., 16 Dec. 1941.

[3] *BBC Handbook, 1942*, p. 82; E. Barnouw, *The Golden Web* (1968), p. 152.

by Night, since the phoney war and the dark days of 1940, with the fullest co-operation of the BBC.[1] In exchange, Raymond Gram Swing, Elmer Davis and Alistair Cooke had broadcast their commentaries from New York to large British audiences, along with feature programmes produced by the CBS Workshop or specially made in the New York offices of the BBC. According to one historian, the day-to-day ramifications of the struggle about isolationism in the United States were better known and more vividly appreciated by Britons than by Americans.[2] Swing, in particular, was an influential mediator on both sides of the Atlantic. In London he had his 'Swing Club', and when he visited Britain in the summer of 1941, 267 guests attended a lunch in his honour: they included eighteen Ministers. He met Churchill privately and George Bernard Shaw, of all people, said that he always listened with 'special interest' when Swing broadcast. In Washington he had the ear of Harry Hopkins, Stimson, Ickes and the President himself.[3] Murrow, too, was dining with Roosevelt on the night of Pearl Harbour.

British broadcasts to America had established a new pattern by the time of Pearl Harbour. BBC Empire programmes had given way to a new North American Service intended for Canada, Newfoundland and the West Indies as well as the USA. Listeners to it heard the same News as listeners to other Empire Services, but they were offered a quite different kind of 'radio technique.' In the case of entertainment programmes the difference was even more marked. 'The primary audience to this Service,' it was recognized, 'is accustomed to the American way of putting over radio shows, and that way has been developed for the last twenty years by all the resources that commercial enterprise can command. It would be of little use trying to attract the audience with broadcasts based on the conventions that have become popular here with listeners at home.'[4]

The critical decisions in relation to the Service had been

---

[1] See above, pp. 292–3.   [2] Barnouw, op. cit., p. 147.

[3] R. G. Swing, *Good Evening! A Professional Memoir* (1964). Extracts from a Roosevelt 'fireside chat' had been broadcast in BBC Home and European programmes in May 1941.

[4] *BBC Handbook, 1942*, p. 15: Note by Rendall, 'Use of Radio in Anglo-American Relations', 12 March 1942.

taken in August 1940 following a visit to Britain of the General Programmes Organizer of the Canadian Broadcasting Corporation. There had been a Canadian Broadcasting Corporation Programme Unit stationed in London since December 1939, led at first by Bob Bowman and after April 1940 by H. R. Pelletier,[1] and it was under the direction of Canadians, particularly Ernest Bushnell, Programme Organizer of the CBC, that the Service, still modest in scale in 1940 and early 1941, had established a tradition of accurate timing and smooth presentation. News bulletins, organized separately, were shorter than those designed for Britain and Europe. *Radio Newsreel* made its war-time début in this context: timing was slick to the second, and the personal element predominated in content and presentation. Another Canadian, Stanley Maxted, working at Evesham, was responsible for the North American edition; Peter Pooley ran the whole programme which foreshadowed many later developments in radio.[2] Among the other programmes which made their mark were *Front Line Family*, written and produced by Alan Melville, which, like all the BBC serials which were to follow it, had its addicts as well as its listeners,[3] and a weekly programme from the Eagle Club, where American pilots serving in Britain gathered long before the United States entered the war.

To strike the right note with American audiences, it was necessary to know 'what the Americans are thinking'. 'We must know all about America,' a BBC report had stated in the autumn of 1940, 'and keep that knowledge right up to date in relation to our North American policy and programmes.'[4] Rendall, Director of Empire Services, visited Canada and the United States for two months in late 1940. He met there

[1] Pelletier joined the BBC as North American Programme Organizer in Nov. 1942. Gerry Wilmot was one of the most popular BBC recruits from CBC.

[2] See above, p. 49.

[3] *Under the name of *The Robinson Family* the serial was eventually broadcast after 1945 in the Light Programme: it ran continuously, therefore, from 1941 to 1947. At first it was 'designed to portray a middle-class English family standing up to the shocks of war' (de Lotbinière, who was in charge of Empire Programmes, to Melville, 1 Jan. 1942). By May 1942 it was reported that '*Front Line Family* seems to have created more general interest than any programme except the News, the talks by Priestley and Wickham Steed and possibly *Newsreel*' (Davenport to de Lotbinière, 11 May 1942). In June 1942 the Germans produced a programme called 'Our Version of Front Line Family'.

[4] *'Recommendations for an Empire Intelligence Service', 27 Nov. 1940.

Gerald Cock, the lively, highly experienced, but badly over-
worked North American Representative of the BBC, who told
him how much the Americans expected both a speedy flow
of news and official and unofficial comment on it. The
Americans chafed under the censorship restrictions, and when
they set up their own Office of Censorship in January 1942
censorship was voluntary: radio scripts could be submitted
for review if broadcasters wished, but it was not required.[1]
Throughout the war unofficial comment was welcomed, so
that a forthright British speaker, like J. B. Priestley, was an
immediate success in the BBC's *Britain Speaks* series. Rendall
concluded, 'Many people have heard our programmes lately who
never did so before.' 'So long as we can build up our direct and
indirect audience as we have been doing by the ordinary activities
of short-wave broadcasting and re-broadcasting, we shall not
be so open to criticism as a national propagandist agency.'[2]

Rendall's visit to the United States in 1940 was followed by an
even more important visit by Wellington in 1941 and by the
subsequent re-arrangement and extension of the BBC's New
York office. Wellington left London for New York in mid-
May 1941 with a comprehensive brief from the Ministry of
Information in which he had rendered such invaluable service:
Duff Cooper himself stated that 'it is vitally important that
everything possible should be done to achieve the greatest co-
operation between this country and the United States in the
broadcasting field', and added that Halifax, by then British
Ambassador in Washington, was himself fully aware of the
position. Among the specific assignments Duff Cooper gave to
Wellington were to explore the possibilities of co-ordinating
propaganda policy with the Americans and of increasing
American short-wave propaganda, if necessary by re-broadcasting, to Europe. He was also to discuss fully questions relating
to transmitter provision and exchange. He was to ask the
Americans the most important question of all in this context—
whether they would be ready, if necessary, 'to take over broadcasting obligations in the last resort'.[3] Finally, he was to

[1] Barnouw, op. cit., pp. 156–7.
[2] *R. A. Rendall, 'Report on a Visit to Canada and the United States, Oct.–
Nov. 1940'; Overseas Board, *Minutes*, 28 Nov. 1940.
[3] *Monckton to Wellington, 2 May 1941; Overseas Board, *Minutes*, 3 April
1941.

concert plans with the Canadians, particularly in relation to the Canadian short-wave project.[1]

The BBC added to Wellington's brief a whole series of additional questions relating to relays of American broadcasts to Europe.[2] Its new Research Board had agreed in May 1941, indeed, that the United States should be brought far more fully into the war-time picture than hitherto and that Denis Brogan, with his vast knowledge of the United States, should have the task of considering in detail how best to project the United States as an 'invincible ally' in all overseas transmissions.[3] The same policy of 'projection' was followed in Home programmes, quietly and unobtrusively before September 1941 and thereafter quite explicitly.[4] Meanwhile, May 1941 had been an important month in yet another American connection. It was then that Maurice Gorham, who had been editor of the *Radio Times* when war broke out, became Director of the BBC's North American Service. Gorham was a vigorous and enterprising Irishman, the kind of man who wanted to innovate and who never accepted the *status quo* unquestioningly. His Monday meetings brought together all the people working primarily for the Service.[5]

As a result of Wellington's mission to New York and Washington, Colonel Donovan, who was appointed Co-ordinator of Information by the United States in July 1941, arranged for a visit to Britain in September 1941 of his representative, Robert Sherwood, the well-known author, along with the Assistant Chief Engineer of the Federal Radio Commission.[6] Sherwood, who knew more about propaganda than about radio,[7] told Ogilvie and Gorham that he was concerned primarily with 'getting American broadcasts to the European

---

[1] See above, p. 349.

[2] *Note by Tallents, 28 April 1941: 'It would be a mistake to commit ourselves to the re-broadcasting of any American output until we were reasonably satisfied that the necessary quality had been secured.'

[3] *Research Board, *Minutes*, 2 May 1941.

[4] *Overseas Board, *Minutes*, 2 Oct. 1941. The appointment by the Ministry in 1941 of Robin Cruikshank as head of its American Division guaranteed excellent advice.

[5] Gorham, op. cit., p. 112.

[6] *Stephen Fry to Rendall, 8 Aug. 1941, concerning the visit.

[7] *Gorham to Rendall, 1 Oct. 1941. See also M. Gorham, *Sound and Fury* (1948), pp. 119–20.

audience more effectively than was now being done, with a view to raising American radio propaganda ultimately to the level of a military weapon'.[1] He subsequently raised just as bluntly the question of transmitters—could they be shared? how should new ones be distributed?[2] It was clear at this time that the British were well ahead of the Americans in their ideas about radio propaganda, in their organization of monitoring, and in their knowledge of the techniques of short-wave broadcasting. The discussions, therefore, were friendly but somewhat limited in effect. There was a more basic problem also. 'The first job to be done,' Murrow wisely told Sherwood, 'was for American propaganda policy to be decided in Washington, before anybody was sent over here to make plans for carrying it out.'[3] The PWE system, as it was developing in Britain at this time, involved control: the American system involved 'guidance'.[4] It was only after the United States actually entered the war in December 1941 that theoretical issues acquired practical point and a sense of urgency.

In the meantime, Sir Gerald Campbell was appointed Director-General of the Ministry of Information Service in New York,[5] and Wellington left the Ministry in London to become the BBC's North American Director—the post was upgraded from that of Representative—in September.[6] Cock remained attached to the New York office in an advisory capacity:[7] he was later to become Pacific Coast Representative, based on San Francisco, while W. M. Newton, who had been Newsome's predecessor before war broke out, was appointed Middle West Correspondent based on Chicago. Thereafter, the constitutional relationship between Ministry and BBC was

[1] *Notes of the meeting, 9 Sept. 1941.
[2] *Board of Governors, *Minutes*, 11 Sept. 1941; Ogilvie to Monckton, 21 Sept. 1941. The matter was discussed at the Policy Committee of the MoI on 11 and 25 Sept.
[3] *Gorham to Rendall, 1 Oct. 1941.
[4] *Wellington to J. B. Clark, 31 Oct. 1941.
[5] *Bamford to Beadle, 9 June 1941; Beadle to Bamford, 1 July 1941; Control Board, *Minutes*, 11, 18 June 1941. Ogilvie, Graves and Wellington met Campbell on 22 July. (Ibid., 23 July 1941.)
[6] *Graves to Maconachie, 4 Sept. 1941; Cablegram from Wellington, 4 Sept. 1941: 'a change in the N.A.R. appointment might be necessary', Control Board, *Minutes*, 23 April 1941; ibid., 1 Aug. 1941 for Wellington's appointment.
[7] *Internal Promulgation, 8 Sept. 1941.

the same in New York as in London.[1] Thereafter, also, Wellington and Gorham were to establish with great success the kind of relationship based on daily transatlantic telephone link-ups which characterized war-time communication at the highest levels. The circuit cost 28 shillings a minute, and it was clear at once from the delays whether Churchill was in or out of the country. According to Gorham, he (Gorham) and Wellington became 'a perfect telephone pair': 'we never said anything twice'.[2]

The BBC's team in the United States was strengthened also by the appointment in December 1941 of Salt, former head of the European Service, as Deputy Director to Wellington. The formal letter went to him on 5 December:[3] he sailed from Belfast on 27 December. By then, of course, the United States was at war. 'American differences of opinion have completely vanished,' WCBX broadcast optimistically on 8 December. 'The Japanese attack,' Dorothy Thompson, the well-known commentator, declared, 'is a part of the Axis war on the whole world.'[4] The title of the Bulletin of the Government Defence Agencies was changed at once from *Defence* to *Victory*.[5]

This was fine talk, yet by the spring of 1942 two points had become clear. First, the American entry into the war had not suddenly changed bad news into good news: it was followed, indeed, by a gloomy succession of new disasters which caused great uneasiness, particularly in Britain. Second, there was far less of an immediate reaction in Europe, positive or negative, to the American involvement than there had been to the entry into the war of the Russians. There was no pro-American counterpart to the cluster of pro-Russian Communist parties in Europe, and American propaganda to Europe remained relatively ineffective.[6] There was, of course, no American parallel to the grim Russian fight for their bare existence, although General MacArthur's unrelenting struggle in the Philippines soon won the same kind of acclaim.

---

[1] *Ogilvie to J. W. Elwood, Manager of the International Division of NBC, 19 Sept. 1941.   [2] Gorham, op. cit., p. 122.

[3] *J. M. Rose-Troup to Salt, 5 Dec. 1941.

[4] *BBC *Weekly Analysis of Foreign Broadcasts*, 16 Dec. 1941.

[5] *Ibid., 23 Dec. 1941.

[6] See J. de Launay, 'La guerre psychologique' in *Les Dossiers de la seconde guerre mondiale* (1964).

Both of these points were reflected in the pattern of broadcasting. Indeed, broadcasting itself became a factor in the sequence of events. Japan began by securing almost all her strategic objectives in the Far East, and during the first stages of her war her naval and military successes were so striking that radio propaganda was quite unnecessary. A high-ranking Japanese official might comment that 'radio is playing an amazing part in the Greater Eastern Asia war. It is serving as a bomb to crush the basic thought and ideas of enemy countries', but it was never a bomb upon which the Japanese had to depend.[1] At the same time, in face of the stunning Japanese successes in those Asian countries which had been governed by colonial regimes, broadcasting was a very inadequate weapon for the British to use.[2] The surrender of Hong Kong on Christmas Day 1941 to the Japanese and the fall of Singapore in February 1942 were blows which hurt, and since they were accompanied by and followed by disturbing German victories in Cyrenaica and by the escape of two German battle cruisers, the *Scharnhorst* and the *Gneisenau*,[3] through the Channel, they shook even Churchill's political position.

In the very month of February 1942, therefore, when Goebbels noted a 'great inner change' in Germany, the German fanfares could sound yet again. The loss of Singapore was compared and contrasted with Dunkirk: 'it is a mistake in this war,' Fritzsche exclaimed, 'for the British to point out that they often lose the early battles in war but win the last one.'[4] The eclipse of the British Empire was inevitable, part of an 'inexorable historical process'.[5]

Churchill had spent five weeks in the United States from 12 December onwards, and though on his return he won an overwhelming vote of confidence in the House of Commons on 29 January by 464 votes to 1, the sense of tension in the British political climate was not dispelled. Not everyone agreed with as much enthusiasm as Nicolson, himself more critical

---

[1] Quoted in Rolo, op. cit., p. 170.

[2] See R. Bruce Lockhart, *Comes the Reckoning* (1946), p. 146 for the first stunned reactions to the first successes.

[3] Nicolson wrote in his diary (loc. cit., p. 211) that he found people more distressed about the escape of the battle cruisers than by the loss of Singapore.

[4] *BBC Weekly Analysis of Foreign Broadcasts*, 17 Feb. 1942.

[5] *Ibid., 24 Feb. 1942.

than he had ever been before, that Churchill was 'the embodiment of the nation's will'.[1] Churchill's broadcast of 15 February
in which he talked of 'drawing from the heart of misfortune
the vital impulses of victory' was not a success,[2] and throughout
February 1942 Gallup pollsters recorded that only one person
in three expressed satisfaction with the composition of the
War Cabinet. The new man of the hour was Sir Stafford
Cripps, who had returned from Moscow on 23 January. The
fact that he had come from Russia, to which he had been sent
by Churchill in May 1940, seemed in itself the major recommendation. Yet Cripps had a message also: it was as bleak as
the weather, and he proclaimed it crisply in a BBC Postcript
on 8 February. Better organization and harder effort were
needed if the war was to be won. 'Had our efforts in production
been greater, we should not now be retreating in North Africa.'

Cripps's conclusion may not have been based on an accurate
assessment: similarly, his public reputation may not have
rested on an accurate assessment of what he had achieved in
Moscow. Nevertheless, his broadcast had a 'sensational' effect
and was said to have evoked a warmer response than Churchill
or Priestley at their best.[3] His appeal for austerity had similar
symbolic significance to the appeal of Churchill, although it was
couched in completely different language, struck completely
different notes, and attracted different sections of the population. When, as part of a Cabinet reshuffle, Cripps became
Leader of the House of Commons on 19 February, his appointment was widely welcomed: it seemed, indeed, to demonstrate
that the country was prepared for tougher action on the home
front than had so far been taken. The logic of long war and of
total war was being explicitly accepted at the very time that
Goebbels was dwelling on the same themes in his diary.
'Austerity regulations' were henceforth to be the order of the
day. As the tale of calamity continued on land and at sea,
there was a leftward trend in home politics. 'The process of

---

[1] H. Nicolson, *Diaries and Letters* (1967), p. 205, entry for 14 Jan. 1941.

[2] Ibid., p. 211. This also was the American view (*BBC *Weekly Analysis of
Foreign Broadcasts*, 24 Feb. 1942), although Collingwood of CBS stated that
'Churchill was still the pre-eminent leader; the country still wants him as Prime
Minister'.

[3] See E. Estorick, *Stafford Cripps* (1949), p. 293; Mass Observation Report,
No. 1166, Sir Stafford Cripps, 23 March 1942.

Bolshevizing England has taken on an almost official character,'
Deutschlandsender stated.[1] In such circumstances most Britons
continued to pay far more attention to Russia than to the
United States. The demand for the opening of a 'second front',
backed by Beaverbrook, grew in volume until it reached a
great climax at a London rally held in June 1942 to celebrate
the anniversary of the entry of Russia into the war. Cripps
was the main speaker, and as the Russian Ambassador left
the meeting with some of his Russian colleagues, one of them
said to him 'Almost like Moscow'.[2] Churchill himself had
publicly welcomed the second-front agitation as a sign of the
'militant, aggressive spirit of the British nation', and a 'Twenty
Year Pact' between Russia and Britain had been signed on
26 May.

Yet at this very time there was something of a reaction:
counter-currents sprang up. Inside the BBC itself Maconachie
had long been worried about 'the demand for nothing but
praise of the Russian way of life': during the summer of 1942
he reiterated what he had said earlier with increasing force.[3]
G. M. Young was among the outside critics who complained
that the BBC was in danger of devoting more attention to
Russia than to the Commonwealth.[4] George Orwell from the
opposite pole was accusing people who 'hated Russia like
poison' up to 22 June 1941 of now forgetting everything that had
happened before that date: 'is there no one who has both firm
opinions and a balanced outlook?'[5] Yet the official attitude
remained one of circumspect co-operation rather than of full
alliance, and Nicolson told Maconachie in June 1942 that
Bracken objected strongly to the idea of a BBC series on 'the
truth about Russia'. 'He says that if we once started on that
Maisky would send a band of dynamiters to blow up Broadcasting House.'[6]

---

[1] *BBC *Weekly Analysis of Foreign Broadcasts*, 24 Feb. 1942.

[2] I. Maisky, *Memoirs of a Soviet Ambassador* (1967), p. 299.

[3] *Notes of a meeting, 4 Dec. 1941; Maconachie to Nicolson, 2 June 1942.
The matter had been discussed at the Ministry of Information Policy Committee
as early as 4 Sept. 1941, when it was agreed that the easiest course was not to
attack Communism but positively to stress the merits of 'our own democratic
institutions'.   [4] See above, p. 392.

[5] S. Orwell and I. Angus (eds.), *The Collected Essays, Journalism and Letters of
George Orwell, Vol. II* (1968), p. 423.

[6] *Nicolson to Maconachie, 17 June 1942.

Although during this same period Anglo-American co-operation behind the scenes was quietly increasing in scope and through personal relationships gaining in intensity, there was little real opportunity for American propaganda either in Europe or in Britain. Likewise British 'propaganda' in the United States was proving difficult, even when the United States was at war, because of the system of commercial broad-casting and the multiplicity of companies. It had to depend upon live 'publicity and promotion', and for opposite reasons to those in the case of Russia, where everything depended on government, it was impossible to secure any 'general reciprocal arrangement of broadcasting facilities'. Stephen Fry, a son of the great cricketer C. B. Fry, was active in New York arranging re-broadcasts of BBC programmes by American stations, but Gorham failed on legal grounds to arrange for the broadcasting of BBC entertainment programmes by American stations in sponsored time.[1]

Economic and institutional factors were not the only problem. Stance and mood counted also. Gorham was discovering what the Americans would and would not take and catering for it deliberately, but the Americans were not always as sensitive to what the British would take. Very soon after Pearl Harbour it was decided in London that a broadcast talk recorded in New York by Dorothy Thompson, one of the best-known of American commentators, was 'unsuitable for a British audience on the grounds that it was "too optimistic and overconfident"'.[2] Phrases like 'Germany is in a desperate situation, externally and internally' were felt to be calculated to do far more harm than good. In general, American propaganda to Europe throughout the war was both too distant and yet too brash, too unsophisticated and yet too contrived to challenge the propaganda forces already at work on the Continent. Problems multiplied, indeed, as the volume of American broadcasting increased substantially in 1942.[3]

For all these reasons attempts to 'co-ordinate' British and American propaganda activities were bound to be difficult

[1] Gorham, op. cit., pp. 118, 127.
[2] *The talk was recorded on 24 Dec. 1941. Barnes recommended at once that it should not be broadcast (Note of 26 Dec.) and Maconachie concurred (Maconachie to Wellington, 6 Jan. 1942).
[3] See Rolo, op. cit., pp. 185 ff.

even after June 1942, when Donovan's office became a part of the newly created Office of War Information under the direction of Elmer Davis and Sherwood became Chief of Overseas Broadcasting, managing a group of old and new short-wave stations.[1] The sense of urgency was plain, as the Director-Generals put it in a solemn joint statement made in July, in which they talked of 'a parting of the ways'. 'It is a matter of common knowledge that deep misunderstandings exist on both sides of the Atlantic. It is also generally accepted that the removal of these misunderstandings is an essential preliminary to promoting a proper understanding. This clearly should be the permanent policy of the two countries and it is vital, if the combined war effort of the United States and Great Britain is to be completely effective, and if the peace that follows is to be one that really achieves the objectives of the Atlantic Charter.' To make such an understanding possible 'more can be done by a proper use of broadcasting than by any other means'. 'The BBC will be neglecting its duty if it does not tackle the problem in the broadest possible way.'[2]

Before turning to the later story, which was to prove as tangled as the earlier, it is necessary to examine more fully how institutional re-arrangements in Britain affected the position of the BBC as an international broadcasting agency and how its own sense of duty, something still independent of Government, not only survived, but was strengthened.

[1] Except to Latin America which was under the separate jurisdiction of the Co-ordinator of Inter-American Affairs.

[2] *Note for the Governors by Foot and Graves, 6 July 1942; a few weeks later plans were made for Newsome to visit Washington. (Cables between Foot and Graves, 25 and 26 Aug. 1942.)

V

TOTAL EFFORT

━━━━━

The war can be lost by people who will
not exert themselves; it will be won by
those who try hardest.

GOEBBELS, January 1943

1. Propaganda and Intelligence

THE first and most far-reaching British development during 1942, a year of further great changes in structure and procedures, was the reorganization of propaganda and Intelligence which followed from the creation and growth of the Political Warfare Executive. On 21 February 1942 Dalton moved from the Ministry of Economic Warfare to the Board of Trade. Handing over SOE 'twanged his heart strings'.[1] Thereafter, however, the operation of PWE became more straightforward, since the number of ministers responsible for it was reduced from three to two. There had been a number of 'futile, infuriating and time-wasting rows'[2] between Dalton, Eden and Bracken between June 1941 and February 1942, although at the official level relations between Bruce Lockhart, Leeper and General Brooks had steadily improved.[3] February 1942, therefore, marked the end of 'a thoroughly bad compromise'.[4] Under the new arrangement, Eden was made directly responsible for policy and Bracken for administration. At the same time Bruce Lockhart became Director-General of PWE.[5] The fortnightly meetings of the two committees of ministers and officials were abolished, and thereafter Bruce Lockhart answered directly to Eden and Bracken.

Most important of all, from the point of view of the BBC, Kirkpatrick was brought into the team.[6] At the end of February 1942, Bruce Lockhart and Brooks moved their London headquarters from Fitzmaurice Place and the Foreign

---

[1] H. Dalton, *The Fateful Years* (1957), p. 384. He was replaced by Lord Selborne who remained responsible for SOE but who took no responsibility for propaganda.

[2] Ibid., p. 382.

[3] Steps were taken to improve liaison. Brooks, for example, began to attend weekly meetings of the Ministry of Information's Executive Board in Nov. 1941 to report on the weekly activities of PWE. (*Ministry of Information Policy Committee, *Minutes*, 6 Nov. 1941.) It was decided that the Policy Committee should cease to meet after 12 Feb. 1942. It did, in fact, meet in March 1942.

[4] R. Bruce Lockhart, *Comes the Reckoning* (1947), pp. 117, 143.

[5] The announcements were made in the House of Commons on 25 March 1942 (*Hansard*, vol. 378, col. 1983). Bruce Lockhart's name was not given.

[6] *Bruce Lockhart to Powell, 13 Jan. 1942.

Office to Bush House, where they were placed, appropriately enough, on the floor above Kirkpatrick, Newsome and the members of the BBC's European Service. Kirkpatrick became a member of Bruce Lockhart's Executive Committee in March. 'The change to Bush House,' Bruce Lockhart wrote later, 'was like a journey from an old-world English home into a brand new skyscraper in a Middle West American township.'[1]

The skyscraper was crowded and cosmopolitan, but much more comfortable than it had been in 1941.[2] It accommodated not only the members of the BBC's European Service and the London sections of PWE, including central research workers and a 'broadcasting studies' group, but most of the old PID staff who had worked hitherto at Woburn, except for those engaged in secret Intelligence and 'black broadcasting' work.[3] Its layout encouraged improved liaison procedures, informal and formal. Kirkpatrick could talk informally to Bruce Lockhart, who was in touch with all the media of Intelligence, and equally informally with Newsome, who continued vigorously and enthusiastically to make his own propaganda, caring less for PWE than for winning the war in the way he thought most efficient and speedy—'through the weapons of responsible journalism and through the instruments of the clever advertiser'.[4] In the late autumn of 1941 Kirkpatrick had promoted him to the new post of Director of European Broadcasts. With Ritchie as his assistant and with W. R. Elston as European News Editor—Elston was to be replaced in July 1943 by Donald Edwards—he now enjoyed a position of exceptional strength. Kirkpatrick told Foot proudly in June 1942 that he had successfully changed the whole situation. When he arrived 'the News Editor could elect to shout white whilst the Programme officials could shout yellow'. He, Kirkpatrick, had ensured that 'the whole cumbrous and highly paid Programme staff appointed by Salt were eliminated'.[5]

[1] Bruce Lockhart, op. cit., p. 163.
[2] See above, p. 353.
[3] *Note of 10 Jan. 1942.
[4] *Note of 9 Dec. 1941.
[5] *Kirkpatrick to Foot, 25 June 1942.

Although formal policy, still often a matter of debate, was laid down at weekly meetings between PWE's regional directors, supported by regional information officers,[1] and representatives of the regional sections of the BBC, the BBC's European Service maintained a substantial degree of independence both of PWE and of Broadcasting House itself. There were five main reasons for this. First, and most important, PWE, apart from its work with the 'black' stations, did not broadcast directly itself. Whatever directives it issued needed to be implemented, therefore, by broadcasters who had their own language and their own techniques. Second, there were differences within PWE itself: it never proved an 'easy team',[2] and in Bruce Lockhart's frequent absences through illness there were often sharp divergences of viewpoint. Although the establishment of an important new post in August 1942, that of Director of Plans and Campaigns, taken over by Ritchie Calder, led to a marked improvement in the co-ordination of propaganda, overseas political warfare was never quite divorced from domestic political warfare.[3] Third, each of the different language sections of the BBC retained its own identity and its own ethos, and its relationships with PWE varied according to the experience and character of the individuals concerned; and it is certainly untrue to generalize that after February 1942 'PWE was able to effect the control of policy over the European broadcasts which was its by right'.[4] When the heads of BBC regional sections were unassertive—as in the Hungarian section, for example—PWE control was effective: in other cases, as in the Polish section, Gregory Macdonald, Polish Editor from 1942 onwards, had a substantial share in the preparation of PWE directives which were written by Moray Maclaren. Several of the heads and many of the members of the different foreign-language services of the BBC were too

[1] *'These,' it was envisaged, 'will be the chief channel through which the specific needs of a regional microphone are met.' (Note of 10 Jan. 1942.) Regional Intelligence units were to continue to operate in the country. They were to continue to propose 'target studies' and they were to continue to deal with 'black broadcasting'.

[2] Bruce Lockhart, op. cit., p. 155.

[3] There were other key appointments in 1942 and significant changes of organization in 1943. Leeper announced his departure in Jan. 1943. He later became British Ambassador in Athens. See below, p. 688.

[4] J. Bennett, *British Broadcasting and the Danish Resistance Movement* (1966), p. 20.

independent to follow a line determined elsewhere, sometimes by people whom they felt knew less about the facts of the situation: 'the Very Free French' had been a not inappropriate title of a Home Service programme in 1941.[1]

Fourth, the staple item in broadcasting to Europe was news— 'straightforward news good or bad, told simply but with a punch'[2]—and it was very difficult for PWE to control this key sector even if it wished to do so. Newsome's team of sub-editors, working around the clock at the Central Desk in Bush House, were in a strategic position to acquire and distribute what everyone else in Bush House needed—news. They alone had access to agency tape machines; they could use the British Press as a source in an uninhibited way that the BBC Home News service could not copy; they alone in Bush House had a direct link by tape with the BBC's Monitoring Service. The news material they prepared, including an account, revised several times each day, of the position on the Russian war fronts, was available in English for the regional editors of the BBC's different European services to use in the making up of their regional news bulletins in foreign languages. All these regional bulletins, when completed, had to be approved by the Central Desk. The Duty Editor in charge would frequently suggest changes, for example, in the order of items or in particular items included: only when he had stamped the script could the bulletin go on the air.

In the selection and presentation of news, therefore, PWE, which had its own 'news creation' department, had no part to play. The sole directives came from Newsome himself. His daily news conferences, held at 11 o'clock in the morning and at 5 o'clock in the afternoon, were attended by all regional editors as well as by Central Desk staff. The daily directives were prepared immediately after the morning conference. Leaving out of the reckoning the force of Newsome's person-ality, the independence of the BBC depended upon the speed of the daily news operation and on the sense of immediacy which everyone in Bush House, whether favourably or unfavourably disposed to Newsome, personally felt. It was a matter of pride to all BBC staff to get news on to the air in the

[1] *Home Board, *Minutes*, 11 July 1941.
[2] *Weekly Note, 31 March–6 April 1942.

briefest possible time after it had been collected by the Central Desk, and it was frequently the case that a news bulletin was interrupted while it was being read in order to thrust into the announcer's hand a translation of some item which had come over the tape machines only five minutes before. The sense of competition with the Germans or with other countries broadcasting news was always strong. PWE, the Foreign Office or the Ministry of Information—the Foreign Office was always the most difficult of the three—might protest after the event, even demand an inquest on what had happened. By then, however, it was too late. Nor were prohibitions for the future very effective. The role of the BBC in providing information for Europe's extensive clandestine press can scarcely be overestimated.[1]

It was Newsome's task as Director of European Broadcasts to maintain consistency and to ensure that BBC broadcasts to Europe followed a common policy reflecting their British origin. He was very unhappy about the thought of the BBC operating simply as a transmitting agency for groups of foreign nationals, whether or not they were acceptable to PWE. At the same time, there was an extremely difficult problem in maintaining the consistency of BBC News policy as a whole, in keeping Bush House and Broadcasting House in harness. In September 1942, for instance, Maconachie drew the attention of his colleagues to discrepancies in the interpretation of the military situation in Russia in European and Home output.[2] Different sources were being used for the news, yet it was clearly not an adequate reply to point to how difficult it was to keep in step when different departments of the fighting services did not always speak with the same voice.[3]

Newsome acquired in addition to his News team a small Central Talks staff which included a European Talks Editor,

---

[1] The first broadcast specifically designed for the clandestine press was on 12 July 1943.

[2] *There had been complaints from the Soviet Embassy in March 1942 about the reporting of the Russian military situation. They were carefully sifted (Graves to Bracken, 11 March, 3 April 1942), but part of the trouble lay in the Russian communiqués themselves (Graves to Bracken, 11 March 1942). For Maconachie's later worries about consistency, see below, pp. 489–90.

[3] *Programme Policy Committee, *Minutes*, 18 Sept. 1942. In this respect the Navy came out well compared with the Army and the Air Force.

Alan Bullock, Military, Naval and Air Correspondents—
General S. R. Wason, Brian Tunstall and Air Commodore
J. A. Chamier—and the European Productions Supervisor,
W. Gibson Parker. Tunstall's role was particularly important in
that most of the BBC's foreign-language sections were less
interested in the long and wearing war at sea than they were in
land operations on the Russian front. Newsome also insisted
that in addition to his strategically important news bulletins
in English, a separate English-language service, *London Calling
Europe*, should be operated directly under his control. He
broadcast frequently himself as 'The Man in the Street' and
also used the service to carry talks which he could not get
into the foreign-language service programmes. His Talks
Editor 'vetted' the scripts of all talks given in foreign languages
to make sure that they followed the Newsome directive: this
process produced friction inside the BBC, but once again it did
not depend on PWE initiatives.

The fifth reason for the BBC's effective 'independence' in its
European broadcasting was Kirkpatrick himself. To some
officials, at least in PWE, he seemed to have become 'more
BBC than the BBC'. He enjoyed his new responsibilities and
did not intend to see them eroded, particularly when very little
control over what he was doing was imposed from the old
and relatively distant BBC citadel in Broadcasting House.
Powell thought that his work with PWE would not 'leave him
free for the general administrative work of the Branch', yet
this was far from the case.[1] As far as PWE was concerned,
Kirkpatrick battled successfully in the first few months after
PWE was created to ensure that no PWE directive should be
given to any section of the BBC unless he or his deputy had
'passed' it. He and Grisewood insisted uncompromisingly
that the directives should not be out of character with the
BBC's reputation as an open broadcasting service, operating
without deception and free from political gerrymandering.[2]
On at least one occasion, also, Kirkpatrick withheld copies
of Newsome's directives from PWE.

As for the Ministry of Information, it probably played a

[1] *Powell to Bracken, 18 Sept. 1941.
[2] For an outsider's view of the conflict, see J. Baker White, *The Big Lie* (1955),
p. 65.

smaller role than had been anticipated. In August 1941 K. G. Grubb took the place of Sir Maurice Peterson as Controller of the Overseas Publicity Division, dealing with all parts of the world except the United States and the Empire. It was recognized from the outset, however, that his functions would have to be re-defined as PWE took shape,[1] and although Grubb set himself at once the task of investigating 'what at present are the aims and objectives of our propaganda in different countries and the resistances encountered in achieving them?', this was obviously a task for PWE once it established itself. A subsidiary question put to Grubb—'Is the relationship between the regional sections—or the foreign section as a whole—with such related bodies as the BBC satisfactory?'— raised the most fundamental questions of regionalism versus centralization, questions to which there was never and never could have been any fully satisfactory answer. A small working party was set up inside the Ministry to examine this and other questions concerning propaganda themes and priorities, but its work was overtaken as PWE developed its own routines.[2]

Vis-à-vis PWE, Kirkpatrick did not disband the Intelligence services of the BBC as was suggested in October 1941 by the small sub-committee headed by Sir Leonard Browett, who had been appointed by the Government to investigate 'over-lapping'.[3] Kirkpatrick also insisted with success that Browett's proposals to 'co-ordinate' all Intelligence through PWE should not entail the abolition of the BBC's own European Intelligence section, which had been set up earlier in the war as a by-product of the Monitoring Service.[4] Although there was some restriction in its output—'intake' reports ceased to be prepared

---

[1] Monckton to Bamford, 25 Aug. 1941 (Ministry of Information Papers). Radcliffe's appointment as Deputy Director-General was announced on 3 Sept. 1941. Radcliffe became Director-General in Dec. 1941, when Monckton moved to Cairo as Director-General of British Propaganda and Information Services. Bamford, formerly Controller (Administration) became Deputy Director-General on 5 Jan. 1942. This new top management survived, along with Bracken, until the end of the war, when the staff of the Ministry had risen to over 3,000.

[2] It was decided in March 1942 that there was no longer any need for a BBC Liaison Officer with PID. Until Feb. 1941 H. J. Dunkerley had served in this post which was later filled by Lindley Fraser. It was at Leeper's suggestion that the post was abolished.

[3] See above, p. 344.

[4] *See above, p. 278. The organization of the Intelligence section is set out in a paper of 8 Oct. 1941 by Griffin, its head.

after 1 November 1941—and although PWE made an effort to raid some members of its staff,[1] the BBC's Intelligence section survived. Kirkpatrick wrote impressive memoranda on the subject[2] and was fully backed by the Board of Governors.[3] They argued that efforts to implement the Browett Report by Walter Adams, the Secretary of PWE, were making the position worse than it had been and would cut off broadcasters from all adequate sources of Intelligence rather than add to their knowledge.[4] At the beginning of April 1942 Bruce Lockhart agreed that the European Intelligence section would remain a part of the European Service of the BBC,[5] and the Treasury, keen as it was to secure economies, reluctantly and provisionally concurred.[6] The one casualty of these often tense and acrimonious discussions—and they covered people as well as issues—was the BBC's Research Unit which had been set up with the highest hopes in April 1941. Its staff members were dispersed after months of uncertainty[7] in February 1942, and the unit was formally dissolved, after a brief but illustrious career, on 21 March 1942.[8] With the dissolution, the *Daily Synopsis*, the *Weekly Analysis* and the Research reports produced by the Unit came to an abrupt end.

The work of the Intelligence section was cut later during the war when it was felt desirable to concentrate more directly on 'working more to the individual requirements of Regional Editors'.[9] According to Griffin, relations with PWE were by

[1] *Conner, Acting Director of the Overseas Central Department, complained of this in a note to Clark on 5 Dec. 1941. On 30 March Griffin grumbled that a member of his staff had been approached so often by PWE that she 'felt like a lemon being squeezed' (Griffin to Kirkpatrick, 30 March 1942).

[2] *Memoranda of 23, 26 Jan. 1942; Kirkpatrick to Stephens, 31 Jan. 1942.

[3] *Board of Governors, *Minutes*, 26 Feb. 1942.

[4] *Kirkpatrick to Stephens, 31 Jan. 1942.

[5] *Sir Guy Williams to Dunkerley, 2 April 1942; Board of Governors, *Minutes*, 26 March 1942: 'The Intelligence Service would not now be taken over by PWE . . .' The members of the Board expressed 'their satisfaction with this arrangement'.

[6] *Notes on a meeting at the Treasury, 8 May 1942. The matter was raised again in 1943 (Woodburn to Beadle, 10 Feb. 1943).

[7] *They had written a memorandum to J. B. Clark expressing their concern on 4 Feb. 1942. See also Conner to Grisewood, 30 Jan. 1942.

[8] Denis Brogan moved to the North American Intelligence Unit and Edgar Lustgarten to the Empire Department. (*Schuster to Foot, Graves and others, 14 April 1942.)

[9] *Note by Grisewood and Dunkerley, 11 June 1943.

then 'good and are getting better pretty quickly'.[1] Nonetheless, the staff of the section was reduced from about seventy at the end of 1942 to fifty by the end of 1944 and both the range and circulation of its productions were reduced. Kirkpatrick continued to defend the section against persistent PWE criticisms.[2] 'The aim of audience research is not to dictate policy [that was the task of PWE], but to find out how broadcasts can best "put across" the policy given to them. . . . Why should not those who have to decide on the policy of broadcasts as well as those who carry out their decisions on the shape of broadcasts, want to know who will be listening and what he will accept?'[3]

Regional Intelligence work, concentrated in four units— Europe, the Empire, Latin America and the Near East— was an essential part of the pattern of operational broadcasting by the BBC's foreign-language sections. Each section, however, went its own way in many matters, dependent though it was on the Central Desk for the supply of news. It is extremely difficult to generalize about European broadcasting, therefore, almost as difficult as it is to generalize about conditions in the different countries to whom the sections were broadcasting. Each section had its own editor and its own staff, and each section was free within the limits already described to produce its own programmes and to arrange its own talks. In the two 'giants' among the sections—the French and the German— there was marked distaste for too much 'centralization'. Gillie, the head of the French section, was an outstanding personality, a man of great experience who was genuinely anxious to look at Europe through French as well as through British eyes. Carleton Greene, the head of the BBC's German section, was exceptionally clear-sighted about what could and could not be achieved: 'a beast—but a just beast', one member of his staff described him. Neither head quite saw things Newsome's way, nor did they see eye to eye with each other. Both men had on their staffs broadcasters of independent views and

[1] *Griffin to Kirkpatrick, 19 June 1943.
[2] *There were even criticisms from PWE (e.g. 28 June 1943) that some titbits of Intelligence were withheld in order to provide padding for the section's surveys.
[3] *Memorandum of 5 July 1943, unsigned.

forceful personality. There was, indeed, an interesting and creative interaction, potentially explosive. There were also quite distinct problems and strategies.

The freedom granted to the French section was greater than that allowed to the German section, and, given the unwillingness to use German refugees, there could be no German parallel to the superbly spontaneous *Les Français parlent aux Français*. The eleven programmes broadcast each day to Germany in the summer of 1941 were thought of as 'raids', not as 'a full-scale offensive', 'psychological and moral attrition, not political warfare'.[1] In the meantime, 'black broadcasting' to Germany was obviously considered more important in some official quarters than white broadcasting,[2] and Delmer, who was strongly supported inside PWE, made the most of the transmissions of *Gustav Siegfried Eins*, the black station which first went on the air on 23 May 1941.[3] The Russian war gave him an opportunity which he was clever enough to seize to the full through the exploitation of the character of *Der Chef*, a voluble German who shared most Nazi prejudices.[4] 'The war against Russia was the making of *Der Chef*.'[5]

Delmer was anxious and ready to exploit further broadcasting possibilities through the medium of 'Aspidistra', the huge 500-kilowatt medium-wave transmitter which had been purchased in America at the orders of the Ministry of Economic Warfare in 1941, unknown to the BBC, and which was transferred later in the year to PWE. This 'Dreadnought of the Ether', which fascinated Churchill far more than the BBC ever

---

[1] *BBC *Monthly Intelligence Report, Europe*, 17 Jan. 1942.

[2] See J. Baker White, *The Big Lie* (1955).

[3] See S. Delmer, *Black Boomerang* (1962), pp. 42 ff. Delmer, who could make the fullest use of German refugees, clearly preferred the skills of 'black broadcasting' to straight radio, disliked the BBC's 'stodgy' ways and would have liked to 'pep it up' in the 'sharp and vivid style of my side of Fleet Street' (see ibid., p. 78). There were other 'black' radio stations broadcasting to Germany, including a 'left-wing' station, *Sender der Europäischen Revolution*. The staffs of each station were wisely segregated from each other. *Gustav Siegfried Eins* went off the air in Oct. 1943 (ibid., p. 76).

[4] In 1942 an English listener had written to the BBC (*13 Jan. 1942) about picking up a broadcast from the station. 'As the "Chef", as he calls himself, attacks both the Soviet regime and the National Socialist Government with particularly venomous reference to the SS, I was puzzled as to where it could conceivably come from.' The letter would have pleased Delmer.

[5] Delmer, op. cit., p. 64.

did, was designed, once again against BBC and Ministry of Information policy, to drown the voices of the German medium-wave foreign-language broadcasts and to intrude into their frequencies. 'Aspidistra' did not come into service until 30 January 1943, and by then the BBC, once it knew of the purchase, had been able to stake its own claim for its partial use.[1] Delmer went ahead with his own independent plans, waiting for the right moment to act.[2]

The BBC's German Service was handicapped by the Government's unwillingness to seek to create or encourage a German 'resistance' or to hold out any definite hopes to the Germans in the future.[3] It began to function far more efficiently as a team, however, and with a far greater sense of enterprise, as a result of changes made during the course of 1941. Early in the year it had been decided that there should be a daily meeting, with Greene in the chair, at which the whole German output, news, news talks and features, would be reviewed.[4] It was decided also that a weekly meeting, attended by Crossman of PID, would be held to ensure that 'technical support' could 'keep pace with what is required from a policy point of view'.[5] It was after careful discussion at the daily meetings that it was decided in the summer of 1941 first to rely less on translation and more on original German composition and second that subbing both of news and talks was to be done in German.[6] More editors had to be appointed in consequence, a move strongly backed not only by Crossman but Kirkpatrick. Unless more staff were appointed and better accommodation secured, Crossman warned, German programmes would have

---

[1] *Board of Governors, *Minutes*, 5 Feb. 1942. [2] See below, p. 434.

[3] *See above, pp. 322–3. BBC European Department, *Monthly Intelligence Report, Europe*, 21 Jan. 1941. 'Until Britain is ready to issue peace aims and unless these offer the Germans some satisfactory inducement to throw Hitler overboard, British propaganda to Germany is at a fatal disadvantage.' When Germany invaded the Soviet Union, the BBC was given no direct guidance as to whether Churchill's phrase that 'any man or state who marches with Hitler is our foe' included in its scope anti-Nazi Germans. Bruce Lockhart replied so vaguely to this and other related questions that the German Planning Committee felt that there was 'adequate latitude for developing the lines of propaganda desired by the Committee' (*Minutes*, 19 July 1941).

[4] *Salt to Lindley Fraser, 1 Feb. 1941.

[5] *The first of these meetings was held on 5 Feb. 1941. The *Minutes* survive.

[6] *Note by Salt, setting out a proposal by Carleton Greene, 25 Aug. 1941, following a meeting on 7 Aug.

to be cut by 35 per cent. 'Why,' he asked, 'should not this country be able to organise itself as adequately as, for example, Russia, in the expansion of its broadcasting services?'[1] When the 'Hess story' had broken upon the world the German Editor had been away on leave, and since he had no deputy the bulletins in the morning and the early afternoon had had to be composed by one sub-editor.[2]

By the autumn of 1941 the position had been substantially improved. 'The German Service has lately been completely reorganised,' it could be announced in November. 'First, geographically: the News Editors, Talks Assistants, Translators, Features Section, Language Supervisors, etc., have all been brought together on the fourth floor, Bush House. Secondly, technically: a new system of preparing the News has been instituted by which the functions of a language supervisor and a sub-editor are merged. The stories are written in English and translated and are then checked with the translating shift-leader by the man who actually wrote the story and not by a third person. In this way it is possible to get the final German version to sound much less like a translation. Cutting and final editing are done on the German text and the editor is able to make quite certain that the translated news item conveys the exact meaning he wants. This system is only possible in a section where the news editors have the requisite language qualifications, and where the supervisors can write news stories.'[3]

The team Greene gathered together was a strong one. Leonard Miall dealt with German talks until he left to take up a new post in the United States in October 1942: imaginative and sensible, he introduced many new broadcasters to the microphone. Hubert Gregg and Stephen Haggard were accomplished actors; James Monahan was to be a future

---

[1] *German Planning Committee, *Minutes*, 16 July 1941.

[2] *Memorandum on 'Existing Conditions of German Broadcasting', 6 June 1941. The difficult problems of what to say or not to say on the Hess case were discussed in a paper by A. E. Barker, 1 July 1941. No talks in German had been given on the story on 12 May, and only one talk was broadcast on 13 May. Yet there were seven talks on the subject on 14 May and nine on 15 May. All in all, four hours of talks were broadcast between 12 May and 4 June. Neither Kris and Speier nor Bramsted refer to the somewhat cumbrous German handling of the affair.

[3] *BBC European Service, *Weekly Bulletin of the BBC Broadcasts to Europe*, 6 Nov. 1941.

Controller of the European Services. Lindley Fraser gained in experience and in authority as a commentator as the war went on. His wit and humour were of a kind that his German listeners could share; his mastery of the German language was obvious; his words were chosen carefully and his style was economical and direct. Above all, what he said was credible. He was as different from Haw-Haw in his approach and in his impact as any war-time broadcaster could have been. Germans certainly knew of him and remembered what he said. 'I have listened to BBC news since about September 1939,' an East German listener wrote to the BBC in 1968, 'and I still remember Lindley Fraser.'[1] Within the BBC's German section there were people who could judge Fraser's efforts and place them in perspective even at the time: outstanding among them was Carl Brinitzer, translator and announcer, who has recently told the story of the BBC's 'battle against Goebbels' for post-war Germans in his lively and informative book *Hier spricht London*.[2] There were many people, too, who were quick to exploit ideas and techniques. Martin Esslin, for example, who had joined the German section from the Monitoring Service early in 1941, developed the brilliant notion of recording Hitler's speeches and those of other Nazi leaders to save them for 'another day'.[3] The records were saved and studied so that when the tides of war turned, they could be used for programmes based on contrasts between 'then and now'. 'Whatever Goebbels may change with his blue pencil,' it could be stated, 'we have the words of Göring, Goebbels and Hitler in our record collection. And we shall see to it that the German people will hear them when the time comes.'[4]

Policies of restraint followed earlier during the war began to pay off. So too did the 'sober, confident tone' of the broadcasts[5] and the willingness, as at the time of the fall of Singapore,[6]

---

[1] *German Audience Research Report, 17 Dec. 1968.

[2] This book, published in Hamburg, gives an excellent account in ch. XII of Fraser and his influence; it has a foreword by Greene.

[3] Maurice Latey and David Graham had prepared for this possibility as early as Sept. 1939.

[4] *BBC Feature, 'Censored Reichsmarschall', 5 Feb. 1943.

[5] R. H. S. Crossman in D. Lerner, *Sykewar, Psychological Warfare Against Germany* (1949), p. 335. 'Exaggeration, excitement, threats and extravagance in all forms were avoided,' it was stated at a Press interview on 25 March 1942. 'It was a trap into which the Russians were inclined to fall.'   [6] See above, p. 409.

to admit defeats. By then an audience had been patiently built up. It could be vilified by Goebbels,[1] and as the war went on, increasingly savage penalties could be imposed for listening.[2] Yet it grew in numbers rather than declined. The listeners, regular or spasmodic, were attracted 'by the sincere voices, the calmness of the speakers, the straight-forward matter-of-fact tone of the commentaries which made such an enormous contrast to the hectic shouting and neurotic heroism of the Nazi broadcasts'.[3] Truthful news, along with the 'Kommentare zur Lage', particularly about the situation on the Russian front, were most in demand.[4] The audience was thought to cover a rough cross section of the German people rather than to be concentrated in particular groups. In mid and late 1942 and in early 1943 it was thought to reach its peak between 8 o'clock in the evening and midnight.[5]

The pattern of BBC German programmes in 1942 provided considerable variety of fare:

The Daily Schedule of the German Broadcasts	
GMT	
0400–0500	Workers' Programme
0900–0915	News
1200–1230	Miscellaneous
1300–1315	Miscellaneous
1400–1415	*Aus der Freien Welt*
1600–1615	Forces' Programme
1745–1800	Seamen's Programme
1800–1830	News and Commentary
2000–2020	News and Talks
2100–2115	Austrian Programme[6]
0000–0015	News

[1] See Brinitzer, op. cit., p. 171, for three categories of listeners as identified by Goebbels.

[2] G. Reitlinger, *The SS, Alibi of a Nation* (1956), pp. 251–2. Himmler admitted that 'we have forbidden listening-in to enemy stations, but we have not been able to punish all who have listened'.

[3] *Contribution by H. Wiedermann to the 21st Anniversary Programme of the German Service, Oct. 1959.

[4] *BBC *Bi-monthly Surveys of European Audiences, Enemy Countries*, 11 May 1942.

[5] *Ibid., 20 Jan. 1943.

[6] The Austrian Programme was not very successful, at least in its early separate stages, and badly needed an Austrian Editor (*Stephens to Kirkpatrick, 5 Feb. 1942).

Of these, the early morning Workers' programmes, arranged by Patrick Gordon Walker, undoubtedly had an audience. The programmes for the German Forces were more contentious.[1] They were listened to chiefly after the first British successes in the North African campaign, when details were broadcast concerning German prisoners of war: indeed, German prisoners of war often took part, in fifteen-minute programmes of talks and features, largely political, which had the blessing of PWE. Special programmes were also planned for German seamen (on the opening night the chief announcer, who came from Hamburg, must have somewhat startled his audience, not to speak of BBC officials, with his opening words, 'Hier ist Hamburg') and, in late 1942, for German airmen. The second of these series of programmes was said to have a 'definite aim'—'to undermine the morale of the German air force'—and an effective 'bait'—the speedy announcement of the names of dead and captured airmen and of the circumstances in which their planes had been brought down.[2] The Austrian Service ran into difficulties of its own. Kirkpatrick thought that 'the nostalgic strain was somewhat overcharged',[3] while others believed it was 'so vulgar as to be incomprehensible to all except Viennese cab drivers'.[4] There was a marked change for the better when Patrick Smith became its editor in August 1942.

In the changing circumstances of 1942, when Goebbels was being forced to introduce a new light entertainment programme as an alternative to the German Home Service,[5]

---

[1] *Overseas Board, *Minutes*, 13 Feb. 1941, refer to Duff Cooper complaining of 'vulgarity' in the German Forces Programme. There were other complaints that there was too much ranting in the programme and that it had something of the style of Workers' Challenge (German Planning Committee, *Minutes*, 29 Jan. 1941). The Forces Programmes at that time were under the general direction of Aylmer Vallance (War Office), Donald McLachlan (Admiralty) and Clifford Troke (Air Ministry).

[2] *BBC European Services, *Output Report*, 6–12 Dec. 1942.

[3] *German Planning Committee, *Minutes*, 18th June, 1941.

[4] *BBC *Monthly Surveys of European Audiences, Enemy Countries*, 28 Aug. 1941. In contrast to the German Service, it accepted talks from the Central Talks Unit.

[5] *BBC European Department, *Weekly Analysis of Foreign Broadcasts, Europe*, 3 March 1942; *Völkischer Beobachter*, 28 Feb. 1942. See also above, p. 18. Goebbels said that Forces listeners had to come first. Dance music was necessary because 'this type of music is liked by workers and soldiers'. Those 'prudes who have objected to coarseness . . . cannot be considered, because that is soldiers' language, and soldiers must come first'.

perhaps one of the most effective BBC programmes put out was the afternoon *Aus der Freien Welt* which carried hot jazz and swing, forbidden in Germany. It consisted at first of gramophone record programmes introduced by Spike Hughes, interspersed with news and short talks, written by James Monahan; later, 'live' dance bands were presented, and Sefton Delmer was one of the commentators. Radio Luxembourg was the model rather than the BBC Home Service, and Mischa Spoliansky, a composer of light music in Berlin during the 1920s, wrote songs with political words which were played by Geraldo, Victor Sylvester and other dance orchestras. Some of the songs were sung by Lucie Mannheim, the wife of Marius Goring, who had originally broadcast in the Armed Forces programme and was brought into the series as young 'Sergeant Richardson', along with Hans Buxbaum, a producer from the Municipal Theatre in Bochum. In the arrangement of such 'features' Walter Rilla, the former film producer who had directed Elizabeth Bergner, found ample scope for his talents, although he was replaced as head of features by Goring in the autumn of 1941.

Kurt and Willi was one of the most popular features: the dialogue, written in Berlin dialect, was slick and clever, and the idea behind the programme still persisted in the 1960s in the German Service programme, *Zwei Genossen*. Another popular programme, *Der Gefreite Hirnschal*, based on *The Good Soldier Schweik*, was written by yet another distinguished member of the BBC team, Robert Lucas (Ehrenzweig), and was played by Fritz Schrecke. When it was published in book form in Switzerland after the war, it proved a best seller,[1] and was subsequently translated into other languages. When also after the war the distinguished German film producer Wolfgang Staudte produced a film on life in war-time Germany he had a scene showing a typical German family listening to Hirnschal on the BBC. The programme is said to have been one of the war-time favourites of Dr. Adenauer.

News and talks programmes remained of the utmost importance, and the BBC was most anxious that the effects of German jamming on these programmes should be carefully investigated.

[1] R. Lucas, *Teure Amalia, vielgeliebtes Weib! Die Briefe des Gefreiten Hirnschal an seine Frau in Zwieselsdorf* (Zürich, 1946).

With this object in view, Greene was sent to Stockholm in August and September 1942 to report fully on the position. He found to his satisfaction that even intense jamming did not render BBC transmissions inaudible when the speakers were clear and did not try to speak too fast and when presentation was simple and straightforward. As a result of this important visit, the more elaborate feature programmes in the BBC's German Service were eliminated. News and talks were simplified in style and the number of words per minute reduced; speakers with deep resonant voices were selected rather than those with voices of higher pitch; and two announcers were employed alternately in the reading of news bulletins to maintain the listeners' attention and to counteract the tiredness induced in even the most attentive listeners by regular jamming.

While the BBC was exploring as carefully as it could the technical and the psychological aspects of its work in relation to Germany and making what use it could of such special sources of information as the intercepted *Hellschreiber* service, which included a teleprinter version of the weekly article by Goebbels for the periodical *Das Reich*, the 'black' broadcasters continued also with their activities. They were sometimes able, for example, to use the intercepted material to pre-release news of awards made to German soldiers, sailors and airmen before their recipients were aware that they had been conferred. Delmer's general policy was directly opposed to that of the BBC. 'Never lie by accident, only deliberately' was the motto of the 'black' broadcasters. Delmer also maintained that heavy jamming might encourage rather than discourage listening. On 5 February 1943, after prolonged rehearsals, he launched a new 'black' enterprise, *Deutscher Kurzwellensender Atlantik*.[1] He had been backed by a brilliant, supremely loyal, motley band of writers and broadcasters: they included Karl Robson of the *News Chronicle*, seconded from the War Office, Clifton Child, a young education officer from Manchester, C. E. ('Tom Brown') Stevens, the most ingenious of Oxford Ancient History dons, and a team of Germans. The political idiom of the new station was that of Goebbels himself. The news was designed to subvert: the entertainment to titillate. Goebbels

---

[1] The story is well told in Delmer, op. cit., *passim*.

himself conceded that the station did 'a very clever job of propaganda'.[1] The station was eventually displaced—and it was one of Delmer's triumphs—by *Soldatensender Calais*, broadcasting on a medium wave with the help of 'Aspidistra', and competing not only with the German radio but with the BBC. It was the BBC, indeed, which concluded that 'by its mere existence *Soldatensender Calais* is damaging our reputation'.[2] Looking backwards, Greene has written that 'the programmes of *Soldatensender Calais* were so funny that I have sometimes wondered whether they did not raise rather than depress morale'.[3]

Relations between Delmer and Greene were so strained in late 1942 and 1943 that Richard Crossman has claimed that 'feuding' led him to leave PWE and take refuge in Eisenhower's headquarters first at Algiers and then in SHAEF.[4] In retrospect, it is perhaps most sensible, if unsensational, to draw the conclusion that both 'black' and 'white' broadcasting had their part to play in the war just as both 'regionalization' and 'centralization' were necessary within the BBC's own European Services. There was even to be a place for 'grey' broadcasting as *Soldatensender Calais* widened its appeal. Such a conclusion, however, must be extended. If the BBC had tried to behave in any other way than it did in 1942 and 1943, it would have contradicted everything which PWE asked it to do. More seriously, it would have broken faith with itself and the objects for which it stood. In consequence, it would have found it difficult, if not impossible, to play a constructive part in the post-war world. Imitating Goebbels, outdoing him, might have its place in 1942 and 1943 within the context of war and in relation to the enemy: in the long run, it was corrupting and in conflict with everything implied in the term 'responsible broadcasting'.

There was 'black' broadcasting not only to Germany but to Italy, to France and to other European countries. Evidence about its impact is just as difficult to collect as evidence in the case of Germany. There was obviously more room to manœuvre

---

[1] *The Goebbels Diaries* (1948), p. 439, entry for 28 Nov. 1943.
[2] *European Divisional Meeting, Minutes*, 30 May 1944.
[3] Lecture on 'Psychological Warfare' delivered at NATO Defence College, 9 Sept. 1959.
[4] *New Statesman*, 9 Nov. 1962.

in broadcasting to Italy, 'black' or 'white', however, than in broadcasting to Germany, since an explicit distinction was always drawn between the Fascist leadership and the Italian people: 'Fascism,' it was argued, 'does not hang as naturally on Italian shoulders as Nazism hangs on German shoulders.'[1] Mussolini was separated out as a special, personal target. Differences between the Italians and the Germans, never far from the surface, provided one of the main themes which could be exploited by 'black' radio:[2] 'white' radio, *Radio Londra*, also allowed scope for programmes introducing this subject. Even before Montgomery's victory in the desert war at El Alamein in October 1942, when 30,000 prisoners, mostly Italian, were taken, there was ample material to work with in the news itself, for the Italians seldom had much to rejoice about. On the home front, despite price and wage controls, there was severe inflation, and black markets flourished in the midst of a bureaucratic rationing system.[3] It is not surprising, therefore, that scepticism about Italian radio propaganda was strongest in Italy itself or that large numbers of people risked arrest to listen to the heavily jammed BBC broadcasts.[4] Churchill thought of Italy as the 'soft underbelly' of the Axis crocodile, and this appraisal influenced broadcasting tactics.

Despite some difficulties in recruiting full-time Italian personnel,[5] Italian exiles took a more prominent part in broadcasting from London to Italy than that allowed to German exiles (with the exception of Thomas Mann). PID and later SOE employed

---

[1] *Note to Kirkpatrick, 3 Oct. 1941.

[2] For some of the differences, see E. Wiskemann, *The Rome-Berlin Axis* (1949); E. Anchier, 'Les Rapports Italo-allemands' in *Revue d'histoire de la Deuxième Guerre Mondiale*, vol. 26 (1957).

[3] See R. G. Massock, *Italy from Within* (1943).

[4] C. F. Delzell, *Mussolini's Enemies: the Italian Anti-Fascist Resistance* (1961), p. 184. By Feb. 1942 penalties for listening to enemy stations had been increased to imprisonment for six months to three years and fines of between 4,000 and 40,000 lire. The system of control was fortunately inefficient. (L. Salvatorelli and G. Mira, *Storia del Fascismo* (1952), p. 912.) Jamming was bad enough, however, for many Italians to try to pick up the British Home Service. There was also widespread scepticism about any kind of propaganda, foreign as well as Italian.

[5] *In Feb. 1942 Sir Guy Williams, Overseas Establishment Officer, made an effort to recruit Italians from the Pioneer Company at Maidenhead. This led to correspondence with the Deputy Adjutant-General, but it was not until later in the war that a few of them could be used.

Max Salvadori, who had dual Anglo-Italian citizenship, and from the end of 1942 Ruggero Orlando;[1] the BBC encouraged Paolo Treves, son of Claudio Treves, the former Socialist leader who died in exile in 1933, and his broadcast scripts were published in Italy soon after the end of the war.[2] Umberto Calosso was also a regular broadcaster. During the final stages of the British-Italian war, indeed, London became something of an Italian 'resistance' centre.[3] It was not always easy to co-ordinate 'resistance' in London with clandestine movements in Italy, but Salvadori himself attaches most importance in retrospect to the British contribution to the Italian resistance story, with that of the Americans coming second.[4]

The star English broadcaster was still Colonel Stevens, and by September 1942 his broadcasts, along with the commentaries of 'Candidus' (John Marus), were so popular that the Italian radio broadcast a satirical commentary by 'Mr. X' at the same time. Stevens, of course, was a 'voice', and the author of his scripts, admirably suited to Stevens' style of delivery at the microphone, was Aldo Cassuto from Trieste. Like Stevens, he had strong Conservative views and was deeply suspicious of the Left, Italian or otherwise. Marus, born in London of Italian parents but educated in Italy where he lived most of his life and went to goal before 1939 for anti-Fascist activities, was bitter, sarcastic and biting. Strongly anti-monarchist in his views, he insisted that the whole system of Fascism had to be destroyed, along with its philosophy, if Italy were to have any future. While Stevens became known for his benevolence, therefore, as much as for his cleverness, Marus attracted the support of those Italians who put their faith in democracy. Not surprisingly, as the war proceeded, the broadcasts by 'Candidus' gained in political importance while those of Stevens diminished. Nonetheless, Stevens retained his personal

---

[1] See M. Salvadori, *Resistenza ed Azione* (1946).

[2] P. Treves, *Sul Fronte e Dietro il Fronte Italiano* (1945). Elio Nissim also gave popular talks under the title 'L'Omo Qualunque'.

[3] See Pentad, *The Re-making of Italy* (1941). Four periods of broadcasting time each week were granted to the Free Italy movement, which was backed by Ivor Thomas, a Labour M.P. who was associated with PID.

[4] M. Salvadori, 'Gli Alleati e la Resistenza Italiana' in *Fascismo e antifascismo, ezioni e testimonianze* (Milan, 1962). This article includes a brief assessment of the role of SOE.

following throughout and remained something of a legend. An Englishman talking to an Italian friend in the town of Ascoli in 1942 was interrupted by the Italian saying 'see those people rushing home: they don't want to miss the Colonel'.[1] When at last British forces invaded Sicily in 1943 some of them were puzzled to read chalk inscriptions on walls 'Viva il Colonnello Stevens'.[2]

Efforts were made to appeal from London to particular Italian audiences. 'Black' radio made the most of differences between Catholics, Radicals and Socialists, but 'white' radio always rejected the idea of a specifically Roman Catholic programme.[3] Talks to Italian workers were started only in 1943 and news bulletins for the clandestine press only in May 1944. An Italian Forces programme had been launched in the spring of 1941, however, at the request of the Ministry of Information. The main thirty-minute Italian programme, organized by F. L. M. Shepley, was called *La Voce di Londra*. It began early in 1941, at first directed by G. R. Foa, who later became producer. It included 'Axis Conversation', written by Shepley, a scripted dialogue between a German industrialist with official business in Italy and his Italian counterpart (George Weidenfeld played the part of the German with outstanding, if at first unsuspected, skill as a comedy actor); *Sottovoce*, a fictional conversation, supposedly in Italy, between three Italians—a 'reasonable' Fascist, an extreme anti-Fascist (Paolo Treves took this part), and a moderate anti-Fascist, played by Shepley; *Politica in Pantofole*, a discussion between two Italians, an uncle and his nephew, the latter an employee of the Ministry of Propaganda; *Osteria del Buon' Umore*, light-hearted dialect discussions on politics, intermingled with light music; commentaries by Livio Zeno, the 'Osservatore Londinese'; and a serialization of Silone's *Fontamara*.

'Axis Conversation' and *Sottovoce* were the two main regular programmes, running week by week until the Italian collapse. They made good use of information collected from the Italian Press, and were at their liveliest when they revealed the

---

[1] *BBC European Intelligence Papers, *Surveys of European Audiences, Italy*, 20 Jan. 1943.

[2] I. Kirkpatrick, *Mussolini, Study of a Demagogue* (1964), p. 508.

[3] *European Divisional Meeting, *Minutes*, 26 May 1942; Memorandum by Kirkpatrick, who was a Roman Catholic, 21 May 1942.

insensitivities of the Germans. In 'Axis Conversation', for example, the Italian businessman, unable because of his position to stand up openly to the German, frequently scored off him by innuendo and ridicule, with the German failing to understand just what was happening. *La Voce di Londra* programme had composite signature tunes written by Spoliansky, based on Garibaldi and Mameli hymns, with an undercurrent of 'Tipperary'. Musical parodies were also an element in the programmes, particularly in the *Osteria del Buon' Umore*, but there was less use of slogans than there was in the French Service, and the 'features', while effective with their audience, were less interesting in terms of radio technique and intellectual content than the parallel French programmes.

The head of the Italian section, C. F. Whittall, who succeeded Sprigge in January 1941,[1] had made his way to Bush House via Reuters (he was correspondent in Rome from 1932 to 1938), Woburn and the Ministry of Information. The Ministry was nominally responsible for broadcasts to Italy even after the entry of Italy into the war, but both between 1940 and 1941 and during the period after PWE had taken over, the section retained a very free hand in formulating its policy. There were a few cases of disagreement with PWE, but both Kirkpatrick and Grisewood were stalwart supporters of a relatively independent line. Newsome also was keenly interested in the Service, and wrote interesting memoranda to PID in February and March 1943 during the critical period when the Tunisian campaign was drawing to a close and the desert war in North Africa was ending. He set out, as in his broadcasts to other parts of Europe, to sketch 'a new European order'. He also made a vigorous 'appeal to youth'. 'We should show the Italians that we aim at a world in which men will be proud to think of themselves not only as good Englishmen or Italians but as good Europeans.' There should be no 'sneering' in the BBC's Italian programmes, only a sense of hopefulness.[2]

There were, of course, enormous changes in the military and political situation which influenced the whole patterning

[1] See above, p. 273. Eden himself took an interest in the Italian section, and wrote to Ogilvie about the need 'to intensify propaganda to Italy' early in 1941 (*Letters of 12, 30 Jan. 1941).

[2] *Note on the 'Italian Psychological Crisis', 7 Feb. 1943; General Directive, 31 March 1943.

of programmes to Italy. The German war was to be protracted and resistance was to continue to the end. For Italy, however, the turning point of the war was November 1942, when Eisenhower's forces landed in Morocco and Algeria and began their eastward push to meet Montgomery's Eighth Army which had already broken through Axis defences at El Alamein.[1] 'Henceforward,' as Mussolini himself put it, 'the strategic initiative passed to the Allies and in Italy every enemy of Fascism promptly reared his head.'[2] The Allied invasion of Sicily followed on 10 July 1943 and Mussolini's fall on 25 July.

Yet the royal-military regime, presided over by the seventy-four-year-old King Victor Emmanuel III and the seventy-two-year-old Marshal Badoglio, confronted both the Italians and the Allies, not to speak of the Germans, with more difficult political problems than they had hitherto faced. The war continued—in Badoglio's phrase—until an armistice was announced on 8 September, and during the interlude, and for several days afterwards, there were sharp differences of opinion as to what to say in broadcasts, with Churchill and Roosevelt themselves intervening from afar.[3] Crossman, who had moved to Eisenhower's GHQ in Algiers—he was the new Director of Political Warfare to the Enemy and Satellites—has written memorably of the day on which Mussolini fell. 'It was one of the great psychological opportunities of the War. . . . We waited for three days and three nights while London and Washington disputed about what should be done. They could reach no agreement on the attitude to be adopted

---

[1] At the request of Crossman and Ritchie Calder, Lindley Fraser was sent to Tunisia for the last stages of the campaign to broadcast in German (*European Divisional Meeting, *Minutes*, 16, 30 March 1943). No BBC representatives were present at the fall of Tunis. Later A. H. Rasmussen was appointed Mediterranean Naval Correspondent.

[2] B. Mussolini, *Memoirs, 1942–3* (1944), p. 3. PWE issued a general directive on 21 March 1943 emphasizing the need to explain to the Italians that a continuation of the struggle would merely prolong a war which was already lost, that the Italians should get out of it, and that it would not be dishonourable but in their interests to do so.

[3] The American Office of War Information broadcast a message on 26 July referring to the 'moronic little King' and to Badoglio as 'the high-ranking fascist' (*New York Times*, 28 July 1943) which, along with a later broadcast promising the immediate return of prisoners of war if Italy surrendered, infuriated Churchill and Roosevelt. See R. E. Sherwood, *Roosevelt and Hopkins* (1948), p. 744; W. S. Churchill, *The Second World War*, vol. V, pp. 55–9; Delzell, op. cit., ch. VI.

towards Italy. After three days and nights we British and Americans in Algiers got fed up waiting for a directive from home. Within a few hours we had worked out a common policy, and when that was cabled back to Washington and London it was accepted by the State Department and the Foreign Office because they were unable to reach agreement themselves. Throughout the War it tended to become a fact that the integrated Anglo-American team under General Eisenhower formulated Anglo-American directives. . . . The mere fact of putting men together in a single headquarters was a major factor in achieving a common solution to psychological warfare problems.'[1]

It was certainly a fact, in other parts of Europe as well as Italy, that once the war entered its last phases, propaganda on the spot was to prove more relevant to operational needs than distant propaganda; and by the end of 1944 integrated staffs overseas had chains of wireless stations under their control. The Italian political situation was sufficiently complicated to involve the Allied controllers of the local stations—the captured Bari station, for example—in many intrigues and adventures. There were enough active political groups in Italy, some of them emerging for the first time, for there to be arguments passing backwards and forwards between London and 'the front'. The situation became even more complicated after Mussolini's escape, engineered by German paratroopers on 12 September, the division of Italy into two, the growth of an aggressive, widespread partisan movement, *resistenza armata*, and the deposition of Victor Emmanuel and Badoglio in the spring of 1944. The BBC played little part in the mobilization of this resistance[2]—this, indeed, was not its role—although the British Ambassador noted 'the almost universal listening on the part of all classes of Italians in the months which

---

[1] R. H. S. Crossman, 'Psychological Warfare' in the *Journal of the Royal United Service Institution*, vol. XCVIII (Aug. 1953).

[2] There has been ample discussion in Italy of whether or not, or to what extent, the Italian resistance was 'spontaneous'. Studies have also been made of its size and age and occupational composition. See *inter alia* M. Salvadori-Paleotti, 'The Patriot Movement in Italy' in *Foreign Affairs*, vol. XXIV (1946). There is a summary of the role of SOE and OSS in Delzell, op. cit., pp. 306–14. Churchill's support of the monarchy was an obstacle, though not an insuperable one, to effective influence. For the relations of a British liaison officer with a Communist brigade, see H. W. Tilman, *When Men and Mountains Meet* (1946).

preceded liberation' and the ability of London broadcasters 'to reach classes which had always been beyond the influence of other media of British penetration'.[1] Likewise, Benedetto Croce in a widely noted speech of September 1944 used the fact that during the last stages of fighting Italians had listened eagerly to 'the British radio' to hear of their own defeats as an argument for treating Italy as an ally: 'the greatest and bitterest battle the Italians had to face was in their own hearts, when they had to . . . desire and hasten the defeat of Italy . . . which alone could bring them the victory of restored independence and liberty'.

Although coded messages were sent to Italian partisans and the work of the BBC in spreading information and accurate news has its place in most novels and films about Italian partisans (from Beppe Fenoglio's *Il Partigiano Johnny* and Gordon Lett's *Rossano* to *Paisà* and *Roma, Città Aperta*), the strength of the BBC's Italian Service was, in fact, curtailed in 1944, when there was a significant shift in emphasis, to be noted later in other parts of Europe, from propaganda towards 'projection of Britain and discussion of general ideas'.[2] English lessons were also being broadcast. Meanwhile there were complaints from the British generals who were still having to fight the Germans through Italy long after the Italian collapse that listeners in England were hearing too much about the new fighting in Normandy and too little about Italy.[3]

In the story of the French section of the BBC, the most remarkable of all the stories, some of the most important dates were the same as those in the Italian story, particularly the American landings in North Africa in November 1942. Yet while these landings assisted propaganda to Italy—they were, indeed, the prelude to the invasion of Italy and to the Italian collapse—they produced a serious *crise de conscience* in relation to France, a crisis which had widespread repercussions, not least inside Bush House. To understand the BBC's place in the development of a French resistance movement, it is necessary to take account of the special place in it of de Gaulle

[1] *Report of an interview between Shepley and Sir Noel Charles, Oct. 1944.
[2] *Whittall to Clark, 3 Nov. 1944; Bruce Lockhart to Charles, 2 Dec. 1944.
[3] *See above, p. 42; Lord Burnham to Haley, July 1944.

—Italy, of course, had no de Gaulle—and of the very early
development of resistance organization and techniques in
France, some of which were borrowed later by the Italians.
It is necessary also to note the role of SOE, which encouraged
specific acts of sabotage and subversion, but sought to restrain
resistance groups from indulging in activities 'which would lead
to their premature destruction'. If the V campaign had been
pushed much further, it might have done this.[1] As it was, SOE
policy was to try to persuade groups, ideologically united or
divergent, 'to organise a common front, and secretly to build
up a disciplined force whose operations could be connected
at a later stage directly with those of the Allies'.[2]

By the end of 1941 the BBC's French section had established
itself so successfully that its operations completely overshadowed
those of the 'black' stations, *Radio Inconnu, Radio Gaulle, France
Catholique* and *Radio Travail*,[3] all of which posed as genuine
'freedom' stations. When André Diethelm arrived in London
from Paris in the late summer of 1941—he was later to become
de Gaulle's Commissioner for the Interior—he commented
that almost the whole of France looked to the BBC for news and
guidance.[4] Frenchmen in France continued to draw no
distinction between Free France and the BBC's *équipe*, an
équipe which had grown in size and strength with the arrivals,
among others, of Geneviève Brissot, a friend of Oberlé, Frank
Bauer, Roger Chevrier, Paul Bonifas, Louis Rochet, Jean-
Pierre Granville, Paul Bouchon, Jean Vacher-Desvernais,
Jean Pecheral and Pierre Dac.[5] In the meantime, only one
member of the original team had left—Jean Marin, who
joined the Free French navy in 1943.[6] The standard of broadcasting remained remarkably high. Ian Black, who became
French Talks Organizer in March 1941, was a powerful and
resourceful new recruit, and Darsie Gillie, whose work came

---

[1] See above, pp. 376–84. De Gaulle himself was most anxious, in the face of
Communist pressures, not to encourage premature sabotage.

[2] See J. Ehrman, *Grand Strategy, Vol. V, August 1943–September 1944* (1956),
pp. 77 ff.

[3] See J. L. Crémieux-Brilhac, 'Les émissions françaises à la BBC pendant la
guerre' in *Revue d'histoire de la Deuxième Guerre Mondiale*, vol. 1 (1950).

[4] Ibid. See also P. Novick, *The Resistance versus Vichy* (1968).

[5] Dac, a well-known comic actor, reached Britain in 1943 after having been in
prison for a year.

[6] *Board of Governors, *Minutes*, 18 June 1942.

to be greatly appreciated first by Duff Cooper[1] and then by Bracken, was just as successful in establishing a large measure of independence vis-à-vis both PWE and Newsome as he had been vis-à-vis the Ministry of Information. 'Whatever directives are issued must in the main be put over by Frenchmen, and by intelligent Frenchmen,' Russell Page had pointed out in the autumn of 1940, 'and they will not do anything without thrashing out every detail first.'[2] When the Ministry insisted that its directives should be circulated to members of the *équipe* in May 1941—'with almost disastrous results', according to Salt—Monckton defended Duchesne and his colleagues.[3] The general view in the French section was that the directives were both vague and contradictory.[4] 'Directives of the French Service,' Salt wrote again a month later, 'come from both the Ministry of Information and the Foreign Office, but these are sometimes diametrically opposed.'[5] When PWE was formed, however, there was sufficient mutual trust, even admiration, for the French section to operate with vigour and drive. The Regional Directors with whom the BBC had to deal—in turn, Colonels Sutton, Gielgud and Fairlie—were sympathetic, and at the weekly meetings between BBC and PWE, which took the place of the old weekly meetings at the Ministry where Oliver Harvey had usually taken the chair, the draft PWE directives prepared before the meetings were often substantially revised.

Relations with Newsome were less smooth. Gillie was not only determined not to be 'centralized', but he also took strong exception to the establishment in October 1943 of a service in French, on the lines of the European Service in

[1] *In a conversation with Duff Cooper on 8 Oct. 1940 Ogilvie had told Duff Cooper that Gillie was a key man 'if the objectives which he and we had at heart were to be achieved'. Duff Cooper visited the French section early in 1941. (*Overseas Board, *Minutes*, 16 Jan. 1941.) In Feb. 1941 the Governors heard a playback of recent French programmes and congratulated the team. (Ibid., 27 Feb., 6 March 1941.)

[2] *Page to Salt, 15 Nov. 1940.

[3] *Salt to Tallents, 13 May 1941; Ogilvie to Tallents, 24 May 1941. A Ministry of Information official said on this occasion that he hoped for 'Duchesne's resignation which would be immediately accepted'. Nothing more was heard of the matter.   [4] *Salt to Tallents, 13 May 1941.

[5] *Note by Salt, 4 June 1941; German Planning Committee, *Minutes*, 29 Jan. 1941: 'Foreign Office directives had on several occasions directly contradicted the E.H. directives.'

English, for listeners in Europe whose second language was French, and there were fierce verbal battles between him and Newsome on this issue.[1] The new service, Gillie wrote, meant

...A DIT LILY MARLÈNE

6. Three drawings by Jean Oberlé from *Les Chansons de Pierre Dac à la Radio de Londres*, published in 1945

reducing the time available to the French Service just 'when our relations with the French people will be exceedingly delicate. We are either going to disappoint them by not

[1] *Gillie to Grisewood, 18 Aug. 1943; Newsome to Grisewood, 19 Aug. 1943; Note by Kirkpatrick, 30 Sept. 1943. Gillie sent a copy of the first memorandum to Colonel Gielgud of PWE which in itself annoyed Newsome. Newsome replied

liberating them before winter or else we are going to land in France and enter upon the extremely difficult chapter of relations between an Anglo-American military authority and the French civil population.'[1] The new service was launched, notwithstanding, and was placed under the direction of Tangye Lean. Matters were not made easier when it took into its employment a number of anti-Gaullist Frenchmen. Programmes were chosen with care, however, and concentrated on creating a bridge between Britain and Europe; they had more in common with the BBC's service for France after the war than they had with the war-time French Service.

In the broadest terms, the 'chief purpose' of British broadcasting to France during the war was defined as seeking 'to restore the self-respect of the French people by assuming that they have never accepted defeat, and to rearm them for a renewal of the struggle by persuading them of the certainty of an Allied victory'. France had lost a battle, but she had not lost the war. Underlying all British propaganda, therefore, there ran the steady refrain: 'la France est toujours présente à la bataille; elle sera présente à la victoire'.[2] This purpose was translated into one of the BBC French section's songs, sung to the tune of *J'attendrai:*

> 'Attendez toujours
> Not' retour
> La victoir' un beau jour
> Nous ramènera
> Tous chez vous
> Près de nous'[3]

Englishmen might complain at times that there was a touch of 'parochialism' in the French programmes or that 'the BBC

---

[1] *Gillie to Grisewood, 18 Aug. 1943.

[2] *BBC European Services, *Output Report*, 13–19 Dec. 1942.

[3] For a full collection of later songs, see *Les Chansons de Pierre Dac* (Paris, 1945) with a moving preface by Duchesne. Sometimes the songs got out of date. 'Le Père Musso qui a perdu Tobrouk' suddenly ceased to be sung. Lefèvre wrote in the margin 'À ne pas utiliser. Pas d'actualité,' but he had a brainwave and added 'Pour l'instant!' (*BBC French Service, 21st Anniversary Programme, 27 Sept. 1959.)

---

with heavy irony that 'the French Editor considers that he possesses a mandate to correct not only in transmissions directed to France but in those directed to a general French-speaking European audience the errors both in fundamental approach and technical detail habitually committed by the "Central" Director of the European Division'.

seems to speak with the voice of Frenchmen in England rather than with the voice of Britain itself',[1] yet such complaints indicated how favourably the programmes were likely to be received in France itself. A programme called *Courrier de France*, broadcast by Brunius between January 1941 and July 1943, dealt with the sizeable stack of correspondence from France which continued to grow until the total occupation of France in November 1942.[2] Many of the letters were carefully examined in the BBC's *Intelligence Reports*. They clearly revealed that although there was some dissatisfaction in France early in 1942 after the failure of the British to open 'a second front' to help the Russians—'What is England doing? Are we to live again in the fine days of Chamberlain's policy?'[3]—there were growing 'resistance' movements in all parts of France.

In September 1941 de Gaulle had constituted his *Comité National Français*.[4] It was not recognized as a government by the British, and there were a number of Frenchmen in London, including a few militants of the old Popular Front, who were uneasy about it. So too was Admiral Muselier, who was later to break with de Gaulle.[5] Yet it quickly established contact with the 'resistance' in France. The 'Deuxième Bureau des Forces Françaises Libres', with Passy (Dewavrin) at its head, organized eleven missions to France during the course of 1941, and in January 1942 Jean Moulin was sent to Unoccupied France as 'a delegate of the Committee' to make contact with a number of groups working in the south of France. Moulin, the former Prefect of Chartres, who had only recently arrived in London in September 1941, made contact with Georges Bidault, the chief resistance leader on the spot, and later arranged for the distribution of radio sets, for the exchange and diffusion of information and for the systematic listening to the BBC for personal messages. He was able, not without initial difficulty, to fulfil the bigger political mission of unifying competing resistance groups, all of whom wished to 'liberate'

---

[1] *BBC European Services, *Output Report*, 13–19 Dec. 1942.

[2] See below, pp. 455–7; Brunius's programme was replaced from July 1943 with *Chronique de France*, a similar programme based on information from other sources, including Frenchmen who had escaped across the Channel.

[3] *BBC *Intelligence Report, Europe*, 14 Feb. 1942.

[4] H. Michel, *Histoire de la France Libre* (1963), pp. 25–6.

[5] See Admiral Muselier, *De Gaulle contre le Gaullisme* (1946).

(a) Programme Parade. *Daily Express*, 26 June 1942

(b) Featuring Radio Westminster. *Sunday Dispatch*, 25 January 1942

13. Broadcasting Fantasies

(*a*) J. B. Clark

(*b*) Robert Foot (right) and Sir Cecil Graves

14. The High Command

(a) Major Longland
Talks it Over

"Here is your request number, Sergeant Smart—'The Teddy Bears' Picnic'!"

(b) 'Record Time.'
Punch, 17 November
1943

(c) The Forces
Programme

15. The Forces Listening

(*a*) 'Private Smith Entertains'

(*b*) An Army Discussion Group

16. The Army Entertains—and Learns

France, but some of which disliked or mistrusted each other almost as much as they disliked or mistrusted Vichy.[1]

The BBC played a big part in Moulin's plan, as Bidault, France's first post-war Foreign Minister, later eloquently recorded. 'In the depths of the sheltering forests, in the undergrowth of the watching moors, in the friendly streets of shadowy towns, a word arrived from across the Channel and spread in miraculous fashion; and so a web was woven, invisible to the enemy. Patiently, dangerously, the network spread, closely and firmly knit vast coils which at the appointed time brought about his fall.'[2] Yet while 'the BBC was the only messenger whose testimony could calm anxiety after long impatience',[3] it was de Gaulle who sought consistently and tenaciously to control the web. He conceived of the struggle of the Free French outside France and of the resistance movement inside France as inextricably associated with each other. With this end in view, he created an autonomous body BCRAM, later BCRA (the Bureau Central de Renseignement et d'Action), with its headquarters in Duke Street: it was charged with dealing with special operations, missions, escapes, the supply of information and counter-espionage.[4] To his chagrin, it was dependent on the British SOE for transport and equipment— he was extremely bitter about those SOE activities which were organized independently of him—but, nonetheless, its continuing existence, inefficient, costly and controversial though some of its activities proved to be, eventually guaranteed that he would be accepted as leader of the French people.[5] Most of the French resistance groups which emerged spontaneously

---

[1] There is a good account of political currents and counter-currents in the resistance in A. Malraux, *Antimemoirs* (English edn., 1968), pp. 86 ff.

[2] G. Bidault, 'The Voice of Liberty' in *BBC Year Book, 1945*, p. 13. Moulin himself was arrested in June 1943 and killed by the Germans.   [3] Ibid.

[4] See M. R. D. Foot, *SOE in France* (1966), pp. 137 ff., for a detailed account of relations between SOE and de Gaulle.

[5] Even in the short run its existence was important. See an important letter from Pierre Brossolette to André Philip, 30 May 1942, quoted in Colonel Passy, *Souvenirs* (1947), vol. II, p. 227, which noted that BCRA was 'the only service which could meet the needs of information in France, whether the information and action were para-military, political or semi-political'. When Philip, a Socialist, became Commissioner of the Interior in de Gaulle's Committee, in 1943, this provided a considerable accession of strength. So too did letters from prominent French politicians, including Georges Mandel and Léon Blum. Brossolette, a man of immense courage, who was to die in the cause of the resistance, also wrote a

[*cont.*

were as ignorant of the difference between SOE and BCRA as they were of the differences between BBC broadcasts and 'Free French' broadcasts,[1] yet de Gaulle himself was aware of every nuance and moved inexorably and indomitably to the position where he could announce in July 1942 that *France Libre* had become *France Combattante*.

The British recognized him as its leader, and so too did the Russians, thereby ensuring the invaluable adhesion of French Communists to his side.[2] As token of his leadership, he addressed a mass meeting in the Albert Hall on 1 April 1942 in which he spoke of 'an entirely new France rising' and 'the greatest revolution in the history of France that was to be'.[3] On 18 June 1942, the second anniversary of his first broadcast appeal, he addressed a further rally of 10,000 Frenchmen in the Albert Hall, and in the same month he issued a declaration which was published in most French clandestine newspapers, beginning with the stirring words: 'Le peuple français s'assemble pour une révolution.'[4]

There were differences, however, between Frenchmen, even while they were increasingly belligerent. De Gaulle wanted the French to show caution, to wait for the appointed hour to strike: not all 'resisters' on the spot agreed with him.[5] He also found it difficult to avoid argument, often bitter, first with the British[6] and then, more seriously, with the Americans, who did not recall their ambassador from Vichy until April 1942.[7] These wrangles influenced the BBC. Duchesne and most of his colleagues, all of whom longed for

[1] H. J. Michel, *Histoire de la France libre* (1950), p. 32.

[2] F. Grenier, the Communist leader, described his first encounter with Gaullist activity in the summer of 1942 (see his *C'Était Ainsi* (1959), pp. 112 ff.). See also J. Lafitte, *Ceux qui Vivent* (1947) and Rémy, *Mémoires d'un Agent Secret de la France Libre* (1947). [3] C. de Gaulle, *Mémoires, Documents*, pp. 277–8.

[4] Ibid., pp. 424–9. [5] Grenier, op. cit., p. 119.

[6] He has left an unforgettable, if one-sided, account in his *Mémoires*, vol. I, pp. 231–2, of his dealings with Churchill whenever they came into collision.

[7] When American rebroadcasts to France (in the *America Calling Europe* series) were permitted on BBC wavelengths in Jan. 1942, the BBC felt that it was necessary to secure 'further policy coordination on the Vichy angle'. (*European Divisional Committee, Minutes, 17 Feb. 1942.)

most interesting report to London in Jan. 1942 (quoted in Crémieux-Brilhac, loc. cit.) in which he argued that the role of radio was not to tell the French that the Germans would lose the war—they knew that—but to prepare them for the part hey would have to play in the final and decisive stages of the struggle.

the liberation of France, were not 'Gaullists' in the sense of wishing to pledge their unqualified loyalty to the General; and Bourdan, in particular, was deeply concerned about de Gaulle's 'personal politics'. The fact that they went on continuously broadcasting to France through thick and thin, paid by the BBC,[1] while de Gaulle regularly and wearingly tussled with Churchill was bound to irritate de Gaulle. There was no contact between Duchesne and the General, and although a representative of the Free French attended the daily French Service meetings, it was decided that the Foreign Office must stamp Maurice Schumann's scripts beforehand. The Free French broadcasts were suspended for a time in September 1941 (for example) on account of political differences between the Free French and Britain about Syria, and for three weeks the BBC made no reference of any kind to de Gaulle in any of its programmes.[2]

Not surprisingly, de Gaulle, who believed above all else in sovereignty, was anxious to build up his own independent network of radio communication. Radio Brazzaville was of key importance to him.[3] Yet he also secured a daily five minutes in Mexico City, two quarter-of-an-hour broadcasts twice a week from New York, regular programmes in Cuba, Haiti, Puerto Rico and South America, half an hour a day in Ethiopia,[4] and so on. In December 1942 the French had access to seven hours a week of broadcast time in five continents.[5] In March 1942 de Gaulle also started his own monitoring service to listen to Vichy, Paris, Algiers and other French-speaking stations, and in May 1942 he set up an Executive Committee for Propaganda, composed of six people, including Georges Boris and Schumann, who met three times a week, once with a PID representative joining them. In

[1] Robert Mengin was so irritated by this kind of taunt that he decided to forgo a salary paid to him by the British. He points out that the salaries and expenses of de Gaulle's team were financed on a loan basis by the British (see R. Mengin, *No Laurels for de Gaulle* (1967), pp. 254–5). Mengin gives a somewhat misleading impression of the kind of advice given by the General in 1942 on the need not to rise prematurely.

[2] *Circular by Nicolls, 2 Sept. 1941. The instruction was cancelled on 24 Sept.

[3] C. de Gaulle, *Mémoires*, vol. II, p. 170.

[4] The Free French had taken part in the Ethiopian campaign. Leclerc's exploits in the Sahara also began in 1941.

[5] H. Michel, *Histoire de la France Libre* (1967), p. 33.

June 1942 he went on to institute a new non-military section in BCRA charged with exchanging instructions, messages and documents between France and London; and in July 1942 he created a Commissariat of Information under the supervision of Jacques Soustelle.

Given this complex new structure, it was tactful of Soustelle to write to a very sympathetic Harold Nicolson in September thanking the BBC for the way in which it had handled the Free French anniversary programmes.[1] The BBC had, in fact, been very co-operative throughout 1942. It had taken an active part, for example, in the planning of demonstrations on 1 May and 14 July, on both occasions responding to requests from resistance groups in France. On the former occasion the request came from the Mouvement Ouvrier Français, on the latter from resistance organizations in the south.[2] On the first of these occasions even the Russians showed that they were willing to collaborate, for after they had been told that different instructions concerning what to do on 1 May had been broadcast to Frenchmen by the BBC and by Moscow's *Radio France*, they concerted their advice with that given in London. On the second occasion a most intensive BBC campaign was mounted with the full support of the Free French Executive Committee for Propaganda, and de Gaulle himself broadcast on the evening of 13 July.[3]

There were successes, therefore, as well as complications, as the BBC became more and more involved in broadcasting to the resistance. Apart from its formal programmes, it broadcast specific resistance messages from the summer of 1941 onwards. In SOE's earliest days Sir Frank Nelson had contemplated using broadcasts of Slav folk tunes to warn agents in Eastern Europe about forthcoming military operations.[4] It was in relation to France, however, that agents learned

[1] *Board of Governors Meeting, 3 Sept. 1942.

[2] The BBC's broadcasts to French workers organized by William Pickles were increasingly effective in 1942 and 1943. Towards the end of 1943 Pickles co-operated with Patrick Gordon Walker, who organized workers' talks to Germany (see above, p. 431), in a general programme for workers in the Todt organization and for foreign workers who had been deported to Germany.

[3] See Crémieux-Brilhac, loc. cit.

[4] Foot, op. cit., p. 110. It is extremely difficult to assess how many of the messages actually got through. They represented an interesting use of mass radio as a means of personal point-to-point communication.

to listen to the BBC for family greetings of such apparent nonsense as 'Romeo embrasse Juliette'. Such messages announced the safe arrival or exchange of couriers and agents or gave warnings about impending operations. Wireless sets were distributed to the resistance, therefore, as a necessary weapon of war.[1] The Germans tried hard to understand what the messages meant—just as one of the sections of the BBC's Monitoring Service watched carefully for German messages, for example in song titles[2]—but they were never able to get very far with them in 1942. As for the members of the French section of the BBC, the messages meant nothing to them: they were not told whether all of them or only a few were operational. They were tempted to resent, therefore, the encroachment on valuable time which otherwise might have been devoted to programmes or to urgent news.

Before 'Operation Torch', the American landing in North Africa, began in November 1942—and it was to have profound effects on radio propaganda to France—the BBC began repeatedly broadcasting the words 'Allo Robert, Franklin arrive, Allo Robert, Franklin arrive'. It did not need elaborate decoding skills on this occasion to deduce that Robert was R. D. Murphy, that Franklin was Roosevelt, and that an American landing was imminent. A number of Frenchmen in North Africa, indeed, had quite clear-cut instructions as to what to do when this message was broadcast. As events turned out, both the reaction to the operation and the operation itself were to prove far from clear-cut, and the Americans, at best innocent about French politics, at worst cynical, were quickly drawn into an 'imbroglio' which exposed all the latent difficulties in the Free French situation.

De Gaulle had not been officially informed of the American landings before they took place—they were not a complete surprise to him—and the Free French took no part in them. The Americans had planned instead to rely on General Giraud who had escaped from a German prison camp earlier

---

[1] H. Michel, *Histoire de la Résistance*, ch. VII.

[2] Listening to girls' names in German song titles had been a recognized monitoring activity from 1940 onwards. In 1941 and 1942 particular songs were under close observation. They included 'J'attendrai', 'Bayerische Hochzeit', and, perhaps not surprisingly, 'Kleine Moewe, flieg nach Halgoland' ('Little Seagull, Fly to Heligoland').

in the year. On 9 November, one day after the landings took place, de Gaulle proposed to send a mission to Algiers. Before he could take any action, however, the Americans, represented by Robert Murphy, turned as a 'temporary expedient' to Admiral Darlan who by a coincidence happened to be in Algiers 'in the name of the Marshal'. Darlan proved himself as willing to collaborate with the Americans as he had been to collaborate with the Germans since 1940. De Gaulle had very little support in French North Africa at that time,[1] but Murphy probably underestimated the significance of the little support he had.[2] De Gaulle was certainly right to tell Churchill that any reliance on Darlan constituted an 'error of strategy . . . in contradiction to the moral character of the war'. To him, as to everyone on his Committee and many people who had nothing to do with it, Darlan was simply a traitor.[3]

On 13 November, therefore, the *Comité National* in London issued a statement that it would take no part in and accept no responsibility for any negotiations with Vichy. This was to dissociate itself from Allied strategy. It had immediate repercussions for PWE and the BBC. After a delay of twenty-four hours Schumann was allowed to broadcast the statement to France at dictation speed, but a speech along the same lines by de Gaulle, planned for 21 November, was vetoed, as was a further speech set for 3 December. Soustelle was able to use Brazzaville, almost inaudible to France, to expound the Free French message, but on Soustelle's instruction Schumann

[1] *The BBC had made a study of its French audience in North Africa (BBC European Intelligence Papers, *The French Audience in North Africa*, 25 June 1942). There were then about 100,000 radio sets in Algeria in the hands of the French and 5,000 in the hands of Arabs. Jamming of BBC broadcasts, which were the same as the broadcasts to metropolitan France, was serious, and the BBC had received no letters from North Africa during the whole of the previous year. The report concluded that 'a positive appeal to the leading elements . . . might, if it inspired them with respect for Anglo-Saxon policy, help to re-create that unity of thought and feeling, the absence of which was partly responsible for North Africa's failure to back the Allied cause in 1940. The rest is a matter for tanks and planes in action rather than for broadcasts.'

[2] For British foreign policy on the eve of the landings, see Sir Llewellyn Woodward, *British Foreign Policy in the Second World War* (1962), pp. 206 ff.

[3] Darlan was, of course, a traitor to Pétain and Hitler also, and was treated as such. See E. Jäckel, *La France dans l'Europe d'Hitler* (1966), pp. 351–2. The BBC itself had often broadcast lines by Van Moppès:

'Un amiral nommé Darlan
Est garanti pro-allemand.'

suspended his series of *Honneur et Patrie* broadcasts. So did
Marin and all those members of the BBC's French Section
who thought of themselves as 'Free French'. The fact that
Duchesne and the other members of the *Les Français parlent
aux Français* team continued to broadcast profoundly irritated
de Gaulle. So, too, did the news that Lord Swinton had suspended Free French broadcasts from distant Dakar. So,
finally, did monitored reports of broadcasts by André Gillois
from a British 'black' station, *Radio Patrie*, which de Gaulle
believed was threatening the unity and independence of the
French resistance.[1] *Radio Gaulle*, a second 'black' station, about
which the Free French knew and approved, had had to go off
the air on 10 November. The launching of the new station was
taken sufficiently seriously by de Gaulle for Boris, his emissary,
to see Colonel Sutton of PWE and later for de Gaulle himself
to write to Eden.[2]

There is evidence that the French refusal to broadcast was
well understood by Kirkpatrick, even though he knew, as
did de Gaulle and Soustelle, that it might interrupt the
continuity of the flow of news and propaganda to France.
Yet two interviews between Colonel Sutton and Soustelle
suggested no way out of the *impasse*. For their part, the Free
French knew first that it was the Americans rather than the
British who were the authors of the North African policy[3]
and second that Anglo-American solidarity was essential to
the general war effort. They knew, too, that considerable
sections of British public opinion, including opinion inside the

[1] Gillois, who had been brought over to London by SOE, did not realize that
the *Radio Patrie* station fell completely outside the de Gaulle set-up.

[2] The story of *Radio Patrie*, which began to broadcast on 8 Oct. 1942, is linked
with the 'visionary schemes of anti-Gaullist resistance groups' in the south of
France led by André Girard (Carte) and the work of SOE. (See Michel, *Histoire
de la Résistance*, p. 21, and Crémieux-Brilhac, loc. cit., p. 87.) The station ceased to
broadcast on 9 May 1943. The Free French did not know in 1943 that 'Aspidistra'
was used to boost Radio Rabat during the early stages of the Algerian moves: this
would certainly have been another cause of complaint.

[3] The British knew nothing of Murphy's negotiations with Darlan, and on
11 Nov. Churchill telegraphed Roosevelt that the British Government were 'under
quite solemn and definite obligations to de Gaulle and his Movement' and 'must
see they have a fair deal' (Woodward, op. cit., p. 209). Diplomatic relations
between Free French and British actually improved during this period on other
fronts. Réunion rallied to Free France on 28 Nov., with full British support, as
did Somaliland on 28 Dec. On 14 Dec. an agreement was signed about Madagascar, which had long been a bone of contention.

BBC, supported their viewpoint, in some cases going even further than they did, and that the Russians, whom they might have used as a counterweight, did not. There were threats, indeed, of resignations inside the BBC and great anxiety in PWE itself.[1] Duchesne succeeded in holding together most of the members of his broadcasting team by telling them of the disastrous effect that a break in broadcasting to France would have on the whole of Allied propaganda, yet something of the fire went out of the team when it became necessary to think not only of France but of the reconciliation, if possible, of British and American ideas about the future of France. There was never again quite as much spontaneity about BBC broadcasts to France after January 1943 as there had been between June 1940 and November 1942.

It is important, nonetheless, not to simplify the propaganda significance of what happened in November 1942. BBC Intelligence Reports put the situation in a somewhat different light. There had been evidence earlier in 1942 that Frenchmen resented the fact that Britain had seemed to be doing little positive to win the war. 'London,' according to one report, 'was no longer in the front line.' What was happening in Russia appeared to have far more point, particularly after Stalingrad was in danger. In this context, the North African landings, coupled with a renewed British offensive further east, offered both an excitement and a hope which not even Darlan's actions could cancel out. 'The BBC has never had so many listeners in France as since the events in North Africa,' the leader of an underground resistance movement wrote on 23 November.[2] 'Anxious curiosity,' it was argued in London, had made French listeners, 'who were more and more tending to switch off without waiting for the *Porte-Parole* or for *Les Français parlent aux Français*', keen to listen all through the programmes in case anything might be said which would throw light on 'the positions of Darlan and de Gaulle'.[3] Moreover, while German propagandists naturally made the

---

[1] The Dieppe raid of 19 Aug. 1942 had been a failure and had entailed heavy losses. It had shown that Britain was not ready for a planned general landing in France. There were signs of French scepticism also about the effects of bomber attacks on France, for example a thousand-bomber raid on St. Nazaire.

[2] *BBC Surveys of European Audiences, France*, 18 Dec. 1942.

[3] *BBC Bi-Monthly Intelligence Report*, 15 Dec. 1942.

most of these divergencies of opinion over Darlan which found an echo in the British Press,[1] the situation had changed dramatically before they could exploit it. First, the Germans occupied the whole of France (Operation 'Anton') on 11 November, scarcely a successful propaganda move, whatever else it was. Second, the French fleet at Toulon was scuttled on 23 November, an event which lent itself to a variety of interpretations. Third, Darlan was assassinated on 24 December, a murder which removed the most controversial character from the stage. Fourth, in the light of the changed circumstances, de Gaulle, who had heard the news of Darlan's death from a friend of Duchesne at Glasgow station,[2] resumed his London broadcasts four days later.

Yet the situation, if less complicated, remained difficult, for during the first months of 1943 sharp disagreement between de Gaulle and Giraud was forced into the open—temperamental, political, even ideological disagreement. It was not until June 1943, after many orthodox and unorthodox diplomatic manœuvres and many dramatic encounters and exchanges, that de Gaulle at last reached an accommodation with Giraud. A new *Comité Français de la Libération Nationale* was set up, with the two generals as co-Presidents. The Committee was recognized by the British on 26 August, and as it gradually established itself Giraud's position became untenable. In turn he lost his co-Presidency and his position as Commander-in-Chief, and soon he had faded completely into the background. Algiers became the temporary capital of a Free France which was under the direction, if not the full control, of de Gaulle.

Duchesne and the team associated with *Les Français parlent aux Français* soon realized that Giraud, who spoke for the first time for the BBC on 21 July 1943,[3] in the time allotted to the Free French, was not a satisfactory alternative leader to de

---

[1] *BBC *Summary of Bi-Monthly Survey of European Audiences*, 25 Feb. 1943.

[2] When Duchesne's friend told him the 'interesting news', de Gaulle replied 'ça pour une nouvelle, c'est une nouvelle' and went on his way. Schumann was due to go to Brazzaville when the news of the assassination was received. The news arrived at Broadcasting House when many senior officials were away, and the newsroom had a somewhat 'chaotic' night, as one member of the staff put it. The Home Announcer had to begin the news bulletin on 25 Dec. with the words 'Good morning—and a very Happy Christmas to you all. Last night Admiral Darlan was assassinated.'

[3] *BBC French Service 21st Anniversary Programme, 27 Sept. 1959.

Gaulle. As de Gaulle established his authority in Algiers, however, they were concerned about the relationship between what was broadcast by Radio Alger and what was broadcast from London.[1] Invasion of France looked to be the obvious next step on the road to victory, yet 'paradoxically', as Brunius was to write later, 'our role became more difficult to sustain the closer victory came into view'. There were reports of some 'slackness', even of war weariness, in the French Service during the summer of 1943.[2] In such circumstances de Gaulle's Executive Committee for Propaganda demanded in June 1943 that there should be an increase in the amount of time allowed to the Free French—a daily ten minutes, as against the thirty minutes allotted to L'Amérique vous parle and the BBC's own programmes of nearly five hours.[3] The request was unsuccessful, although they were able to participate on agreed terms in the management of a new 'black' station, Honneur et Patrie, which took the place of Radio Patrie after the latter closed down in May 1943. Grenier and later Waldeck-Rochet—both Communists—were among the members of its directorate, and Grenier, who had been prevented from talking freely about francs-tireurs and partisans in his BBC broadcasts,[4] doubtless welcomed, with others, the greater freedom of the new station. It was the BBC, however, which continued to hold the vast majority of the French audience, and not surprisingly first Boris and then Pierre Viénot continued to press for more free time on the BBC wavelengths.[5] De Gaulle, it was stated in January 1944,

[1] *European Divisional Meeting, Minutes, 23 Feb. 1943. Kirkpatrick reported a proposal that Duchesne visit Algiers to contact Radio Alger and to report whether the time was ripe for the transfer of Les Français parlent aux Français to Algeria. Shortly afterwards Duchesne left for Algiers, where he met Giraud and quickly decided for himself that Giraud had no political future.

[2] *European Divisional Meeting, Minutes, 31 Aug. 1943.

[3] Crémieux-Brilhac, loc. cit. The Executive Committee, which by then was a powerful body, including among others Boris, Soustelle, Chevrier, Grenier, Brisson and Brossolette, pointed to the Dutch and Belgian examples. At the end of 1943 Boris became General Delegate of the Commissariat of the Interior in London and civil representative of the Comité d'Action in France. General Koenig was the military representative.

[4] Grenier, op. cit., p. 147, where he quotes a letter from Colonel Gielgud. He writes fully also about his difficulties with Carlton Gardens.

[5] *See a memorandum by Gillie to Col. Gielgud, 8 June 1943. Kirkpatrick thought that it was necessary to 'walk warily'.

had not been heard on the BBC for eight months. After consulting PWE, Gillie agreed that broadcasts by de Gaulle might be relayed from Algiers, but warned Viénot that censorship applied to speeches even by Heads of State and that Duff Cooper, who had replaced Harold Macmillan as British Minister in Algiers, would have to approve de Gaulle's texts first.

In Algiers there had been a confused situation in relation to broadcasting since January 1943, with political responsibility ultimately resting with the Psychological Warfare Board which operated as an adjunct of the United States War Department. PWB supervised *Radio France* broadcasts and ran a United Nations Radio which was extremely slow to develop a constructive broadcasting policy of its own. It was in this milieu that Crossman developed his views about the conditions for effective integration of propaganda.[1] There was certainly a need for more effective integration in relation to broadcasting to France. PWB received directions from both the Americans and the British; and Ian Black, who visited Algiers on behalf of PWE and the BBC in September 1943, expressed himself extremely unhappy about the set-up, describing Algeria as more like an occupied than a liberated country. He also had a frank interview with Henri Bonnet, the Commissioner of Information of the *Comité Français*, who made it clear that he was very suspicious of the BBC's French team. The only consolation for the BBC was that he was told by a French friend that Pierre Bourdan's name was as well known in France as that of General de Gaulle himself.[2] When Black visited Algiers for a second time in 1944, he once again noted considerable prejudice against the French broadcasting team in London. He concluded, however, that whatever happened in Algiers, London would remain until the end of the war the centre of all major decisions relating to propaganda and that it was to London that most people in occupied Europe would

---

[1] See above, pp. 439–40.
[2] For Bourdan's views, which were plainly anti-Gaullist, in the middle of the war, see Mengin, op. cit., p. 261. Another strongly anti-Gaullist broadcaster was Héron de Villefosse, who had quarrelled with de Gaulle over his attitude to Admiral Muselier.

choose to listen almost to the exclusion of any other station.[1]

Early in 1944 Bonnet once more raised the question from Algiers of whether the amount of time devoted to 'Free French' broadcasts could be increased, and in April 1944 he sent over as a delegate Jean-Jacques Mayoux to discuss a proposition that both Schumann's *Honneur et Patrie* broadcasts and *Les Français parlent aux Français* should be submitted to a common control by the British and by the *Comité Français*. The BBC's team would be allowed full freedom of expression and treatment, but there would be integration of policy on the eve of a possible Allied invasion of France. Agreement was eventually reached in May 1944, and thereafter Boris, Mayoux and Gillois attended the weekly meetings of the French section at which PWE directives were discussed.

After all the bickering, the new agreement was announced in the most friendly fashion in a BBC broadcast to France by Gillois on 9 May: 'Great events are in preparation. The *Comité Français* will communicate by radio to Frenchmen information and guidance from London. Since 1940 the BBC has given the most fraternal hospitality to the members of the French team whose voices are so familiar to you and thanks to whom you have kept confidence and have retained even in the most sombre circumstances a hope which the events of today justify. We render homage to the spirit of liberty and sympathetic understanding which our English friends have proved to us. . . . Alongside French news bulletins edited and directed by the British, the programme *Les Français parlent aux Français* has permitted the team to which you have listened for almost four years to express the voice of France. It is necessary that liaison between this team, whose independence has been and will be respected by all, and the *Comité Français* shall be more intimate and more strict. Representatives of the Committee sit today with members of the team associated in their labours. . . . It is necessary to affirm this unity at a time when advice and orders from London must be addressed direct to Frenchmen in France. In listening to *Les Français parlent aux Français* you hear responsible voices who carry to you decisions taken by your government.'

[1] Information derived from extremely perceptive notes by Ian Black. Although new transmitters were installed in Algiers they were not powerful enough to allow its programmes to be picked up throughout France.

There is ample evidence that by the time of D-Day French listeners, some of whom were associated with the Forces Françaises de l'Intérieur, the unified resistance agency brought into existence in February 1943,[1] were ready for a new round of messages which would announce imminent invasion. There was a serious shortage of wireless sets and of spare parts[2]—and in some places the Germans confiscated them[3]—but most Frenchmen in the south continued, even after the total occupation of France, to listen to Vichy as well as Paris radio stations.[4] There was little listening to American broadcasts, some to Swiss broadcasts and more, particularly in the north, to Russian broadcasts. Yet it was the BBC which counted for more than the rest put together. 'People who have grown so accustomed to getting not only their news but their comment from London,' one French businessman commented, preferred going on listening to London to experimenting with other stations 'the weight of whose views they have not been able to judge'. 'The French Section of the BBC does well to continue speaking French in the great Allied capital,' wrote a listener from St. Cloud.[5]

Yet there was impatience inside France during the last few months before D-Day when the Germans were hurriedly building the Atlantic Wall and were transporting all dangerous 'politicians' to concentration camps in Germany.[6] Not surprisingly, therefore, there were more criticisms of the BBC's French Service at this time than there had ever been before. 'All arose from the impatience of a nation weary of words of encouragement and advice. . . . Even young and enthusiastic resisters reported personal boredom with *Les Français parlent*

[1] See H. Michel, *Histoire de la Résistance*, pp. 98, 106.

[2] *BBC Surveys of European Audiences, France*, 2 Feb. 1944, quoting an article in the *Dépêche de Toulouse*, 8 Dec. 1943. The official number of licences, which had risen continuously since Dec. 1940, had fallen between Dec. 1942 and July 1943. The price of what sets were available put them beyond the reach of any but the rich. There was a further fall in the number of sets between July 1943 and April 1944 (ibid., 2 Oct. 1944).

[3] There was confiscation both in Paris and in parts of the provinces. As late as Aug. 1944 an Alsatian was sentenced to death for listening to foreign broadcasts (*Mülhauser Tageblatt*, 11 Aug. 1944).

[4] Some listeners had said that Radio Vichy was 'about half way between Radio Paris and London'. [5] *BBC Surveys of European Audiences, France*, 9 Feb. 1944.

[6] Jäckel, op. cit., ch. 17. It was estimated that 4,000 persons a month were moved during this period to German concentration camps via a transit camp in Compiègne.

aux Français and warned us that people in France were "tired of the BBC". Accusations of over-angling for French consumption, of over-optimism, of instructions and advice impossible to carry out, of too highly coloured accounts of Maquis activities, of unnecessary padding of news commentaries "drowned in the mass of political material" were more and more frequent, and several careful observers reported a definite drop in listening to all London broadcasts other than news bulletins.'[1] At the same time Phillippe Henriot, the new Vichy Propaganda Minister, a former Paris broadcaster who had offended Pétain,[2] was skilfully winning an audience for himself, playing on pre-invasion hopes and fears.[3] If invasion had not come when it did, propaganda to France might well have played itself out.

In other branches of the BBC's European Services, there were quite different problems associated with both propaganda and Intelligence. Relations between the BBC and some of the Allied Governments were far closer than they were between either the BBC or PWE and the Free French, a fact which in itself annoyed Carlton Gardens. The Norwegian Government, for example, was on such close terms with the BBC after the agreement of August 1940 came into effect in the October of that year that the Norwegian section under Winther could rightly claim that it was 'the happiest and most harmonious section in the European Service'.[4] The Norwegian Government never felt it necessary to ask for 'free time', and when PWE suggested that it might wish to review its arrangements, the Norwegians replied that they already had excellent relations with the BBC.[5] King Haakon's broadcasts throughout the

---

[1] *BBC *Surveys of European Audiences, France*, 2 Oct. 1944.

[2] See Jäckel, op. cit., p. 418. Pétain tried to resist Henriot's appointment: he felt that he had insulted the French Army in his Paris broadcasts. Henriot was nonetheless appointed with Darnand, the Police Chief, from 1 Jan. 1944.

[3] For the invasion and its consequences, see below, pp. 671 ff.

[4] *Article by Winther, Dec. 1943.

[5] *Letter from the Norwegian Government to Kenney (Ministry of Information), May 1941; Winther to Grisewood, 7 May 1943. Relations with SOE were more complex, and there were differences between the Norwegians and the British about the Lofoten Islands raids in May and Dec. 1941. (See S. Kjelstadli, 'The Resistance Movement in Norway and the Allies' *in European Resistance Movements, 1939–1945* (1964), pp. 327–8.) Agreement between SOE and the Norwegian resistance was not reached until 24 Sept. 1942.

war were extremely effective in consolidating Norwegian unity.

The history of the Greek section was in complete contrast. Its members were for the most part anti-royalist Liberals, who feared that the liberation of Greece might be followed by the imposition of a new dictatorship, and their views were very different from those both of the exiled King in Cairo and of the British Foreign Office. In May 1941, when the King fled the country, the Greek Minister in London handed over to the BBC the identification and interval signal of Athens Radio —cow and goat bells and a shepherd's flute—which were used by the Greek Section until 5 November 1944, but the section's Editor, Angeloglou, was out of sympathy with the regime, as were some of its other members.[1] The King of Greece divided Greeks as much as the King of Norway united Norwegians.[2] Tensions persisted even after he had moved back from Capetown to London in June 1941 and Angeloglou was replaced in March 1942 by D. E. Noel-Paton, former Director of the British Institute in Athens and a Foreign Office nominee. The result was that whereas the Norwegian Government never felt it necessary to ask for 'free time', the Greeks, with some British official support, began to ask for it in April 1942.[3] Michaelopoulos, the Greek Under-Secretary of State for Information, maintained that he had the right 'to give all Greek news in his own way',[4] and 'free time' was conceded in July 1942.[5] There were further tussles which became more serious after the Greek Government left London and established itself in Cairo in April 1943. By then it was having to concern

---

[1] *S. N. Soteriades, a member of the section, complained to Newsome in a letter of 22 Nov. 1941 about the King not being truly representative of the Greek nation. His objections to having to include in the news bulletins a great deal of 'news and views of the Greek authorities or about them' were sustained by Newsome. Soteriades also objected to PWE directives, and was backed by Kirkpatrick who objected to 'angled news' (Ralph Murray (PID) to Kirkpatrick, 13 Dec. 1941; Kirkpatrick to Murray, 15 Dec. 1941). There were more disputes early in 1942, and Kirkpatrick wrote 'bosh' against one of Murray's letters (19 Feb. 1942).

[2] For King George's broadcasts, the first of which was given on 23 Sept. 1941, see C. M. Woodhouse, *Apple of Discord* (1948).

[3] *European Divisional Meeting, *Minutes*, 14 April 1942; Kirkpatrick to Bruce Lockhart, 6 May 1942.

[4] *Noel-Paton to Kirkpatrick, 19 June 1942. At a meeting held in April 1942 and attended by Noel-Paton, Murray and Miss Dilys Powell, Michaelopoulos had asked for ten or fifteen minutes' free time in the daily Greek half hour.

[5] *Noel-Paton to Kirkpatrick, 25 June 1942.

itself directly with the complex politics of resistance movements in Greece which had, indeed, begun to assume increasing importance from the autumn of 1941 onwards.[1]

The fact that the resistance movements were themselves bitterly divided added to the complications.[2] ELAS, the military counterpart of EAM, included a core of Communists and was the only militant organization left in Greece after the dictatorship in 1936 had put an end to all political opposition, while EDES was positively anti-Communist. Neither EAM nor EDES included royalists, a fact which itself led to tussles between SOE, anxious to support guerrilla resistance in a country where six German divisions were required to keep order, and the Foreign Office, resolutely backed by Churchill himself, which was sympathetic to the King.[3] In such circumstances broadcasting to Greece from London was never easy. While the Greek section not only reported what was happening as fairly as it could but also instigated passive and active resistance to the Germans inside Greece and encouraged able-bodied Greeks to escape to join the Greek forces in North Africa, the section was always unhappy about the policy of the Greek Government, and the Greek Government itself never found it easy to fill its free time.[4] The difficulties were to come to a head during the autumn of 1944 when the Germans left Greece and British forces entered the country. Point was added to the problems by the fact that by then Leeper, who knew so much about propaganda and its organization, had become British Ambassador to Athens.[5]

Broadcasting to Yugoslavia was caught up in an equally intricate political tangle. H. D. Harrison, who was Balkan Editor until September 1944,[6] had to deal with a continuous

[1] The word 'resistance' had been used in Greece in 1938—in relation to the political opposition to General Metaxas, the Greek dictator.

[2] See D. G. Kousoulas, *Revolution and Defeat* (1965); C. Pyromaglou, 'La Résistance Grecque et les Alliés' in *European Resistance Movements, 1939–1945* (1964), pp. 304 ff.

[3] See Brigadier E. C. W. Myers, *Greek Entanglement* (1955) and Woodhouse, op. cit., p. 152. 'It was futile on the part of the King's adherents to blame this fact upon the British authorities for supporting republican organisations in Greece: there had been no other organisations in Greece visible without a microscope.'

[4] *Kirkpatrick to the Greek Ambassador, 21 Sept. 1943.

[5] See his book, *When Greek meets Greek* (1950).

[6] See above, p. 264.

flow of complaints from the Royal Yugoslav Government before and after it moved to Cairo in October 1943. Twice, indeed, the Government threatened to call up key members of his staff; on another occasion suggestions were made that there should be a completely new panel of announcers and translators, a move which Kirkpatrick described as 'a Yugoslav ramp to get back into the BBC two of the staff with whose services we have dispensed'.[1] Linguistic disputes, forced by national rivalries,[2] often produced impossible situations. Thus, when the Royal Government rejected the idea of a separate daily Croatian bulletin in August 1942 on the grounds that it would emphasize 'the breaking up of Yugoslavia and the growth of separatist tendencies',[3] one of its Ministers, Dr. Krnjević, who wanted such a bulletin, not only refused to broadcast thereafter himself but set out to persuade others to follow his example. A British diplomat who tried to get him to change his mind made no headway, writing disconsolately: 'I rather doubt if Chrysostom himself could do much with him.'[4] Some of the Ministers took the opposite line and wanted to broadcast too often, and some of them were so long-winded that Kirkpatrick threatened to ban them if they exceeded six minutes.[5]

All the time, the future of Yugoslavia was being determined not in London—or in Cairo—but in Yugoslavia itself. Mihailović, a pan-Serb, never believed in a general rising against the enemy; and he allowed his subordinates to collaborate with the Germans and Italians to secure food and to obtain arms which they were prepared to use in the first instance against Tito's Partisans. The courage and enterprise of the Partisans won them the support of a distinguished series of British military officers sent out by SOE for purposes of military liaison. The BBC, knowing little of the situation on the spot, could do little to determine its own policy: indeed, it sometimes attributed resistance activities in Yugoslavia to the wrong groups. Yet after Mihailović had been appointed Minister of War by the Royal Government in London in January 1942,

[1] *Kirkpatrick to Foot, 15 Sept. 1942.
[2] See above, p. 381.
[3] *Kirkpatrick to Greenway, 4 Aug. 1942.
[4] *Greenway to Kirkpatrick, 6 Aug. 1942.
[5] *Kirkpatrick to Murray, 17 Dec. 1941; Kirkpatrick to Vilder, 22 July 1942. On another occasion the Prime Minister failed to turn up for a broadcast.

every effort was made to project him, 'even to build him up into something which he never seriously claimed to be',[1] and the Yugoslav 'Military Cabinet' in London was allowed to broadcast to him each Wednesday weekly messages, including coded instructions.

Whatever the effect of the messages in Yugoslavia, they caused considerable alarm in Bush House. There was a shift of emphasis in August and September 1942, however, as the final assault on the German positions in North Africa was being planned. When, for instance, the Royal Government took exception to a broadcast by Harrison, in October 1942, in which he stated that 'all the best Yugoslav fighters, whether under Mihailović or under Partisan leadership, are fighting for the same ideals of liberty and cooperation', his broadcast was commended by Kirkpatrick, who said that it tallied closely with, even if it anticipated, the full implications of the kind of policy being pursued by PWE. Murray of PWE explained that the Royal Yugoslav Government had not been consulted about this change of line because PWE feared that there would be prolonged discussions which would end in deadlock.[2] 'I am sure you will agree that the problem of the treatment of the Partisan question is a very delicate one,' Kirkpatrick wrote to the Yugoslav Prime Minister later in November. 'The policy of our broadcasts in this matter is to present the facts after the most careful checking possible; and we deal with the Partisan resistance to the Axis, of which there is considerable evidence in the light of that policy. Our broadcasts are, of course, made in conformity with His Majesty's Government's basic policy of full support to General Mihailović in his fight against the Axis.'[3]

The British Government's efforts to bring together the two different and diametrically opposed wings of the Yugoslav resistance had, in fact, clearly failed by the summer of 1942;[4]

[1] F. Maclean, *Eastern Approaches* (1949), p. 438. See also F. W. Deakin, 'Britain and Jugoslavia', written for the Oxford Conference on Resistance Movements, 1942.

[2] *Harrison gave his commentary on 18 Oct. 1942. Sir George Rendel, Ambassador to the Royal Yugoslav Government, expressed their objections. Murray (PWE) welcomed the broadcast as fully authorized on 5 Nov. 1942.

[3] *Kirkpatrick to the Yugoslav Prime Minister, 10 Nov. 1942.

[4] Woodward, op. cit., p. 336.

and during the spring of 1943 Eden insisted that if Mihailović did not abandon his 'collaboration' with the enemy help to him would cease. The warning, which did not lead to any change in Mihailović's tactics, was followed by the dropping by parachute of Captain (later Colonel) Deakin into Monte-negro and in July by the appointment of Brigadier Maclean as head of a liaison mission with Tito. Maclean reported in November that Mihailović would never unify the country even in the most favourable circumstances and that in the short run the only hope of large-scale military action lay with Tito's Partisans; and, though efforts continued to be made to call upon Mihailović to redeem his reputation as a fighter, support began to swing to Tito. On his way to the Teheran Conference, Churchill told the new Yugoslav Prime Minister, M. Purić, that Mihailović was collaborating with the enemy, and Purić in reply claimed, quite wrongly, that British propa-ganda was responsible for the rise of the Partisans to power.[1]

Tito's rise owed nothing to BBC propaganda from London. When, earlier in the year, Kirkpatrick had once again defended Harrison after Harrison had argued that support for Mihailović was being 'over-done'—the letter found its way into the hands of the Royal Yugoslav Government—he had made it quite clear that the BBC was not biased in favour of the Partisans, but was faced with the necessity of reporting as accurately as possible on the success of their efforts.[2] Relations between the BBC and the Royal Yugoslav Government were clearly strained at this time.[3] In any case, the Russians were extremely active in their broadcasting to Yugoslavia, and in December 1943 a broadcast from a 'free Yugoslav' station on Russian territory, the existence of which had been known by the BBC's Monitoring Service from November 1942, demanded recogni-tion of Tito's Supreme Legislative Council, set up in November, as the sole government of Yugoslavia not only after the war

[1] Ibid., p. 339.
[2] *Letter from Kirkpatrick, 18 Feb. 1943.
[3] W. S. Vucinich in R. J. Kerner (ed.), *Jugoslavia* (1949), p. 372. 'Relations between the BBC and the Yugoslav Government deteriorated during this period as the BBC continued to credit the Partisans with their contribution against the German army.' The BBC service hitherto called the Serbo-Croat Service was renamed the Yugoslav Service in Jan. 1943. (*European Divisional Meeting, *Minutes*, 19 Jan. 1943.)

but during it.[1] Through all the subsequent political difficulties —and most of them were to prove insuperable—the BBC remained essentially a reporter of the Yugoslav situation rather than an active agent in Yugoslav politics.

The broadcasters to Poland had a more active role, although, as the war went on, the political situation in Poland was such that it registered every kind of Anglo-Russian difference. The contrasts between the Yugoslav and Polish sections were, indeed, substantial. There was no parallel to the Mihailović-Tito problem, and no British military team operated in Poland until after 1944. Moreover, the Polish Government in London had good communications with the Polish underground 'Government Delegation' and the Polish Home Army. Just because Polish/Russian differences were deep-rooted, the BBC felt it had a duty to acquaint the Poles with what was happening: it knew also that it was addressing Poles scattered throughout the battle areas of Europe and North Africa and the Middle East.

The Polish Government in London had tried to shape the policy of the Polish section even before Russia came into the war, but failed completely when Winch, its Editor, who took no pains to hide his dislike for it, was backed by Newsome and Kirkpatrick.[2] Newsome thought of the members of the Polish Government as feudal reactionaries, and on the Polish side there were elements strongly opposed to co-operation. Ritchie did his best to iron out difficulties—he was adept at this— but it was not until Winch was replaced as Editor by Gregory Macdonald in February 1942 that relations improved. By then the Polish Government had been allowed the 'free time' (through Radio Polskie) for which it had been pressing,[3] partly on grounds of prestige, partly to put the Poles on parity with the Czechs.

The quarter-of-an-hour a day placed at its disposal from 9.30 to 9.45 a.m. was restricted, however, to news concerning the Polish Forces in Britain and the activities of the Polish Government, and scripts, prepared in English as well as Polish,

---

[1] Woodward, op. cit., p. 339. The BBC used broadcasts from this station with caution as a source of news about Partisan activities.

[2] *Lawrence to Salt, 5 May 1941.

[3] *Kirkpatrick to the Polish Minister of Information, 19 Dec. 1941; European Divisional Committee, *Minutes*, 23, 30 Dec. 1941.

had to be scrutinized before they were broadcast, in normal circumstances by nine o'clock on the evening before they were delivered. Very precise instructions were laid down. 'Where a news commentary differs from ours merely in its expression of opinion, no objection need be taken to it . . . but where the commentary deals wrongly with facts, as we know them, it should be amended.' In relation to talks, the question was always to be asked whether or not the argument of a particular talk cut across major lines of British policy. 'We could not agree to a talk expressing the opinion that Germany should be partitioned after the war, since this would cut across our German broadcasts. We could not pass a talk claiming Czech or Russian territory for Poland, since this would involve us with the Czech or Soviet Governments.'[1] The switch-censor was to inform Kirkpatrick at any time of minor deviations from script, and the programme was to be cut if there were any major deviations.[2] Certain members of the Polish Government disliked these restrictions: they had set up a 'Radio Section' in their Ministry of Information;[3] they wished to take up more BBC time (their opponents thought that this was encroachment) and they continued to press the Polish Minister of Information to seek for control of all broadcasts from London to Poland.[4]

Kirkpatrick was acutely conscious of 'the lack of a concerted plan' in broadcasting to Poland[5] and of the atmosphere of mutual suspicion. He welcomed, therefore, the sense of renewed co-operation when Macdonald took over. So, too, did Count Balinski, the Polish Government's Liaison Officer, who was a sensible go-between.[6] Balinski recognized and appreciated that Macdonald believed that the most important duty of the Polish Service was to report truly and faithfully both news and comment about the war, whatever the political situation.

[1] *Note by Kirkpatrick, 31 Dec. 1941.
[2] *European Divisional Meeting, *Minutes*, 30 Dec. 1941.
[3] Its head, Kisielewski, figured in a scene with Winch on 24 Dec. 1941.
[4] *Unsigned note, 28 Jan. 1942.   [5] *Ibid.
[6] For Balinski's first appointment, see above, p. 272. There were weekly meetings at Bush House attended by Macdonald, Savery, the BBC's East European Language Supervisor, Balinski and a representative of PWE. 'The Polish representatives,' it was stated (*Undated Memorandum by Macdonald, 1943) 'express their complaints as well as their appreciation.'

Macdonald's views were radically different from those of many of his colleagues in Bush House, and he refused throughout the war to seek to bombard Poland either with the kind of anti-Russian broadcasts which 'black' stations might have initiated or with optimistic Allied propaganda which assumed that there were no political differences between Britain and Russia. In addition, he acquainted his listeners with the kind of debate in the Press and in informal conversations which was taking place in Britain itself.[1] He was strongly supported by his superiors when he set out to follow this policy, and he was relatively free of harassment from PWE. It was thanks to the good relations which he established with Radio Polskie that when the schedules for 1942 were being drawn up a second period of free time was added to meet the needs of the Polish underground Press.[2] Listening conditions in Poland were appalling, and it was less through listening to broadcasts from London than from reading clandestine newspapers carrying news and views broadcast from London in the dawn transmission of the BBC—including editorial quotations from the British Press— that the Poles were kept in touch with London and with the BBC. The letters BBC meant little. 'London radio' was the usual term employed, and it covered equally the BBC broadcasts and those of Radio Polskie. The radio was also used to broadcast private messages and 'musical codes' each evening for the use of the Polish resistance: 'Lieutenant Peterkin' of the Polish General Staff (George Zubrzycki) was the officer in charge. He worked with SOE, and every morning took round to Bush House records identified by code numbers.

Politics were too important to the Poles for the relationship with the BBC ever to be completely free from difficulty, and there was enough wild talk in Polish circles in London about a Baltic littoral controlled by Poland or about expansion in Eastern and Central Europe for passages from particular broadcasts to have to be cut.[3] Attempts were made also to discourage the Poles from following a different line and

[1] Each week there was a talk by an English commentator, 'a kind of Westminster Diary', read by an Englishman in Polish.

[2] After long negotiations a third free period was added in April 1944, primarily for Polish Forces in Italy, to whom the Germans, who had ignored Polish broadcasting in 1939, were directing two evening broadcasts.

[3] *Undated Memorandum by Macdonald, 1943.

multiplying references to the role of 'small nations' against 'great powers'. Critical episodes in the relations between Stalin, Churchill and Roosevelt were bound to have their repercussions, but the Poles were asked to avoid a 'controversial, disputatious or provocative tone'. In April 1943, after Sikorski had told Churchill about German reports of the discovery of a large number of bodies of Poles in a common grave at Katyn and had demanded a Red Cross investigation, Radio Polskie, with PWE approval, reported what was happening.[1] But there was no attempt to start any kind of 'radio war' after the Soviet Government broke off diplomatic relations with Poland. The news of the tragic death of General Sikorski in an aeroplane accident in July 1943 was reported with the deepest sympathy, and a moving message from Churchill was read in translation by the famous Polish broadcaster, Jozef Opienski.

Sikorski had been a frequent broadcaster from London, as was his successor Mikolajczyk. It was not until the Warsaw rising of August 1944, which was fully reported in and supported by BBC broadcasts from London, that the full implications of Russo-Polish relations became plain. Between Mikolajczyk's taking office and then, however, there was an increase in the number of PWE directives relating to Polish affairs. 'Policy directives with regard to Polish affairs,' Macdonald wrote in June 1944, 'are now frequent and explicit both in the PWE Central Directive and in the weekly PWE Directive for BBC Polish Services.'[2] They covered not only political complexities but the military situation on the Polish Front where the Poles were seeking to convince the Western governments of the strength of their military organization.

The story of the BBC's Czech section offered almost as many contrasts to that of the Polish section as did the Yugoslav. Newsome admired the Czechs as much as he distrusted the Poles, and Beneš and the head of the Czech Department of Information, Dr. Hubert Ripka, were encouraged to express general views on Europe's future which were far more comprehensive than those permitted to Polish speakers. As Beneš drew closer to the Soviet Union, the Polish leaders in London felt that he was losing 'the objectivity necessary to the part of a

[1] For the incident, see Woodward, op. cit., pp. 203–4.
[2] *Macdonald to J. B. Clark, 23 June 1944.

mediator' and became increasingly uneasy about the emphasis on the role of Russia as a liberator. This uneasiness influenced the pattern of relationships in Bush House. The editors of the Czech section—Sheila Grant Duff, who became Czech Editor in May 1942, and the historian, Professor R. R. Betts, who replaced her in September 1943[1]—had a very free hand in compiling news bulletins in Czech, and did not feel in any sense inhibited in programme policy by PWE, which did not in fact appoint a separate Regional PWE Director until September 1943: up to that date the same Director dealt with Poland and Czechoslovakia.

Broadcast programmes other than news were planned with the full co-operation of Dr. Josef Körbel, the official responsible for broadcasting in the Czech Government. By the end of 1942 the number of news bulletins had increased to four, and the Czechs, like the Poles, were given free time in March 1943, even though they did not ask for it.[2] There had been differences of opinion between Ripka and the BBC about a possible complete amalgamation of the BBC's Czech section and the Wireless Department of the Czech Ministry of Foreign Affairs; and it had been made clear, before free time was offered, that the Czechoslovak section as a whole remained an integral part of a BBC European Service, following basic directives issued by PWE.[3] Yet when the Czech Government took over a ten-minute period in the early morning and a fifteen-minute period in the evening, they were subjected to very little control. Certainly few listeners in Czechoslovakia could distinguish between the 'official' offering and the BBC's offering, and the Czech Government a year later willingly borrowed both Czech and Slovak announcers from the BBC to maintain its service.[4] The political side of the Service

[1] Miss Grant Duff married Newsome in July 1942. Betts, who resigned from his editorship in April 1944 on grounds of ill health, joined the Central News Desk as a policy editor. He was replaced by Michael Roberts, the poet and writer, a man of remarkable gifts, who had been editing the clandestine Press news for Poland. Roberts stayed until Aug. 1944, when he was replaced by Duckworth Barker who stayed in the post until the end of the war.

[2] *European Divisional Meeting, Minutes, 23 Feb. 1943.

[3] *Miss Grant Duff to Körbel, 8 March, 1943; Report of a Conference, 10 March; Aide-mémoire by Ripka, 6 April; Ripka to Kirkpatrick, 6 April; Betts to Grisewood, 5 May.

[4] *J. B. Clark to Ripka, 3 Oct. 1944; Ripka to Clark, 16 Oct. 1944.

continued to be of great importance—Masaryk's broadcasts were as lively and effective as ever—yet as the Russian armies advanced there was also a military side. Code messages continued to be sent to SOE and Czechoslovak agents throughout the last phases of the war.

Broadcasts to Czechoslovakia had something in common with broadcasts both to Eastern and to Western Europe. In the East, the Roumanian and Bulgarian Services played a relatively minor part in influencing the course of events. The Bulgarian Press seldom missed the opportunity of attacking 'mischievous London propagandists',[1] and at the end of the war the Metropolitan Stefan of Sofia told a British correspondent that BBC broadcasts 'had been Bulgaria's safety valve during the past three and a half years'.[2] Yet, apart from one fighting speech on Bulgaria by L. S. Amery on 3 March 1941, two days after the Bulgarian Prime Minister had signed a pact with Germany, and a number of speeches by Churchill,[3] there was little scope for anything more than news bulletins and 'projection of Britain'. The Foreign Office had stated firmly in August 1941 that no encouragement should be given in propaganda to Bulgarian aspirations or to a Free Bulgarian movement,[4] and every effort was made to improve relations between Bulgaria and Yugoslavia and Greece.

The Roumanian Service was constantly troubled by spokesmen of different and rival brands of nationalism, and Newsome, among others, was opposed to trying to encourage from London any kind of popular movement against the Antonescu Government.[5] Bucharest, nonetheless, appealed to all

---

[1] *BBC Handbook, 1944,* p. 76.

[2] *BBC Handbook, 1945,* p. 122.

[3] The Bulgarians declared war on Great Britain and the United States in Dec. 1942. British propaganda stressed, however, that there was a difference between the Bulgarian people and the Government. In Aug. 1943 there were appeals to the Bulgarian people to resist and a speech was made by the former Bulgarian Minister in London on 24 Aug. 1943 appealing to his compatriots to act against the Germans. Bulgarian radio immediately denounced him as a traitor.

[4] *BBC Balkan Weekly Service Meeting, *Minutes*, 27 Aug. 1941. Two Bulgarian speakers on the BBC—Matzankiev and Mrs. Karastoyanova—were sentenced to death *in absentia* by the Bulgarian Government and Mrs. Karastoyanova's elderly widowed mother was put in a concentration camp.

[5] *Memoranda of 7 Feb. 1943. A Roumanian Bureau had been set up in London in 1942 with the co-operation of the Foreign Office, PWE, SOE and the BBC. It tried to bring together Roumanians anxious to forget their political divisions and
[*cont.*]

Roumanians not to listen to the BBC.[1] The Hungarians were treated differently still.[2] The Hungarian section was notorious for its intrigues and quarrels, with anti-Semitism complicating personal rivalries. Two members of the section were dismissed in 1941,[3] and there were intermittent allegations both of bribery and of infringements of security. There were also problems relating to the content of the broadcasts. In May 1942, for example, the Board of Governors heard that some of the talks to Hungary had been described as of 'an appeasing nature'.[4] PWE itself was at that time following a less 'tough' line than that in relation to some other Balkan countries.[5] The complexities of the Hungarian domestic situation made it difficult to strike the right notes, yet certain speakers, notably C. A. Macartney, acquired a reputation in Hungary which survived the vicissitudes of the war. Certainly Hungarians listened eagerly to BBC broadcasts throughout the war, and after the war was over Lady Haire, a Hungarian who had been employed by the BBC, was told by people in Budapest that while the war lasted the BBC knew more of what was happening in the country than the Hungarians themselves.

In the West, the Belgian and Dutch Services also provided a number of interesting contrasts. Radio Oranje had great freedom if not 'complete liberty',[6] and the Dutch Editor had to take steps in 1941 to ensure that discrepancies were avoided in BBC and Radio Oranje programmes.[7] Later during the war the Dutch acquired a bigger share themselves in programme making. Thus, in October 1942, they took over the most

[1] *BBC Handbook, 1944*, p. 76.

[2] *Bracken to Powell, 8 June 1942.

[3] *Duckworth Barker to Cameron, 1, 2 Sept. 1941; Newsome to Cameron, 3 Sept. 1941; Ogilvie to Pym, 2 Oct. 1941.

[4] *Board of Governors, *Minutes*, 7 May 1942. They were said, notwithstanding, to have been produced with the approval of the Foreign Office. (Ibid., 14 May 1942.)

[5] *Bracken to Powell, 8 June 1942.

[6] *Letter from Kirkpatrick, 4 Aug. 1941.

[7] *Dutch Service Meeting, *Minutes*, 30 July 1941. Pelt agreed that 'facts in both services must be identical', but stressed the advantages of diversity in presentation and interpretation.

support the Allied war effort. Members of the Bureau broadcast regularly, although it proved 'very difficult to reach common agreement on the contents of each individual talk' (*Kirkpatrick to Orme Sargent, 30 Dec. 1943).

important programme in Dutch, *De Brandaris*, a broadcast for seamen, which they themselves had first asked for early in 1941[1] but which the BBC produced.[2] Beginning with a well-known Dutch song as a signature tune, *De Brandaris* had as its leading broadcasting figures M. Van den Broek, 'Der Rotter-damer', and A. den Doolaard, a well-known Dutch novelist who escaped from Holland in the spring of 1941. The team was later joined by a radio operator from the Dutch merchant navy who had escaped after being torpedoed. Queen Wilhel-mina and Prince Bernhard often figured in its programmes, and its hundredth performance was relayed from a London theatre. Listening in Holland was severely restricted—an attempt was made to confiscate all wireless sets in May 1943[3]—yet BBC broadcasts undoubtedly attracted a wide audience. Despite serious difficulties in the organization of SOE activities —fourteen SOE transmitters in Holland were actually taken over and operated by half-a-dozen German operators[4]—BBC programmes were used to send codes and to assist resistance groups.

The Belgians, despite great pressure, secured no free time until 1943,[5] when additional BBC transmitters became available. They were able, however, to increase the power of their African station at Léopoldville, which rebroadcast some British programmes. There was no English Editor of the Belgian Service, and De Laveleye did his best to gain increases in available broadcasting time for the Belgian Government, pointing out that both the Dutch and the French had 'an unfair advantage': he argued also that as 'the man who originated the V sign' he was entitled to special attention.[6] Broadcasts to Belgium continued to have an operational slant in 1942 and 1943, and instructions to resistance movements

---

[1] *Ibid., 2 Jan. 1941.

[2] *European Divisional Meeting, *Minutes*, 5 Oct. 1942. Yet the suggestion had been opposed in May (ibid., 19 May 1942).

[3] *BBC Handbook, 1944*, p. 78.

[4] Foot, op. cit., p. 109. For 'Operation North Pole', see H. G. Giskes, *London Calling North Pole* (1953); P. Dourlein, *Inside North Pole* (1953).

[5] *European Divisional Meeting, *Minutes*, 5 Jan. 1943; Delfosse, the Belgian Minister of Information, to Kirkpatrick, 4 March 1943. The Belgians tried un-successfully to get Churchill to broadcast at the opening of the new Léopoldville service. They also at one stage planned broadcasts of their own from Eaton Square.

[6] *De Laveleye to Dunkerley, 30 Jan. 1942.

were given both in the Radio Belgique and in the post-1943 free-time Radiodiffusion Nationale Belge broadcasts. In relation to the Belgian, as to the other 'free' nationally sponsored services, the Foreign Office, at Kirkpatrick's instigation, explained that Allied Governments had to conform to BBC policy in their 'free time'.[1]

In BBC broadcasting to the European 'neutrals', there were no problems in operational broadcasting of the kind that sometimes created difficulties in the belligerent countries after the war,[2] but each neutral country constituted a special case with problems of its own. The only broadcasts to Switzerland were transmitted for one month in April/May 1941, after which it was decided, correctly, that the time allotted to such broadcasts could be more properly used 'in other directions'.[3] Sweden, however, actually secured two extra daily fifteen-minute programmes, the first in November 1941. Alf Martin ('Commentator'), the London Correspondent of *Handelstidningen*, took over weekly political commentaries previously given by Erik Rydbeck; and a successful series of short-wave broadcasts from the United States by Nobel prize winners, including Einstein and Thomas Mann, was supplemented by panel discussions about points raised in letters received from Swedish listeners. In September 1943 Margaret Sampson, who had joined the Swedish Service in 1941 and had become its Editor, paid a visit to Stockholm during which she corroborated the fact that large numbers of Swedes listened to London: the head of the Swedish Workers' Educational Association told her, for example, that 'the Swedish working classes are very peculiar. They seem to consider it a patriotic duty to listen to *your* broadcasts.' There was, nonetheless, an almost universally evident distaste for propaganda, both British and German, and it seemed to Miss Sampson that

[1] *Board of Governors, *Minutes*, 21 May 1942.

[2] After the war, attempts were made by a number of Belgians accused of summarily killing collaborators to maintain that instructions had been given in broadcasts from London (*Memorandum of 9 Aug. 1951). There is only one reference, however, in the surviving *Minutes* of the Belgian Weekly Programme Meeting to broadcast attacks on *individual* Belgians known to be working for the Germans.

[3] *Hansard*, vol. 371, cols. 1204–5.

the Swedes were carefully and critically scrutinizing 'actual political behaviour' rather than allowing themselves to be drawn into the war of words.[1]

Denmark was a different case. It was the only German-occupied country which was ruled by a government the legal status of which was not in doubt, and the problems of pursuing a consistent broadcasting policy in relation to the Danes derived largely from the uncertainties of British foreign policy. In May 1942 it was stated bluntly in a BBC output report that 'we do not attempt to preach open resistance, still less revolt against the orders of the Danish Government, but we give full details of the heroism shown by the other oppressed peoples, particularly by the Norwegians'.[2] News had always enjoyed pride of place in the Service, including news of the Danish Council in London which was set up in October 1940 and which received open support from the British Government in February 1941.[3] Yet from the summer of 1941, the scope of the news was widened. There had been some 'stiffening' of the tone of the broadcasts to include biting criticisms of the Government;[4] Denmark's signature of the Anti-Comintern Pact in November 1941 had been vigorously attacked; and the 'entire propaganda' of the BBC was felt to have played some part, if not a crucial one, in the popular demonstrations which followed.[5] The first agents to be parachuted into Denmark arrived in December 1941.[6]

By May 1942, however, PWE was more cautious in its approach to the activities of resistance movements everywhere, and broadcasts to Denmark were more muted. It was in that month also that J. C. Møller, leader of the Danish Conservative Party, arrived in London under the auspices of SOE. Møller had immediate talks with the members of the BBC's Danish Service. He said that 'Danish-language broadcasts were good, even praiseworthy' and that the Danes admired Britain's

---

[1] *Report on a visit to Sweden, Sept. 1943–Jan. 1944, 1 Feb. 1944.

[2] *BBC European Services, *Output Report*, 17–23 May 1942.

[3] See J. Bennett, *British Broadcasting and the Danish Resistance Movement*, p. 33. A brief propaganda battle followed.

[4] Directive of 18–24 June 1941, quoted ibid., pp. 48–9.

[5] For Danish reactions, see *The Times*, 28 Nov. 1941. Count Reventlow, the Danish Minister in London, resigned on 2 Dec. 1941, stating that he could no longer accept orders from the Danish Foreign Ministry.

[6] Bennett, op. cit., p. 56, quoting J. Haestrup, *Kontakt med England* (1954), ch. 7.

willingness to tell the truth as Churchill had told it after the
fall of Singapore. 'Any kind of exaggeration' was to be deplored.
At the same time, he suggested, the impression should never
be given 'that opinion is made in London and projected on
the Danes'. 'If the situation arose', the BBC could extend its
operations deliberately to include the provocation of demonstrations and 'even sabotage', but care should be taken to
avoid irresponsibility.[1] Møller was not taken into the confidence
of SOE,[2] which had brought him to the country, nor was he
advised of the factors influencing official British attitudes
towards acts of sabotage.[3] He was not allowed to say what he
wished on the BBC's Danish Service until there had been yet
another veering of official policy in late August and September
1942. Then, at last, he told his compatriots that there was no
such word as neutrality.[4] 'Action is required of us all, of each
one of us. Not Denmark but the Danish people as such are
Allies. . . . The outcome of this gigantic struggle concerns
us all.' While Møller was preparing, delivering and testing
reactions to his speech, Newsome in his general directives was
laying increased emphasis on Danish resistance.[5]

In October 1942 'the situation' as Møller had envisaged
it appeared to have arrived. It was in that month that the
Germans put great pressure on the Danes and almost forced
a crisis. Yet once again Møller was curbed on the advice of
PWE, and the Danish section of the BBC seemed to be unable
to give clear advice.[6] It was not until the final crisis in 1943
that the BBC could follow a definite policy of encouraging
resistance.

The crucial months in war-time Danish history were March
1943, when a general election showed the world how little

---

[1] *Notes on a discussion between Møller and T. M. Terkelsen, 2 June 1942.
Møller added that there was virtually no Danish listening to Bremen.

[2] His complaint to Commander Hollingworth, head of the Danish section of
SOE, on 19 July 1942 is printed in Bennett, op. cit., pp. 63–4.

[3] See ibid., pp. 65–6, for links between Danish Army Intelligence, 'the League'
and SOE.　　　　　　　　[4] Ibid., p. 80.　　　　　　　　[5] Ibid., p. 81.

[6] *There were differences between Newsome and PWE (ibid., pp. 84 ff.), and
at a meeting on 15 Oct. the Danish Section was accused by Brinley Thomas,
head of the Northern Department of PWE, of mismanaging its broadcasts. An
inquiry followed. The Danish Editor, R. J. Jørgensen, in a memorandum of
15 Oct. 1942, objected to criticism of 'our output' which was based simply on 'a
matter of opinion'. There had been previous differences in June 1942 about
broadcasts by the Danish Minister in Washington.

support the Nazis had in Denmark, April 1943, when SOE decided to go ahead with the full mobilization of resistance, and August 1943, when after a wave of strikes and demonstrations, the Danish Government refused to accept an ultimatum from the Germans asking them to impose the death penalty on saboteurs, to ban all strikes, to censor all news and to introduce a curfew. The 'Model Protectorate' came to an end in that month, and power passed fully into the hands of the *Wehrmacht*. Broadcasts from London contributed to this sequence of events. July broadcasts, particularly those of Hørsholt Hansen, a Danish journalist in London, were deliberately aimed at Danish workers, and played an important part in precipitating the August crisis. Møller himself broadcast on the day of the German ultimatum, stating categorically that 'whatever happens in Denmark . . . there is no doubt that the people will act'.[1] On 29 August, when the Government resigned, a broadcast of a Danish resistance leader, Dr. Fog, recorded on disc in Copenhagen and smuggled out to London, was played in the BBC's Danish programme.[2]

A Freedom Council of seven resistance leaders was set up in Denmark on 16 September 1943, but because of PWE directives it did not receive the full support of the BBC until 31 October.[3] In the meantime, it was a measure of BBC influence in Denmark that the Council had tried to make direct contact with London through a message to the BBC. From November 1943 onwards —not without criticism from inside Denmark[4]—the BBC set itself the task of seeking to gear its broadcasts to the actions of the Freedom Council so that 'minor isolated acts of resistance' could be linked in a general campaign. The use of broadcasting to Denmark as a weapon became as necessary as in broadcasting to France.[5]

Spain, Portugal and Turkey were quite different cases. British policies towards all three countries were bound to take

[1] Bennett, op. cit., pp. 131–5.
[2] Earlier in the year *Faedrelandet*, 3 April 1943, had written of the London broadcasts booming 'through the quiet streets and spreading poison and incitement in thousands of Danish homes'. Quoted op. cit., p. 137.
[3] Ibid., p. 143.
[4] See below, pp. 690–1.
[5] See above, pp. 458–9.

account of the changing pattern of war, and first one and then the others assumed sufficient importance to interest both the Armed Forces and public opinion. In the case of Spain, there had always been room for disagreement between Sir Samuel Hoare in Madrid, 'a sort of Presence behind the scenes', and the BBC.[1] In 1941 Hoare wanted all references to the Spanish Civil War to be deleted from BBC broadcasts and the likely return of a Republican regime to be played down or even dismissed, yet later in the year he was anxious that attacks on 'Fascism' should be permitted. Clearly the case of Spain touched on every issue related to the 'real nature' of the war. Was it a 'people's war' or was it a war where support for the Allies had to be found where it could? Kirkpatrick himself objected strongly to Hoare's 'reckless and hysterical' outbursts:[2] Newsome was just as resentful. At the same time Douglas Woodruff, well-known as a Catholic writer, broadcast frequently to Spain during the early stages of the war along lines that were thought to carry weight even with pro-German listeners.

Attacks on Italian 'Fascism' figured from time to time in broadcasts to Spain, but it was not until the fortunes of war began to favour the Allies that the Nazis were satirized in an interesting programme *La Intuición*, which poked fun at Hitler's intuition and Dr. Goebbels's propaganda directives. Hitherto severe restraint had always been exercised. The dangers implicit in Franco's decision to send the Spanish Blue Division to fight against the Russians were clearly identified, but it was insisted that the 'guiding principle' behind BBC broadcasts was 'to appeal to Spaniards of all shades of political opinion and to avoid the appearance of taking sides in matters of domestic controversy'. No mention had been made of 'the plans for a new and better post-war world which have played a part in our propaganda elsewhere. The Atlantic Charter and its implications in fact received relatively little attention, perhaps for the reason that on the international side our proposals were too vague to appeal to the concrete-minded

---

[1] *Marks to Stewart, 31 Oct. 1941. See above, p. 262. There are references to the Service—but not in the index—in Lord Templewood, *Ambassador on Special Mission* (1946) and the book by C. J. H. Hayes, the American Ambassador to Madrid, *War-time Mission in Spain* (1945).

[2] *Kirkpatrick to Roberts, 26 Nov. 1942.

Spaniard, and that on the domestic side they raised precisely these questions of economic and social reconstruction such as land reform, we have been so consistently determined to avoid.'[1]

It proved very difficult in practice to steer clear of Spanish controversies or even to eschew all talk about what would happen after the end of the war. Franco's name was never mentioned, yet Hoare complained again in November 1944 about deviations from non-interventionism. He had been alarmed in 1943 about BBC broadcasts which, in his view, encouraged the Spanish Government to continue exporting wolfram to Germany.[2] The Foreign Office also was worried about the composition of the Spanish section of the BBC, even though the BBC pointed out that the 'émigrés' it employed had different shades of political opinion:[3] it suggested, indeed, in 1942 that all Spanish staff should sign an undertaking not to participate in Spanish refugee politics in Britain.

The outstanding regular Spanish broadcaster, R. M. Nadal, was not a political refugee. He broadcast under the pseudonym of Antonio Torres, and was not afraid to deal with views as well as news. He debunked Hitler and Mussolini, counteracted through ridicule German victory fanfares by using a Walt Disney tune himself, and dealt with letters from Spain which he did everything to encourage. He was very popular with a considerable Spanish audience. He too ran into political difficulties, however, in 1943 when the Allies were beginning to get the upper hand and the German victory fanfares had ceased. He was withdrawn from the microphone at Hoare's insistence in December 1943,[4] reinstated in April 1944, but so heavily censored in June 1944, when it was believed he was campaigning for a return of the Spanish monarchy, that he himself refused to broadcast in future. There were difficulties also in connection with Salvador de Madariaga, the greatest Spaniard in exile. Although he broadcast regularly to Latin America—his broadcasts were also relayed to Spain prefaced with the words that they were 'specially written for the Latin

[1] *BBC European Services, *Output Report*, 15–21 March 1942.
[2] Hayes, op. cit., p. 214. The American OWI stopped its broadcasts to try to facilitate negotiations.
[3] *Duckworth Barker to Kirkpatrick, 7 April 1942.
[4] *Memorandum by Dunkerley, 8 Dec. 1943.

American Service'—he was never permitted to broadcast
direct to Spain on any political subjects.[1]

Colonel Casado, who had commanded the troops defending
Madrid during the Civil War, broadcast a weekly military
commentary, however, under the pseudonym of Coronel
Padilla, while Alejandro Raimundez, formerly Professor of
Political Economy at the University of Barcelona, deliberately
selected programme material designed to project British
institutions and ways of life in the hope that they 'might be
an example to the Spain which had to be rebuilt after the
Civil War'. He also emphasized with tact and prudence the
need for 'dialogue' in Spain between victors and vanquished
and the need to take legal and political dispositions in order
to guarantee an orderly succession after Franco's death.[2]

Portuguese broadcasts also were concerned mainly with the
projection of Britain. Their control was separated from control
of the Spanish broadcasts late in 1941, when Winch, who had
previously been Polish Editor, was transferred to the Portuguese
section.[3] The stars of the service were F. L. de O. Pessa, who
had been an announcer in Lisbon, and Antonio Pedro, who,
whatever the limitations, often strayed into politics. The
Portuguese were officially not allowed to listen to foreign
broadcasts in public, but discipline was far less strict than in
Spain, where people were arrested and fined or imprisoned for
reading or possessing the BBC's guide to its programmes.[4]
There was talk as early as 1940 of the BBC stationing a permanent representative in Lisbon—Salt suggested two—but no
representative ever took up residence there.[5]

There was no BBC representative, either, in the other great
neutral capital, Ankara, although David Mitchell, the BBC's

[1] *Daily Telegraph*, 18 June; madariaga to Monahan, 3 Aug. 1962. He broadcast
in a historical series on the millennium of Castile and other non-political topics.

[2] Note by Raimundez, 1967.

[3] *J. B. Clark to Macgregor, 20 Sept. 1941; Dunkerley to Kirkpatrick, 14 Nov.
1941; *Latin American News*, 15 April 1942. Winch was later replaced by B. S.
Willmore. J. H. P. Marks, appointed Spanish Programme Organizer in Nov. 1940,
became Spanish Editor, to be succeeded by R. H. C. Papworth in Feb. 1942 and
C. H. C. Guyatt in Dec. 1943.

[4] Templewood, op. cit., p. 203. The Spanish Press never printed times of BBC
broadcasts, while it regularly printed those of *Voz de Alemania*.

[5] When Marks left the Spanish Service in 1942 he went out to Lisbon as
Ministry of Information representative.

Turkish Editor, served as Press Attaché there from the autumn of 1942 to the spring of 1943. The Turkish Service, organized as a part of the Near East Services of the BBC under Hillelson and Stephenson, was seldom free from disputes both with the Ministry of Information and the British Council. 'I doubt if there is any service over which there has been so much vacillation, in both policy and practical fields,' J. B. Clark complained, 'on the Ministry side.'[1] There were also difficulties of recruitment. The most zealous and able recruit was a young Turkish student, A. Kartal, who was described during the war as a kind of Turkish Ed Murrow, but his zeal and ability led the Turkish Ambassador to accuse him of appealing over the heads of the Turkish Government direct to the Turkish people.[2] The employment of other Turkish students raised further difficulties with a different Ambassador.[3]

Sir Wyndham Deedes, a retired Army officer, whose credentials were beyond reproach[4] and who was regularly employed by the BBC as a commentator on every kind of subject, was felt by the head of the British Council in Ankara, Michael Grant, to speak the wrong kind of Turkish. 'He does not talk modern Turkish and he uses too many Arabic and Persian words.'[5] To try to deal with the awkward problem of language, the BBC's Turkish Language Supervisor was changed, yet the argument about what, if anything, constituted 'common correct Turkish' continued throughout the war. The content of the programmes aroused equal argument, not least because of the uncertainties concerning British foreign policy, even greater uncertainties than there were in the case of Denmark. Not even Kirkpatrick knew how to deal with them.[6]

This account of the complex pattern of propaganda and Intelligence shows how difficult it is to generalize about the BBC's European Services as a whole and about relationships

---

[1] *Clark to Graves, 4 June 1942. Further intrigues are outlined in a memorandum from Stephenson to Hillelson, 3 April 1943.

[2] *Barbour to Hillelson, 7 Oct. 1941; Notes on an interview, 3 Oct. 1941.

[3] *Clark to Hillelson, Notes on a Meeting, 30 Aug. 1942.

[4] See J. Presland, *Deedes Bey* (1942).

[5] *Note of 11 June 1941.

[6] *Clutton to Kirkpatrick, 2 Oct. 1943; Stephenson to Hillelson and others, 5 Oct. 1943.

with PWE. Individuals counted, and many of them had their own sense not only of what broadcasting could and could not do in a protracted war but of what mattered and did not matter. Where 'high policy' was thought to be lacking or contradictory, there was obviously a place for independent judgement, and it is not surprising to read in the Minutes of a European Divisional Meeting, held in the period before D-Day, that 'it was reaffirmed that no PWE directive applied—until it had been formally accepted by the BBC. Editors were entitled to challenge any directive with which they were not in agreement and circulation should not take place until such disagreements had been thrashed out.'[1]

Whether or not a detailed scrutiny of the history of PWE itself would also reveal tensions between 'centralizers' and 'regionalists' or between 'planners' and 'improvisers' is a question which cannot be answered in the light of existing available evidence. Within the BBC, however, it is clear that Newsome, with so many assets at his disposal, could never push 'centralization' as far as he and possibly Kirkpatrick would have liked. He put down his views on paper far more than most of the regional editors. 'We are wandering off the target,' he complained in June 1942, 'not just sometimes but nearly always. . . . Not only do some editors follow their own line, but they actually adopt a line directly contrary to that which has been laid down. Now that clearly cannot go on. The principle has been accepted in the highest quarters that the European Service shall act as an entity, as an army attacking clearly defined objects, and using a strategy laid down broadly by the Commanding Officer, and not as a series of guerilla bands or groups of partisans, with no cohesion and entirely self-ordained plans and aims.'[2]

Such arguments were always resisted within Bush House, a house with many mansions, not to speak of the corridors: feelings still remain strong about them after nearly thirty years, to such an extent that perspectives can still be warped. At the same time, the arguments were also resisted by the Regional Officers of PWE, some of whom felt that if the war were to be fought all over again the BBC would have to be

---

[1] *European Divisional Meeting, *Minutes*, 30 May 1944.
[2] *Directive of 18 June 1942, quoted in Bennett, op. cit., p. 83.

given a very different place in it. They were aware of aspects of Intelligence, without an appreciation of which they did not think any adequate broad strategy of propaganda could be laid down. 'It is legitimate to point to good Intelligence as the foundation of good propaganda,' Ivor Thomas wrote in a wartime Pelican book, *Warfare by Words*. The intelligence, however, had to be comprehensive as well as good. The operations of SOE had to be taken into account as well as the economic, social and political facts which arrived in Bush House via the BBC's own Intelligence section. Kirkpatrick was in the picture, but he had come to the conclusion even before PWE routines were established that the most important thing for the BBC to do was to seek to tell the truth.

The greatest special skill of the BBC lay in its provision, with the help of highly efficient engineers, many of whom still remain anonymous, of a daily programme of broadcasts which deliberately started in the early dawn. The idea of a 'dawn cycle' was originally Salt's[1], and through rapid switches of short programmes in different languages throughout the day the maximum audience was attracted.[2] Attention was paid to four relevant factors—the number of potential listeners; the availability of transmitters; the psychology and sociology of listening, given that listening conditions were often difficult and that hard evidence was sometimes equally difficult to come by; and priorities as between the different services.[3] Every readjustment of the schedule, whether on account of a change in wavelengths or of German summer-time, involved the most searching discussion about relative needs. The kind of modification which took place as discussion and bargaining continued may be illustrated from the table on p. 484.

The Blue Network was one of a number of different 'colour' networks which together constituted the nexus of overseas broadcasting. Each network comprised studios, switch-gear, lines and a group of transmitters. In late 1941 there were four

[1] *Wellington to Salt, 29 Dec. 1940; Salt to Wellington, 3 Jan. 1941; Note by Newsome, 17 Feb. 1941.

[2] *Lawson-Reece to Grisewood, 10 March 1942: 'There is evidence that listeners in Europe find it difficult to concentrate for long periods on a continuous broadcast in any one language, and the continual increase of jamming will not improve this situation.'

[3] *Lawson-Reece to Dunkerley, 26 Nov. 1941.

networks, Red, Blue, Green, and Yellow, the second of which carried broadcasts to Central and Western Europe and the Mediterranean and the third of which carried services *inter*

BLUE NETWORK: CHANGES IMPLEMENTED IN 1942

First Planned Schedule 12 Dec. 1941		Revised Schedule after discussions 26 Jan. 1942	
0345	Announcements	0340	German News (dictation speed)
0350	Polish News	0350	Polish
0400	German	0400	German
0415	French	0410	Czech
0430	Italian	0415	French
0440	Dutch	0420	Danish
0450	Polish	0430	Italian
0500	German	0440	Dutch
0510	Czech	0450	Polish
0515	French	0500	German
0530	Italian	0510	Czech
0540	Flemish	0515	French
0550	Polish	0530	Italian
0600	German	0540	Dutch
0610	Czech	0550	Polish
0615	French	0600	German
0630	Italian	0610	Czech
0640	Dutch	0615	French
0650	Radio Belgique	0630	Italian
0700	German	0640	Radio Belgique (on Sundays
0710	Czech	0700	German Luxembourg)
0715	French	0710	Czech
0730	Radio Oranje	0715	French
		0730	Radio Oranje
		0745	Entertainment period

Under Existing Schedule			Under Revised Schedule
Germans	1 hr.	(lose 10)	50 mins.
Italians	30 mins.	—	30 mins.
Poles	15 mins.	(gain 15)	30 mins.
Czechs	15 mins.	(gain 5)	20 mins.
French	30 mins.	(gain 20)	50 mins.
Dutch	—	(gain 20)	20 mins.
Belgians	15 mins.	(gain 5)	20 mins.
Danes	15 mins.	(lose 5)	10 mins.

alia to Turkey and the Near East.[1] In 1942 a further network, Brown, was added to deal with the Near East and Latin America, and the Yellow Network was reorganized to provide

[1] The system was first described to the public in the *BBC Handbook, 1942*, pp. 9 ff.

the channels for additional European Services for Spain, Portugal, the Balkans and Scandinavia.[1] Further changes took place in relation to Europe when Grey was added to Yellow and Blue. The first idea had been to call it 'Black', but Dunkerley pointed out that 'black' had different connotations.[2]

As the networks were constructed, the total output of BBC programmes to Europe increased substantially, as had been planned when 'triple expansion' was envisaged. The following table sets out some of the relevant figures: the fact that minutes are given shows in itself how nicely the relative proportions were judged:

EUROPEAN SERVICE OUTPUT, 1939–1945
(Hours and Minutes each Week)

Service	Year						
	Sept. 1939	Sept. 1940	Sept. 1941	Sept. 1942	Sept. 1943	Sept. 1944	May 1945
English Language	66.51	61.36	24.44	19.15	21.05	27.15	25.15
French	3.30	17.30	28.00	35.35	39.30	43.45	38.15
German	7.00	17.30	28.35	32.05	34.40	34.25	32.55
Austrian	—	—	—	—	8.45	12.15	14.00
Italian	3.30	14.00	15.45	19.50	29.45	30.45	21.00
Polish	—	5.15	7.00	12.15	15.10	16.55	18.40
Czechoslovak	—	7.00	8.45	11.05	15.10	15.10	16.55
Belgian	—	—	3.30	5.50	8.45	8.45	3.30
Dutch	—	8.45	9.55	12.15	17.30	16.30	15.45
Norwegian	—	6.25	7.35	8.10	12.15	14.00	14.00
Greek	—	3.30	5.15	8.45	12.15	12.15	12.15
Yugoslav	—	3.30	6.40	6.05	11.20	12.05	9.35
Albanian	—	—	0.35	0.35	2.55	2.55	1.45
Bulgarian	—	1.45	1.45	4.40	6.00	8.45	8.45
Hungarian	—	1.45	2.55	5.15	8.45	8.45	8.45
Roumanian	—	3.30	3.30	4.40	9.20	9.20	8.10
Danish	—	1.45	2.20	5.15	7.00	10.30	8.45
Finnish	—	1.45	1.45	3.30	7.00	7.00	7.00
Swedish	—	1.45	1.45	3.30	5.15	7.00	3.30
Spanish	1.45	3.30	7.00	9.00	10.30	12.15	12.15
Portuguese	1.45	3.30	7.00	8.45	8.45	12.15	12.15
Icelandic	—	—	0.15	0.15	0.15	—	—
Luxembourg	—	—	—	—	1.00	1.45	1.45

---

[1] *BBC Handbook, 1943*, pp. 9 ff.
[2] *Dunkerley to Hayes, 5 June 1942.

It is impossible to secure comparative figures about changing German foreign-language output during the war, although the BBC's Monitoring Service, by 1942 a lynch-pin of the whole BBC war-time organization, watched carefully what was happening. It had always to be ready to respond to the demands from 'important consumers of our material', wherever they were. The Armed Forces counted on the service, for example, to monitor all receivable lists of prisoners of war; the Intelligence agencies called on the Y Unit to monitor all 'Freedom Stations'; and the one Hellschreiber machine available in 1942 was put to good use, as we have seen, by PWE and the BBC's German Service.[1] In the middle of 1942 the Monitoring Service employed 550 people and was seeking to secure an additional hundred. Both PWE and the Ministry of Information attached the utmost importance to its growth and to the full co-ordination of the service with that of other related agencies inside or outside the BBC.[2]

It is scarcely surprising, therefore, that the *haute politique* of monitoring counted for so much in 1942.[3] Yet the move to Caversham, which had caused so much controversy and had contributed to Ogilvie's resignation, was successfully accomplished in April 1943. The Treasury had approved the move in April 1942, and the delay in moving was caused not by any further argument inside the BBC but by dilatory behaviour on the part of the authorities.[4] The move was immediately

---

[1] *R. Burns, 'Monitoring Service Development', Memorandum to J. B. Clark, 20 Aug. 1942.

[2] *Note by Clark on 'Coordination of Monitoring Services', 10 Dec. 1941, following a meeting at the Ministry of Information on 19 Nov. 1941.

[3] See above, p. 361.

[4] *Treasury approval is noted in the Director-General's Meeting, *Minutes*, 17 April 1942. The main reasons for the move were stated clearly in a letter from Foot to Radcliffe, 16 March 1942: 'our proposal is to move Monitoring to properties near Reading, at Caversham Park, for the accommodation of the headquarters and main body of the unit, and at Crowsley Park for the erection of special aerials for reception of very distant stations. The district in which they are situated has several technical advantages over Evesham. It is a greater distance from any high power broadcasting station, Droitwich being only about 12 miles from Wood Norton, the present location of Monitoring. There is greater space for the erection of the special aerials and more suitable land for the lay-out. The lines to London are shorter, thereby allowing for a simpler organisation, and there is ample space for expansion of technical or other facilities. Furthermore, it will no longer be necessary to maintain a monitoring office in London, and this will save money and staff.'

successful on technical grounds, for many stations which had not been 'readable' at Evesham could now be heard, and others which had been difficult to receive were now received with far greater clarity.[1] On the social side, despite all the worries expressed earlier, there had been 'a few minor billeting problems' but all had been 'settled satisfactorily'.[2] Nicolson, as a Governor, was very happy about the 'excellence of the set-up'. 'I never miss a single report,' he wrote in May 1943, 'and find them immensely useful and informative.'[3] There is no evidence, however, as to whether members of the Cabinet spent much time reading the 'Report on World Broadcasts for the War Cabinet'[4] and a much-discussed project to print the *Digest* was turned down on financial grounds in September 1943.[5] By then it may be said that the enterprise, like many other enterprises concerned with Britain and Europe, had reached its highest level. The peak effort, however, was still to come. There must have been great excitement when, at last, in April 1944 the Director-General sent a personal message to each member of the staff impressing upon them 'the supreme necessity for the strictest observance of security measures during the next few weeks and months'.[6] D-Day was imminent.

2. The World Map of Radio

THE European Service of the BBC, which by 1942 had developed to an extent never envisaged in 1939, had to deal with the most difficult war-time problems both of Intelligence and of propaganda. It was a fair, if ironical, indication of the pressures on it that it was agreed in April 1943 that the staff were too busy to take part in a discussion on the international

---

[1] *Note by Foot, 21 Sept. 1943.

[2] *BBC Monitoring Service, *Editorial Bulletin*, 7 April 1943.

[3] *Ibid., 11 May 1943.

[4] *Monitoring Service Liaison Committee, *Minutes*, 1 June 1942.

[5] *Ibid., 29 Sept. 1943. Specimens had already been printed (ibid., 25 Aug. 1943) and there was great enthusiasm for the project. R. S. Baker, who had been head of the Editorial Unit since Dec. 1940, was transferred in June 1943.

[6] *BBC Monitoring Service, *Editorial Bulletin*, 28 April 1944. See below, pp. 660 ff.

uses of radio.[1] Critical moments like the Allied landings in North Africa in November 1942 or the Russian success at Stalingrad in January 1943 influenced what could be and what had to be said in Europe. Yet Europe was only one area on the map of war. Middle Eastern and African events were directly related to events in Europe; broadcasting to the United States was broadcasting to the most powerful of the Allies; Latin America was influenced throughout the war by rival propaganda emanating from both the United States and Europe; and in Asia the European powers, particularly Britain, had great possessions, many of them occupied by the enemy. India, in particular, played its part in domestic British politics, particularly at the time of the abortive Cripps mission of March 1942 which followed the Japanese conquest of Burma and what appeared to be a mounting threat to Ceylon and to India itself.

'The Ministry of Information is using us to co-ordinate monitoring all over the world,' the Director of the Monitoring Service wrote in August 1942. 'We are already receiving material from Istanbul, New Delhi, Mauritius, the United States West Coast and other places, and we expect in the near future to have a unit in Washington and a service is being set up in Australia.'[2] The global preoccupations of the monitors were shared by the engineers on whom they depended. At the end of 1943 the Governors were congratulating Bishop on 'the completion of . . . great and complicated expansion'.[3] Three new short-wave stations had been brought into use—two of them situated a mile apart on a common site at Skelton, near Penrith, one near Ludlow in Shropshire.[4] The Brown Network was shared between the Near East and Latin America. The Red Network covered the Pacific Service, the

---

[1] *European Divisional Meeting, *Minutes*, 13 April 1943. In Nov. 1943, however, de Laveleye became chairman of a committee to consider an international staff association after the war (ibid., 16 Nov. 1943).

[2] *R. Burns to Clark, 'Monitoring Service Development', 20 Aug. 1942.

[3] *Board of Governors, *Minutes*, 2 Dec. 1943. For 'triple expansion', see above, pp. 345–65.

[4] See H. Bishop, 'The War-time Activities of the Engineering Division of the BBC' in the *Journal of the Institute of Electrical Engineers*, vol. 94 (1947). One of the stations at Skelton was designed for the European Service, the other for world coverage. Woofferton, near Ludlow, was for world coverage, but certain aerials were provided for the European Service.

African Service and the North American Service. Sometimes
'freak' conditions permitted the most unlikely programmes to
be picked up in the most unlikely places. In August 1942,
for instance, it was noted that the BBC's African Service
was being picked up in Northern Russia, and Clark was
asked in consequence to consider making occasional references
to British convoys and troops assisting the Russians.[1] This was
an even more remarkable phenomenon from the broadcaster's
point of view than Miss Sampson of the BBC's European
Service being told by a Russian diplomat on her official visit
to Sweden in 1943 just how good he thought the BBC's broadcasts in Bulgarian were.[2]

There were anomalies as well as surprises in the organization
of the World Service, some irritating rather than inspiring.
Thus, the use of Home Service wavelengths for the early
and late morning Norwegian news bulletin continued throughout the war, and it was not until 28 March 1943 that Home
wavelengths ceased to be used for the early evening news in
Norwegian.[3] 'It just makes hay of our programmes,' Nicolls
had protested in October 1941. 'When your audience suddenly
drops to nil, it takes quite a lot of time to pick it up again.'[4]
A quite different kind of conflict of interest arose in 1942.
Ritchie complained about a passage in a Home Service talk
which conflicted with a comment in the European Service
News in English the same night, and the passage was duly cut.
Yet Maconachie brought all his guns to bear in further discussion of the issues raised. Hundreds of listeners in Europe,
he pointed out, chose to listen to the Home Service rather than
to the European Service of the BBC 'partly because they
regard this service as comparatively free from propaganda
and partly because the European Service in English suffers
from jamming'. In France 'moderate and sensible people often
said that when they wanted news they listened to the British
Home News from which they got accurate facts without
any embroidery; no encouragement, but truth'; in Belgium
eight out of ten Belgians who spoke English listened to the

---

[1] *Controllers' Conference, *Minutes*, 5 Aug. 1942.
[2] *Report of 1 Feb. 1944. See above, p. 474.
[3] *Board of Governors, *Minutes*, 25 March 1943.
[4] *Nicolls to Kirkpatrick, 29 Oct. 1941.

BBC's Home Service. 'To modify the Home Service in order to bring it into line with the European Service would, therefore, be not merely making the foreign tail wag the British dog, but also destroying the qualities in the Home Service which cause it to be so widely listened to in Europe.'[1]

Given the vast amount of radio eavesdropping which went on during the war, this was fair comment. The second of two big studies of 'eavesdropping', completed in April 1944, concentrated on Europe. 'In almost every part of Europe,' it began, 'people overhear, either at a set or second hand, British broadcasts not meant for them.' The practical problem posed by this was how to maintain consistency while tolerating necessary divergences of emphasis.[2] The problem was accentuated since the German overseas services frequently indulged in polemics against all the different British services in English, setting one off against the others. There were some parts of the world where there was a very wide choice of BBC programmes in English. Thus, of listeners in French North Africa who reported 'eavesdropping' on programmes in English in 1943, six listened to the British Home Service, five to the BBC's African Service, which could be picked up more easily, three to the Pacific Service, two to the European Service, and one to the North American Service.[3] From the Portuguese African colonies, where sets were few, there were reports of people listening to the BBC's Latin American Service as well as to broadcasts designed for Portugal itself.[4] In the Middle East there were many Arab listeners who felt that they were 'more likely to get the truth from the material provided to the British audience than from that specifically aimed at themselves'.[5]

---

[1] *Maconachie to Foot, 23 Sept. 1942. Cf. a comment made by Radio Paris, 1 March 1942: 'If one listens to transmissions in English for home consumption and not for "the negroes of the Continent" one can realise the uneasiness in England.' (Quoted in 'Radio Eavesdropping'.)

[2] *BBC Special Studies of European Audiences, 'Radio Eavesdropping', 24 April 1944. The first report had been issued on 15 Dec. 1941. They are both remarkable reports, thorough, comprehensive and persuasive. See also Programme Policy Committee, Minutes, 18 Sept. 1942. There was a discussion on this occasion of differences in the interpretation of the Russian military situation in Home and Overseas broadcasts: the cause of the difference was thought to be 'divergent sources of specialised advice'.

[3] *BBC Special Studies of European Audiences, 'Radio Eavesdropping', 24 April 1944. [4] See above, p. 480.

[5] *Report by E. G. D. Liveing, 18 Sept. 1942. For the Report, see below, p. 526.

The European Service of the BBC was, as we have seen, a microcosm of its own centred in Bush House. The core of broadcasting to the rest of the world was the BBC's Empire Service. On Christmas Day 1932, six days after the opening of this pioneering service, King George V had told his listeners that 'it may be that our future will lay upon us more than one stern test'. There were certainly many 'stern tests' during the middle years of the war. However great and scattered the new world audience and however strong the arguments for treating the needs of the United States in a specialized fashion, Empire needs continued to be given particular attention. Large numbers of soldiers, sailors and airmen from all parts of the Empire were serving in the Allied Forces, and there was immense interest in Toronto, Sydney and Johannesburg in what was happening in London. Kirkpatrick's opposite number, J. B. Clark, Controller (Overseas), played an important part in the transformation of the Empire Service into a world service with distinctive regional sections, and late in the war he was to succeed Kirkpatrick as Controller (European). Yet he represented the continuity of the service: he had done much to establish its standards before the war,[1] and the Corporation's insistence in 1941, not without difficulty at the time, on giving the key Overseas post to him and not to a new person recruited from outside,[2] was of the utmost long-term importance. His main assistant was R. A. Rendall, also very much a BBC man (a good example of the proverbial 'old head on young shoulders'),[3] who always drove himself very hard; and Rendall in turn worked very closely with Marjorie Wace, an indomitable organizer whose friendly assistance was appreciated by everyone who came to the microphone. Miss Wace died young during the war, in 1944.

Although the Ministry of Information had an Empire Division and was expected to maintain close liaison with the BBC,[4] particularly with the Empire News Editor, the Ministry exercised far less control over Empire broadcasting than over broadcasts to Europe; and although the Dominions Office—

---

[1] See Briggs, *The Golden Age of Wireless* (1965), p. 648.
[2] *Powell to Bracken, 27 Sept. 1941.
[3] M. Gorham, *Sound and Fury* (1948), p. 97.
[4] *Control Board (Overseas), *Minutes*, 13 Nov. 1941.

through Lord Cranborne—for a time arranged weekly meetings 'to give general guidance on treatment of Empire affairs',[1] the guidance given was usually general rather than specific. It seldom involved the BBC in difficulties similar to those which it encountered because of the intervention of the Foreign Office. Nonetheless, Vernon Bartlett complained in Parliament in May 1942 that when Cripps visited India 'the directives came only from an official in the India Office and not from the BBC'. He grumbled also that it had been decided earlier 'by Heaven knows what Government Department' that the BBC should never refer to the development of British trade routes across Africa, 'one of the most romantic things which have happened in this war'.[2]

During the middle years of the war, the Empire Service was transformed into a universal service in English, catering not only for Dominion and Colonial audiences but, amongst others, for British and Commonwealth forces operating in very different conditions in the different theatres of war. The transformation began with the launching in November 1942 of a service for British forces in North Africa and the Middle East; it was re-named the Overseas Forces Programme on 10 January 1943. By then programmes were being broadcast for six hours a day. On 13 June 1943 output was doubled, and the range of the service was extended to cover listeners from the Burmese frontier of India to the west coast of Africa. Finally on 21 November 1943 BBC engineers, the indispensable agents without whom there could have been no world service, provided it with new beams to cover the South Atlantic shipping lanes, South America and the United States and Canada, and output rose to 20 hours a day.[3] This General Overseas Service, as it was eventually called, was listened to both by soldiers and civilians, often in the most remote places. It was designed, above all else, to provide a link with Britain: propaganda played a very minor part.

It was supplemented zealously and imaginatively, under Rendalls' direction, by services of a regional character specially

---

[1] *Board of Governors, *Minutes*, 5 Feb. 1942.

[2] *Hansard*, vol. 380, col. 168.

[3] *BBC Yearbook, 1944*, p. 83. For these changes in a different context, see below, p. 589.

designed for North Africa, the Caribbean, Africa, India, South-East Asia and the Pacific. The policy of 'increasing specialization' both of staff and programmes had been enunciated in 1941 before the General Overseas Service came into existence.[1] 'As the regional specialists come to learn more about broadcasting,' Rendall wrote privately then, 'so we find it possible to give them greater executive responsibility without any serious loss in standard.'[2] By 1943, when the number of transmitters available had increased as planned, the policy became explicit. 'A salient feature of war-time broadcasting,' it was stated, 'is that programmes in these services are specialised as far as possible to suit various groups of listeners for which they are primarily intended.'[3]

The number of foreign languages used had increased substantially by the spring of 1943 to include Afrikaans, Bengali, Burmese, Chinese (Cantonese, Hokkien and Kuoyü), French (for Canada), Greek (for Cyprus), Gujerati, Hindustani, Malay, Marathi, Maltese, Sinhalese, Tamil and Thai. There had also been a substantial increase in the amount of re-broadcasting of BBC programmes by independent Dominions' radio services and by Colonial stations. Twenty-five countries in all were involved. The Australian Broadcasting Commission re-broadcast a weekly average of 112 hours, including *Radio Newsreel* and three BBC news programmes each day. The Canadian Broadcasting Corporation broadcast on an average 11 hours a week, All India Radio 3½ hours, the South African Broadcasting Corporation 12 hours, and the New Zealand Broadcasting Service as much as 16 hours, including seven news bulletins each day. Barbados, Gold Coast, Nigeria, Sierra Leone and Trinidad relied almost exclusively on British programmes.

The 'unity of the Commonwealth'—and the word 'Commonwealth' was beginning to replace the word 'Empire'—was expressed not only in a sense of interest in and concern for common themes, given all the necessary differences of presentation,[4] but in the building up of a team of broadcasters

[1] *Rendall to A. S. Bokhari, 28 Aug. 1941. [2] *Ibid.
[3] *BBC Brief for the Minister of Information, 2 April 1943.
[4] M. Barkway, 'Twenty-five Years of the BBC Overseas Service' in the *Birmingham Post*, 15 Dec. 1953: 'presentation had to vary. . . . But at least the theme was common and simple and absorbingly interesting. And the market was eager.'

from different Commonwealth countries. The North American Service, as we have seen, depended on people from the Canadian Broadcasting Corporation; R. C. McCall of the Australian Broadcasting Commission was called in to run the first Pacific Service; and Z. A. Bokhari of All India Radio was selected to manage the services for India. At the same time, the London Transcription Service, LTS, which had been started in 1941,[1] went much further than the Joint Broadcasting Committee had done in despatching round the world recorded programmes of all kinds on 'virtually unbreakable discs'.

There was one development which did not take place during the war, although it was advocated with fervour by a number of people inside and outside the Ministry and the BBC— the creation of a large-scale 'Empire Broadcasting Network'. As early as May and June 1939, before the outbreak of war, the Empire Service Director, then J. C. S. Macgregor, had prepared a paper for Ivison Macadam, then a key member of the staff of the embryonic Ministry of Information, entitled 'Communication by Broadcasting: World Network for Defence'. It set out details of an ambitious development plan, including the building of a high-power short-wave relay station in Singapore and a medium-wave transmitter in Cyprus to serve the Middle East.[2] By 1941 nothing had happened,[3] though there had been further talk of the construction of a Canadian short-wave station when Britain was in danger.[4]

Even after an Overseas Sub-Committee, under Clark's chairmanship, had produced a report on the need for an extended Empire network which won the Board's blessing,[5]

[1] See above, p. 344, and *London Transcription Service, First Progress Report, 10 Nov. 1941.

[2] In Parliament Sir Frank Sanderson gave notice in Oct. 1939 that he was pressing for 'a chain of wireless stations throughout the Empire . . . to counteract subversive tendencies'. R. H. Scott of the Ministry of Information pressed consistently for the building of the Singapore transmitter.

[3] See above, p. 347; *Clark to Rendall, 21 Dec. 1940. U.K. High Commissioners had been advised of the recommendations of the Plymouth Committee of 1936 on the encouragement of Colonial broadcasting and there had been talks between Ogilvie and Malcolm Macdonald about the possibility of obtaining grants from the Colonial Development Fund for this purpose.

[4] *Ogilvie to Lee, 24 June 1940. For the station, see above, p. 349.

[5] *'Empire Broadcasting Network', 13 Aug. 1941. The Committee had met in June and July. Its report was considered by Control Board and approved with

the plan which it proposed never secured the support of the Government. It urged the installation of more Empire transmitters on a co-operative basis, the establishment of a relaying network for distribution purposes, the improvement of reception of the Empire broadcasts and the fostering of local development of broadcasting services, particularly in the Colonies: it ended with the stirring words—'to leave this development to proceed unplanned and unco-ordinated, evolving by its own slow processes, is to acquiesce in a spasmodic and unequal growth always lagging far behind imperial and local needs and to prolong a situation in which the exchanges between Great Britain and the rest of the Empire are inevitably far too one-sided.' Macgregor, then at the Ministry of Information, welcomed this extension of his own plan: indeed, he thought that as the war spread to all parts of the world it was an essential element in what he called 'a world strategy of broadcasting'.[1] His new Minister, Bracken, sympathized with him. 'The formation of PWE marked a notable step forward by combining under one control all broadcasts directed to those territories which are now under enemy rule; but similar co-ordination of transmissions for other parts of the world is badly needed.'[2]

Yet, once again, nothing happened. Talk of a co-ordinating committee to include representatives of PWE, the Foreign Office, the Ministry of Information and the Dominions and Colonial Offices with an independent chairman—Reith was suggested—broke down in face of the Prime Minister's 'aversion to committees'.[3] Thereafter Bracken is said to have lost interest.[4]

[1] *Note by Macgregor, 'The Strategy of Broadcasting', 8 Sept. 1941. He complained of the multiplicity of agencies taking decisions about propaganda. 'All broadcasting projects,' he urged, 'should pass through a single filter.'

[2] *Draft Paper by Bracken, 28 Oct. 1941.

[3] *Note by Miss Benzie, 25 Aug. 1942.

[4] *Note by Lawson-Reece, 15 Sept. 1942. Lord Hood was as keen as ever. 'I suggest some form of inter-Allied Broadcasting Committee . . . such a body would also be able to view the Far East from a broad angle and decide where transmitters could best be erected and how they should best be employed.' (Hood to Macgregor, 14 Aug. 1942.)

some modifications (*Minutes*, 3 Sept. 1941), and later by the Board (*Minutes*, 11 Sept. 1941). Ogilvie then sent the details of the plan to Radcliffe. Before he did so, he had written earlier to Monckton (15 Aug. 1941) that 'various recent developments have suggested here the need for an authoritative Government Committee which should handle problems of broadcasting developments overseas'.

The problem, said Radcliffe, involved so many interdepartmental jealousies and difficulties that it was 'just one of those things over which any co-ordination cannot be achieved. In the circumstances, even if a committee could be established, several vital interests would either remain outside or would just go their own sweet way.'[1] A number of Members of Parliament continued from time to time to ask questions about the subject, but got no support.[2]

The result was 'unplanned and unco-ordinated growth' in scattered parts of the Empire with friction on the way, particularly after the Americans entered the war. A small station was erected at Lusaka in 1941. Broadcasting services in the Gold Coast were started under the control of the Public Relations Department. Independent plans were put forward, like those of Captain Watterson of the Inter-Services Research Bureau, for a propaganda station in the Near East.[3] Nairobi continued to broadcast in French even though its transmissions could not be heard in Madagascar for which they were intended.[4] Lord Gort went ahead with the building of a low-power station in Gibraltar, assisted by a Marconi Company engineer: he had been told by Bracken he could do what he liked and that he would get 'full support'. Yet Sir Samuel Hoare had not been consulted at that stage about the implications for Spain of British broadcasting from Gibraltar, and the broadcasts, when they began in the spring of 1942, were inaudible in French North Africa where they might have been useful.[5]

Macgregor's dream of a Mediterranean link-up within an Empire network (Gibraltar, Malta, Cyprus) never came true, and there was no adequate machinery for deciding on the rival claims of Cyprus and Palestine to a 100 and a 50 kilowatt transmitter which became available in 1943. In Gibraltar itself, demand for a 50 kilowatt medium-wave station continued

[1] *Clark to Graves, 31 July 1942.

[2] Captain Plugge, who was prominent in discussion of all matters relating to broadcasting, had asked about Mediterranean links in 1941 (*Hansard*, vol. 370, col. 572); Granville raised the question of an Empire chain in 1944 (*Hansard*, vol. 398, col. 465).

[3] *Ashbridge to Ogilvie, 10 Oct. 1941; Ogilvie to Radcliffe, 17 Oct. 1941.

[4] *Minutes of a meeting at the Ministry of Information, 2 June 1942.

[5] *Minutes of a meeting at the Ministry of Information, 1 Sept. 1941; Monckton to Ogilvie, 5 Sept. 1941.

to be pressed when it was by no means clear that it would serve as useful a purpose as a new station located elsewhere.[1] Nor did Macgregor's dream come true of a link-up between the Americans and the British and Dominion Governments. There were complications and compromises instead of co-ordination. He drew attention to the fact, for instance, that the United States was offering broadcasts in French to South-East Asia 'though it was ill-placed technically to serve Indo-China'.[2]

The most frustrating case of all was Singapore, the city on which the whole idea of 'imperial broadcasting' had pivoted in pre-war days. The demand for a station there had been described as 'urgent' six months before war broke out.[3] When a transmitter was eventually shipped out there, early in 1941, it was sunk on the way, and a second transmitter of smaller power which was sent from the United States had not been put into use before the Japanese arrived. The city fell with heated complaints still arriving in London from Singapore that the project had been handled in a 'slipshod' and 'short-sighted' way. 'One delay after another has occurred, some unavoidable, some not.'[4]

The same might have been said of a broadcasting service from London to the Far East. R. A. Butler had written to Ogilvie from the Foreign Office in February 1941 pressing for the appointment of BBC staff capable of broadcasting to the Far East,[5] staff whom Sir John Pratt, an expert on the Far East then working in the Ministry of Information, had also been demanding.[6] For some reason, possibly connected with linguistics, the BBC preferred to look for a Director of Eastern programmes 'as a whole'—from the Persian Gulf to the China seas—rather than to take a Chinese or Japanese specialist. Tallents and Clark both had their eyes not on China or Japan but on India, where there were already so many difficult

[1] *Memorandum of 21 May 1942.
[2] *Note of a meeting, 2 June 1942.
[3] *Memoranda of May and June 1939.
[4] *R. H. Scott to Macgregor, 23 June 1941.
[5] *Butler to Ogilvie, 26 Feb. 1941.
[6] *Tallents to Butler, 27 Feb. 1941; Clark to Tallents, 28 Feb. 1941; Overseas Board, *Minutes*, 27 Feb. 1941.

broadcasting problems that officials were in danger of being overwhelmed by them.[1] In early March 1941, plans for broadcasting in Japanese were abandoned,[2] a decision supported by Kirkpatrick who told the Foreign Office that the BBC should not be pressed to broadcast in Japanese unless such broadcasts would be 'of great value'.[3] Doubtless the difficult problem of just what to broadcast was in his mind as much as the more fundamental problem of how many or how few would listen or the technical difficulties of broadcasting to Japan. Butler was not happy about this decision,[4] but he and Pratt welcomed the start of weekly newsletters in Thai, Malay and Chinese (Kuoyü and Cantonese) which began in April and May.[5] When Pratt continued, notwithstanding, to press for a Japanese service, he was told that the BBC would consider it further 'when the Government had made up its mind':[6] Pratt believed that broadcasts in Japanese might well influence Japanese policy—they would be listened to by monitors, if by no one else, and their contents would be summarized for the benefit of government officials—and whether or not everyone in the Foreign Office agreed with this assessment, it accepted the view in May 1941 that a single weekly programme should be initiated as soon as possible.[7]

By this time, Rendall himself was convinced that a new range of Far Eastern services was needed, but he was seriously concerned about the implications in terms of manpower and finance. 'I am worried,' he wrote in May 1941, 'lest a sudden dramatic turn of events in the Far East should cause us to be

---

[1] See below, pp. 504–12.

[2] *Overseas Board, *Minutes*, 13 March 1941.

[3] *Ibid., 10 April 1941. Kirkpatrick had had an accident in March and was away from the BBC for a time.

[4] *Butler to Ogilvie, 20 March 1941. He wrote again on the same lines on 3 June 1941. 'I feel that nothing should be left undone to encourage resistance to Japan and to prevent her becoming actually involved in war against us.' A further letter followed on 24 June in which he suggested that the BBC should be represented in talks at the Ministry of Information.

[5] *See above, p. 493. The Thai Service had been requested in a letter from Macgregor to Conner, 26 Nov. 1940 (see Rendall to Macgregor, 5 Dec.), but it had proved very difficult to find a suitable speaker. The Thai newsletters were increased to three a week in Aug. 1941.

[6] *Report of a conversation between Pratt and Clark, 29 April 1941.

[7] *Rendall to Pratt, 6 May 1941.

faced with an urgent demand for starting a Chinese news service, possibly even a Japanese news service too, and certainly an increased number of broadcasts in Japanese and Thai. The history of the development of the European Department suggests that one can foretell little about such demands except that when they do come they will be extremely urgent. What I do know is that the Empire Department is simply not equipped suddenly to cope with a demand so exotic and so obviously outside its proper sphere.'[1]

Once again, progress was extremely slow. When an Eastern Service Director was appointed in September 1941, he was an Indian and not a Japanese or Chinese specialist, Professor Rushbrook Williams, who was working in the Ministry of Information.[2] Meanwhile, there had been great difficulties in finding Japanese staff who were both good broadcasters and acceptable to the Aliens' War Service Department.[3] Pratt had left the Ministry of Information, and his successor was more doubtful about the value of going ahead with Japanese. The problem of how to switch-censor Japanese broadcasts was also raised,[4] along with the point that short-wave listening in Japan was in any case prohibited except by special permit, and a special permit was rarely granted.[5] Finally, Singapore was suggested as a better broadcasting centre than London.[6] The station there actually broadcast in Japanese from the beginning of December 1941.

By then the 'sudden dramatic turn of events' had taken place, perhaps more sudden and dramatic than Rendall had foreseen. As the Japanese struck their rapid blows—Penang was evacuated on 19 December, Hong Kong surrendered on 25 December, and Singapore followed on 18 February—the possibility was considered of transferring broadcasts in

---

[1] *Rendall to Tallents, 19 May 1941.

[2] Rushbrook Williams was appointed on 29 Sept., with A. F. N. Thavenot as Assistant Director. See below, p. 505. Efforts had been made earlier to secure J. R. Firth of the School of Oriental Studies. (*Ogilvie to Butler, 14 June 1941.)

[3] *Ormond Wilson, Empire Talks, to M. E. Denning, Foreign Office, 4 July 1941; Overseas Board, *Minutes*, 1, 8 May 1941.   [4] *Note of 18 July 1941.

[5] *Clark to Rendall, 8 March 1941; Note by F. J. Daniels of the School of Oriental Studies, 30 July 1941. Short-wave sets, he reported, were on sale in Japan, but they were expensive and they were supervised by the police. 'Short-wave broadcasts would have no effect at all.'

[6] *Clark to de la Valette, Ministry of Information, 17 Sept. 1941.

Japanese from London to Rangoon, Batavia, Manila or New Delhi.[1] Yet Rangoon fell on 10 March, the Japanese landed in Java on 28 February, Corregidor surrendered on 6 May, and on 4 April three British warships were sunk in the Bay of Bengal. In such times of flux and disaster Rushbrook Williams and many of his colleagues in the BBC thought of broadcasting in Japanese as at best 'a stunt', with broadcasting in Korean, which was also mooted, as an even bigger stunt.[2] As the possible alternative stations—with the exception of New Delhi—fell one by one to the Japanese, Clark, in particular, remained sceptical of Japanese broadcasting from London and pressed the case for concerted Allied broadcasting from the United States and Australia as well as India.[3] 'This is a case,' he argued, 'in which we should not blindly be the obedient servants of H.M.G., but should point out firmly, as we have done on previous occasions, the reasons for restraining action on the many practical grounds of which we can take a much truer measure in the broadcasting field than anyone in the Ministry of Information or the Foreign Office.'[4]

Operational needs, however, suggested that the BBC should be doing something more than it was doing, and Wavell from New Delhi joined the Foreign Office and the Far Eastern Section of the Ministry of Information, which was in charge of PWE work, in demanding political warfare by radio.[5] Accordingly, C. J. Morris, who had been a Professor of English in Japan before the outbreak of war, was appointed as an assistant in the Eastern Service in February 1943. Morris sensibly advocated directing BBC broadcasts at the Japanese forces rather than at the few wealthy and influential Japanese who had short-wave receiving sets and permission to listen. Among the Forces, he noted, 'there has always been a great desire to know what is really happening on the European and African fronts. If it is proposed to comment on the news,

[1] *Note of a meeting at the Ministry of Information, 11 Dec. 1941. The Dutch had an excellent radio system in the Dutch East Indies with a large number of short-wave stations.

[2] *Rushbrook Williams to Rendall, 19 Feb. 1942; Rushbrook Williams to Clark, 18 March 1942. 'The Ministry of Information have asked us to arrange a broadcast in Korean to annoy the Japanese.'

[3] *Clark to Rendall, 24 Nov. 1942.

[4] *Ibid.

[5] *Rushbrook Williams to Clark, 18 March 1942.

commentaries should, in the first instance, be devoted to placing European events in their proper perspective.'[1]

During the spring and summer of 1943 the first really serious talks took place between the different interested parties about an adequate broadcasting plan for the Far East and how to finance it. They started with a meeting at the Ministry of Information which was attended by Foot, Clark and Morris of the BBC, Radcliffe, Grubb and H. V. Redman of the Ministry, General Brooks of PWE and Denning of the Foreign Office. 'Stages of development' were laid down, with considerable expansion envisaged during the first stage, particularly in Japanese broadcasting—News was to be the main element—and with the second stage leading into the period after the fall of Germany. There was naturally considerable discussion of what was being done or could be done by the Indians and the Australians, but the lack of the kind of Imperial or Allied Broadcasting Committee, which had so often been talked about but, as we have seen, had never been implemented,[2] made detailed cross-reference difficult.[3] Liaison with the Americans was being organized through the PWE Mission to Washington, headed by David Bowes-Lyon, and eventually British broadcasts once a week were transmitted in Japanese from San Francisco. The BBC also tried to recruit suitable staff in the United States for broadcasting in Japanese from London, and Morris subsequently paid a visit to Canada and the United States during the spring of 1944, looking for recruits.[4] Three Americans whom he discovered at a Military Language School were willing to come, with the full blessing of the State Department, but the War Department did not allow them to do so. At last two suitable Japanese broadcasters were found in September 1944, and daily transmissions in Japanese and English were started on 31 December. The war in Europe was drawing to a close, therefore, when the first effective action was possible.

Yet there had been big organizational changes. In March 1944 policy control of the London broadcasts passed from the

[1] *Morris to Rendall, 6 April 1943.   [2] See above, p. 495.
[3] *Notes of a meeting, 12 April 1943. De la Valette had gone to Australia, however, as Liaison Officer for Far Eastern Affairs.
[4] *Morris to Rendall, 23 March, 4 April 1944.

Ministry of Information to PWE,[1] and in July 1944 Morris succeeded Rushbrook Williams as Eastern Service Director. At the same time, the Regional Editors of the different Eastern Services were given greater control over their output on much the same lines as the Regional Editors in the European Service had enjoyed for several years. Unfortunately, the Americans were never willing to offer broadcasting time to the British from stations in the United States at the right broadcasting hours:[2] the co-operation which the BBC had offered to the Americans in Europe was not fully reciprocated, and there were no direct relays of broadcasts recorded in Britain. No one knew, of course, in mid-1944 how long the Japanese war would last, and the British were obviously going to have to depend not on London but on stations in India or in recaptured territories.

The BBC played little part, therefore, in the pattern of propaganda in relation to the war in the Far East; far less, indeed, than the Germans played. There had been three main obstacles—first and foremost, lack of linguists, a natural if deplorable failing; second, divided counsels which led to procrastination and uncertainty; third, intrinsic difficulties in finding propaganda themes which were comparable in appeal with those employed in Europe. In Europe it was possible to speak with the voice of liberators: in Asia it was impossible to avoid the entanglements of Empire. This is not to say that BBC news bulletins did not constitute a source of reliable and relevant information in Eastern countries, but the context in which the news was received was completely different from that in Holland, France or, for that matter, Germany. There were two countries in the East, however, China, an ally, and India, a dominion, which had somewhat different stories which deserve to be examined separately.

The Chinese Service had started in May 1941 with weekly letters in Cantonese and Kuoyü.[3] This service was not controlled by the Ministry, although it was later under the direction of PWE.[4] By February 1942 British transmissions in Chinese

[1] *Rendall to Bowes-Lyon, 26 March 1944.
[2] *Clark to Rendall, 12 May 1944.
[3] See above, p. 498.
[4] *Rendall to Pennethorne Hughes, 28 June 1945.

had increased to six a week and in July to seven. By then, the daily programmes included a news bulletin and a commentary, although it was felt that there was 'no concrete indication of what Chungking wants'.[1] Nearly a year later in May 1943 the British Ambassador reported from Chungking to the Foreign Secretary that 'intellectual broadcasts would be welcome'. He had been given this advice by Dr. Joseph Needham and Professor E. R. Dodds, who were on a visit to China dealing with Sino-British scientific and academic relations. Already the BBC's Chinese Service had put on a whole range of interesting programmes, including readings of contemporary English poetry. William Empson, the poet and critic and ex-monitor, was a Talks Producer, who according to George Orwell 'wore himself out' trying to get the BBC 'to broadcast intelligent stuff to China', and succeeded, in Orwell's highly critical opinion, 'to some small extent'.[2] It was some encouragement to know that the BBC's service in Kuoyü was regularly relayed by Chengtu, a station controlled by the Chinese Minister of Communication, which was listened to by university students.

Chungking Radio, by contrast, was controlled directly by the Chinese Minister of Propaganda.[3] For this and other reasons, it always proved extremely difficult to extend political co-operation. Efforts to secure direct BBC representation in Chungking, where there was a Ministry of Information office, were abortive, American broadcasting influence was thought to be extremely strong,[4] and the Chinese censorship was known to be so strict that it was difficult to get news out.[5] Reception of BBC programmes was poor,[6] there were few

---

[1] *Rendall to Rushbrook Williams, 10 Aug. 1942.

[2] S. Orwell and I. Angus (eds.), *The Essays, Journalism and Letters of George Orwell*, vol. II (1968), pp. 304–5. The comment was made in a letter written in July 1943. See also *London Calling*, 21 Oct. 1943, 'BBC's Service to China Breaks the Intellectual Blockade'.

[3] *Bonwit to Lawson-Reece, 23 Aug. 1943. There were direct links between the Ministry, the Kuomintang (the Party) and the Secret Police.

[4] *Lawson-Reece to Rushbrook Williams, after an interview with Erik Watts, British Press Attaché, 15 Dec. 1943.

[5] *D. Stephenson, 'Report on a Visit to Chungking, 30 Dec. 1944–21 Jan. 1945', 29 Jan. 1945. OWI operated a radio-photo circuit to San Francisco, and there were many star American reporters in the city.

[6] Reception of Australian stations was good, as was reception from SEAC's Z OJ station in Colombo.

receivers—only 300 in the Chungking area, it was estimated, and only 6,000 in 'Free China' as a whole[1]—and electricity supplies often failed. Moreover, Chungking Radio was reluctant at any time to re-broadcast BBC programmes in English as part of its regular service.[2] Finally, late in the war, when proposals for programme exchange were being made more seriously at the suggestion of the Ministry of Information, it was from the British side that Haley insisted on proceeding with caution. 'We cannot commit ourselves to even a five-minute weekly dose of Chinese propaganda in the Home Service,' he declared. He was perhaps less worried about Voice of China relays than with what he thought was a Chinese wish to nationalize all foreign news going into China.[3]

Throughout the war years, therefore, there were suspicions all round in Chinese-British broadcasting relations, despite Chinese courtesy and British charm.[4] For all these reasons, China, the ally, one of the Big Four at most of the war-time international conferences, played almost as small a part in the pattern of British war-time broadcasting as Japan, the enemy. There is very little evidence, either, as to whether BBC programmes were heard by Chinese communities outside China, particularly in Hong Kong, Singapore and Malaya.

India was the heart of the Empire. For a time, indeed, it seemed to be at the heart of the war. The story of the BBC's Indian Service was complex and often turbulent. In February 1940, Sir Malcolm Darling, a retired Indian civil servant, had been recommended by the Viceroy of India to be Editor of

---

[1] *Memorandum of 1 July 1942.

[2] On XGOY there was a fifteen-minute spot each day, *British Interlude*, provided by the Ministry of Information: it did not use BBC programmes excepting occasionally London Transcription material. XGOA, the other Chungking station, relayed the BBC science talk in Kuoyü once a month. The most powerful out-station Kunming (XPRA) broadcast no British programmes at all, and was restricted in any case to broadcasting four hours a day because of fuel shortage. (*Report by Stephenson, 29 Jan. 1945.)

[3] *Haley to Macgregor, 5 Feb. 1944.

[4] *When Stephenson visited China in 1945, he found 'a profound admiration for the BBC'. 'I spoke,' he wrote, 'with several Chinese of standing who sang our praises, though more than one, on questioning, revealed that he had rarely if ever heard a BBC transmission, and knew our excellence only by hearsay.' (Report of 29 Jan. 1945.)

the new Hindustani Service,[1] with Lionel Fielden, who had been Controller of Broadcasting, New Delhi, as the Viceroy's first choice as Sub-Editor.[2] Fielden arrived in April and Darling a month later. Z. A. Bokhari had already been seconded as an adviser by All India Radio,[3] and had produced two interesting memoranda on 'Publicity Plans for India' in which he discussed Indian attitudes towards the war and how to exploit anti-Hitler feeling. From India itself there was a demand for 'something which we can't get out here, something fresh, authentic and arresting'.[4]

The Hindustani Service started on 11 May with a ten-minute daily broadcast. Within a few weeks, however, there were such differences of thought and feeling between Darling on the one hand and Fielden and Bokhari on the other that co-operation was impossible. Fielden left the team in August 1940 and the BBC in November,[5] and Darling, anxious to control, and Bokhari, a gifted and imaginative programme organizer, were temperamentally hostile to each other. In September 1940, Darling moved to Wood Norton and Bokhari stayed in London, but a new division of labour between them proved unsatisfactory. There were further arguments, still more bitter, in 1941 when the BBC proposed to make the Indian Service directly responsible to the new Eastern Service Director. Before Professor Rushbrook Williams was appointed to this position in September,[6] Darling had threatened to resign, not for the last time, if Bokhari's powers were extended, and the Government of India had supported his demand for

[1] *Cable from F. H. Puckle, Director-General of Information, New Delhi, to Sir Findlater Stewart, Under Secretary of State for India, 28 Feb. 1940. See also above, pp. 493–4.

[2] Fielden, who had worked with the BBC before going to India (see Briggs, *The Golden Age of Wireless* (1965), pp. 143, 147), was not acceptable to the BBC as Editor. (*Cable from Stewart to Puckle, 12 Feb. 1940; Graves to Fielden, 8 March 1940.) It was he, nonetheless, who first suggested BBC broadcasts in Hindustani (Fielden to H. V. Hodson, Ministry of Information, 24 Sept. 1939), and he was corresponding with Ogilvie from Dec. 1939 onwards.

[3] *Ogilvie to Findlater Stewart, 18 Jan. 1940.

[4] *Puckle to Stewart, 4 Jan. 1940: 'I want it to be a quarter-of-an-hour to which every Indian will feel he must tune in.' For the inception of the service, see above, p. 494.

[5] *Note by Tallents, 23 Aug. 1940; Rendall to Tallents, 26 July 1940; L. Fielden, *The Natural Bent* (1960), p. 219.

[6] See above, p. 499. The idea of this appointment had been first mooted in Feb. 1941.

'firm political control of the Service'.[1] It was Rushbrook Williams, however, not Darling, who was to be responsible from September 1941 until his resignation in July 1944 'for ensuring that the output in all sections of Eastern Services accords appropriately with Government policy and directives in both a general and specialised sense'.[2] He was chairman of an Eastern Service Committee which met each fortnight and included representatives of the Ministry of Information, the India Office and the School of Oriental Studies. He was also in close touch with the Indian High Commissioner, who broadcast regularly to India. The Government of India sent fortnightly cables, and in these and other messages it 'maintained a constant stream of suggestion, criticism and advice'.[3]

India had been such a cause of contention in British politics during the 1930s and its political future was so uncertain during the early years of the war that these personal struggles behind the scenes had more than local significance. After reading one file on the subject, one BBC official wrote, 'I shudder to think what will happen when Japan gets to India'.[4] The *New Statesman*, which under Kingsley Martin's editorship had always been keenly interested in Indian nationalism, complained openly that neither the BBC's English nor Hindustani programmes were appealing to Indians. They 'prefer the racy style of Berlin to the British solemnity. . . . The Germans, who have made a special study of India, well understand how to meet Indian tastes and susceptibilities.'[5] Such talk was anathema to Darling, and he was, if possible, even more alarmed when Fielden wrote an article in the paper a few weeks later demanding a wholesale reorganization of propaganda to India and everywhere else.[6] Fortunately for

---

[1] *Ogilvie to Tallents, 24 March 1941; Tallents to Darling, 31 May 1941; Darling to Tallents, 7 June 1941.

[2] *Clark to Darling, 14 Nov. 1941. Rushbrook Williams made Darling's position quite clear in a memorandum of 29 April 1942.

[3] *Note by Foot, 22 June 1943.

[4] *Note by L. Schuster, 21 Feb. 1942.

[5] *New Statesman*, 5 July 1941. Tallents replied vigorously on behalf of the BBC (ibid., 19 July 1941), but the editor, while admitting that some improvements had been made, stuck to his general charges.

[6] Ibid., 19 July 1941. The article is called 'That Bad Word'. 'Hitler, in *Mein Kampf*—I am sorry, but there it is—makes two interesting points about war propaganda . . . it must not be swamped by the mass of the mediocre . . . and it

the BBC, an extremely interesting collection of other distinguished people came to the defence of its Indian Service. The first of these, E. M. Forster, who had broadcast himself on more than one occasion, said that he had found 'no traces of British parochialism in its office' and that he had been much impressed by 'the intelligence and initiative of its Indian staff'.[1] A second, Desmond Hawkins, claimed that the Indian department was a 'much more enterprising and—to borrow your word—"serious" team than some other limbs of that great Elephant of Culture': he went on to draw attention to the fact that among the literary men who had recently broadcast in English to India were Edwin Muir, V. S. Pritchett, Herbert Read, T. S. Eliot, Louis MacNeice and George Orwell.[2] A third, T. M. Pande, sub-editor of the *Sunday Standard Bombay*, dismissed German broadcasts to India as 'a cheap propaganda stunt' and argued that 'the Indian listener to-day wants news, just as it is, without any superfluous sugar-coating . . . exactly what he gets from the Hindustani Service of the BBC'. 'I still remember,' he added, 'how people in a metropolis like Bombay and a small town like Dehra Dun eagerly await to hear the announcer begin his bulletin with [the words] "London salutes India".'[3]

In this round, open to the public or at least to a small sector of it, the BBC had won. It was not the last round, however, and the Corporation's Indian programmes were to provoke argument throughout the war, including argument in the House of Commons. Not all the criticism came from the Left. The India Office also was strongly critical of 'the presentation and content of the Hindustani bulletins' in 1942, a point which would certainly have been registered in the BBC's favour in some quarters.[4] Given the challenge to the service and the importance of the Indian audience, it was a matter of national concern that conflicts inside the BBC were not stilled. When the Wood Norton group returned to London, Darling's

[1] Ibid., 2 Aug. 1941.
[2] Ibid., 26 July 1941.
[3] Ibid., 9 Aug. 1941.
[4] *Rushbrook Williams to Clark and Rendall, 14 May 1942.

must never be decided by "Committees" but must be the responsibility of producers.' Fielden also wrote a letter in reply to a letter from Tallents, which had appeared in the same number as his original article.

responsibilities were limited to concentrating on the Hindustani News and News Talks—he appealed to Foot against this decision—and Bokhari, who was spared from the BBC to spend six months in India in 1943, somewhat oddly dealt not so much with programmes in Hindustani as with broadcasts in English.[1] On the positive side, Bokhari gathered round him, not without difficulty,[2] an able group of Indians;[3] and an increased flow of information began to reach London about the Indian reaction to what was being broadcast.[4] Indeed, in April 1942 an Intelligence Officer, Laurence Brander, was sent to India to investigate the possibilities of a comprehensive listener research service. He was assisted by Ahmed Ali, a well-known writer and a lecturer in English at Lucknow. This time it was Rushbrook Williams who was sceptical, and he complained about 'ill digested material which contains a good deal of grain among heaps of chaff'.[5] Some of the difficulties were apparent enough to Brander. When he sent out a questionnaire to listeners in India he got a nil return from Indians, a 4 per cent return from Europeans, and a 60 per cent return from the Army, 'fresh from England mostly and wireless minded'.[6]

It was clear from Brander's report, as from the evidence, that the BBC's effort needed to be supported and extended in India itself. There was, indeed, as strong a case for the setting up of a BBC Office in India as there had been in the United States.[7] Not only was Indian opinion considered to be of special importance in relation to a world war effort, but after the Japanese advances, which threatened India itself, the large numbers of troops, British and American, in India were

[1] *Memorandum of 8 July 1942.

[2] *J. B. Clark to Joyce, 9 Feb. 1942.

[3] In June 1943 he had eight staff Programme Assistants and a Hindustani Repertory Company. 'Many Indians resident in Britain render valuable unpaid assistance.' (*Memorandum on the Indian Service by Foot, 22 June 1943.)

[4] In 1940 he had described the All India Radio figure of 120,000 wireless licences as a gross understatement, 'an average figure of about 10 per cent'. (*Bokhari to Stephen Fry, 12 Oct. 1940.)

[5] *Rushbrook Williams to Rendall, 4 July 1942. Brander's interesting and valuable report was dated 11 Jan. 1943.

[6] *Note by Brander, Oct. 1942. Brander made it clear that publicity was needed. Some people told him that if 'we knew what your programmes are, we could reply to the questionnaires'.

[7] See above, p. 405.

a problem on their own.[1] It was only after they had begun to be catered for as a distinct group from the time of the extension of the General Forces Programme in 1943[2] that the Indian Service was left free to concentrate on India itself.

There were four main problems. The first was institutional, the existence of All India Radio, which was controlled, at least on paper, by the Indian Government through its Department of Information and Broadcasting.[3] AIR did not choose to re-broadcast the BBC's Hindustani news and, unlike the Australian Broadcasting Commission and the Canadian Broadcasting Corporation, was carrying relatively few BBC programmes in 1942, 'despite the fact that these items are chosen with the utmost care, and with expert advice, as being of a kind likely to appeal especially to India'.[4] Relations between it and the BBC were described then by Rushbrook Williams as 'a bit nebulous'. 'We should like to give them more: they say that they cannot take more without discouraging local talent.'[5]

The second problem also was institutional. As the war went on in Asia there were separate British centres of authority. GHQ India had an organization distinct from the South-East Asia Command (SEAC) under Mountbatten. In addition, there was a Far Eastern Bureau (FEB), a branch of the Ministry of Information, and it was FEB which reinforced the international services of AIR: Allington Kennard was in charge of their international programme in 1943 and in the following year E. D. Robertson was appointed Special Officer, Far East, in charge of AIR broadcasts in all the major languages of the East, from Burmese to Japanese, and responsible jointly to AIR and FEB. The BBC felt, not surprisingly, that it needed its own Director in New Delhi if it were to maintain and

[1] Through an agreement with OWI, All India Radio re-broadcast considerable American material, including two twenty-minute shows a week for American troops, a *Voice of America* broadcast, thirty minutes of American Variety, 'American Women's Club on the Air', and thirty minutes of music. (*Rushbrook Williams to Joyce, 5 Feb. 1943.)   [2] See above, p. 492.

[3] Puckle was replaced as head of this department in Dec. 1943 on going to a post in Washington. His successor knew nothing of radio and its problems. (*Ryan to Foot, 17 Dec. 1943.) The Delhi Government had little direct control over All India Radio broadcasts from Calcutta, Bombay and Madras. (*Ryan to Haley, 24 April 1944.)

[4] *Note by Rushbrook Williams, 12 Feb. 1942.

[5] *Rushbrook Williams to Brander, 24 June 1942.

strengthen its own position in the context of this substantial development.[1] Yet there were delays in getting this idea accepted in London. The Ministry of Information thought that Foot's proposal to appoint a BBC Director in New Delhi was too ambitious and expensive, and it was only after Ryan had visited India towards the end of 1943 and reported that 'we cannot afford to be without a man here of reasonable seniority',[2] that a modified proposal went ahead. Accordingly, Donald Stephenson became first New Delhi Director on 1 February 1944. Already by then post-war developments as much as war-time issues were in everyone's mind. It was clear, as Ryan put it, that politics would soon 'come to life again in an atmosphere highly embittered by the imprisonment of the Congress leaders'. It was regarded as most important in official quarters, Ryan added, 'that the voice of Britain shall be listened to to the fullest extent through the BBC, and this will not happen unless we have planned our programmes on a realistic basis'.[3] The task was not made easier by the fact that 'the Indian mind' seemed 'prejudiced against us'.[4]

This raised the third problem—politics. The Indians themselves were increasingly divided between Muslims, many of whom were working for an independent State, and Indian nationalists who turned to the Congress Party whose leaders were in prison. To militants in both groups BBC broadcasts often seemed too literary—what was good enough for the small Chinese Service was not right for them—while AIR was politically suspect and, given all the uncertainties about the role of the BBC, seemed to 'lack the authority' attaching to the BBC.[5] Early in the war Bokhari had been concerned about the relationship of language to politics— the desire for a Hindi language which eliminated all Arabic

---

[1] The proposal was put forward by Rendall, who also recommended the appointment of a Press Officer and other staff. (*Clark to Rendall, 7 Jan. 1943.) Foot sent details of the request to Radcliffe on 5 April 1943. A few weeks earlier Macgregor had reported 'the increased activities of American correspondents' in India (*Memorandum to Rendall, 3 March 1943), a point that was to be made in other contexts.

[2] *Ryan to Foot, 17 Dec. 1943. The stock of *The Times*, he said, was high.

[3] *Ryan to Haley, 24 April 1944.

[4] *Brander to Rushbrook Williams, 21 July 1943.

[5] *'Note on the Necessity for the Expansion of a BBC office in India', 7 April 1943; Ryan to Haley, 24 April 1944.

or Persian words.[1] In the middle of the war the main issue was the relationship of security to politics, a problem which the BBC could scarcely touch. And during the last years of the war the problem was communication.[2] It says much for the BBC that, though it could be criticized by the Viceroy for giving 'undue prominence' to speeches by Congress leaders,[3] it tried extremely hard to recruit speakers who were not afraid of 'controversial' broadcasting. Thus, at the end of 1943 it transmitted a series of discussions, 'India and the Four Freedoms', with Wickham Steed, one of its most experienced broadcasters—'the old fox of journalism', German radio called him[4]—as chairman.[5]

Among the other speakers whom it regularly employed, George Orwell, broadcasting under this name, was prominent as a full member of the Corporation from late 1941 until November 1943. The BBC did not consult the Government of India about this. A. H. Joyce in the India Office told Rush-brook Williams that it would be a mistake to refer the matter directly to the Government of India. 'If *asked*, the Government might feel called upon to adopt a critical attitude. If the question is not raised, Mr. Joyce thinks they are very unlikely to object.'[6] Nor did they. Orwell was blunt about the kind of speakers *he* chose. 'Most of our broadcasters are Indian left-wing intellectuals, from Liberals to Trotskyists, some of them bitterly anti-British. They don't do it to "fox the Indian masses" but because they know what a Fascist victory would mean to the chances of India's independence.'[7]

The fourth problem was the Axis propaganda assault on India. The hope of turning India into 'an advance base for United Nations propaganda activities in the Far East' was

[1] *Memorandum from Bokhari to Clark, 'The Type of Hindustani Used', 30 March 1940. He added that the Muslims were introducing 'more and more high-flown Arabic and Persian words into their language'.

[2] *The BBC complained of unsatisfactory guidance from the India Office during the Bengal famine of 1943 (B. Moore to Macgregor, 29 Oct. 1943).

[3] *Rendall to Moore, 4 July 1942. Wavell also had been concerned to restrict the selection of news items for India. (Clark to Foot and Graves, 19 March 1942.)

[4] *BBC Year Book, 1945*, p. 28. Wickham Steed wrote an article in this number (pp. 26–8) with the dramatic title 'Dr. Goebbels called me "International Assassin".' [5] *Radio Times*, 7 July 1944.

[6] *Rushbrook Williams to Clark, 29 Oct. 1942. Orwell wrote an introduction to a selection of talks broadcast in English to India in 1943.

[7] Quoted in S. Orwell and I. Angus, op. cit., p. 229.

never fulfilled. Instead, German and Japanese radio remained a challenge within India itself, and in the autumn of 1942 Brander stated unequivocally that 'at the moment we are not winning the radio war that rages every night'. 'The Axis are concentrating on this field with skill and energy, following the old Crewe House propaganda rule—concentrate on the enemy where he is weakest.' 'A tremendous amount of stuff had been pumped into India' by the Germans in 1942 'to offset Cripps's visit', and the volume did not diminish. There was always a sizeable Indian contingent working with the Germans, and a second group with the Japanese. In late 1943 and early 1944 the Japanese were ahead in the assault as the table on p. 513 shows: their main attack was in Hindustani, Bengali, Tamil and Punjabi.[1]

The BBC took up Tamil in May 1941—the service was expanded to three broadcasts a week in May 1944; Bengali in October 1941—a second period was added each week in January 1944; Gujerati in March 1942—the service was withdrawn in September 1944; and Marathi in March 1942—this service was also withdrawn in September 1944. Sinhalese programmes, first broadcast in March 1942, were given twice the original time in May 1942 and stayed at this level throughout the rest of the war. How many people listened to these programmes it is extremely difficult to say. At least the Indians were not in the position of the Burmese, for in December 1942 the Japanese in Burma prohibited listening to any station other than Rangoon under the threat of very heavy penalties.

There was far less scope for the kind of broadcasts George Orwell made to India in the BBC's war-time African Service, which had a straightforward and relatively uncontroversial history. Broadcasting to Africa meant in the first instance broadcasting to South Africa, a Dominion, where there was a battle with the German radio for the support of the

---

[1] *Brander to Rushbrook Williams, 21 Jan. 1944. It is interesting that Brander and Rushbrook Williams had few fears about Russian broadcasts to India. 'The USA stations cannot be heard well,' Rushbrook Williams had written on 24 June 1942. 'The USSR is, I am glad to say, just starting; and this may do a deal of good.'

Afrikaners, but where the South African Broadcasting Corporation took twelve hours of BBC broadcasts each week. Next came the Rhodesias, from which contingents of soldiers and airmen had come in impressive numbers to join the

SHORT WAVE BROADCASTING IN INDIAN LANGUAGES FROM ENEMY STATIONS: OCTOBER 1943

	Tokyo		Japanese-controlled		Axis		Daily Total	
	hrs.	mins.	hrs.	mins.	hrs.	mins.	hrs.	mins.
Hindustani		45	2	55	2	41	6	21
Urdu		30						30
Bengali		15		50	1	5	2	10
Tamil		15	1	10		30	1	55
Gujerati		20				3		23
Marathi				10		3		13
Punjabi			1	25		15	1	40
Pushtu				45				45
Assamese				15				15
Telugu				15		30		45
Gurkhali				10				10
Andhra				15				15
Malayalam				10				10
Canarese						3		3

war. Third came 'the Colonies', last but not least, since John Grenfell Williams, a bilingual South African who had become African Programme Organizer in December 1940, was said to have been interested more than anything else in 'the development of colonial peoples'.[1] Grenfell Williams believed that his task was fourfold. First, he had to describe what was happening

[1] M. Gorham, Sound and Fury (1948), pp. 105-6.

in the war as vividly as possible to people who knew little of the circumstances in which it was being waged. Second, he had to 'project the United Kingdom to the Colonies' as 'faithfully' as he could. Third, he had to ensure that the BBC made 'a contribution to the solution of colonial problems': he was in fact responsible for programmes to Cyprus and to the West Indies as well as to Africa. Fourth, he 'just had to be friendly'.[1]

Grenfell Williams became Deputy Director of Empire Services in January 1941. He had as his South African Programme Organizer Etienne Amyot, who 'knew everybody in the worlds of arts and letters and had great knowledge and unerring taste. It was only natural that he should help to launch the Third Programme when it began in 1946.'[2]

It is possible to see in retrospect that the events of the war, at least the participation of black African troops in it, marked a new phase in the development of African politics. Between 1939 and 1945, however, it would have been difficult to predict from the pattern of broadcasting the shape of things to come. Africa, indeed, scarcely figured in any of the war-time briefs prepared for the Minister of Information by the BBC except in relation to the campaigns in North Africa and the morale of the troops. In Germany there was considerable talk of Africa, during the early stages of the war, as an Eldorado richly endowed with war materials which would strengthen Germany's new European Order, but as the German armies were pushed out of Africa the talk ceased abruptly. Both the British and the German programme schedules for Africa in 1942 record how limited the framework was, as the table opposite shows.

In 1943, however, there were moves towards greater specialization. The inauguration of a separate Forces programme for troops in North and East Africa and in the Middle East made it possible to introduce at the end of the year a special programme for the East African colonies and to increase the

---

[1] *BBC Year Book, 1945*, p. 92. *Graves in a letter to Radcliffe, 12 March 1942, urged in addition the importance of familiarizing listeners with what British Ministers were doing. 'Apart from the Prime Minister and one or two of his colleagues it is doubtful whether British Ministers are as well known as they should be overseas.' It is true to say that he related this responsibility as much to the United States and Australia as to the African Empire.

[2] Gorham, op. cit., p. 131.

Sample Day's Programmes to Africa:
September 1942

	BBC*	ZEESEN	ACCRA (local)
0500		Call sign. Day's programme announcements	
0600		Concert	
		Concert	
0700		News in English	
0715		Close down	
1100			News in French
1510–40			Schools programmes
1530	Call sign. Day's programme announcements		
1535	War Review		
1540		Call sign. Day's programme announcements (German and English)	
1545	Dance music		
1550		Deutschland Echo (German)	
1615	Calling South Africa	News in English	
1625	Military band		
1630		Blinkfever Heimat (German)	News in Twi
1650		News in Afrikaans	News in Hausa
1700	News		News in Ga
1715	Song time in the Laager		
1722		Musical interlude	
1730		Review of the week ('Haw-Haw')	
1745		News in Portuguese	News in Ewe
1800	Radio Newsreel	News in French	BBC News relayed
1815		Organ recital	French programme (till 1920)
1830	Front Line Family	News in Afrikaans and talk	
1845	Music feature		
1915	American commentary	News in English	
1920			Gold Coast news and talk
1930	Music	Orchestral concert	
1945	News	Deutscher Volkskonzert	
1955	Commentary	News in Portuguese	
2000	Forces Favourites		
2015	Music		* In addition parts of the Eastern and Pacific transmissions of the BBC were audible in North and West Africa.
2050	London Calling Day's programmes		
2100	Close down	News in German	
2115		News in English	
2130		Close down	

number of broadcasts to West Africa. Between then and the
end of the war more and more talks were given on such subjects
as the growth and organization of trade unions in Great Britain,
the development of Women's Institutes and Co-operative
movements, educational and social changes and the procedures of parliamentary government. Speakers included
Victor Feather on trade unions, Dr. Arthur Lewis on Co-
operation and Miss Elizabeth Christmas on Women's Institutes.[1] Broadcasts of this kind anticipated the new post-war
pattern.[2] The Afrikaner programme was also extended by
fifteen minutes every evening in 1943. The mid-term influence
of the new African programmes may have been substantial,
yet any verdict on the war-time influence of the Afrikaner
programme must be inconclusive. There was so little evidence,
Grenfell Williams wrote in 1944, 'as to the size of the Afrikaans
audience in South Africa, or of its reactions to the programmes,
that it is impossible to say whether or not we have in fact a
steady audience at all'.[3]

Africa, like Asia, was a relatively new preoccupation of
the BBC, at least in detail. The two pioneering pre-war
foreign-language services to Latin America and to the Middle
East retained their importance during the war, particularly
the latter, for the war itself directly involved the Middle East.
In the case of Latin America, the main problem was not
involvement but distance. How could the BBC handle a
potential audience of 130 million people which, in the words
of Zimmern, a war-time Director of the Latin American
Service, extended from Rio Grande in the north to Cape Horn
in the south, and thus included 'the ten republics of South
America, the six in Central America, Mexico, Haiti and the
Spanish-speaking islands of the Caribbean'.[4] There were

[1] *BBC Year Book, 1945*, p. 92.
[2] So, too, did some of the Home programmes on the Empire, notably a series
Brush up your Empire broadcast in 1944, described as 'one of the most successful
features of its kind the Talks Department has ever undertaken'.
[3] *Grenfell Williams to Rendall, 22 May 1944.
[4] *Note by Norman Zimmern, 22 June 1943. Zimmern, a cousin of Sir Alfred
Zimmern and an active member of a family business dealing with Latin America,
succeeded C. A. L. Cliffe as Director of the Latin American Service on 5 Jan.
1942. He remained in the post until after the end of the war. J. A. Camacho, who
was to have a distinguished post-war career in the BBC, was Latin American
Programme Organizer.

variations in language, culture and politics, not to speak of the most important variations of clock time, and if the policy of increasing specialization recommended by J. B. Clark[1] was to apply to Latin America, it was clear that there would have to be substantial changes in the organization of the service as it operated in 1940 and 1941.[2]

The big change came in November 1943 when the service was split into two transmissions—Spanish and Brazilian Portuguese—and programme hours were consequently almost doubled.[3] Henceforth, there was a continuous programme in each of the two languages: its contents could become more varied and its timing could be better adapted to peak listening hours in different parts of the continent. Programmes could be repeated, and in this respect, as in others, the BBC secured for the first time a substantial lead over the German Latin American Service. Far greater publicity was secured in the Latin American Press, and BBC Representatives were appointed to take up residence in Buenos Aires, Bogotá, Rio de Janeiro and Mexico City.[4] Largely as a result of their efforts, there was a great increase in the volume of medium-wave re-broadcasting by Latin American stations of BBC material, including material supplied by the London Transcription Service, so that by the end of 1943 nearly a hundred stations were broadcasting BBC News each day.[5] Another result of the appointment of Representatives was an improved flow of information about Latin American audiences.

The members of the BBC's Latin American Service in England, who started the war in Broadcasting House and were moved to Evesham in October 1940, were somewhat isolated after June 1942, fifteen miles away from Bush House, at Aldenham House, Elstree.[6] They were subject to 'guidance'

---

[1] See above, p. 480.   [2] See above, pp. 280–1.

[3] The total time on the air was increased from 5 hours to 9 hours 15 minutes each day (Brazilian, 3 hours 45 minutes; Spanish, 5 hours 30 minutes).

[4] The first appointments were those of T. P. Gale in Mexico City in Dec. 1942, G. B. Gorton in Buenos Aires in Feb. 1943, S. Annan in Rio de Janeiro in May 1943, and W. G. L. Linsell in Bogotá in July 1943 (*BBC Year Book, 1944*, p. 93).

[5] Ibid., p. 94.

[6] *For the problems, see a memorandum from W. J. Breething, Latin American News Editor, to A. B. Oldfield-Davies, the Overseas Services Establishment Officer, 2 Oct. 1944. The service had a publicity office in Great Castle Street and a talks office at 200 Oxford Street.

from the Ministry of Information—for a time Philip Guedalla, the historian, headed the Latin American Section there, to be followed by Oliver Bonham Carter—but in practice they were allowed a very free hand. They were proud of the fact that during the early years of the war they had resisted Foreign Office pressure to broadcast extracts from Vansittart's *Black Record* which they were sure, rightly, would never either impress or convince Latin American listeners. They believed, indeed, that it was during this period that their service had acquired a distinctive character—quietly confident but frank about failures; unbombastic; above all, credible, accurate and reliable. The increase in the amount of programme time available to them was seen as an opening for widening the range of the programmes, with a greater emphasis on history, art and music. They were able without difficulty to recruit full-time members of their team from Latin America and to employ both Spanish and Portuguese speakers who, for political reasons, were difficult to use in the Spanish and Portuguese Services[1]—de Madariaga, for example, who was used as regularly as J. B. Priestley in the BBC's North American Service. Another leading speaker was J. A. Camacho, who directed the schedule and content of programmes and broadcast under the pseudonym of 'Atalaya' (Watchtower),[2] a pseudonym he also used in commentaries for film news reels. P. Xisto (Martins Pinheiro Neto) and later Aimberé (Manuel Antonio Braune) were regular commentators in Portuguese for Brazil.

The group did not regard themselves as propagandists, yet there were many occasions when the course of broadcasting was influenced by political factors. Suggestions were made, for example, in the words of the Director, 'to send Argentine to Coventry' in December 1943, when Argentine policy towards the Axis was equivocal,[3] a different solution from that which would have been adopted in relation to countries in other parts of the world whose policies were also equivocal. From 1943 onwards a special news bulletin was broadcast at 1400 GMT to reach Mexico at 0800 local time.

[1] See above, p. 479.
[2] Another speaker was the ubiquitous Wickham Steed.
[3] *Zimmern to Clark, 20 Dec. 1943.

For technical reasons it had to be relayed via Brazzaville. It was picked up at an official Mexican telecommunications centre (Mixoac) and a transcript was supplied to the Mexican Government less than an hour later.[1]

Special attention was always paid to people of German origin in Latin America, and programmes based on monitoring of the German Home and Latin American Services were broadcast from 1941 onwards. For the most part religion was deliberately left out.[2] The whole tone of the broadcasts remained restrained throughout the war, since it was known that a large part of the audience consisted of people with intellectual and cultural interests; and many of the greatest successes of the service were the dramatic and feature programmes of Angel Ara, a Spaniard who was in Britain at the outbreak of war and proved to be 'one of the leading exponents of dramatic radio production'.[3] A new note was struck in 1944 and 1945, however, after Francis Hallawell, 'Chico Alabem', had been appointed as special correspondent with the Brazilian forces in Italy. His war reports were as popular in Brazil as any of the cultural programmes.

This successful record must be seen in perspective. Some jealousy and suspicion was shown by the Office of the Co-ordinator of Inter-American Affairs in Washington.[4] Not all the programmes which were transmitted to Latin America during the war and certainly not all the items sent out by the London Transcription Service were appreciated in Latin America. Nor was there much knowledge in war-harassed Britain of what was happening in Latin America, a condition of reciprocal understanding.[5] The BBC did as much as any

---

[1] American influence in Mexico was strong, of course, and the main broadcasting interest, that of Emilio Azcarraga, which enjoyed a near monopoly, had close relations with United States interests.

[2] *Zimmern to Clark, 26 Feb. 1942; Latin American Services Committee, *Minutes*, 4 March 1942, which recommended 'restrained use of Catholicism from a Protestant country'.

[3] *BBC Year Book, 1945*, p. 104.   [4] *Report by Rendall, 27 July 1943.

[5] Some efforts were made to inform the British public, and missions from Latin America (Brazil, Mexico, Guatemala, Peru and Uruguay) visited London. In 1941 there was a major series of talks about Latin America in the BBC's Home Service, and a pamphlet based on the talks by Camacho and Guedalla sold 75,000 copies. It was an exceptional event, however, when Dr. Santos, ex-President of Colombia, broadcast at a peak time in the BBC's Home Service in 1943 (*BBC Year Book, 1944*, p. 94).

other agency to extend and develop relationships which were
not always as well cultivated as they might have been, and
after the war it was to extend them still further. Yet, as
Zimmern himself put it in 1944, after D-Day, 'it is in no way
derogatory to those responsible for the output to Latin America
during the war to say that the reputation of the BBC in Latin
America is by no means entirely due to the quality of that
output. In a large measure it is due to the fact that London
has been the centre of resistance to Germany as well as the
centre from which the present offensive has been planned.
London has been to a greater extent than ever before the real
metropolis of the world. In consequence, whatever has been
broadcast from London has been listened to with more respect
and more sympathy than would otherwise be the case.'[1]

'Respect and sympathy' were not always the reactions to
BBC programmes in the divided Middle East, where, nonetheless, it is important to remember that there were always
Arabs fighting on the British side in bodies like the Sudan
Defence Force, the Arab Legion and the Senussi Auxiliaries.
For the armies, as for the politicians, it was true, as the *BBC
Year Book, 1944* put it, that 'our victories in the field in 1943
were more eloquent than words in convincing a critical
audience of the certainty of Allied victory, and the battle of
words against enemy propaganda was no longer the uphill
struggle of 1941'.[2] Italian broadcasts in Arabic, the main
inducement to the BBC's pre-war involvement in foreign-
language broadcasting, ceased after the armistice in 1943,
and German broadcasts lost something of their punch[3] and
much of their credit at the same time.

Nevill Barbour, the BBC's Near East Intelligence Officer,
had noted in December 1941 that there were constant complaints from Cairo that BBC news bulletins were 'unimaginative
and insufficiently dramatic'.[4] Yet in late 1941, 1942 and 1943

---

[1] *Zimmern to Clark, 20 Sept. 1944.   [2] *BBC Year Book, 1944*, p. 94.
[3] *At a meeting with Ministry of Information officials in the summer of 1940
it had been said that the BBC programmes in Arabic 'lacked punch' and that 'the
news was not woven enough into the programme' (Minutes of a meeting, 2 July
1940). Yet 'policy guidance' from the Government was often lacking (Barbour to
Tallents, 12 May 1941).
[4] *Barbour to Hillelson, 1 Dec. 1941.

there was certainly no shortage of drama. In May 1941
Donald Stephenson, then responsible for news bulletins in
Arabic,[1] was rung up in the middle of the night, at the request of
the British Ambassador in Baghdad, Sir Kinahan Cornwallis,
to arrange a special broadcast to Iraq on the Rashid Ali
rebellion. Very soon afterwards the British entry into Iran
in August 1941 and the subsequent abdication of the Shah
seemed to prove the power of broadcasting—a Press correspondent described it as 'the first instance in history in which a
ruler has been hurled from his throne by radio'[2]—and there
was the closest co-operation between the BBC and the British
Ambassador in Teheran, Sir Reader Bullard, who fully
appreciated what Clark called 'the general potentialities of
our medium'.[3] That there was some strain in the relationship
later[4] was far less important than the fact of co-operation at
the critical moment; and it was a sign of the influence of radio
that in November 1941 a leading Iranian politician sent to
London the script of a broadcast which he wanted to have
delivered anonymously because he thought the BBC was the
best instrument for putting across to the world what he wanted
to say. The talk was, in fact, broadcast in the BBC's Persian
Service on 5 November 1941 and attributed to 'a distinguished

[1] Stephenson later moved to New Delhi (see above, p. 510). In 1944 he was
replaced by Barbour. G. L. W. Mackenzie, a senior sub-editor, became Near East
News Editor on 1 April 1944.

[2] *'I doubt if the power of broadcasting has ever been shown in such a way
as by the success of these transmissions,' Dimbleby said in a despatch. (*Near East
Bi-Monthly Service Report*, 6 Nov. 1941.) Eden told Ministers that he accepted this
kind of interpretation. (Note by Stephenson, 23 Sept. 1941.)

[3] *Clark to Graves and Ogilvie, 27 Sept. 1941. There had, however, been some
difficulties at the London end. The immediate effect of the invasion of Iran was a
refusal by some of the Persian staff to collaborate in BBC broadcasts. They agreed,
however, to go on translating bulletins (Stephenson to Barker, 25 Aug. 1941).
When the Shah accepted the presence of Allied Forces, the Persian staff resumed
their duties and the Chief Announcer stated on the air that he had been allowed
to absent himself while the situation remained obscure but now returned of his
own free will. (Clark to Rendall, 29 Aug. 1941.)

[4] Fears were expressed in 1942 that the Ambassador was expecting the BBC to
follow his instructions too closely. 'In the Arabic Service,' the Near East Service
in London stated, 'it has never been held to be axiomatic that a Diplomatic Post
is inevitably the best judge of the specific use to be made of broadcasts from
London.' (*Minutes* of the Near East Service meeting, quoted in a letter of 16 May
1942.) There were differences of opinion between the Ministry of Information
and the Foreign Office about broadcasting policy later in 1942. (*Stephenson to
Hillelson and Clark, 5 Aug. 1942.)

Iranian student of foreign affairs who is also a friend of Great Britain'.[1]

The vicissitudes of the North African campaign, with El Alamein as the climax, produced drama of a different kind. After the fall of Tobruk in June 1942 there had been urgent discussions as to what should happen if ESB, Egyptian State Broadcasting, ceased to operate.[2] Special transmissions for Egypt were started, in fact, in December 1942 after the crisis was over. By then the Near East Service was congratulating itself that it had 'never allowed its strategy to be dictated by the enemy'[3] and was broadcasting in Arabic three times a day (2 hours), in Turkish four times a day (1 hour) and in Persian once a day (15 minutes). The first programme—Koran and News—was broadcast at 0445 GMT, and the last, a news bulletin in Arabic, at 1745. The news bulletins included a very full and topical service of local Arab news items provided by the Arab News Agency. Each week these were supplemented by weekly newsletters from Iraq, Aden, Syria and Palestine, cabled by Information Officers, and by an Egyptian newsletter read by an Egyptian commentator and transmitted for a BBC re-broadcast by beam from Cairo. There was also a War Review by Al-Raqib ('Onlooker')[4] every Saturday, re-broadcast on medium wave by Egyptian State Broadcasting.[5]

The general programmes included a wide range of material—propagandist, instructional and cultural. According to E. Marmorstein, who was a Senior Assistant in the Arabic Service during the war, the best of these programmes were songs and recitals from the Koran, some of them specially recorded for the BBC in Egypt, like the morning recitals 'by Shaikhs of world-wide repute', and 'elegant and scholarly talks on Arabic culture',[6] designed to gain the ear of 'leaders of thought'[7] and

[1] *Clark to Ogilvie, 14 Nov. 1941.

[2] *Note of a meeting, 3 July 1942. ESB had been founded in 1934. The supervising staff, including the General Manager, were British.

[3] *BBC Year Book, 1945*, p. 101.   [4] There were different speakers in this series.

[5] *Statement of Broadcasts to the Middle East, 22 Dec. 1942.

[6] *The first phrase is taken from ibid.; the second is Mr. Marmorstein's. By contrast, colloquial Arabic broadcasts had been introduced in 1941 for Egypt, Palestine and Syria, including a popular programme *Café Chaos* set in a Cairo coffee shop. Such humorous programmes were more successful than serious colloquial programmes (*BBC Year Book, 1945*, p. 100).

[7] See S. Hillelson, 'Broadcasting to the Near East' in the *Journal of the Royal Central Asian Society*, vol. XXVIII, July 1941.

subsequently reprinted in the widely circulated *Arabic Listener*.[1] The features, plays and magazine programmes in Arabic were far more imaginative and ambitious than those from any other station.[2] There were also annual poetry competitions and, from 1944 onwards, play competitions.[3] The poetry was judged by a panel consisting of Professor H. A. R. Gibb, the Egyptian Ambassador, the Saudi Arabian Minister, and, from 1943 onwards, the Iraqi Chargé d'Affaires; and the set subjects always included a war topic (1941—air; 1942—sea; 1943—underground front; 1944—'soldier on battlefield'), an Arab subject (1941—Arab Spain; 1942—Arab Unity) and an 'abstract' subject (1942—Democracy; 1943—Youth Movement and Blessings of Peace; 1944—East and West meet; 1945—The World of Tomorrow).[4] Preliminary contests were arranged by local stations—Cairo, Jerusalem, Baghdad, Khartoum, Aden, Singapore (in 1941 only!), Bahrein (from 1942), Beirut and Damascus (from 1943), and Jiddah (from 1944). Alongside these exercises in traditional Arabic culture brought up to date, the pattern of English-language lessons, first introduced in 1939, was revised in April 1941:[5] such lessons were broadcast throughout the war, and they subsequently played an important part also in the BBC's European Service in the form of 'English by Radio'. Discussion programmes were also greatly appreciated, and the introduction of *Listeners' Forum* (*Nadwat al Mustami'in*) quadrupled in one year the BBC's correspondence from the Middle East.

One of the indirect effects of the BBC's broadcasts as planned by Hillelson, the Director, was the enhancement of a sense of unity in the Arab world: 'it was in the nature of things that

[1] The first number of this fortnightly paper had appeared on 4 April 1940. By July 1943 10,000 copies were being circulated.

[2] *A special birthday programme for King Feisal of Iraq in April 1942 was thought to have been particularly successful. The young King asked for 'fierce music', and riddles and 'Advice from a Caterpillar' from *Alice in Wonderland* (Clark to Foot and Graves, 21 April). The *Alice* extract was done in Arabic. A model of a Hurricane fighter was hidden in the palace as a surprise present (Hillelson to Clark, 28 April 1942).

[3] See *London Calling*, 13 Jan. 1944.

[4] In 1943 the three prizes went to a Syrian in Beirut, an inhabitant of Mecca and a Moslem Syrian residing in West Africa. Hausa scholars in Nigeria also competed. (*BBC Year Book, 1944*, p. 95.)

[5] *A. E. H. Paxton to Hillelson, 7 April 1942. Basic English was used in 1941 after consultation with C. K. Ogden, although the term was not employed.

an Arabic Service from London should be metropolitan rather
than regional and should thus work in harmony with the Arab
urge towards the strengthening of their common nationhood.'[1]
Viewed from this angle, BBC programmes to Arab countries,
socially limited though their appeal often was, were far more
successful than BBC programmes for the occupied countries
of Asia. This is not to say that there were no complications,
particularly before the tide of war turned. Thus, in July 1942
there was friction between PWE and the BBC about the BBC's
Arabic and Moroccan broadcasts, when 'the pan Arab appeal
of the Arabic broadcasts' seemed to conflict with PWE directives
concerning the French Empire.[2] Stephenson was extremely
unhappy about the written directives which he received, and
on mentioning the Atlantic Charter at a meeting at the
Foreign Office, uncovered such 'coyness' that he was driven
to the conclusion that 'the Foreign Office might have set more
importance by this document if it had been signed at Runny-
mede'.[3] After the reconquest of North Africa and the re-
establishment of French authority, the separate Moroccan
Service was, in fact, abandoned in the course of 1944.[4] There
was a still bigger political difficulty in the Middle East itself.
In September 1941 it was noted that 'British propaganda was
hampered in answering allegations about Zionism by the
Government's policy which discouraged the mention of Zionism
in Arabic broadcasts. The effect of enemy references to Zionism
had been particularly noticeable in Iraq and Syria.'[5] Surface
appearances were quieter during the last stages of the war,
but the issue could not be indefinitely shelved, and it was to
erupt again, far more violently, after 1945.[6]

From 1942 onwards, the BBC had had its own Middle
East Director on the spot in Cairo. Once again, the New York

[1] *BBC Year Book, 1945*, p. 101.

[2] *Minutes* of a meeting, 30 July 1942.

[3] *Stephenson to Hillelson and Clark, 7 Sept. 1942. The meeting had taken
place on 2 Sept. under the chairmanship of William Strang.

[4] *See a note by Hillelson, 6 Sept. 1944. 'There is no longer a case for the
maintenance of a separate service directed to that area. The BBC has already
integrated the former Moroccan Service into its main Arabic transmission' (it had
done this on 28 May 1944) 'and the time is now ripe for the abolition of the news
bulletin in Moroccan dialect which still survives.'

[5] *Overseas Board, *Minutes*, 25 Sept. 1941.

[6] *Paper by Barbour, 15 Aug. 1944.

Office set the precedent.[1] E. G. D. Liveing, at that time the BBC's West Regional Director, was sent out to Cairo in August 1942.[2] He was expected not only to sound out local Arab opinion but to maintain liaison, which had never hitherto been easy, with the Resident British Minister of State, the Services HQ, and the Middle East Bureau of the Ministry of Information. It was the latter function, indeed, which was stressed in official quarters, for it was hoped that 'the BBC Cairo Office would be kept down to a size consistent with [its being] a focal point of contact with the Minister of State's [Casey's] office' rather than turn into another 'Arabist' organization. ('Amateur Lawrences of Arabia grew on every bush.')[3] Liveing's proposals for the development of the Cairo Office were accepted,[4] and he took up his post in February 1943, with C. J. Pennethorne Hughes, the West Regional Programme Director, as his Assistant. They were soon helped by Frank Gillard, who had come out to the Middle East as a war correspondent, and by BBC programme producers borrowed from the Army.[5] Despite the worries in official circles before the Cairo Office came into existence, it proved easier in practice thereafter to maintain liaison with the Minister of State and with the local Controller of the Ministry of Information[6] than it was to find Egyptian and Arab staff and to develop necessary broadcasting links. All efforts to find a Near East Organizer failed, and Arabic programmes had to be arranged through the Egyptian State Broadcasting Corporation. The scope of the office's work increased, however,

[1] *Hillelson to Rendall, 9 July 1941; Graves to Clark, 17 July 1941. The project had first been mooted in Dec. 1940. See above, p. 284.

[2] D. F. Aitken, an Empire Talks Assistant, had been there since the spring of 1942 and had been in contact with Monckton. Liveing wrote a fascinating report on his visit, dated 18 Sept. 1942. In it he warned that 'a swing of opinion in the Levant towards the Axis may occur at any time', though there was 'at least a fairly general temporary antipathy to the Axis Powers'.

[3] *Note by Stephenson on a meeting at the War Cabinet Offices, 18 Dec. 1942. The Minister of State had begun to interest himself in 'the number and variety of broadcasting organisations in the Middle East in September 1942 and had given Lord Moyne supervision of broadcasting propaganda' (*Notes of a meeting, 14 Sept. 1942). PWE was specifically brought in.

[4] *Director-Generals' Meeting, Minutes, 23 Dec. 1942.

[5] *Liveing to Foot, 20 March 1943.

[6] In April 1943 Curteis Ryan was appointed Controller of the Ministry of Information's Services in the Middle East (*Programme Policy Committee, Minutes, 16 April 1943).

particularly after Liveing returned to London on sick leave in August 1943 and Pennethorne Hughes took over, first as Acting Director and then from 1 April 1944 as Director.[1] That there was a question mark against the future of the Office was merely a pointer to a bigger question mark, for a Minute of the Director-Generals' Meeting in October 1944 included the telling phrase, 'if the Arabic Service continues after the War. . . .'[2] The future pattern of overseas broadcasting was already a major preoccupation of the BBC.

3. Reorganization

ALL this vast effort required organization. 'Whenever I find organization I break it,' Lord Beaverbrook is reported to have said—to Reith's awe—when he was driving as hard as any man could do the new improvised machinery of the Ministry of Aircraft Production.[3] Yet Foot, when he became 'General Adviser on War-Time Organisation' in October 1941,[4] was faced with the task not of breaking organization, in this case what was still substantially, despite all the muddles, Reith's organization, but of producing a tidy and acceptable pattern which would save the BBC from incessant Treasury intervention. He approached his task step by step, talking to a representative group of individuals inside the BBC and separately to each Governor 'in order that each one might ask me any questions on any points of doubt which they might have'.[5]

Ryan had used the term 'reorganisation' in a letter to Radcliffe in September 1941 in which he had complained that

---

[1] *For the work of the office in 1944, see a Note by Rendall, 21 Oct. 1944. Pennethorne Hughes left to become Director, New Delhi, on 16 April 1945, when Wing-Commander A. H. Marsack, who had been running the Sharq al Adna station, became Director.

[2] *Director-Generals' Meeting, *Minutes*, 25 Oct. 1944.

[3] Quoted by J. C. W. Reith, *Into the Wind* (1949), p. 5.

[4] See above, p. 359.

[5] Foot Manuscript, p. 130.

18

within the existing set-up 'policy is not always considered as it should be at the planning stage',[1] and even earlier he had referred to 'the anomalous divorce between Administration and Finance'.[2] The two BBC officials to consult, he suggested to Foot, were Lochhead and Beadle, and it was to them, as we have seen, that Foot turned. From the start Lochhead, a man of immense experience, was his main consultant on financial problems and Beadle his main consultant on questions of administration. Beadle, indeed, has claimed that even before Foot's inquiry began he had reached the same conclusion as Foot was to reach. 'A few days after Foot had been appointed he came to see me and asked me what I thought we ought to do about organisation. I took a scheme of organisation out of my drawer and I told him this was what I had tried to get Ogilvie to adopt but without success. Whereupon he produced from his pocket an almost identical scheme which he had worked out for himself. In other words, there was, on this issue, an identity of view which made the writing of reports or recommendations quite unnecessary. All we had to do was to work it out in detail and to put it into effect.'[3]

The reorganization was designed first to establish financial control and second to reform 'the highly centralised pre-war administrative machine built up by Reith in peace-time'.[4] The first task was the subject of an independent report by R. Kettle of Deloitte, Plender, Griffiths and Company. 'Prior to the war,' Kettle concluded, 'the Finance Controller [in BBC terminology he was not, in fact, Controller] by virtue of the limitation of aggregate expenditure, was in a position to exercise a close control over annual estimates and the expenditure in the various divisions of the Corporation.[5] War-time conditions of finance have abolished the limitation of aggregate expenditure and, in consequence, the Finance Controller [in December 1941 there was such a post] has been

---

[1] *Ryan to Radcliffe, 22 Sept. 1941.
[2] *Ryan to Monckton, 25 Aug. 1941.
[3] Beadle to D. H. Clarke, March 1965 (letter in Mr. Clarke's possession).
[4] G. C. Beadle, *Television, a Critical Review* (1963), p. 29.
[5] This was perhaps too favourable a retrospective judgement. For the financial problem of the BBC in 1939 and for the special difficulties caused by the development of overseas broadcasting and of television, see Briggs, *The Golden Age of Wireless* (1965), pp. 613–18.

deprived of this standard whereby he might control the expenditure of the different divisions. He is now placed in the difficult position of trying, by stressing financial considerations, to influence the decisions of the Controllers of rank equal or senior to himself. In effect, he is still held responsible for controlling the expenditure of the Corporation, but he has been deprived of the standard upon which this control was formerly based and which provided him with some measure of authority over the financial transactions of other Controllers.'[1]

The pre-war 'limitation of aggregate expenditure' described by Kettle was determined by Treasury and Post Office decisions concerning the proportion of wireless licence revenue handed on to the BBC. Income from this source was augmented, of course, by net profit from publications.[2] In war time, however, BBC income depended not on a freely disposable share of licence receipts but on grants-in-aid which were made by the Government after the BBC had presented estimates which were discussed directly with the Ministry of Information and the Treasury.[3] 'The Minister [of Information],' it was stated in the key constitutional document, 'shall pay to the Corporation such annual sum as from year to year the Lords Commissioners of the Treasury, on representations made by the Corporation to the Minister, shall approve as sufficient for the adequate conduct of the services provided by the Corporation, having regard to the conditions existing from time to time.'[4]

Graves had expressed 'some disappointment' at this formula in January 1940 and had suggested that the word 'representations' was an inadequate safeguard to the Corporation, but he had given way when Waterfield had told him that 'it would be difficult to ask the House of Commons to approve the payment of annual sums on the basis of "agreement" with the Corporation'.[5] When the new formula was accepted on 14 February 1940—it took effect from 1 April[6]—Waterfield assured Graves

---

[1] *Memorandum of 23 Dec. 1941.
[2] For the pre-war system, see Briggs, op. cit., pp. 420–1, 483–4, 500–2, 613–19.
[3] See also, pp. 359–60; *Memorandum of 26 Sept. 1939; Cmd. 6117, 1 March 1940.
[4] Agreement of 14 Feb. 1940.
[5] *Graves to Waterfield, 31 Jan. 1940; Waterfield to Graves 27 Jan. 1940.
[6] It was to last until 1 April 1946. (*Bamford to Haley, 13 March 1946.)

that it would be so construed 'as not to prevent the Corporation from having an independent point of view and maintaining that point of view in the course of the consultation for which the clause provides, though the approval of the Treasury will ultimately, in accordance with the Agreement, be the determining factor'.[1]

Clearly by the end of 1941, when Kettle reported, the Treasury had tightened its detailed control, sometimes against the best interests of broadcasting; and this was the main point which Bracken made to Foot when he asked him to become General Adviser. The Treasury was also unhappy about the fact that BBC estimates bore little relation to actual expenditures.[2] According to Bracken, there had not always been the 'formal consultation' envisaged in the Agreement of 14 February 1940.[3] The Kettle Report was followed, therefore, by detailed discussions between the BBC and the Treasury which culminated in June 1942 in a document setting out 'a code of procedure for the future'. Each year, not later than 15 January, the BBC was to provide a 'forecast' of the following year's expenditure divided into two sections, the first concerned with maintenance of existing services, the second with new development.[4] Home and Overseas expenditures were to be separated. 'The amount of the forecast,' it was agreed, 'will constitute the first limit within which the Corporation's expenditure on the approved services covered within the forecast will be made good to them by issues from the Grant-in-Aid.' Capital expenditure was to be treated separately and no net savings on recurrent grant could be transferred to capital.

This 'code' was similar in some respects to that followed by the University Grants Committee, and, like a university, the BBC was to have certain 'delegated powers' to 'incur

[1] *Waterfield to Graves, 2 Feb. 1940.
[2] See above, pp. 359–60.
[3] *Bracken to Powell, 5 Nov. 1941.
[4] *Forecasting procedures were worked out in 1942 (Director-Generals' Meeting, *Minutes*, 24 June 1942). Three forecasts, A, B and C, were planned, the second dealing with increases in costs over which the BBC had no control and the third with development. Kettle set out in his report the details of existing procedures in late 1941. The Board of Governors considered estimates of expenditure on a quarterly and a yearly basis, but could exercise little direct control over the position.

expenditure on additions to existing services within moderate limits to be agreed'. For its part, the Treasury conceded that it would 'admit in the forecast for the year a global figure to cover the contingency of increases in costs, rising prices, etc. which hitherto they have rejected'. There was a 'fight' about the extent of the 'delegated powers', but the discussions were amicable and constructive, and Foot paid a warm tribute to Sir Alan Barlow of the Treasury who throughout a series of meetings had shown that he was genuinely anxious 'to allow us to operate with as much freedom as possible'.[1] Later, Barlow was to tell the Public Accounts Committee that the BBC estimates before 1942 had been 'very wild indeed', but that after 1942 the system became methodical and 'reliable'.[2]

There is no doubt that Foot was largely responsible for securing an unprecedented upsurge of confidence in the Treasury, and there were no more major arguments about the finance of broadcasting during the rest of the war. Foot, indeed, used the 'reorganization' as Bracken had told him to do, as a means of pressing the BBC's claim to 'freedom'. He lost no time in submitting details of his reorganization plans, through Bracken, to the War Cabinet.[3] Much, therefore, that had been a matter of argument earlier during the war now became a matter of routine. Yet the general situation inevitably involved continuing pressures on the BBC—from outside as well as from inside—to extend the scale of its operations. While Home Service outlay remained at much the same level as it had been in peace time, the main growth of expenditure was concerned with overseas broadcasting. Estimates of recurrent expenditure actually fell after reaching a peak figure in 1942; grant-in-aid income fell with them, even though on the basis of the number of current wireless licences, the main pre-war criterion determining BBC income, there would have been a small annual increase in revenue. Overseas developments, particularly in relation to the Monitoring Service, were so large, however, that they necessarily overshadowed

---

[1] *Memorandum by Foot, 16 June 1942; Barlow to Foot, 29 Oct. 1942.

[2] First report of the Select Committee on Estimates, Session 1945–6, Sub-Committee D, April 1946. This report provides a most useful summary.

[3] *Note on a telephone conversation between Foot and Bamford, 8 June 1942.

everything else.[1] The relevant statistics are set out in the
table on p. 533.

It is interesting to compare this table, reflecting an unanticipated increase in the scale and range of broadcasting activity,
with the original modest forecasts of the 'estimated cost of
broadcasting in war-time', prepared in July 1939 and based on
a detailed breakdown of the relevant recurrent items. At this
stage television was still envisaged as a claim on resources:

ESTIMATED ANNUAL COST OF BROADCASTING IN WAR-TIME, 1939

	Sound £	Empire £	Foreign £	Television £	Total £
Programmes	888,000	53,000	16,000	10,000	967,000
Engineering	214,000	56,000	28,000	—	298,000
Premises etc.	175,000	12,000	10,000	10,000	207,000
Administration	56,000	—	—	—	56,000
Public Relations	14,000	4,000	14,000	—	32,000
Salaries/Pensions	949,000	88,000	70,000	41,000	1,148,000
Replacements	170,000	20,000	10,000	—	200,000
Income Tax	40,000	—	—	—	40,000
TOTAL	2,506,000	233,000	148,000	61,000	2,948,000

In his report Kettle recognized how 'the abnormal conditions encountered in war-time' tended to reduce the value
of annual estimates as a means of controlling expenditure.
He suggested, therefore, that there should be a rearrangement
and redefinition of individual responsibilities within the
Corporation. The Director-General should have expert advice
on financial questions. Each major Departmental Head
should accept full responsibility for the direct expenditure
which the work of his Department entailed, and Programme
Units should relate programme hours to programme costs.
The Buying Department should be separated from the Finance
Division. Likewise, the Staff Administration and Staff Accommodation and Legal sections of the Administration Division
should be independent departments responsible directly to
the Director-General for the control of a 'BBC Establishment'.
Above all, each set of departmental estimates should be so
drafted that 'the financial effect of changes of the volume of

[1] The salary bill rose from £1,200,000 in 1939 to £3,800,000 in 1945.

BBC FINANCES 1939–1946

(Net Licence Income for fifteen months to 31 March 1940 was £4,745,000: an overspending of £69,000 was reimbursed in the grant-in-aid for 1940–1941, which amounted to £4,855,000)

Year	Paid Licences in Force	First BBC Estimate Submitted	Revised BBC Estimate	Grant in Aid	Publications and Other Income	Operating Expenditure	Capital Expenditure	Surplus or Deficit (—) for year
		£	£	£	£	£	£	£
1941–42	8,635,642	6,233,000	6,648,000	6,700,000	345,000	6,607,000	869,000	−431,000
1942–43	9,193,641	11,010,000	10,000,000	8,400,000	515,000	7,432,000	1,610,000	−127,000
1943–44	9,506,714	10,000,000	9,800,000	8,400,000	875,000	8,316,000	627,000	332,000
1944–45	9,663,369	9,500,000	9,300,000	8,300,000	693,000	8,541,000	148,000	304,000
1945–46	10,347,831	9,700,000	8,500,000	8,300,000	797,000	9,002,000	102,000	− 7,000

work in a department due to varying conditions could be easily determined'.[1]

The second object of reorganization in 1942—'decentralization'—was directly related, therefore, to the first, the achievement of financial control. Yet its implementation had far wider ramifications. When Reith had carried out his great reorganization of 1933,[2] the Corporation employed only 1,750 people: in 1942 there were nearly three times as many engineers alone. Moreover, the staff, most of them quite new to broadcasting, were scattered, as we have seen, in places as removed from each other as Bristol and Bedford, Evesham and Manchester. In each of these new centres there were difficulties in finding accommodation, equipping studios and offices, and arranging billeting and welfare services. Centralization of administration added to the difficulties of management. The staff records system of the Staff Administration Department, for example, found it difficult to provide full and up-to-date information to the Salaries section of the Accounts Department. There was often a geographical separation, moreover, between departmental executives of the Programme Administration Department and the actual programme workers themselves. The Director of Programme Administration, responsible to the Controller (Administration), found it far from easy to organize 'the system', particularly when Nicolls, the Controller (Programmes), had himself graduated to his job from the job of Controller (Administration) and when Maconachie, the Controller (Home) had graduated to his job from the Indian Civil Administration.

Reith had set great store in 1933 on the deliberate separation of 'creative' and 'administrative' functions inside the Corporation with a view to liberating the creators and streamlining the administrators. The attempt at separation had become increasingly unsatisfactory. Controller (Administration) and Controller (Programmes) shared top-level responsibility very uneasily, and in the lower echelons of the Corporation the initial simplicity of the 'system' had given way to intricate complexity. The heads of programme departments responsible to Controller (Programmes) were necessarily responsible for

---

[1] *Memorandum of 23 Dec. 1941.
[2] Briggs, op.cit., pp. 441 ff.

the allocation of work, the assessment of quality and the formulation of policy within their own departments, yet the Programme Executives, who worked by their side, were responsible to the Controller (Administration). The allocation of finance for programmes, the central task in any broadcasting corporation, was the responsibility of the Director of Programme Planning who was himself responsible to Controller (Programmes). It was easy to bypass the Programme Executives: it was equally easy for misunderstandings at the top to percolate through to the lower levels of the organization. Even before the outbreak of war Graves, the Deputy Director-General, had wrung his hands in horror, crying piteously, 'it's the system; it's the system'.[1] In such circumstances, a Beaverbrook in Broadcasting House would certainly have had ample scope.

There were several important changes in organization between 1939 and 1942, most of which have already been described, but they did not affect the 'system' as a whole. The old Public Relations Division, which Tallents had built up before 1939, had been abolished in May 1940 when the Home and Overseas Divisions were created, although a Director of Publicity, Kenneth Adam, who was to have an influential future in the post-war BBC, was appointed in August 1941.[2] The removal of the Accounts Department from the Administration Division in November 1940 to form a new Finance Division had marked the first attempt to get out of the financial mix-up. The splitting up of the Overseas Services and the European Services in October 1941[3] had been associated, as we have seen, with the creation of a News Co-ordination Division with one key man, Ryan. Controller (Administration) retained his powers, however, and dealt with both Home and Overseas broadcasting staff and equipment. He had a foothold also in the most independent of all

---

[1] Quoted in Harman Grisewood, op. cit., p. 121.

[2] *Control Board, *Minutes*, 27 Aug. 1941. 'The PR Division,' Graves wrote in an important note of Dec. 1940, 'was expected to be a buffer between the Corporation and the public, yet was not in a position to speak with the necessary authority because it had to refer to the Division whose work was under discussion. It was, in fact, mainly a channel of communication.' In Jan. 1941 Ryan (letter to Regional Directors, 1 Jan.) stated firmly, 'it is felt here, and I think you will agree, rightly, that in the stress of war we have not kept before the public, as emphatically as we might, what the BBC has been doing'.

[3] See above, p. 342.

the divisions, Engineering, which had its own chain of command from Controller (Engineering) down to Engineers-in-Charge of transmitters and studio centres. Staff and Establishment was the responsibility of an Engineering Establishment Officer under the Director of Staff Administration in the Administration Division; alongside him was a General Establishment Officer.

Until the post of Director of Office Administration was abolished in March 1941 and a new Business Management (Legal) Department was created, there was as much scope for criticism of the set-up from subordinates as there was from senior officials. The Director of Office Administration had been responsible for the acquisition, planning and equipment of premises, for studio accommodation both in London and in the provinces, a most onerous task as war-time financial and physical controls multiplied, and for the maintenance and furnishing of existing accommodation and services, including Library and Catering. On the one hand, he had to meet complaints from users; on the other hand, to cope with the tangled mass of official regulations. He had to be equally at home with architects and joiners, and he had to supervise travel and subsistence allowances and entertainment expenses, along with cleaning and archives. His clients included the Director of Programme Administration, Heads of Departments in the Administration and Engineering Divisions and Regional Executives who managed their own services. The changes of March 1941 were inevitable. They included, *inter alia*, the transfer of the Library and Registry to the Secretariat.

The Director-General could not hope to know much in detail about this cumbrous 'system'. His tasks were complicated, indeed, by the increase in the number of Controllers directly responsible to him. In 1939 there had been four: Administration, Programmes, Public Relations and Engineering. In 1942 there were eight: three geographical—Home,[1] European and Overseas; three functional—News Co-ordination, Engineering and Programmes; and two general—Administration and Finance. Foot was determined from the moment

---

[1] This was a strangely assorted Division which included Talks (Home), News (Home), School Broadcasting, *Radio Times* and *The Listener*: it was no more Home than Programmes was. This makes the geographical classification somewhat misleading.

that he arrived in Broadcasting House to change this central core of BBC organization. In his step-by-step review of functions and of job specifications he produced a completely different pattern which allowed for greater de-centralization of initiative as a concomitant of greater financial control.

He was able to make rapid progress not only because of the help given him by Beadle and Lochhead, but because what he was proposing was generally acceptable to large numbers of people who had been frustrated before January 1942. He could concentrate on his administrative tasks after February 1942, however, because he had as Joint Director-General an experienced BBC man, Graves, who was particularly concerned not with 'machinery' but with 'output'. Graves had been ill when Foot arrived in November 1941, and he took no part in the initial review. Yet while it proceeded, he watched what was happening sympathetically. He and Foot soon established mutual understanding. It was easy as well as tempting to satirize 'the diarchy', gently or savagely—'Tweedledumgee' and 'Tweedledeegee', for instance—but Foot was right to insist on the complementarity of the two Directors-General. 'Together Graves and I commanded more confidence both inside and outside the BBC than at that time either one of us alone would have been able to command—he with his long and successful experience in the control and direction of BBC programmes of all kinds—and I with my equally long, and I hope equally successful, experience in management of a large Public Utility like the Gas, Light and Coke Company, which in a more limited sense had also its public duties and responsibilities both to its millions of consumers and to the Government.'[1]

There was no doubt about the goodwill of Government. In June 1942 Bracken wrote to Foot telling him that months ago he had undertaken to produce a paper for the War Cabinet showing the organization of the BBC and the changes that had been made.[2] Foot responded at once,[3] yet Bracken decided equally quickly that there was no longer any need to tell the War Cabinet about how the BBC was run.[4] Although a second paper was eventually prepared in March 1943 and

[1] Foot Manuscript, p. 143. See also above, p. 363.
[2] *Bracken to Foot, 5 June 1942.   [3] *Foot to Bracken, 22 June 1942.
[4] *Bracken to Foot, 13 July 1942; Note by Foot, 12 Aug. 1942.

on this occasion presumably made its way to the Cabinet,[1] there were no signs of any of the tensions which had accompanied similar exchanges earlier during the war.

The main outcome of the 'reorganization' carried out by Foot was the reform of the BBC's committee structure and, far more important, the abolition of the old Administration Division with its own Controller. Although there had been changes in the nomenclature of BBC committees earlier during the war—thus for example, the Home Broadcasting Committee had changed its name in November 1939 to the Home Service Board and in January 1940 to the Home Board[2]—Ogilvie, supported by Tallents, had resisted and eventually ruled out an attempt made by Ryan in February 1941 to merge the Home and Overseas Boards.[3] In face of Ryan's complaint that because of the welter of internal meetings it was difficult for Controllers to keep important appointments with senior officials outside the BBC,[4] he argued that attendance at committees was vital and that the titles of the Boards should remain as they were.[5] This was very much Tallents's view. Ryan continued to press for reorganization, and in a series of papers revealed clearly just how dissatisfied he was with the existing arrangements. 'Policy is not always considered as it should be at the planning stage. It is apt to be left to the eleventh hour, when much work has already been put into a programme, and even until publicity about it has been issued.'[6]

Changes were made in October 1941, when the work of Control Board was sub-divided—Control Board (Administration) meeting on Wednesdays, Control Board (Overseas) on Thursdays, and Control Board (Home) on Fridays[7]—but the crucial changes in this connection took place, like the other big changes, only after the appointment of Foot and Graves as joint Directors-General in January 1942. On 2 February 1942 Control Board in its old form was abolished,

---

[1] *Bracken to Foot, 15 Jan. 1943; Foot to Bracken, 16 Jan. 1943; Foot to Bracken, 1 March 1943, enclosing memorandum. Bracken suggested that one of the BBC's 'bright young men' should write it.

[2] See above, p. 105.   [3] *Control Board, *Minutes*, 12 Feb. 1941.

[4] *Ryan to Ogilvie 30 Jan. 1941.   [5] *Note in ink by Ogilvie, 2 Feb. 1941.

[6] *Note by Ryan, 22 Sept. 1941, headed 'BBC Reorganisation'.

[7] *Note by Ogilvie, 14 Oct. 1941.

on the grounds that it 'created a lock in the direct responsibility from Controllers to the Directors-General',[1] and in its place three committees were planned. On Wednesday mornings there was to be a Director-Generals' Meeting at which both Foot and Graves would be present and to which any Controller could bring up questions for discussion. On alternate Wednesday afternoons there was to be a 'Controllers' Conference' to deal with 'general policy matters'. On Fridays at 2.30 there was to be a weekly meeting of the Directors-General with the output Controllers (Programmes, Home, European, Overseas and News Co-ordination).

The abolition of the old Administration Division was a far more radical change than any proposed in the Kettle Report. Thereafter there was no longer to be a central administrative unit of the Corporation with officers who owed no responsibility or allegiance to the Division in which they actually worked, although there was to be a small group dealing centrally with staff recruitment and employment. The new scheme, totally different in conception from that which it supplanted, laid down that each Division was responsible for its own administration and was to be staffed accordingly.[2] Its administrative officers were made directly responsible to the Controllers of their Divisions.

'In addition to the firm intention to decentralise,' Sir William Haley was to write later, 'there was also the feeling that administration and what may be loosely called production would no longer be so apt to get at loggerheads if they were brothers within a Division rather than being divisional rivals.'[3] In the case of Programme Departments within the Programme Division, each Departmental Head was to have the services of an Administrative Assistant.[4] The Controller of each

---

[1] *Note of a meeting between the Directors-General and the Controllers, 2 Feb. 1942.

[2] There were, however, common grades, salaries and procedures relating to recruitment, promotion and transfer. See below, p. 547.

[3] W. J. Haley, 'The War-time Administration of the BBC', Address to the Institute of Public Administration, 2 Feb. 1946.

[4] *Memorandum of 30 March 1942: 'The Reorganisation of Five Operational Divisions'. The title 'Administrative Assistant', a new one within the BBC, was accepted in April 1942 (Director-Generals' Meeting, *Minutes*, 1 April, 1942). The acceptance of the reorganization is recorded in Board of Governors, *Minutes*, 16, 23 April 1942.

Division was also to be made directly responsible for its finances. The estimates which he prepared were to be passed on to the Controller (Finance), who was to retain responsibility for records and for the supervision of the overall finances of the BBC, but it was for the Controller of the Division to watch unit costs and to relate new developments to existing commitments. Any variations in the estimates which he had prepared were to be submitted—in the first phase after the reorganization took place—to a weekly Director-Generals' meeting or 'tribunal' at which Controller (Finance) was present as the Director-Generals' principal adviser on financial questions. At the same time, all staff establishments were to be reviewed, and a statistical unit was to be attached to the Director of Staff Administration's Office.[1] Each separate divisional or departmental establishment could be varied thereafter only by central agreement, and each post within each Division or Department had to be registered and graded.[2]

When the outline of the new organization was set out in diagrammatic form, decentralization was emphasized above all else:

	Engineering Programmes News Home Overseas European	Operational Divisions
Directors-General +2 Principal Assistants— +Secretariat (Management)	North Midland West Scotland Wales Northern Ireland	Regions
	London Southern Bedford Bangor	Area offices
	North American Office	
	Publications Management Publicity Catering	Departments

---

[1] *Note by W. St. J. Pym, Director of Staff Administration, 28 Nov. 1941.

[2] *Memorandum of 29 May 1942, 'Reorganisation—Control of Establishments'; Memorandum of 24 June 1942, 'Establishment Control'. 'We are determined that once the reorganisation has become effective and the Establishments

It was clear from this diagram that while some of the BBC units it described would have purely war-time significance— the Area Offices, for instance—others, notably the Regions, would have a somewhat different role in future peace-time organization. The Regional Directors, indeed, had their role specified in the most general way. 'Regional Directors are responsible for the welfare and discipline of all Corporation personnel working within their regions, and any actions or behaviour not in the best interests of the Corporation and its Staff come within the scope of their responsibility.' 'It is intended that everything which goes on within a Region shall be regarded as within the scope of the Regional Director.'[1]

The emphasis was to persist after the war when the Regions regained their freedom fully to develop their programming. During the early stages of the war, the importance and influence of the Regional Directors had been seriously curtailed as a result of the reduction in the number of wavelengths, and at the time of reorganization both Foot and Graves were anxious to restore 'as much of the pre-war autonomy and local importance as was possible under war conditions'.[2] The Regional Directors were not only given greater administrative responsibilities, therefore, but were invited to monthly meetings at Broadcasting House where they met the Central Controllers. Every attention was paid to the free expression of their wishes. Foot was aware of 'the danger of the BBC becoming a top heavy and remote organisation looking at its policy and its performance with what I may call the eyes of the Londoner'.[3]

[1] *Memorandum of 5 May 1942. The diagram as printed above leaves out other specifically war-time responsibilities, e.g. defence. G. S. Strode was appointed Defence Adviser (the title Defence Director was dropped), and defence became the direct responsibility of Regional and Area Directors and, for the larger transmitters, of Controller (Engineering). In so far as office routine required regulation by management, this was to be undertaken by the Secretariat. There was also to be a Legal Department with Jardine Brown as its Director. The New York office was to be allowed great freedom. 'Geographical considerations make it necessary for this unit to be more completely decentralised than any other in the Corporation.'   [2] Foot Manuscript, p. 172.   [3] Ibid., p. 173.

have become self-contained units, the Heads of these Establishments will not only be able but encouraged to act with a real sense of responsibility and authority. . . . But just as it is obvious that the Management, through the medium of the Accounts Department, must keep an overriding check on expenditure as compared with approved estimates, so also it is necessary for there to be a supervisory control on establishments generally throughout the Corporation.'

He paid careful attention, therefore, to outside writers on post-war broadcasting who were almost unanimous in urging that a Regional scheme should become 'the basis of a reorganised BBC',[1] and doubtless welcomed Press comment that the 'centralisers' who had had their way earlier during the war had been checked and that the regions had 're-asserted themselves and kept the nation vividly aware of its essential diversity'.[2]

Complaints from the Regions about 'under-representation' continued, nonetheless, to be made. In June 1942, for example, Edgar, the Director of the Midland Region, and Denis Morris, Midland Regional Programme Director, urged that because of the key importance of the Midlands in the war effort, the Midland Region should be recognized as an area of strategic importance in programme making. They put their case to Nicolson,[3] yet they were still complaining more than a year later that 'the Regions have been badly treated in the war-time set up'.[4] Early in 1943 the local Ministry of Information Committees in the North of England were demanding 'the full restoration of regional broadcasting as early as possible';[5] and in 1944 John Coatman, the North Regional Director, strongly criticized the fact that 'the characteristic activities of the North of England hardly enter into our programmes'.[6] In an exchange of letters with the Director-General both correspondents were drawn into the pre-war debate about 'merit' and quality being the test of a devolved regional contribution to national broadcasting,[7] while at the same time

---

[1] See, for example, P. P. Eckersley, *The Power Behind the Microphone* (1941), p. 179. See also below, pp. 716-18.

[2] *Birmingham Mail*, 12 April 1944.

[3] *Nicolson to Graves, 24 June 1942.

[4] *Morris to Nicolls, 17 Sept. 1943.

[5] *Notes on a meeting of the Advisory Committee to the North Region of the MoI Newcastle, 19 Jan. 1943. 'The meeting was extremely valuable from the BBC standpoint,' it was stated, 'in disclosing as it did a strong feeling in important quarters in the North East of England that regional representation in BBC broadcasts is not sufficient under the present system of centralisation.' Four months later the Board of Governors turned down a request from Lord Derby for a Northern half hour on the lines of the Scottish half hour and for projected Ulster and Wales half hours (Board of Governors, *Minutes*, 20 May 1943), while agreeing that there should be more regional items in the News.

[6] *Coatman to Foot, 21 Feb. 1944.

[7] See Briggs, *The Golden Age of Wireless*, pp. 293 ff.

(*a*) Parents in London talk to their Children in Australia
and New Zealand

(*b*) Nursing Sisters in the Middle East record for 'Messages Home'

17. Messages Across the Seas

(a) A Sussex Farmworker in 'Transatlantic Call'

(b) The Radio Allotment

18. Back to the Land

(*a*) W. J. Haley in Italy with Denis Johnston (left) and
Frank Gillard (right)

(*b*) Margaret Hubble announcing in the AEF Programme

19. With the Forces, 1943–4

(a) Booklet of Songs by Maurice van Moppès dropped over France

(b) Some Members of the 'Team', 1944

From left to right, with pseudonyms in brackets: Paul Bouchon (Paul Boivin), Pierre Lefèvre, J. B. Brunius (Jacques Borel), Michel Saint-Denis (Jacques Duchesne), Jean Vacher (Jean Desvernais)

20. Les Français parlent aux Français

they touched on new war-time themes, like the numbers of
Northcountrymen serving in the Forces overseas. By the end
of 1944, the Director-General himself was involved in public
debate about the place of regionalism in post-war broadcasting.[1]

There was one other important aspect of the changes
made in 1942 which was to have peace-time significance. A
News Division was set up in September 1942. Home and
Empire News and News Talks services which had hitherto been
managed separately, with Ryan as Co-ordinator, were in future
to be fused, with Ryan as Controller:[2] European News still
remained outside the machine, with Newsome retaining his
independent power in Bush House. At the same time, the
specialist knowledge of the regional sections of the Overseas
Services Division was explicitly recognized, as J. B. Clark had
always insisted,[3] and it was agreed, first, that no news commentator would be introduced into any Overseas Service
until his name had been approved by the Overseas Services
Division and, second, that the Overseas Services Division,
which had recruited an impressive group of reporters and
had pioneered exciting new programmes like *Radio Newsreel*
and *Listening Post*,[4] would state its requirements concerning the
number of news bulletins to be broadcast in each service,
their timing and their presentation. In this connection, News
Division would act as 'service agents'.[5] Eleven days after the
announcement of the impending change, it was also announced
that J. C. S. Macgregor, who had been seconded to the

[1] This followed an address he gave to the Radio Industries Club on 'Post-War Broadcasting' on 28 Nov. 1944. See below, p. 722.

[2] *Board of Governors, *Minutes*, 6 Aug. 1942. The policy in embryo was set out in a paper by the Joint Directors-General on 5 March 1942.

[3] *Memorandum of 11 Nov. 1941; Clark to Ogilvie, 12 Nov. 1941; Memorandum of 13 Feb. 1942. Clark's last statement on the subject was made on 17 Aug. 1942, the day before the changes were announced (Note of 18 Aug. 1942): his view throughout was that there should be what he called 'differential' treatment.

[4] News commentators included Robert (later Sir Robert) Fraser, who was to become first Director-General of ITA, Tahu Hole, who later became Editor, News, BBC, Thomas Cadett, later Paris Correspondent of the BBC, and Edgar Lustgarten. Among people working at various times for *Radio Newsreel* were Alan Melville, Terence de Marney, Audrey Russell, Vera Lindsay, George Weidenfeld, Peter Quennell and Michael Goodwin.

[5] *Promulgation of 18 Aug. 1942, 'News Division'.

Ministry of Information, would become Assistant Controller (News).[1]

The rearrangements came into effect on 14 September. They involved a crucial change which affected the whole approach of the BBC to news collection and dissemination. 'Up to the outbreak of war,' Farquharson had written earlier in 1942, 'our News work escaped public attention to a remarkable degree as compared with other matters which loomed large in Parliament and elsewhere.'[2] Ryan had long been concerned that in war-time conditions the Home and Empire Services of the BBC had not followed the same rules. 'Home invariably checks with the three fighting Services, the Foreign Office, etc. Empire does not go so far as this, limiting itself to consultation with the Services when in the opinion of the Editor on duty, such a step is desirable. The more tight hold on Home has been necessary for political rather than for more general reasons.'[3] He wanted to see the two separately organized services brought into line with each other. By 1942, indeed, it had been clear for more than two years that the News work of the BBC, Home or Overseas, was bound to create public, parliamentary and governmental interest to such an extent that it would directly influence all general judgements about the BBC. Between 1942 and 1945, as we have seen, the BBC greatly strengthened its News services. It was being drawn inevitably into that unremitting quest for 'topicality' which most sharply distinguishes post-war from pre-war patterns of broadcasting.

Ryan was the main individual behind the immediate moves which were to have such long-term repercussions. He had urged since 1940 that the Ministry of Information should have control of news independent of all other Government Departments.[4] He had also argued since 1940 that the BBC News Editors were absurdly restricted: 'it is as though the

---

[1] *Note by Foot, 29 Aug. 1942. For Macgregor, see above, p. 101.

[2] *Farquharson to Foot, 5 Feb. 1942. See also above, p. 47. There had been eighty parliamentary questions relating to the BBC's handling of news bulletins between Sept. 1939 and Feb. 1942.

[3] *Ryan to Foot, 6 Aug. 1942.

[4] *See above, pp. 48–9. His most important Memorandum, 'The Handling of News as a Weapon of War', was dated 16 April 1940. See also his Memorandum of 4 June 1941.

Editor of *The Times* could only make up his front newspage after the War Office had approved every line he proposed to print about military affairs and the Admiralty, the Air Ministry, the Foreign Office, etc., had done the same.'[1] If the BBC were to secure greater freedom, it would have to work, in his opinion, in the closest co-operation with the Ministry, and it would have to follow a common News policy, deliberately conceived and effectively implemented. 'At present,' he noted, 'it is possible for Home and Empire independently to send men, and even recording vans, on the same job.'[2] 'Official' news was inadequate for public needs in both cases: what was needed was 'a variety of sources'. Equally important, there had to be scope for 'flexibility in treatment'. Yet it was from the daily meetings at the Ministry of Information, at its Executive Board, that 'the freedom' of the BBC ultimately derived[3] and it was from sections of the Press that the main hostility or suspicion often came.[4]

Ryan's dissatisfaction with the machinery of 'coordination'[5] and his desire to achieve more effective control lay behind the decision to set up the News Division. From early in 1942 onwards a daily meeting had been held in Ryan's room at which BBC News policy was discussed: Ryan was now given the chance, as he wished, to extend its size to include 'the sending out of correspondents and comparing of notes as to how this or that story had been handled in the various services'.[6]

---

[1] *Ibid.   [2] *Note of 22 Sept. 1941.

[3] *Ryan to Graves, 10 Feb. 1942; Ryan to Radcliffe. 31 Dec. 1942. 'We get at the Board authoritative Ministry of Information rulings on a miscellany of topics on which we need guidance . . . [in addition] the meetings (and their informal prologues and epilogues) give a chance for comments on BBC programmes to be aired.'

[4] *Rendall to Ogilvie, reporting a Press Conference by the Minister of Information with representatives of the Empire Press, on 15 Oct. 1941; there was a protest from the Newspaper and Periodical Emergency Council when the BBC announced news of damage to the *Scharnhorst* and *Gneisenau* on 3 May 1942. CBS broadcast the news at 4.30 p.m. on 3 May, although there had been an embargo until 3 a.m. on the 4th. As a result, the BBC broadcast the news at 9 p.m. on the 3rd. In a memorandum to Hodge on 7 May, Ryan stated that Radcliffe, with whom he had had several discussions, agreed that 'British official communiqués should be given to the world, including the people of this country, at least as quickly by British as by foreign radios'.

[5] *Ryan to Foot and Graves, 27 May 1942; Ryan to Foot, 17 July 1942.

[6] *Ryan to Graves, 10 Feb. 1942; Ryan to R. T. Clark 4 July 1942. Difficulties still persisted (Ryan to Graves, 27 May 1942).

Changes were made in consequence in the composition of the new News Division. R. T. Clark remained in charge of Home News, but his title was altered to Editor (Home News Broadcasts) in June 1943, when Donald Boyd, who had been appointed Home News Talks Editor in April 1942, assumed responsibility for home-based news reporters. A. E. Barker was appointed Foreign Editor in December 1942,[1] and in June 1943 Bernard Moore Editor (Overseas News Broadcasts) and Peter Pooley Editor (Overseas News Talks). Europe remained outside the set-up. Meanwhile, steps were taken to build up a corps of BBC foreign correspondents.[2] The BBC, it was felt, should no longer be dependent either on official handouts or on messages from Reuters and other News Agencies: it had 'to recruit its own resident and "string correspondents"'.[3] The first attempt to appoint a United States correspondent was taken in December 1942, when Michael Barkway, formerly Chief Editor (Empire Services), was sent as a special correspondent to Washington.[4] A. H. Wigan later replaced him. Although it was not until 1944 that Kenneth Matthews became BBC Cairo Correspondent, that Norman Macdonald was sent to Sweden, and that Thomas Cadett went to Paris, all the essential policy decisions had been taken by the middle of 1943.[5] After the reorganization, Ryan himself continued to have wider responsibilities than those of a Controller. He continued 'to act as Home Adviser in the political field, passing on any necessary policy directions to the other Controllers concerned'.[6]

The BBC's foreign correspondents were to become something of a *corps d'élite*, achieving what Ryan wished—the highest standards in handling news and, in their case, interpreting

---

[1] *Ryan to Foot and Graves, 25 Nov. 1942.

[2] *Report of the Foreign News Committee, Oct. 1942. Barker was Chairman and Moore and Clark were members. Before the war such a News service had been considered far too costly. (*A. E. Barker to Farquharson, 25 Sept. 1943.) Yet there had been an increase in the number of News commentaries and talks from overseas.   [3] *Rendall to R. T. Clark, 8 April 1942.

[4] Barkway was given this title on 1 July 1942.

[5] *Macdonald was to go to Germany after the end of the war in 1945, becoming the BBC's first Berlin Correspondent. The BBC's first News Division Diplomatic Correspondent was not appointed until 1948. There was talk of appointing resident correspondents also in Ankara and Lisbon. (A. E. Barker to Farquharson, 25 Sept. 1943.) The general idea is outlined in Macgregor to Marshall, 1 Feb. 1944.

[6] *Note by the Directors-General, 4 Aug. 1942.

it and setting it in perspective. There were many other changes in 1942 and 1943, however, which influenced the recruitment and organization of BBC staff as a whole for years to come. It was decided in August 1942 that staffing questions should be dealt with in future within six departments, each reporting directly to the Directors-General—a Staff Department, under W. St. J. Pym's direction, dealing with rates of pay and conditions of work, relations between employers and employed, and pensions; an Appointments Department under D. H. Clarke, dealing with recruitment, transfers and release or deferment from military service; a Staff Training Department, under E. A. F. Harding, dealing with the training of all non-engineering staff; an Allowances Department, under J. M. Rose-Troup, concerned with 'the framing and interpretation of allowances regulations';[1] a Welfare Department, with a Welfare Adviser, Miss G. Freeman, 'advising and assisting Heads of Establishments, primarily Regional and Area Directors, in matters of staff welfare'; and a Secretary, Establishment Control, examining all requests for increases and decreases of 'Establishments' and changes in specifications, titles and grades of individual posts. The Directors-General envisaged that while they might wish to intervene directly in the work of any of the six sections of management, they would normally depute their authority to Beadle or Pym.[2]

Each of these departments had its own history. Recruitment continued to be difficult, particularly when foreign languages were essential qualifications.[3] Billeting was often unsatisfactory as a number of eloquent memoranda relating to the sociology of 'billeters' or 'billetors' and 'billetees' demonstrate.[4] Staff training grew greatly in importance in relation to everything

---

[1] The first Allowances Officer had been appointed in April 1941 to deal with regulations for travelling and subsistence allowances and with new problems arising out of dispersal, billeting, and shift working.

[2] *Promulgation of 19 Aug. 1942.

[3] Special language assessors co-operated with the BBC in recruiting.

[4] *There is a fascinating memorandum on the situation at Evesham (Lord Kingsale to Brigadier Horn, 28 April 1942) with a harrowing account of low-quality accommodation, inadequate public amenities, and strained social relations. Some 'billeters' objected strongly to the presence of foreigners. There were unsolved economic disputes about 'wear and tear' of linen. There was, of course, another side to the coin, and some members of staff made good friends with their 'billetors'.

else that followed. The Staff Training Department had been revived in June 1941 several months before general reorganization.[1] Fortnightly courses dealing mainly with 'programme techniques, accompanied by sketches of the main engineering and administrative processes which render them possible in British broadcasting', began in the same month. Lecture One dealt with the constitution of the BBC in war time, Lecture Two with administration, Lecture Three with the Overseas Division, and Lecture Four with the BBC's Intelligence services. There was a place in the general training scheme for the study not only of broadcasting techniques but of the activities of secret agents and sabotage, 'jobs that saved the training staff from developing too academic an outlook'.[2]

The first recruits mustered by the Staff Training Department certainly provided what was most needed—a pool of people available for the needs of 'triple expansion'.[3] Members of two of the early courses included Louis MacNeice and William Empson, poets and scriptwriters, Leslie Perowne, then an Assistant in the Variety Department, J. G. Weightman, Marius Goring and M. Zvegintzov of the European Service, Frank Hardie, the historian of Victorian and Edwardian England, and E. K. Bramsted, the future historian of Dr. Goebbels's propaganda machine. The Engineering Training School had started even earlier in May 1941 with D. H. Schaschke as Chief Instructor. Between then and July 1942 it trained 707 newcomers, 465 of them women, and gave refresher courses for 249 existing staff. It also produced an impressive *Engineering Training Manual* drafted by F. C. Brooker.[4]

Staff 'welfare' was developed more ambitiously throughout the war, so that in the process the BBC was brought more into line with other large organizations.[5] The pre-war

[1] *Memorandum of 11 June 1941. The first staff training courses, 'lavish and leisurely' (M. Gorham, *Broadcasting and Television since 1900* (1952), p. 180), had been given in 1936. They closed down at the outbreak of the war.

[2] E. A. F. Harding, 'The Past and Future of Staff Training' in *BBC Handbook, 1947.*

[3] War-time Staff Instruction, 'Pool of Staff', 18 Oct. 1941, signed by A. C. Cameron.

[4] *Note by R. T. B. Wynn on the Engineering Training School, 4 July 1942.

[5] *The detailed history of 'welfare' is full of interesting episodes. There was a curious little note on 27 Sept. 1939: 'The pages seconded to the Ministry of Information are worried as to whether they will receive their pay on Friday next,

paternalism, which had been strongly criticized outside the Corporation,[1] gave way to recognition of independent technical and non-technical staff associations, later amalgamated, with whom the management of the BBC could deal.[2] When war broke out a drafting committee was at work on a scheme for a Joint Council, but Ogilvie and the chairman of the staff side felt in March 1940 that the introduction of any scheme would have to be postponed until the end of the war.[3] Given the increasing interest during the war in questions of more 'democratic' industrial relations, this decision could not stand, and in September 1940 Ogilvie was told by representatives of 'a thousand staff in a large number of grades' that they had decided in May to set up a new association.[4] 'Will the Corporation recognise our Association?' he was asked. 'May it be assumed that the principle of joint consultation . . . will still apply as far as possible?' 'Will the Corporation let representatives of the "Management" in centres outside Broadcasting House know that representatives of local groups have status corresponding to that of the representatives of groups in Broadcasting House?' Ogilvie gave the necessary assurances, and the BBC's Staff (Wartime) Association, with H. Lynton Fletcher as Chairman, came into existence 'as a war-time substitute for the full Joint Council Scheme upon which the Drafting Committee was engaged at the outbreak of war'.

On 11 June 1941 a Staff Association intended exclusively for Electrical Engineers of the BBC was also formed: it quickly enrolled 620 members.[5] It too was recognized by the Corporation,[6] although there were obvious disadvantages in having to deal with two overlapping organizations which showed many signs of antagonism.[7] The two bodies between them

[1] See Briggs, *The Golden Age of Wireless*, pp. 449–58.
[2] Ibid., p. 515.
[3] *Memorandum by Ogilvie, 20 March 1940.
[4] *H. L. Fletcher and eight other signatories to Ogilvie, 5 Sept. 1940.
[5] *W. T. Milsom, its Secretary, to Cruttwell, 2 July 1941.
[6] *Ogilvie to Milsom, 2 Oct. 1941.
[7] *Record of Interview (by Cruttwell) between Milsom and Cruttwell, 21 July 1941.

September 29th. They understand that, while the Ministry of Information is paying the overtime which they earn, the BBC is paying their wages.' On 29 Sept. it was reported that 'the lads' were 'not altogether happy' about their hours of work and had to pay too much for their tea and biscuits. The issues were settled by 2 Oct.

established the principle of independent representation and when they eventually amalgamated just after the end of the war, the Director-General expressed the hope that the new BBC Staff Association would be fully supported by 'all sections and grades of the staff'.[1]

In the meantime, other trade unions were tolerated, and in a paper written in August 1942 Foot maintained that 'the Corporation has to a large extent met Mr. Attlee's contentions [when he was a member of the Ullswater Committee] in that the right of every employee to join the union of his choice has always been recognised and this has been made plain to staff'.[2] When the two Staff Associations were created, the right of employees to join any union was still explicitly recognized along with 'the willingness [of the Corporation] to receive the Unions' representations on any point and to satisfy the appropriate Union that conditions of work and rates of pay by the Corporation are at least equal to those obtaining in comparable circumstances outside'.[3]

Such an approach to trade-union questions showed that Foot was open-minded and co-operative. In the meantime, he had made a different kind of assault on 'paternalism' from the management's side in 1942. Hitherto in each staff member's 'personal file' there had been a variety of comment on individual qualities and defects, some of it 'unauthenticated'. Maconachie raised the issue of whether such comment could be justified in July 1942.[4] Foot took it up at once, and Pym not only worked out a new scheme to ensure that only 'official' comments made their way into the files, but ordered the destruction of a considerable amount of material already present in the files. Foot supervised the operation, quoting the experience of the Gas, Light and Coke Company where 'it was an absolute rule as inflexible as the laws of the Medes and Persians that in the case of an adverse report or even an adverse comment, the individual concerned must be told about it'.[5]

An air of greater efficiency characterized the reorganized BBC. The possibility that it was over-staffed was seriously

[1] *Haley to Chairman BBC Staff Association, 6 Nov. 1945.
[2] *Note by Foot, 21 Aug. 1942, 'The Policy of the BBC towards Trade Unions'.
[3] *Ibid.
[4] *Director-Generals' Meeting, Minutes, 8 July 1942.
[5] Foot Manuscript, pp. 134-5.

discussed inside the Corporation.[1] So, too, was the possibility
that it circulated too much paper.[2] By March 1943 it seemed
abundantly clear that 'the principle of decentralisation' had
been 'justified in practice'. It was possible then, indeed, to
make a number of adjustments within the new system. A
Finance Division was re-established, and the establishment
procedures for central control were somewhat relaxed.

Yet to assess in proper perspective just what had happened
during the progress of reorganization,[3] it is necessary to emphasize three points. First, by the time that the reorganization took
place the BBC had already ceased to grow. The hectic expansion
of the first and second years of the war had come to an end.
The total number of effective staff in June 1942 was 11,409:
in March 1945 it had risen only to 11,543. Developing formal
routines in such circumstances was far easier than it had been
earlier during the war when there were large numbers of
newcomers and life was often very hectic. Second, in the light
of subsequent experience after the war, the pattern of 1942
can be criticized on the grounds that it was 'excessively
fragmented': 'any attempt to exercise control tended to be
regarded as an attempt to sabotage the principle of decentralisation'. More seriously, 'the enormous span of control at the
top' could be held to impose 'an intolerable burden on the
Director-General'.[4] These comments were, of course, illumin-
ated by hindsight. The 'decentralization' lasted in fact for six
years, and it is best thought of, perhaps, like all 'reorganizations',
as a successful attempt to deal with a particular situation
rather than as an exercise in organizational logic.

Third, however effective the new 'system' was in winning
outside confidence in the short run, its smooth operation

---

[1] *Directors-Generals' Meeting, *Minutes*, 7 Oct. 1942.

[2] *Ibid., 14 Oct. 1942.

[3] *Memorandum by Foot of 16 March 1943, 'Financial and Administrative
Reorganisation'.

[4] *Memorandum, 'An Historical Outline of BBC Organisation', Aug. 1960.
Foot commented on his own experience as follows: 'The number of Departments
which under my plan became directly responsible to the Director-General may
seem at first sight to have been both too many and too diversified . . . in fact,
they were no worry to me at all. Each one of them was in charge of a highly
qualified and responsible Director who knew that he need only come to me in my
room or more officially to the Director-General's weekly meeting if he had some
special problem on which he wanted my advice or decision.' (Foot Manuscript,
pp. 133–4.)

depended on people, and several important changes took place which had certainly not been premeditated. Beadle cracked a spinal disc and after convalescing had to leave London to return to his old post as West Regional Controller, where he was to stay until 1956.[1] Graves, who had been dogged by illness throughout his long years of service with the BBC, which he joined in 1926, retired from the Joint Directors-Generalship in September 1943, leaving Foot, who had been in sole charge for most of the year, to reign alone.[2] Foot took steps at once to have Ashbridge, the Controller (Engineering), appointed as Deputy Director-General. He did this in the knowledge that Ashbridge's Assistant Controller, Bishop, had every qualification to become Controller (Engineering) and that the Engineering Division as a whole had always responded conscientiously and alertly to the needs of war. Foot felt, however, that he needed an additional senior colleague on the programmes or 'output' side, where Graves had always taken a special interest. After Bracken had told Foot that there was much to be said for a continuation of the diarchy, if he could find the right man, the Chairman and the Governors of the BBC expressed the opposite view with great firmness and urged Foot to find a new 'Editor-in-Chief' from outside the Corporation.[3] They expressed complete confidence in and gratitude to Foot,[4] and assisted him fully, as did Bracken, in his difficult quest to find the right kind of partner.

The quest led to Reuters. William Haley, a Reuters Director, who was also Joint Managing Director of the *Manchester Guardian* and *Evening News* Ltd., was introduced to Foot by Maloney and Chancellor, the two Reuters joint managers. The first meeting was brief and hurried, but according to Foot it was 'long enough to convince me without any doubt that he was the man we had been looking for'.[5] Bracken was delighted with the name: 'Why didn't I think

---

[1] Beadle, op. cit., pp. 29–30.

[2] In his long career with the BBC, Graves had filled many posts including that of Controller (Programmes), 1933–8. It was a great disappointment to him that he had not become Director-General in 1938 (see Briggs, op. cit., pp. 637–9). Graves died in January 1957.

[3] Foot Manuscript, pp. 178–9: *Board of Governors, *Minutes*, 22 July 1943.

[4] Lady Violet Bonham Carter to Foot, 6 May 1943.

[5] Foot Manuscript, pp. 185–6.

of him myself?' he asked. Haley was willing. Haley, therefore, it was.[1] He was then forty-two years old, a man with very different experience from Foot. Above all else, he thought of himself at that time as a Press man. 'It seems to me,' he stated in his first interview, 'that the functions of broadcasting and the Press are complementary. They both have their highly important parts to play in modern civilisation.' Yet Haley was a Press man with a difference. He had as strong and as staunch a sense of responsibility as Reith and almost as complex a character, shy, determined, dominated from the start, as he put it, by one single guiding principle: 'that the BBC by its very nature has one over-riding duty to all spheres—to give its listeners the best in the world'.[2]

Press comment on Haley's appointment stressed that he would be doing a super-editor's job, 'a complete change in the higher direction of British Broadcasting'.[3] This was an inaccurate historical estimate, for Reith had searched hard for an 'output chief' during early 1930s.[4] Yet it was a new idea to relate the BBC directly to the Press as the *Manchester Guardian*, Haley's old paper, tried to do: 'The newspaper and the BBC can both help and learn from each other.'[5] *The Times*, which was to be Haley's next assignment, had little of interest to say, but *The Observer* commented directly on the man. 'The new appointments made by the Governors . . . bring to the surveillance of the BBC's gigantic output of news, views, arts and entertainments, a man of wide tastes and accomplishments, and proved dynamic force in administration.'[6]

The appointment of Haley as Editor-in-Chief had been announced to the Controllers on 1 September 1943 at the same time as they were told of Foot's appointment as sole Director-General. Powell explained that in the view of the Governors Haley would bring with him 'courage and commonsense'. He was 'in no way a nominee of the Government'. Foot had been consulted about all the arrangements.[7] There

---

[1] *Board of Governors, *Minutes*, 26 Aug. 1943. Haley attended his first Governors' Meeting on 4 Nov.
[2] *The Times*, 2 Sept. 1943.   [3] *Daily Mail*, 2 Sept. 1943.
[4] See Briggs, *The Golden Age of Wireless*, pp. 443 ff.
[5] *Manchester Guardian*, 2 Sept. 1943.
[6] *The Observer*, 5 Sept. 1943.
[7] *Statement by Powell at the Controllers' Conference, 1 Sept. 1943.

was talk at once of Haley's provincial background, and the hope was expressed by some of the Regional Directors that there might, in the words of the *Birmingham Mail*, be a swing of the pendulum back to regional broadcasting.[1] In fact, however, almost the first of Haley's assignments was to pay a visit to the Italian battlefront and not only to interview the Generals in command, among whom Alexander, in particular, was keenly anxious to meet a high-ranking BBC official 'to discuss certain misunderstandings and problems affecting broadcasting',[2] but to talk to soldiers about BBC programmes and policies. The outcome of Haley's first mission was not an expansion of regional broadcasting but a new General Forces Programme which started on 27 February 1944.[3]

Foot had anticipated working closely with Haley, but in yet another of the surprises of the war, he decided early in 1944, after very careful thought, to accept an invitation to join the Mining Association as independent chairman. There was much speculation and argument at that time about the future of the coal industry, and Foot as a proven administrator, whose earlier business, the Gas, Light and Coke Company, had been one of the biggest customers for coal, seemed to have exactly the right qualifications if the industry was to reform itself and stay un-nationalized. Bracken did his best to persuade Foot not to go: he told him not only of his hopes for the post-war BBC but of his fears about the coal-owners whom he thought would not want a strong leader and would object to necessary reorganization. Radcliffe added that if the mines were nationalized he hoped Foot would be nationalized at the same time.[4] Powell was openly reluctant to see yet another big change inside the BBC, but he stated generously that 'the coal industry in this country is a vital thing . . . and if any man feels he is called upon to make a contribution to the solving of [the] grave situation it is difficult to imagine a more

---

[1] *Birmingham Mail*, 2 Sept. 1943. The *Mail* spoke optimistically of a 'new tide of local patriotism which has set in as a natural reaction against necessary wartime regimentation'.

[2] *Board of Governors, *Minutes*, 2 Dec. 1943.

[3] *Ibid., 6 Jan. 1944. Haley had told how the other ranks were particularly interested in links with home. See also the script of a broadcast by Foot, 26 Feb. 1944. See below, p. 591; Foot Manuscript, pp. 154–5.

[4] Quoted ibid., p. 195.

important call'.[1] Foot was sure he was right and, in particular, he felt he could do something useful to improve 'the shockingly wrong' relations between capital and labour.[2]

The resignation came as a far bigger surprise to the Governors than Graves's resignation, and the Press devoted more space to Foot's move than to his replacement by Haley, which was logical and anticipated. 'I am sure,' Foot remarked generously at one of the last of his Controllers' Conferences, 'that the management will be in even better hands than mine.'[3]

4. The Pattern of Programmes

WHILE Foot was organizing the administration of the BBC, Graves was dealing with problems of 'output'. Familiar old issues continued to be raised—whether, for instance, *Happidrome* should be broadcast in the Forces Programme 'opposite' the religious service[4]—and the Corporation continued to be judged by most of its listeners, of course, not on the basis of its organization but in terms of the home programmes it provided. General opinions varied, as always. According to *The Times*, 'the whole world appears compressed within the walls of a cosy room'.[5] 'This constant radio listening is rapidly destroying our powers of original thought,' a local newspaper complained comprehensively in the middle months of the war. 'What is our present procedure? Monday—*Monday Night at Eight*: Tuesday—*The Brains Trust*: Wednesday and Thursday alone are free: Friday, *Tommy Handley*: Saturday, *Music Hall*: and Sunday, *Bebe, Vic and Ben*. What a calendar for our descendants of 2043.'[6]

[1] *Statement by Powell at the Controllers' Conference, 31 March 1944.

[2] *Statement by Foot at the Controllers' Conference, 31 March 1944.

[3] *Ibid. Foot's last Controllers' Conference was on 26 April 1944.

[4] *Board of Governors, *Minutes*, 25 Feb. 1943. The Director of Religious Broadcasting had objected to this. Like many other programme matters, it made its way to the top—to the Board of Governors which never abdicated its interest in programmes in war time.

[5] *The Times*, 9 April 1943.

[6] *Prescott and District Reporter*, 8 Jan. 1943. See also *Woman's Own*, 16 June 1944, 'Radio, Blessing or Curse?'

The solution offered by the newspaper—rationing of radio output in small doses only[1]—was one form of rationing not introduced during the war. Instead, radio was ubiquitous and the war-time phrases of radio programmes passed into general use outside the studio and the home—'Good morning—nice day'; 'I must warn you I am going to make a deliberate mistake'; 'why did I open my big mouth?'; 'let me tell you'; 'it's being so cheerful as keeps me going'.[2] Radio personalities were certainly at the height of their influence during the war—not only the comedians, but the talkers. Their words were discussed, compared, if necessary fought over. One of them at least, the Radio Doctor, Charles Hill, 'the doctor with the greatest number of patients in the world', was to have a post-war future in the making of general broadcasting which could never have been anticipated. 'These five-minute talks after the 8 o'clock news,' wrote one admirer in search of the highest possible praise, 'radiate the same unaffected cheerfulness, simplicity and common sense as Mr. Middleton's talks on gardening.'[3]

Yet success with the audience was no guarantee that the 'star' broadcasters were secure in their engagements. Priestley continued to be employed somewhat patchily and never without controversy in war-time home programmes.[4] Joad, who had announced that he would stand as a parliamentary candidate at the next election, was refused permission to broadcast a series of individual talks.[5] Even Middleton was felt at one time during the war to appeal mainly to 'confirmed gardeners', and there was talk in the Ministry of Information, though not in the BBC, of dropping him.[6] He went, instead, from

---

[1] There was, of course, a persistent demand for fuel economy which could imply, directly or indirectly, rationing of radio hours. See above, pp. 356–7.

[2] Watt claims that the first catch-phrase which caught on was Arthur Askey's 'I thang yew' in *Band Waggon*: the phrase in itself almost ensured the success of the programme (*News Chronicle*, 7 July 1945).

[3] *Yorkshire Evening News*, 26 June 1943, reviewing Hill's *Wise Eating in Wartime*.

[4] *Six talks by him were approved in 1943 (Board of Governors, *Minutes*, 11 March 1943), but when he said that he wished them to be delayed until after the opening of the Second Front (ibid., 18 March) the Board demurred. It also refused to support the idea of rebroadcasting in the Home Service two talks he had broadcast overseas, on 'Fair Weather Leaders' and 'Bureaucracy'. Priestley later agreed to do the talks (ibid., 27 May 1943).

[5] *Board of Governors, *Minutes*, 25 March 1943.

[6] *Green to Maconachie, 20 Jan. 1940. Middleton took part in a radio discussion.

strength to strength, and from February 1942 the practical point of his message was illustrated in the BBC's own 'radio allotment' in Park Crescent.[1] His 1942 series was followed up in further series in 1943 and for a short time in 1944: they won the blessing of the Ministry of Agriculture.[2]

'Campaigns' continued to involve government departments in the business of broadcasting. Many of them were concerned with securing the best utilization of 'manpower' and 'woman-power' as the nation was fully mobilized. The Armed Services had always been given special attention, and in late 1942 and 1943 it was the turn of the nurses. Programmes for women—and to a lesser extent for 'youth'[3]—were of increasing impor-tance as the war went on. 'I am not sure,' Miss Quigley had written in February 1942, 'that we are making all the use we can of the power we possess of reaching and influencing women at the present time. . . . This is serious, as I believe that no single factor is at the present moment more important for the war effort than getting the call-up of women to run efficiently and happily.'[4] A year later Miss Quigley was thanked by the WAAF's Director of Public Relations for all that she had done to help recruitment.[5] Thanks were received from many other organizations as the war went on. The BBC became increasingly confident in this branch of broadcasting, so confident, indeed, that Barnes, Maconachie's successor as Director of Talks, vigorously defended *Women's Page* against criticisms from the Governors. 'I find the comments on programmes received from the Governors increasingly discouraging and I now no longer circulate them to my staff since I conceive it to be my

---

[1] *The idea of an allotment had originally been Standing's (Standing to Nicolls, 24 Oct. 1941).

[2] There had been 'Dig for Victory' sermons and services earlier in the war (*Welch to Green, 8 April 1941). There was also a comedy, *Digging for Victory*, written by L. du Garde Peach.

[3] E. G. Francis of the BBC pointed out to a local audience in Feb. 1943 that there was still a gap in BBC programmes for adolescents, 'or as they had been aptly termed, "the under-20s". He was afraid that these programmes had not been entirely successful in bridging this gap.' (*Walsall Times*, 27 Feb. 1943.) *Youth Magazine* was the most important of these programmes. For criticisms of BBC youth programmes, see two articles in *The Times Educational Supplement*, 20/27 Feb. 1943. *Youth Magazine* was withdrawn in Dec. 1942. See also *John Bull*, 5 Dec. 1942, 'Give Youth a Chance'.

[4] *Miss Quigley to Barnes, 12 Feb. 1942.

[5] *Letter to Miss Quigley, 16 Feb. 1943.

job to keep my staff on their toes and interested in their work. To be frank, I attach no more importance to a Governor's opinion of a programme than I do to any other person's.'[1] There was some scepticism also about the comments of civil servants. After attending a campaign meeting in 1943 Maconachie wrote sharply that the discussions had shown 'how little is understood about the actual work of broadcasting by those not concerned with it'.[2]

The details of a carefully organized and highly sophisticated mid-war campaign can be illustrated from the 1942 Fuel Economy Campaign, to which critics of the BBC felt that the Corporation itself could contribute more directly than by propaganda. It was planned that from 29 June onwards 'practical hints on fuel economy' would be given in the *Kitchen Front* programmes on two days out of three. References were also to be made in continuity announcing, particularly at black-out times, and the idea was to be considered of 'building up one personality in connection with these announcements'. On 30 June or 1 July Sir Ernest Gowers, Chairman of the Coal Commission, would mention fuel economy *en passant* in a talk on coal, and the *Industrial War Commentary* on 9 July would be given by Sir Harold Hartley on the subject of the contribution of science to fuel economy.[3] It was also suggested that doctors should refer obliquely to the subject in health talks and that there should be more comprehensive treatment of the main issues in *In Britain Now* in late August and early September. 'The Meaning of Fuel' should be explored in schools programmes and in *Children's Hour*. Even then, this did not exhaust the possibilities. There was to be a 'Fuel Bee' between housewives and experts; a series of feature programmes in July and August dealing with the general problem of waste; an outside broadcast from a power-station at black-out time; and at the end of September a full-scale feature dramatizing the relationship between the coal miner, the housewife, the Government, the factories and the fighting services. All this talk pre-supposed a 'phased' campaign with

[1] *Barnes to Maconachie, 25 Oct. 1943.

[2] *Maconachie to Miss Quigley, 18 March 1943.

[3] *The BBC devoted increasing attention to science as the war progressed. It consulted the Royal Society and the British Association (Board of Governors, *Minutes*, 7 Oct. 1943).

'the curve of the first phase of the campaign . . . carefully regulated and built up towards the opening of the second phase'. Variety was not to be left out. Fuel economy was to figure in a series called *Mr. Cropper's Conscience*, and 'the possibility should be tentatively considered of introducing a theme song in variety programmes at about the beginning of September'.[1]

Not all these possibilities were taken seriously. Some were criticized, others discarded. Criticized or uncriticized, however, not all propaganda campaigns were successful. Clothes rationing, introduced in June 1941,[2] proved very difficult to handle, even when the Board of Trade, alarmed that members of the public were 'using their coupons at too fast a rate', launched a 'Mend and Make Do' campaign. *Beating the Coupon* and *New Clothes for Old* never became popular programmes, and a proposal for a 'Sewing Bee' was turned down by the BBC.[3] Maconachie, sceptical throughout the war about the value of such campaigns, strongly opposed a suggestion that there should be a 'series of talks-cum-music on "Mend and Make Do" for work parties' and withstood continuous pressure for 'talks on such a dreary subject as darning, etc., to such a limited audience'.[4] 'The BBC,' he reiterated, 'would always be willing to consider any likely programme material which is informative, and has entertainment value.'[5] The introduction of *Wise Housekeeping*, broadcast between December 1942 and March 1943, did not appease the Board of Trade, and more talks on 'Make Do and Mend' (the slogan was turned round) had to be introduced later, some of them in time devoted hitherto to *The Kitchen Front*.[6] The script of a talk offered

[1] *'1942 Fuel Economy Campaign: Memorandum for Discussion at BBC Programme Policy Meeting, Friday 28 June 1942.' [2] See above, p. 325.

[3] *Miss Park, Ministry of Information, to Barnes, 11 June 1942; Miss Quigley to Barnes, 1 July 1942; Miss Quigley to Miss Crawshay Williams, Board of Trade, 19 Aug. 1942. [4] *Maconachie to Howgill, 14 Nov. 1942.

[5] *Maconachie to Room, Ministry of Information, 14 Dec. 1942; Board of Governors, *Minutes*, 3 Dec. 1942. The Board endorsed the policy of resisting excessive requests by government departments for propaganda talks.

[6] *Salmon to Barnes 19 June 1943; Simmonds to Maconachie 24 July; Simmonds to Armfelt, 28 June; Armfelt to Simmonds 5, 25 Aug.; Miss Quigley to Simmonds, 14 Sept. The flow of recipes from listeners for *Kitchen Front* programmes trickled in during the autumn of 1943 so that Freddy Grisewood was asked to say 'I hope they'll roll in again as they did all last winter and spring'. (Miss Harris to Barnes, 5 Oct. 1943.)

by the Board of Trade telling how men and women had actually used their clothing coupons was turned down by the BBC on the grounds that it would 'excite a lot of come-back from the listeners and the BBC will take the rap and not the Board of Trade'.[1] Programmes of this kind proved to be surprisingly popular, however, during the last stages of the war.[2]

The most popular programmes, apart from the News, were those with obvious 'entertainment value'. Taking in order the list of weekly programmes which the disgruntled provincial critic claimed were 'destroying our powers of original thought', *Monday Night at Eight* was a revival of a pre-war show specially devised in terms of 'pure radio'.[3] 'Puzzle Corner', an item in the show, was the first radio quiz: Inspector Hornleigh, played by S. J. Warmington, was one of the first radio detectives. No single item in the show lasted for more than six or seven minutes, and each item was rehearsed and timed separately with no complete run-through of the whole show until the actual broadcast. The family appeal of the programme depended not only on the ability of the individual artists but on the imagination and skill of Harry S. Pepper in blending the different elements together. There was something for everybody, and, according to Listener Research, *Monday Night at Eight* was popular with everyone, whereas the Bob Hope and Jack Benny programmes—and even *ITMA*—were immensely popular with most people and equally strongly disliked by others.

The *Brains Trust* had more than entertainment value, and more than any other programme it developed a life, even a folklore, of its own, a life which BBC administrators—and Ministry of Information officials—remained always anxious, sometimes for good reasons, to check and, if goaded, to control. The size of its audience continued to increase steadily through to the end of the war; the Tuesday broadcasts were listened to by 20.7 per cent of the listening public in 1942 and 1943,[4]

[1] *Richard Sharp to Ryan, 9 June 1943.

[2] *Barnes to Maconachie, 7 March 1945.

[3] See Briggs, *The Golden Age of Wireless*, (1965), p. 117. *Monday Night at Seven* was its first title. It had originally been broadcast at seven o'clock so that its 'stars' could, if necessary, go on to a stage performance later in the evening. This was no longer feasible in war time. See also above, p. 109.

[4] The first run of the *Brains Trust* finished in June 1942 after eighteen months. A gap of three months followed before the next series, although a special overseas edition continued to be produced.

when two to three thousand letters were arriving about it each week, by 23.7 per cent in the period from 1943 to the end of February 1944, by 24.9 per cent in the period from February to September 1944,[1] and by 29.4 per cent in the period ending in June 1945.[2] At the time, these figures seemed to need a gloss. 'That the *Brains Trust* is the subject of persistent disparaging comment,' Listener Research noted in 1944, 'is certainly true, yet, paradoxically, its audiences show no sign of diminishing. They remain so large as to be easily the greatest for any regular spoken word programme, other than the News, and the envy of many a programme of pure entertainment. The truth would seem to be that as long as the audience is retained, the sniping at the *Brains Trust* should properly be regarded as evidence that it is doing its job. It was designed as a provocative programme and a provocative programme it has certainly remained.'[3]

Listener Research distinguished between two types of listener to it—those who turned to the programmes for good lively discussion and those who expected definitive answers to set questions. The first group greatly regretted the break-up of the original triumvirate, Joad, Campbell and Huxley[4]; the second thought it made for 'less waste of time'. The first group disapproved of the 'Open Question' and of 'Second Thoughts' on the grounds that they destroyed spontaneity; the second group approved of them 'insofar as they led to more accurate information being imparted'. Yet both groups were dazzled, if not convinced, by verbal brilliance. Neither group liked the Question Master to participate in the discussions, while they both welcomed and paid particular critical attention to his summing up.[5] In 1943 the six best speakers in order of public

---

[1] *BBC Listener Research Report, 6 Sept. 1944.

[2] *Ibid., 17 Aug. 1945. There was, of course, a large audience for the repeat programmes. From the end of Feb. 1944 the Sunday repeat, which had been at 4.15 p.m. in the Forces Programme, was changed to 1.30 p.m. in the General Forces Programme, and the broadcast was abbreviated. This change of plan and form is difficult to justify in retrospect and was unpopular at the time.

[3] *Ibid., 6 Sept. 1944.

[4] *When the second series of Brains Trusts started in the autumn of 1942, the number of resident members was increased, with the Board of Governors continuing to demand 'a widening of the field from which the members should be drawn' (*Minutes*, 14 Jan. 1943).

[5] *BBC Listener Research Reports, 21 Dec. 1942, 29 Dec. 1943, 6 Sept. 1944, 17 Aug. 1945.

approval were thought to be Huxley, Malcolm Sargent, Joad, Commander Gould, Vernon Bartlett, and Commander Campbell. In September 1944 Huxley still had top place, Joad had moved into second place and Campbell into third, with Malcolm Sargent, Barbara Ward—a new name—and Gould following. In August 1945 Barbara Ward, young, vigorous and extremely lucid in everything she said, had moved into first place. Joad was second, Huxley third, and Campbell, Sargent and Gould filled the other three places. There was thus a remarkably consistent appraisal and approval of the main participants. Howard Thomas himself insisted that the success of the programme depended not on its serving as 'a radio university' but on its 'traffic in personalities'.[1] *Punch* concluded that the *Brains Trust* had become a Hearts Trust. Its members had received offers of marriage and had had to be protected by the police lest the buttons should be torn off their mantles.[2]

However wild the enthusiasm for the members—and it was not shared in all circles inside the BBC[3]—there was never full public approval of the policy behind the programme. Some listeners objected on the grounds that the pursuit of knowledge was 'vulgarised'.[4] The main criticism, however, was that not enough questions were devoted to controversial topics, of which politics, religion and sex were frequently mentioned as examples.[5] Until January 1943 Nicolls had weeded out questions which he thought might cause 'irritation in Parliament'. They were removed somewhat arbitrarily, and among them were questions with little party political dynamite in them, like 'Should there be equal pay for men and women?'

[1] H. Thomas, *Britain's Brains Trust* (1944), p. 31.

[2] *Punch*, 19 April 1944, 'Howard Thomas's Wireless Witenagemot'.

[3] *Welch for example objected bitterly to Joad: 'We recently built up Mr. J. B. Priestley as a radio personality, but I do not think I detect in Priestley the exhibitionism which I personally detect in the relish with which Joad trots out slick answers to profound questions.' Joad himself said that he liked to be attacked, for instance after a sharp attack by Quintin Hogg. He welcomed the fact that the *Brains Trust* had broken through, 'if only for a time, the glaze of BBC gentility' (*New Statesman*, 27 May 1944).

[4] See L. Aaronson, 'The Brains Trust—and Guests' in *The Nineteenth Century*, 15 Jan. 1942. 'The very phrase connotes a vulgarisation of language.' 'Everywhere the quiet voice is beset; and, therefore, this is no time for the professors of great—and small—universities, for "experts" of any type . . . to help Demos in its business of denying the authentic ways of seeking truth.'

[5] *BBC Listener Research Report, 6 Sept. 1944.

Others frightened Nicolls more than they would have frightened anyone else. 'Would the *Brains Trust* advocate a moral philosopher in the Cabinet?' was rejected summarily, for example, on the simple ground—'Joad'. 'Will the *Brains Trust* forecast quite firmly what conditions will be like a year after we win the war?' was rejected on the dubious basis that 'the *Brains Trust* are not called upon to be prophets'.[1] Quite specifically Nicolls wrote to Cleverdon on one occasion requesting him to 'avoid all questions involving religion, political philosophy or vague generalities about life'.[2] Not surprisingly, some members of the *Brains Trust* themselves thought that 'censorship' from inside the BBC was turning the programme into a 'polite parlour game',[3] and questions were asked in Parliament about limitations on free discussion.[4]

The Governors relieved Nicolls of his exclusive responsibility only at the expense of solemnly discussing themselves whether or not a question on the profit motive should have been asked and answered: they considered that it was not an 'appropriate question' for that particular programme.[5] They also dealt with a request from the Archbishop of Canterbury for specific Christian representation on the Trust.[6] While they stressed that

[1] *Nicolls weeded out 19 questions in three months before Jan. 1943. They also included 'Do you agree that I am justified in giving up canteen work if I am compelled to fire watch?' which was dismissed as 'involving home security policy'.

[2] *Nicolls to Cleverdon, 11 June 1941.

[3] *Letter from Clark, Joad, Huxley, Gilbert Murray, and Leslie Howard to Powell, 19 Jan. 1943. (Board of Governors, *Minutes*, 21 Jan. 1943.) Foot replied formally, denying a 'ban', on 2 Feb. 1943. 5% of the questions sent in at that time were political and 5% religious. (*Manchester Guardian*, 23 Jan. 1943.)

[4] The Minister of Information replied himself that the *Brains Trust* was entirely a matter for the BBC (*Hansard*, vol. 377, col. 1509). His questioner had objected to the size of their fee, £40 for two sessions. 'Does he think that what they give the public is worth it?' 'It shows that they have brains' was Bracken's characteristic reply.

[5] *Board of Governors, *Minutes*, 18 Feb. 1943.

[6] *Ibid., 21 Jan. 1943. The Archbishop had written to Graves on 15 Jan. 1943: 'If the Christian or at least the religious attitude to the universe is not represented, it is by implication denied.' Graves (letter of 15 Jan. 1943) replied at once that there could not be such representation, but he gave the very unsatisfactory reason that 'the *Brains Trust* is designed essentially as a light-hearted entertainment programme and the approach is more often than not a flippant one'. A more formal reply was sent on 1 Feb. 1943. Religious objections had been raised much earlier (Welch to Maconachie, 4 June 1941), and the Board of Governors decided on 4 June 1942 that the programme was not 'an appropriate setting' for discussion of religious matters. See below, pp. 621–34, for a fuller account of religion and broadcasting.

there should always be 'a reasonable number of questions to which the approach is amusing and light-hearted',[1] their own approach to the *Brains Trust* was far from light-hearted. They objected to a filmed version of the programme,[2] and showed themselves to be tough when the Proprietary Association for Great Britain objected to an answer given on patent medicines and asked for a 'factual' counter-statement to be broadcast presenting their case.[3] They did not want to rule out politics completely, 'though caution in respect to political questions was asked for for a short and limited time'.[4] Later in 1943 they reiterated their view that 'questions which might embarrass the Government in the sphere of foreign policy and the war effort should be avoided'. They decided at the same time that there should be alternating Question Masters and that the average frequency of appearance of every member of the panel should be not greater than once every three weeks.[5] This decision was to sap the roots of the *Brains Trust*, but it did not destroy it.

ITMA, the best-documented as well as the most famous of war-time BBC shows, had not been very successful in peace time.[6] Although it became the most English of English programmes, it had started very differently as an 'attempt to create a British version of the Burns and Allen show' in the United States.[7] The early war-time idea of satirizing the Ministry of Information, which certainly called for satire,[8]

---

[1] *Paper of 2 Feb. 1943.

[2] Board of Governors, *Minutes*, 21 Jan. 1943. Part of their worry was that the film might be shown in Bristol at the time of the Bristol by-election where Jennie Lee, 'the most popular woman member of the Trust we have' (Note by Nicolls 29 Dec. 1942), was an Independent candidate.

[3] *Board of Governors, *Minutes*, 15 April 1943. The newspapers made no mention of this, a point used by Tom Driberg in his review of Howard Thomas's book (*Reynolds News*, 16 April 1944) as an argument against the 'commercialisation of radio'.

[4] *Paper by Powell for Board Meeting, 28 Jan. 1943.

[5] *Board of Governors, *Minutes*, 19 Aug. 1943. Note by Nicolls, 16 Aug. 1943. Nicolls, who had become more open-minded about the programme, suggested experiments with political sessions, but this idea was not approved by the Director-General (Note of 17 Aug. 1943) or by the Governors (*Minutes*, 19 Aug. 1943).

[6] See Briggs, op. cit., p. 118. Only three programmes were, in fact, given before the war broke out.   [7] T. Kavanagh, *Tommy Handley* (1949), p. 96.

[8] The Ministry of Aggravation and Mysteries was housed next door to the Office of Twerps. It was a coincidence that the BBC was a near neighbour of the Office of Works.

had endless possibilities, but it was not until the fourth and fifth series of *ITMA* in 1942 and 1943 that the programme acquired its enormous vogue and prestige. 'Had we decided, after those first three [badly supported and ill-received performances] before the war to cancel it,' Watt, the Director of Variety wrote in 1943, 'we should not have our present success. There must be time to get a show right.'[1] *ITMA* was designed as a vehicle for a particular comedian: in its classic form it also concentrated on a limited set of characters and a limited range of themes.[2]

There was immense energy and vitality in the partnership of Francis Worsley, an extremely able producer, Ted Kavanagh, a brilliant scriptwriter, a New Zealander of Irish extraction, and Tommy Handley, an essentially creative comedian from Liverpool, whose 'quick mind and ear were ever on the alert for a phrase'.[3] The minor characters, stooges though they might be, also lived in their own right—Mrs. Mopp, the Beloved Char (Dorothy Summers), Signor So-So (Dino Galvani), Ali-Oop, the Oriental Pedlar (Horace Percival), who also played the Diver and one of the two odd-job men, with their rhyming dialogue (Jack Train, the *ITMA* veteran, was the other). As Maschwitz wrote after Handley's death in 1949, 'Tommy Handley, together with Kavanagh and Worsley, created more lovable characters than even Walt Disney. Like Disney's enchanting animals, they had a clear-cut comical simplicity that appealed to children of all ages.'[4] W. E. Williams added perceptively that while the characters in the *ITMA* programme were caricatures, Handley was himself, 'a situation which bore some resemblance to the contrast between Alice and the inhabitants of Wonderland'.[5]

The sociology of *ITMA* received almost as much war-time attention as the sociology of the *Brains Trust*. Both programmes

---

[1] *J. Watt, 'Report on Output of the Variety Department', 24 July 1943.

[2] The first series during the Phoney War had introduced 'Funf'. The second series, 'It's That Sand Again', was located in Foaming at the Mouth, with Handley as the mayor. Later series featured Handley as factory manager, landowner, the farmer pestered by 'Min. of Ag. and Fish', post-war planner, and prospective M.P. Each series introduced new characters. Some characters were dropped, like Mrs. Tickle, played by Maurice Denham, who gave way to Mrs. Mopp. The 'classic form' was the form of 1942, 1943, and 1944.

[3] F. Worsley, 'Anatomy of ITMA' in *Pilot Papers*, vol. i. (1946), p. 45.

[4] *Sunday Times*, 16 Jan. 1949.   [5] *The Observer*, 16 Jan. 1949.

depended not only on memorable individuals but on teams ('Why,' asked a writer in *Time and Tide*, 'is it so much more entertaining to hear five people talking together on a subject than one?').[1] Both programmes were supremely 'unofficial'. The 'star' performers in the *Brains Trust* got into as much trouble with the authorities as Handley who loved to guy them. The fictitious characters in *ITMA* were really characters, as were Commander Campbell and, above all, Joad. There were catch phrases in the *Brains Trust* ('it all depends on what you mean by . . .') just as there were in *ITMA* which relied upon them:[2] it relied also on references to unintelligible sets of initials which meant so much in the war-time world of big organizations, and, as was sometimes the case in the *Brains Trust* programmes, on elaborate and speedy word play, including pun play, which was pre-eminently suited to sound broadcasting. The microphone itself was often part of the play. Both programmes combined topicality with 'timelessness'. To listen to the recording of a *Brains Trust* programme years after it was made is to lose almost as much—and it is a great deal—as to listen years later to the recording of an *ITMA* programme. Both programmes refused to leave politics out,[3] and it is interesting to note that Handley, like Joad, ended his war-time performances as a prospective parliamentary candidate. Above all, both programmes appealed to a very broad section of the national audience, cutting across the lines of occupation and class, soldiers and civilians. The Queen is said to have sent a question to the *Brains Trust*—'Why do they call the Italians "Wops"?'[4]—and certainly Queen, King and Royal Princesses were enthusiastic listeners to *ITMA*, which was the first purely radio show to have a Royal

---

[1] *Time and Tide*, 8 July 1944.

[2] Worsley (loc. cit.) collected some of the successful among them; others were less successful. Was there a common denominator? 'This is Funf speaking', 'Don't forget the diver', 'After you, Claude; after you, Cecil', 'Missed him', 'It's me noives', 'He's a great guy', 'Boss, boss, something terrible's happened', 'Nothing at all—nothing at all', 'Can I do you now, Sir?', 'Good morning, nice day', 'I go—I come back', 'I don't mind if I do', 'I'd do anything for the wife', 'I'll forget me own name in a minute', 'TTFN', 'I'll have to ask me dad'.

[3] 'I'll have to ask me dad' was a political phrase introduced into *ITMA* when post-war reconstruction was looming. It had overtones of 'Lloyd George (or Gladstone) knows my father'.

[4] *News Chronicle*, 19 April 1944.

Command performance at Windsor Castle on Princess Elizabeth's birthday in 1942. It was also the most popular show with the Forces. A war-time cartoon depicts a number of soldiers in a slit trench with the NCO in charge looking at his watch and saying, 'Remember boys, we attack immediately after the Tommy Handley programme'.[1]

Music Hall had a predictable formula and a shifting cast. Almost every variety artist of note, good or bad, appeared in it at one time or another, and the quality of each programme depended on the ability of the artists to adapt themselves to the microphone. Sometimes it would reach a very high standard. At other times, like *In Town Tonight*, it was dull and uninspired. It relied on one or two main 'stars' backed by less well-known artists, but it always held its audience. *Bebe, Vic and Ben* was the successor to *Hi Gang*. It had many critics, yet it reached a listening barometer figure of 29.2 per cent. Its American flavour became less distinctive to British listeners, however, as the war went on and as a more direct American influence could be traced in other BBC programmes. Watt sent his Assistant Director, Pat Hillyard, to the United States in 1942 to 'bring back a team of writers and stars to infuse new life and competition into our present set up'. Hillyard won the co-operation of USO (United Services Organization), the American counterpart of ENSA, and signed an American scriptwriter, Hal Block, who arrived in London in February 1943. Block wrote the script of a new Anglo-American series *Yankee-doodle-doo*, prepared and recorded a special Bob Hope programme which was given before an audience of Allied troops and Red Cross nurses 'somewhere in North Africa', and introduced other American artists to Britain. Irving Berlin, for example, brought over his well-known *This is the Army* show in the autumn of 1943. The dummy Charlie McCarthy and his creator Edgar Bergen were familiar to British listeners by the end of the year.[2] A year later there were complaints of too much 'Americanization' of variety, and Haley urged that 'in the entertainment field it is essential to ensure that the use of

---

[1] Quoted in Worsley, loc. cit. See also his book *ITMA* (1948), which includes a large number of photographs.

[2] For the role in the United States of Jack Benny, Bergen and other American stars, see E. Barnouw, *The Golden Web* (1968) pp. 98–100.

. . . American serial broadcasts such as the Bob Hope, Jack Benny and other programmes does not become a Frankenstein'.[1] Norman Collins, the Director of the General Overseas Service, pointed out realistically that while he had been 'constantly and persistently nagging for straight English Variety', . . . 'if any hundred British troops are invited to choose their own records, 90 per cent of the choice will be of American stuff'.[2]

Whether listeners were civilians or servicemen, they were offered not only a regular round of weekly programmes, but quite diverse forms of entertainment, including special programmes like *The Stage Presents* with a galaxy of international talent. Some of the programmes designed with specific audiences in mind, like *Works Wonders* or *Music While You Work*, acquired far bigger audiences than anticipated. So, too, did many programmes prepared in London by Cecil Madden's Overseas Entertainment Unit. The origins of the immensely popular post-war programme *Much Binding in the Marsh* with Kenneth Horne and Richard Murdoch can be traced back to the RAF contribution to *Mediterranean Merry Go Round*; it was sponsored each week by a different branch of the Services and deserves to take its place alongside *Navy Mixture*.[3] So, too, does *Starlight*. At the same time, some BBC programmes, like Leslie Baily's *Everybody's Scrapbook*, a new series of which was introduced in September 1942, were deliberately designed 'to act as a real Empire link'[4] and were as popular in Australia or Canada as in Britain.

Baily was concerned, like many other scriptwriters and, indeed, like ENSA itself,[5] with something more than mere entertainment. The very first of his new *Scrapbooks*, broadcast in July 1940,[6] had ended with Robert Donat declaiming

---

[1] Memorandum by Haley, 16 Aug. 1944. There was to be no increase of American material without reference to him.

[2] *Collins to Alick Hayes, 19 April 1944.

[3] *Madden's scrapbooks are in the BBC Archives. See also feature articles in the *Radio Times*, 16 Nov. 1945, 2 April 1948. Many isolated feature shows were also produced along with parlour games. There is an anthology of appreciative comment in a paper on 'The Empire Entertainments Unit', produced in Feb. 1942.

[4] *Baily to Nicolls, 28 Oct. 1942. De Lotbinière, the Director of Empire Programmes, wrote a special note of appreciation at the end of the series (Memo. to Nicolls, 27 March 1943). Baily also produced a longer series, *Travellers' Tales*.

[5] See B. Dean, *The Theatre at War* (1956), especially chapter 18.

[6] See above, p. 109.

that when he felt 'tired and full of doubt' he turned to 'the rationalising solace and courage of music' and with Kathleen Long playing Bach's prelude 'Sanctify us by thy Goodness'.

'Things of good report' particularly interested Baily.[1] Yet the production of such programmes, which appealed to a large number of listeners, did not save the Variety Department from an immense amount of criticism. Some of the criticism recalled pre-war criticism; some of it pointed to the future;[2] some of it was based on the theory that 'more means worse'. As the war went by, the output of the Department increased enormously:

WEEKLY OUTPUT OF VARIETY PROGRAMMES[3]			
	1939 National, Regional, Latin-American and Empire	1943 Home and Forces	1945 Home, Light, General Overseas and General Forces
Productions (including Dance Band and Theatre Organ Productions)	20	42	72
Dance Music Sessions	23	25	30
Cinema and Theatre Organ Sessions	9	17	17
	52	84	119
Record Programmes[4]	27	1	1
TOTAL	79	85	120

[1] *He wrote a report on the first series of new *Scrapbooks* broadcast between July and Dec. 1940 in which he included in the list of necessary ingredients 'things of beauty', as well as 'things of humour' and 'things of achievement'.

[2] *Daily Mail*, 16 March 1943: 'Your job surely is to study popular appeal: you don't.' Cf. a letter to the *Manchester Guardian*, 25 March 1943: 'If there were an end to monopoly there would be a higher standard in light entertainment.' *Advertisers' Weekly*, 20 Jan. 1944, printed a graph showing how various American industries had used network radio for light entertainment in 1942.

[3] *Memorandum by Standing, 'The Variety Department', Dec. 1945. The weeks were not strictly comparable. The 1939 week was in May, the 1943 week in October, and the 1945 week a post-war week in December.

[4] There was no separate Gramophone Department in 1939 when 'light' record programmes were handled by the Variety Department. This swells the 1939 figure.

The central question raised by such statistics was not a new one. Could such an increase in output be achieved without loss of quality? This question, touching both on the availability of talent and on the danger of the individual artist, however brilliant, becoming stale, frequently became entangled, however, in a mesh of equally familiar questions about 'vulgarity'. In January 1941 Watt had circulated a note to all his producers telling them that Ogilvie was 'insistent that the accusations of vulgarity in our programmes should be ill-founded'.[1] Yet just after the beginning of the Foot–Graves regime a year later, the Board of Governors was still noting tersely, 'Music Hall: low standard deplored', and two months afterwards reached agreement that the standard of Variety was 'still declining, owing to competition of prevailing high stage fees and poor scripts'.[2] On one occasion Foot and Graves decided to pay a visit to Bangor:[3] on another, Foot invited the Archbishop of Canterbury to a private hearing of a *Music Hall* programme. Although they both approved—and laughed —complaints did not cease to come in from outside.[4] One of the most vociferous grumblers in 1943 was Lady Snowden, widow of Philip Snowden and a formidable ex-governor, who wanted not only to eliminate vulgarity but to abolish crooning 'root and branch'.[5]

The critics were not simply a minority of people in positions of established importance who were seeking to judge what Watt somewhat condescendingly called 'the backbone of our output . . . lowest-common-denominator entertainment'.[6] There was also a severe slump in listener satisfaction, as measured by Listener Research Surveys in 1942.[7] And although

[1] *Watt to Regional Directors, 31 Jan. 1941.

[2] *Board of Governors, *Minutes*, 29 Jan., 26 Mar. 1942.   [3] *Ibid., 5 Nov. 1942.

[4] Foot Manuscript, pp. 155–6. The Archbishop concluded that there was nothing to worry about and that it had been a 'good mixed programme' which could continue 'without interference or censorship'.

[5] *Daily Telegraph*, 13 Aug. 1943; *The Star*, 14 Aug. 1943. See also 'The Radio Aunt Sally' in the *Perthshire Advertiser*, 18 Aug. 1943.

[6] *Memorandum of 14 July 1942. Nicolls was in the grip of this kind of argument particularly when he was on the defensive. In a Memorandum of 1 Jan. 1942 he said that while ENSA entertainment was of a 'notoriously low standard', by and large BBC Variety producers were 'everywhere working to keep their material clean— . . . sometimes at the price of dullness'.

[7] *See, for example, Listener Research Bulletin, 10 Oct. 1942: 'Dissatisfaction with existing Variety programmes was expressed with disturbing frequency.'

there had been a marked improvement by 1944,[1] the proportion of listeners who felt that the BBC 'ought to prevent
comedians from being vulgar' increased from 13 per cent in
January 1941 to 20 per cent in August 1943.[2] At the end of the
war, Standing, the new Director of Variety, wrote that the
reputation of the Variety Department was 'very low, pretty well
at the bottom of a decline which set in some two years before'.[3]

From time to time Watt did his best to describe what in
his view was happening. Preoccupied with the practical
problems of managing Variety from Bangor, he must have been
irritated, as Basil Dean was in ENSA, by the far too general
nature of many of the criticisms. Broadcasts from Bangor,
where the Department was made extremely welcome by the
local population,[4] meant a round trip for most artists of about
four hundred miles, yet established artists of the calibre of
Arthur Askey, Jack Buchanan, Jack Hulbert and Cicely
Courtneidge did not hesitate to go there. Harry Korris used
to motor all through the night to Bangor to take part in
Happidrome.[5] By the time that the move to Bangor took place
in April 1941, the staff of the Department had risen from the
22 who had gone to Bristol in 1939[6] to 432—not to mention
17 dogs and a parrot—and a special train had had to be hired.
The move back to London was accomplished in stages in 1942
and 1943.[7]

[1] *Ibid., 2 Oct. 1944. 49% were then enthusiastic about BBC Variety, 28%
favourable, 16% neutral, 4% unfavourable and 3% very unfavourable. The
strongest hold of Variety was on the young (16–19 years old), 61% of whom were
Variety enthusiasts. Its hold was least secure on the 'upper middle class', yet even
within this group 35% were enthusiastic.

[2] *Listener Research Survey, 14 and 20 Sept. 1943. A survey later in the year
(Listener Research News Letter, Nov. 1943) showed that compared with 66% of
civilians, 79% of Forces listeners felt that the BBC was 'careful enough'. Home
listeners had made the point that they were embarrassed when listening with
children to programmes which went 'too far' and some admitted that they 'enjoyed
a good joke after the children had gone to bed'. Many of the listeners who were
critical objected 'not so much to *what* was said as to the *way* it was said'.

[3] *Standing to Howgill, Dec. 1945.

[4] In Oct. 1943 the Mayor of Bangor presented the BBC with a plaque to be
placed in Broadcasting House.

[5] *BBC Handbook, 1945*, p. 49.

[6] See above, p. 107.

[7] *Controllers' Conference, *Minutes*, 6 Jan. 1943: it was reported that the move
to London would be made as soon as possible. Ibid., 3 Feb. 1943: early spring
was to be the date.

It was against this background that Watt had to deal with the Governors of the BBC as well as with artists and listeners. He knew that whatever the criticisms a greater proportion of listeners were 'enthusiastic' about Variety than any other BBC programmes, as a mid-war survey covering the year 1942, which was printed in the Press, showed:[1]

		Enthusiastic	'Neutral'	Hostile
Top Five	Variety	51	13	3
	Cinema Organ	34	23	7
	Dance Music	28	22	11
	Parlour Games	27	22	13
	Talks	26	24	13
Others	Discussions	20	24	16
	Symphony Concerts	10	17	40
	Religious Services	16	30	11
	Poetry	6	23	34
	Chamber Music	5	17	46

Watt himself was always self-critical. 'We have found that we cannot be funny all the time, as we have tried to be,' he wrote in July 1942, 'owing to the lack of writers and material. Let us, therefore, try to be funny half the time and do more musical shows, though they invariably have only half the audience.'[2] Watt also suggested in 1942 that the 'star' system should be abandoned and that the scripts of shows should be commissioned with the casting done later. This was the opposite of the highly successful *ITMA* formula, and it shows how flexible Watt's approach could be. He also believed that it was necessary to 'cast producers even more carefully than

[1] *Manchester Guardian*, 14 May 1943. The Variety figure fell later from 51 to 35 and the Cinema Organ from 34 to 27. Those hostile to Symphony Concerts fell from 40 to 29 and those hostile to Chamber Music to 38. The liking for Parlour Games did not vary with income. The liking for Variety did—29% of the upper middle class were enthusiastic about Variety, 39% of the lower middle class and 56% of the working class. For symphony orchestras the comparable figures were 27, 16 and 6. Such figures must be treated with caution.

[2] *Graves had suggested this in a Memorandum on Variety Programmes, written on 19 Jan. 1941: 'I feel that under the heading "Variety" we could cut out quite a fair amount of the Music-Hall comedian type of stuff, which appears under all sorts of guises and titles, and replace this by more of the Dance Band type of features—*Geraldo's Hour*, etc.—with which I believe people are just as satisfied.'

we cast artists'.[1] Yet there was a serious shortage of able producers and the BBC was not in a position to commission scripts at lucrative fees. Radio never became an accepted 'big money' market for writers. Ogilvie or Foot might complain of stale jokes as well as of blue jokes, but the economics of BBC entertainment did not enable the Corporation to save itself from what Robert MacDermot, the Programme Organizer in Programme Planning, once described appropriately as a 'wasting disease'.[2]

Nicolls, whose job forced him to mediate between different worlds, told the Governors as forcibly as he could that while 'our Variety output might be much better . . . the true picture is of a clever, loyal, and hard-working staff, producing programmes under unprecedented difficulties caused by dispersion, competition, the hostility of the outside managements, the bad influence on taste of the music hall itself and of ENSA, and continued loss of staff and artists through the exigencies of the war'.[3] In such a statement he revealed his own tastes, although he would doubtless have been forced to agree with a statement in the highly critical *Sunday Pictorial*, which did not share his tastes, that 'second-rate Variety is worse than no Variety at all'.[4]

Nicolls drafted the list of difficulties confronting BBC Variety producers after the Governors had invited Edgar, the Midland Regional Director, to submit a 'professional, dispassionate and frank' report on Variety output based on fourteen weeks' intensive listening—a very severe test.[5] Edgar was 'appalled' at the low standard of a great part of the output, at what he considered to be both the dearth and misuse of talent, and at the 'persistent continuation of series which are obviously below standard'.[6] Yet he approached the problems of providing entertainment in a kind of vacuum. Thus, he objected to undue attention being paid to 'audience size' and even to listener research—'it is only natural that men who have

[1] *BBC Handbook, 1944*, p. 49.
[2] *MacDermot to Adams, 2 Nov. 1943.
[3] *Note by Nicolls, 26 July 1943.
[4] *Sunday Pictorial*, 21 Feb. 1943.
[5] *Board of Governors, *Minutes*, 29 July 1943.
[6] *The policy of dropping series had been agreed upon at the Programme Divisional Meeting of 11 Nov. 1942.

come to us from the music hall business or the West End stage should have a very definite eye on these results'—criticized 'the vicious circle into which we seem to be getting by the use of Variety Agents', urged that the theatre should be controlled even to the extent of forcing BBC artists to give the BBC an exclusive call on their services, and demanded an end to artists seeking to give each other publicity in a kind of 'back slapping mutual admiration society'.[1]

His report was in line with the pre-1939 BBC approach to Variety which was as far removed from 'show business' as possible. He quoted with approval, for instance, a remark made in Parliament by Professor Gruffydd, hardly a judge of light entertainment, that 'whatever we think of other parts of the programme, all of us are agreed that the light variety entertainment provided by the BBC does consistently and regularly underrate the mentality of the average Briton'. Finally, while relating Variety output to the immediate needs of the war—'transport difficulties are on the increase, and people are forced to turn more and more to the radio for their general entertainment'; 'conditions next Winter may be even harder than they are at present . . . and broadcasting can play a vital part in preserving morale'—he looked also into the more distant future. 'It would be well to remember that after the war there will probably be a strong bid made for sponsored programmes by a certain section of the public who might use as one of their arguments the poor quality of many of our Variety programmes in the past.'[2]

Watt, like Nicolls,[3] was not prepared to accept this assessment, although the Governors were. 'Greater control,' they reiterated, 'should be exercised over the passing of scripts with a view to the elimination of all innuendos and vulgarity.'[4] Watt, whose views were diametrically opposed to those of

---

[1] *Edgar carried out his own selective listener research on this last subject. 'The BBC is not supposed to advertise,' one listener told him, 'but there is a lot of indirect advertising of artists and films.' (Report on the Output of Variety Department, July 1943.)

[2] *Ibid.

[3] Nicolls was well aware of the financial implications of Edgar's strictures. To employ artists or writers on exclusive contracts would be very expensive. Might not the BBC have to put up its own chain of theatres? This would mean 'war to the knife' with the impresarios.

[4] *Board of Governors, Minutes, 29 July 1943.

some, at least, of the Governors,[1] replied briefly that it was 'a complete myth that there are swarms of unknown talented artists rotting in the provinces, although one does occasionally find something new'. If the BBC were to ignore agents and impresarios it would be left 'high and dry': as it was, the BBC's realistic relations with some of them were good, better than they had ever been. As far as the employment of better script-writers was concerned, the BBC was suffering from 'parsimony in the past' in paying them. After all, whatever the criticisms, it enjoyed many successes of its own, and its regular standard of production was higher than Edgar suggested, particularly when compared with the 'sustaining programmes' used in the American commercial networks.

Much of Edgar's report seemed to Watt to rest, however, not on an analysis of procedures but on a plea for the production of more and more programmes for minority audiences. 'Personal likes and dislikes are no criterion. Opinions passed by people one meets, are, in the main, misleading because, in general, one only meets people in roughly the same income group. The "West End" point of view is the most dangerous of the lot. The taste of Southern England is at great variance with that of the North. Listener research is our sole guide to the popularity of the programme. It is, and was, intended to be the equivalent of a non-commercial box office, and it is highly desirable that we should know and make use of this fact.' A programme like *Happidrome*, 'cheerful and unsophisticated', would never have any chance of pleasing the minority public: this did not mean that it should be dropped. Similarly, a programme like *Northern Music Hall*, which Edgar had criticized, originated in the North Region and was popular with the audience for which it was designed precisely because it appealed to the taste of Dewsbury rather than set out to tell Dewsbury what it ought to want.

Finally, Watt complained, Edgar had ignored a whole range of programmes which had been greatly appreciated by their

[1] *Lady Violet Bonham Carter to Powell, 18 Aug. 1943. Like the other Governors, she had been pursued by telephone inquiries from the journalists about the statement attacking Variety programmes made by Lady Snowden (see above, p. 570). 'My own reaction to the statement officially issued (that the BBC taste had steadily improved) was one of wondering incredulity. *Can* it have been worse in days gone by?'

audiences.[1] *Ack-Ack-Beer-Beer*, which was to run continuously until 1944, had 'created a sense of unity between the personnel of the two Commands'.[2] *Workers' Playtime*, organized by Imlay Watts and compèred by Bill Gates, had been immensely popular, and it had avoided all the pitfalls of becoming a vehicle for popular uplift.[3] *Music While You Work* had won the blessings of the Ministry of Labour on the grounds that it 'sustained morale', increased production and gave workers everywhere 'a sense of kinship';[4] it had also interested sociologists and psychologists at least as much as *ITMA* or the *Brains Trust*. They turned back learnedly to a pioneer experiment carried out in 1937 by S. Wyatt and J. N. Langdon and to later American surveys of the effects of music on work.[5] 'Working processes,' they concluded, 'have an important influence on the popularity or otherwise of these programmes. In general, workers in light industry or those employed on monotonous and repetitive tasks, prefer dance music. Workers in "heavy" industry (machine shops, foundries, etc.) prefer a "heavier" type of programme—music of a more robust nature played by military bands, brass bands, or large light orchestras. A sub-division is necessary, however, to obtain a true balance. Older workers, especially men, show a preference for martial and light music. Younger workers, and many thousands of women are in this group, prefer dance music.'[6]

[1]* Watt to Nicolls, 24 July 1943.

[2] *Nicolls to Watt, 23 Feb. 1944: 'it could never be a real winner at that time of the day but it has run continuously longer than most programmes I can remember . . . and after 320 odd performances can well be proud of its record.'

[3] *Watt to Nicolls, 20 Oct. 1941. Workers in all parts of the country heard it. Thus, in Sept. 1942, a show for harvest workers was broadcast from near Ross-on-Wye. According to Gates (*Nottingham Journal*, 1 May 1944), since the stage had been decorated with hops, all the bees in the neighbourhood gathered inside the hall and made their own contribution to the programme.

[4] *Letter from R. Lloyd Roberts, Ministry of Labour, to Imlay Watts, 18 Nov. 1943.

[5] *Industrial Health Research Board, Report No. 77, 'Fatigue and Boredom in Repetitive Work' (1937); Wheeler Beckett's War Production Board Survey, Washington (1942); *Radio Times*, 10 Dec. 1943; Talk by Wynford Reynolds, who took charge of the programme in May 1941, for the Industrial Recreation Association Conference in New York, July 1943.

[6] *Report by Reynolds, 22 July 1943. Nearly 7,000 factories employing 4 million workers were listening to the programme in May 1943 (Note of 31 May 1943). A year later (Note of 1 June 1944) the comparable figures were said to be 8,000 and 4½ million. In June 1945 the figure was said to be 9,000. These figures did not include many small factories and workshops.

Edgar's report on Variety left out dance music, one of the main features in the Variety Department's output, just as it left out cinema organs. In relation to dance music also there was an attempt on the part of people who sometimes knew little about the subject to pontificate on the need for more 'vigorous' and for less 'sentimental' music. Nicolls, for example, wrote in February 1942 that 'I am sure that we all feel much sympathy with the M.P. who asked the Minister of Information last week for us to cut out the dull spots and "substitute gay and patriotic musical numbers".' He added that he felt strongly that 'we would be more in the mood of the moment if we cut out a lot of our dreary jazz sophistications (D.V. forgive me!) in favour of waltzes, marches and cheerful music of every kind'.[1] There is no evidence that the *we* in this statement included the majority of listeners to dance music, whether civilians or servicemen—women outnumbered men by two to one in this group[2]—yet Nicolls went on a month later to claim more sweepingly that the general standard of playing and musical ability was well below the American standard, that 'crooning'[3] should continue to be barred, that there should be a 'positive policy of encouragement of better and more virile lyrics', and that song plugging should be very carefully watched.[4] In the light of this statement, Nicolls set up a committee to work out a 'new policy' for dance music. At the core of the policy was 'the elimination of crooning,

[1] *Nicolls, Programme Directive, 24 Feb. 1942. See also above, p. 216.

[2] *Listener Research Survey, 26 July 1943. Working-class listeners and young listeners were said to be more numerous relatively than their total numbers warranted.

[3] *He added that 'it was difficult to define, but was easily recognisable in various forms such as sub-tone, falsetto, and other modes of effeminate singing'.

[4] *Draft Note on Music Policy, 1 April 1942. There was a long history of song-plugging. Haley claimed (Note of 1 Dec. 1943) that during the war the BBC had kept 'a firm hand' on the number of times any tune could be played. Yet the hand could never be as firm as the BBC wished. There had been serious difficulties in 1940 (see *The Melody Maker*, 10 Feb. 1940) and a question was asked about song plugging in Parliament. 'All see to it,' wrote Watt in 1941 (Memorandum of 23 June), 'that within the orbit of the programme for which they are responsible, numbers do not get repeated too often. But without an organisation to vet all programmes centrally, I do not think that it is possible completely to guard against the same song going over five or six times, each one emanating from a differing programme unit.' Watt was realistic, and he knew that dance band leaders and song writers did not look at the question in the same way. The issue was raised again in Dance Music Policy Committee, *Minutes*, 3 March 1944.

sentimental numbers, drivelling words, slush, innuendos, and so on', yet there were other points in it also such as 'not jazzing the classics' and barring certain 'offensive' songs from the air.

The policy was announced to the Press[1] and communicated to music publishers and dance band leaders. 'Anaemic and debilitated vocal performances by male singers' were to be barred along with 'insincere and over-sentimental' performances by women singers. Tunes borrowed from 'standard classical works' were to be rejected, and words like 'Chink' or 'Yogi', which might offend 'religious or Allied susceptibilities', were never to be permitted. The music publishers claimed, not without justification, that not only was there no general public demand for this new 'dictatorial' policy, but that the BBC itself had contributed in the past to the promotion and diffusion of music, including 'slushy' music, which it was now condemning. At the same time, the Music Publishers' Association took part in regular talks with the BBC on the subject of popular songs until June 1944.[2]

The Press was more divided than the publishers.[3] Their debate had immediate point. *Sincerely Yours*, the Vera Lynn programme, produced like the *Brains Trust* by Howard Thomas and first broadcast in November 1941, did not appeal to most correspondents of the *Daily Telegraph*, but it was 'solidly popular with the ordinary rank-and-file of the Forces'. There were signs of the same kind of divisions of taste between the young and the old which bedevilled all the BBC's attempts to set common standards. It was not only the rank-and-file or the young, however, who liked the Vera Lynn programmes, and Colonel Stafford, who started the war as the BBC's Defence Director and ended it as Station Director at Plymouth, stated boldly in 1944 that 'in his opinion the British soldier was much more likely to be brought to a fighting pitch after hearing sentimental songs than by martial music'.[4] The debate concerning styles of music never died, and it never went on for long without bringing in Vera Lynn's name.[5]

[1] *Press Release of 21 July 1942.   [2] The meetings then lapsed for two years.
[3] *The Melody Maker*, 22 Aug. 1942 and *passim* during this period; Adam to Howgill, 25 Aug. 1942.   [4] *Western Evening Herald*, 21 Jan. 1944.
[5] *Board of Governors, *Minutes*, 4 Dec. 1941: '*Sincerely Yours* deplored, but popularity noted.' Val Gielgud was concerned about the effect of her songs on

In fact, Vera Lynn triumphed over most of her critics and won her secure place in the history of the war as the 'Forces' Sweetheart', as secure a place as that of Joad or Handley. Graves might not like to listen to her,[1] but millions of people did.[2] Howard Thomas rightly pointed out that she would not be so successful if she sang 'bright' songs of the type some of the older listeners wanted. Other women singers also had their appeal, notably Ann Shelton, whose fans liked both her voice and the 'simple marching songs' which she popularized.[3] Yet the one popular song of the war which crossed all the frontiers, including the enemy frontiers, was not a marching song of the type Nicolls would have preferred, but *Lili Marlene*. The tune had been written in Vienna in 1938 and the words in the distant days of 1923. In its war-time form it made its way from the North African desert to both Germany and Britain. No copies of *Lili Marlene* were available in Britain in October 1942.[4] By the end of 1943, however, everybody was singing it and the BBC was looking for a similar success.[5] 'It's the one real song that the war has produced so far which can be compared with *Tipperary* or *Over There*,' a gramophone compère stated enthusiastically in September 1943. 'It's not a song of the Afrika Korps or the Desert Army, it's the song of the Mediterranean soldier.' The Sicilians, too, were singing it as willingly as the Canadians.[6]

In the summer of 1943 the BBC commissioned Spike Hughes to write a report on dance music. This time, the Corporation had commissioned a real expert who could write with the

[1] H. Grisewood, *One Thing at a Time* (1968), pp. 133–4.

[2] *Her first solo broadcasts were in 1935, and she had appeared on television in 1938. She was already popular with the *Ack-Ack-Beer-Beer* listeners in 1940. From Sept. 1940 she began to appear in *Starlight* in the Overseas Service.

[3] *Madden to de Lotbinière, 5 Aug. 1942. She sang many other sorts of songs, of course, including 'Only for Ever', 'Jealousy', and 'No Love, no Nothing'.

[4] *Howgill to David Miller, 30 Oct. 1942.

[5] *At the Dance Music Policy Committee meeting on 13 Dec. 1943 Howgill said that a song was required for the Forces abroad 'that would have a similar effect to *Lili Marlene*'. The words of a song were written but were not thought to be suitable (ibid., 3 March 1944).

[6] *Recorded excerpts from a despatch by Peter Stursburg, 13 Sept. 1943. See also *The Gramophone*, July 1944 and *Daily Dispatch*, 17 June 1944.

troops hundreds of miles away. In the United States Frank Sinatra, 'the Voice'. made a big hit at New York's Paramount Theatre in 1943 (I. Settel, *A Pictorial History of Radio* (1960), p. 133). There were 'frenzied outbursts from the teenage audience',

kind of knowledge that carried conviction. 'The original object of broadcast dance music no longer applies; it does not provide music for dancing to at home,' he began. 'The roll-back-the-carpet-and-dance era ended long before the war so we must, therefore, presume that this music is designed to serve another purpose.' Hughes, who had spent months listening to dance music 'inattentively' and days 'monitoring' it in a concentrated fashion—the latter experience he said was surely unique, for he could imagine no member of the public doing any such thing—pointed out sensibly that large numbers of people wanted background music: others wanted to 'pick up' lyrics. He commented on the performance of the four BBC contract bands, left a place for 'swing' if it were played by 'specialists',[1] and urged from a far more knowledgeable standpoint than most previous commentators that more attention should be paid to good dance band singing. The standard should be set by Bing Crosby, Mildred Bailey and Dinah Shore.[2]

Howgill, Assistant Controller (Programmes), thought that Hughes had overlooked the fact that sometimes the Forces actually did dance to BBC music; he pointed out also that Victor Sylvester's audience was approximately twice as large as that for any other band. At the same time, he advocated resting contract bands from time to time to avoid staleness and to allow a greater variety of names to be brought before the public.[3] The Board of Governors missed the nuances of this sophisticated discussion. Reverting to its Minutes of June 1942, that 'measures shall be taken to encourage a more robust and virile type of dance music', it demanded that a continued watch should be kept on the quality of vocal items and re-affirmed that dance music should 'meet the demands of the attentive listener'.[4]

Neither jazz nor 'light music' figured in Hughes's report. The former, a subject in which he was an expert, was the province during the war of the Radio Rhythm Club, which had

---

[1] *Listener Research Survey, 26 July 1943, showed that supporters of strict tempo and straight dance music were in a majority, and that supporters of 'sweet' were more numerous than supporters of 'strict'.

[2] *Report on Dance Music, Aug. 1943. The Listener Research Survey of 26 July 1943 showed that dance music enthusiasts greatly preferred vocal to non-vocal dance music.

[3] *Note of 31 Aug. 1943.   [4] *Board of Governors, Minutes, 16 Sept. 1943.

started in 1939 with vigorous support from Leslie Perowne, Charles Chilton and, in the background, Harman Grisewood. The Radio Rhythm Club Sextet, formed by Chilton, led by George Shearing and 'fronted' by Harry Parry, was voted the most popular group in a *Melody Maker* poll. 'Light music' was the subject of a separate BBC report by Eric Coates, the well-known composer of light music, in the protracted inquest on programmes in 1943.[1] Coates pleaded for more Johann Strauss, Massenet, Lehar, Delibes and Bizet, but Fred Hartley, the Light Music Supervisor, believed that the main function of the light music provided by the BBC was to serve as a background to 'talk or food'.[2] He did not consider that there was any need to theorize about it: the sole object should be to please. Hartley did not agree, either, with Coates in his opinion that 'small complements with inadequate strings are the major handicap of light music', and in reply to Coates's criticism of cinema organists on the grounds that they played sentimentally rather than accurately, he remarked that a special committee had been working for over a year to raise 'the programmes and standards of playing of cinema organists'.

Yet Coates was right to note the implications for light music of the development of musical tastes during the war and the moving frontiers of appreciation of 'light' and 'serious' music. To him, light music was 'the public meeting ground in all music'. It was in this spirit that the BBC Symphony Orchestra devoted one of its programmes to 'light music' in 1943, that Stanford Robinson experimented with opera, and that *Tuesday Serenade* and *Music for All* were to show in 1944 'what a high proportion of music is suitable to more than one type of setting'.[3] There was one casualty, however, early in 1943.

---

[1] *Eric Coates, 'Report on Light Music', 22 May 1943. He had listened systematically from 7 Feb. to 8 May. He was very forthright in his general statements. 'If singers were made to understand that if they crooned they would be taken off the air, they would soon get back to a less objectionable style.' Fred Astaire was held up as a model of a singer who never crooned. 'It is a nasty thing to know that the younger-generation-listener is being brought up on this undesirable and slushy sentimentality, and is hearing harmless numbers sung *off the note* and *after the beat* in the most unpleasantly suggestive manner.'

[2] *Note by A. Bliss, 8 Sept. 1943.

[3] *BBC Handbook, 1945*, p. 46. Surprisingly Malcolm Sargent discerned and deplored the decline in public appreciation of 'melodious light music' during the war, while not noting the shift in taste. (*The Spectator*, 20 Feb. 1942.)

The BBC Military Band was dispersed on the grounds that there were so many first-class military bands which were now willing to perform for the BBC that the maintenance of a separate combination was thought to be unjustifiable 'under present conditions'.[1] The Band had been formed in 1927 under its first conductor B. W. O'Donnell, the brother of Major P. S. G. O'Donnell who conducted the band in its last years; and throughout the war, whatever shifts of taste, there were few changes in the numbers of people who were enthusiastic, neutral or hostile to military band music.[2]

Whatever the vicissitudes of light music, 'serious music' gained a wider and more knowledgeable audience during the course of the war.[3] 'The belated discovery has been made,' one critic put it as early as 1942, that 'art is not the privilege of the few but the birthright of the many.'[4] Both in the Home and Forces programmes there was a considerable increase in the time devoted to classical and contemporary music. Two-hour periods were regularly devoted to broadcasts of symphony concerts, and there were fortnightly lunch-hour concerts;[5] a full studio opera was broadcast each month, along with a short opera and a comic opera; and the broadcasting of the 'Proms' was revived after a two-year gap, with Sir Henry Wood conducting his forty-eighth consecutive season and with two orchestras—the London Philharmonic, conducted by Basil Cameron, and the BBC Symphony, conducted by Sir Adrian Boult—for the first time sharing the programmes.[6] Hundreds had to be turned away from the Promenade Concerts and,

---

[1] *Board of Governors, *Minutes*, 4 Feb. 1943.

[2] *Manchester Guardian*, 14 May 1943, noted this interesting statistical evidence.

[3] *The Spectator*, 23 July 1943: 'Whatever else it may have destroyed, the war has undoubtedly re-created music in our midst, affirming it a living force vital to the needs of a great people.'

[4] J. Leeper, 'Art and Music in War-time' in the *Contemporary Review*, Aug. 1942.

[5] For the boom in orchestras in war time, see T. Russell, *Philharmonic Decade* (1944), p. 123. In 1944 and 1945 there were prolonged disputes about broadcasting fees (see *The Times*, 27 April 1945).

[6] *Between 1940 and 1941 the Promenade Concerts series was presented by Keith Douglas under the auspices of the Royal Philharmonic Society. The BBC greatly regretted the break in broadcasting which was decided upon without consultation. (*Note by Nicolls, 25 April 1940; Sir Henry Wood quoted in *The Times*, 5 April 1940; letter by Boult to *The Times*, 9 April 1940.) The 1941 concerts were in the Albert Hall, the Queen's Hall having been destroyed. For the 1942 decision, see Control Board, *Minutes*, 27 Aug. 1941.

as the *BBC Handbook* put it, 'the nightly packed houses were a vivid and tangible sign of the growing demand for good music which has been constant throughout the country since the beginning of the war'.[1] Most encouragingly, there was a lively interest in new works. Ireland's *Epic March* was specially commissioned by the BBC; Rubbra's Fourth Symphony was conducted by himself; Britten's *Sinfonia da Requiem* was broadcast for the first time, along with Shostakovich's 'Leningrad' Symphony performed on the first anniversary of Russia's entry into the war. The symphony was repeated at the 'Proms' a week later; the conductor's score along with the orchestral parts, nine hundred photographed pages in all, had arrived in Britain from besieged Leningrad in microfilm sent by diplomatic bag from Moscow. Among other remarkable, if less dramatic, events of the year were a guest concert conducted by John Barbirolli, who had succeeded Toscanini as conductor of the New York Philharmonic Orchestra; a version of the *Messiah*, edited by Julian Herbage, which broke with Victorian custom and reverted to the original score; a recorded concert by the Toronto Symphony Orchestra, the first special recording of any Dominion orchestra; and six concerts associated with the William Byrd quater-centenary celebrations, which fittingly extolled a continuing tradition in English music.

In April 1942 Arthur, later Sir Arthur, Bliss had succeeded Boult as Director of Music, since at his own request Boult wished to free himself of administration and devote himself entirely, as Chief Conductor, to the BBC Symphony Orchestra.[2] It was Bliss, therefore, who was formally responsible for the still further extended musical output of 1943 and early 1944, an output which critics complained was somewhat lacking in

---

[1] *BBC Handbook, 1943*, p. 42.

[2] The Symphony Orchestra and Music Department had moved to Bedford in July 1941 (see above, pp. 111–12). They were joined there in September by the Music Productions Unit and the Theatre Orchestra. They remained there until 1946. There was one other change of personalities in December 1943, when R. F. Thatcher, who had been Deputy Director of Music since 1936, resigned to take up the post of Warden of the Royal Academy of Music: he was replaced by K. A. Wright. In 1942 Sir Hugh Allen, who expressed doubts as to whether 'a composer, conductor or other executant' should be Director of Music, had suggested a 'triumvirate' to run the Music Department. Graves thought the proposal had 'little to recommend it'. (*Note by Graves, 5 March 1942.)

design and purpose.[1] Particular emphasis was placed during this year on British works, even though James Agate complained that whenever 'he tuned in to the wireless' he got nothing except the piano concertos of Rachmaninov and Tchaikovsky.[2] New works were performed by Arnold Cooke, Britten and Tippett, and a new *Music of Our Time* series included Stravinsky's *Rite of Spring*, Hindemith's symphony, *Mathis der Maler*, and Berg's *Three Fragments from Wozzeck*. Among the new performers Yehudi Menuhin made his broadcasting début in April. At the same time the amount of serious music broadcast from gramophone records increased dramatically from 6 per cent of total output in 1942 to 40 per cent in 1944. Interests of listeners outside Britain were not overlooked. European music was introduced in the BBC's Eastern Service 'with the special object of accustoming the Asiatic ear to Western music in its best forms',[3] and four good concerts of the 'Proms' type were broadcast each week in the main Overseas Service. As for the 'Proms' themselves, they broke all previous records. Sir Henry Wood collapsed on the opening night, 1943, and most of the subsequent conducting had to be taken over by Boult and Cameron. Wood conducted the closing concerts and received a tremendous ovation.

There was a prolonged search in 1943 for the best way of presenting opera, for which John Christie of Glyndebourne believed the BBC should feel some special responsibility.[4] Rudolf Bing prepared an interesting report on broadcast opera in 1943 in which he compared the advantages of stage and radio performances. 'Vitally important things can go wrong on the stage which cannot go wrong on the air,' yet studio performances all too often lacked 'life and vitality'. Romantic opera, in his view, fared better over the air than Mozart, and the performance of *Eugene Onyegin* in May 1943 was

---

[1] William Glock in *The Observer*, 18 Jan. 1944.

[2] *Daily Express*, 12 June 1943. In Oct. 1943 Bliss wrote to the *Sunday Times* that during the course of the year 27% of the music broadcast had been British, of which 17% was by contemporaries. The Governors had decided in 1942 (*Minutes, 15 Oct. 1942) that while the primary consideration in music policy should be quality, 'when the merits were equal as between enemy and British composers, preference should be given to the British'.

[3] *BBC Handbook, 1944*, p. 43.

[4] *Christie to Powell, 30 June 1943.

the best broadcast opera he had listened to in war time.[1] Yet once again, as in the case of the reports on light music, the BBC hesitated, even demurred, when confronted with the opinions of a distinguished outsider. Bing, it was argued, had allowed 'too little for the music itself'. 'Broadcasting gives something of the same scope to opera that lack of scenery gave to Elizabethan drama. Free from restraint of "realism", the drama developed a highly poetic form of expression which made great demands on the visual imagination of the audience. It is possible that broadcast opera might similarly evolve its own technique.'[2]

War-time drama did evolve its own techniques, and its history is at least as interesting as the history of war-time music. 'Just as the symphony has reached over the air a new and larger public who have learned to understand and love it,' a sensitive American critic remarked in 1941, 'so poetry and the poetic drama may be able to win a responsive new audience through radio. But it must be borne in mind that whereas music is perfectly suited to the conditions of radio, poetry will win its hearing only by skilful and realistic adaptation to the new medium.'[3] In fact, poetic drama was only one of the forms of drama which thrived during the war. Louis MacNeice, whose *Christopher Columbus* (1942), specially written for the 405th Anniversary of the discovery of America, created a sensation in artistic circles on both sides of the Atlantic, gets only a brief mention in Gielgud's *British Radio Drama*. His perspectives may well be right. V. S. Pritchett feared, when *Christopher Columbus* came out in book form in 1944, with a valuable introduction, that 'what looks like a new art form may be as transient as the silent cinema was',[4] and

[1] *For a different verdict, singling out *The Force of Destiny*, see *Musical Opinion*, March 1943.

[2] *Report on Opera by Rudolf Bing, May 1943; Note by the Music Department, 12 July 1943. Nicolls (Note of 30 July 1943) pleaded for a 'long view' in relation to institutions and for a closer relationship with Sadlers Wells.

[3] D. Taylor, quoted in A. Bonner, 'Verse Drama and the Radio' in *Poetry*, vol. XLVII, Aug. 1941.

[4] *New Statesman* 1 April 1944: '*Columbus* and *The Rescue* make the claims of radio serious and impressive.' *Punch* (17 May 1944) said that 'the play could stand on its poetry alone'. In *The Spectator* (22 April 1944), however, Henry Reed described the play as 'rather disappointing'. *Columbus*, he went on, 'convinces one that some of the advantages which the radio writer thinks he enjoys are really handicaps'. See also *The Times*, 4 Sept. 1963, for a later assessment.

although the writers of verse drama during the war—Geoffrey Bridson, Patric Dickinson and Edward Sackville-West as well as MacNeice—gained what seemed to be a secure hold over their public and prepared the way for the post-war stage success of Christopher Fry, they did not change either art or taste as much as some of the war-time critics believed that they were doing.

According to Gielgud, who enthusiastically welcomed the return of the Drama Department from Manchester to London in 1943,[1] the most distinguished contribution to radio drama in 1941 was Clemence Dane's series *The Saviours*, seven plays on a single theme; he also found the first performance of Constance Cummings at the microphone in Alice Duer Miller's *White Cliffs of Dover* 'irresistibly moving' in the circumstances of the time.[2] In 1942 he singled out Eric Linklater for his play *The Cornerstones*, which was followed by a sequence of successful discussion plays, one of which, *The Great Ship* (1943), had the unique distinction of being broadcast three times in a single week.[3]

Gielgud had the satisfaction of seeing some of his early war-time worries disappear. During 1942, indeed, the popularity of the radio play rose sharply,[4] and the 1943 programme schedule was accordingly made even more ambitious. *War and Peace* in eight parts was not an unqualified success, although the very fact of performance prompted a cable from the Union of Soviet writers, with Alexei Tolstoy and Ilya Ehrenburg among the signatories; more memorable was Ibsen's *Peer Gynt* produced by Tyrone Guthrie, with Ralph Richardson as Peer. Rearrangements of the timing and organization of plays deserved almost as much attention in 1943 as the plays themselves, for in April *Saturday Night Theatre* was launched, at Nicolls's suggestion, with the deliberate object of interesting the 'average listener'. The suggestion was lively and imaginative, and for many listeners it was to introduce a new fixed point in the listening week. Likewise, a new weekly thriller series, *Appointment with Fear*, introduced by John Dickson Carr,

---

[1] See his *British Radio Drama, 1922–1956* (1957), p. 102.

[2] Lynn Fontanne read the poem in the American broadcast and aroused great enthusiasm.

[3] Gielgud, op. cit., p. 101. John Gielgud was in the main part.

[4] *BBC Handbook, 1944*, p. 46.

an American who remained in England throughout the war, was an immediate success from the evening of its first broadcast in November. Yet another new phrase was introduced to the language in consequence, for newspapers began to use the title *Appointment with Fear* as a caption under cartoons on quite different subjects.

'Features' continued to thrive during this period. '"The Features Department", which wears this foolish name like a clown's mask,' one writer stated in 1942, 'sprouts with uneven and interesting possibilities.'[1] In 1943, however, the interest was far greater than the unevenness. 'Those BBC documentaries are good' was the title of a *New York Times* article in February 1943.[2] In 1943 'Special Nights' were instituted during which there was a planned sequence of programmes in illustration of one central theme. *Workers' Gala Night* on 1 June was thought to be very successful. So, too, was *Army Week* in February which appealed both to the Army and to the Governors of the BBC. One great virtue of the 'Special Nights', it was claimed, was that 'they refreshed the pattern of broadcasting by breaking down the separate compartments into which a normal day's listening is apt to fall'.[3]

We are back again at the concept of a daily or weekly frame with which this study of programmes began.

There was one other question, however, which loomed large, particularly in 1943. What should be the relationship between the two alternative programmes broadcast by the BBC—the Home Service and the Forces Programme?[4] There were some particular programme items of national importance, like speeches by Churchill, which were broadcast simultaneously in both services; there were also some programmes, including Variety programmes, which originated in one service and were subsequently repeated in the other. A large share of the public had taken to the lighter and more 'cheerful' Forces Programme by preference, as a report by Nicolls, backed by evidence collected by Listener Research, had shown conclusively in January 1942. 'This is the first occasion,' Nicolls wrote then,

[1] *The Spectator,* 20 Feb. 1942.
[2] The article was by G. H. Gorey, *New York Times,* 7 Feb. 1943.
[3] *BBC Year Book, 1944,* p. 48.
[4] *The Governors also raised the question of more use being made by the Home and Overseas Services of each other's material (*Minutes,* 12 March 1942).

'on which the BBC has applied the "hot and cold tap" system to its programmes, and apart entirely from the Forces aspect it is a practical recognition of the pre-war situation when the BBC was losing listeners to Luxembourg, Fécamp, Radio Normandie and other stations, merely because its programmes were not meeting this demand.' Critics of the Forces Programme—and in July 1942 they included Brendan Bracken himself[1]—might complain that it was pandering to the worst of tastes;[2] even, as Nicolls wrote, that it was 'filth' or more generally 'tripe'. Yet this was too condescending a view. 'The demand will remain,' Nicolls went on, 'and the sponsored programme stations will crop up like mushrooms again after the war. It therefore should, I submit, be a cardinal point of BBC policy to retain its hold on this popular audience both now and after the war. In this policy, incidentally, the BBC can count on the support of the Press.'[3] It also secured the full support of the Commander-in-Chief Home Forces who stressed the continuing need for 'light entertainment'.[4] The Governors themselves recognized that the Forces needed 'longer unbroken periods of suitable music and light entertainment' and 'less frequent talks at the best listening times'.[5]

Characteristically, however, Nicolls looked backwards to the Reithian BBC as well as forwards to a post-war world. 'Could the Programme be improved culturally without diminishing its acceptability?' he asked. 'The answer to this is probably "yes",' he concluded, 'provided that the improvement is gradual and does not outrun its public or contravene the accepted important policy of the hot and cold taps. In other words, improvement is possible and desirable within rather narrow limitations, and we are consistently attempting it.'[6] This somewhat cautious reiteration of the BBC's pre-war policy—the opposite approach to broadcasting from that which may be called the gradual descent down the slippery slope—was to survive the war, although more attention was to be

---

[1] *Board of Governors, *Minutes*, 16 July 1942.

[2] See above, pp. 137–9.

[3] *Report by Controller (Programmes) on the Forces Programme, 1 Jan. 1942.

[4] *Note by the Director-General, 10 Dec. 1942, summing up the principles relating to the Forces Programme and attitudes towards them outside the Corporation.

[5] *Board of Governors, *Minutes*, 17 Sept. 1942.   [6] *Ibid.

paid after 1945 than before 1939 to the stratification of audiences.

While the Forces Programme retained its popularity in 1942 and 1943, most programmes designed for the Forces overseas, particularly those in North Africa and later in Italy, were broadcast in the General Overseas Service of the BBC. By late 1942, indeed, the BBC was running three programmes rather than two, which large numbers of British listeners were habitually following. It had been decided in October 1942 to increase the General Overseas Service for troops abroad to seven hours a day of continuous broadcasting, and to widen the coverage; and in May 1943 the broadcasting day was lengthened to over twelve hours and the coverage still further extended. This was the situation when at the end of 1943 Haley, the new Editor-in-Chief, went out to Italy to study the reaction of generals, privates and of all ranks in between to BBC output.[1] After discussing the politics of broadcasting with General Alexander, who had issued him with the invitation to visit Italy through the Ministry of Information, Haley went on to study the effect of broadcasting on morale, with much the same objects in view as Ryan had had when he visited the BEF in France during the phoney war.[2] He returned to Britain convinced that British troops fighting in Italy would be far happier if they could hear the Forces Programme, at least between the hours of five and seven o'clock in the evening —they would appreciate a 'link with home', and if the Forces Programme were to be slotted into the General Overseas Programme for this period each day, they would feel that they were listening to the same programmes as their families or friends or sweethearts back in Britain.[3]

This was a relatively straightforward proposal, but it was quickly abandoned, along with an alternative proposal that the Forces Programme should be transmitted to Italy by short-wave at certain times of the day, in favour of a bolder solution. The General Overseas Service had established itself as a smoothly running, perfectly timed operation with

[1] See above, p. 554.
[2] See above, p. 127.
[3] *Programme Policy Meeting, *Minutes*, 21 Dec. 1943; Board of Governors, *Minutes*, 6 Jan. 1944.

many popular, original programmes,[1] and in talks between Haley, Foot and Ashbridge it was decided to scrap the Forces Programme and to turn the General Overseas Service into *the* alternative programme for home listeners and the general programme for all Forces serving overseas in no matter what theatre of war.[2] India was mentioned as well as Italy,[3] and the fact that the opening of what was still called 'a second front' was now imminent introduced a sense of urgency into the deliberations. Logistic issues were involved also. The reduction of BBC general programmes from three to two liberated studio space and saved money. The comparative costs of Home and Forces Programmes had been watched carefully throughout the war:[4] in 1943 the case had been prepared for the Ministry of Information for a doubling of licence fees from ten shillings to one pound.[5] There was to be no increase until after the war, and in the meantime the economics of broadcasting had to be considered along with all the other factors influencing BBC policy.

When Foot told his Controllers' Conference in early January 1944 about what he called a 'revolutionary' change in policy, he dwelt, however, not on economics but on morale, not on post-war but on war-time issues. Everyone in the Services,

---

[1] *Among them *Radio Newsreel, Sandy Calling* (for Ceylon and India), *Talks to Forces Overseas* (a successor to the old John Hilton programmes), *Tommy Handley's Half-Hour*, produced by Pat Dixon, John Morris's *Question Time* (about the Far Eastern war) and *Home Flash* were thought to be particularly suited to Forces everywhere and to home listeners. (Note of 7 Jan. 1944.)

[2] *Programme Policy Meeting, *Minutes*, 28 Dec. 1943, 21 Jan. 1944; Board of Governors, *Minutes*, 13 Jan. 1944.

[3] *Note by Director-General and Editor-in-Chief for the Board of Governors, 3 Jan. 1944.

[4] *There is an interesting note on the subject by G. G. Duffus, 22 Jan. 1941. Problems of expenditure on programmes would have been even more acute had not programme expenditure in the early part of the war been 'regularly less than estimated' in the initial budgets. (Lochhead to Howgill, 13 Jan. 1941.)

[5] *Memorandum to the Minister of Information, 30 March 1943. 'It is frankly admitted,' the Memorandum stated, 'that in supporting the suggested increase in the fee the Corporation has very much in mind its post-war position.' 'If the general policy of raising the licence fee is approved,' the Memorandum also stated, 'the present time would seem to be a favourable one for doing so. Among the general mass of the population family earnings have risen substantially and throughout the country the opportunities for spending money have been greatly reduced. As the bulk of the population affected by this increase work on a weekly budget, it is interesting to note that the total charge for all that a listener gets from the radio will be at the rate of 4½d a week, and the increase will be 2½d a week.'

'from the Adjutant General downwards,' he began, had told him that 'there is a tremendous and deep longing to feel quite sure that their home life is safe, that what they are fighting for is still intact. The link they desire is spiritual and not material, and the feeling is very strong indeed.' One programme only was necessary for Forces everywhere, but it should be a shared programme with Britain itself. Interestingly enough, Foot touched not only on the desire to share the same entertainment but the desire to listen to the same news. There was a 'faint suspicion' on the part of some of 'the more junior officers' overseas that the news was 'faintly doctored': the same news bulletins would eliminate this suspicion for good. Foot anticipated the early opening of a second front. 'The time is coming when we shall have a large number of troops going from this country to Western Europe': they would begin by hearing the Home Service, but as they advanced it would become less audible. In such circumstances 'the link' with home would be of vital importance.[1]

In making this statement, which was inspired by Haley, Foot admitted that the decision to turn the General Overseas Service into the alternative programme had not been unanimous.[2] He emphasized, however, the importance of acting without delay. It was decided, therefore, to change the system on 27 February 1944.[3] In the short interval the maximum amount of publicity was to be given to the reasons for the change and what it would imply. There was an early Press leak,[4] but thereafter Press publicity was very efficiently managed by a Publicity Sub-Committee directed by Kenneth Adam, the BBC's Director of Publicity. So too was direct BBC publicity. 'For the first time in BBC history,' Adam proudly

---

[1] *Statement by the Director-General at the Controllers' Conference, 5 Jan. 1944.

[2] *In a letter to Powell, 10 Jan. 1944, Foot wrote that there had been 'objections, particularly at the outset, on the part of some of the Controllers concerned, but following the many conversations I have had with all concerned, I am satisfied that they will apply themselves with a real sense of loyalty to making the change a success'. At a Controllers' Conference on 2 Feb. 1944 Regional Directors expressed concern that the new programme would involve serious loss of regional time.

[3] *Programme Policy Meeting, *Minutes*, 21 Jan. 1944.

[4] See *Daily Express*, 6 Jan. 1944; *Report of a telephone conversation between Miss Fuller, the Director-General's secretary, and Hodge of the Ministry of Information, 6 Jan. 1944.

20

proclaimed, 'we shall make use of our own medium to publicise a major development in BBC policy.'[1] Both the wireless and the *Radio Times* were used to inform people of what was to happen. So also was *Broadcasting News*, a stencilled paper. 'The General Forces Programme,' it was stated—and this was the name eventually chosen for the transformed new service—'will present to Home listeners many old friends in a new dress —battle-dress—and some quite new ones. The most notable change will probably be not so much in programme items as in presentation. For General Forces is a world-wide service, addressing itself not to one country or area but to a succession of them. For this is a global war, and British Forces are scattered far and wide as never before.'[2]

Behind the scenes, Foot and Haley were settling the details of the new service, with the help of a specially created sub-committee.[3] They believed that the service should be directed with 'autonomy' under the Overseas Services Division, headed by J. B. Clark, 'working directly to us'.[4] 'Provided the Home and Overseas programmes retain their individuality,' they told the Governors, 'a sense of competition will be engendered—not only within the BBC (providing a stimulus to creativeness, to originality, and to the improvement of technique), but also in the mind of the listener.' Undoubtedly Haley had his eye on the problems of the post-war BBC even before he became Director-General. 'In time,' he and Foot stated, 'the provision of genuine contrast, the feeling of competition and choice in the BBC's programmes, should cause what present demand there is for commercially provided competition to subside.'

In retrospect, there was irony in the fact that soon after the introduction of the new service, its direction was handed to Norman Collins, one of the most able and enterprising young men in the BBC, who was to play a main part in the introduction of commercial television into Britain ten years later.

---

[1] *Adam to Hytch, 29 Jan. 1944.

[2] *Broadcasting News*, 22 Feb. 1944.

[3] *Programme Policy Meeting, *Minutes*, 28 Dec. 1943. Its main work was to decide which particular programmes from the old Forces Programme would be relayed in the new service. The sub-committee met on 29 Dec. 1943 and 3 and 6 Jan. 1944.

[4] *Note by Director-General and Editor-in-Chief, 3 Jan. 1944.

Collins had joined the BBC as a talks producer: he was to become the Head of the post-war Light Programme in 1946.

In the meantime, the new service went ahead,[1] not without continuing criticism. First reactions from troops overseas were as lukewarm as those from many people at home. 'There was certainly some disappointment because at the listening end,' Frank Gillard reported from Italy and North Africa, 'the GFP was simply the General Overseas Service under another name. The disappointed men were those who have been accustomed, through many years of peace-time listening, to the Home Service type of programme and presentation as typifying British broadcasting. They still feel that the GFP does not carry them back in imagination as they would like it to. In fact, their quest for nostalgia will not be satisfied until they hear Stuart Hibberd, or Frank Phillips, or some other voice with home associations reading the News. These men still strain their sets trying to catch the Home Service bulletins.'[2] Even the Request Programmes were beginning to become stale: 'all that talk for one paltry tune' was one disillusioned comment.

Gillard reported, indeed—and it was before the fall of Rome —that there still remained a Forces audience for enemy programmes. 'When I said goodbye to General Hawksworth one morning, he took me into the mess for a farewell drink, and his own radio set in there was pumping out light music from Rome interspersed with short propaganda quips in English.'[3]

The new service had its 'winners', however, and among the familiar programmes it included were *ITMA*, the *Brains Trust, Happidrome, Songs from the Shows, Forces' Favourites, Music While You Work*, Doris Arnold's *These You Have Loved* and the *Epilogue*. New programmes included a daily five-minute review of the British Press, an entirely new feature for British

---

[1] See below, p. . 713
[2] *Notes from Gillard to Haley, 27 March 1944.
[3] *Ibid. Cf. T. W. Chalmers, Overseas Presentation Director, to Norman Collins, 28 March 1944: 'We ought to do something to prevent the German radio having it all their own way during our shut down period.' Even in England the Regional Directors reported a tendency for listening to foreign programmes other than the BBC to be on the increase. (*Controllers' Conference, *Minutes*, 26 April 1944.)

home listeners. The idea of sharing cares and delights was represented in the timetable of the service. Broadcasts before 5 p.m. were to be shared with listeners east of Suez, some of them in the 'forgotten areas' of the war: broadcasts after 5 p.m. were to be shared with listeners in the Middle East, the Mediterranean area and West Africa.[1] The right martial note was struck each time *Lilliburlero* was played before the news bulletins. Everything was to be ready for the opening of the 'second front', and a brisk, unsigned, undated, early note about the service reads: 'The Second Front is assumed to open not later than the second week of May. The General Forces Programme begins in February—that gives ten weeks for the execution of a planned sequence.'

On the eve of D-Day—6 June—the ten most popular programmes (some of them broadcast in both the Home Service and the General Forces Programme) are shown in the table opposite. Nearly all of them were weekly programmes in a regular series. The percentages given in brackets represent the largest single audience for the programme in question.[2]

The changing balance of different programme constituents during the war was not calculated by Listener Research, but it is interesting to make such a calculation and to compare the details with those of the pre-war period.[3] Rigid lines of demarcation are, of course, extremely difficult to draw, and some items, like News, might include such different elements as News in Dutch, French and German in the Forces Programme in 1940 and Norwegian in the Home Service[4] which very few British listeners would ever have chosen to hear. Outside broadcasts were few in number, and in the week chosen most of them came from the BBC's allotment. Weather forecasts were banned until May 1945. The weeks chosen were autumn weeks when audiences in Britain were settling down to the thought of another long winter of blackout: it was not until the last of the autumns that there was much thought, not of the blackout, but of bright lights, and even then there were still to be surprises in store before the war was won.[5]

---

[1] *Notice issued with contracts to artists contributing to the GFP, 27 Feb. 1944.

[2] *Memorandum for the Director-General from Listener Research, 22 May 1944. Five weeks were taken.

[3] For the pre-war pattern, see Briggs, *The Golden Age of Wireless* (1965), p. 54.

[4] See above, p. 489.   [5] See below, pp. 698 ff.

The Top Ten Programmes: April and May 1944

Home Service	%	%	General Forces Programme	%	%
ITMA Thurs. 8.30 p.m.	39·7	(43·3)	It was Fun While It Lasted (T. Trinder) 5 April 8.30 p.m.	28·3	
Monday Night at 8	36·3	(40·0)	Old Town Hall Thurs. 8.00 p.m. (3 broadcasts)	23·4	(23·5)
Vaudeville of 1944 Sat. 8.00 p.m.	28·7	(31·6)	Palace of Varieties Sunday 8.30 p.m.	22·9	(25·9)
Saturday Night Theatre Saturday 9.20 p.m.	28·6	(30·7)	Songs from the Shows Friday 10.00 p.m.	21·2	(24·6)
Brains Trust Tuesday 8.15 p.m.	27·9	(30·2)	Bandstand Wed. 8.00 p.m.	20·9	(24·9)
Combined Operations 15 April 1944	27·7		Forces' Favourites Friday 9.30 p.m.	19·9	(21·7)
The Lilac Domino 8 May 1944	26·7		Music While You Work Friday 10.30 p.m.	19·1	(22·3)
That's a Good Girl 24 April 1944	25·8		These You Have Loved Thurs. 9.50 p.m.	18·5	(21·6)
Workers' Playtime Thursday 12.30 p.m.	25·4	(28·0)	ITMA (recording) Sunday 4.30 p.m.	18·1	(20·4)
Sunday Postscript Sunday 9.20 p.m.	20·0	(27·2)	Med. Merry-Go-Round Friday 7.15 p.m.	16·5	(19·5)

Programme Constituents One Week in October 1939–44 Inclusive

	1939	1940 Forces	1940 Home	1941 Forces	1941 Home	1942 Forces	1942 Home	1943 Forces	1943 Home	1944 General Forces	1944 Home
Total Transmission Time	120h. 45m.	98h. 10m.	121h. 20m.	116h. 10m.	121h. 20m.	115h. 30m.	121h. 20m.	115h. 30m.	121h. 20m.	115h. 30m.	121h. 20m.
	%	%	%	%	%	%	%	%	%	%	%
CLASSICAL MUSIC											
Opera (whole or part, not excerpts)	—	—	—	—	—	—	—	—	1·26	—	—
Orchestral (with soloists)	9·73	0·50	9·62	0·43	9·20	5·13	9·35	3·62	10·87	4·59	5·09
Chamber Music	2·56	—	2·13	—	1·17	—	0·62	0·30	0·63	0·72	0·84
Instrumental Recitals	2·97	1·02	2·89	0·21	2·03	0·43	1·24	0·60	2·42	—	2·08
Song Recitals	0·71	1·02	2·27	0·64	1·11	0·22	0·77	0·23	0·70	—	0·57
Cantatas, Oratorios, Church Music	—	—	0·89	—	—	0·22	0·29	—	—	—	1·04
Total:	15·97	2·54	17·80	1·28	13·51	6·00	12·27	4·75	15·88	5·31	9·62
LIGHT MUSIC											
Orchestral, Band, Small Combination (with Soloists)	15·74	20·46	10·51	19·87	11·34	20·74	8·39	22·45	9·63	17·34	10·04
Operetta, Comic Opera, Musical Comedy	1·37	2·12	0·63	1·00	1·66	0·43	2·07	0·67	0·42	0·70	0·77
Ballad or Chorus	2·83	2·88	1·73	3·65	0·83	2·24	0·63	3·20	0·42	2·85	1·45
Café, Restaurant, Cinema Organ	6·21	6·11	3·34	5·60	2·69	3·61	2·44	4·56	1·67	2·21	1·40
Total:	26·15	31·57	16·21	30·12	16·52	27·02	13·53	30·88	12·14	23·10	13·66
DANCE MUSIC	5·10	11·97	6·39	12·43	6·47	12·27	4·00	14·08	7·30	8·93	8·68
GRAMOPHONE RECORDS	4·22	18·34	5·08	16·47	6·05	17·69	8·88	17·94	9·23	19·08	11·72
DRAMA	2·76	0·43	3·34	0·40	4·34	0·73	3·04	0·23	2·91	—	4·97
FEATURES	4·07	3·74	2·95	0·40	3·51	2·97	7·71	1·75	4·93	1·74	2·00

LIGHT ENTERTAINMENT Music Hall, Vaudeville, Cabaret	5·66	13·75	4·45	16·93	4·47	12·34	3·50	10·62	3·94	14·83	6·40
Revue	1·38	1·44	1·52	1·00	—	0·43	0·42	0·44	—	0·90	0·42
Star Entertainer or Celebrity	—	0·51	0·41	1·72	0·28	2·24	0·63	1·02	0·43	1·34	—
Total:	7·04	15·70	6·38	19·65	4·75	15·01	4·55	12·08	4·37	17·07	6·82
CHILDREN'S HOUR	2·89	—	3·78	—	4·20	—	4·00	—	4·08	—	4·08
SPOKEN WORD News and Official Announcements	12·49	11·46	13·47	10·11	13·88	10·75	14·02	10·19	12·51	13·28	12·19
Talks, Discussions	5·04	2·46	9·07	7·24	10·38	5·41	11·34	5·79	9·70	7·74	10·20
Poetry and Prose Readings	1·03	—	0·40	—	0·76	0·29	0·55	0·23	1·33	—	1·27
Appeals	—	—	0·08	—	0·08	—	0·08	—	0·08	—	0·08
Total:	18·56	13·92	23·02	17·35	25·10	16·45	25·99	16·21	23·62	21·02	23·74
O.B.s Running Commentary	1·24	0·77	—	1·00	0·22	0·66	0·23	1·09	—	1·30	—
Ceremonies	—	—	—	—	—	—	—	—	—	—	—
Speeches	—	—	—	—	—	—	—	—	—	—	—
Total:	1·24	0·77	—	1·00	0·22	0·66	0·23	1·09	—	1·30	—
RELIGION	3·52	1·02	4·88	0·90	4·93	1·12	5·00	0·99	5·08	2·45	4·39
SCHOOL BROADCASTS	8·28	—	9·62	—	9·76	—	10·31	—	10·46	—	10·32
INTERLUDES 'Fill-ups' advertised in *Radio Times*	0·20	—	0·55	—	0·64	0·08	0·49	—	—	—	—
TOTAL:	100·00	100·00	100·00	100·00	100·00	100·00	100·00	100·00	100·00	100·00	100·00

5. Politics, Religion and Society

I T was impossible in planning war-time programmes to leave politics out. When J. B. Priestley was in the thick of his private and public controversies about his Postscripts in 1941, he received hundreds of letters of an abusive character from people who charged him with 'turning the classes against each other'. 'Don't struggle about post-war problems,' said the critics, 'until the war is won. Don't distract the public mind from the war. These things of which you have complained can be settled in their own time.' Priestley's reply was twofold. First, the war, he claimed, would not be won unless big changes took place both in national mood and in social structure. Second, 'the terrible years' which had followed the First World War and led to the war of 1939 were the direct result of 'a failure to plan the post-war world in time'.[1]

Such an approach was completely different from that of Churchill and the leading members of his Government, including Ernest Bevin, his Minister of Labour. The longer the 'catalogue of catastrophes', the more important it was, they felt, both for M.P.s and for solid citizens to stay loyal. Churchill, in particular, as Eden noted, was always loath to turn his mind to matters not immediately connected with the winning of the war.[2] For him, 'controversy' would merely divide the nation. Energies which it was necessary to harness to the war effort would be dissipated in the process. 'The most painful experiences would lie before us . . . if we fell to quarrelling about what we should do with our victory before that victory had been won.'[3] Churchill was backed by other

---

[1] See J. B. Priestley, *Out of the People* (1941). Use is also made in this paragraph of a characteristically pro-Priestley review in a Northern newspaper (*Bootle Times*, 5 Dec. 1941). Cf. the *News Chronicle*, 28 March 1942, which spoke of 'a widespread sense of frustration. . . . The call is everywhere for *action*. For more vigour; more initiative, a ruthless extermination of waste, muddle and decay.' See also H. J. Laski, *Reflections on the Revolution of Our Time* (1943).

[2] Earl of Avon, *The Eden Memoirs: The Reckoning* (1965), pp. 441–2.

[3] *The War Speeches of Winston Churchill*, vol. II (1952), p. 370. See also an intervention he made in Parliament in 1943 (*Hansard*, vol. 392, cols. 921, 924, 932): 'Everything for the war, whether controversial or not, and nothing controversial that is not *bona fide* needed for the war.'

members of his Government. In the House of Commons Cripps, for example, stated firmly in the autumn of 1942 that 'the times are clearly inappropriate to bring forward legislation of a character which is likely to arouse serious controversy between the political parties',[1] and Bevin, even more than Cripps, felt strongly that once the Labour Party had joined Churchill's Coalition Government, it would have to show both loyalty and restraint until the war was won.[2]

Priestley, however much he spoke for the 'nation', always challenged such politics of consensus. So, too, in his very different style, did Joad. In Joad's view, it was a mistake that the *Brains Trust* had to approach politics with circumspection and religion not at all.[3] In fact, the borderline between religion and politics seemed to be one of the most dangerous frontiers to argue about during the war. The question confronting the BBC was how far it should allow controversy to affect broadcasting. Should it seek, within the limits open to it, to maintain reasonably free access to the microphone or should it exercise self-discipline in what the Government believed were the interests of the nation?

The critical year in political and social terms was 1942. It began with the news of disaster, and stimulated many questions. Why had Singapore fallen? Why had it proved so hard to sink the *Bismarck* when the Japanese had destroyed the *Prince of Wales* so easily? It ended with the highly controversial assassination of Darlan. Why were the Allies, fighting in the cause of human freedom, prepared to do a deal with a man whose career showed that freedom meant nothing to him? It was during this year, not surprisingly, that Churchill's reputation was most seriously challenged inside Britain.[4] Although during this year some, at least, of the shifts of national policy were being made which advocates of a more strenuous war effort had demanded in 1940 and 1941—the implementation of a 'manpower budget' made possible a total war effort; rationing was extended; the Board of Trade's 'utility' scheme

---

[1] Ibid., vol. 385, cols. 40–1.

[2] See A. Bullock, *Ernest Bevin*, vol. II (1967), *passim*.

[3] *Radio Times*, 22 Sept. 1944. 'Religion languishes for lack of air, the cold but stimulating breath of contradiction. She is rather like a Victorian lady confined to her sofa in an over-heated drawing room.'

[4] See above, p. 409.

began to operate; and Dalton promulgated his 'austerity regulations'—nonetheless, sharp political disagreement was never far from the surface. Four independent candidates won by-elections, the greatest swing against the Conservatives of all the war years. Mass Observation reported in August that one in three citizens had changed their political views since the war began. *The Times*, with E. H. Carr writing bold leaders both on social justice and on nationalization, made the most of the 'reconstruction' theme. 'Let Churchill win the war quickly,' was one of the slogans of the early summer, 'then let Cripps win the peace.' There were debates behind the scenes as to whether planning was 'here to stay', debates which were sharpened in tone as the German 'Baedeker raids' of April, May and June brought the war directly into Britain's smaller towns and as the U-Boat campaign imperilled Britain's food supplies.

Not surprisingly, this was the year when the *Daily Mirror* was in trouble for what Churchill a few months earlier had called 'rocking the boat', awaking 'class and party dissensions', spreading the idea that the Government was incompetent, and creating a spirit of 'despondency and resentment, of bitterness and scorn' which 'at the proper moment' might be 'suddenly switched over into naked dejection'.[1] George Bartholomew and Cecil Thomas were summoned to see Morrison in March 1942 and told that just as one newspaper— the *Daily Worker*—had already been banned and there was no possibility of its reinstatement, so if the *Daily Mirror* were closed down, it would be 'for a long time'.[2] 'Reasonable criticism on specific points and persons is one thing,' Morrison said later in Parliament, 'general violent denunciation, manifestly tending to undermine the Army and depress a whole population is quite another.' Not everyone agreed with Morrison. Indeed, a full-scale parliamentary debate on the subject revealed a wide spectrum of attitudes. So too did statements in the Press. All these attitudes, boldly contrasting or gently nuanced, were present throughout the war, but they were seldom expressed so explicitly or dramatically as in the spring of 1942.

[1] See H. Cudlipp, *Publish and Be Damned* (1953), for the exchange of letters between Churchill and Cecil King in 1941.   [2] Ibid., p. 180.

Because of its direct links with the Ministry of Information, the BBC was as much concerned during 1942 as it had been earlier in the war not only with 'controversy' but with the maintenance of 'morale'. 'The policy of the Governors,' it went on to reiterate in 1943, 'is that the microphone is not the place in wartime for persons antagonistic to the war effort and further that the special facilities of the microphone, whatever the speaker desires to say there, should not be accorded to those persons whose words and actions are calculated to hamper the nation in its struggle for life.'[1] In 1942 efforts were being made by the Ministry of Information to carry out yet another 'morale campaign'. Accordingly Foot told the Governors in the early autumn, by which time Churchill had done much to buttress his position as Prime Minister and 'war leader',[2] what steps the BBC had taken 'by talks and features' to bring home to the people of this country the reality of the war and in particular the sufferings of those in occupied countries.[3] There was evidence of renewed increased listening to German broadcasts in English during the winter of 1942, when once again the size of the audience did not seem to depend greatly on what particular BBC programmes were competing with 'Haw-Haw'.[4]

Yet the military tide was beginning to turn.[5] While the Russians were holding out at Stalingrad, General Montgomery, the new commander of the Eighth Army in the desert war, overwhelmed Rommel at El Alamein in a battle which began on 23 October and ended triumphantly on 2 November 1942. Two days later the BBC, warning its listeners not to switch off since they would hear the best news for years, broadcast a

[1] *Brief for the Minister of Information, 1 July 1943.

[2] After the fall of Tobruk on 21 June 1942 various anti-Churchill moves had been made. Beaverbrook broadcast on the same day, charging that 'people in high places' who had approved helping Russia in 1941 were opposed to opening a second front now. A parliamentary motion of no-confidence in the 'central direction' of the war, proposed by Sir John Wardlaw-Milne, a Conservative backbencher, and supported by Bevan, was defeated by 476 votes to 25 with 40 abstentions, and it was clear from the debate that there was no alternative to Churchill.

[3] *Board of Governors, Minutes, 24 Sept. 1942.

[4] *Controllers' Conference, Minutes, 2 Dec. 1942.

[5] The first battle of El Alamein was being fought when Wardlaw-Milne's motion was being debated.

special Cairo communiqué from General Alexander—Bruce Belfrage, who read it, said he would never forget the day, which was also the day when he sent in his resignation to the BBC—revealing that the Germans were in full retreat from Egypt.[1] More good news followed. The Allied landings in North Africa, however much political controversy they opened up,[2] marked, in Churchill's felicitous phrase, if not the end, 'perhaps the end of the beginning'. On Sunday 15 November, the church bells rang again all over England announcing 'Monty's victory'.

'Morale', as always, depended more upon good news than upon the solicitude of the Ministry of Information. Yet given the differences of opinion, muted though they often might be, between Left and Right, along with the existence of the party political truce, there were many people of a conservative frame of mind who believed that the BBC should do nothing but emphasize national consensus. The BBC itself took no steps to notice the Labour Party's publication *The War and Peace, Problems of Reconstruction*.[3] A few months later General Sir George Jeffreys, a Conservative M.P., objected when the BBC broadcast a play dealing with the situation which might arise if Germany defeated Britain. 'What is wrong in occasionally reminding the public that we might be defeated?' another Conservative asked, while Sydney Silverman, the Labour M.P., added tartly, 'If the BBC issued nothing which was likely to lead to differences of opinion might they not just as well close down altogether?'[4]

Members of Parliament were extremely suspicious of their opponents being given too much time or notice on the radio in 1942: they were also very sensitive to their own claims as potential broadcasters. However much the BBC insisted first that it kept a balance and second that it was interested above all else in the quality of M.P.s not as M.P.s but as broadcasters, M.P.s pressed in 1942 for details of just how many of their number had broadcast since September 1939.[5] They also asked

[1] B. Belfrage, *One Man in His Time* (1951), p. 129; S. Hibberd, *This—is London* (1950), p. 223.   [2] See above, pp. 451 ff.

[3] *For the Labour Party's protest, see Board of Governors, *Minutes*, 5 March 1942. The Board was told that the BBC had acted according to precedent.

[4] *Hansard*, vol. 383, cols. 1624–5.

[5] Ibid., cols. 1982–3.

in vain for details of how much had been paid to them in fees.[1]
Bracken gave the numbers.[2] One hundred and sixty M.P.s
had broadcast on 1,321 occasions, although some of the broadcasts were repeats. Vernon Bartlett was well ahead with 115,
and only three other M.P.s had broadcast more than 50
times—Philip Noel-Baker's figure was 75, Commander Stephen
King-Hall's 61, and Walter Elliot's 51. Among the Ministers
Churchill had broadcast 33 times, Amery 39, Morrison 27,
Eden 21, Bevin 21 and Attlee 17. Among the regular or intermittent critics of the Government, Bevan had broadcast
twice, Shinwell once,[3] Hore-Belisha twice[4]—though in distant
times—Wardlaw-Milne once, and Winterton twelve times.[5]

There were to be many queries and more than one debate
in the House of Commons about the political role of the BBC
in 1943. It was not the case in 1942 itself, however, that the
BBC avoided all controversial broadcasting. As early as
February of that year Maconachie was prepared to argue
that *As I See It* programmes should be broadcast by people
whose views were different from those of the Government,
provided that the BBC made it clear that 'the opinions
expressed were neither official nor those of the BBC nor
anything but the speaker's own personal views' and that it
ensured that 'a general balance of political complexion should

[1] Ibid., vol. 385, cols. 331–2, 740–1. Related questions of a critical kind were
being asked regularly around this time about the system of deducting half the
broadcasting fee paid to members of H.M. Forces. 'Do professors who broadcast
have to return half the fee to their universities?' Thurtle was asked, to which he
replied, 'No Sir, because they have not acquired their knowledge in the service of
the Government.' (*Hansard*, vol. 383, cols. 2249–50.) An important concession
was made by the Chancellor in December 1942 (*Hansard*, vol. 385, cols. 2068–9)
allowing all Crown servants, both members of the Forces and civilians, to retain
full fees up to £50 a year. Above that figure the 50% rule was still to operate.

[2] 'I felt myself,' he frankly told the House later, 'that this enormous list was a
great waste of time.' (Ibid., vol. 385, col. 332.)

[3] Shinwell had asked to broadcast in Feb. 1942. (*Board of Governors, Minutes*,
12 Feb. 1942.)

[4] Hore-Belisha complained on more than one occasion of the reporting of
his parliamentary speeches, e.g. in June 1941 and July 1942 (*ibid., 23 July 1942).

[5] Thurtle gave the names of 92 members of the House of Lords who had broadcast since Sept. 1939: they included the two Archbishops and 9 Bishops (*Hansard*,
vol. 385, cols. 740–1, 25 Nov. 1942). The matter was raised again in June 1943
(ibid., vol. 390, col. 1143) when Bracken said that he had nothing to do with the
BBC's choice of M.P.s except that 'occasionally I am asked by Members of this
House why their talents are overlooked, and I often promise to pass on their
suggestions to the BBC'.

be maintained'. Such broadcasts, he argued, would 'bring back into our talks an element of vitality and independence which they sadly lack at present'.[1] In the same month, Norman Luker of the BBC's Talks Department saw Harold Wilson, then in the Ministry of Supply, and Frere of the Ministry of Labour about a series of programmes to be chaired by John Hilton called *Industrial Forum*, the counterpart on the industrial front of *War Commentary*;[2] and in March plans were drawn up for what was potentially at least a highly controversial discussion series on India, to be chaired by Sir Frederick Whyte: the first discussion was to be about Indian nationalism.[3]

Later in the year there were talks about a series on planning —'its purpose, its limitations and the risks involved in making it at once as comprehensive and as effective as its advocates seem to aim at making it'[4]—and a very general but lively discussion was broadcast dealing with free speech itself, in which Francis Williams, Maurice Webb and Harold Nicolson took part. Nicolson as a Governor and as an ex-Parliamentary Secretary of the Ministry of Information felt it necessary to insist that 'the BBC is not like a newspaper which can express its editorial opinion or repudiate responsibility for what it publishes.[5] . . . It must be inspired throughout by the utmost carefulness, which is something wholly different from timidity. And that carefulness must take constant account of the fact that when an idea or an opinion is broadcast it at once loses its true proportion and becomes magnified or amplified beyond life size.' Nicolson went on to advocate 'a round table method' of discussion, in which speakers of different persuasions would take part: this, he thought, would be a guarantee of 'responsibility'. Webb, however, a more dedicated party politician and a journalist, while welcoming the opportunity of frank controversy, permitted, as he said, for once by

---

[1] *Note by Maconachie for the Governors, 27 Feb. 1942.

[2] *Ibid.

[3] *Note by Maconachie, 11 March 1942.

[4] *Note by Maconachie, 27 Oct. 1942.

[5] Cf. an exchange of views in Parliament on this subject in 1941 when Maxton, the ILP member, asked, 'Have we not got a right to expect from the BBC, a publicly owned Corporation, the same kind of freedom for its employés [*sic*] as is granted by a publicly owned newspaper?' Duff Cooper replied, 'That is an entirely different matter', to which Maxton replied, 'I hope so'. (*Hansard*, vol. 369, cols. 1270–7.)

the BBC in war time, argued that 'the desire to achieve a balance leads to a quite unnecessary restriction on controversy. . . . The Left and the Right would both attack you less if you let them hammer away at each other more on the air than you do. Most of us, I am sure, would prefer good, honest red-blooded argument to some of the anaemic stuff which is so obviously designed to avoid treading on anyone's toes.'[1] Webb ended by admitting that 'the BBC has certainly given us considerable freedom in this series', and, in retrospect, Harold Nicolson touched on perhaps the most controversial long-term issue of all when in reply to a question as to whether it was a good thing for the BBC to have a monopoly he answered, 'That is for Parliament to decide. If they don't like the system, they can abolish it.'[2]

Within less than a month the BBC was involved in the most difficult set of 'controversial' issues which had arisen since the war began, issues which concerned not only ministers or M.P.s but the general public. The publication of the Beveridge Report in December 1942 is a key date in the social history of war-time Britain. 'Here at last,' as Alan Bullock has written, 'was a programme, more than that, a manifesto, on which people could fasten. For or against "Beveridge" became the test of allegiance to the future or the past, and those who were "for" were in no mood to listen to qualifications or doubts whatever the Government, caught up into other problems, might say.'[3]

The BBC was interested in the Report both as a document bearing on home affairs and because of what was thought to be its international significance. Bracken, moreover, as Minister of Information, was responsible more than any other minister for the spate of publicity which surrounded the initial publication of the Report.[4] Perhaps he was unaware of the furore it would raise, for while the Report quickened more intense political feeling than any other domestic issue since the outbreak of the war and for a time challenged the politics of consensus associated with the war effort, it was in no sense a

[1] *BBC script, 'Westminster and Beyond: Freedom of Speech', 12 Oct. 1942.
[2] See *The Listener*, 22 Oct. 1942.
[3] Bullock, op. cit., p. 225.
[4] The Ministry's Overseas Planning Committee produced a Special Issues Paper on the subject as early as 23 Nov. 1942.

revolutionary document. The philosophy behind it—the need for a comprehensive plan to enable all sections of the community to share in mutual insurance against want—was the same philosophy which had become associated with the war effort itself. 'I've been up the last three days and nights reading the first chapter of a book called *Gone with the Want* by that stout fellow Beveridge,' Tommy Handley explained, appearing as 'His Fatuity the Minister of Social Hilarity' in the current *ITMA* programme.

The timing of the Report ensured its topicality. Enormous numbers of it were sold, and the Gallup Poll investigators calculated that within two weeks of its publication nineteen out of twenty people had heard of it—an exceptionally high proportion—and nine out of ten believed it would be adopted.[1] Beveridge himself, well known as an occasional member of the *Brains Trust*, broadcast on the Report one day after it appeared[2] and took part in a radio discussion about it with Maurice Webb in *Westminster and Beyond* five days later.[3] The most was made of the Report also by the European and Overseas Services of the BBC.[4] Alan Bullock, Acting European Talks Editor, directed the attention of all European News Editors to it one day before it was published, and announced a

---

[1] See British Institute of Public Opinion, *The Beveridge Report and the Public*.

[2] The broadcast 'Security for All' is printed in *The Listener*, 10 Dec. 1942. Beveridge began and ended with a somewhat unconvincing reference to the Atlantic Charter. He paid a tribute to Churchill. 'I should like to see him complete . . . the work that he began in social insurance thirty years ago.'

[3] *The BBC was criticized later for introducing into its news bulletins on 1 Dec. 1942 what was said to be a misleading comparison between the cost of the Beveridge proposals and the cost of the war. This comparison, which was not made in the 6 o'clock News, had been drawn in order to try to make the financial figures more meaningful to the man in the street. The Governors were worried about this (Foot to Farquharson, 3 Dec. 1942), but there was nothing really wrong about the comparison as such. For M.P.s' views about the news reporting on an earlier occasion (22 Nov. 1942), see *Hansard*, vol. 385, cols. 1146–7.

[4] *There was an argument about the timing of news of the Report. The Government proposed to release the news abroad by cable at 6.0 p.m. on a Tuesday with an embargo on publication and on broadcasting until 3.0 a.m. the day after: this was to help the morning newspapers. Yet Ryan pertinently asked what should happen if the embargo were to be broken by someone else? Should the BBC give the news in its foreign-language bulletins but not in its English bulletins or in its English-language bulletins for overseas and not in its Home Service bulletins? 'The fact comes down to this,' he stated. 'Stories must be released as soon as they are issued, and if the Government wishes to hold up publication until this or that hour, then it must also hold up the release.' (Note of 27 Nov. 1942.)

series of talks on it by himself, Patrick Gordon Walker, Frank Hardie and William Gerhardi.[1]

There is no doubt that the propagandist use of the Report in broadcasts to Germany, in particular, worried Goebbels. The first German reaction was straightforward. 'British stocks of food are declining,' Breslau radio warned, 'British trade is slipping away . . . and all the factors in operation at the present are of a nature to make her economic position progressively worse. In these circumstances 100,000 words from Sir William Beveridge are most unlikely to make any difference to the people.'[2] Yet, when it was clear that there was enormous British interest in the plan, the first of the post-war plans to appear in what Beveridge himself was later to call 'the White Paper Chase',[3] German ground shifted somewhat. It was stated then that the Report was 'nothing more or less than a belated British attempt to imitate the social security programme of the National Socialist Party'.[4] Finally, it was pointed out that 'it is not yet known whether the Government will adopt the Report or any section of it'.[5]

[1] *Memorandum by Alan Bullock to all Editors, 1 Dec. 1942. Crossman also broadcast to Germany on the Report on 6 Dec. 1942, and on 5 Dec. Bullock broadcast a reply, 'Ley and Beveridge', to an article in Der Angriff. Beveridge himself was interviewed by Gordon Walker in the series Britain Today in the European English Service on 7 Feb. and in the German Service on 15 Feb. Beveridge also was interviewed for the North American Service on 6/7 Dec., for the Pacific Service on 16/17 Jan. and for the Empire Service on 21 Feb. 1943.

[2] *Broadcast from Breslau in English, 1 Dec. 1942. Cf. Workers' Challenge on the same day: 'What a bright and merry pastime for the long winter evenings. If you can't get a drink in a pub, or if the beer is too lousy to drink in any case, gather round the empty fireplace and discuss ninepence for fourpence in the good old style of 30 years ago. That's the way to keep the workers' spirits up.'

[3] A. Marwick, Britain in the Century of Total War (1968), p. 314.

[4] *Talk in English from Calais, 2 Dec. 1942. A later broadcast from Calais claimed that the German schemes were much better. 'Even in the 1880s Bismarck did not stoop to such half measures as those proposed by Beveridge when he started to tackle the social problem in Germany.' There were abundant further references to Beveridge's 'plutocratic' dependence on the big insurance companies.

[5] *NBBS (2 Dec.) deliberately took the line that 'we [i.e. the British, whom the Germans were claiming ran the station] cannot afford to chase shadows. Until we know if, how and when we are going to win the war, we have no right to speculate on post-war reconstruction.' This, interestingly enough, was not very different from Churchill's own position. Churchill made no mention of the Report in his Memoirs, although in Appendix F of vol. IV, pp. 861–2, he reprinted a paper, circulated to the Cabinet on the day he left for the Casablanca Conference (12 Jan. 1943), in which he stated that 'a dangerous optimism is growing up about the conditions which it will be possible to establish here after the war'.

The Government, in fact, became uneasy almost at once about the public reaction to the Beveridge Plan, and the more uneasy it became, the more uneasy large sections of the public became about the Government. There had been immense pre-publication publicity concerning the Report, and Beveridge, who loved publicity, had not improved matters in relation to the Right by telling the *Daily Telegraph* with stirring exaggeration that his proposals would 'take the country half way to Moscow'.[1] Although the Government had made it clear months earlier that the Report was Beveridge's own and that he alone must sign it, the Government had, after all, commissioned it.[2] Churchill might remain convinced—indeed grow more convinced—that it was dangerous to direct energies away from the war effort to discussions of social policy, but his *bête noire*, the *Daily Mirror*, warned him, even before the Report appeared and its contents were known, that it dealt with 'a subject which the mass of the people recognise as of vital interest to the welfare of the country as a whole. Vested, sectional or personal interests cannot be allowed to intervene.'[3]

As the Report became 'a symbol of the new Britain',[4] a right-wing reaction, extremely unpopular with most sections of the public, set in. Many Conservative newspapers, like the *Yorkshire Post*, had supported it: so did the *Daily Express*, *The Economist* and *The Times*. Conservatives, indeed, were divided. Some agreed with the spokesmen of the big insurance companies that it was 'a very bad report'. Some, the members of the Tory Reform Group, warmly approved of it. Others were lukewarm, 'welcoming it in principle but whittling it away by detailed criticism'.[5] When at last it was debated in Parliament in February 1943, Sir John Anderson, Sir Kingsley Wood and Oliver Lyttelton, as Government spokesmen, 'welcomed' it

[1] *Daily Telegraph*, 16 Nov. 1942. Cf. Attlee's comment quoted in F. Williams, *A Prime Minister Remembers* (1961), p. 57: 'Beveridge seemed to think the war ought to stop while his plan was put into effect.'

[2] Cmd. 6404, *Social Insurance and Allied Services* (1944), p. 19.

[3] *Daily Mirror*, 16 Nov. 1942. The article ended with the slogan 'Hands off the Beveridge Report'.

[4] Ibid., 16 Feb. 1943. Three days later the paper tried to put the issue in perspective: 'too much has been made of the Beveridge Report. . . . It is a beginning, not an end, and it must not be confused with reconstruction in the largest sense.'

[5] H. Nicolson, *Diaries and Letters, 1939–1945* (1968), p. 264.

but added, at Churchill's insistence, that legislation to implement it must await the advent of a new Government elected at the end of the war.[1] Their advocacy was so unconvincing to M.P.s that a Labour amendment introduced by James Griffiths and supported by a number of Conservatives, including Quintin Hogg and Lord Hinchingbrooke, and several Liberals, secured 119 votes. Only one member of the Parliamentary Labour Party who was not a minister voted with the Government; and Arthur Greenwood, an ex-minister, was prominent in the revolt. So, too, was Lloyd George who returned to Westminster to protest against 'the watering down' of Beveridge. The day before the debate, the *Manchester Guardian* had rightly summed up popular feeling when it wrote that 'unless we get the Beveridge Plan or something at least as comprehensive and bold, we shall not escape without injury to our national reputation abroad and without far-reaching damage at home'.[2]

The ramifications of the Report went further than a debate in the House of Commons, however, just because the Government had used it as 'a powerful weapon of propaganda' abroad.[3] Maconachie had noted before the debate that Captain Pickthorn, the Conservative M.P. for Cambridge University, had foreseen 'that the line taken in our European Service would be used by the Left as a lever on the Government to swallow the Beveridge Report'.[4] Yet more even than the BBC's European Service was involved. Indeed, the only veto influencing the BBC related to the Forces Programme.[5] On 5 November Barnes, the Director of Talks, had written to

---

[1] They said that in the meantime the Coalition Government would prepare the legislation.　　　　　　　　　　[2] *Manchester Guardian*, 15 Feb. 1943.

[3] See also the *Daily Herald*, 13 Feb. 1943. 'Acceptance in principle will not be enough unless it is accompanied by the promise of legislation during the war. The Government would lose immensely in prestige if it tried to confine itself to a vague benediction. That loss of prestige would not be confined to Britain. For, from the day of its appearance, the Beveridge Report was grasped and wielded by the Government as a powerful weapon of propaganda. It was proudly broadcast through the world as an advertisement of our Democratic accomplishments and aims.'

[4] *Maconachie to Barnes, 14 Feb. 1943; Farquharson to Grisewood, 2 April 1943.

[5] There was an interesting *Freedom Forum* discussion in the Overseas Service on the subject, reprinted in *The Listener*, 21 Jan. 1943. G. M. Young, H. J. Laski, Beveridge and F. W. Morgan, General Manager of the Prudential Assurance Company, took part. Ed Murrow was in the chair.

Maconachie stating that the War Office had long been pressing him to get John Hilton to discuss the Report in the first of his talks after its publication, but Maconachie, after consulting Radcliffe, said that there should be no such broadcast until after the debate in Parliament.[1] This was the view of the Secretary of State for War, Sir James Grigg, who made himself very unpopular with large numbers of soldiers for expressing it. Hilton, nonetheless, broadcast on the subject to Forces overseas on 2 December, when there was something of the same muddle as was to occur on 21 December, when the War Office withdrew an ABCA pamphlet on the Report which had been issued only two days before.[2]

Bracken and Grigg were obviously pursuing quite different tactics in relation to the Report, and Bracken never expressed any regret for the publicity he had given to it, even when hostile critics attacked him forcefully in the spring of 1943. When Captain Pickthorn asked him, for instance, in April 1943 whether he agreed that by allowing the Overseas Service of the BBC to devote so much attention to the Report he had taken a risk in encouraging people overseas to think that 'we are more interested in social reform than in questions of strategy and frontiers', he had no hesitation in replying that 'as continual publicity was given at the same time to the strategic results of the Allied landings in North Africa and to General Montgomery's triumphal progress along the shores of Libya, the hypothetical risks which my Hon. Friend has in mind did not arise'.[3]

The Beveridge Report had more than the symbolic interest which was noted at the time. In retrospect it is possible to see that its publication marked one critical stage in the social history of the war. Thereafter, it was never possible again to push post-war issues of reconstruction completely into the background. The Government was to produce its own White Paper on *Social Insurance* in 1944 and to set up a Ministry of National Insurance in the same year.[4] Beveridge was to go on

[1] *Barnes to Maconachie, 5 Nov. 1942; Maconachie to Barnes, 16 Nov. 1942.

[2] See W. Beveridge, *Power and Influence* (1953), p. 332.

[3] *Hansard*, vol. 388, cols. 1673–4; *Farquharson to Grisewood, 2 April 1943: 'I don't think that this propaganda [on Beveridge] has ever taken priority over our insistence that our national aim is to bring military aid to the Continent just as rapidly as we can.'   [4] Cmd. 6404 (1944).

to examine the economics of full employment, the subject also of an important White Paper in 1944, in many ways more important than the Beveridge Report.[1] R. A. Butler, the President of the Board of Education, was to produce not only a White Paper, *Educational Reconstruction* (1943),[2] but an important Act of Parliament (1944). There was to be a vague paper on an issue which everyone claimed needed attention, *A National Health Service* (1944).[3] Following the Uthwatt paper (1942),[4] which had dealt with land and development problems, Sir Patrick Abercrombie was to draw up his *Greater London Plan* (1944) at the request of the Ministry of Works and Buildings; other new Acts of Parliament, the Town and Country Planning Acts of 1943 and 1944, were to be passed; and a new Ministry, the Ministry of Town and Country Planning, was to be set up in 1943.[5] Finally action was to be implemented to build new houses—the first of them the

---

[1] W. Beveridge, *Full Employment in a Free Society* (1944); Cmd. 6527 (1944), *Employment Policy*. There is an excellent account of the background and implications of this report in Bullock, op. cit., pp. 225–31. In the *Freedom Forum* discussion for overseas listeners on the Beveridge Report on Social Security (see *The Listener*, 21 Jan. 1943), G. M. Young had suggested very pertinently that Beveridge should have concentrated on employment first and insurance second. 'The Government's first enquiry ought to have been with the possibilities of the employment of labour . . . [answering] the question not "What am I going to get?" but "What am I called upon to do?" That would be the positive side.' 'Don't you feel,' he asked Beveridge, 'that there is something of the Maginot Line in the minds of certain people that your plan is a defence against poverty and not an attack?'

[2] Cmd. 6458 (1943). When Butler expressed a desire to broadcast on the subject before a debate on education had taken place in Parliament, the Board would not agree. (*Board of Governors, *Minutes*, 8 July 1943.) Bracken objected to this decision, saying it was his prerogative to decide on this question of timing, but the Board's reasons were, in fact, accepted by the War Cabinet at a meeting on 13 July 1943. (*Note by R. N. Armfelt, 13 July 1943, after a telephone call from the Board of Education.) There was little that was controversial about the White Paper. Indeed, when Parliament debated the subject, it was, as *The Times* put it, 'of one mind to a degree rare in Parliamentary annals. . . . Not a single voice was raised in favour of holding up or whittling down any of the proposals for educational advance.' (*The Times*, 31 July 1943.) The Board of Governors passed a resolution at Nicolson's suggestion, however, on 10 Feb. 1944, stating that 'when a debate on a major matter of public policy is imminent or is actually taking place in Parliament, the BBC cannot allow the broadcasting of Ministerial or other *ex parte* statements thereon'.

[3] Cmd. 6502 (1944). See H. Eckstein, *The English Health Service* (1959), pp. 139 ff., 155 ff.

[4] Cmd. 6386 (1942). 'Uthwatt now' had become a popular cry, rather like 'Beveridge now', when it seemed likely that the Report would be shelved.

[5] See P. Abercrombie, *Greater London Plan*, Cmd. 1944 (1945).

prefabricated 'Portal' temporary houses—as well as to make 'new towns', and a first step was to be taken with the passing of the Housing (Temporary Accommodation) Act of 1944.[1] In the middle of these changes Lord Woolton became Minister of Reconstruction, with a seat in the War Cabinet, in November 1943. The public certainly expected all this debate about post-war policy to lead directly to action, as it had expected the discussions on the Beveridge Report to do. Aspirations had to be translated into blueprints. 'There is a rapidly growing interest in post-war problems,' Mann wrote in a memorandum circulated to the other Governors of the BBC in March 1943. 'The BBC has, I submit, a valuable service to perform in stimulating healthy discussion on these matters to help the nation to reach agreement in true democratic fashion.'[2]

Mann believed that most of the problems could and should be tackled in 'an all-Party or non-Party spirit'. He wanted the BBC to arrange for discussion of controversial subjects on a 'comprehensive basis' with more emphasis on what different people held in common than on 'comparatively minor points of difference'. He felt that this was necessary if the country was not to be thrown into violent disagreement at the end of the war, 'at a time when it is vital that we should offer Europe wide leadership in regard to still greater problems of an international character'. Yet this view was impossible completely to uphold. The party system in Britain was not dead, but rather in suspended animation. While there was a substantial measure of agreement about future social policy among people from different parties—the Liberal Action Group, the Tory reformers and Herbert Morrison, for example —and such agreement was to lay the foundation of a tacit post-war consensus, there was also scope for renewed party controversy once it was clear that the war was being won. The cry which had been raised by 'independents' in 1941 and 1942 that the pre-war idea of 'party' was obsolete, the cry of independents both of Left and Right, proved no more than a cry in the night. At that time it had been the 'independents' who grumbled about lack of access 'nationally' to the

[1] Cmd. 6609 (1945).
[2] *Note by Mann, 10 Mar. 1943.

microphone[1]—at a time when party spokesmen, tied by the war-time political truce, were grumbling about the fact that they were being outbid by 'independents' locally in their own constituencies. From late 1943 onwards, however, the men of the parties came back into their own. 'Nationalization', in particular, was to divide the main parties sharply and, so it seemed at the time, irrevocably. Beveridge himself, an oppo-nent of nationalization, was eventually to become associated with the Liberal Party and a candidate at the first post-war elections.[2]

All this was far ahead early in 1943, as Bracken implied, yet Churchill had to respond immediately to the new mood as reflected in the response to Beveridge's Report. On 21 March 1943, therefore, he broadcast for once not on the war but on a 'Four Year Plan'. He ranged back in time to his own work as a promoter of national insurance before the First World War and declared himself a supporter of compulsory insurance in the future 'for all classes for all purposes from the cradle to the grave'.[3] *The Economist* welcomed his 'conversion',[4] but on the whole the speech was not a great success. It did not follow the line of the Right,[5] and it did not give much satisfaction to the Left. 'Eager reformers,' the *Manchester Guardian* stated, 'are asked to pipe down and trust the Government.'[6] Churchill still believed firmly and stated categorically that winning the

[1] 'We cannot suit all tastes in the House unless we get someone like the Admir-able Crichton to enter the BBC,' Bracken exclaimed (*Hansard*, vol. 388, col. 174). It was in these circumstances that the ILP member, John McGovern, gave notice in February 1943 (ibid., vol. 386, cols. 899–900) that he would move that 'more opportunities should be given to the propagation of the different shades of opinion on political, social, religious and medical questions so that the Corporation should be used as an instrument of democracy instead of one for the creation of an authoritarian regime in this country'. (Ibid., vol. 388, col. 835.) See above, pp. 58–9. Bevan, Shinwell, Sir Herbert Williams, Hore-Belisha and Sir John Wardlaw-Milne were among those who did not vote.

[2] Party pressures were immediately apparent when the BBC dealt with the White Paper on the National Health Service in 1944. Both Labour and Conserva-tive M.P.s attacked the BBC in relation to a talk by 'the Radio Doctor', who was an organizer of BMA resistance. (*Hansard*, vol. 399, cols. 363, 495–6.)

[3] The speech is printed in full in C. Eade (ed.), *War Speeches*, vol. II (1952), pp. 424 ff.

[4] *The Economist*, 27 March 1943.

[5] The right-wing attack on Beveridge, more represented in periodicals than in Parliament, made much of the need for 'individualism' and assailed what it called 'the fusty muddle-headed Beveridge mentality' (*Truth*, 2 June 1944).

[6] *Manchester Guardian*, 22 March 1943.

war against Germany was the prior task on which everything else depended. It was untrue, he warned his hearers, that 'we shall soon all be able to get back to the politics and Party fights of peace-time'. Suspicions lingered. Such a return to the past was not what the supporters of the Beveridge Report wanted, and they found it difficult, given Churchill's qualifications, to accept his argument that he was merely enabling 'all our political forces to march forward to the main objective in unity, and so far as possible in step'. His language, moreover, when he talked about education, for instance, bore little relation to theirs: it reflected a quite different cast of mind, a divergent experience.[1]

Beveridge heard Churchill's broadcast in Oxford and welcomed the reference to himself as a 'friend', even though there was no reference to his Report. He rang up Lady Violet Bonham Carter and asked her whether he could now have the chance of giving a broadcast on the subject himself. A reference by Churchill to 'people not working all-out at the moment' made him feel he could do something to get people to work harder. Lady Violet, who was sympathetic, replied that whether or not Beveridge could broadcast was a matter of high policy; Foot, who described the whole topic as 'very tricky', was doubtful whether Beveridge was the right man to do what he said he wanted to do; Maconachie felt that the BBC in any case had given too much publicity both to the Report and to Beveridge himself;[2] and Bracken declared more simply that he had no objection to Beveridge broadcasting provided that he confined himself to the main war-time theme he had mentioned. When the Board of Governors considered the matter formally, they resolved that while 'they would not, on their own initiative, have extended an invitation to any speaker to broadcast a comment on the Prime Minister's recent speech, they consider in this matter of high policy affecting the war effort [that] the Government should accept the full responsibility for such a broadcast, if given, including full approval of the script'.[3]

---

[1] Churchill went to the microphone again in May 1944 to describe what the Government had already done to achieve the objectives of the 'Four Year Plan'.

[2] *Maconachie to Foot, 24 March 1943.

[3] *Board of Governors, Minutes, 25 March 1943.

The matter was settled when Beveridge made it clear to Foot that he did not wish to give a broadcast on these restricted lines. Beveridge, Foot told Bracken, 'was more than satisfied with the Prime Minister's speech, but was doubtful whether the Government as a whole had the same feeling as the Prime Minister'. He intended to concentrate on this theme, which was clearly unsuitable for the BBC, in an article in *The Observer*.[1] A few months later, when Shinwell asked Bracken why no M.P. had been invited to broadcast on social policy following Churchill's speech and whether he agreed that M.P.s should be given the chance 'to propound views on reconstruction', he was told that 'though I am sure that every member of this House has interesting views on reconstruction, I doubt if the Governors of the BBC could accommodate all of them in their overcrowded programmes'.[2]

Members of the House became more rather than less restive about their own position in relation to the BBC after the Beveridge debates.[3] They continued to ask for further details of how M.P.s were chosen to broadcast by the BBC;[4] to criticize *The Week in Westminster*;[5] to complain about the way in which they had been reported or to grumble that they had not been reported;[6] to claim the right to answer Ministerial

---

[1] *Record of telephone conversation, 25 March 1943.

[2] *Hansard*, vol. 391, col. 906.

[3] See, for example, questions by Tom Driberg in *Hansard*, vol. 389, cols. 158–9.

[4] 57 M.P.s, other than Ministers, broadcast during the twelve months beginning 1 Oct. 1942. Liddall asked why Conservatives had given only 70 out of 174 broadcasts; Moelwyn Hughes, a Labour M.P., asked why they had given so many. Thurtle pointed out that some of the broadcasts were quite non-political (e.g. *Desert Island Discs*, then a new programme), and when pressed by Labour members, replied—he was, of course, a Labour M.P. himself—'that my Hon. and Learned Friend must face this fact: for good or ill nearly two-thirds of the members of the House are members of the Conservative Party' (ibid., vol. 397, col. 845).

[5] Ibid., vol. 391, cols. 2288–9. Shinwell said some of the programmes had been 'incompetent and not at all objective' and asked why journalists could not be used. Bracken replied that a competent journalist was not always a good broadcaster and that he had no intention of interfering with the BBC's right to choose speakers. If he did, 'Hon. Members would say "Why was I not asked to speak?"'

[6] The BBC, as Bracken pointed out, had three or four minutes to give to Parliament while *The Times* had six or seven columns. The following complaints were made against its reporting in 1942 and 1943: John Parker, 3 Feb. 1942; J. J. Davidson, 26 Feb. 1942; R. R. Stokes, 13 April 1942; L. Hore-Belisha, 2 July, 1 Oct. 1942; L. Silkin, 5 Oct. 1942; E. Granville, 17 Dec. 1942; Sir Herbert Williams and T. Levy, 25 Mar. 1943; L. Silkin, 12 May 1943; Alfred Edwards, 11 June 1943; Russell Thomas, 16 June 1943; the Minister of Information, 5 Aug.

[cont.

broadcasts;[1] even to challenge the BBC's constitution.[2] Bracken had told the BBC specifically in October 1942 that he wished it to be quite free to choose its own speakers in the well-established *The Week in Westminster* series and to decide for itself on the number in the panel and the rotation in which the members would speak. He admitted, however, that there was a difference of opinion between himself and the Labour Chief Whip on this issue. Bracken would have preferred that M.P.s should not be used in the series, although he did not press his case: Whiteley requested that the party whips should be consulted.[3]

The BBC continued to use M.P.s and to exclude journalists.[4] It also managed its own rota. From September 1939 until May 1943 the BBC had followed the rota Conservative, Labour, Liberal, Conservative, Labour, National Liberal, but in May 1943, after the Minister had said that he did not

[1] *Hansard*, vol. 396, col. 203.

[2] See below, p. 619.

[3] *Hansard*, vol. 387, cols. 166–7. When Granville asked, 'Now that the Brains Trust has become controversial, does the Rt. Hon. Gentleman not think that it would be better if this feature were controversial, or would it be better to allow Lobby correspondents to become radio reporters of Parliament?', Bracken replied, 'I have yet to discover that a report of the proceedings of Parliament should be made controversial. I thought the object of a report was to give an accurate account of the Debates in the House.'

[4] *Maconachie to Armfelt, 10 Jan. 1942: 'M.P.s are in a better position to speak freely without causing offence and getting us into P.R. trouble than any other class of speakers.'

1943; Capt. Cunningham-Reid, who argued that he was being left out because he did not always 'see eye to eye' with the Minister, 22 Sept. 1943; Quintin Hogg, 23 Sept. 1943; Miss E. Rathbone, 27 Sept. 1943; F. Messer, 23 Nov. 1943. *In April 1943 the following table was prepared, based on reporting since 19 Jan. 1943:

SPEAKERS MENTIONED BY NAME

	Conservatives	Labour	Liberals	Others
BBC	113 (46%)	88 (36%)	31 (13%)	13 (5%)
The Times	413 (46%)	324 (36%)	79 (9%)	83 (9%)
Daily Express	73 (52%)	54 (38%)	4 (3%)	10 (7%)

Ryan rightly pointed out (*Memorandum to Foot, 9 Oct. 1943) that 'the suggestion that we should give more time to Parliament would not . . . save us from the criticism of members. The longer we made our summary, the more M.P.s would be liable to complain that we had left something out that we ought to have put in. For even the most optimistic view of what the public would stand does not envisage more than half an hour's summary.'

think the BBC need invite National Liberals as such,[1] the rota was simplified to read Conservative, Labour, Liberal. It was also decided in April 1943 that one out of twelve talks should be open to an M.P. outside the main political parties,[2] and Willie Gallacher, the Communist M.P., duly spoke in the series on 12 June 1943. The idea of supplementing such talks with comments from a full-time lobby correspondent was frequently made inside the BBC,[3] yet it was decided not to appoint one on the grounds that 'he would be liable to be challenged on every half sentence'.[4] From January 1941 onwards the BBC had had at its disposal a small gallery holding six people at Westminster, and it was to be consulted by the Select Committee of the House on the rebuilding of Parliament.

The choice of speakers for Postscripts, which had been such a highly controversial matter earlier during the war,[5] was gradually handed over to the BBC. A 'freer hand' was asked for in October 1942,[6] and in March 1943 it was accepted that sole responsibility for the broadcasts lay with the BBC.[7] Although many Postscripts had very little to do with politics— and Maconachie at least came to believe that they no longer need have anything to do with morale[8]—M.P.s were jealous of their 'rights' here also. One member, Austin Hopkinson, quipped, for instance, that a Postscript by an M.P., 'a careful paraphrase of the Sermon on the Mount, had been turned down on the grounds—first that it was fascist, second that it was anti-working-class, and third that it was anti-Christian'. Bracken, who was well able to deal with jokes of this kind, replied aptly that the BBC did not like repetition.[9] On this kind of question he was very forthright indeed in all his parliamentary answers: only rarely did he show any signs of

---

[1] *Graves to Maconachie, 22 July 1942.

[2] *Board of Governors, *Minutes*, 15 April 1943.

[3] *See, for example, a Memorandum by Mann, 4 July 1943.

[4] *Ryan to Foot, 9 Oct. 1943. See also an important background paper, 'Parliamentary Reporting'.

[5] See above, pp. 320–2. As late as May 1941, Duff Cooper insisted that Ministers should have a 'first call' on Postscripts. (*Ryan to Maconachie, 21 May 1941.)

[6] *Board of Governors, *Minutes*, 8 Oct. 1942.

[7] *Controllers' Conference, *Minutes*, 3 March 1943.

[8] *Note by Maconachie, 28 Jan. 1943.

[9] *Hansard*, vol. 385, cols. 330–1.

losing his patience, and he was sharp only when it was necessary. When a pacifist M.P. asked him, for example, as he had often been asked, whether a few minutes out of the BBC's twenty-four hours schedule should be devoted to 'minority opinions', he replied, 'if those who take a minority view are anxious to impede the war effort, the BBC will give them no time whatever'.[1]

Political controversies continued to centre not only on M.P.s but, as earlier in the war, on the *Brains Trust* and on J. B. Priestley. When, for instance, in August 1943 the *Brains Trust* was revived after a brief pause, the Governors still insisted that political questions should not be discussed by the team.[2] They had decided a year earlier that the team should not include M.Ps.[3] They refused also to introduce a new 'political question and answer' programme, on the grounds that it was not wise policy to emphasize party divisions in broadcasting in war time.[4] When proposals were put forward for a *Questions for Tomorrow* series in November 1943, they asked for a more explicit title and for a list of speakers.[5]

The last struggle about Priestley also came in 1943. In February of that year Priestley had proposed that he should give 'not fewer than six talks to strengthen public morale at an hour of great tension': he was anxious, knowing nothing of the military time-table, that his talks should coincide with the opening of 'the Second Front'. Priestley had broadcast regularly and with great success in the North American Service of the BBC from 17 July 1941 to 4 September 1942 and from 24 December 1942.[6] When the BBC decided that

---

[1] Ibid., vol. 400, col. 747.

[2] *Board of Governors, *Minutes*, 19 Aug. 1943.

[3] *Ibid., 27 Aug. 1942.

[4] *Ibid., 23 Sept. 1943. See above, pp. 563–4. The first question asked about political bias in the *Brains Trust* dated back to 21 May 1941 (Ryan to Ogilvie). On 18 June Nicolls prepared a memorandum showing that so far 22 left-wing, 25 right-wing and three 'doubtful' broadcasts had been given, though 'the political balance . . . is, of course, offset by the fact that two of the three members of the Permanent Brains Trust are left'.

[5] *Board of Governors, *Minutes*, 18 Nov. 1943.

[6] He gave 40 talks (*Britain Speaks*) in the Overseas Service in 1942, one Overseas Christmas Day broadcast, one New Year Resolution, five *Answering You* talks, two feature programmes—*St. George and the Dragon* and *The Ships*—and one contribution to *Radio Newsreel*. Part of his Christmas Day broadcast was rebroadcast in the Home programme, *The Town that Stayed at Home*. Some of the broadcasts were

he should be allowed to do six talks, but that they should not await an Allied invasion of Europe—it said that it considered him 'one of its most able broadcasters to English-speaking audiences overseas'—a number of Conservative M.P.s— Liddall, Lees-Jones, Commander Bower and Capt. Alan Graham—gave notice of a parliamentary motion stating 'that in the opinion of this House, the continuing practice of the BBC in giving excessive preference to Left Wing speakers, such as Mr. Priestley, calls for censure'. The BBC retorted that no preference was shown for left-wing speakers, but full consideration was given to 'good broadcasters of the schools of thought able to hold the listener's attention at home and overseas'.[1]

Two amendments to the motion, both favourable to the BBC, were tabled by other M.P.s. A rival Conservative group— Hogg, Molson, Tree, Sir Alfred Beit and Viscount Hinchingbrooke, the nucleus of the Tory Reform Committee—suggested deleting everything in the motion after the first 'that' and replacing it with the diametrically opposed resolution that 'this House applauds the present impartiality of the BBC in the selection of speakers, approves of the principle that the primary qualification should be broadcasting ability and not political opinion, and supports the policy of editorial freedom from political interference embodied in the Charter of the BBC and respected by the present Minister of Information'. Silkin went further, and his proposed motion stated flatly and concisely that 'this House welcomes the increased opportunities offered by the BBC for the expression of varied points of view on matters of public interest and, in particular, congratulates the BBC upon the revival of broadcasts by Mr. J. B. Priestley'.

The motions were not debated, nor would the Clerk at the Table accept a question asking in effect that the Minister should arrange for six talks by a speaker with an opposite

[1] *The motion was down for 29 June 1943. For the story, see the BBC's Brief for the Minister, 1 July 1943.

criticized in Parliament. On 29 July 1942, for example, a Conservative accused him of broadcasting to America 'views tending to show that the Nazi Party and the rest of the German people are different', while upholders of the opposite thesis were not allowed to broadcast. Bracken denied that this was so (*Hansard*, vol. 382, cols. 522–3).

viewpoint to that of Priestley.[1] If the motions had been debated, the discussion would doubtless have followed the same line and ended in the same kind of outcome as the discussion initiated from the Left by McGovern a few months earlier.[2] In the month when it might have been debated, there was a diverting side issue. Howard Thomas had designed a new programme series, *Everybody's Mike*, an 'audience participation' show of a new type, in the first of which six M.P.s, three women M.P.s pitted against three men, were to answer questions put to them by the comedian Naunton Wayne. The M.P.s had anticipated taking part in a kind of Brains Trust, and when they learned of what was intended, they refused to participate. Quintin Hogg, one of the six, said not only that they had been misled but, in more general terms, that 'although most Members of Parliament are anxious to get in touch with people and not in the least anxious to stand on their dignity, there is a point at which it becomes highly improper for them to allow themselves to be guyed innocently or intentionally. . . . It rests with all bodies responsible for the dissemination of information, to treat our democratic institutions with a certain amount of respect, and the fact that in this case no disrespect was intended in some ways constitutes an aggravation and not an excuse, because it shows, on the part of those responsible for the programme, a complete failure to understand the nature of our constitution.'[3]

The Governors agreed with Hogg,[4] and Foot duly wrote him a letter saying that even if M.P.s had agreed to take part in *Everybody's Mike* 'with their eyes completely open', it would have been quite wrong for the BBC to provide an opportunity for them to do so. 'The House of Commons is the

[1] *Note by Farquharson, 24 June 1943. The Clerk at the Table acted on the advice of the Minister, and different Ministers, unlike the pre-war Postmasters-General who were consistent in their behaviour, had taken up different positions about such questions throughout the war. G. Strauss had been restrained by the Speaker from proceeding with a motion on the adjournment on the question of the banning of Sir Hugh Roberton and the Glasgow Orpheus Choir (19 Dec. 1940) simply because the Parliamentary Secretary had advised him that the Minister believed the BBC to be directly responsible. Yet Duff Cooper had made himself answerable when Sir Archibald Southby on another motion on the adjournment had raised the Narvik episode on 11 June 1940. (See above, pp. 602–3.)

[2] See above, p. 213.

[3] *Hogg to Foot, 9 June 1943.

[4] *Board of Governors, *Minutes*, 10 June 1943.

greatest democratic institution in the world, and the BBC has a clear and obvious duty to democracy in general and to democracy in this country in particular to present the House of Commons (and this of course includes all its Members) to listeners only in such a way as is consistent with its true position, dignity and importance.'[1]

The background to this exchange, with its Whiggish overtones, was mentioned in *The Star*,[2] and Howard Thomas was called before Foot to explain himself. He satisfied the Director-General that there had been no intention to deceive.[3] 'There should be a Corporation rule running through all output Divisions,' Foot told Nicolls, 'with regard to the procedure to be followed if it is desired to invite Members of either the House of Lords or House of Commons to broadcast, and it seems to be my responsibility that no such rule is apparently in force at the moment.'[4] Somewhat to redress the balance suggested by this story, at one of the two meetings at which the Governors considered the case, they decided also, by a coincidence of timing, to reaffirm the maintenance of freedom of political activities of all members of the BBC's staff qualified only by 'the interests of broadcasting'.[5] Charles James Fox would have understood all the issues at stake on these two contrasting occasions far more easily than J. B. Priestley.

Religious broadcasting involved even older issues, and frequently during the war it was as much caught up in controversy as politics. Particularly after William Temple left York and became Archbishop of Canterbury in 1941,[6] the frontiers between religion and politics became blurred. Archbishop Garbett of York spoke language that raised no problems. He believed that the war was a 'war of religion, like the wars of the sixteenth or seventeenth centuries', 'a struggle to determine which of two sharply contrasted notions of the right

---

[1] *Foot to Hogg, 15 June 1943.
[2] *The Star*, 9 June 1943.
[3] *Board of Governors, *Minutes*, 17 June 1943.
[4] *Foot to Nicolls, 9 June 1943.
[5] *Board of Governors, *Minutes*, 17 June 1943.
[6] The enthronement ceremonies of Temple at Canterbury and at York of Garbett, former Bishop of Winchester and an important figure in earlier broadcasting history (see Briggs, *The Golden Age of Wireless*, pp. 227–49), were both broadcast in 1942.

way to order human life shall have scope and influence in the next period of history'.[1] Temple, by contrast, dwelt not on comparisons with the past but on dreams of the future; 'he now openly preaches Socialism', 'Chips' Channon wrote in his diary, 'from a platform which he shares with Cripps'.[2] When he was criticized from the Right, his friends on the Left complained that the criticisms, like those of Beveridge, were calculated to raise doubts as to the 'genuineness in some quarters' of the demand for a new post-war world.[3] 'Neutrality in religion is impossible,' Temple once told Graves, 'because religion covers the whole field of thought and conduct.'[4]

In stating this, Temple, of course, was not speaking only for himself. The Malvern Conference of clergymen and laymen in January 1941 had advocated the enunciation of a Christian social programme which by its nature was bound to provoke right-wing opinion as much as any political statement on the part of the 1941 Committee. Yet such a programme had great appeal to many of the same kind of people who followed Priestley in turning hopefully from the tattered past and the stormy present towards a new post-war society. Temple's own Penguin book, *Christianity and Social Order* (1942), sold 139,000 copies.[5] There were echoes of all these developments inside the BBC; more than echoes, indeed, for whoever the Archbishop of Canterbury had been, there had always been close co-operation between him and the Director-General. Moreover, Temple's biographer, Iremonger, had been the predecessor of Welch as Director of Religious Broadcasting.

Welch himself believed that 'religion is concerned with men in society, and therefore with politics and economics', but he accepted the argument put before him by some of his colleagues in the BBC that this concern should relate to 'the moral and religious principles which Christians believe should test and guide these two activities of mankind' rather than to 'details of planning'.[6] This, indeed, was one of the points set out in what

---

[1] *Script for Transatlantic Discussion, 7 Jan. 1942.
[2] R. Rhodes James (ed.), *Chips: the Diaries of Sir Henry Channon* (1967), p. 337.
[3] *The Times*, 2 Nov. 1942.   [4] *Temple to Graves, 15 Jan. 1943.
[5] F. A. Iremonger, *William Temple* (1948), p. 435.
[6] *'Broadcasting Policy', No. 6, Religious Broadcasting, Feb. 1943. In a sermon before the University of Cambridge on the subject of religious broadcasting, delivered on 8 Nov. 1942, Welch dwelt on this theme.

came to be called 'the Concordat' of August 1941 after talks between Nicolls and Maconachie, who were both uneasy about 'controversial' religious broadcasting. There was an obvious need for clarification if not for definition. Duff Cooper had told the House of Commons in March 1941 that it was not 'considered desirable that politics should enter into religious broadcasts',[1] and although Harold Nicolson had issued a gloss that 'politics' in this phrase meant 'political controversy or party politics and nothing more',[2] doubts remained. How much control should the BBC exercise over its religious speakers? Already it more or less excluded pacifists and representatives of 'non-orthodox' religions like Christian Science.[3] Was it now going to control, if not to exclude, Christian Socialists as well as clergymen like the Bishop of Chichester who had their own ideas both about the conduct of the war and the kind of 'social order' which would emerge at the end of it?

The Concordat laid down that Ministers of Religion as such had 'no competence to speak on the detailed working out' of matters relating to politics or economics, but only on 'the moral and religious principles and criteria by which political and economic situations, proposals and policies should, according to their belief, be decided'. Those religious speakers who were 'competent' in politics or economics should make it clear when they preached a sermon or gave a talk whether they were speaking as 'experts' or not, and whether their views were 'controversial' or not. This formula was accepted by Ogilvie and approved by Powell on 23 September 1941; and from that date onwards all scripts of war-time religious broadcasts were scrutinized by Maconachie, whose comments were then passed on to Nicolls for such action as he considered necessary. The BBC's Central Religious Advisory Committee, CRAC, accepted 'the Concordat' at its meeting in October 1941.[4]

---

[1] *Hansard*, vol. 370, col. 569–70. Hely-Hutchinson had complained against religious talks which included 'controversial political diatribes'.

[2] *Maconachie to Nicolson, 28 March 1941.

[3] Different views had been expressed on the Board of Governors about religious broadcasting in 1942. 'Some thought the Director of Religious Broadcasting was choosing speakers who were lukewarm in their support of the war effort.' (*Minutes*, 11 June 1942.)

[4] *Central Religious Advisory Committee, *Minutes*, 2 Oct. 1941.

Temple's position was somewhat different. He wrote in his Penguin book that 'it is of crucial importance that the Church acting in its corporate capacity should not commit itself to any particular policy. . . . The Church is committed to the everlasting Gospel and the Creeds which formulate it; it must never commit itself to an ephemeral programme of detailed action.'[1] The key words here were 'in its corporate capacity'. Difficulties were bound to arise when Temple spoke not as Archbishop but as a 'Christian citizen' advocating particular policies. Should the BBC treat his opinions simply as news or should it allow him to explain them over the air? The Governors turned to this issue in October 1942, and after their Vice-Chairman, Millis, had drawn critical attention to a speech delivered by the Archbishop at the Albert Hall expressing his own distinct views on politics and economics, the Governors decided that 'if this tendency were developed in religious broadcasts, adequate representation should be given to opposite views'.[2]

'The Concordat' had by no means settled everything, therefore, and some Governors, like some BBC officials, continued to worry about religious programmes; for example, a series of Friday evening talks, planned in 1942, which were designed 'to bring the Christian revelation to bear on contemporary social and political issues, both national and international'. Among the speakers suggested, there were several known critics of the shape of Britain as it was—Maurice Reckitt, Canon V. A. Demant and H. A. Mess.[3] Two months later in December 1942 the Governors approved every proposal put forward for future programmes by the Director of Religious Broadcasting except that for a series on religion and politics.[4]

Most religious talks avoided such controversial themes. They dwelt instead on prayer and worship or on theological or ecclesiastical questions, controversial perhaps in a different sense. To consider war-time religious broadcasting in proper perspective, it is necessary to take account not only of talks but of programmes with an enormous popular following, like the

---

[1] W. Temple, *Christianity and Social Order*, p. 19.
[2] *Board of Governors, *Minutes*, 8 Oct. 1942.
[3] *Ibid., 1 Oct. 1942.
[4] *Ibid., 3 Dec. 1942.

Sunday Half Hour of community singing which continued to be broadcast at 8.30 p.m. in the Forces Programme and Selby Wright's highly successful broadcasts, also in the Forces Programme on Wednesday evenings after the 9 o'clock News.[1]

There were also series of talks like C. S. Lewis's eight talks on 'Christian Behaviour', broadcast in September and October 1942, which created widespread interest, and there were others which set out to bring together Christians of different denominations in 'united witness', like another series of 1942 broadcasts called *How Christians Worship*.[2] One of the most interesting aspects of this activity was that as the war went on religious programmes were no longer concentrated so much on Sundays but were spread throughout the whole week.[3]

There was, however, one specifically and deliberately controversial religious programme, *The Anvil*, which early in 1943 took the place of the religious service hitherto broadcast on Sunday evenings. The chairman was a layman, Professor Victor Murray—Crossman was the first person to be approached to fulfil this task[4]—and the team of four represented 'the three main strands in British Christianity'—Anglican (Canon F. A. Cockin), Free Church (Professor R. D. Whitehorn), and Roman Catholic (Father Agnellus Andrew). The fourth member, Mary Trevelyan, was an Anglican. The team endeavoured 'to give honest Christian answers to listeners' doubts, difficulties and enquiries', and the purpose was said to be 'to help, not to entertain'. The BBC, which had accepted the idea of the programme only after prolonged discussion and insisted that it should contain nothing that smacked either of triviality or of humour,[5] was at pains inside its walls as much as outside to insist that 'there were no grounds of comparison of *The Anvil* with the *Brains Trust* programmes'—since the technique was necessarily different[6]—yet such comparisons were, in

---

[1] The Rev. Ronald Selby Wright was seconded by the Army to become the BBC's Radio Padre in April 1942.

[2] In the planning of this series, which was introduced by Temple, Welch was assisted by an inter-denominational team inside the BBC, including the Rev. Eric Fenn, a minister of the English Presbyterian Church, A. C. F. Beales, a Catholic layman, and the Rev. Cyril Taylor, a talented musician. There was also an oecumenical service on Whit Sunday 1942 in which continental Protestants took part.

[3] *BBC Year Book, 1945,* p. 42.   [4] *Fenn to Crossman, 27 Aug. 1942.

[5] *Board of Governors, *Minutes*, 3 Sept. 1942.

[6] *Controllers' Conference, *Minutes*, 3 Feb. 1943.

fact, drawn within the Corporation itself. An early paper on the subject began with the words, 'The experience of the present Brains Trust shows that there are many listeners who look to it for guidance on religious questions with which it cannot properly deal.'[1] In fact, some of the same difficulties arose as in the case of the *Brains Trust*, not least the difficulty of ensuring that the main differences of opinion were genuinely and openly expressed. One real difference between the two programmes was that questions put to the *Anvil* team were seen beforehand by the members—this disappointed part of the audience— although the answers were not written out. Nonetheless, in a war-time society where concern for religion was real, the programme created great interest, and some four thousand questions were submitted during the first series of six programmes.

The Anvil was not as controversial as Dorothy Sayers's remarkable cycle of religious plays, *The Man Born to be King*, had been. In February 1940 Welch approached Miss Sayers, the well-known writer of detective stories, to ask whether she would write a series of plays on the life of Jesus to be broadcast in Children's Hour programmes on Sundays. Miss Sayers had already written a Nativity play, *He That Should Come*, which had been broadcast at Christmas 1938. She replied that she would do a new series only on condition that she could break with stage convention and introduce Jesus as a character: 'in broadcasting we are freed from some of the obvious objections which attend the visual representation of Christ by an actor'. She wished to choose language for the plays 'which is neither slangy on the one hand, nor Wardour Street on the other'.[2]

Her acceptance, however, was merely the first of a number of hurdles which Welch had to surmount. First, Ogilvie secured the agreement of the Lord Chamberlain, the Earl of Clarendon, whether or not this was strictly necessary.[3] Second, there were problems about the producer Miss Sayers wished to have chosen,

[1] *Religious Broadcasting: Programme Schedule for Oct.-Dec. 1942, Appendix 3, 'The Anvil'. [2] Miss Sayers to Welch, 18 Feb. 1940.

[3] *The Earl of Clarendon to Ogilvie, 28 Aug. 1940. The Lord Chamberlain added ominously that 'if . . . you were intending at some future date to televise any programmes of this description . . . it would create a very difficult position, in view of our existing regulations'. (See also Control Board (Home), *Minutes*, 14 Nov. 1941.)

and after arguing with Children's Hour organizers she said
that she would cancel the contract unless Val Gielgud produced
the cycle: only when Nicolls agreed that Gielgud should do so
would she co-operate.[1] Third, Welch himself insisted that the
Brains Trust would have to be re-timed so that it did not
provide the alternative programme on the Forces wavelength.[2]
Fourth, an actor had to be found to play Jesus who was 'a
believing active Christian and a member of the Church':
eventually Robert Speaight was selected. Fifth, although the
BBC had not expected a row, there was a row following a
lively Press Conference on 10 December, when Miss Sayers
read a long prepared statement explaining what she wanted
to do—'to present the story not in the form of a devotional
exercise, but primarily as a piece of real life, enacted by human
beings against the stormy social and political background of
first-century Palestine'. She was anxious, she said, to avoid all
kind of 'genteel piety in the stained glass manner'.[3] When she
had finished, the reporters present asked her to read extracts
from the dialogue, and some of the extracts they heard were
subsequently used by some of the popular newspapers to
attack Miss Sayers. In one case the attack was so violent that
Miss Sayers threatened to bring a libel action.[4]

As soon as the public read the incomplete accounts of what
was being planned, large numbers of people, none of whom of
course had read the script, protested directly to the BBC, to
the Minister of Information, to the Archbishop of Canterbury,
or even to the Prime Minister.[5] The Lord's Day Observance
Society not only complained to Ogilvie, describing the project
as 'an act of irreverence bordering on the blasphemous',[6]
but printed a full-page hostile advertisement in the *Church*

[1] *Nicolls to McCulloch, 28 Feb. 1941.
[2] *Welch to Nicolls, 17 Oct. 1941.   [3] *Press Statement, 10 Dec. 1941.
[4] For one of the reports, see the *Daily Mail*, 11 Dec. 1941. It had the headline
'BBC *Life of Christ* Play in U.S. slang'.
[5] *Statement by Welch for the members of CRAC, 19 Dec. 1941.
[6] *H. H. Martin, Secretary of the Lord's Day Observance Society, to Ogilvie,
12 Dec. 1941. For good measure, Martin added that 'the BBC by its recent
continentalising of Sunday broadcasts with Music Hall and Jazz programmes has
already distressed multitudes of good citizens'. There were other institutional
protests from the Religion and Morals Committee of the Free Presbyterian Church
of Scotland and from Northern Ireland. Some protesters were worried about the
slang: others objected more fundamentally to any tampering with the Word of God
in the Scriptures.

of England Newspaper[1] and declared that it was willing to spend £1,200 on a further campaign.[2] The editor of the *Church of England Newspaper* agreed with Welch, however, that 'the Christian influence of these plays on the vast multitudes who are outside the Church will be great'.[3] 'You will notice,' he wrote realistically, 'that Mr. Martin of the Lord's Day Observance Society has broken out, but I cannot help feeling that all this is to the good because it attracts attention to the broadcasts.'[4]

The row was so fierce that the Minister of Information told Ogilvie that 'he did not want religious controversy at this moment' and asked him to call together the members of CRAC to decide whether or not the play cycle should be performed. CRAC was the only one out of a whole cluster of pre-war BBC Advisory Committees which continued to meet regularly in war time,[5] yet it proved impossible on this unique occasion to collect enough members to hold an extraordinary meeting. Copies of the first play in the cycle had to be circulated to members, therefore, for their comments. Thirteen out of the fourteen opinions received were entirely favourable, but the Governors were somewhat disconcerted that the replies of the Chairman of CRAC and of three other of its members had not been received by the time they had to decide.[6] Since the Minister of Information was unwell, it was left to Radcliffe to approve of the BBC going ahead with the first programme as scheduled on 21 December 1941.[7] The Governors were themselves hesitant about what their future policy should be. They decided cautiously that CRAC should meet before the later programmes in the series were broadcast, that any slang phrases in Miss Sayers's script should be omitted from the broadcast version of the plays, and, more comprehensively, that no opinion on human conduct or on religious doctrines

[1] *Church of England Newspaper*, 19 Dec. 1941.
[2] *Sunday Dispatch*, 28 Dec. 1941.
[3] *Welch to the Bishop of Winchester, 19 Dec. 1941.
[4] *Herbert Upward to Welch, 19 Dec. 1941.
[5] At a meeting on 5 March 1942 CRAC decided that a sub-committee should be set up, under the chairmanship of the Archbishop of York, consisting of members living in or near London who could meet to discuss urgent questions. For the earlier history of CRAC, see Briggs, *The Golden Age of Wireless*, pp. 227 ff., 467 ff.
[6] *Board of Governors, *Minutes*, 18 Dec. 1941.
[7] Radcliffe saw Powell on 19 Dec.

should be attributed to Christ which was unsupported by Biblical evidence. At a somewhat lower level, they agreed that in future the Chairman of the Governors should always be consulted before a Press Conference was called.[1]

CRAC met on 7 January, when 243 letters of opposition had already been received about the first broadcast, more than half from adolescents, parents and teachers.[2] The Committee 'was unanimously of the opinion that the Corporation should proceed with the broadcasting of these plays'.[3] The Bishop of Winchester, who was soon to move to York, agreed to read all the later scripts.[4] For his pains he was subjected to a flood of abusive letters from the Lord's Day Observance Society.[5] Yet the public furore died down as quickly as it had started or had been started. The plays, produced by Gielgud and acted by what Miss Sayers called a 'wonderful company' of well-known broadcasters (among them Laidman Brown as the Evangelist, Cecil Trouncer as Herod, Valentine Dyall as one of the Wise Men, Bryan Powley as Joseph and Lilian Harrison as Mary), were an immediate success. The performance of Robert Speaight by itself dispelled all fears about the reverence and devotion of the production. One writer remarked enthusiastically that he had learned more about religion in half an hour than he had done in all his years at Sunday School. Another stated that he had been 'thrilled to the core'. 'The very language used shocks us out of worn conventional terms. I was moved and helped by the last Sunday's broadcast more than ever in my life.'[6]

[1] *Board of Governors, *Minutes*, 18 Dec. 1941, 5 Jan. 1942.

[2] Nearly 26 per cent of the correspondents expressed the hope that the BBC would not allow itself to be influenced by the protest of the Lord's Day Observance Society. Large numbers of letters of criticism came in also, but of the correspondents only 80 had actually heard the broadcasts. Some letters were from people who normally supported the Society but did not do so on this occasion. 'The phrasing of the protest is extravagant and hysterical,' one writer put it, 'and I am sure that it completely fails to interpret the beliefs of the majority of Christian people.'

[3] *The Bishop of Winchester to Powell, 9 Jan. 1942; Board of Governors, *Minutes*, 15 Jan. 1942. In his summing up at the CRAC meeting the Bishop of Winchester stressed how remarkable it was that representatives of the different Christian confessions from all parts of the country were 'united on the main issue'.

[4] His offer to resign the chairmanship of CRAC was not accepted and he was pressed to stay (*Board of Governors, *Minutes*, 5 March 1942).

[5] *The Bishop of Winchester to Graves, 6 Feb. 1942.

[6] Dorothy L. Sayers, *The Man Born to be King* (1966), p. 14.

The controversy about *The Man Born to be King*, like the continuing pressure of the 'Big Ben Movement',[1] reveals that not all the divisions about religious broadcasting in war time bore on political issues.[2] However much caution the Governors of the BBC had displayed, Miss Sayers's efforts were preeminently successful. Welch thought she had produced her *magnum opus* and that the project was 'the most important venture in religious broadcasting the BBC had ever undertaken'.[3] The venture was, in fact, repeated, first complete in the Home Service in 1942 and 1943 and then in part only, the Passion sequence, in 1944 and 1945. Religious drama as a whole was given a new lease of life as a result. *Paul*, *A Bondslave*, *Job* and *Pilgrim's Progress* were only some of the plays which followed. *The Man Born to be King* was broadcast also during the war in Canada, Australia, South Africa and New Zealand.[4]

Religious issues, like political issues, were international in character, and the question of how to treat the enemy was at least as basic to Christian behaviour as it was to political warfare. Welch believed that in contrast with the First World War, when religion was exploited, often crudely—what would broadcasting have meant then?—the Second World War had seen no attempt 'to use religion to serve a merely national end'.[5] At the same time, he maintained that 'our religious broadcasting is rooted in the conviction which is the conviction

---

[1] *See above, p. 300. The issue was raised again in 1943. (Board of Governors, *Minutes*, 25 March, 1, 15 April 1943.) 'Although the arrangement reached in 1941 commended itself to CRAC it had never satisfied the Big Ben Council. They had continuously pressed for definite pauses before and after Big Ben, brief microphone reminders, regular references in published programmes, regular weekly talks.' (See also A. Dakers, *The Big Ben Minute*, which was published in 1943. For a later reference, see the *Kensington News*, 30 June 1944: 'Would it not be a timely gesture on the part of the BBC if a few words were broadcast to remind its listeners of the Silent Minute observance which follows the chimes of Big Ben at the nine o'clock news?') The last time the Governors discussed the subject was in March 1944 (*Minutes*, 2, 9 March) when representations were made from a group including the Archbishop of Canterbury after the BBC had introduced the General Forces Programme (see above, pp. 589–93). It was agreed generally that the BBC would not allow its programme arrangements to be influenced by the fact that an outside body had identified itself with some item in the programmes.

[2] The religious and political issues were sometimes linked. Thus, Sir Waldron Smithers, a right-wing critic of the BBC at home and abroad, was also chairman of the Big Ben Committee.

[3] *Welch to the Bishop of Winchester, 19 Dec. 1941.

[4] *BBC Year Book, 1945*, p. 43.

[5] *Sermon to the University of Cambridge, 8 Nov. 1942.

of Christian leaders in this and other countries that the Allied cause is righteous'.[1] Most humanists, who were left out of this whole dialogue or were confined to the *Brains Trust* where they could not talk about religion, shared this conviction.

The story was not without its twists of fortune. During the early stages of the war, the policy was quite deliberately followed of not seeking to use religion as a weapon of war in broadcasting to Germany: 'it was felt that we should do more harm than good if we broadcast anything which might be interpreted as implying a British God'.[2] By the spring of 1941, however, Newsome and many people inside the European Service—as in the Ministry of Information—were saying that there should be religious broadcasting to Germany and Europe, broadcasting which would project 'the part played by Christianity in our history, the part it plays in our national life today and the role it is likely to occupy in the future'.[3] Soon afterwards, in August 1941, a German Religious Advisory Committee was set up in the Ministry—on Crossman's initiative —with Nigel Law as Chairman: it included the Bishop of Chichester, who was keenly interested in the position of the German Christians and of anti-Nazi German pastors.[4]

Welch was not a member of this Committee nor had he been given any responsibility for religious broadcasting to Europe other than the organization, intermittent rather than regular, of religious services. He was unhappy about these restrictions, for he was personally concerned about what was happening to Christians in both France and Germany and urged that the BBC should appoint its own officer specifically concerned with religious broadcasting to Europe.[5] There were, he knew, quite different situations and problems in different countries,[6]

---

[1] Cf. Ivor Thomas, *Warfare by Words* (1942), p. 17: 'There is no need to apologise for the phrase "righteous cause". . . . The name of God came trippingly from the tongue of the Kaiser . . . but perversion of the name of God cannot alter the fact that Great Britain for all her national apostasy, is today upholding the noblest cause for which any nation has ever unsheathed the sword.'

[2] *Miall to Tallents, 3 Jan. 1941.

[3] *Newsome to Kirkpatrick, 5 May 1941.

[4] *German Religious Advisory Committee, *Minutes*, 20 Aug. 1941; CRAC, *Minutes*, 2 Oct. 1941.

[5] *Welch to Nicolls, 6 Oct. 1941.

[6] *According to a BBC paper of March 1941 no religious broadcasts had been allowed in Belgium since the Occupation, but such broadcasts were allowed in Holland. Services were broadcast in Norway, but not in Occupied France.

[cont.

but it was broadcasting to Germany which raised the most
central, if the most difficult, issues. He believed that both
religious services and religious talks had their place in any
extended plan. 'It is clear,' he wrote, 'that although religious
services are not to be used in propaganda,[1] religious talks are.'
He pressed for more of each. 'We are not allowed to broadcast
acts of worship we could share with fellow Christians in
Germany through the medium of broadcasting.' Talks, too,
were legitimate, because, after all, 'the issue of this war is a
spiritual one'.

Yet Welch never found it easy to exert the influence in this
connection which he wished. At a meeting at the Ministry of
Information in October 1941, at which Crossman was present,
he made his position clear and won Crossman's support for
regular religious services in German and regular religious
talks,[2] but he was complaining soon afterwards that he was
making little headway inside the BBC itself. Nor had he found
it possible to persuade the Corporation to appoint a new officer.
On the first point, Marius Goring, to whom he turned for
advice on programme timings, remarked cryptically that 'the
responsibilities of the various people in the German section
are none too clearly defined and it would take a clever man to
say exactly who can determine what'.[3] On the second, the
idea of employing the Rev. Nathaniel Micklem as a part-
time director of religious broadcasting to Europe broke down
for a number of different reasons.[4] It was not until there had
been further discussions at almost every level—even Anthony

[1] *Welch to Nicolls, 29 Aug. 1941. The Archbishop of York had written to
Welch on 28 June 1941 arguing that 'it would be shocking to broadcast an act of
worship as a means of propaganda'.   [2] *Welch to Salt, 9 Oct. 1941.
[3] *Goring to Welch, 21 Jan. 1942. He added, 'Crossman has no title as he is
outside the BBC, but it is fairly safe to say that Crossman is in a position to decide
most difficult issues. Köppler is his assistant with regard to religious matters as he
has a very special knowledge of inside conditions in Germany.'
[4] *At a meeting in Nov. 1941, Kirkpatrick had queried the need for an appointment and had said that in any case it was a matter for PWE. Ogilvie thought
it was a matter for the Ministry. Welch came to believe a part-time appointment
was not enough.

(Memorandum by J. Tudor Jones, the European Programme Director, urging that
British religious broadcasts should be increased, 6 March 1941.) Tudor Jones
referred to the value of hitching some religious broadcasts to the Five Peace Points
of the Pope, points which had clearly raised domestic controversy and in the jargon
of the day 'jeopardised national unity'. (Welch to Tudor Jones, 24 March 1941.)

Eden was brought in—that regular Lutheran services in German began to be broadcast in November 1942.[1] A month earlier the Rev. F. A. House, who had been recommended by Dr. Visser 't Hooft of the World Council of Churches, was appointed to the long debated new post.[2] Yet these important changes coincided with an increase in the responsibilities and powers of the Religious Division of the Ministry of Information under the Rev. Hugh Martin, and it was under the Ministry's aegis rather than Welch's that policy continued to be formulated.[3]

As the war went on, it continued to prove extremely difficult to draw fine distinctions between religion as propaganda and religion as a spiritual force in its own right. 'Will our war-time broadcasts,' Welch asked, 'bear the scrutiny of an impartial Christian mind when peace has given us disengagement from threatened interests and has set our work in wider context?'[4] The question continued to haunt him. Because of the formula of 'unconditional surrender', less effort was made to separate German Christians from the rest of the German community —the distinction between 'Nazis' and 'Germans' involved religious as well as political factors—than would have been the case if a more flexible national policy had been pursued. Yet even when the distinction was accepted, Christian dilemmas did not disappear. When some, at least, of the German Bishops showed themselves to be openly critical of the Nazis, there was a tendency in PWE and in official circles at large to think of them not as religious leaders but simply as useful political allies. Parliament itself took a growing interest in this subject. After Sir Patrick Hannon had asked Bracken in February 1943 whether he had read the Christmas Pastoral Letter of Count von Preysing, the Bishop of Berlin, Bracken assured him that he had and that it had been broadcast to the

[1] *Welch to the Rev. F. A. House, 17 Aug. 1942. When Welch asked Kirkpatrick, a Roman Catholic, why Lutheran services had been chosen, the reply he received was scarcely spiritual. It was that 'we give less time in our present schedule to Protestant Germany than to Catholic Germany, and this proposal was intended to redress the balance'. Occasional Roman Catholic masses had already been broadcast at times of Christian Festival. (Kirkpatrick to Welch, 18 Sept. 1942.)

[2] He resigned in April 1944 and was replaced by the Rev. R. S. Lee. He returned to Broadcasting House as Director of Religious Broadcasting in Oct. 1947.

[3] *Memorandum by Fenn, 14 July 1942. The BBC retained responsibility for the Empire and the United States.

[4] *BBC Year Book, 1945*, p. 41.

German people. He did not reply to a question as to whether he would arrange to send a copy to Vansittart. The last word was with the Labour M.P., Sorensen, who wanted copies of anti-Nazi documents circulated by the German Bishops to be placed in the House of Commons Library. The parliamentary exchange on this occasion deserves to be quoted in full:

'Hannon: Has the Rt. Hon. Gentleman any information as to what effect these broadcasts have upon the German people?

Bracken: It is very hard for us to estimate what effect broadcasts by German Bishops have upon Germans.

Sorensen: What effect do broadcasts by English Bishops have here?'[1]

A few Members of Parliament were concerned not only with religion and politics or with domestic political issues in Britain itself but with the broader aspects of British propaganda to Europe and with European as well as with British society. A few M.P.s on the Right were worried about the employment of aliens by the BBC, and, like Sir Waldron Smithers, asked frequent questions on the subject, often absurd in implication or unpleasant in tone.[2] A number on the Left demanded more militant support of liberation movements and were not afraid to relate, sometimes very superficially, what they believed was happening inside Britain to what was happening inside Europe.[3] A different group on the Left were unhappy about instructions being given about sabotage.[4] Many asked for more

---

[1] *Hansard*, vol. 387, col. 166.

[2] Bracken dealt with these queries fairly. See ibid., vol. 380, cols. 1049–50. When Smithers asked whether it would not be better to use British experts than to rely upon 'aliens in the BBC and the Ministry of Information' and 'thus stop German infiltration?', Bracken replied, 'It is a great pity that this House should be used as a sounding board for this mean campaign against decent Germans who left their country because of their opposition to Hitler, and who can and are playing a most worthy part in the war effort.'

[3] There was a thread of complaint about British foreign policy which influenced approaches to propaganda. It began with criticism of British 'support' of Darlan (see above, pp. 452–5), continued with an attack on British 'appeasement' of Badoglio and Italian Fascists (see above, pp. 439–40), and reached its climax in noisy opposition to British policy in Greece in 1944. The 'Second Front' agitation influenced both the content and the mood of this pattern of protests until AMGOT, Allied Military Government of Occupied Territory, was criticized by sections of the Right as well as of the Left.   [4] *Hansard*, vol. 393, col. 643.

information—a weekly broadcast on the continental Press, for instance, the advertising of BBC European Services programmes in *Radio Times*, and the placing of BBC European and Overseas Service scripts in the Library of the House of Commons.[1] Many had complaints. Sir Irving Albery, for instance, who before the war had been a member of a small BBC panel of M.P.s advising on political broadcasts,[2] asked in 1943 why on 1 October 'The Man in the Street' (Newsome) had made a broadcast to Europe of 'a controversial nature damaging to the prestige and unity of this country'.[3] Bracken told him then in very definite terms, which he might not have employed later in the war, that 'it is most undesirable that partisan political opinions should be aired by the section of the BBC controlled by His Majesty's Government'.[4]

That 'section of the BBC' was keenly aware, indeed, as the year 1943 unfolded, that the key to the winning of the war lay in Europe, where the war had begun; and Kirkpatrick told the Governors in December 1943 that the BBC was moving into a new political phase which greatly increased the problems of the opportunities open to the European Service. Routines had by then been established, but it was incumbent on the European Service to behave flexibly and to deal promptly with whatever new political happenings arose.[5] Whatever the criticisms made of it—or the differences within it—the Service was prepared. So, too, were the officers in charge of Home broadcasting. Maconachie looked further ahead than the war itself when he suggested a series of talks on international reconstruction. The object was 'to convince the ordinary man and woman that, if they want freedom from fear and want they will have to undertake certain obligations and sacrifices in peace as well as in war'; the first programme in the series was to be called 'What do we want after the war?'[6]

[1] Ibid., vol. 388, cols. 1672–4; vol. 391, cols. 210–11.

[2] The panel also included Miss Megan Lloyd George, A. P. Herbert and George Isaacs. It was in abeyance, however, during the period of party truce which very quickly began to break down after D-Day.

[3] *Hansard*, vol. 392, col. 890. Bracken said that the script of the broadcast might have been 'better phrased'.

[4] Ibid., vol. 392, col. 1392.

[5] *Board of Governors, *Minutes*, 16 Dec. 1943.

[6] *Note by Maconachie, 4 May 1943.

VI

VICTORY AND RECONSTRUCTION

———

Beginning at 12.40 a.m. last Tuesday, and on through the day you had a feeling that radio, in its capacity as an informant, had grown up. . . . The service of the British Broadcasting Corporation, as D-Day listeners know, was not less than superb.

The *New York Times*, 10 June 1944

It is hoped that all the enthusiasm and enterprise that has gone to make this war-time news service really radiogenic will not be abandoned when peace comes again. The feeling of being in touch with events as they occur is exhilarating, and it can only be achieved by radio.

Birmingham Post, 22 June 1944

I look back with regret and forward with hope to those peaceful days when we sat around whilst Stuart Hibberd or Alvar Lidell read the old type of bulletin from the weather forecast to the fat stock prices. . . . Will there ever come a time again when 'No News' will be the standard news?

H KEMBALL COOK in the *Manchester Guardian*, 5 April 1944

1. Prelude

IN 1943 and the early months of 1944 the war was moving towards its climax. At the Casablanca Conference of January 1943 important decisions were taken to prepare for a landing in Northern France in such strength that the invading armies could liberate western Europe and strike at Germany itself. The Chiefs of Staff made it clear that an operation of such magnitude could not be undertaken until the spring of 1944. 'Operation Overlord', as it soon became known, was to be organized from Britain by a joint Anglo-American staff under the direction of Generals Morgan and Barker. They began planning in March 1943, and at Washington in May the target date was fixed for 10 May a year later.[1] In the autumn of 1943 SHAEF (Supreme Headquarters Allied Expeditionary Force) was set up, and General Eisenhower, who had made his reputation in North Africa, was appointed Supreme Commander. General Montgomery was given operational control of land forces in the assault phase, but it was understood that Eisenhower would assume direct command of land operations when an American Army Group took the field under General Bradley. In January 1944 Eisenhower reluctantly asked for the invasion to be postponed until June to give an 'adequate margin to secure success'. Thereafter planning proceeded through sustained team work. Given what was often said about the power of German planning earlier during the war,[2] it was ironical that Rommel, who worked hard to take practical counter-measures, was essentially an improviser, while it was the Allies who put their trust in planning. There was no shortage of controversies within the Allied team—some were acute, some were prolonged—but preparations went forward relentlessly and enthusiastically.

The setting up of SHAEF had three main sets of implications, quite different from each other, for the BBC. First, SHAEF

---

[1] See Sir F. Morgan, *Peace and War* (1961).
[2] See above, p. 16.

created a Psychological Warfare Division of its own, what has been called 'one of the most efficient apparatuses of psychological warfare ever set up':[1] this had obvious ramifications for the BBC's European Services. Second, it demanded a new international broadcasting service for troops serving under the SHAEF Command, and turned directly to the BBC for assistance. Third, its very existence seemed a guarantee that the opening up of the 'Second Front' was merely a matter of time: the BBC, therefore, along with other broadcasting agencies, had to make preparations for its own reporting of D-Day, the biggest event in the history of the war.

Psychological Warfare, which had played its part in North Africa and in the Italian campaign, was recognized from the earliest days of SHAEF as a separate division of Supreme Headquarters, and Crossman returned from the Mediterranean area to the new H.Q. in London.[2] It was taken for granted that what had been learnt in Algiers would be applied in France and Germany. Soldiers and civilians, the former headed by the American General Robert McClure, the latter recruited mainly from journalism and from advertising, sought to ensure that policy directives coming from either the Americans or the British—OWI or PWE[3]—were integrated with the strategic requirements of the Command. This task of co-ordination was supplemented by an Intelligence function, broader in scope and more varied in purpose than military Intelligence.

PWD/SHAEF was concerned from the start, as PWE had been, but in conditions which usually allowed for greater opportunity and demanded immediate tactical skill, with policies and propaganda designed to demoralize the enemy.[4] There had to be liaison, therefore, with the air forces for the distribution of leaflets—two squadrons of Flying Fortresses were devoted exclusively to the distribution of leaflets—and with

[1] R. H. S. Crossman, 'Psychological Warfare', a paper printed in *The Journal of the Royal United Service Institution*, vol. XCVIII, November 1953. This is one of three extremely interesting papers given by Crossman to the Institution.

[2] See above, p. 434.

[3] OWI was not a secret organization. Its activities were public.

[4] PWE had appointed Ritchie Calder as Director of Plans and Campaigns on 17 Aug. 1942. It also appointed a Director of Political Warfare Intelligence. See above, p. 419.

both 'white' and 'black' broadcasting organizations.[1] In addition, when necessary, new radio stations had to be launched, like new newspapers. Finally liaison had to be established with SOE and the American OSS to assist their operations, and an interrogation service had to be provided to obtain the maximum amount of relevant information from prisoners of war.

Below PWD at Supreme HQ, where William Paley, the President of CBS, worked alongside his Company colleague, Davidson Taylor, there was a PWD in each Army Group and in each Army Headquarters: the Americans were to interpret SHAEF's directives to the American Army Group and the British to Montgomery's 21st Army Group. Yet views were passed upwards as well as downwards, and were often concerned with strategy as well as tactics.[2] 'We constantly found in SHAEF,' Crossman has written, 'that it was our duty to say to London or Washington, "if you give us this political directive, we must point out to you that it will postpone or hamper our achievement of victory in this particular area". The soldier must have the right—and the competence— to point out what are the consequences of carrying out a certain political directive.'[3]

By the end of the war, the effective control of the day-to-day operations of psychological warfare passed from London and Washington to SHAEF, although administrators and broadcasters had to work closely within the general outlines of policy—particularly the formula of 'unconditional surrender',

---

[1] Delmer's role was to use *Soldatensender Calais* before the Allied invasion to suggest that Hitler's soldiers in France were 'written off', 'deserted' and 'second-class'. See S. Delmer, *Black Boomerang* (1962), pp. 119-20: 'The true defence of the German Fatherland is on the Eastern Front.' He also dwelt on new American wonder weapons. During the preparation for 'Overlord', Delmer moved to a new office in Bush House (ibid., p. 125). He was appointed Director of Special Operations in June 1944.

[2] Crossman's argument that radio is an instrument ill-suited for tactical use, on grounds that there is no way of preventing people who are not meant to hear it from hearing it, is not entirely sound. The role of the BBC in sending out operational messages in code, while it carried with it dangers, was important in tactical as well as strategic terms. Crossman himself recognizes the tactical value of small 'black' or 'grey' stations, like the short-wave stations in California which broadcast programmes in Japanese that were picked up almost entirely by Japanese monitors, a highly specialized audience.

[3] Crossman, loc. cit., p. 531.

a phrase invented by Roosevelt,[1] which became official Anglo-American policy after the Casablanca Conference of January 1943.[2] This formula inhibited many exercises in psychological warfare. Nonetheless, the whole idea of operational PWD was sufficiently exciting for it to attract to SHAEF many people who had previously been employed in other branches of political warfare. Among them was Newsome, whose secondment was arranged in May 1944.[3] 'We have now passed through the supreme political crisis of the war,' he had written in May 1943, 'and are now approaching its supreme military crisis. We are now in the aftermath of the climax of the Nazis' great political forestalling counter-offensive and in the preliminary stage of the great Allied military offensive.'

While Newsome was as unhappy as Crossman about the formula of unconditional surrender, he believed that the Allies could and should exploit 'the double failure' by the Nazis in the West and in the East 'in order to hearten our friends to further efforts, to accelerate their liberation, and to undermine our enemies' last hopes of avoiding defeat'.[4] 'Our friendly listeners had lived through the phase when their morale was tender and fragile,' he wrote a few months later, 'when they needed and wanted to be encouraged and flattered and reassured. . . . Now they want to *know* . . . what we think is going to happen.'[5] Newsome did not move to SHAEF until after D-Day, but directives and broadcasts along these lines reveal his conviction that broadcasting should now concern itself directly with action. In an interview with Haley he was told that he was too much of a crusader to have a future in post-war broadcasting, and he never forgot these words during the last months of what to him had always been a great crusade.

Ritchie, who succeeded Newsome in Bush House, wrote a paper for PWD/SHAEF in April 1944, at the invitation of Kirkpatrick, emphasizing how important it was to state clearly in advance what the anti-Nazi forces in Europe were expected to do in the case of an Allied invasion.[6] Character-

[1] R. E. Sherwood, *The White House Papers of Harry L. Hopkins* (1949), pp. 692–3.
[2] Chester Wilmot, *The Struggle for Europe* (1959 edn.), pp. 136 ff.
[3] *European Divisional Meeting, *Minutes*, 30 May 1944.
[4] *Notes on a New Phase of Broadcasting in Europe, 4 May 1943.
[5] *Special Standing Directive, 1 Oct. 1943.   [6] Ritchie MSS.

istically he went on to suggest that the BBC had a particularly important part to play. While 'Colonel Britton' was never brought back to life, Ritchie himself was to broadcast on several occasions as the 'No. 1 Voice of SHAEF', for the first time in May 1944. Yet the BBC was at pains to insist on these and other occasions that its 'orders' came not from SHAEF but from PWE. 'We do not take orders from SHAEF, but we do give consideration to their suggestions.' When any SHAEF suggestion involved 'substantial policy questions', it had to be referred direct to the Controller (European Services).[1] While there were some understandable suspicions inside the BBC of 'the creative planners' inside SHAEF—Greene accused them of wanting to scrap the staple BBC programmes in German and to substitute programmes based on psychological repetition of themes involving pain, fear of bombs and homesickness[2] —the more integrated the PWD team became, the easier it was for the BBC to deal with Anglo-American questions which had hitherto often involved conflicting advice. 'C. Eur. S. to try and induce PWE and OWI to improve position,' a Minute of the European Divisional Committee had read in November 1943. 'Not considered fruitful to send another man to Washington at this juncture.'[3] Tom Hamilton of OWI was appointed to work inside the BBC at the end of 1943,[4] and by the time of D-Day it was acknowledged that there had been a 'simplification of technique and an establishment of proper organisation on the PWD side which had led to smooth working.'[5]

There had also been increased co-operation between BBC engineers and programme staff and SHAEF, and five engineers, including F. C. Maclean, who became Chief Engineer PWD/ SHAEF (he was later to become Director of Engineering of the BBC), were seconded to SHAEF in April 1944. 'Their task,' wrote McClure, 'will be to assess the condition of

[1] *European Divisional Committee, *Minutes*, 27 June 1944.

[2] H. Carleton Greene, 'Psychological Warfare', a Lecture to the NATO Defence College, 4 Sept. 1959. By contrast, Delmer remained extremely critical of the BBC. In Nov. 1962 he wrote that he did not think the BBC had performed its task 'as well as it might have done' (*New Statesman*, 16 Nov. 1962).

[3] *European Divisional Committee, *Minutes*, 16 Nov. 1943. See above, p. 501.

[4] *Ibid., 14 Dec. 1943.

[5] *Ibid., 27 June 1944.

remaining radio facilities and make recommendations about their repair or replacement; to conduct mobile radio units, which will, so far as possible, take the place of damaged installations; and to conduct public address systems which, together with the mobile radio units, will be at the disposal of the military authorities for distributing information and instructions to the civilian populations.'[1]

Direct BBC relations with the Americans had, of course, long preceded the setting up of SHAEF; they had been concerned from the start both with political warfare and with 'straight broadcasting' to inform and to entertain American soldiers in Europe. After the meeting of Ogilvie, Ashbridge, Gorham and Sherwood in September 1941,[2] when decisions were taken in principle to grant the Americans a number of fifteen-minute daily broadcasting periods on BBC wavelengths for transmissions in English, French, German and Italian for European audiences,[3] the number of *Voice of America* broadcasts, with the full approval of PWE, increased considerably during the year 1942. In December 1941 Colonel Donovan had asked for enough time to broadcast in twelve languages,[4] and though this was not possible, German and French output was doubled in 1942, and Polish and Finnish added to the number of languages. By March 1943, fourteen languages were being employed, and many programmes were re-transmissions from the United States itself.[5]

The increasing use of re-transmissions reflected American reaction to German claims that 'American broadcasts to Europe were nothing more than subsidiary to the BBC's'.[6] Although some people inside the BBC had doubts about the

---

[1] *McClure to Haley, 24 April 1944.

[2] See above, p. 406. *Board of Governors, *Minutes*, 11, 18 Sept. 1941; M. Gorham, *Sound and Fury* (1948), p. 119.

[3] *Earlier exploration of the possibilities is set out in a Note by Tallents, 1 May 1941, and in Kirkpatrick to Tallents, 2 May 1941.

[4] *Cable of 4 Dec. 1941 (see D. Stephens to Whitney, 11 Dec. 1941).

[5] The re-transmissions started on 4 Jan. 1943, at a time when there was evidence of increasing interest in American broadcasting. (*Bruce Lockhart to Kirkpatrick, 22 Nov. 1942.) 'At the Ministerial Meeting on November 19th, Mr. Bracken formally approved the direct re-transmission of American broadcasts.'

[6] *Note by Graves, 9 Nov. 1942. The German claims had been picked up in Intelligence Reports.

quality of the American broadcasts[1] and on the eve of D-Day
Paley was pressing for an increase in their quantity,[2] there
was no lack of co-operation. The PWE Mission headed by
Bowes-Lyon in the United States, to which Miall and Russell
Page were attached from October 1942,[3] had established
useful working relations. There was co-operation also in the
Monitoring Service, as Americans went to work alongside
BBC monitors at Caversham.

It was against this background that the Americans also
developed an impressive network of radio stations for their
own Forces. In January 1943 the Armed Forces Radio Service
(AFRS) had 21 outlets: in December 1943 it had 306. The
first new AFRS station had been built in Casablanca in March
1943, and it was not until four months later in July that American
Forces Network (AFN) programmes began to be transmitted
in Britain.[4] The studios were in London, the transmitters, all
low-power, were scattered locally at American bases, and
miles away in Santa Monica Boulevard, Los Angeles, there
was 'a bustling program factory'. AFN output included BBC
programmes, re-broadcasts of American commercial radio programmes and material of its own, as well as programmes specially
prepared in the United States for the troops.[5] It emphasized,
of course, that it was in no sense a competitor of the BBC.[6]

While AFN was developing its activities, plans were also

[1] *'The dominant impression,' one BBC expert wrote (Memorandum of 20
April 1943), 'is that American broadcasts are not nearly sufficiently related to
Intelligence evidence of the audience. This applies not only to the general conditions and reactions of a given audience, but also to the particular political or
economic situation which affects propaganda.'

[2] *Paley to Bracken, 11 Feb. 1944.

[3] See above, p. 501. Mark Abrams and Basil Thornton were also attached for a time.

[4] The idea had been first mooted early in the summer of 1942 in talks by
Generals Mayhill, Eisenhower and Hughes and representatives of the OWI.
Pending the start of the programme, the BBC included material specially designed
for American Forces in its own programmes (*Programme Policy Committee,
Minutes, 27 Feb. 1942; Note by Nicolls, 17 July 1942.) On the instructions of the
Ministry of Information Foot met Whitney in Feb. 1943 to discuss future plans.
The BBC agreed to waive its de facto monopoly rights in favour of OWI, and the
Post Office provided wavelengths and licences for the new network. Seven trans-
mitters were in use in July 1943, twelve by 1 Sept.

[5] There is an unpublished University of South California thesis by T. S. de Lay,
'An Historical Study of the Armed Forces Radio Service' (1951). See also E. H.
Kirby and J. W. Harris, Star-Spangled Radio (1948).

[6] See Lt.-Col. C. H. Gurney and Capt. J. S. Hayes, This is the American Forces
Network in the European Theatre of Operations, 1 Nov. 1943.

being made by the Americans to schedule an extension of their broadcasting services after the invasion of Western Europe. In October 1943 they proposed to create a new station, ABSIE (American Broadcasting Station in Europe), which would reach the population of Europe at the critical psychological moment.[1] ABSIE first went on the air (using both medium and short waves and employing eighteen languages) on 30 April 1944 with a message from Sherwood that 'we shall give you the signal when the hour comes for you to rise up against the enemy and strike'.[2] Sherwood also paid a tribute to the BBC. 'All of us in OWI,' he stated, 'have ample reason to know and appreciate what a superb job the BBC has done in helping to keep alive the fire of hope in the darkness of the past few years in German-occupied Europe.'[3] It was as a gesture of co-operation and of friendship, indeed, that Haley as well as Sherwood contributed to the first day's talks. The BBC was expected to provide 1 to 1½ hours of the 8½ hours of the new ABSIE daily time-table of broadcasts. 'Thus,' Sherwood added—and what he said echoed everything that was being said in SHAEF—'broadcasting to Europe becomes more and more a joint Allied operation in support of our joint military operations.'[4] ABSIE continued to broadcast until July 1945: its last programme included contributions from General McClure and from Haley.

ABSIE raised fewer questions than the continued development of AFN. In welcoming AFN the BBC had been cautious, granting it unique facilities but recognizing that there were aspects of further development which needed vigilant super-vision. Several danger signals were noted as the scheme went ahead—difficulties likely to arise with the Canadian Government and Allied Governments in London, as the Americans employed their own transmitters, something which no other Allies had been allowed to do;[5] problems of policy and censorship;[6]

---

[1] *Wallace Carroll (OWI) to Ashbridge, 26 Oct. 1943.
[2] Kirby and Harris, op. cit., pp. 123-4.   [3] *Press Release of 26 April 1944.
[4] *Ibid.; Sherwood to Haley, 30 May 1944; Paley to Ashbridge, 25 April 1944. An OWI section was established at Bush House, and studios were taken over in Wardour Street.
[5] *Ashbridge to Foot, 25 Feb. 1942; Programme Policy Committee, *Minutes*, 27 Feb. 1942.
[6] *Ashbridge to Foot, 25 Feb. 1942; Chief Censor to Foot, 22 May 1942.

possibilities of technical interference with the BBC's own group of H Transmitters;[1] a likely diversion of restricted equipment to the Americans from the BBC's own services;[2] a possible switch of interest by American commercial broadcasting companies from the BBC to AFN when they were looking for programmes about Britain;[3] complications if the Americans became involved with British radio relay interests— a long-standing *bête noire* of the BBC—or if they began their own outside broadcasts on a large scale;[4] the likely effect on the British home audience, since AFN provided in parts of the country, though not in London, an alternative programme, particularly for teenagers;[5] and, not least in a long list, the 'dangers of separatism'.

This last point was shared by many people who were not afraid of American 'competition'. AFN was a programme designed for Americans living on foreign soil far away from their homes. As Allied Forces were being drawn closer and closer together in the common war effort, of which Eisenhower became the symbol, the question began to be asked whether it would not be sensible after D-Day to have one single broadcasting service for SHAEF troops. Could there not be a recognition of common interest? Winant, the American Ambassador, was believed to share the feeling that AFN was not the only answer. So too were a number of high-ranking American officers. In their view, what was needed was genuine 'integration'.

When the 'Overlord' plans were well in hand, the American General Barker called on J. B. Clark, with Eisenhower's full authority, to discuss how one single programme could best be organized for the united forces in 'the North West', principally American, British and Canadian. Clark, 'thinking aloud', suggested 'something in the nature of a composite programme drawn from the General Forces Programme and the American Forces Network': Barker, who praised the BBC News service

---

[1] *Ashbridge to Foot, 22 May 1943; for the H transmitters, see above, p. 63.
[2] *Statement by Gorham, 24 May 1943.
[3] *Gorham to Clark, 17 May 1943.
[4] *Ashbridge to Foot, 22 May 1943; see also below, p. 715.
[5] The programme could never be heard, in fact, by more than 10 per cent of the civilian population. From the start advocates of commercial radio pointed to AFN programmes as far more 'popular' than those of the 'highbrow' BBC. (M. Gorham, *Broadcasting and Television since 1900* (1952), p. 193.)

and implied that AFN would go out of business if the new programmes were started, stated that Eisenhower himself would be 'directly interested in its general policy and lay out'.[1]

Both men agreed that any new arrangements would apply exclusively to Britain and to German occupied areas entered for the first time after D-Day. They knew that there had been a remarkable growth of AFN broadcasting in Italy—with a Fifth Army Mobile Station following General Mark Clark's Forces north. They knew also that British troops in the Mediterranean were being served not only by the new BBC General Overseas and Forces Programme but by Army stations. A Middle East Broadcasting Unit had established itself in Cairo, initially under the direction of Major Peter Haddon and later managed by Colonel R. L. Meyer, who before the war had been associated with commercial radio. Meyer negotiated the first Army arrangements with local broadcasting authorities for the transmission of 'Forces Hour' programmes.[2] As the Eighth Army left the desert and made its way through Italy along with other British and Allied troops, new broadcasting possibilities had been opened up. It was even possible to employ artists like Gigli and Tito Gobbi, though some of the time had to be devoted to undermining the influence of 'Axis Sally', the German propaganda girl who had a remarkable collection of American song hits in her possession.[3]

After the meeting in London between Clark and Barker, further talks about the pattern of broadcasting in new battle areas of Europe went ahead between representatives of SHAEF, of the 21st Army Group, of the AFN and the BBC. The negotiations were intricate, and Norman Collins, head of the new General Overseas Programme, played a leading part in them. As a result, Lt.-General W. Bedell Smith, U.S. Army Chief of Staff, SHAEF, wrote to Haley on 28 April 1944 formally proposing 'the establishment of a joint radio service for the AEF engaged in operations in the European theatre, such radio service to consist of news, music and entertainment, designed to be, as far as possible, of mutual interest to the

[1] *Clark to Haley, 30 March 1944.

[2] The first full-time Forces station at Quartina did not begin to operate until Aug. 1944.

[3] See G. Pedrick, *Battledress Broadcasters* (1964), pp. 8 ff., for an interesting account of the growth of Army broadcasting.

Anglo-American-Canadian Forces': programmes were to be radiated from a medium-wave transmitter and to continue from 6 a.m. to 11 p.m. News broadcasting was to be strictly objective, and entertainment programmes—at the insistence of Eisenhower himself, with a characteristic touch—were to be apportioned in such a way that they would 'reflect the relative strength of American, British and Canadian Forces participating in the operation'. There was to be a Director, Broadcasting Services, SHAEF, who would act as Liaison Officer with the BBC and AFN, and an Advisory Council would meet 'weekly or oftener to review progress'.[1]

The BBC's Board of Governors wished operational control of the new SHAEF programme to rest with the BBC.[2] They were not entirely happy about the idea of the Advisory Council or about the multiplicity of partners, each of whom would seek to influence the content of the new programme. At every level, indeed, there was scope for possible misunderstanding. Thus, the BBC's Director of Religious Broadcasting, forthright as ever, sharply criticized ideas tentatively put forward about religious broadcasting. It had been suggested informally that religious services and 'Sunday Half Hours' would be provided on alternate weeks by the BBC and the American chaplain responsible for 'Radio Chapel'. After hearing part of a 'Radio Chapel' programme—music by a boys' choir, a 'pep talk' and a number of highly emotional hymns—Welch said that he would take no responsibility as Director of Religious Broadcasting or as an Anglican parson for 'this appalling mush' which seemed to him to be 'a travesty of religious broadcasting'.[3] The fact that the programme would be listened to by soldiers and airmen in moments of crisis added to its dangers. There were similar, if less profound, crises of conscience on the part of many other BBC programme officials. Yet Bracken told Haley bluntly on 22 May that if the BBC would not produce the new SHAEF programme, then SHAEF would do so on

---

[1] *Memorandum for the Board of Governors, 28 April 1944.

[2] *Haley to Lt.-Gen. W. B. Smith, 5 May 1944.

[3] *Welch to Gorham, 18 April 1944. 'By giving a BBC "cover" to this programme,' he added, 'we are seriously lowering the whole standard of religious broadcasting which has been carefully built up by Stobart, Iremonger and myself, under the control of Nicolls and the advice of the Central Religious Advisory Committee.'

its own. Churchill himself was aware of Eisenhower's plans, and promised that if discussions with the BBC failed, transmitter facilities such as 'Aspidistra' would be immediately offered to SHAEF. Extra transmitter facilities would certainly not be given to the BBC to radiate its General Overseas and Forces Programme in competition with a SHAEF service.[1]

There was little left to do except to discuss terms. The BBC asked for 'control' of programmes. It also demanded that the BBC's World News would be that used by the new service—Eisenhower is said to have had the highest opinion of the trustworthiness of BBC News—and that any Advisory Council should have no executive powers. The Minister made it clear that the programme would be at the disposal of the Supreme Commander for issuing instructions to his troops: this, indeed, was said to be 'the over-riding consideration'.[2] The BBC asked in addition for the release of British, American or Canadian servicemen whom it wished to have associated with the new service either as advisers or as producers. The cost of the programmes was to be shared equally between the Government of the United States and the Government of Great Britain. All these points were accepted. It was agreed also, however, that the BBC was committed to the programme only for as long as the joint campaign in Western Europe continued. When the armies of invasion became the armies of occupation, the project would be reviewed.[3]

On 23 May Haley sent for Gorham, who for a short time had been Acting Controller (Overseas), and asked him to be Director of the new service. Gorham agreed and was told that liaison with SHAEF was to be provided by Colonel E. M. Kirby, SHAEF's Director of Broadcasting Services, whom he had met previously when Kirby was Radio Chief of the Public Relations Division of the War Department in Washington. The two men were to have adjacent offices in Broadcasting House. Gorham proved an excellent choice: he enjoyed his new job and was to describe it in retrospect as 'a unique experiment amongst all the radio innovations of the war'.[4]

---

[1] *Note on a meeting between Bracken and Haley, 22 May 1944; Gorham, *Sound and Fury*, p. 140.   [2] *Sendall to Haley, 25 May 1944.
[3] *Haley to Gen. Barker, 24 May 1944.
[4] Gorham, *Broadcasting and Television since 1900* (1952), p. 206.

Yet the first few days were very uncertain. Kirby was uneasy about the arrangements which had been agreed upon with the BBC and tried to re-open everything. General Barker[1] had to be called in, and there were more talks with Haley.[1] The arrangements stood. Barker had expressed the view to Haley that the programme was in good hands and the hope that it would be a huge success:[2] later he was to become a fervent admirer of the BBC.[3] He was enough of a diplomat, however, to suggest that despite 'the splendid objectivity of the BBC News Bulletin', Eisenhower could be placed in 'a tricky position' if, as Commander of the American Forces, he were not to enjoy the right to make 'deletions and additions'.[4]

Once the constitutional position had been reaffirmed, a high-level Policy Council supervised the operation. Gorham's main immediate task, however, was to recruit staff. He very quickly got his 'old friends', the engineers, to find him a transmitter—at Start Point—a wavelength and a diagram of the service area of the new station. He also acquired studios in Broadcasting House. Madden, who was to be his only male civilian, joined him at once with Miss McBride. For the most part, however, Gorham had to rely on uniformed men and women from the three nations. The first of them arrived at Broadcasting House with their bedrolls, revolvers and ammunition, not knowing in the least what their new assignment was. They included experienced broadcasters and producers, some of them released, often unwillingly, from other military jobs, like Franklin Engelmann, a former BBC announcer, who had been serving as an instructor in an RE school in the North of England and Royston Morley, an experienced broadcaster who was serving as a Battery Commander. Major More O'Ferrall had been in television before joining up, and Major Max-Muller had invaluable experience of War Office procedures. The American and Canadian staff included Broderick Crawford, a film actor, Vick Knight, a Hollywood scriptwriter, and later Glenn Miller with the whole of his deservedly well-known and universally acceptable Air Service Corps Band.

---

[1] Gorham, *Sound and Fury*, pp. 144–5.
[2] *General Barker to Haley, 25 May 1944.
[3] Gorham, op. cit., p. 145.   [4] *Barker to Haley, 25 May 1944.

Details of the new service, including programme schedules, had to be marked 'secret'—the diagram of the service area of the new station gave 'a very good outline of the invasion area'[1]—and even people in the Broadcasting House offices next to Gorham and Kirby did not know what was afoot. It was agreed from the start that details of the service when it was inaugurated either on D-Day or D-Day plus one would not be published in the *Radio Times*. Inquirers were to be told that the programme was directed at a 'specialised audience'.[2]

The first Programme Planning Meeting was held on 25 May, and on 30 May the first 'dry run' was made.[3] Further rehearsals went on for a week. On 6 June a further 'dry run' was cancelled. 'D-Day' itself had dawned. It had long been anticipated. As the American magazine *Broadcasting* had put it at the beginning of May, 'For all of us alive today, the biggest story since Creation is about to break.'[4]

The preparations for D-Day had also brought in quite different sections of the BBC. As early as 1942, before SHAEF was established, Michael Standing, the Director of Outside Broadcasts, had written to Nicolls suggesting that a plan should be drafted for using the microphone for 'actuality recordings' connected with war-time operations instead of relying upon official dispatches and eye-witness accounts.[5] During the same month, C. Lawson-Reece, Supervisor of Overseas Planning Liaison, wrote about 'a movement in the War Office and Ministry of Information to bring about a closer relationship between broadcasting and the armies in the field' and described an abortive attempt by the War Office itself, independently of the BBC, to organize, somewhat on PK lines, direct reporting

---

[1] Gorham, op. cit., p. 143.

[2] *Programme Policy Meeting, *Minutes*, 25 May 1944. Gorham wrote a fascinating 'Background story on AEFP for the North American Director' on 13 June 1944. I have used this account in my narrative.

[3] A final official meeting between Haley, Ryan, Clark and Gorham, on behalf of the BBC, and Barker, Kirby and Col. DuPuy, was held on 29 May.

[4] *Broadcasting*, 1 May 1944.

[5] *Standing to Nicolls, 13 Aug. 1942. On 3 April 1942 Ryan had written to Graves that 'we have been criticised by the Board of Governors, by the Minister of Information and by No. 10, for not having a high standard of news observing. We must, you will agree, admit that this criticism is justified.' In a note of 10 Feb. 1942 Arthur Mann had urged 'a spirit of healthy rivalry' with the Press.

designed as part of 'a big plan to bring civilians into closer touch with the Army'.[1] The work of the German PK units was the subject of a special monitoring report prepared in September 1942:[2] curiously enough, by this time, the amount of time devoted to *Frontberichte* in Germany had been drastically curtailed and 'the jubilant myth of 1940 and '41 had died for good'.[3] The American example was also studied, for the Americans were already broadcasting special programmes describing the activities of their troops in Europe.[4] J. B. Clark was particularly anxious that the British should produce a small portable recorder before the Americans did.[5]

After detailed inquiries had taken place, covering both technical and institutional questions—'a major obstacle' was said to be 'the Services' natural fear of interference with operational messages'[6]—plans went ahead to equip both programme producers and engineers with the necessary apparatus and knowledge to report 'on sorties or on the Second Front'.[7]

The lessons of North Africa were also diligently studied: after the Allied landings the BBC had not been taken into the confidence of the Army, the Americans were in sole control of transmitting facilities in Algiers, and the war correspondents were short both of equipment and transport.[8] It was in these

---

[1] *Lawson-Reece to J. B. Clark, 14 Aug. 1942.

[2] *Monitor's Special Report on Outside Broadcasts on the German Home Service, 28 Sept. 1942. The report referred not only to the *Frontberichte* but also to *Zeitspiegel* ('Mirror of the Times') reports. Three hours a week were allotted to the latter.   [3] *Ibid.

[4] *Programme Policy Meeting, *Minutes*, 21 Aug. 1942.

[5] *Clark to Graves, 6 Oct. 1942. He pointed out that while there had been effective BBC recording by Charles Gardner of an air battle in 1940 (see above, p. 220) and by Dimbleby of the British entry into Bardia, a small recording machine would be necessary 'for the proper reporting of future operations'.

[6] *Report on Broadcasting Facilities in the Field, 23 Oct. 1942. It had always been difficult to deal adequately with commando raids. Thus in a memorandum of 9 Dec. 1941 Ryan had complained of the 'subfusc atmosphere' in which Sir Roger Keyes had worked.

[7] *Report on Broadcasting Facilities in the Field, 23 Oct. 1942.

[8] *Report by Robert Dunnett, BBC correspondent, 16 Feb. 1943. 'For future operations,' Dunnett maintained, 'it appears to be absolutely essential that at least one person in Broadcasting House with a full practical knowledge of the Corporation's requirements should be taken into the complete confidence of the Imperial Staff—it is not good enough just to know how to broadcast or how to make a recording or write a script. Every BBC man reporting a campaign should be part of the pattern of it before it begins, and a force within it thereafter to tell its exploits roundly to the world.'

circumstances that Mann, the BBC Governor with the greatest experience of journalism, pressed his case for a new and bolder approach to BBC reporting,[1] and Graves and Ryan won the support of Radcliffe in the Ministry of Information for a considerable extension of BBC reporting 'to get the quickest, widest and most vivid approach to the public (in and out of uniform) through broadcasting'. Mann's stress on the need to 'involve' the public in war news was accepted. So too was Clark's point about the Americans, this time from a different angle. Unless Britain went ahead on its own, Graves insisted, 'there is a real danger that British prowess will be swamped by American stories'.[2]

In January 1943 Howard Marshall was appointed BBC Special Correspondent concerned with 'front line broadcasting' and was sent to North Africa;[3] and in the same month bomber crews taking part in a big RAF raid on Berlin were accompanied both by BBC and Press representatives. The Press rightly hailed the inclusion of reporters as 'a commendable departure from official practice'.[4] Yet the Air Ministry was so slow in allowing reports of the mission to be broadcast that the Germans, who bombed London by way of reprisal the following night, were able by 'a propaganda boob' to get in with the news first.[5] There was a similar delay in September 1943 when Wynford Vaughan Thomas recorded a commentary in another bomber raid on Berlin. Obviously the value of 'the quickest, widest and most vivid

---

[1] *There are many memoranda by Mann in the BBC files on this subject, e.g. a letter to Powell, 2 May 1943, and a general statement of 4 July 1943. 'The American broadcasting systems are all far ahead of us in the quality of their own reporters and commentators. . . . On the battle fronts only an occasional BBC representative proves equal to an impressive word picture worthy of the deeds of our fighting men.' The first reference to Mann's interest is mentioned in a letter from Graves to Ryan, Feb. 1942. By 26 July 1943 Mann was able to write, 'Mr. Ryan satisfied me that when an offensive on the Continent started, better descriptive talent would be available.'

[2] *Graves to Radcliffe, 2 Oct. 1942. The same point about air battles was taken up by the Board of Governors, 8 July 1943. 'American claims were less restrained than the British and it should be made clear that such claims were from American communiqués when they were quoted in News bulletins.'

[3] *Programme Policy Committee, Minutes, 22 Jan. 1943.

[4] The Scotsman, 18 Jan. 1943.

[5] The Aeroplane, 22 Jan. 1943. On 24 April 1943 a recording was broadcast of orders given and the conversation between members of the crew of a big bomber jockeying for position over Stettin.

approach to the public' was not fully accepted in official circles.[1] In the meantime, Howard Marshall had become involved in acrimonious disputes with General Alexander in North Africa which were not sorted out until Haley visited Italy late in the year.[2] Harold Macmillan, British Minister resident in North Africa, was 'very friendly disposed to the BBC and most helpful', but the BBC was under regular attack in Algiers.[3]

London was less difficult than Algiers, and the idea of a 'Radio Commando Unit' soon took shape.[4] An 'Army Week' was successfully planned in February 1943 in co-operation with the Army Liaison Units[5] and a pioneering exercise for BBC reporters (Operation 'Spartan') was held in co-operation with the Army in March 1943,[6] during which a mock battle was fought out across the Thames and up beyond Oxford. This was an event of considerable importance, and a fascinating account of it was written by Dimbleby who took part in the exercise and drew out of the experience what seemed to him to be the relevant lessons concerning future techniques and organization. He emphasized *inter alia* the need for 'a sense of military discipline and bearing' on the part of the correspondents: 'we . . . must fit ourselves into the landscape and conduct ourselves in accordance with the rank whose privileges we enjoy'.[7] It was no longer possible, he argued in addition,

[1] *Talks behind the scenes about Army co-operation are mentioned in Foot to Bracken, 9 Feb. 1943; Grigg to Bracken, 26 Feb. 1943.

[2] See above, p. 554. *Marshall's report is discussed in Marshall to Ryan, 27 March 1943.

[3] *Macmillan to Bracken, 30 March 1943. 'The technical arrangements for improving relations between the Army and Press and the BBC is a matter which is a task of the soldiers, and there will doubtless be an improvement. I feel sure that any change will be in the direction of tightening up rather than letting out the news more freely.' The BBC's case was set out in Ryan to Radcliffe, 21 April 1943. The Governors congratulated Ryan on his handling of North African news on 13 May 1943. In Oct. 1943, Hayes, Head of the Overseas Engineering and Information Department, visited North Africa and reported on transmitting stations, the type of material broadcast, listening conditions and the consequences of the Psychological Warfare approach.

[4] *Nicolls to Foot, 26 Jan. 1943.

[5] *Board of Governors, *Minutes*, 14 Jan., 11 March 1943.

[6] *Ibid., 4, 25 March 1943; Controllers' Conference, *Minutes*, 26 March 1943, in which Foot reported that teams of correspondents would be attached to the British and Canadian Forces 'for the duration'. For comments on 'the idea of a team in the field', see Dimbleby, op. cit., p. 31.

[7] His report is reprinted in *Richard Dimbleby, Broadcaster* (1966), pp. 31–5.

22

for the same man to provide both 'situation' material and eye-witness reporting. In mobile warfare more than one kind of reporting was necessary.

Dimbleby's report was supplemented by recorded reports on the exercise while it was in progress, and these were played back soon afterwards to the BBC Governors, Sir James Grigg and the Adjutant-General. They were all immensely impressed by the graphic 'sound photography'.[1] They were also beginning to learn how necessary it was to depend upon fully trained and fully fit men. Being a first-class war correspondent meant having many of the virtues of the soldier as well as the capacity to fit into the landscape. The point was made unequivocally at a conference at the War Office attended by Foot and Ryan at the end of March 1943.[2] It was recognized by S. J. de Lotbinière, Director of Empire Programmes, who was appointed to select teams and to take charge of plans, with G. J. B. Allport responsible for administration. Less than two months later, in May 1943, the BBC's front-line unit was christened 'the War Reporting Unit';[3] and after de Lotbinière took up the post of BBC Representative in Canada in November 1943, Howard Marshall was chosen as Director, with Malcolm Frost as Deputy Director.[4]

The Unit was charged somewhat verbosely with 'the responsibility for getting active service war material in any theatre of war and for meeting the demands of all consumers with sure regard for the interests of programmes as a whole'. At that time, Marshall was still worried about the fact that the Unit was well below strength—'we have not even two full teams, let alone a reserve team'—and about the suspicions of the Press.[5] Within a few months he was worried also about suspicions inside the BBC itself and long and wearing arguments

[1] *Note by Foot, 25 March 1943.

[2] *Programme Policy Meeting, *Minutes*, 2 April 1943.

[3] *Ibid., 14 May 1943.

[4] *Note by Foot, 1 Nov. 1943. De Lotbinière took up his new post on 1 Jan. 1944.

[5] *Memorandum by Marshall, 19 Oct. 1943. Yet see an important article in *World's Press News*, 11 Nov. 1943, 'What Portland Place owes to Fleet Street', pointing out the contribution to broadcasting of Ryan, R. T. Clark, Newsome, Ritchie, Greene, Edwards, Tangye Lean, Hodson, Gillie, Hulme, Harrison, Adam, A. E. Barker, Dunnett, Talbot and Dimbleby, all associated with the Press during earlier stages of their careers.

involving departmental jurisdiction. The main difficulty came from the Foreign News Department which had special responsibilities for the selection and training of staff, and Haley had to use all his weight to prevent 'undue rigidity'.[1] In March 1944 Dudley Perkins, then an Assistant in the BBC's Legal Department, was appointed Manager of the Unit to assist with administration.

Notwithstanding the troubles, plans went ahead. The first full-scale invasion practice, 'Operation Pirate', was held in October 1943, and the first special training course was held at Wood Norton in March 1944. The BBC's war correspondents were placed under the supervision of a physical training instructor (he called them his 'War Commandos') and underwent courses in reconnaisance, weapon training, signals, aeroplane and tank recognition and map reading. They learned how to live rough and to work in the field. They were quite deliberately being taught to think of themselves as 'men of the army who had an unusual and specialized job'.[2] Once this degree of involvement had been achieved, most of the difficulties of the past were forgotten. Army reporting, indeed, now became more straightforward than reporting of air operations which was still controversial. The Governors disliked all signs of 'gloating' in reference to bombing attacks,[3] and when the idea was put forward of a 'live' broadcast from a bomber over Berlin it was rejected both for home and overseas audiences. The grounds were well stated by Haley: according to him, 'the BBC's policy regarding the bombing of Germany is that it is a scientific operation, not to be stunted, to be gloated over, or to be dealt with any other way than the most objective factual reporting arising from the communiqués and from material obtained from Air Headquarters or Bomber Stations'.[4]

[1] *Note by Haley, 7 Feb. 1944.
[2] *War Report* (1946), pp. 17, 44; S. MacPherson, *The Mike and I* (1948), pp. 62–9.
[3] *Board of Governors, *Minutes*, 24 June 1943.
[4] *Haley to Macgregor, 6 April 1944. At the Trades Union Congress of 1943 Sir Walter Citrine had reinforced an appeal for increased production by referring to Vaughan Thomas's commentary of Sept. 1943. Cf. a letter to *The Spectator*, 4 June 1943, 'let us look upon these raids as a necessary evil . . . and not as copy for heartless rejoicing'. Goebbels often noted the terrible effects of the bomber attacks (see entries in his Diary; for example, for 6, 14 March 1943, 16 May 1943), yet because of his own fearless attitude to the raids and his willingness to travel through Germany to see air raid damage, he personally gained in popularity as a result of them (R. Semmler, *Goebbels, The Man Next to Hitler* (1947), p. 111). See also D. Irving, *The Destruction of Dresden* (1963).

While the Army training schedules were in progress and the reporters were learning not only about war conditions but about the intricacies of military censorship, BBC engineers were perfecting a new so-called 'midget recorder'—it weighed forty pounds, carried twelve double-sided discs and was simple to operate[1]—and BBC programme planners were considering the most effective way of organizing *War Report*. Gilliam, the brilliant Assistant Director of Features, recommended in April 1944, 'after discussions with the interested parties', either that *War Report* should take the place of the 9 o'clock News or that it should immediately follow it. The second alternative was chosen, although the first had its attractions— a statement of facts, including the communiqué; colour; front line recordings edited and linked by the announcer; explanation and comment; and 'the rest of the news'.[2] *Frontberichte* techniques were explicitly rejected. 'The material used in the supplement will be actual. Once the invasion starts there will be no dramatisation or studio production of war incidents such as *Into Battle*, etc. This will not preclude specially written and devised programmes using War Report Unit material on occasion, but these programmes will be considered individually and will in any event be outside the evening news and supplement period.'[3]

The last stages of the preparations before D-Day were as carefully worked out as the military preparations for D-Day itself. The correspondents had to be deployed so that they could immediately cover every phase of the landings; and they had to be placed in a position in which they could speedily get their despatches and messages back to Broadcasting House. Given the need for the utmost secrecy, they were provided with special security bases on the South Coast—the most important of them on a hillside near Fareham—from which

[1] It was first used at Anzio. For the midget recorder and its use, see *War Report* (1946), pp. 20 ff., which includes a vivid broadcast by Chester Wilmot on the subject.

[2] *Gilliam to Nicolls, 25 April 1944. There had been some impatience shown with 'rest of the news' items earlier in 1943. See, for example, *Dundee Courier and Advertiser*, 15 Feb. 1943: 'Why cannot the BBC keep to real news in the news bulletin and not waste people's time with parliamentary backchat?' Members of Parliament were naturally quite unsympathetic to this approach.

[3] *Minutes of a meeting, 2 May 1944.

they were able to send their messages 'up the line' back to Broadcasting House.[1] Monitoring channels were to be held open night and day, and a telediphone unit was to be available at all times to convert verbal messages into typewritten scripts for censorship and subsequent circulation to news departments and programme editors. The Unit was reinforced almost at the last moment by a shipment of equipment from America which 'had almost to be kidnapped': during the first hectic stages of the invasion it was manned by volunteers.[2] Improvisation and planning thus went on together, indeed, in a characteristically British way.

Ryan issued his final instructions to the team of correspondents on 8 May. 'All BBC men in the field are serving the Corporation as a whole. There must be no question of any man regarding himself as a member of this or that Division: still less of being primarily concerned with serving this or that part of the programmes. The team is a BBC one. The material it supplies will be used on its merits as good broadcasting material . . . we shall edit hard at this end and kill anything that is not worth using, judged by the following standards. There are no back pages in a broadcast. Everything we put out is in the nature of front-page stuff . . . everything we broadcast is liable to be heard by the troops in the field and you will hear about it if you say anything of their doings which rings false . . . let pride in the achievement of our armies come through—but never seek to "jazz-up" a plain story. . . . It is a very good broadcast that stands up for more than five minutes. . . . Be chary of sound effects. Sounds that might have been hatched in the studio read phoney nowadays. . . . You will meet practical difficulties in the field. Censorship, when it is on your plate and off ours, will sometimes seem to you slow or unreasonable, or both. There will be arguments about the issue of information, about Conducting Officers, about transport, maybe of favouritism. Your line in coping with

---

[1] The transmitting station was available for the use of Allied broadcasters of all nationalities.

[2] *War Report* (1946), p. 31; *World's Press News*, 17 Aug. 1944, 'How the BBC Planned its Invasion'. Four BBC monitors were seconded for a week to the Telediphone Unit. (*BBC Monitoring Service, *Monthly Report*, June 1944.) 61 official queries were answered by the Monitoring Service on D-Day itself.

these difficulties must be a commonsense one. Field service is no picnic. The soldiers with whom you work will make mistakes and get het up, the same as you will. So don't shoot demands to us in London to raise Cain unless you are quite certain you have a case. But, if you are certain, then report your difficulties to us without delay and you can rely on us to fight your battles up to the highest levels. . . . Finally, good luck. There will be times when you will get bored and depressed . . . but by and large you handful of men have been chosen to undertake the most important assignment so far known to broadcasting. Good luck.'[1]

2. D-Day and After

BEFORE the War Reporting Unit went into action, there was exciting news from the Italian front. On 4 June, less than a month after General Alexander had started a new offensive against the Monte Cassino line, Rome fell to the Allies. The following evening British listeners could hear the cheers of the citizens of liberated Rome with the bells of St. Peter's ringing in the background. The excitement was very quickly eclipsed, however, when the long-awaited news of the Allied landings in France arrived two days later. The Germans with all the resources of modern communication at their disposal had guessed neither the day nor the place.[2] Yet during the previous weeks, while SHAEF was completing its plans, the whole of the South of England had become one vast military camp. 'England is expectant, almost hushed,' a diarist wrote in the last week of May. 'Every time we turn on the radio we expect to hear that the great invasion of Europe has begun.'[3]

---

[1] *Ryan to all Correspondents, 8 May 1944.

[2] This is not strictly true. Hitler guessed right but, as A. J. P. Taylor says, 'he hesitated to back his hunch' (*English History, 1914–1945* (1965), p. 581). For Rommel's reactions, see below, pp. 670–1. The Allies, of course, made every effort to deceive the Germans.

[3] J. L. Hodson, *The Sea and the Land* (1945), p. 145.

The BBC had begun to make many other preparations for D-Day besides the new SHAEF programme and the planning of *War Report* long before the beginning of 1944. On 6 June itself, however, it forestalled the first Allied communiqués and on the basis of German reports monitored at Caversham announced at 8 a.m. the invasion of Europe, which had been postponed for one day because of the weather.[1] J. B. Clark had spent most of the previous hour resisting official efforts to prevent the news being broadcast: he said that he would not budge unless there was a censorship stop, and this never came.[2] The official news was broadcast at 9.30 a.m. when both Home and Overseas General Forces programmes were interrupted in order that John Snagge could read a broadcast by Eisenhower to the peoples of Europe.[3] Eisenhower told resistance leaders to follow the instructions they had received and stated firmly that 'effective civil administration of France must be provided by Frenchmen'; he ended by saying that the landing was 'but the opening phase of the campaign in Western Europe'. Recorded exhortations by the King of Norway and the Prime Ministers of the Netherlands and Belgium followed in their own languages.

As the day went by, information of early successes began to reach London from Allied sources. The first eye-witness accounts were broadcast from a Mitchell bomber after the one o'clock News.[4] During the afternoon it was announced that de Gaulle had arrived in England and would send a message to the people of France: this was broadcast later in the afternoon. Among people returning home from work there was an almost desperate demand for authentic news. 'That night,' another war-time diarist wrote—from the bustle of a Land Army hostel—'was the first and last time that there was

[1] *BBC Monitoring Service, *Monthly Report*, June 1944. According to BBC records the beginning of operations in Normandy on 6 June was first announced on the German radio in voice and on Hellschreiber at 7.0 a.m. According to Delmer, *Soldatensender Calais* picked up a German flash and interrupted dance music to broadcast the news at 4.50 a.m. on 6 June (Delmer, *Black Boomerang* (1962), p. 161).

[2] J. B. Clark, Day Book, 6 June 1944.

[3] *The speech was read simultaneously by Colonel DuPuy in the ABSIE programme (Note from Haley, 5 June 1944).

[4] *War Report* (1946), p. 61. This 'record of dispatches' broadcast by BBC correspondents between 6 June 1944 and 5 May 1945 is invaluable.

complete silence during the six o'clock News.'[1] After the nine o'clock News, the King spoke to the nation and the first BBC *War Report* was introduced by John Snagge. Unlike the bulletin which preceded it and the official communiqués which placed it in perspective, it was 'essentially personal and informal'. Such *War Reports* were listened to regularly during the months that followed by ten to fifteen million listeners in Britain and thousands overseas.[2] Indeed, *War Report* became the most important and effective link between 'the civilian and the services': 'it took the microphone to places where things were happening, and let it listen—as one would one's self like to listen—to the sounds of battle, to the voices of men just returned from the fighting line, to observers who spent that day touring the scene of action.'[3]

The day ended with a short religious service—with a sermon from the Archbishop of Canterbury—*Songs from the Shows*, an Albert Schweitzer recital on gramophone records, and yet another news bulletin at midnight. The casualties of the day had included a scheduled Delius concert and *Sportsmen's Corner*. Behind the scenes, J. B. Clark's office in Bush House had become something of a clearance centre for information. The Security Section of PWD/SHAEF had the highest respect for him and turned to him with confidence when it was anxious that arrangements for releases of scripts and news should be handled more efficiently and responsibly than had been the case in North Africa.[4] It was from this office that news flashed round the world. It was estimated, indeed, that 725 out of a total of 914 United States stations carried BBC programmes on 6 June.[5]

[1] S. Joseph, *If their Mothers Only Knew* (1946), p. 101. The demand for newspapers was also unprecedented. See a note in *World's Press News*, 15 June 1944: 'Amazing demand on D-Day newspapers—harassed vendors have a busy and hectic time. Even experienced old-timers of the circulation game were amazed by the exceptional rush and demand for evening papers on D-Day. In some cases the police had to protect the vendor from the almost overwhelming surge of the public towards the news seller.'

[2] Haw-Haw's comment that 'the place and time of the invasion could not be better from the German point of view' received little attention. In fact, the Germans gave considerable coverage themselves to the events of 6 June.

[3] *War Report*, p. 10.

[4] *Clark to Haley, 12 June 1944.

[5] *BBC North American Service, 'American Stations, Use of BBC Invasion Broadcasts, June 6th to 11th', 19 June 1944.

Interest could not be sustained to this degree during the day that followed, although it is remarkable how *War Report* retained its initial popularity. It is still illuminating to compare these programmes with the German *Frontberichte* of 1940 and 1941, when the Germans were on the offensive.[1] These programmes also had been designed to appeal to the widest public and to provide 'a solid link between Front and Homeland in order to forestall any danger of estrangement or rift such as, in Hitler's view, lost Germany the First World War'.[2] The *Frontberichte* were far more contrived, however, and far less intimate than *War Report*, and in the process of sub-editing background noises were inserted when it was felt that they would heighten dramatic effect.[3] One of the very first British eye-witness reports of 6 June brings out the difference of style and approach. 'We're coming down right low to attack our target,' an Air Force Observer reported—he was using a so-called midget recorder—'I don't think I can talk to you while we're doing this job, I'm not a blinking hero. I don't think it's much good trying to do these flash running commentaries when you're doing a dive bombing attack.'[4]

The cross reference to 'running commentaries' was apt, for it was on the 'running commentary' technique, developed before the war by the BBC's Outside Broadcasting Unit, that the new programmes were based. Little attempt was made to rely on *montage* or to contrast, as in *Frontberichte*, the natural and often halting voices of 'the men' with the slick professional voices of the named full-time reporters. Yet Gilliam had a hand in the editing of *War Report*, taking responsibility for the programme on alternate nights. His opposite number, Boyd of News Talks, was in charge on the other nights. The tempo was alarmingly quick and the business of cutting tricky and exhausting. As much professionalism had to be displayed

[1] See above, p. 20.

[2] *BBC Monitoring Service, 'The Nazi Wireless at War', July 1941.

[3] Dr. Raskin, a close associate of Goebbels (see above, p. 225), developed his theory of 'the dramaturgy of propaganda' as part of 'total wireless' (see *Handbuch des Deutschen Rundfunks* (1939)). 'Raw material' had to be sifted, 'produced' and re-set, while at the same time its topicality had to be maintained.

[4] *War Report*, p. 61. Compare Field-Marshal Montgomery's very different style. 'We have a great and righteous cause. Let us pray that the Lord, mighty in battle, will go forth with our Armies and that this special providence will aid us in the struggle.' (Quoted ibid., p. 74.)

by the backroom boys, therefore, as by the men at the front.

Many of the men at the front had a very tough time, and a few never returned. Marshall sent back his first report on 6 June, 'sitting,' as he put it, 'in soaked through clothes with no notes at all': two of the boats in which he had travelled had capsized.[1] Another reporter, who had travelled up Channel with a convoy to a point three miles off-shore, managed to reach the Isle of Wight by ship's picket boat; there he persuaded a Wren running a motor launch to take him across to Hamble, and from there he hitch-hiked to Fareham. Despite these devious modes of transport, his report was ready for transmission from London two hours after he had left his ship.

Very soon Marshall was to fade out of the picture, with Gillard, who had served with distinction as a war correspondent in Italy, taking increased responsibility in Normandy and Dimbleby in London. Immediately after D-Day itself, however, the operational difficulties received less attention than the superb journalistic achievement. 'Congratulations on putting over this morning's historic programme,' Haley told his colleagues. 'No one hearing it will have realised the alarms and excursions we were subjected to up to the very last moment. The programme matched the occasion.'[2] This was certainly a widely held opinion. G. M. Young was excited as a historian:[3] a reluctant ordinary listener in the provinces was equally enthusiastic. 'The BBC is an institution to which, like many other people, I am chronically allergic,' he wrote to the *Daily Mail*, 'and it therefore gives me all the more pleasure to borrow a slogan from its frightful vocabulary and to exclaim "Salute to the BBC" for the really amazingly high standard of its *War Reports* from Normandy.'[4]

In the meantime, the first SHAEF programmes had gone out on D-Day plus one. *Oranges and Lemons*, the signature tune,

---

[1] Ibid., p. 68. See also *Newspaper World*, 10 June 1944 and MacPherson, op. cit., ch. vi.

[2] *Haley to Nicolls, Ryan and Clark, 6 June 1944.

[3] See above, p. 57.

[4] *Daily Mail*, 27 June 1944; for other praise, see the *Manchester Guardian*, 7 June 1944; *The Star*, 7 June 1944 ('We should like to add a tribute to the BBC for their masterly handling of the news'); *The Weekly Scotsman*, 10 June 1944 (a 'special word of praise'); *Birmingham Post*, 22 June 1944 ('no falling off in the high quality of the nightly War Report').

was played, and at 5.55 a.m. Engelmann read a special message from SHAEF. This was broadcast by British and American voices five times during the first day. A prayer by an American Army Chaplain followed, then news headlines, then the first of a series of two-hour early morning programmes called *Rise and Shine*, in which two well-known broadcasters took part—Ronnie Waldman of the BBC and the American Dick Dudley, then a Sergeant in the United States Air Force. The News, which was broadcast every hour on the hour, was read by a rota of American, Canadian and British announcers in turn: as Gorham noted later, this 'resulted in a standard of news reading probably more erratic than anything previously broadcast under the aegis of the BBC'.[1] At the time, he wrote feelingly on 13 June, 'we are still aiming at parity between British and American voices in the reading of news headlines, but it is a great relief to be authorised to put accuracy first'.[2]

The SHAEF programme soon established itself, despite all the difficulties at its inception and the 'lack of reliable information on the listening habits and tastes of the AEF overseas'.[3] Close liaison was maintained with ABSIE, with the European and Overseas Services of the BBC and with the Psychological Warfare Department of SHAEF, but no attempt was made by SHAEF to impose any broadcasts on Gorham.[4] Indeed, he received no material directly from SHAEF between the arrival of the first orders on 6 June and 13 June.[5] AFN proved somewhat more difficult to deal with: it had access both to men and to programmes, the latter in abundance, but Gorham always felt that he had to have his eyes 'wide open' in his discussions with its Director, Johnny Haynes. His weekly planning meetings were tough affairs in which everyone came out 'battered'. 'If this isn't inter-allied co-operation,' Major Max-Muller once said, 'I don't know what it is—unless it's murder.'[6] One of the most successful AEF programmes was *Combat*

[1] M. Gorham, *Broadcasting and Television since 1900* (1952), p. 207.
[2] *Gorham to Rendall, 13 June 1944.
[3] *Ibid.
[4] *Ibid.
[5] This must have been a surprise. 'Programmes are liable to be broken into for news flashes or cancelled to make up for more important special reports', *The Melody Maker* wrote on 10 June 1944. Robin Richmond and his sextet were the first to be interrupted by the first Eisenhower communiqué.
[6] M. Gorham, *Sound and Fury* (1948), p. 149.

Diary, prepared by Royston Morley in Broadcasting House: it lasted for a quarter of an hour and prided itself on items in which a broadcaster of one nationality was reporting on the actions of troops of another.[1]

During the first week of the fighting, the BBC's War Reporting Unit improved its communications. A mobile medium-wave, low-power transmitter, Mike Charlie Oboe, which had been moved to the South Coast a week before D-Day mounted in a three-ton Army truck, had been carried with difficulty across the Channel. For the first night after its arrival in France it was housed in a tent near the beaches so that it could go into immediate action. The following day it was transferred to the tower room of the fourteenth-century castle at Creully near Bayeux, which was converted into a studio.[2] The transmitter was used for a variety of broadcasts—French, American and Canadian as well as British (Pierre Lefèvre's broadcasts among them)—but as the Allies moved across Europe, 'Mike Charlie Oboe' proved too low-powered to move with them. High-power transmitters MCN and MCP then came into full use.

Before the war in France opened up after the Americans broke through on 25 July 1944, the War Reporting Unit had run into trouble with Montgomery. He had been under sharp criticism for 'lack of progress',[3] and after he had launched an offensive on 18 July he objected to the BBC sending detailed information to London and placed an embargo on all news from the front. He told Howard Marshall that the BBC's up-to-date situation reports in the 9 o'clock news gave valuable information to the Germans about how the battle stood. Certainly German military communications were in some cases less effective in July 1944 than those of the BBC—a reversal of the 1940 position—and the Germans were able to use *War Report* as a cheap Intelligence service.[4] Montgomery was also disturbed

---

[1] Ibid., p. 146.

[2] In 1960 Sir Hugh Greene as Director-General of the BBC unveiled a bronze plaque to commemorate this story in the banqueting room of the castle: the tower room itself had been converted into a small war museum.

[3] H. C. Butcher, *My Three Years with Eisenhower* (1946), p. 617.

[4] *Marshall to Ryan, 19 July 1944. They also used the 'situation reports' of *Soldatensender Calais* (Delmer, op. cit., p. 167), as did Jon Kimche of the *Evening Standard*.

by the broadcasting of parts of a speech which he delivered to men of the Sixth Airborne Division which he did not wish to have generally released, and Chester Wilmot, the tough Australian war correspondent, who had made a recording of it, was ordered home.[1] This was all part of the fortunes of war, yet it was only after the BBC had made it clear that it had no intention of replacing him that Wilmot was allowed, with all speed, to return. Montgomery apologized to him personally for the misunderstanding.[2]

During the next month another correspondent, Robert Dunnett, who had reported the campaigns in North Africa,[3] had difficulties with the Americans. General Bradley was as critical of the BBC as Montgomery had been: he told a Press Conference, indeed, 'that the BBC had cost the lives of American soldiers by making a premature announcement closing the Falaise gap'. At this time, Dunnett felt that Bradley's attitude was calculated to undermine confidence in BBC News and make it impossible for a BBC reporter at American Army Group to carry out his job. 'Reid and I are repeatedly, and publicly, countering accusations wherever we meet them,' he wrote boldly, 'and whatever the rank of those who make them.'[4] True to the promise of high-level assistance which he had given to his war correspondents, Ryan reported Dunnett's difficulties to the Public Relations Division of SHAEF. He received in reply a letter quoting the Chief Press Censor SHAEF as stating that 'clearly the error was one by Censorship here and the BBC is entirely without fault'.[5]

Given the speed and complexity of the fighting, it is not surprising that there were such incidents. Protests continued to be made from time to time about BBC 'compromisers of

[1] *Wilmot to Ryan, 28 July 1944.

[2] *Dimbleby to Ryan, 24 Aug. 1944.

[3] *In an interesting report of 16 Feb. 1942 he had emphasized how important it was to co-operate with the Americans. 'We have now been three months in North Africa and still from day to day we cannot be certain that American facilities will be available to the best advantage of British broadcasters. This attitude is not due to malice but to naive enthusiasm for their own interests and to the irresponsibility of inexperience.'

[4] *Dimbleby to Ryan, 24 Aug. 1944. Robert Reid had formerly served as North Region Publicity Officer. Newsome also had his difficulties with Bradley when he took over his job in SHAEF: he was accused of being 'too pro-BBC'.

[5] *Butcher to Ryan, 8 Sept. 1944.

security', and there was more than one threat of 'pre-censorship'.[1] The protests continued, indeed, until the very last stages of the war, when in April 1945 the American Director of the Public Relations Division of SHAEF, Brigadier-General Allen, complained that the BBC had broken an embargo on the news of the link-up between the American and Russian forces. In this case, however, the BBC had relied not on its own reporters but on messages from Associated Press.[2]

Difficulties in Europe were only part of the story. Press correspondents were sometimes irritated by what seemed to be preferences shown to the BBC. Before the BBC War Reporting Unit moved into France, it had often been said that newspapermen were far more enterprising than BBC reporters: the BBC had frequently been criticized, as we have seen, for 'dullness' and 'secondhand' reporting.[3] Now there were signs of envy that the BBC had so many correspondents, complaints that BBC correspondents had better opportunities of getting their messages back to Britain more quickly than newspapermen, criticisms even of Montgomery for favouring the radio as a method of reaching his troops direct.[4] William Hickey in the *Daily Express* recalled Northcliffe's words about infant radio that 'there is our deadliest enemy': the BBC, he went on, is 'a Corporation by a Government and not a revelation by a God'.[5] From a quite different angle, a listener complained that 'it is not well that the BBC, an official body, should join the scoop merchants of the Press'.[6]

Whatever the criticisms—and few of them were made or shared by the general public[7]—the members of the BBC team

[1] *Lord Burnham to Ryan, 3 Jan. 1945; Cyril Ray to Ryan, 4, 5 Dec. 1944.

[2] *Haley to Allen, 3 May 1945.

[3] See, for example, an article by T. Harrisson in *The Observer*, 16 April 1944. See also above, p. 194.

[4] *Newspaper World*, 19 Aug. 1944. Montgomery gave several broadcasts to 'all soldiers in the group of armies under my Command'.

[5] Ibid., 13 May 1944; cf. *World's Press News*, 18 May 1944.

[6] *Weekly Review*, 7 Sept. 1944.

[7] There was a small minority which objected to *War Report* on different grounds. 'Most of the broadcasts direct from the battlefield are to be grievously deplored, for their effect is very largely to give us seats in a gigantic amphitheatre in which gladiators are fighting and killing one another before our eyes. Not even in the days of pagan Rome were such mighty thrills due to such encounters awaited each evening in quiet homes throughout the country.' (*British Weekly*, 24 Aug. 1944.) Cf. the reaction to the reporting of air battles in 1940: see above, p. 220.

were greatly admired for their energy, their courage, their resourcefulness and, not least, their command of the English language. They filled hundreds of the 5,000 or more blank discs issued each week by the BBC.[1] Montgomery himself paid a tribute to them for their 'crusading spirit': 'this spirit,' he declared, 'had many and deep sources and the BBC was one of the means by which this spirit was fostered.' He also remarked that 'when the history of these times comes to be written, they will prove of great value and importance'.[2] A member of the BBC's team, Chester Wilmot, trained before the war as a historian, was later to write 'one of those enduring works of military history—which have enduring value both as an eye-witness account and as an authoritative survey of a large and complex campaign', *The Struggle for Europe* (1952).[3] Another member, Richard Dimbleby, then thirty-one years old, was to become perhaps the best-known of all post-war television commentators. Yet another, Frank Gillard, was to become post-war Director of Sound Broadcasting.

A mere catalogue of names does too little justice to the qualities of the team: their achievements, in many cases, belong not only to the war years but to the years before and after. Michael Standing, Wynford Vaughan Thomas, Edward Ward, Stanley Maxted and Stewart MacPherson had already established their broadcasting reputations before D-Day. Robin Duff was the first producer and narrator of *Radio Newsreel*, the pioneer topicality programme which set a new style.[4] Godfrey Talbot had already published before 1944 a volume of his African broadcasts, *Speaking from the Desert*. Denis Johnston, the playwright, who worked with Gillard in Italy, had made his mark with an *Inside Yugoslavia* programme which included partisan songs and a Yugoslav version of *Tipperary*. The full list of Western Front reporters also included Robert Barr, David Bernard, Guy Byam (reported missing), Rupert Downing, Alfred Fletcher, Alan Melville, Richard North, Cyril Ray, Robert Reid, E. Colston Shepherd, Kent Stevenson (also reported missing), Douglas Willis, Colin Wills,

---

[1] In July 1944 the figure reached 6,600 (*Haley to Controllers, 28 July 1944).
[2] Foreword to *War Report*, p. 3.
[3] Introduction by Michael Howard to the 1966 paper-back edition of *The Struggle for Europe*, p. v. [4] See above, p. 49.

and Ian Wilson. Their broadcasts were supplemented by broadcasts from the Italian front by Reginald Beckwith, Francis Hallawell, John Nixon, Michael Reynolds and Patrick Smith; from the Balkans by Kenneth Matthews; and from distant Burma by Richard Sharp, who had arrived in New Delhi in January 1944.[1]

Apart from Pierre Lefèvre, there were no reporters from the European Language Services of the BBC in France during the early weeks of the invasion. When Kirkpatrick, who was to leave the BBC for PID on 1 September 1944, complained about this, Brigadier Neville replied briskly, 'I have just returned from the other side, where there are *1.85 corres-pondents per mile* of front. The result of this magnificent system is that there is no room for them to get back to their communications and get their stuff off. . . . My great difficulty is trying to run the show out there from here, which, in fact, cannot be done, and the flocks of correspondents in France are undoubtedly out of hand.' The most he could suggest was that some of Kirkpatrick's 'polyglot party' could be taken out for short visits later on.[2]

The 'polyglot party' had, of course, its own part to play in the events of D-Day, the great day for which the resistance movements throughout Europe had waited for so long, often with impatience. General Rommel had noted 'increased transmissions on enemy radio of warning messages to French resistance organisations' in his weekly *Estimate of the Overall Situation* on 5 June, but he concluded on the basis of previous experience that the increase did not indicate that invasion was imminent.[3] The same conclusion was reached by von Rundstedt's Chief of Staff, General von Blumentritt. Von Rundstedt's headquarters had monitored an exceptionally long list of coded messages at 9.15 p.m. on 5 June in the BBC's French programme: the list took twenty minutes to read instead of the usual five to ten. During the course of the programme a BBC spokesman declared that 'today the Supreme Commander directs me to say this: in due course, instructions of great importance will be

---

[1] *Controllers' Conference, *Minutes*, 5 Jan. 1944. The Japanese invaded northeast India in March 1944. They were pushed back after the decisive battle of Imphal early in July.   [2] *Neville to Kirkpatrick, 6 July 1944.

[3] Quoted in Chester Wilmot, op. cit., p. 257.

(a) V. A. de Laveleye (Belgian Programme Organizer) and
Nand Geersens (Flemish Programme Organizer)

(b) British Soldiers in France listen to a Receiver hidden
from the Germans, June 1944

21. The Resistance Vindicated

(*a*) Stanley Maxted recording 'War Report' at Arnhem

(*b*) Pierre Bourdan and Pierre Gosset after their Escape
from the Germans

22. At the Front, September 1944

23. Sir Henry Wood amid the Ruins of the Queen's Hall

24. Broadcasting House on VE Day

given to you through this channel, but it will not be possible always to give these instructions at a previously announced time. Therefore you must get into the habit of listening at all hours.' Although this programme put the Germans on the alert and they collected related evidence from other sources—radio jamming and weather reports, for example—no special precautions were taken. Even when Rommel's HQ sent out a 'Most Urgent' signal at 10 p.m. telling German troops to stand by ready for urgent action, the signal was transmitted to the German Fifteenth Army alone, the divisions between the Orne and the Scheldt. To the Seventh Army guarding the coast towards which the Allied invasion fleet was already heading Rommel's HQ gave no warning at all.[1]

Resistance messages had indeed increased greatly in volume during the early days of June 1944, after orders had been given in May by Dr. Leslie Beck of PWE to Boris, Brilhac, Mayoux, Serreulles and Colonels Vernon and Manuel to prepare a code of instructions for use by the French resistance on D-Day.[2] In March 1944 de Gaulle, whose dispute with Giraud had by then passed into history, had decreed the formation of FFI, the *Forces Françaises de l'Intérieur*, and had given the order that 'at the right moment' they had to launch a 'national effort', firm and consistent enough 'to play a part in Allied strategy'.[3] On 1 May 1944 SOE had been re-named Special Force Headquarters (SFHQ), 'a convenient cover name to make relations between the directing body and the more regular formations engaged in the coming invasion of France more secure'.[4] Nonetheless, before the invasion started, there was another sharp *contretemps* between Churchill and de Gaulle, who was summoned back to London from Algiers on 3 June.[5] On the following day he was informed by Churchill for the first time that the invasion of France was timed to

---

[1] Ibid., p. 258. See also L. F. Ellis, *Victory in the West* (1962), vol. I, p. 198.

[2] J. L. Crémieux-Brilhac, 'Les Émissions Françaises à la BBC pendant la Guerre' in *Histoire de la Deuxième Guerre Mondiale*, no. 1, Nov. 1950.

[3] C. de Gaulle, *Mémoires de Guerre* (1959 edn.), vol. II, p. 312.

[4] M. R. D. Foot, *SOE in France* (1966), p. 32.

[5] He had been invited to London, with no definite date given, on 23 May, and Churchill's new invitation to come at once reached him on 2 June. He travelled alone, since he said it would be useless for him to bring members of his Government unless the Americans were prepared to recognize him. (E. L. Woodward, *British Foreign Policy in the Second World War* (1962), p. 265.)

start the following day. Asked at such short notice whether he would allow a French commando troop and a small party of French SAS to take part in the expedition—the commandos were, in fact, already at sea and the members of the SAS party were briefed and 'sealed' in a Gloucestershire aerodrome—he had no alternative but to say yes. The security arrangements had been so strict that de Gaulle felt that he had been deliberately left out. There was as much mutual rancour between Churchill and de Gaulle on this occasion, indeed, on the eve of the climax of the whole war, as there had ever been.[1]

Irritation expressed itself, as it had done so many times in the past, in relation to arrangements for a de Gaulle broadcast to the French people. J. B. Clark had spent 3 June preparing for the recording of D-Day broadcasts. Eisenhower had already recorded a message,[2] and Clark discussed with Paley of PWD and others, how best to obtain a recorded message from de Gaulle. They decided to send a recording car to Eisenhower's headquarters at 7 a.m. on 4 June. The car duly arrived, but L. F. Lewis, the senior recording engineer, who distinctly remembers the noise of de Gaulle's and Churchill's altercations, returned without a de Gaulle recording. He reported, moreover, that the General strongly disapproved of the cautious wording and tone of Eisenhower's message which did not mention himself or the *Comité National* and which did not, in his view, include a sufficiently rousing general call to the French resistance.[3] De Gaulle went on to propose certain alterations in the text which he then sent to Eisenhower, but he was told on 5 June that they had arrived too late.[4] It was not until 2 a.m. on D-Day itself, 6 June, that the BBC made

[1] For one version of the events of 4 June, see W. S. Churchill, *War Memoirs*, vol. V, pp. 553 ff.

[2] See above, p. 661. It included the words, 'To members of Resistance Movements, whether led by nationals or by outside leaders, I say "follow the instructions you have received". To patriots who are not members of operational resistance groups, I say "continue your passive resistance, but do not needlessly endanger your lives".'

[3] C. de Gaulle, op. cit., p. 342.

[4] See a quotation from Alanbrooke's diary on 5 June, quoted in A. Bryant, *Triumph in the West* (1960 edn.): 'A long Cabinet at which it was explained how tiresome de Gaulle was being now that he had been fetched back from Algiers. He is refusing to broadcast unless Eisenhower alters the wording of his own broadcast.' He also was threatening to withdraw French liaison officers attached to the Allied Forces (Woodward, op. cit., p. 266).

contact with de Gaulle at his bedside after Churchill, through Charles Peake, had approached Pierre Viénot, the General's Diplomatic Representative in London, asking him to intervene. In the middle of the night de Gaulle promised at last to record a broadcast.[1] News of it was 'trailed' in the early D-Day programmes to France, and it was recorded in the late morning of 6 June at 12.30 p.m. Michel St. Denis, who met him on this occasion, introduced André Gillois to him as 'your representative at the BBC': Gillois had, in fact, recently replaced Maurice Schumann as de Gaulle's *porte-parole*. There followed a preposterous but not uncharacteristic muddle about transcription and translation:[2] there were mechanical defects in the first recording, and there was delay in getting an English text of the message to be approved by PWD/SHAEF. The BBC had planned to transmit the address at 2.30 in the afternoon, but it could not be used until 5.30 in a News period in the French Service. It was subsequently repeated in programmes at 6.30 p.m., 7.30 p.m., 9.35 p.m. and 12.30 a.m. and 1.30 a.m. on 7 June. The record still exists in the BBC sound archives.

Behind these bizarre events there were real issues of principle. Not only did Roosevelt remain chary of recognizing de Gaulle as head of a 'Provisional Government': Eisenhower, also, placed little confidence in support from the French resistance, except on a limited local scale. The Allied Air Forces, not the members of the French resistance, were thought to offer the most effective means of preventing the movement of German reinforcements to the Normandy bridgehead. Yet the resistance did stir. The persistent labours of the BBC—and of SOE[3] —during the previous years, culminating as they did in de Gaulle's broadcast, produced something like a French national uprising. Radio messages from Pétain and Laval stating that France was not at war were treated everywhere with contempt.[4]

---

[1] It was a busy night. Viénot told Eden at 1 a.m. that he would not change his mind about the officers. Duff Cooper eventually persuaded him to send some officers.

[2] J. B. Clark, *Day Book*, 6 June 1944.

[3] Foot, op. cit., p. 397.

[4] E. Jäckel, *La France dans l'Europe d'Hitler* (1968), p. 455; R. Aron, *Histoire de Vichy* (1954). Pétain's message had been recorded earlier in the year (ibid.) on the grounds that 'he will probably be asleep at the moment of the invasion' (Jäckel, p. 425). See also R. Aron, *Histoire de la Libération de la France* (1959), pp. 140 ff.

BBC messages giving orders to the resistance led to the implementation of 950 out of a planned 1,050 interruptions of railway traffic. During the next few weeks resistance support for 'Overlord' was a good deal more effective than had been expected in London, although the price was a large number of French casualties. As the insurrection grew, de Gaulle could say, in the style of the Italians of 1848, *Francia farà da sè*.[1]

Two members of the BBC's French *équipe* in London, Pierre Bourdan and Pierre Gosset, who were sent to Brittany on 2 August,[2] were captured by the Germans near Rennes[3] and were transported south by train, moving very slowly because of resistance sabotage. They were impressed by the fact that everywhere the train stopped, there were cries of *Courage*. The two men escaped to tell their story in the BBC's French Service. 'Nous avons découvert les trésors de générosité d'une France qui n'était pas encore libérée, et qui jamais n'a été aussi digne, aussi fraternelle, aussi solidaire.'[4]

The Germans, like the British and Americans, might attach far less importance to the activities of the resistance than they did to the Allied advances in Normandy,[5] but French spirits were high, and the liberation of Paris, after the German bomb plot against Hitler on 20 July had briefly thrown the Germans in Paris into confusion,[6] was the result of a popular uprising. The American breakthrough in Normandy, beginning on 25 July—'une Blitzkrieg, American style', Larry Lesueur, the CBS radio reporter, called it in appropriate international language[7]—was the prelude to the German evacuation of France, which proceeded as quickly as their initial conquest in 1940. They began to leave Paris on 16 August, the day the Canadians entered Falaise. On the 19th several French gendarmes seized the Police Prefecture, and during the night of the 19th/20th the FFI gained control of the heart of the city.

---

[1] Foot, op. cit., pp. 389–90.

[2] Pierre Lefèvre arrived in Granville on 12 Aug. and gave a vivid broadcast on conditions there (*War Report*, pp. 182–4).

[3] Rennes was captured by the Allies on 4 Aug., and after a rapid movement south Brittany was sealed off.

[4] *BBC Script, 12 Aug. 1944. For correct German assessments of what was happening, see Jäckel, op. cit., pp. 457 ff.

[5] Ibid., p. 466.

[6] Ibid., pp. 470 ff. See below, pp. 692–3.

[7] *War Report*, p. 158.

A three-day armistice was signed with the German Military Commandant on the morning of the 20th, whereby the members of the FFI were recognized as belligerents and the Germans were allowed to withdraw from the capital unmolested. Fighting broke out again, however, in the evening, and Radio Paris, still controlled by the Germans, warned that 'revolt' would be 'rigorously suppressed'. On the 21st the FFI sent envoys to the Americans warning them of the serious plight of the FFI, and on the 22nd General Bradley ordered his troops to enter Paris as soon as possible after the armistice expired.

Before the Allies entered Paris on the 24th, General Koenig prematurely announced the liberation of the city, and Carlton Gardens put pressure on the BBC to reveal the 'news', which was unconfirmed by SHAEF, to Europe and the world. The announcement was made by the BBC—Gillie regarded it as 'one of the few mistakes of news inside France during the war'—while fierce fighting was still going on inside and outside the city. On the 25th and 26th, however, the Allies, led by General Leclerc's troops, began to pour into Paris, with General de Gaulle in their midst. BBC reporters made the most of this great occasion. Two of them, indeed, Marshall and Duff, were later to be suspended by the Public Relations Division of SHAEF for broadcasting messages from a Paris radio station on 25 August, messages which they knew would be monitored by the BBC, before SHAEF facilities for transmitting were made available.[1] Although they later handed over copies of their broadcasts to SHAEF in duplicate, they were suspended for sixty days. The suspensions were later cut to thirty days after the opinion had been freely and forcefully expressed that if correspondents could get into Paris so could the censors.[2] One of the first Americans to rush to the Paris radio stations to try to capture the transmitters and studios intact was Colonel David Sarnoff, pioneer of American broadcasting, then in the Signal Corps. With pistol on hip he took over CTSF, the French short-wave station.[3]

The British public was as excited by the first broadcasts from Paris as it had been by the news of the first Normandy landings.

[1] *The Times*, 2 Sept. 1944.
[2] *World's Press News*, 21 Sept. 1944.
[3] E. Lyons, *David Sarnoff: A Biography* (1966), pp. 259-60.

'The war scenes in Normandy were admirably pictured, but it was when Paris was approached and entered that the real triumph was obtained,' wrote the *National Review*. 'There can never have been anything more dramatic than the entry of General de Gaulle on foot into Paris amidst the delirious joy of a liberated people, with whose cheers and songs were mingled the shots of Germans and Pétainist assassins. The broadcast of Mr. Robert Dunnett from the Place de la Concorde was thrilling, but it was surpassed by the broadcast of Mr. Robert Reid from the doors of the Cathedral of Notre Dame where General de Gaulle went, escorted by all Paris, to attend a Te Deum.' The sound of the Paris bells 'ended a notable description of a wonderful scene'.[1] Dunnett had mingled his commentary with sounds of gunfire: Reid was in the midst of what he called 'one of the most dramatic scenes I've ever seen'. His report is breathless even to read. 'And now here comes General de Gaulle. The General's now turned to face the square and this huge crowd of Parisians (*machine-gun-fire*). He's being presented to people (*machine-gun-fire*). He's being received (*shouts of crowd—shots*)—even while the General is marching (*sudden sharp outburst of continued fire*)—even while the General is marching into the Cathedral . . . (*break on record*).' The broadcast ended as dramatically as it had begun. 'Four snipers have been caught inside the Church. They were all in civilian clothing. . . . And even more firing is still going on here (*shot*). That was one that just came over us.'[2]

With the liberation of Paris and the establishment of de Gaulle's Provisional Government,[3] which was fully recognized by the British and Americans in October 1944, the role of the BBC's French *équipe* in London obviously became far less important.[4] News bulletins were what counted now, hard facts concerning further victories, rather than topical commentaries. Clandestine French radio was prominent in local

---

[1] *National Review*, Oct. 1944. The *National Review* got the dates of the broadcasts wrong, a sign that historical inaccuracies can creep into the most immediate accounts.

[2] *War Report*, pp. 202–4.

[3] On 15 August Allied troops, mostly American, had landed also in the south of France.

[4] *This had been envisaged earlier (European Services Divisional Meeting, *Minutes*, 22 Aug. 1944).

resistance activities and often continued to depend on information from London, but *Les Français parlent aux Français* was broadcast for the last time on 22 October 1944.[1] The time previously devoted to it was now offered to the newly constituted *Radiodiffusion Française* which some people in France insisted on calling 'la BBC française'. For Gillie the phrase-makers were taking over,[2] although it was in the finest possible phrases that the inaugural transmission paid the warmest of tributes to the BBC. 'During the long dark four years, the BBC was a torch in the darkness and the embodiment of the promise of liberation. The world was in agony; but the BBC played its life-giving music. The world was submerged in lies; but the BBC proclaimed the truth. This tradition of truth and honour will be continued here.'[3]

There had been no more discussion inside the BBC about the long-term objectives of broadcasting to France than there had been about the long-term objectives of broadcasting to Germany, and there was little certainty about British policy towards France at the very moment of liberation. The easiest way out—and the one actually taken—was to seek to 'project' Britain. Henceforth, the task of the French section of the BBC,

[1] In his last remarks Duchesne thanked 'our English friends who, having welcomed General de Gaulle, the first "resistant" of France as he is called now, allowed us to speak to you each day. Above all, we thank the Englishmen of the BBC, with whom we have been able to work in the saddest and most difficult times—and there were some of those—because they knew not only how to respect our freedom but also how to organise it.'

[2] Note from Darsie and Cecilia Gillie to the author, 13 Jan. 1969.

[3] Quoted in *BBC Year Book, 1945*, p. 114. The BBC received many letters from France on this theme, 4,000 in Dec. 1944 alone. 'To you, BBC, I want to write my first letter to England,' a Paris schoolteacher exclaimed, 'for you have been Life, Truth and Freedom to me through the fifty terrible months we have had to live.' An electrician on the staff of the Paris Opera House remarked that 'I believe that the French owe their liberty and all it means, to the BBC, for without you how could we have known about our General de Gaulle?' Another letter from Dieppe described the BBC as our 'moral salvation', while a letter from Lyons described how a faithful listener who had smuggled out letters to the BBC throughout the occupation was shot by the Gestapo one day before the Allies entered Lyons. See also the tribute from Georges Bidault, then one of the most prominent resistance leaders: ' "Ici Londres, les Français parlent aux Français". These were the words which, in the silence of occupation, when every mouth was gagged, helped the French to surmount and overcome the lies of the enemy. Like a compass to the sailor, the wireless was to them the guide and the assurance which, at the height of the tempest, saved them from despair. It is partly, indeed largely, thanks to you, dear familiar voices, that our minds stayed free while our limbs were bound.' (Ibid., p. 14.)

it was said, would be to inform the French about the opinions of the British—on politics, society and culture—'illustrating in a variety of fields the manner in which our democratic institutions and authorities are dealing with current problems of war and the prospects of peace'.[1] A programme called *Angleterre en Mouvement* described the processes of continuous adjustment in British society; a programme called *Institutions Anglaises* dealt with law and punishment; *Lettres Anglaises* brought to the French public well-known British writers, including H. G. Wells, Rosamond Lehmann and V. Sackville-West; for children there was a serialization in French of *Alice in Wonderland*.[2]

As the Allies moved east to liberate other European countries in a great campaign of movement, the same shift took place. Brussels was liberated on 5 September: Chester Wilmot gave a lively broadcast about it, reaching his audience by means of a secret transmitter fitted in a suitcase and dropped by the RAF for the use of the Belgian underground during the occupation. The wavelength he used was outside the BBC's normal range, and the broadcast was picked up not by the BBC's Monitoring Service but by an Army receiving station.[3] Throughout Belgium, Wilmot and his fellow reporters were greeted with enthusiasm, and as the whole country was liberated there was the same shift in BBC broadcasting to Belgium as there already had been in broadcasting to France. 'Our work is done,' de Laveleye, the initiator of the 'V' sign who became Minister of Education in the Belgian Government, told his compatriots in the last broadcast of 16 September. 'You are free and have no more need of the voices that reached you from London and gave you reasons for hope.' To the British he gave thanks for the chance of working 'in an atmosphere of absolute independence'.[4]

When American Forces reached Luxembourg in the late summer of 1944, a valuable radio asset was acquired in the form of Radio Luxembourg. The Germans tried to destroy the wireless station before they left, but their dynamite charges

---

[1] Ibid., p. 111.
[2] Ibid., pp. 115–16.
[3] The broadcast is printed in *War Report*, pp. 210–12.
[4] *BBC Year Book, 1945*, p. 112.

failed to destroy the transmitter. A Luxembourg engineer who had encouraged them to shoot holes in transmitter valves—to divert them from more ambitious schemes of destruction—dug up a set of transmitter valves which he had buried four years earlier in the expectation of the eventual day of liberation.[1] From 22 September 1944 onwards the station was in full operation under the control of PWD/SHAEF. The station was discovered to have a valuable collection of discs, including recordings of Benny Goodman, the Dorsey Brothers and Glenn Miller, which the Germans would have used had they landed in Britain in 1940. Very quickly PWD could make effective use of these; and although it was decided not to broadcast bulletins in German based on material and guidance from London,[2] PWD also employed the station for 'black' broadcasting to Germany during the last stages of the war. Every night from 2 a.m. to 6 a.m. the transmitter operated on a changed wavelength in the guise of a German-language station, 'Twelve Twelve'. It was the object of this service, which was operated secretly and quite independently of the other Luxembourg services, to create confusion in Germany as the Allied armies advanced.

Newsome worked with Radio Luxembourg throughout this period, and among other members of BBC staff seconded there for periods were Patrick Gordon Walker and Leonard Miall: in addition, Carleton Greene, Lindley Fraser and Marius Goring of the BBC's German Service paid brief visits there. Reports from Luxembourg certainly helped the German section at the moment when the operational needs of the service were beginning to become paramount. Yet the BBC was worried about the drain of staff to Luxembourg, and on occasion there were somewhat acrimonious exchanges between J. B. Clark and Paley.

Holland was not liberated until 1945, and it was from Arnhem, where British parachutists were unsuccessful in September 1944 in their bold attempt to seize German-held bridges over the Rhine, brilliantly described in *War Report*,[3]

[1] E. Barnouw, *The Golden Web* (1968), p. 201, quoting *Yank*, 11 May 1945.

[2] *Programme Policy Meeting, *Minutes*, 24 Oct. 1944.

[3] *War Report*, pp. 254–5. See also *News Review*, 5 Oct. 1944. 'Crawling between the mortars and the shell fire', Stanley Maxted made recordings of the sounds and impressions of the men. Unfortunately most of the records were smashed when a
[*cont.*

that the Germans operated their own 'deceiving station'—
Radio Arnhem, a station which was neither 'black' nor 'grey'
but resorted to a new technique of deception. It relayed AEFP
and BBC Home Service programmes from 6.25 in the morning
until 11 o'clock at night, interspersing them with its own
material, consisting of music, headline news and messages from
British and American prisoners of war. It had sufficient power
and was near enough to the installations of Allied troops to be
heard quite clearly, and it caused considerable trouble when
on 8 January 1945 it broadcast a statement, purporting to
emanate from the BBC, praising Montgomery and disparaging
the Americans. Despite the fact that, as the BBC put it, 'such
attempts by the enemy to mislead listeners can generally be
detected if the substance is weighed with a little commonsense',[1]
the incident was taken sufficiently seriously for Bracken to send
a personal message to Eisenhower.

Meanwhile, Dutch listeners continued throughout the long
hard winter of 1944/5, when they were desperately short of
food, fuel, electricity and transport, to listen whenever they
could to BBC broadcasts. 'One underground paper even
arranged to record all our transmissions.'[2] Although a free
Dutch station in Eindhoven began to broadcast in September
1944 under the name of *Herrijzend Nederland,* it was *via* the
BBC that the Dutch were warned of the final German round-ups
of forced labour and of the German bombing of the Walcheren
dykes which flooded the Zeeland Islands. A programme for
Dutch workers was broadcast twice a week, encouraging them
to acts of sabotage, but there were differences of opinion as late
as April 1945 about a 'call to arms' which was broadcast by
Radio Oranje without the prior approval of SHAEF.[3]

By the end of September 1944 the German defences in
Western Europe had been stabilized, and the Allied armies

[1] *BBC Announcement to Press Agencies, 10 Jan. 1945.
[2] *Undated unsigned paper, 'Some Notes on the Dutch Service'.
[3] *BBC European Divisional Meeting, *Minutes,* 3 April 1945.

near miss by a mortar peppered the recording unit, but Maxted was able to save
three discs which he tucked inside his battle blouse. The other reporter, Guy
Byam, was a Fetcham man, and there is an account in his local newspaper, the
Dorking and Leatherhead Advertiser (6 Oct. 1944), of how he and Maxted had kept
Britain 'in direct and intimate touch with the men of that amazing drama'.
Johann Fabricius, a Dutch broadcaster, gave a moving epilogue to the report.

were strung out in Europe from Antwerp to the Swiss frontier. From 7 November 1944 onwards, therefore, it was decided that *War Report* could no longer be maintained as a daily feature and would have to be restricted to certain days each week.[1] There was a further twist of fortune when the Germans started a powerful counter-offensive, their last of the war, on 16 December. Within three days they had advanced forty-five miles and were dreaming of recapturing Antwerp. Although their push had lost its momentum by Christmas Day 1944, these were dispiriting days. For the first time, indeed, *War Report* had had to report withdrawals, consoling its listeners with the words, 'Hitler wants to make as much propaganda out of it as he can, to bolster the spirit of his people at home.'[2] A BBC news analyst was very cautious even on New Year's Day 1945. 'It would be wise,' he said, 'to abstain from prediction . . . that this year will see the end of the fighting either in Europe or Asia.'[3]

From 4 February 1945 until the Allied crossing of the Rhine on 23 and 24 March, *War Report* was suspended as the Allies accumulated men and materials for their final assault. The decision to take this step was made in late January.[4] The programme was replaced by a fifteen-minute period which included *War Commentary*,[5] one of the oldest war-time programmes, and topical material not related to the war. There was also a daily Forces War Review.[6] The SHAEF radio service by then had comfortable offices in Paris and Brussels, directed by Charles Brewer and Franklin Engelmann, and employed a greatly increased range of captured transmitters. This was 1940 in reverse. Some of the first people associated with the service, notably Kirby, had left and been replaced; and its brief history had been darkened by a broadcasting

---

[1] *Programme Policy Meeting, *Minutes*, 7 Nov. 1944.

[2] *War Report*, p. 297, Report of R. Hottelet (CBS). In fact, while the German offensive was progressing, PWD/SHAEF was engaged in a most effective propaganda exercise, designing four leaflets for the future advance. It knew exactly which line that advance would take. (See R. H. S. Crossman, 'Psychological Warfare' in the *Journal of the Royal United Service Institution*, Aug. 1953.)

[3] *BBC Year Book, 1946*, p. 8.

[4] *Programme Policy Committee, *Minutes*, 30 Jan. 1945.

[5] *War Commentary* had been reinstated in Aug. 1944, when a decision had also been taken to simplify *War Report* (*ibid., 15 Aug. 1944).

[6] *Perkins to D. Hawkins, 14 March 1945.

tragedy, announced to the radio audience on Christmas Eve 1944—the disappearance of Glenn Miller, whose single-engined plane had been lost crossing the Channel to visit Paris after the liberation. Miller had left so many recorded programmes behind him that it had been possible to go on broadcasting them between the time of his disappearance and Christmas as if he were still there.[1]

Although AEFP secured the services of many other top-class broadcasters, notably Bing Crosby,[2] it faced increasing competition during the winter of 1944/5. AFN had its Paris headquarters in a former residence of Napoleon III, and it had an increasing number of stations in the field, while AFRS, the American Army's short-wave service from Hollywood, was putting out programmes specially designed for use by U.S. Army relay stations in the SHAEF area in their local option time. Within SHAEF itself Colonel Niven was pressing for more American time on the SHAEF service on the grounds that an increasing proportion of American troops were involved in the military campaigns.[3] There were, moreover, considerable difficulties in picking up the SHAEF programme in the Vosges area and in the South of France.[4] Something of the same kind of problem was confronting the Allied broadcasters as was confronting the Allied generals, squabbling about future strategy.

By then also the BBC was thinking hard about its own strategy, looking to the future, when the SHAEF programme would terminate and when the scale and content of broadcasts in European languages would be determined less by operational needs. On 20 November 1944 Radcliffe had written to Haley proposing that they worked out 'an acceptable understanding' to cover relations between the BBC and the Ministry of Information[5] for the future, as political warfare needs were changing. 'I note,' wrote J. B. Clark, who had succeeded Kirkpatrick, 'that Radcliffe does not contemplate

---

[1] M. Gorham, *Sound and Fury* (1948), pp. 152–3.
[2] Ibid., pp. 156–7. Crosby had arrived in Aug. 1944.
[3] *Gorham to Rendall, 'The Future of the AEF Programme', 20 Dec. 1944.
[4] *Programme Policy Meeting, *Minutes*, 16 Jan. 1945.
[5] *Radcliffe to Haley, 20 Nov. 1944; Board of Governors, *Minutes*, 14 Dec. 1944. The first BBC reference to broadcasting in re-occupied countries is in Board of Governors, *Minutes*, 15 July 1943.

the maintenance by the Ministry of Information of day to day, or weekly directives (such as we have had in the past from PWE but which have now lapsed) but does ask for regular contact and consultation with us.' He went on to express the hope that 'our relationship with them can be as informal as possible' and that direct contacts with the Foreign Office could be 'preserved and possibly extended'. The likelihood that Kirkpatrick might return to the Foreign Office would greatly facilitate this.[1] There were further discussions between Haley and Radcliffe, during which it was agreed that there would in future be no standing committees and no directives, that instead there would be 'general personal consultations between the various regional broadcasting heads of the BBC and their opposite numbers in the Ministry of Information', that 'final responsibility for broadcasting' rested with the BBC, and that all foreign-language services outside the control of PWE would be 'objective and non-propagandist'.[2]

On 19 January 1945 Tangye Lean, who, following the departure of Gillie, had taken over the position of Acting French Editor, was told that control of broadcasts to France had finally passed out of the hands of PWE.[3] Belgium passed from the control of PWE in March, and Yugoslavia, most parts of which, including Belgrade, had been liberated during 1944,[4] in early April.[5] The BBC's own Intelligence department was liquidated in December 1944, Griffin left the BBC, soon afterwards to become Radio Officer to the British Embassy in Paris, and those members of the Intelligence staff who were still retained worked to the direction of Regional Editors.[6]

[1] *J. B. Clark to Haley, 27 Nov. 1944.

[2] *Haley to Radcliffe, 13 Dec. 1944; Radcliffe to Haley 19 Dec. 1944; Board of Governors, *Minutes*, 14 Dec. 1944. 'The Board noted that D.G. was pursuing the question of appointing an expert to advise on Foreign Affairs, to which the Board attached great importance.'

[3] *Clark to Lean, 19 Jan. 1945; Radcliffe to Haley, 12 Jan. 1945. 'PWE do not now wish to retain any control over BBC broadcasts to France, and the Government's interest in their contents is now vested in the Ministry of Information.'

[4] In liberated Yugoslavia, BBC broadcasts were taken down by special monitors and reproduced not only in newspapers but on wall posters. (*BBC Year Book, 1946*, p. 118.)

[5] *European Divisional Meeting, *Minutes*, 3 April 1945.

[6] *The changes took effect from 1 Jan. 1945. In a Promulgation of 16 Jan., J. B. Clark stressed the need in future to avoid political Intelligence work and severely to cut documentation.

Haley, who was opposed to the BBC 'spawning in Europe', as he put it, had complained sharply in July 1944 about a paper called 'Wireless Receiving sets in Europe: Roumania'. 'I do feel,' he had written then, 'that all these things must add up to a tremendous amount of misplaced effort.'[1]

The war was still not won, however, and while the Allies were preparing in the early months of 1945 for their final offensive, the Russian armies were smashing their way forward in the East and in the Balkans. Roumania, the first of the German satellites to detach itself from the Axis, announced its intentions on 23 August. The news reached the Bush House studio from the Monitoring Service just as the BBC's News in Roumanian was about to go on the air. 'Roumania's decision to break with Germany,' the announcer interpolated, 'gives the Roumanian nation and army a chance to rise and drive the Germans out of their country . . . action for which Britain, in common with Russia and America, has urgently called.' The overthrow of the Bulgarian pro-Axis government in September was described in the Bulgarian Service as a vindication of 'the line consistently pursued in talks and comments from London' in face of mounting German propaganda.

By the end of the year Finland had signed an armistice with the Russians (on 19 September) and in Hungary Admiral Horthy had ordered the end of hostilities—his proclamation of 15 October was repeated frequently by the BBC—and a new provisional Government had been formed which declared war on Germany.

The BBC spent much of its time during these months encouraging the countries of Eastern and Central Europe—and Finland—to put their trust in the Russians.[2] This was a very important and neglected aspect of BBC policy. On his

---

[1] *Haley to Clark, 19 July 1944. By March 1945 the peak total of daily broadcast hours to Europe (nearly 50 in June 1944) had fallen to 43—20 to Western and Central Europe, 13 to Italy and South-Eastern Europe and 10 to Scandinavia and the Iberian Peninsula (Note on European Services, April 1945).

[2] *When Smollett of the Ministry of Information visited Moscow in May 1944 he told the Chairman of the All-Union Radio Committee about 'the wide use of Soviet material by the BBC' (Record of an interview, 29 May 1944). The Russians showed great interest in BBC output and techniques. Miss Kallin, who had been transferred from European Intelligence to the Transcription Service, had achieved remarkable results within the BBC, although 'effective liaison' was still weak (J. B. Clark to Grubb, 3 July 1944).

visit to Moscow in October 1944 Churchill had recognized that Bulgaria and Roumania fell within the Russian sphere of influence; and the BBC, not surprisingly, argued thereafter that they had become 'so much a Russian concern' that the 'modest' services still provided for them posed no special problems.[1] It had already been agreed that when there were clashes of times between London and Moscow broadcasts 'of particular interest to the Balkans', 'the BBC should consider rearranging its own schedules', subject to the proviso that this should be done only where there was a persistent rather than a temporary clash.[2]

In the case of Czechoslovakia, there was more positive action. As Czechoslovak territories were liberated by the Russians during the course of 1944—the first territory to be handed back to them was the sub-Carpathian Ukraine—the new Czech authorities found themselves without radio transmitters of their own. The BBC decided, therefore, to give full accounts of what was happening in the liberated territories, and offered advice as to how best to frustrate German attempts to devastate the countryside. The popular uprising in Slovakia in August 1944 was felt to provide 'the best evidence of the success of the BBC's broadcasts': it was certainly planned in co-operation with the Czechoslovak Government in London, and a delegate of the Slovak National Council, who arrived in London in November 1944, expressed the view that 'were there no London broadcasts there would have been no national uprising in Slovakia'. Day after day communiqués from the Slovak commander had been broadcast from London a few minutes after their arrival in code: news was also given of Czech troops fighting in the West, particularly their siege of Dunkirk. The BBC also increased the number of programmes addressed to Czech trade unionists and to Czech writers and granted more 'free time' to the Czech Government. President Beneš spoke on Christmas Day 1944 of the future constitution and foreign policy of his country and addressed his fellow-countrymen for the last time from London in March 1945 before proceeding back home to Kosice.

The pro-Russian tone of the Czech broadcasts obviated any

[1] *J. B. Clark to Haley, 27 Nov. 1944.
[2] *European Services Divisional Meeting, *Minutes*, 31 Oct. 1944.

arguments with the Russians. 'Czechoslovakia will become a neighbour of Russia and must get on to good terms with her,' Masaryk, a very frequent and a very eloquent broadcaster, told Harold Nicolson. 'At the same time Czechoslovakia does not wish to lose her contacts with Mother Europe.'[1] During the Battle of Prague in May 1945 all the BBC's Czech bulletins were re-broadcast by Prague Radio, a service which continued until 3 June, and loudspeakers in the streets both of the capital and of provincial towns and villages were used to diffuse BBC broadcasts as widely as possible. On 15 May, after the war against Germany had ended, the liberation of Prague was celebrated by a special hook-up between London and Prague, the first to be arranged between London and a liberated European capital. On this unique occasion Lord Mayor Zenkel broadcast greetings to Prague from a Bush House studio.

The tensions within the Czech situation were not to become apparent until after 1945. In Poland, however, there were real and extremely disturbing signs of the shape of things to come in 1944 itself. On 23 July 1944 Moscow Radio broadcast a manifesto to the Polish nation issued by the Committee of National Liberation: the publication coincided with the arrival of Russian troops on the Vistula. Seven days later further appeals were made, this time more specific, to the people of Warsaw to fight.[2] Attempts had been made earlier to discredit the Polish Government in London, the Polish Home Army and its Commander, General Bor-Komorowski; and when the Poles in Warsaw, directed by the Home Army, decided to rise against the Germans on 1 August, with the Russians less than a score of miles away, the Russians made no effort to assist them.[3] Despite all Churchill's entreaties,

---

[1] H. Nicolson, op. cit., p. 392.

[2] The BBC had hitherto shown the same caution in its Polish broadcasts as it had done in other broadcasts. Its advice, 'Be patient, do not strike too soon', was in sharp contrast to a Russian campaign of incitement. For Polish activities which were directly co-ordinated with the Red Army's drive, see S. Okecki, 'La Résistance Polonaise et les Alliés' in *European Resistance Movements*, vol. II (1964), pp. 435 ff., which gives a completely distorted picture of the Warsaw rising, describing it as a prolonged anti-Russian demonstration.

[3] For Bor-Komorowski's account of the rising, see T. Bor-Komorowski, *The Secret Army* (1950). There is an account of the rising by Colonel Ivanek-Osmecki in the *History of the Second World War*, vol. 5, No. 13. See also A. Pomian (ed.), *The Warsaw Rising: A Selection of Documents* (1945).

Stalin refused to act. Warsaw withstood valiantly for sixty-three days, but in the process 250,000 lives were estimated to have been lost, including 50,000 members of the Home Army, and the city was almost totally destroyed.

During the Battle of Warsaw the Polish resistance set up two underground broadcasting stations of its own, reported BBC News bulletins from London, communicated with London in code, and transmitted messages to the Polish section of the BBC. London Radio had been the first to report the rising,[1] and there was regular contact between the 'open' station, *Blyskawica*, monitored at Caversham, and the BBC. The world heard of what was happening in Warsaw mainly from the BBC, for when the rising started Mikolajczyk, the Polish Prime Minister, was in Moscow, and Stalin claimed that he knew nothing of events in the Polish capital. Communists everywhere followed the lead of the Union of Polish Patriots in Moscow and played it down.[2] When the German radio announced on 17 August that the revolt had been crushed, Bor-Komorowski, broadcasting from *Blyskawica*, denied the report:[3] from then until the day before he surrendered on 5 October, there were daily broadcasts in Polish, English and German. As the Germans closed in on different sectors of the city, communication between the different suburbs was carried out by short-wave transmitters *via* London, and when the struggle was near its end, *Blyskawica* thanked a number of BBC broadcasters by name for the help they had given.

The Warsaw Rising has its place not only in the history of the Second World War but in the history of the 'cold war' which followed it. So, too, does the Yalta Conference of February 1945, when there were keen arguments between Churchill and Stalin about the future of Poland. The arguments did not lose their point even after the Conference ended

[1] The news of the rising was given on 2 Aug. at 5.45. At that time Bor-Komorowski's own transmitter was out of action (*The Secret Army*, p. 227). The Russians did not report the news until 13 Aug., but the Germans reported it on 4 Aug.

[2] *The Daily Worker*, 7 Aug. 1944, said, for example, that the battle was 'a product of the imagination of Polish émigré circles in London'. The British Ambassador in Moscow cabled Bruce Lockhart later in the year on 30 Sept. 1944 about the anti-Soviet character of British propaganda.

[3] Bor-Komorowski's appointment as Commander-in-Chief of the Polish Armed Forces was announced by the BBC on 30 Sept.

in a blaze of goodwill and Russia, the United States and Britain accepted in principle the setting up of a new Provisional Polish Government. The BBC reported the bare facts of Yalta, insofar as they were known, with a minimum of comment in Polish. The obvious object of the Allies was to finish the war in Europe as quickly as possible, with the military and political issues of the Far East still to be decided. The independently organized Radio Polskie broadcasts from London did not come to an end until 5 July 1945, the eve of Britain's recognition of the new post-war Polish Government.

Poland was not the only storm centre of international politics in the autumn and winter of 1944. In Greece also, which the Russians told Churchill in October 1944 lay '90 per cent' within the British sphere of influence, the political troubles which had been present for years[1] reached a climax following the German withdrawal from the country. Civil war between the opposing Left and Right political forces led to Churchill dispatching sixty thousand troops to Greece, to his visiting Greece himself, along with Eden, on Christmas Day 1944, and to the imposition of a provisional government. Considerable sections of the British Press were opposed to Churchill's intervention, and there were angry protests both from Rex Leeper, the British Ambassador in Athens, and the British Commander-in-Chief about the BBC broadcasting a daily survey of British Press reactions.[2] The issue was examined at the highest level, and the BBC retained its freedom to broadcast details not only of facts but of opinions.

Troubles in the Spanish section later in 1945—after the end of the war—were not handled so successfully,[3] and the political direction given to it was thought to be not too forthright but too vague. Clark had been anxious to work directly with the Foreign Office, and reached agreement with the Foreign Office in November 1944 that they would establish direct contact 'on occasions when the use of the Ministry of Information as an intermediary involved undesirable delay'.[4] Clark wanted in relation to all countries to get rid as quickly

[1] See above, pp. 461 ff.
[2] The Corporation handed back the symbolic interval signal of Athens Radio on 5 Nov. 1944 (see above, p. 461).
[3] *Oliver Harvey to O. A. Scott, Ministry of Information, 25 June 1945.
[4] *J. B. Clark to Haley, 27 Nov. 1944.

as possible of the ramifications not only of PWE 'control' but
of Ministry of Information 'guidance' which he felt was for
the most part 'unconstructive'.[1] He was anxious, indeed, about
the activities of the Ministry of Information's Broadcasting
Attaché in Paris and wanted the BBC, through its newly
established European Liaison Office, to which Miss Reeves
returned, to work directly with *Radiodiffusion Française*.[2] 'The
liberation of European countries,' he told Bamford of the
Ministry of Information a few weeks later, 'has, of course,
made possible the restoration of our BBC contacts with fellow
broadcasters on the Continent, and we have, therefore,
revived our European Liaison Office which has, of course,
been in abeyance throughout the war.'[3]

Denmark and Norway remained very much within PWE's
sphere of influence until the end of the war, and independent
broadcasting was not resumed in the two countries until the
5th and 9th of May respectively. There was a possibility
during the very last stages of the war, indeed, that Norway
might become the final German fortress. It was not until the
spring of 1945 that BBC Norwegian transmissions became
frankly operational in character. Many fears had hitherto been
expressed by the organizers of the Norwegian Service of
prematurely raising false hopes.[4] Nonetheless, the Norwegians,
while still under German occupation on Christmas Day 1944,
paid a generous tribute to the BBC in the Christmas Number
of a Norwegian newspaper, *Norges Nytt*, published in Stockholm.
'At the turn of the year, all listeners, and in particular
Norwegians, wish to send their warmest thanks to the BBC,
which in its whole-hearted understanding of the importance
of victory over Nazism, has placed all its resources at the
disposal of the occupied countries.'

[1] *Yet see a note by Haley to Clark, 8 Jan. 1945: 'No country will be considered
officially liberated until Radcliffe informs me in writing.'

[2] The Director of *Radiodiffusion Française*, Jean Guignebert, had been in London
during November 1944. He took up the same themes as his compatriots. 'The
whole of France was dependent upon the transmissions of the BBC. You provided
a miraculous tonic administered by the best doctors in the world.' He invited all
the members of the French Service to a dinner in the Savoy Hotel, where they
dined on a whole turkey. It was during these talks that the BBC decided to appoint
John Sullivan as its own Representative in Paris.

[3] *Clark to Bamford, 6 April 1945.

[4] *BBC Year Book, 1946*, p. 122.

The Danish section, however, still had its troubles. It was not until February 1944 that the BBC established direct contact with the Danish Press Service (DPT), which had been set up in a hotel in Stockholm after the collapse of the Danish Government and which acquired most of its information from the Danish underground newspaper *Information*.[1] Although DPT made sure, thereafter, that the BBC had access to its news service before Stockholm radio and Swedish newspapers did— the Germans tried in vain to persuade the Swedes to suppress DPT—it was highly critical of the BBC for not making the best use of its material. Persistent complaints arrived in London that Danish news of the utmost importance to the Danes did not appear to interest the BBC's Danish Editor. On 26 June 1944 DPT went so far as to cut off completely, without warning, its news service to London.[2] The Foreign Office responded at once with a telegram stating that it was in agreement with DPT's objections and that it was pressing for 'immediate reform at high level', while the BBC—also by telegram—promised radical changes.[3] Sporborg of SOE argued with great insistence for a new broadcasting policy which would ensure that 'the Danish resistance should have the moral support of the BBC so that the people of Denmark may know that their present mood, attitude and actions are highly appreciated and approved in this country'.[4]

Although some of the allegations against the BBC were subsequently withdrawn,[5] Newsome insisted on a full report and found out that some members of the staff of the Danish section were unhappy, particularly about their Editor.[6] More disturbing still, reports continued to come from members of the Danish resistance that 'the BBC is out of touch with

[1] J. Bennett, *British Broadcasting and the Danish Resistance Movement, 1940–1945* (1966), pp. 162 ff.

[2] Ibid., p. 184.

[3] Telegrams of 30 June 1944, referred to fully ibid., pp. 184–5.

[4] *Sporborg to Brooks, 5 July 1944.

[5] *Clark to Newsome and Jørgensen, 10 July 1944. A BBC/PWE/SOE meeting had been held a few days earlier. There was a second meeting on 2 Aug. Jørgensen had made it clear earlier in the year that he received less Danish material from the BBC's Central Desk than the amount of Dutch material accessible to Radio Oranje or of Belgian material available to Radiodiffusion Nationale Belge.

[6] *Edwards to Newsome, 24 July 1944.

popular feeling at home'.[1] It is difficult to say in the light of the evidence available whether or not PWE was following a deliberate policy of *not* seeking at this time fully to mobilize the Danish resistance.[2] Denmark was still not recognized as an ally. There was no Danish Government in London. In June and July 1944, when the complaints came to a head, there were more urgent matters to worry about on the Western Front.

Yet by the autumn of 1944, when the Allies had advanced in the West, the situation improved. Newsome, who was opposed to any kind of 'local parochialism' in reporting, had left the BBC for SHAEF,[3] SOE activity in Denmark increased, and after fears had been expressed of strong American competition from ABSIE,[4] the proportion of Danish news in BBC Danish broadcasts significantly rose. Co-operation between BBC and DPT was restored and the prestige of the BBC was regained. Two broadcasts in Danish on an RAF attack on the Gestapo Headquarters at Aarhus in late October 1944 were thought to constitute 'first-class political warfare'.[5] During the last months of the war, 'the BBC was used to its full capacity as a means of communication between Britain and the Danish resistance'.[6] Scores of special messages were broadcast, and even though the Allied armies never undertook any military action in Denmark against the enemy, there were close links between BBC, SOE and SHAEF.[7] A special message from Churchill was broadcast in Danish on the last day of 1944. It began, 'I cannot promise you that the end is near; but I can say that the Nazi beast is cornered and that its destruction is inevitable.'

---

[1] *BBC European Intelligence Report, 16 Aug. 1944, quoted in Bennett, op. cit. Six young fishermen had stated bluntly, 'If we want a pack of lies we listen to the Danish radio; if we want to hear the Allies we listen to London; if we want to hear the truth we listen to Sweden.'

[2] J. W. Varley of PWE, quoted in Bennett, op. cit., p. 177, had written in May 1944 that 'the primary purpose of the Danish BBC is to project British views on the war to the Danish people'.

[3] Terkelsen to Varley, 5 Oct. 1944, quoted ibid., p. 192.   [4] *Ibid.

[5] Terkelsen to Varley, 7 Nov. 1944, quoted in Bennett, op. cit., p. 200. The attack was described in the Danish Service eighteen hours before it was described in the Home Service and five minutes before the Germans put out their version from Radio Kalundborg.   [6] Bennett, op. cit., p. 203.

[7] On 27 Nov. 1944, for example, Terkelsen broadcast on 'Transport Sabotage', and on 5 March 1945 Eisenhower's HQ issued a communiqué in appreciation of work by Danish saboteurs. *The Times* had articles on the subject in December 1944 and May 1945.

Until the Nazi beast was cornered, British broadcasting to Germany continued to follow PWE rules. In August 1944 'political guidance' had been given to the BBC's European Service that an extended service in German would be needed during the last months of the war, while, at most, French and English programmes had to be maintained at their existing level. The amount of time devoted to other European countries would have to be cut down to half of its peak allotment, and the 'dawn cycle' could be brought to an end. A continuous service in German for fifteen hours a day was contemplated at first, but after 'a change of thought' a 'minimum schedule' was set, beginning at 6 a.m. and ending at 11 p.m., with bursts of broadcasting—6 a.m. to 8 a.m., 12 to 2, and 6 p.m. to 11 p.m. This new phase in the history of the extended German Service, it was suggested, might last over a month or two, and only after a broadcasting service had been established on German soil would it be possible to reduce the amount of broadcasting in German to three or four hours a day.[1]

During the autumn of 1944 the estimated audience for the BBC's German broadcasts amounted to as many as between ten and fifteen millions a day, several millions of them, however, outside the Reich itself.[2] The pattern of broadcasting earlier during the war no longer seemed relevant, despite the skill of Greene and his colleagues in exposing false German prophecies about the course of the war:[3] Newsome, indeed, complained to Greene just before he left for SHAEF that there were too many 'anachronistic features' in relation to a 'final phase' when 'the clock has already struck twelve and is now ticking away Germany's future'. Even if the formula of

[1] *J. B. Clark to Grisewood, 19 Aug. 1944. This important memorandum also stated that 'over the schedules generally we are asked to assume that broadcasting to Europe both during the transition period and in peace time will have two main purposes (a) to provide a first-class and objective news service and (b) to provide in a form attractive to listeners a reflection of the life, culture and thought of Britain'. The post-war pattern of broadcasting to Europe and the plans made to prepare for it will be discussed more fully in the next volume of this History.

[2] Address by Lindley Fraser to the Royal Empire Society, 18 April 1945, 'The BBC versus Dr. Goebbels'. The title was a tribute to the fact that the sense of a contest still continued.

[3] Three short features, *Nazi Prognosen*, broadcast on 6, 7 and 8 April 1944, made the most of false German prophecies and of a statement made by Goebbels in *Das Reich* (2 April 1944) that 'our prediction for the course of this war has been fulfilled with an almost sinister exactitude'.

unconditional surrender made it impossible adequately to exploit the opportunities open after the Bomb Plot attack on Hitler on 20 July 1944—the attack, in fact, actually strengthened the position of Goebbels[1]—the continued broadcasting of 'funny and entertaining' programmes like *Kurt und Willi* seemed to Newsome to be psychologically wrong. 'On their home radio the Germans will be hearing the grim story of the Generals' trial in the People's Court: they should not get jokes when they tune in to London.'[2] There were similar complaints about the programmes on *Soldatensender Calais*, even though some at least of the conspirators against Hitler had listened to them.[3]

In fact, Greene was sensitive to the shifts of mood during this last period of the war. He had allowed himself an unusual degree of latitude on the night of the Bomb Plot when he began the German news bulletin with the deliberately dramatic statement, 'In Germany civil war has broken out'.[4] He believed that there might still be resistance groups which the BBC with such words might encourage to hold on. During the last months of 1944 and the early months of 1945 the maximum use was made of broadcasts by captured German prisoners of war. Scripts were vetted for security, not for the views which they contained.[5] A twice-weekly religious service was introduced also, and talks on ethical subjects were planned for Sunday nights.[6] 'We shall not forget the few courageous Germans who were filled with a real love of their country,' it was stated in a broadcast of November 1944.[7]

As the Allied armies pushed forward through France, the number of German listeners to the BBC and to the black stations undoubtedly increased, despite heavy jamming and,

---

[1] E. K. Bramsted, *Goebbels and National Socialist Propaganda* (1965), pp. 335 ff. Goebbels became 'Reich Plenipotentiary for the Total War Effort' on 25 July 1944. According to Delmer, Bracken treated the first news of the Bomb Plot as a Goebbels propaganda move (Delmer, op. cit., p. 174). 'White' radio was inhibited from any effective action. 'Black' radio had greater freedom, and soon after the plot Dr. Otto John, one of the conspirators, joined Delmer's team.

[2] *Newsome to Greene, 8 Aug. 1944.

[3] Delmer, op. cit., p. 121.

[4] *Script of a Broadcast Interview between Greene and Lindley Fraser.

[5] *Note on Prisoner of War Broadcasts, 7 Feb. 1945.

[6] *Clark to Bruce Lockhart, 9 Feb. 1945.

[7] *BBC Feature, 'The Good Germans', 9 Feb. 1945.

later on, sabotage of electrical power and equipment. 'It was in the second half of 1944 that my friends and I began listening regularly to the German news bulletins emanating from London,' H. P. W. Wagner, than a young *Luftwaffenhelfer*, wrote in 1954. 'We relied on this source for accurate and trustworthy information regarding the change in military situations.' 'In August 1944,' wrote a young anti-Nazi German after the war, 'I had the opportunity of hearing the BBC reports of the liberation of Paris and of the landing of the Allied armies on the Mediterranean coast, so I knew there was good hope.'[1] If the Allies had been able at this time to appeal directly and in specific terms to German anti-Nazis, established or incipient, they might well have been able to rally a German resistance and to shorten the war. 'Roosevelt,' according to Gerhard Ritter, 'had presented Goebbels with the best of all his propaganda slogans'—unconditional surrender:[2] it was in late 1944 and early 1945 that this proposition was most true. Yet if any serious attempt had been made to produce a resistance movement sympathetic only to the Western Allies, there would undoubtedly have been grave difficulties with the Russians.[3]

From the time of the failure of the German counter-offensive in the Ardennes, which had for a moment offered new hope to a for once over-optimistic Goebbels,[4] the Allies had little need to do more than issue orders to the Germans. On 7 March American forces crossed the Rhine at Remagen; on 23 March Montgomery's armies crossed the river further north and entered the Ruhr; and with the Russians pressing in the east Germany ceased to be one Reich under one Führer. During the whole of this period, a leaflet campaign backed by popular daily broadcasts at noon and at five o'clock was directed at Germans living in areas under Allied control. These broadcasts included instructions, mostly issued in Eisenhower's name, as well as news and comment. Though the Allies were in some doubt themselves as to whether or not to advise German

---

[1] *Note by Heinrich Wiedemann. See above, p. 10.

[2] G. Ritter, *The German Resistance* (1958), p. 219.

[3] During 'the softening-up period' there had been at least two black stations, G8, 'Christ the King', using religious arguments—Delmer did his best to plant the idea that it was run from the Vatican (op. cit., pp. 122–3)—and a Workers' Station using *Lili Marlene* as its call sign.

[4] See Bramsted, op. cit., p. 359.

civilians to stay put,[1] there was ample evidence, in Lindley Fraser's phrase, that 'the average German' eagerly listened to the instructions and tried his best to carry them out. Recaptured Radio Luxembourg was one of the stations used in this campaign. At the same time, Delmer and his colleagues broadcast counterfeit instructions on German frequencies, those of Radio Cologne and Radio Frankfurt, thereby employing one of the devices designed to confuse which the British themselves had feared would be used against them in 1940.[2] Delmer had spent months training German refugees, one of them an ex-Gauleiter, flawlessly to imitate German announcers. By conveying counterfeit instructions—for example, that party leaders should be the first to be evacuated from danger zones—they made it very difficult for the Germans to use their own radio stations.

If it was Delmer's task to confuse, it was the BBC's task to provide reliable instructions which Germans could trust. The latter task had long-term implications for post-war Germany. Fraser always tried to set tactical broadcasting in its bigger frame. 'We do not waste time proving that the war is lost—but we do emphasise that every day it continues means extra useless death and destruction. . . . We do not indulge in much *overt* "counter propaganda" (i.e. answers to what the Nazis are now saying) but we do see to it that their protestations of innocence and of the justice of their cause are dealt with by recalling the facts about the origins of the war and the aggressive speeches made by the German leaders when things were going well. Whenever possible, we play back discs of Hitler's own voice. . . . We seek to establish clearly in the mind of the average German that he is coming under an Allied Military Government to whose authority he must give unquestioning obedience. The Allies will be fair to those who obey and merciless towards any who try to carry on the struggle by underground methods. . . . The Allies do not intend to destroy Germany, but they do intend to destroy not merely National Socialism but also German militarism; the sooner the ordinary German realises this, abandons all dreams

---

[1] Delmer, op. cit., pp. 200 ff., reports Churchill's dissatisfaction with a SHAEF directive which was followed by the BBC, the Voice of America, and Radio Luxembourg, telling the Germans to stay put. Churchill was anxious to add to confusion by telling them to take to the woods.

[2] See above, p. 205.

of further aggression and revenge, understands that he too shares in the responsibility for what he allowed the National Socialists and the militarists to do in his name, the sooner the time will come when Germany can begin to be regarded again as a member of the community of civilised nations.'[1]

German morale did not crack under this barrage. The war of words was by itself never decisive. Almost until the last, when the Russian and American armies met at the Elbe on 25 April 1945, Goebbels, however discredited his propaganda might be, made what he could of the increasingly desperate German military situation, at times peering into the future to forecast further political conflicts, particularly between the West and Russia, at other times seeking to stand outside or above history. At the last he resorted, not unwillingly, to nihilism. The ultimate German failure was military—defeat in face of massed Allied power, Western and Russian—however bankrupt, bizarre and perverse were the last days of the regime.[2]

One by one the German radio stations were captured or became silent. On 23 April the German *Hellschreiber* and morse services ceased abruptly. Three groups of stations continued to broadcast along with a few new Nazi outpost stations, like *Werwolf* and *Festung Holland*. Munich Radio was seized for a few hours by German 'partisans'. Queries poured in to the BBC's Monitoring Service as German output diminished or became increasingly difficult to pick up.[3] As the Russian armies were moving into Berlin, Kurt and Willi made their last appearance for the BBC. The programme ended with Willi saying to Kurt, 'I must go out now and see if there is any news'. There was, for as soon as the programme was over a breathless announcer rushed to the microphone with the message 'Hamburg radio has just announced that Hitler is dead'.[4]

Hitler killed himself on 30 April and Goebbels went with him. On 4 May the German forces in north-western Germany surrendered to Montgomery on Lüneburg Heath. Three days later on 7 May the German Supreme Command surrendered

---

[1] 'The BBC versus Dr. Goebbels', 18 April 1945.
[2] See H. R. Trevor Roper, *The Last Days of Hitler* (1947).
[3] *BBC Monitoring Service, Monthly Reports*, April, May 1945.
[4] *BBC Year Book, 1946*, p. 130.

at Rheims. On the same day the war ended for Germany, as it had begun for Britain, with a broadcast.[1] At 2.3 p.m. Count Schwerin von Krosigk, the recently appointed German Foreign Minister, broadcast a message by German radio from RRG's Flensburg station, stating that Grand Admiral Dönitz, the Führer's successor, had declared Germany's unconditional surrender. He talked in his broadcast as much of German unity in tribulation as of freedom and law. 'After a heroic fight of incomparable hardness, lasting almost six years, Germany's strength has succumbed to the overwhelming power of her enemies.'[2]

The news of the broadcast made its way around the world before Eisenhower, Churchill and Roosevelt were prepared to admit to the formal German surrender at Rheims, where a complete cessation of hostilities had been ordered for 8 May. The embargo which they tried to impose on the news from Flensburg, rightly described by Drew Middleton as 'the most colossal "snafu" in the history of the war',[3] could not be enforced. In the evening of 7 May, when the London crowds were already celebrating the great victory, the Ministry of Information announced solemnly that 'VE Day' would start officially in a few hours on 8 May.

3. A Year of Climax

VE Day on 8 May began with a fanfare of British trumpets, followed by a personal message from Churchill. Thomas Cadett gave an eye-witness account of the German

---

[1] See above, p. 77.

[2] *BBC Monitoring Service, *Daily Digest*, 8 May 1945. Schwerin von Krosigk had given his first broadcast from Flensburg, referring to 'the iron curtain in the east' moving closer, soon after his arrival there on 2 May. Dönitz had broadcast from Hamburg on 1 May, announcing that he had been appointed Hitler's successor. Bolshevism was the main theme of his speech also (J. Toland, *The Last Hundred Days* (1966 edn.), pp. 545–7). For Goebbels's use of the 'iron curtain' theme—he first used the phrase in February 1945—see Bramsted, op. cit., pp. 366–7 and *Das Reich*, 25 March 1945. Europe had not—and has not—heard the last of the last propaganda appeals and broadcasts of Goebbels.

[3] Toland, op. cit., p. 579.

surrender at Rheims. Sixty-two per cent of the listeners to the programmes expressed themselves as 'completely satisfied', the highest proportion ever recorded. 'Only the most jaundiced eye,' Listener Research remarked, 'would attribute this figure to nothing more than indiscriminate benevolence engendered by the joy of victory.'[1]

The BBC had begun to consider as early as October 1943 what form its programmes should take in the days immediately following an armistice with Germany;[2] and in August 1944 Haley had written, 'we must seek to balance rejoicing, thanksgiving, tribute and warning; and if we can rise to greatness so much the better'.[3] Between August 1944 and May 1945 there were enough excitements in Britain itself to make 'the year of climax', as J. B. Clark called it, as challenging as any wartime year which had preceded it. While the British public was sharing its listening with the Forces overseas or hearing in detail of the unfolding of great events across the Channel— there were six Home news bulletins a day in January 1945 and four *Radio Newsreels*[4]—it had ample preoccupations of its own. It is true, as A. J. P. Taylor has well put it, that already by the summer of 1944 the British people had decided, rightly or wrongly, that the war was as good as won,[5] yet, notwithstanding, civilians as well as soldiers were still in danger. The first V1, on which Goebbels had pinned many of his hopes,[6] fell on 13 June, and on 3 July there was the longest general alert of the war in London from 11.51 in the morning until 8.34 at night. The 'flying bombs', as they were called by

---

[1] *Listener Research Bulletin, 23 May 1945.

[2] *Draft by Nicolls, Oct. 1943. The draft was based on the assumption that there would be an 11 a.m. armistice as in 1918.

[3] *Comment of 31 Aug. 1944 on a Memorandum from Maconachie to Nicolls, 30 Aug. 1944; Programme Policy Meeting, *Minutes*, 29 Aug. 1944.

[4] *A. P. Ryan, 'Post-war News', 2 Jan. 1945.

[5] A. J. P. Taylor, *English History, 1914-45* (1965), p. 583.

[6] Goebbels had first heard of Hitler's plans for building guided missiles and rockets on 23 March 1943. He was extremely irritated by the long delay in producing them. He made the most of the *Wunderwaffen*—coining the slogan 'V for Vergeltung' (retaliation)—but was irritated when Otto Dietrich, with whom he was in bitter rivalry, issued a Press Directive in June 1944 exaggerating German hopes about the opportuneness of the new weapons. See E. K. Bramsted, *Goebbels and National Socialist Propaganda* (1965), pp. 316 ff. See also O. Dietrich, *12 Jahre mit Hitler* (1955). British Intelligence was aware in advance of the attack (see S. Delmer, *Black Boomerang* (1962), pp. 168 ff.).

the Cabinet—'doodle-bugs' by the public—continued to fall day and night: even when they were shot down over built-up areas, they caused as much damage as if they had proceeded on their relentless way. The menace was not overcome until anti-aircraft guns had been moved to the coast and Montgomery had overrun the VI launching sites in the Pas de Calais on his triumphant offensive from the Seine to Antwerp.[1] Even then, a V2 attack—this time with rockets—continued to batter London, and plans were made to abandon the capital.[2] There was talk, indeed, of a 'Second Battle of Britain'.[3]

The situation was very different, however, from that of 1940: although there were no less than sixteen 'flying bomb' incidents involving BBC premises, an effective 'alarm within the alert' system, installed in December 1942, warned of the imminent approach of danger, and less than seventeen hours of working time were lost. Symbolically, also, the full national black-out ended on 17 September, and in early December the Lord Mayor of London gave a dinner at the Mansion House, from which the speeches were broadcast, to mark the standing down of the Home Guard. However much listening there might be to enemy stations overseas, Haw-Haw could make little of the last desperate German attacks.[4] He was concentrating instead on what the United States would do to Britain and British interests after the war; and when he said in the last months of the war that he could not 'bear to see the city dying: she is dying and will never be saved',[5] he was referring not to London but to Berlin.[6]

Morale in Britain was high as the war came to an end, and neither the V attacks—portents of the shape of wars to come—

[1] On 8 Sept. 1944 Duncan Sandys announced that 'the battle is over'.

[2] The V2 impressed Goebbels far more than the VI, and he believed it would bring England to its knees (diary entry of 11 July 1944).

[3] B. Collier, *The Battle of the V Weapons, 1944–1945* (1964).

[4] Yet nonetheless BBC officials noted that on 5 July 1944 there was a spate of 'Haw-Haw' rumours about places laid flat by doodle-bugs.

[5] J. A. Cole, *Lord Haw-Haw—and William Joyce* (1964), p. 222. His last broadcast on 3 April 1945 sounded 'hysterical', and it was said he had 'a drunken voice' (ibid., p. 232).

[6] Heavy attacks not only on Berlin but on other German cities—for example, the devastating attack on Dresden on 14 Feb. 1945—were a feature of this period of the war. The bomber offensive did not end until 16 April 1945. See H. Rumpf, *The Bombing of Germany* (1963); C. Webster and N. Frankland, *The Strategic Air Offensive against Germany* (1961).

nor signs of conflict between the Allies—portents of the future 'cold war'—greatly disturbed confidence. It was a sign of the return to normalcy that on 19 October 1944 the ban on all reference to the weather was lifted. Information could now be given about the weather of the day before yesterday. 'Most people,' the first BBC bulletin stated, 'will have cause to remember it because in most parts of the country it just rained and rained. . . . So far this month we've had three times as much rain as we had last year.'[1] Yet just as the black-out gave way at first not to bright lights but to a 'dim-out', so while it was possible to talk about recent weather there were still to be no weather forecasts. 'On the whole,' wrote *The Listener*, 'it seems that just as the much-advertised "dim-out" has made no genuine difference to the discomfort of the black-out, so equally in weather reporting this "concession" is rather a portent of jam tomorrow than something very substantial here and now. We shall have to wait some time yet before those old friends, the deep depression over Iceland and the areas of high pressure round the Azores, return to their ancient splendour.'[2]

The demand for other moves towards peace-time broadcasting had begun as early as 1943, the year of the reintroduction of the Bow Bells interval signal (on 30 May), and many of them had been resisted by the BBC itself. Thus, for example, when in May 1943 Lord Sefton had asked for the broadcasting of racing results to be resumed, the Board had decided cautiously that 'any extension of the existing practice of giving only the more important racing events would be inopportune'.[3] More seriously, controversial broadcasting was still held very firmly in check.[4] The turning point came in June 1944, the month of D-Day, and the Governor who initiated the change was Lady Violet Bonham Carter. So far, she said, all debates on controversial broadcasting—and there had been many—had been fruitless. The war-time inhibitions which had affected the Home Service far more than the Overseas Service[5] should no longer be allowed to influence policy. The Minister

---

[1] *BBC News Bulletin, 8 a.m., 19 Oct. 1944.   [2] *The Listener*, 26 Oct. 1944.
[3] *Board of Governors, *Minutes*, 27 May 1943.   [4] See above, p. 618.
[5] *She had written to Powell on 26 Jan. 1943 urging that the Home Service and the Overseas Service should be treated in the same fashion. She had complained, as she had done before, about censorship of *Brains Trust* questions on politics, economics, ethics and 'the future'.

of Information himself at the luncheon held on 5 June, the eve of D-Day, to honour Sir Henry Wood's seventy-fifth birthday, had actually encouraged the BBC 'to be more controversial, to be a public forum'. Do not be intimidated by parliamentary questions, he had added, nor by 'political publicity hounds'. 'I will take care of them.'[1] Lady Violet believed rightly that if the Governors did not respond to this challenge, 'the responsibility will rest with us alone and it will be justly laid at our door'.[2]

The Director-General prepared a memorandum on the history of controversial broadcasting to enable the Governors to make up their minds about the next step. One of the Governors, at least, Sir Ian Fraser, had always been very uneasy about 'stirring up opinion' in war time: others were just as uneasy as Lady Violet was about the policy being followed. Haley's memorandum was purely factual, but it put the issue in a nutshell. 'The question which now arises is whether, in view of the altered state of national affairs, the public demand for education on important issues, and the need for informing the nation of the problems which lie ahead, a wider field of discussion should be encouraged.'[3] This time, the Governors had no doubts. They agreed at their next meeting that 'a wider field of discussion on controversial issues should be covered'.[4]

The talks prepared for the autumn of 1944 included 'Full Employment' or 'Jobs for All' and a series on 'Reconstruction', describing Britain's post-war plans as set out in White Papers and ministerial statements. On foreign affairs, there was to be a series on 'Europe and Ourselves': its object, perhaps a little surprisingly, if not controversially, was 'to show that Europe has ceased to be the political entity that it was and must be thought of in connection with the rest of the world'.[5] In the following quarter the number of discussion programmes was increased. A debate between Beveridge and a Labour Party

[1] *Manchester Guardian*, 6 June 1944.

[2] *Memorandum of 12 June 1944.

[3] *'Controversial Broadcasting', June 1944.

[4] *Board of Governors, *Minutes*, 15 June 1944; Programme Policy Meeting, *Minutes*, 1 Aug. 1944: 'controversial broadcasting would be given a trial later in the year.'

[5] *Memorandum by Barnes, 8 July 1944.

speaker on 'Can we get full employment without socialism?' was one of the topics suggested.[1] Every Friday there was to be a 'Friday Discussion', not unlike the Overseas Service's *Freedom Forum*, and among the speakers suggested were eminent controversialists like A. J. P. Taylor, Vansittart and Kingsley Martin.[2]

There were, in fact, many discussions going on not in front of the microphone but behind the scenes, all of them indicating a shift in mood. The Governors argued, for example, whether it was 'controversial' or not to encourage people to buy British, even to push an export drive,[3] and Haley boldly told the Ministry of Labour that he would not give publicity to the promise that there would be no unemployment as a result of demobilization after the war. 'It is no part of the BBC's duty *on its own volition* to give such an assurance,' he laid down, 'and it would have no authority to do so. If in fact unemployment did in due course ensue it would then rightly be accused of having taken part in a campaign to mislead the public and the most we can do in this sphere is to reflect and report. We can point out *how* full employment may be assured but not that it *will*.'[4]

Controversy could not go on for long without raising the issue of religious broadcasting and without bringing to the surface the whole range of questions relating to the full return to party politics and to the BBC's role at the next general election. On the first point, Welch reported in October 1944 that his Department had become convinced that the ban on the freedom of religious discussion was doing harm to broadcasting and that it was time to remove 'the impression it gave of one-sidedness and dogmatism'. There should be debate between Christians and non-Christians on such issues as what was meant by words like 'reason' and 'reasonable' in religion.[5] On the second point, it was once again Lady Violet

---

[1] *Memorandum by Barnes, 6 March 1945.

[2] *BBC Year Book, 1946*, p. 69. *Freedom Forum* was to experiment in 'new techniques'. Scripted and unscripted discussions were to be compared. (*Note by Haley, 8 July 1944.)

[3] *Note by Haley, 17 Oct. 1944.

[4] The Ministry of Labour's expectation had been set out in a paper issued on 8 Feb. 1945 by the Public Relations Branch, Ministry of Information.

[5] *Paper by Welch, Oct. 1944.

Bonham Carter who introduced the subject at a Board meeting in February 1945, reminding the members that it was not being raised for the first time.[1] Both the Labour and Liberal parties had announced in 1944 that they would fight the next election independently, and it was a sign of the growing public demand for livelier politics on the radio that after W. S. Morrison, Minister of Town and Country Planning, had broadcast in November 1945 on urban problems, the *Daily Herald* complained that his speech was delivered in 'an expansive mood of self congratulation' and pressed that it should be answered at once by Lord Latham, a Labour spokesman. 'This is the course the BBC should be instructed to take if the blitzed cities are to know the meaning of a square meal and if the BBC Directors know the meaning of a square deal.'[2]

'We all recognise,' Lady Violet wrote in February 1945, 'at least when we are in public, that it is one of our primary duties to inform, to educate and enlighten. . . . I am not suggesting for one moment that we should engage on behalf of all, or any, of the political parties in a "raging, tearing propaganda" nor that we should attempt directly or vicariously to exhort or to persuade. I am suggesting that an opportunity be given for a cool, factual, objective statement defining the policies of the various parties, under certain agreed headings, so that the vast, uninformed Electorate who will have it in their power to decide the future of this country in one of the most crucial periods of its history may do so with a mind as clear and as informed as we can make it.'[3]

The General Election of July 1945 falls outside the scope of this volume. Nonetheless, the prologue to it covers the last months of the war—the holding of the postponed Labour Party Conference in December 1944; the endorsement of most of its future candidates in January 1945; the setting up of a party election campaign committee under Morrison in February; the holding of the Conservative Party Conference in March 1945; noisy but straight party political argument between Ernest Bevin and the Minister of Information himself

---

[1] *Note by Lady Violet Bonham Carter, 20 Feb. 1945.
[2] *Daily Herald*, 20 Nov. 1944.
[3] *Note by Lady Violet Bonham Carter, 20 Feb. 1945.

in April. These events led inexorably to the rejection by the Labour and Liberal parties in May 1945 of Churchill's invitation to stay in a coalition government until Japan had been defeated and, in turn, to Churchill's rejection of their demand that the general election should be delayed until October; to the resignation of Churchill as Prime Minister on 23 May; and to the setting up of a new, essentially Conservative, 'caretaker Government' under his leadership.

Broadcasting was to play an important part in the election, with the BBC allotting time to the different parties, as it had done at the last general election ten years before, according to a formula agreed upon between the parties.[1] Broadcasting arrangements were being made, thoughtfully and meticulously, in March 1945 as the parties made their respective positions clear.[2] Yet Maconachie, at least, approached the new period of party contention with some distaste. After Ryan had drawn Haley's attention in December 1944 to the imminence of party conferences and had suggested that there should be 'licence to overrun' the times devoted to news bulletins if their proceedings were particularly interesting or even to cancel talks arranged after the News, Maconachie replied that 'this sort of thing not only upsets our relations with speakers but makes it extremely difficult to maintain a good standard of talks'.[3] A few weeks later he wrote that while the BBC should not shirk presenting election issues to its great audience, 'there is another service which we could render to our audience and which seems to me important: that is to immunize them against the narcotic effect of the woolly clichés which will be

---

[1] See Briggs, *The Golden Age of Wireless* (1965), pp. 140–1.

[2] *Controllers' Conference, *Minutes*, 7 March 1945, when the Director-General reported that he had been authorized by the Board to start discussions with the parties with a view to arranging organized programmes of party statements for broadcasting after the German war was concluded or at such earlier period as the National Government considered desirable. On 2 May he gave details of the schedule. Party warfare had already been whipped up in Parliament. See *Hansard*, vol. 408, cols. 212–13, 14 Feb. 1945, for a Labour question on why the BBC had given publicity to the report of a Conservative Party Sub-Committee. Bracken replied accurately that similar publicity had been given to Labour and Commonwealth publications earlier during the war. Gallacher then raised the Communist position, and McGovern the ILP position. Bracken replied bluntly that 'one of the great virtues of the BBC is that extremists on both sides of the House dislike it so much'.

[3] *Maconachie to Haley, 7 Dec. 1944.

slung about in such quantities by speakers of all parties during the election period'. A ten-minute programme should be arranged at 'goodish though non-peak times' in the course of which two speakers ('not Conservative and Labour but of more or less opposing views') would discuss such terms as 'democracy' and 'balance of power'.[1]

Although Maconachie was expressing his case very much in his own personal terms, the BBC as a whole was extremely conscious of its 'educative role' during the last phases of the war. Indeed, it continued, as it always had done, to attach as much weight to education broadly interpreted as to the stimulation of controversy. The term 'educative' is far broader in scope than the term 'educational', and there was ample evidence of a concern both for public 'enlightenment' and for education as such. The Central Council for School Broadcasting had met on 25 February 1944 for the first time since 3 April 1939, and it was able to report proudly that the number of schools listening to BBC school broadcasts had increased substantially during the war.[2]

LISTENING SCHOOLS

School Year, beginning September	Beginning	End
1937/8	5,612	8,543
1938/9	7,511	9,953
1939/0	—	—
1940/1	5,206	7,022
1941/2	9,960	11,299
1942/3	10,429	12,112
1943/4	10,829	

Modern language broadcasts had been abandoned during the war and so too had the admirable pre-war pamphlets accompanying all courses, but current affairs programmes,

[1] *Maconachie to Barnes, 30 Dec. 1944.
[2] *Central Council for School Broadcasting, *Report on the Work of the Council since April 1939.*

news commentaries and health talks had all flourished. While experiments had continued to be made in school broadcasting, particularly in an attempt 'to allow more precisely for differences of age and type of ability', it seemed gratifying to know that in a war which had changed so much, the 'principles' of school broadcasting had 'remained substantially the same as they were in peace'. There had perhaps been only one major sign of change: the sense of 'immediacy' in school broadcasting had been enhanced. 'School broadcasts have "immediacy" in common with the News broadcasts . . . they have, therefore, peculiar advantages for referring school subjects to an "insistent present" which during the last four years has been insistent as never before.'

Mary Somerville, the outstanding pioneer of school broadcasting, was clearly responsible for this balanced account of what had been achieved between 1939 and 1944. Yet in all her writings, in war as in peace, she attached as much importance to 'perspective' as to 'immediacy'. Current affairs broadcasts were 'an exercise in relating an event to a wider framework of reference', not an attempt 'to impart a body of knowledge likely to be remembered in relation to a particular event'.[1] Although Haley was unwilling to link school broadcasting with 'other so-called educational broadcasting . . . youth, other educational groups, etc.',[2] the same kind of approach to the adult education of the listener can be traced in 1944 as to the education in 'perspective' of the boy and girl at school. The Corporation was keen to go ahead with plans which had been approved by the Treasury to appoint political correspondents abroad, 'men of high integrity and craft, trained in the special needs of wireless, able to present accurate, dispassionate, informative background to the news'.[3] 'The BBC must play an important part', it was maintained, 'in

[1] *Note by Miss Somerville, 24 Jan. 1944.
[2] *Note by Haley, 26 Jan. 1944.
[3] *Note by Haley, 13 July 1944. Treasury approval was granted on 16 Sept. Haley suggested 2 in the United States, 3 in Germany, 2 in France, 1 in Italy, 1 in the Balkans ('It is undesirable he should have a fixed base . . . because men who stay too long in any Balkan capital invariably seem to lose balance and to become partisans of one nation against another'), 1 in the Middle East, 1 in India, 1 in Russia ('if ever the Soviet Radio Committee, in whose hands the matter curiously appears to lie, will agree'), and eventually 1 in Canada, 1 in South Africa and 1 in Australia.

informing and educating the public in foreign affairs, and through a corps of correspondents throughout the world, must be a source of information and enlightenment to the British people, to the Commonwealth and to other peoples.'[1]

At a quite different level, the BBC felt that it had a duty to broadcast information to soldiers on demobilization schemes, on pensions and gratuities (*War Office Calling the Army*), and on personal difficulties: it ran a service called '*Can I Help You?*', with Douglas Houghton and John Morgan dealing with practical questions of every kind within the range John Hilton had specialized in so successfully earlier during the war. It was the absence of guidance of this kind at the end of the First World War which had produced the first signs of disillusionment on the part of returning servicemen.

Above all, the Corporation began a great drive to extend its programme of Forces education. The original initiative for Forces Educational Broadcasting had come from the War Office in May 1943—Sir Ronald Adam, the Adjutant-General, was a keen advocate—when it was suggested that wireless should be used for general educational purposes during the demobilization period; and between then and 1945 plans went ahead for the start of the service as soon as possible after the end of the war. An Inter-Services Committee on Educational Broadcasting was formed, with W. E. Williams, the Director of the Army Bureau of Current Affairs, as chairman: it met for the first time on 31 July 1944, and produced its first set of proposals on 31 October.

Although the scale of suggested operations was subsequently reduced, the BBC went ahead at once with the formation of a special Services Educational Unit, appointed as its Director N. G. Luker, then a Pilot-Officer training as a navigator in Bomber Command, and, most important, secured Treasury sanction for a scheme which entailed eighteen twenty-minute broadcasting periods each week at the rate of three a day.[2] For their part, the Services undertook to provide sufficient receiving sets of suitable type in camps and barracks, to make themselves responsible for securing the best listening conditions,

---

[1] *Memorandum for the Postmaster-General, 12 Oct. 1944.
[2] It was hoped that they would be placed at a time which would not entail clashes with school broadcasts.

to advertise programmes and times to their 'constituents', to arrange for the training of instructors in the use of the broadcasts, and to keep the BBC informed to the fullest possible extent about the reactions of the audience. One thing could not be planned or predicted: how long would the scheme last? It seemed reasonable early in 1945 to think of a minimum period of one year and a maximum period of two years between 'the armistice' (with 1918 in mind, this was the word used in March 1945) and final demobilization. The starting date was to be one month after the collapse of Germany.[1]

While all this preparatory work for the future was going on—and it was hopefully designed to direct the attention of the Forces not only to problems that mattered, but to prepare them for a richer and fuller life—the actual range of BBC talks and discussions for the Home audience in 1945 was wider still. Ralph Wightman, 'Dorset Farmer', was establishing his reputation as a broadcaster on rural England;[2] *Country Magazine*, first broadcast on 3 May 1942, was at the height of its popularity; and regional broadcasters were preparing, not without some misgivings about the degree of freedom they would be allowed, for the resumption of peace-time broadcasting.[3] Dylan Thomas gave his first talk from Wales in March 1945—'Reminiscences of Childhood'. *Strike a Home Note*, relayed from the North Region, carried in the General Overseas and Forces Programme the sound of children's choirs, colliery bands, works orchestras and northern folk songs.

Meanwhile, Val Gielgud in the Drama Department was welcoming Wellington's new appointment as Controller of Programmes in October 1944,[4] and the BBC's new Director

---

[1] *See an important mimeographed paper, 'BBC Forces Educational Broadcasts, The Record of an Adventure in Education, 3 Sept. 1945 to 21 Dec. 1946' (1946).

[2] *Note by Haley, 8 July 1945. His talks were said to be 'increasingly popular'. There is a further relevant Note of 29 March 1945.

[3] *For example, Note from Controller, Scotland, 4 Aug. 1967. 'After D. Day and continuing in 1945, much thought and effort was given to the preparation for the re-starting of Scottish broadcasting. One measure of the success of the planning was that on 29 July 1945 the Scottish Home Service went into operation with an output of 28 hours a week.'

[4] 'To be given some credit, and to have one's advice taken made a most agreeable change.' (*Years in a Mirror* (1965), p. 121.) On Wellington's appointment Nicolls was given the new post of Senior Controller.

of Music, Victor Hely-Hutchinson, who replaced Arthur Bliss in June 1944,[1] was preparing the first post-war music programmes. Walton, Bax, Ireland and Vaughan Williams figured prominently in the last war-time programmes,[2] and Benjamin Britten wrote the music for Edward Sackville-West's *The Rescue*. Bartok's Violin Concerto was broadcast for the first time. So, too, was Shostakovitch's Eighth Symphony. This also was the birth year of what was to prove one of the BBC's most interesting, successful and distinctive music programmes, *Music Magazine*, described modestly at the time as 'one more step in the search for the most effective way of talking about music'.[3] Charles Münch was the first foreign musician to conduct for the BBC since 1939 when he came over from Paris early in 1944; and in March 1945 the BBC Chorus, conducted by Leslie Woodgate, gave the first performance of Poulenc's *Figure Humaine*, written in Occupied France and inspired by the struggle for freedom.[4]

The big musical event of 1944 was the Jubilee of the 'Proms'. For the first time three orchestras were engaged—the London Philharmonic, the London Symphony and the BBC Symphony —and all three were scheduled to take part in the closing concert on 12 August. What followed constituted a drama in itself. The German V Bomb attack on London led to the Albert Hall season being suspended, but Wood and his colleagues carried on magnificently 'amidst so much hazard'.[5] 'I must say,' Wood wrote to Haley, 'there were occasional moments which created most un-musical thoughts as, for instance, when one of the "devils" landed nearby, during a long *pianissimo* in an Aria, and on another occasion during a rehearsal of a Violin Concerto, when Mr. Basil Cameron asked would they like to stop for the time being, bringing forth a definite No! from everyone.'[6] All the concerts designed to be broadcast from the Albert Hall were broadcast instead from Bedford, including two on 10 August, the last of the series. Nine days

---

[1] Hely-Hutchinson had been Professor of Music at Birmingham University. He had served on the BBC's staff from 1926 to 1934.

[2] The series in which their works were broadcast was called *British Composers of our Time*.   [3] *BBC Handbook, 1945*, p. 46.

[4] The programme was relayed to France by *Radiodiffusion Française*. It was the first music programme to be transmitted in this way since 1940.

[5] *Haley to Wood, 1 July 1944.   [6] *Wood to Nicolls, 8 July 1944.

later, Wood died suddenly. The Jubilee, therefore, was 'at once the most splendid and saddest musical event that had ever taken place in England'.[1] On 5 June at a Jubilee Commemoration lunch given by the BBC—and attended by Solomon, one of the greatest pianists of the war years, and a large number of distinguished non-musicians, including Joad and James Agate—Wood had invited the BBC to become a 'curator' of the 'Proms' and to accept the right to carry them on for as long as it felt fit. 'I hope with all my heart,' he added, 'that the BBC will carry on my concerts as a permanent annual institution for all time.'[2]

Out of the welter of war, therefore, there was to be a new permanence. In the autumn and winter of 1944/1945 the 'struggle for freedom', as conceived by Poulenc, went on. *War Report* described the closing scenes of the war as movingly as it had described the first weeks of the invasion. In addition, a series of feature programmes—*In Normandy*, *The Rebirth of Paris* and *The Harbour Called Mulberry*—provided brilliant documentary. The last of these was written by Cecil McGivern, later to become Deputy Director of post-war BBC television, who had proved one of the outstanding war-time script writers.[3] His *Bomb-doors Open*, *The Air is Our Concern* (about the aircraft industry) and *Junction X* (about the war effort of the railways) were triumphs of feature producing. 'If ever an Oscar is awarded for an outstanding radio production,' Stuart Hibberd, a discriminating judge, declared, 'Junction X should surely have first claim.'[4] Gilliam had started the war wondering with Gielgud how he could justify his personal 'reservation' from military service on the grounds that he was essential to a country at war;[5] by 1945 he was able to see in retrospect

[1] *BBC Handbook*, *1945*, p. 46.

[2] *Manchester Guardian*, 6 June 1944. *Wood had written to Haley making this proposal on 26 May 1944 and Haley on behalf of the BBC accepted the exclusive right to the title 'The Henry Wood Promenade Concerts' on 30 May.

[3] For discriminating praise of *The Harbour Called Mulberry*, see W. E. Williams in *The Observer*, 11 March 1945, who called it 'an all round triumph'. It had been the revelation of an all-out effort 'in which the admirals and generals played no more decisive a part than the concrete mixers and the steelworkers'.

[4] S. Hibberd, *This—is London* (1950), p. 251.

[5] Quoted in V. Gielgud, *British Radio Drama*, *1922–1956* (1957), p. 106. One of the last of the war-time *Transatlantic Call* feature programmes had dealt movingly with the death of President Roosevelt, the first of the big political changes of 1945.

how features had come to be 'the striking force of radio in war time'.[1] It was fitting, indeed, that the war was to end not only with a sequence of well-prepared Victory feature programmes broadcast nightly in the week after VE Day, with the title *Their Finest Hour*, but with the formal separation of the Features Department from the Drama Department on 31 July 1945, a well-deserved tribute to Gilliam and his staff.[2]

War Report had described on 27 April how in the picturesque medieval town of Torgau the Americans had linked up with the Russians[3] and how on 4 May the north-west German armies had surrendered to Montgomery. On 2 May Gillard had reported at length a conversation with General Dietmar, the German radio commentator, who gave his last commentary on the war not to the Germans but to a BBC reporter. Another broadcast on 4 May, not sponsored by the BBC, was from Hamburg. It began, 'This is Germany calling . . . and tonight you will not hear views on the news by William Joyce who has been most unfortunately interrupted in his broadcasting career.'[4] The last BBC *War Report* was on 5 May. Everything had drawn to its final climax for the listener as for the soldier.

On the night of VE Day, Broadcasting House, bedecked with the flags of twenty-two Allied nations, was floodlit for the first time since Coronation Day, May 1937. It was a changed Broadcasting House—muddy grey in colour instead of gleaming white, and pitted with bomb damage. Tudsbery, the BBC's Civil Engineer, who had been associated with the BBC from its earliest days, wanted the 'battle scars' on Broadcasting House to remain 'as a memento to those days',[5] and they are still there on the western face of Portland Place. Yet while there was pride there was little nostalgia. 'With the end of the war,' the *BBC Year Book* for 1946 stated, 'a whole phase of broadcasting, we may hope, has come to an end; that phase in which deliberately false and misleading propaganda has been loosed upon the world with the express purpose of enslaving public opinion and causing strife among

---

[1] *BBC Year Book, 1945*, p. 58.
[2] Feature scripts were often changed at the last moment: drama scripts were read long in advance and carefully rehearsed.   [3] *War Report*, p. 418.
[4] Ibid., p. 425.
[5] *Note by Tudsbery, 8 Nov. 1954. See above, pp. 293–5.

nations.'[1] The carefully prepared VE Day programmes themselves were in the sharpest possible contrast with the carefully
prepared programmes which the BBC had produced at the
beginning of the war. 'Warmest congratulations to everyone
concerned with a most remarkable week's broadcasting,'

FROM: Director-General   TO: Distribution A
                                          Copy to all Notice Boards

---

On this day of Victory in Europe and rejoicing everywhere,
a message of thanks and congratulation must be sent to every member
of the BBC's staff. Six long, weary and perilous years are behind
us. It is easy to look back now on the dangers we have come
through and the rigours men and women have undergone, both at their
work and in their homes. But those perils and rigours were great,
and the spirit which doggedly and undemonstratively overcame them
was great. And through them all, British broadcasting was kept on
the air. Today's victory is one in which everyone in the BBC can
feel he or she has played a part.

Broadcasting is the newest of the great instruments of
peace which can also be used to wage war; and at home, overseas,
and in the enemy and enemy-held countries we have used it as well,
as efficiently, and as vigorously as each one of us knew how.
Tomorrow we must turn that same energy to the problems of peace.
But today, thanks.

W. J. Haley

Director-General

8th May 1945

FW

8. The Director-General's Message to BBC Staff on VE Day

Haley wrote to Wellington when the celebrations were over.
'The public heard nothing of our difficulties: they heard
plenty of our qualities. It has all been a grand effort.'[2]

The SHAEF programme was broadcast for the last time on
28 July 1945; it survived, therefore, for a shorter time than
'the sixty to ninety days' after the end of hostilities which
Haley had agreed upon with General Barker.[3] During the

---

[1] *BBC Year Book, 1946*, p. 7.

[2] *Memorandum by Wellington, quoting Haley, 14 May 1945.

[3] *Programme Policy Committee, *Minutes*, 16 Jan. 1945. See above, pp. 647–52.
It had had many civilian listeners. 'I am sure that most people listen to the AEF
instead of the Home and Forces Programmes,' one listener wrote in Sept. 1944
(*News Review*, 21 Sept. 1944). Yet it also had had its soldier critics. 'What about us
highbrows? Can't we have Caruso or Clara Butt. Ten minutes a night of Beethoven
. . . would satisfy me' (*Evening News*, 12 July 1944).

last weeks of the war, however, at the instigation of General Eisenhower himself, the amount of 'free time' available to AFN stations increased and the monopoly of BBC News came to an end.[1] From 4 July onwards the BBC provided short-wave facilities to AFN stations in Europe which were able to serve American troops entirely with their own programme.[2] Before the SHAEF programme went out for the last time General Barker thanked Haley for all the work the BBC had done. 'Personally,' he added, 'I shall be sorry to see the end of the AEF Programme because it has been a splendid "institution" throughout.'[3] In his reply Haley stated more generally that 'we will always remember with pleasure our collaboration with you and your fellow countrymen through one of the most momentous years in history'.[4]

The General Forces Programme remained in existence until 29 July 1945, when the BBC introduced the new Light Programme. If it had not proved as successful with civilian listeners as had been hoped at first, it had liberated men and studio space as it had been planned to do. It had also speeded up the pace of broadcasting. Surprisingly there had been a switch from the GFP to the Home Service. Whereas the old Forces Programme had been listened to on average by 60 per cent of the civilian listeners and the Home Service by 40 per cent, the GFP averaged 40 per cent against 60 per cent for the Home.[5] Yet Norman Collins, the Director of the Service, was rightly felt to have done 'a good job' constructively and, when necessary, self-critically. In January 1945, for example, he passed on to Controller (Programmes) a comment from a Corporal in Italy saying that 'the lads out here are particularly vehement in asking why British variety programmes are not of the same standard as those provided for their American comrades'.[6] Collins pressed hard during the last months of the war for more 'top-line scripted Variety'.[7]

In the public mind, the GFP was still particularly associated with Haley. When he became Director-General in April 1944,

[1] *Haley to Niven, 20 April 1945.
[2] *Programme Policy Committee, *Minutes*, 10 May 1945.
[3] *General R. W. Barker to Haley, 23 May 1945.
[4] *Haley to Barker, 25 May 1945.
[5] M. Gorham, *Broadcasting and Television since 1900* (1951), p. 202.
[6] *Note of 8 Jan. 1945.   [7] *Note of 21 Nov. 1945.

most commentators in the Press and elsewhere had referred to his initiative in starting the new Service.[1] Whatever the criticisms made of it,[2] he continued to regard it as a guarantee for the future—'the millions of British men and women serving overseas are the BBC's licence holders of tomorrow'.[3]

4. Reconstruction

I N March 1945 Haley carried his vision of the future further. He told listeners that 'the BBC had wiped Goebbels off the ether' and promised them that within ninety days of the end of the war, the BBC would provide listeners in the United Kingdom with two full-scale alternative programmes and that the regional services which had been 'interrupted' for security reasons would also return.[4] From the time that he had become Editor-in-Chief, months, indeed, before he became Director-General, he had been deeply concerned with the peace-time future of broadcasting, particularly home broadcasting.[5] Foot's mind had already moved in the same direction.[6] As early as

[1] See, for example, News Review, 13 April 1944.
[2] See above, pp. 590–4. Foot had to insist that 'the discontinuance of the old Forces Programme was not an artful dodge' (*Report of Press Conference, 23 Feb. 1944).
[3] *Paper of 10 Jan. 1944.
[4] The Times, 16 March 1945.
[5] *A Commonwealth Broadcasting Conference was held in February 1945. The earliest reference to the idea of such a Conference was a Memorandum from Rendall to Clark, 7 Sept. 1943. The implications of this Conference, the story of the planning of a new European and Overseas structure inside the BBC, the history of frequency allocations and of BBC relations with UIR (the Union Internationale de Radiophonie) and later the European Broadcasting Union are dealt with in the fourth volume of this History.
[6] As early as April 1942, soon after he and Graves took over, A. R. Burrows, a pioneer of British broadcasting, who had been working until 1940 with UIR in Geneva, was invited to collect relevant information on the subject of post-war planning and to co-ordinate views. Earlier still, indeed, in January 1941, Graves and de Lotbinière were discussing plans (*de Lotbinière to Graves, 1 Jan. 1941), and in July 1941 Control Board had begun to discuss the problems of post-war organization in broad outline 'to forestall any attempt to present us with a cut and dried scheme prepared by some Government Department or, worse still, by some dominant party interest' (*Control Board, Minutes, 30 July 1941; Coatman to Graves, 11 Aug. 1941).

March 1943, when reports were reaching London of 'increasing initiatives' on the part of the relay companies, old pre-war adversaries of the BBC, Foot stated that the time had come for the BBC to give a lead: it should be ready, he said, for the post-war period.[1] Later in the year the Governors were noting that the BBC's Charter would expire on 31 December 1946. Nicolson believed that there would be no threat after the war to the monopoly—M.P.s were aware 'that sponsored pro-grammes mean advertisements and that advertisements mean Big Business'[2]—and argued, with the support of several other Governors, that the most important task the BBC would have to face in the meantime would be to strengthen the Board.[3] Foot foresaw more realistically, however, that there would eventually be an attack against the continuation of the mon-opoly.[4] Relay companies figured in most of these discussions. In a paper of June 1943, circulated to all Controllers and Regional Directors, Foot argued that the BBC 'must maintain its sole rights within the United Kingdom to originate pro-grammes for distribution by wire or wireless. It should not seek to intervene in the actual operation of relay exchanges. It should use its influence to secure for the relay listener the widest possible freedom of choice between the various alterna-tives available to the wireless listener and, as an important element in this freedom, full access to BBC programmes.'[5]

[1] *Special Controllers' Meeting, 19 March 1943.
[2] *Memorandum by Nicolson, 9 Sept. 1943.
[3] *Note by Lady Violet Bonham Carter, 18 Sept. 1943; Note by Mann, 3 Oct. 1943.   [4] *Note by Foot, 12 Oct. 1943.
[5] For the relay companies before the war, see Briggs, *The Golden Age of Wireless* (1965), pp. 356–60. In 1928 the BBC had contemplated taking over the relay exchange system in co-operation with the Post Office (ibid., p. 358). The Ullswater Committee (Cmd. 5091) (1935) recommended that they should be owned and operated by the Post Office and that their programmes should be supplied by the BBC. Licences to operate exchanges had been required from 1930. The existing system was extended, however, after controversy, in 1936 (Cmd. 5207) (1936), although it was stated that the Post Office would carry out experimental work in distributing programmes by wire. In March 1939 the companies' licences were extended for another ten years—to 1949. There was a meeting at the Post Office in August 1942, at the instigation of the Minister of Information, between repre-sentatives of the BBC and the companies, when the BBC representatives reported that while they were in favour of existing relay services being maintained they could not express any views about the desirability of extension. The new activity of 1943 included efforts to transmit special programmes. The BBC itself gave outside broadcasting and line facilities to one company to produce a programme for a war factory.

Relay companies had increased their *clientèle* during the war to 435,000 subscribers, the biggest proportion of them in the North and Midlands, with South Wales and East Anglia next in importance. Local authorities had a close interest in the system, and some of them profited financially from it.[1] The policy of the exchanges was to please and attract the greatest number of subscribers, and before the war they had been the biggest patrons of Radio Luxembourg. Foot elaborated his approach to the provision of 'the widest possible freedom of choice' in this context. The BBC should ensure that when relay companies offered a choice of four programmes after the war, as did the Post Office's own radio-by-phone service, three of them should be BBC services. The figure 'three' was soon to acquire great significance.[2] Ashbridge, whom Foot was obviously consulting regularly and closely, had assured him in 1943 that the BBC 'might be in a position to offer a total of three alternative programmes with something approaching national coverage (including certain Regional alternatives). In practice, this would mean that all listeners would have a minimum choice of three programmes. The average listener would get two "National" and one "Regional", at least— and some would get two "National" and two "Regional", i.e., a choice of four alternative programmes. Television would be additional.'[3]

It is fascinating to see how this engineer's blueprint, which provided the necessary foundation of future broadcasting policy, was adopted by Haley without major alteration and

[1] *Memorandum on Relay Exchanges, 18 June 1943. When Foot asked Controllers for their views on the future of the BBC in 1943 (*Controllers' Conference, *Minutes*, 19 March 1943), one at least had expressed an interest in local radio. Foot said that no encouragement should be given to the idea that broadcasting time should be granted to 'individual cities since it was questionable whether this would be desirable on policy grounds and in any event was likely to be impracticable technically' (ibid., 6 Oct. 1943).

[2] *At an earlier stage of the war Beadle had suggested six different channels: (1) News, (2) Music, (3) Light Music, (4) Variety and Light Drama, (5) Non-topical information and Serious Drama, (6) Local Affairs, using wireless continuously with ample repeats. (Memorandum of 29 Jan. 1942.)

[3] *Memorandum on Relay Exchanges, 18 June 1943: 'A massive development of television on a popular basis would seriously affect the industry, since the distribution of television programmes by wire need not be taken into account for a considerable number of years to come in view of the amount of technical development and outlay of material that will be necessary (though it will ultimately come).'

given new policy implications. Technical and policy questions were always intricately interrelated, as they had been during the earliest years of broadcasting. Yet the foundation itself seemed firm. Ashbridge, like Foot, believed without doubts in the BBC's monopoly. 'The distribution of wavelengths would be quite wasteful if not centrally organised and controlled, and the same applies to the use of equipment and the organisation of staff, music lines and research. The existence of two broadcasting systems in this country is, in fact, incompatible with essential standards of economy and efficiency.'[1] Given the monopoly, however, there had to be variety in programming: this was the condition, indeed, of 'the widest possible freedom of choice'. When Foot told the Controllers and Regional Directors of the way his mind was moving in July 1943, Ryan told him at once that the best safeguard of the BBC was the provision of more attractive programmes than continental sponsoring stations.[2] Foot replied that the successful operation of a sponsored system outside Britain would undeniably result in strong pressure for microphone facilities for British advertisers in the home market.

By February 1944 Foot and Haley had prepared a considered statement about the future BBC, relating technical questions to questions of 'output'. The BBC should retain its monopoly, and the whole cost of the services should be met from licence revenue. 'The United Kingdom should retain protection against commercial radio.' 'The BBC should be responsible for all broadcasting in and from this country and to this country by reciprocal arrangements.' Overseas broadcasting from London should not stop, but there should be some kind of international broadcasting code, 'a kind of Atlantic Charter'.[3] Inside Britain 'there should be a strong programme staff in the Regions with as much independence of production as is consistent with the maintenance of overall BBC standards'.

---

[1] *Ibid. 'The introduction of frequency modulation would not alter this fact.'
[2] *Controllers' Conference, Minutes, 7 July 1943.
[3] An interesting PEP Report ('The Future of Foreign Publicity', Broadsheet 213, 1943) had suggested also that inside Britain there should be a co-ordinating centre of policy at the highest level and 'some means for giving guidance to the foreign side of the BBC. It cannot be left entirely free, but its directives should be much broader and its freedom from day-to-day control much greater than is necessary in war time.'

Indeed, there should be 'a constant stimulus to enterprise by internal competition through Programmes' within the BBC. The figure three then came back again into the argument. Three competing programmes 'which we have called (a), (b) and (c)' should be introduced. What was called Programme (a) should be 'a programme of the highest possible cultural level devoted to artistic endeavour, serious discussions, educational broad-casting and the deeper implications of the news, corresponding in its outlook to a *Times* of the air'. What was called Pro-gramme (b) should be 'the real Home programme of the people of the United Kingdom, carefully balanced, appealing to all classes, paying attention to culture at a level at which the ordinary listener can appreciate it, giving talks that would inform the whole democracy rather than an already informed section; and generally so designed that it will steadily but imperceptibly raise the standard of taste, entertainment, outlook and citizenship'. What was called Programme (c) should be 'a programme made up more specifically of the different voices of the United Kingdom, in which Regional enterprise will play the major part; all Regions contributing to the whole with every kind of programme'.

The selection of 'the right men' to take charge of these three programmes and of the two main overseas services, Foot and Haley went on, 'will be a matter of the greatest importance, and the five people appointed will form a vital part of the composition of what can properly be called the Central Executive. Each one will have his own responsible job to do, and they will meet together under us as frequently as may be found desirable to make their full contribution to the common pool of thought, knowledge and enterprise.'[1]

After the Governors had considered this plan at their meeting in April 1944, they accepted it in principle, although Mann demanded that the character of the proposed three programmes needed 'close and careful examination'. Did not *The Times* analogy with 'Programme (a)' imply 'too rigid a division of the nation into highbrows and lowbrows'? Might not 'Programme (b)' be 'too low and trivial'? Should not the proposed 'central executive' be free from departmental duties?,[2]

---

[1] *Memorandum of 14 Feb. 1944.
[2] *Memorandum by Mann, 18 Feb. 1944.

a question which had often been put by the Governors during the war. Most of the Governors wondered just how Foot and Haley could 'protect the United Kingdom from commercial radio'. They asked whether an international broadcasting code was feasible. Foot replied that if it were not feasible, other steps might be necessary at home. 'The BBC had the support [against commercial radio] of the whole of the Press of the country.' 'If ever'—and the big *if* was stressed—'commercial advertising must be done (for the British audience), then the BBC and no other should do it.' The future of television, however, was left more open. Foot and Haley had not dealt with it in detail 'because the situation at the moment is not sufficiently clear to justify us doing so', and the Governors agreed to leave the matter unresolved. Sponsoring had been discussed before the war,[1] and while Foot believed that television would establish itself in post-war conditions 'without any question of advertising', at least one Governor, Fraser, said that he 'might find himself in favour of sponsoring if that were the only way to get television'.[2]

There was no open talk of commercial television in 1944 and 1945, yet there were some signs of pressure to introduce commercial sound broadcasting either at home or, if that was impossible, from overseas bases.[3] Nonetheless, the BBC's twenty-first birthday celebrations in 1943, which had inspired a whole anthology of editorial comments on the Corporation, particularly in the provincial newspapers, passed off in a round of congratulations[4] which started with the BBC and ended with 'the system'. 'What the BBC does well it does superlatively so, and that applies with special distinction to its war effort.'[5]

---

[1] For the attitude to 'sponsored television' in the Ullswater Report, see Briggs, op. cit., p. 503. For a discussion on the subject just before the war, see ibid., p. 644.

[2] *Board of Governors, Minutes*, 20 April 1944. In his memorandum of 29 Jan. 1942, Beadle had envisaged that television should 'be partly, at least, commercial'.

[3] *Controllers' Conference, Minutes*, 7 July 1943; *Hansard*, vol. 401, cols. 821–929, 29 June 1944. Gammans was an advocate of commercial radio in competition with the BBC, and Captain Plugge, with substantial commercial broadcasting interests, re-stated the case he had made before the war. In this debate on the estimates Bevan advocated the abolition of the licence fee and the conversion of broadcasting into a free service.

[4] Yet the *Daily Mirror* had an article, 'Too Much BBC', 17 Nov. 1943. 'From half-past six in the morning until twelve o'clock at night, entertainment (?) goes on . . . would not the public be better served by less in quantity and more in quality?'

[5] *Edinburgh Evening News*, 13 Nov. 1943.

'The BBC has become utterly efficient . . . it is discharging
its task brilliantly, both on the home front and in the theatres
of war where propaganda is vital.'[1] 'The BBC has continued to
hold its prestige despite the restrictive effect of four years of
war. The constitution of the BBC as a public corporation
created by Royal Charter is an example of that genius for
happy compromise which is enshrined in many older British
institutions.'[2] 'It may be that British broadcasting would have
gained in entertainment value if it had been developed on the
American model with sponsored programmes, but we believe
it would have suffered greatly as a public service.'[3] 'From time
to time criticisms are levelled at the BBC. There are people
who envy the more gaudy attractions of commercially
sponsored broadcasting. But I have been a professional listener
throughout the life of the BBC. I have listened to its growth
from a few squeaky notes in a welter of atmospherics, to the
great public service of today, and I am convinced for our
particular circumstances the British system is the best in the
world.'[4] 'The BBC has served the public taste without pandering to it, and there could be no better tribute to its coming of
age.'[5]

Bracken at the twenty-first birthday lunch of the BBC in
1943 agreed that 'no coming of age is more deserving of
celebration than the BBC's'. He went much further than
platitude, however, and after paying a tribute to the BBC's
war record and acknowledging its war-time difficulties, which
Powell had stressed,[6] he completely underwrote the BBC's
own plans for the future. 'Though I am no prophet, I shall be
surprised if the British public will approve of the introduction
of commercial broadcasting in Great Britain. . . . As an

---

[1] *Birmingham Mail*, 15 Nov. 1943.

[2] *Eastern Evening News*, 15 Nov. 1943.

[3] *Yorkshire Post*, 13 Nov. 1943.

[4] *Birmingham Post*, 16 Nov. 1943. Cf. the Aberdeen *Bon Accord*, 18 Nov. 1943:
'Most of us turn away in horror from the only possible alternative—free trade in
the air for everyone who has the money to pay for it. A combination of peptonised
culture and the latest bargains in gentlemen's underwear.'

[5] *The Statist*, 20 Nov. 1943.

[6] *'I am sure it will be remembered (when the Charter is reconsidered) that the
very substantial part of our life under the present Charter has been spent in the
difficult conditions of war, conditions which were hardly touched upon when
the Ullswater Committee indicated the lines which broadcasting in this country
should follow in times of peace.'

old and trusty Tory, I naturally object to monopolies. But I
see no reason why healthy competition should not be developed
within the structure of the BBC.'[1]

This categorical statement—coupled as it was with a reference, popular in the circumstances of the time, to the need to
stimulate regional broadcasting after the war, a main theme
of war-time writing on broadcasting[2]—went further than some
of the Press comment.[3] There is no evidence, however, as to
whether Bracken had or had not consulted five of his colleagues
who had become members of a Government Committee to
review problems of post-war broadcasting in January 1944.
The Committee consisted of Lord Woolton in the chair, Attlee,
Bracken, Capt. H. F. C. Crookshank, the Postmaster-General,
and the Minister of State for Foreign Affairs. This Committee,
which held several meetings, produced a draft report but failed
to reach unanimity on a number of important questions and
broke up with the fall of the Coalition Government.[4]

In the meantime, while the Government hesitated, the war-
time BBC was beginning to disintegrate. 'Months before the
Germans acknowledged defeat, there was an air of packing up
in the corridors and offices.'[5] Many of the temporary war-time

---

[1] *Script of the Minister's Speech, 8 Dec. 1943. Among the broadcasters present
at the lunch were Handley, Hill, Bartlett, King-Hall, Middleton, Jack Payne,
Rhoda Power and Sir Henry Wood. The menu comprised fish, chicken, and fruit
cup.
[2] See, for example, P. P. Eckersley, *The Power Behind the Microphone* (1941), pp.
175 ff., and E. G. D. Liveing 'The Future of British Broadcasting' in the *Fortnightly
Review*, Sept. 1944, where a former Regional Director argued that broadcasting
should take its place as 'the mirror of the rich kaleidoscope of national culture and
local characteristics in this widely diversified country'. In a manuscript, *A Policy for
Broadcasting*, written by Coatman and sent to the Director-General on 10 May 1945,
the same case was argued. See also *The Scotsman*, 29 Nov. 1944: 'True regional
development means not simply accepting local standards as we find them, but
creating conditions and opportunities in such a way that the life and interests of
the community will be adequately reflected and its standards as far as possible
raised.'
[3] *The Scotsman*, for example, 13 Nov. 1943, wrote that 'the question is often
raised whether British broadcasting would be better if it were not a monopoly.
We should keep an open mind, remembering, however, that competitive broadcasting lives by its highly paid advertising space.'
[4] Herbert Morrison to Lord Listowel, 23 Aug. 1945 (Post Office Papers). The
aftermath of this story will be a main theme in the fourth volume of this History
which will also be concerned with the reorganization of European and Overseas
broadcasting.
[5] H. Grisewood, *One Thing at a Time* (1968), p. 151.

staff—Kirkpatrick outstanding amongst them—moved out almost as quickly as they had moved in. The Ministry of Information also drastically cut the size of the staff it had so laboriously acquired.[1] Haley, however, was in his element preparing his first public statements on the pattern of post-war British broadcasting. There were two of them, both made in the period between his appointment as Director-General in April 1944 and the end of the war, the first addressed to the Radio Industries Club on 28 November 1944 and the second, far away from London, to the Cardiff Business Club on 15 March 1945. 'The most hopeful thing in the world today,' he began on the first and more significant of the two occasions, 'is the zest and eagerness with which the British people are arguing about the future.' After moving quickly over the world scene and at greater length over what was happening in Europe, he turned to the home listener and promised after the war 'three programmes designed entirely for himself'. He still called them (a), (b) and (c), but the order and the scope had been changed. Programme (a) was to be the Home programme 'capable of regionalisation'—this equivocal phrase produced some unfavourable press comment;[2] Programme (b) was to be 'of a light character'; and Programme (c) was to be a 'third programme'. There was still an element of mystery about 'Programme (c)'. 'It will enable us to do many things which mere considerations of space have denied to us before, things which ought to find a place in any properly constituted broadcasting service.'[3]

Haley's peroration was in line with what he was to dwell upon in an essay in a later *BBC Year Book*. 'Behind British

---

[1] Its authorized complement on 8 May 1945 was 2,374 at HQ, 524 in the Regional Offices and 145 in the Film Units. This figure, substantially lower than the war-time peak, was to be reduced to 2,602 by 8 Aug.

[2] See, for example, *Yorkshire Evening News*, 29 Nov. 1944. Yet *The Birmingham Post* (1 Dec. 1944) wrote that the phrase 'seems to indicate a larger measure of decentralisation, with all the regions contributing the best that is in them to the common pot. Such a system will put the regions on their toes and avoid the waste of material that was caused when "peak" programmes of each area were confined to the local transmitters.' Haley dwelt on the importance of regional contributors to broadcasting in his Cardiff speech, but reiterated that regional broadcasting must be good and not merely regional and that regions should compete with each other nationally.

[3] *Press Release, 28 Nov. 1944. Details of the subsequent planning of the programmes and their scope was given to a Controllers' Conference on 2 May 1945.

broadcasting there has always been a philosophy.'[1] Reith, 'that very great and deeply inspired leader', had enunciated it: the war had vindicated it. 'Broadcasting has grown up. It must be adult. In our post-war plans we shall sacrifice nothing in the quality or quantity of our entertainment, but we shall safeguard broadcasting from becoming a glorified juke-box. By news, by discussions, by talks, by documentaries, by still new forms which we will seek and perfect, we shall play our part in making this country the best informed democracy in the world. Broadcasting can play its part in doing this—if it is well founded and wisely run.'[2]

There were to be far more challenges to this philosophy after the war than there had been during the war, far more indeed than had been anticipated during the war and at a far greater number of points. Very quickly, however, much more quickly than most prophets had predicted, the country was to move from the age of wireless into the age of television. At the very heart of the war, the future of television had been referred to an official committee of inquiry. In September 1943, the year that the last German television transmitter at Witzleben was bombed out of existence,[3] Lord Hankey had been appointed chairman of a Government Committee charged with the task, first, of preparing a plan 'for the provision of a service to at any rate the larger centres of population within a reasonable period after the war', second, with studying problems of research and development, and third—a phrase with a post-war ring—to consider 'the guidance to be given to manufacturers, with a view specially to the development of the export trade'.[4]

Hankey is associated in the history books mainly with the

---

[1] *BBC Year Book, 1946*, p. 8.

[2] *Press Release, 28 Nov. 1944.

[3] J. Swift, *Adventure in Vision* (1950), p. 116. The German station had been broadcasting not for the general public but to the wounded in hospitals. Television research was carried on in Paris under German supervision at a later stage of the war, as Ed Murrow reported in a broadcast of 4 Nov. 1944.

[4] The appointment of the Committee was announced in the House of Commons on 18 Jan. 1944. It had held its first meeting on 26 Oct. 1943. It subsequently met 30 times and examined several witnesses, with the exception of those from the BBC itself, and from the Ministry of Education, all representatives of the electrical industry and of government departments. They included I. Schoenberg of Marconi/EMI, Gerald Cock and H. L. Kirke of the BBC, J. Arthur Rank, C. O. Stanley and, not least, J. L. Baird.

First rather than the Second World War, but his Report, published in March 1945, looked forward to a time not only when there would be popular television, but colour television, possibly with stereoscopic effects.[1] 'The extension of the service to large centres of population outside London will greatly increase the demand for receivers; their price, which at first will be higher than before the war, should fall, particularly when the stage of mass production is reached. In the educational field, also, we believe that television opens up considerable possibilities. But it is the televising of actual events, the ability to give the viewer a front-row seat at almost every possible kind of exciting or memorable spectacle, that television will perform its greatest service.'[2] 'Television has come to stay.'[3]

Hankey's colleagues on the Committee were Sir Stanley Angwin, Engineer-in-Chief of the Post Office, Sir Edward Appleton, Secretary of the Department of Scientific and Industrial Research, Sir Noel Ashbridge, Sir Raymond Birchall, Deputy Director-General of the Post Office, Professor J. D. Cockcroft of Air Defence Research, who was absent for several meetings on what was described as 'other government business'—it was, indeed, work on the atomic bomb[4]—and first Foot and then Haley. The Committee, in other words, was strongest on the scientific and technical side. Yet it was forced to note such economic and social issues as the development during the war of television across the Atlantic, the problem of sponsored programmes, and the need for an advisory committee to watch the public interest.

All three points were important. Britain had enjoyed a lead in the provision of regular television programmes between 1936 and 1939: as war-time work on television in Britain almost reached a standstill,[5] the United States pressed ahead. In May 1941, before Pearl Harbour, the Federal Communications Commission had announced that full commercial television would start on 1 July; it did, albeit quietly, and by

---

[1] *Report of the Television Committee 1943* (1945), §25.
[2] Ibid., §74.
[3] Ibid., §78.
[4] See M. Gowing, *Britain and Atomic Energy, 1939–1945*, pp. 321–7, 330–2.
[5] Baird continued work throughout this period on all-electronic systems of colour reproduction. He gave a demonstration on 16 Aug. 1944 (Swift, op. cit., pp. 118–19).

1945 the way was prepared for future expansion, although there were still only 6 stations and 7,000 receiving sets.[1] Other public hearings had been held in the United States on the future development of the service. The Americans were clear that sponsored programmes were the answer to the financing of a new service: Haley and his colleagues were circumspect. 'It is quite clear that until the television service is well developed, commercial interests would not be willing to incur large expenditure for this purpose owing, for example, to the limited audience served. In the early stages, therefore, we could not expect sponsored programmes to provide a substantial contribution towards the cost of the television service. In these circumstances and without prejudicing the matter for the future, we feel it would be premature to come to a conclusion on this question.'[2] An advisory committee would be necessary to determine technical standards, to co-ordinate or initiate research and 'to watch all future developments . . . at home and abroad, including its use in cinemas': it was to be very much an advisory committee, however, not a committee of management or control.[3] There was further talk about the possibility of 'the cinema industry and the BBC working together in collaboration and not as competitors in the exploitation of television'.[4]

The Hankey Report is more interesting in retrospect than contemporaries found it at the time. The *Investors' Chronicle*, a shrewd judge, noted that it had created 'surprisingly little' attention.[5] The *Liverpool Daily Post* from the distant north expressed fears that a television development programme would mean that the BBC would spend money received from millions of listeners for the benefit of a few viewers.[6] Yet *The Star* had a headline 'Television in Colour (£1 a year) planned' and *The Birmingham Post* pointed out significantly and correctly

---

[1] C. A. Siepmann, *Radio, Television and Society* (1950), p. 318.

[2] *Report of the Television Committee*, §70.

[3] Ibid., §62.

[4] Ibid., §34.

[5] *Investors' Chronicle*, 17 March 1945. Yet see the *Financial Times*, 12 Aug. 1943: 'There is general agreement that radio is destined to be at once one of the major industries of the future and one of Britain's post-war export-winners. . . . It is understood that a great deal of the development work on the new television in this country has been done by EMI and Cossor . . .'

[6] *Liverpool Daily Post*, 9 March 1945.

that television had already made far greater progress by 1939 than sound broadcasting had made by 1914. 'By 1919,' it went on, 'wireless telegraphy had advanced to a stage when it was ripe for the purposes of public recreation. And the war-weary public was more than ready—it was avid—for the new wonder and the new hobby. Within three years of the Armistice . . . there was, so to say, a radio rush. Will there not be a comparable "boom" in television?'[1]

The last word was with the scientists and engineers—and with Haley. 'There are some people who call themselves realists when they are merely being short-sighted, who believe that television is in its toddling steps. One day it will stride out, not only across countries and states, but also, we hope, across oceans. After the things which the scientists, and above all the radio scientists, have achieved in the past six years, who dares to say that anything is ultimately impossible?'[2]

[1] *The Birmingham Post*, 9 March 1945.
[2] Quoted in Swift, op. cit., p. 119.

BIBLIOGRAPHICAL NOTE

VERY little has been published concerning the detailed history of British broadcasting during the Second World War, although there is a useful outline in the longer history by M. GORHAM, *Broadcasting: Sound and Television since 1900* (1952), a valuable pamphlet by T. O. BEACHCROFT, *British Broadcasting* (1946), and a shorter pamphlet written during the war by ANTONIA WHITE, *BBC at War* (n.d.). Technical history is covered thoroughly in a valuable article by Sir HAROLD BISHOP, 'The War-time Activities of the Engineering Division of the BBC', in the *Journal of the Institution of Electrical Engineers* (1947), and the BBC *Year Books*, published throughout the war, are indispensable. Comparative American broadcasting experience is examined in E. BARNOUW, *The Golden Web* (1968).

The main source material for Volume III of this History has been the same as for Volumes I and II—primary material in the BBC's own voluminous archives. There are over 7,000 BBC files covering the war period, and of these 2,000 have been analysed or consulted. Board of Governors' *Minutes* and *Papers* deal with BBC 'high policy', but there is an immense amount of rich information relating to broadcasting activity in the files of other committees and departments and in the personal files of some of the most prominent broadcasters. Programmes as broadcast have also been studied when thought to be relevant, along with news bulletins and Listener Research Reports. Some information has also been gathered from programmes broadcast since the war, particularly programmes of personal reminiscences. One wide range of BBC material is new to this volume—Intelligence Papers and Reports, Monitoring Digests and special papers written by monitors. Unfortunately a great deal of primary material has been destroyed, particularly concerning the BBC's Overseas Service, and many files of key papers are incomplete. The difficulties of using this voluminous material are immense, but efforts have been made both to cross-check and to ferret out missing material.

Because of war relationships, *Hansard* and the papers of

Government Departments are more relevant to BBC history than they otherwise would be. I have been able to make some use of Ministry of Information papers and a number of other related papers, but some central aspects of Government policy can only be uncovered when there is full access to all official papers. Even then, as Professor Rushbrook Williams pointed out in a letter of 22 December 1941, 'I think you are perfectly right in your conjecture that there is a great deal of information bearing upon the BBC Services in the files of the various Government Departments. . . . My experience leads me to believe that this information is rarely, if ever, embodied in specific reports. It is found principally in brief paragraphs, two or three sentences, or even a mere side reference . . . in documents dealing with quite other matters.'

BBC sources have been supplemented not only by official papers, wherever possible, but by several important private papers. The most important of these is an autobiographical manuscript by Mr. ROBERT FOOT, which he very generously allowed me to see. I have also used, as I did in Volume II, a collection of Sir STEPHEN TALLENTS's papers, very kindly placed at my disposal by Mr. T. W. Tallents, and Mr. RALPH WADE's vivid, unpublished manuscript, *Early Life in the BBC*.

The following biographies and autobiographies, only a selection from the far bigger list referred to in footnotes, deal with personalities and issues described in this book:

T. BARMAN, *Diplomatic Correspondent* (1968)
G. C. BEADLE, *Television, A Critical Review* (1963)
B. BELFRAGE, *One Man in His Time* (1951)
A. B. CAMPBELL, *You Have been Listening to . . .* (1940)
DUFF COOPER, *Old Men Forget* (1953)
H. DALTON, *The Fateful Years* (1957)
L. FIELDEN, *The Natural Bent* (1960)
I. FRASER, *Whereas I was Blind* (1942)
C. DE GAULLE, *Mémoires de Guerre* (1959)
V. GIELGUD, *Years in a Mirror* (1967)
M. GORHAM, *Sound and Fury* (1948)
F. GRENIER, *C'était ainsi* (1959)
F. GRISEWOOD, *The World Goes By* (1952)
H. GRISEWOOD, *One Thing at a Time* (1968)

H. HALL, *Here's to the Next Time* (1935)

T. HANDLEY, *Handley's Pages* (n.d.)

S. HIBBERD, *This—is London* (1950)

W. HOLT, *I Still Haven't Unpacked* (1953)

F. A. IREMONGER, *William Temple* (1948)

T. KAVANAGH, *Tommy Handley* (1949)

E. LYONS, *David Sarnoff: A Biography* (1966)

J. MACLEOD, *A Job at the BBC* (1947)

S. MACPHERSON, *The Mike and I* (1948)

L. MIALL (ed.), *Richard Dimbleby, Broadcaster* (1966)

E. NIXON, *John Hilton* (1946)

E. MASCHWITZ, *No Chip on My Shoulder* (1957)

R. MENGIN, *De Gaulle à Londres* (1965)

H. NICOLSON, *Diaries and Letters, 1939–1945* (1967)

W. PICKLES, *Between You and Me* (1949)

J. B. PRIESTLEY, *Margin Released* (1962)

J. C. W. REITH, *Into the Wind* (1949)

W. SHIRER, *Berlin Diary* (1941)

Other books dealing with particular aspects of broadcasting, often at considerable length and with revealing frankness, are:

E. BLISS (ed.), *In Search of Light: The Broadcasts of Edward R. Murrow* (1968)

A. C. CAMERON, 'School Broadcasting' in R. W. Moore (ed.), *Education, Today and Tomorrow* (1945)

A. DAKERS, *The Big Ben Minute* (n.d.)

B. DEAN, *The Theatre at War* (1956)

P. P. ECKERSLEY, *The Power Behind the Microphone* (1941)

V. GIELGUD, *British Radio Drama* (1957)

J. GREEN (ed.), *Green Pastures*, a Series of Agricultural Education and Technical Broadcast Talks (1945)

A. HURD, *A Farmer in Whitehall* (1951)

E. TANGYE LEAN, *Voices in the Darkness* (1943)

N. NEWSOME, *The 'Man in the Street' Talks to Europe* (1945)

S. ORWELL and I. ANGUS (eds.), *The Collected Essays, Letters and Journalism of George Orwell* (1968)

R. PALMER, *School Broadcasting in Britain* (1947)

G. PEDRICK, *Battledress Broadcasters* (1964)

J. B. PRIESTLEY, *Postscripts* (1940)

J. Swift, *Adventure in Vision* (1950)

H. Thomas, *Britain's Brains Trust* (1944); *The Brains Trust Book* (1942)

F. Worsley, *Itma* (1948)

At every stage in this volume it has been necessary to study broadcasting history within the context of the general history of the war. Volume III was written before the appearance of the fascinating general survey, *The People's War* (1969) by A. Calder, but the following is a brief list of some other general books used:

J. R. M. Butler, J. M. A. Gwyer and J. Ehrman, *Grand Strategy*, 6 vols. (1956–64)

W. S. Churchill, *The Second World War*, 6 vols. (1948–54)

B. Collier, *A Short History of the Second World War* (1967)

D. Flower and J. Reeves (eds.), *The War, 1939–1945* (1960)

A. Marwick, *Britain in the Century of Total War* (1967)

A. J. P. Taylor, *English History 1914–1945* (1965)

C. Wilmot, *The Struggle for Europe* (1959 edn.)

E. L. Woodward, *British Foreign Policy in the Second World War* (1962)

The Central Statistical Office produced a *Statistical Digest of the War* in 1951, and Mass Observation produced a number of surveys of opinion including: *War Begins at Home* (1940), *Home Propaganda* (1941), *People in Production* (1942) and *The Journey Home* (1944).

Other books dealing with particular war-time personalities, periods or problems include:

Alan Bullock, *Ernest Bevin* (1967) (extensive in scope and far more than a biography)

H. Cantrill (ed.), *Public Opinion, 1935–1946* (1951)

B. Collier, *The Defence of the United Kingdom* (1957); *The Battle of Britain* (1962); *The Battle of the V Weapons* (1964)

H. Cudlipp, *Publish and be Damned* (1953)

H. Dalton, *The Fateful Years* (1957)

P. Fleming, *Invasion 1940* (1957)

T. H. Hawkins and L. J. Brimble, *Adult Education—the Record of the British Army* (1947)

N. SCARLYN WILSON, *Education in the Forces 1939–1946* (1949)

E. S. TURNER, *The Phoney War on the Home Front* (1961)

D. WOOD and D. DEMPSTER, *The Narrow Margin* (1961)

On scientific and technological history the following books include directly relevant sections or notes:

R. CALDER, *Profiles of Science* (1951)

R. W. CLARK, *The Rise of the Boffins* (1962)

T. G. CROWTHER and R. WHIDDINGTON, *Science at War* (1947)

M. HENSLOW, *The Miracle of Radio* (1946)

A. PRICE, *Instruments of Darkness* (1947)

A. P. ROWE, *One Story of Radar* (1948)

SIR R. WATSON WATT, *Three Steps to Victory* (1957)

For British propaganda and intelligence see:

J. BENNETT, *British Broadcasting and the Danish Resistance Movement* (1966) (the only detailed monograph on such a subject and extremely valuable for its detailed survey)

R. BRUCE LOCKHART, *Comes the Reckoning* (1947)

S. DELMER, *Black Boomerang* (1962)

M. R. D. FOOT, *SOE in France* (1966)

B. SWEET-ESCOTT, *Baker Street Irregular* (1966)

IVOR THOMAS, *Warfare by Words* (1942)

General books on intelligence and propaganda, which touch on radio, include:

H. BERNARD, G. A. CHEVALLEZ, R. GHEYSENS and J. DE LAUNAY, *Les Dossiers de la seconde guerre mondiale* (Paris, 1964)

H. L. CHILDS and J. B. WHITTON (eds.), *Propaganda by Short Wave* (1943)

L. DE JONG, *The German Fifth Column in the Second World War* (1956)

D. LERNER (ed.), *Sykewar, Psychological Warfare against Germany, D. Day to V.E. Day* (1949)

A. J. MACKENZIE, *Propaganda Boom* (1938)

M. MÉGRET, *La Guerre Psychologique* (1956)

C. J. ROLO, *Radio Goes to War* (1943)

The German propaganda machine is described and discussed in the following books, many of which include sections specifically concerned with radio:

E. K. Bramsted, *Goebbels and National Socialist Propaganda* (1965)

C. Brinitzer, *Hier Spricht London* (1969)

J. A. Cole, *Lord Haw-Haw—and William Joyce* (1964)

E. Kris and H. Speier, *German Radio Propaganda* (1944)

R. Semmler, *Goebbels, The Man Next to Hitler* (1947)

D. Sington and A. Weidenfeld, *The Goebbels Experiment* (1942)

Z. A. B. Zeman, *Nazi Propaganda* (1964)

An invaluable source is the record of the confidential meetings Goebbels held with his propaganda team. Unfortunately the record does not cover the whole war. See:

W. A. Boelcke, *Kriegspropaganda 1939–1941, Geheime Ministerkonferenzen im Reichspropagandaministerium* (1966); *Wollt ihr den Totalen Krieg? Die Geheimen Goebbels-konferenzen, 1939–1943* (1967)

APPENDIX A

Establishment and Staff Numbers
1939-1945

BEFORE the war and after 1943 there was an authorized staff 'establishment'. The outbreak of war caused such dislocation in the Staff Records Section that there was confusion as to who held an established post and who did not. Many pre-war posts were abolished, many new departments were created, and many services had to build up at immense speed. By 1943 staff numbers as given bore little relationship to pre-war 'establishment' lists. There were indeed three categories of employees:

(1) those in an approved post, i.e. one which belonged to the pre-war establishment or one which had been approved after the outbreak of war;
(2) those in a temporary post,

    (*a*) awaiting official approval, or
    (*b*) created for some immediate purpose; or

(3) those in a post on an approved reserve, normally involving training.

The figures which appear in the following table must be accepted with reserve, but they set out rough numbers

3 Sept.	1939	4,889
31 Oct.	1940	5,579
31 Dec.	1941	10,504
30 Sept.	1942	11,329
31 Aug.	1943	11,521
31 Dec.	1944	11,600
April	1945	11,479

In August 1941 Controller (Administration) prepared the following table setting out the functional distribution of BBC Staff.

I *Direction*			
1. Central Direction		32	
2. Direction and Management of			
Regions and Areas		83	
3. Finance Direction		41	
		——	156
II *Broadcasting Operations*			
4. Home Programme Service ..		779	
5. Overseas Programme Services:			
i European Service	698		
ii Empire Service	357		
iii Latin-American Service ..	102		
iv Near Eastern Service ..	90		
	——	1,247	
6. Engineering Operational Staff		1,744	
		——	3,770
III *Other Operations*			
7. Monitoring Service		495	
8. Publications		159	
		——	654
IV *Staff Management*			
9. General Management and Re-			
cruitment		154	
10. Welfare		43	
11. Instructional Staff		12	
12. Pay and Records		136	
		——	345
V *Services*			
13. Secretariat		56	
14. Publicity		68	
15. Technical Research, Installa-			
tion and Equipment ..		371	
16. Construction and Management			
of Premises		118	
17. Transport		119	
18. A.R.P. and Fire Services ..		374	
19. Armed Watchmen		64	
20. Catering and Domestic ..		779	
21. Office Services:			
i Buying, Stores and Miscel-			
laneous	123		
ii Registry	73		
iii Telephone Operators ..	139		
iv Duplicating	94		
v House Engineers	133		
vi Other House Staff (includ-			
ing Part-time Charwomen)	1,220		
	——	1,782	
		——	3,731
VI *Others*			
22. Unposted Staff in Training ..		210	
23. Staff serving with the Forces			
and seconded to Government			
Departments, Civil Defence			
etc.		827	
		——	1,037
			9,693

Throughout the war the proportion of Engineers remained constant at two-fifths and the staff as a whole fell into three roughly equal categories: (*a*) manual, (*b*) clerical, (*c*) monthly-paid; (*a*) and (*b*) each represented rather less and (*c*) rather more than one-third.

In 1945 employees in the Overseas Services numbered 400 monthly-paid staff, 300 clerical and 1,200 engineers.

Staff were scattered at various times over 250 sets of premises in and out of London. The pay-roll in 1945 was £4,000,000, and the great variety of professions and trades within the BBC may be illustrated by the fact that in the Ministry of Labour Schedule of Reserved Occupations BBC Engineering staff alone fell into 100 different categories.

APPENDIX B

Wireless Licences, Sales of *Radio Times* and *The Listener*

	*The Listener**	*Radio Times*	Licences at 31 Dec.	Percentage of readers of the *Radio Times* to Licences
1938	50,478	2,880,747	8,856,494	32·53
1939	49,692	2,588,433	8,893,582	29·10
1940	60,270	2,302,399	8,852,363	26·01
1941	85,606	2,282,422	8,577,354	26·61
1942	91,527	2,718,654	9,019,419	29·90
1943	107,091	3,181,095	9,387,827	33·89
1944	122,907	3,679,859	9,602,137	38·32
1945	131,425	4,058,650	9,940,210	40·83
1946	138,167	5,202,937	10,769,957	48·31

*From 1940, figures for *The Listener* relate to the financial year, e.g., 1940/41, 1941/42, etc.

APPENDIX C

Radio Sets in Europe, 1938/1946

	1938	1946	
Albania		20,000	
Austria	600,000	820,000	
Belgium	857,000	802,000	
Bulgaria	34,000	205,000	
Czechoslovakia	1,000,000	1,618,000	
Denmark	704,000	1,064,000	
Finland	232,000	550,000	
France	4,164,000	5,577,000	
Germany	9,087,000	8,000,000	
Greece	23,000	52,000	
Hungary	383,000	300,000	
Italy	995,000	1,648,000	
Luxembourg	Not known	33,000	
Netherlands	1,072,000	1,053,000	(453,000)
Norway	305,000	340,000	
Poland	869,000	405,000	(100,000)
Portugal	69,000	134,000	
Roumania	216,000	150,000	
Spain	300,000	400,000	
Sweden	1,074,000	1,877,000	
Switzerland	549,000	749,000	
Turkey	46,000	182,000	
USSR	4,550,000	9,300,000	(?6,000,000)
Yugoslavia	113,000	180,000	
	27,242,000	35,459,000	(6,553,000)

Figures in brackets refer to wired broadcasting. They are part of the totals.
Information supplied by BBC External Broadcasting Audience Research Officer.

INDEX

ABERCROMBIE, SIR PATRICK, 611.
Abetz, Otto, 223.
Abrams, Mark, 148, 156, 645.
Abyssinia, 66 n., 187, 327.
Ack-Ack, Beer-Beer, 314, 318, 576.
Acland, Sir Richard, 322 n.
Adam, Kenneth, 535, 591–2.
Adam, General Sir Ronald, 707.
Adams, Godfrey, 30, 126, 151, 310.
Adams, Mary, 124 n.
Adams, Walter, 345 n., 424.
Adenauer, Konrad, 432.
Adler, Bruno, 278.
Admiralty, 42–3, 95, 163, 192 n., 279;
    and Forces Programme, 128–35;
    shipping losses, 147 n., 191; with-
    holds news, 191 ff.; and Scapa
    raid, 193–4.
Adolf in Blunderland, 108, 110.
Africa, *see* North *and* South Africa.
African Service, 490, 493, 512–16;
    broadcasts in Afrikaans, 493;
    heard in N. Russia, 489. *See also
    particular countries.*
Agate, James, 584, 710.
Agronsky, Martin, 386.
Aimberé (Manuel Antonio Braune),
    518.
Ainley, Henry, 114.
Air Log, 135.
Air Ministry, 42–3, 191, 215, 293; and
    Forces Programme, 125–30; Battle
    of Britain, 287–9, 290; war losses,
    147 n.; fifth column, 233–4; news
    delayed, 654.
Albanian Service, 265.
Albery, Sir Irving, 635.
Alexander, F. W., 53 n.
Alexander, Field-Marshal Sir Harold,
    42, 554, 589, 602, 655, 660.
Ali, Ahmed, 508.
Alice in Wonderland, 678; in Arabic,
    523 n.
Allen, Chesney, 299.
Allen, Brig.-Gen., F. A., 668.
Allen, Sir Hugh, 583 n.
Allport, G. J. B., 656.
Al-Raqib (Onlooker), 522.
American Commentary, 301.
Amery, L. S., 168, 305–6, 471, 603.
Amyot, Etienne, 514.
Anderson, Bruce, 327.

Anderson, Sir John, 608.
Andrew, Father Agnellus, 625 n.
Angeloglou, George, 265, 461.
Angwin, Sir Stanley, 724.
Annan, S., 517 n.
Anvil, The, 625–6.
Any Questions, 318. *See also Brains
    Trust.*
Appleton, Sir Edward, 724.
Appointment with Fear, 586–7.
Ara, Angel, 519.
Arabic Service, 6, 81, 522–7; and
    Zionism, 524; news bulletins, 281,
    521–2; criticized, 281–4, 331, 520.
    See also particular countries.
Arberry, A. J., 282 n.
Argentine, 518.
Armfelt, Roger, 335 n., 559 n.
Army Broadcasting Liaison Com-
    mittee, 42.
Army Bureau of Current Affairs, 311,
    610, 707.
Army Week, 587, 655.
Arnold, Doris, 136, 593.
Artist in the Witness Box, The, 117.
Ashbridge, Sir Noel, (b. 1889), 23, 105,
    123, 174, 176–7, 192 n., 395; and
    technical developments, 62–7,
    327; against jamming, 66 n., 238–
    9; triple expansion, 347–8; on
    War Cabinet Committee, 68;
    appointed DDG, 27, 552; and
    Forces Programme, 590; co-
    operation with USA, 644; blue-
    print for the future, 716–17, 724.
Askey, Arthur, 108, 299, 302, 571.
Asquith, Cyril, 313 n.
As I See It, 603.
Associated Press, 280, 668.
Astaire, Fred, 581 n.
Astor, J. J., 300.
At the Armstrongs, 317.
At the Billet Doux, 109.
Atlantic Charter, 36, 382, 413, 478,
    524, 606 n.
Attlee, C. R., 89, 98, 233, 550, 603,
    608 n.; for 'opposition time', 119;
    on BBC 'class voice', 207 n.; future
    of broadcasting, 721.
Australia, 178, 500, 630.
    Australian Broadcasting Commission,
    327, 493–4.

Reynolds, Michael, 328, 670.
Reynolds, Quentin, 325.
Reynolds, Wynford, 576 n.
Rhodesia, 513.
Ribbentrop, Joachim von, 8, 191, 400.
Rich, Roy, 136, 316.
Richardson, Ralph, 586.
Richmond, Robin, 665 n.
Rilla, Walter, 432.
Ripka, Hubert, 469–70.
Rise and Shine, 665.
Ritchie, Douglas, 398, 466, 489; as
    'Col. Britton', 371 ff., 643; and V
    campaign, 367, 372, 376–81; and
    Newsome, 418; and SHAEF,
    642–3.
Ritter, Gerhard, 694.
Roberton, Sir Hugh, 620 n.
Roberts, Michael, 470 n.
Robertson, Eric, 509.
Robertson, Sir Malcolm, 56 n.
Robinson Family, The, see *Front Line
    Family*.
Robinson, Stanford, 581.
Robinson, Vincent, 314.
Robson, Karl, 433.
Rochet, Louis, 442.
Roumania, 71, 176 n.; breaks with Axis,
    684; and USSR, 386, 399, 685.
    Roumanian Service, 471–2.
Rommel, Field-Marshal Erwin, 306,
    400, 601, 639, 660, 670.
Roosevelt, Franklin D., 5–6, 36, 253 n.,
    301; Hitler on, 6 n.; as 'gangster',
    402; his broadcasts, 323, 402–3;
    and Italy, 439; and USSR, 469;
    and France, 453 n., 673; uncon-
    ditional surrender formula, 641–2,
    694; on VE-Day, 697; his death,
    710 n.
Rose-Troup, J. M., 547.
Rossi, Tino, 223.
Rothstein, Andrew, 396.
Rowse, A. L., 299.
Rubbra, Edmund, 583.
Rundstedt, Field-Marshal G. von, 670.
Russell, Audrey, 543 n.
Russell, Sir John, 393.
Russia, *see* Union of Soviet Socialist
    Republics.
Russian Commentary, 393.
Ryan, A. P. (b. 1900), 43, 141, 216,
    365, 391, 717; as Home Adviser,
    25; at MoI, 185, 219–20; as
    Controller (Home), 195–6, 335;
    and Government, 31–2; and
    G. M. Young, 56–8; and Electra
    House, 87, 188; returns to BBC,
    195–6, 340–1; and the French,
    173–5; and Forces Programme,

127–31, 133–4, 589; appointed
    Controller (News Co-ordination),
    352 n., 535; and Priestley, 320–2;
    in reorganization, 25, 527–47; as
    Controller, News, 543; on News,
    48–9, 308, 543–6; in India, 510;
    and War Report, 654–7, 659–60;
    in conflict with SHAEF, 667; and
    post-war politics, 704.
Ryan, Curteis, 526 n.
Rydbeck, E., 474.
Rytter, Olav, 270–1.

SACKVILLE-WEST, EDWARD, 586, 709.
Sackville-West, Miss Victoria, 678.
Saint-Denis, Michel (Jacques Duch-
    esne), 248–9, 443, 454, 677; and
    Churchill, 250; and de Gaulle,
    448–9, 453, 673.
Salt, J. S. A. (1905–1947), 66 n., 362,
    370, 480; and European Services,
    260–2, 264, 271, 277; on News,
    261; and dawn cycle, 483; in
    reorganization, 341–2, 344 n., 418;
    and broadcasts to Russia, 397–8;
    on French Service, 443; in USA,
    343, 408.
Salvadori, Max, 436.
Sampson, Margaret, 474–5, 489.
Sanderson, Sir Frank, 494 n.
Sandford, Jack, 253.
Sandy's Half Hour, 136.
Sandys, Duncan, 182, 699 n.
Sargent, Sir Malcolm, 562, 581 n.
Sarnoff, David, 675.
Saturday Night Theatre, 586.
Saviours, The, 586.
Savoy Hill, 29.
Sayers, Dorothy, 626–30.
Scandinavia, 260. *See* Denmark, Nor-
    way, Sweden.
Schaschke, D. H., 548.
Schellenberg, W., 225.
Schoenberg, I., 723 n.
School Broadcasting, 317; output and
    policy, 115–17, 705–6; and reli-
    gion, 111 n.; Central Council for,
    705–6.
Schrecke, Fritz, 432.
Schumann, Maurice, 244–6, 253, 256,
    452–3, 458, 673; and Foreign
    Office, 449.
Schweitzer, Albert, 662.
Scorgie, Colonel N. G., 211, 332 n., 337 n.
Scott, R. H., 494 n.
Scottish Half Hour, 216.
Scrapbook, 109, 568.
Second Front, 14, 401 n., 440, 590–1,
    594, 618, 640; agitation for, 393,
    411, 634 n.